THE WESTERN HERITAGE

TEACHING AND LEARNING CLASSROOM EDITION

BRIEF FIFTH EDITION

VOLUME ONE: TO 1740

Donald Kagan
YALE UNIVERSITY

Steven Ozment
HARVARD UNIVERSITY

Frank M. Turner
YALE UNIVERSITY

PEARSON
Prentice
Hall

Upper Saddle River, New Jersey 07458

Library of Congress Cataloging-in-Publication Data

Kagan, Donald.
  The western heritage / Donald Kagan, Steven Ozment, Frank M. Turner—Teaching and learning classroom ed., brief 5th ed.
    p. cm.
  "Combined volume."
  Includes bibliographical references and index.
  ISBN 0-13-221107-6
  1. Civilization, Western—History—Textbooks.   I. Ozment, Steven E.   II. Turner, Frank M. (Frank Miller), 1944-   III. Title.
  CB245K28 2006b
  909'.09821—dc22

                                                    2005036328

Vice President/Editorial Director: Charlyce Jones Owen
Executive Editor: Charles Cavaliere
Associate Editor: Emsal Hasan
Editorial Assistant: Maria Guarascio
Editor-in-Chief/Development: Rochelle Diogenes
Media Editor: Deborah O'Connell
**Vice President/Director of Production
  and Manufacturing:** Barbara Kittle
Senior Managing Editor: Joanne Riker
Production Liaison: Louise Rothman
Prepress and Manufacturing Manager: Nick Sklitsis
Prepress and Manufacturing Buyer: Benjamin Smith
Director of Marketing: Brandy Dawson
Assistant Marketing Manager: Andrea Messineo
Marketing Assistant: Jennifer Lang
Creative Design Director: Leslie Osher

Cover and Interior Design: Laura Gardner, Amy Rosen,
  Kathy Mrozek
Electronic Artist: Carey Davies
Cartographer: CartoGraphics
Director, Image Resource Center: Melinda Reo
Manager, Visual Research: Beth Brenzel
Cover Image Specialist: Karen Sanatar
Photo Researcher: Teri Stratford
Image Coordinator: Robert Farrell
Color Scanning Service: Joe Conti, Greg Harrison,
  Cory Skidds, Rob Uibelhoer, Ron Walko
**Composition and Full Service
  Project Management:** Caterina Melara/Prepare, Inc.
Printer/Binder: Courier Companies, Inc.
Cover Printer: Phoenix Color Corporation

Cover Art: Queen Tiy, from Kom Medinet Ghurab (Near el-Lahun). Dynasty 18 C. 1390–1352 B.C.E. Boxwood, Ebony, Glass, Gold, Lapis Lazuli, Cloth, Clay, and wax, Height 3 3/4" (9.4 cm). Staatliche Museen zu Berlin, Preussischer Kulturbesitz. Agyptisches Museum. Photo by Margarete Busing.

Credits and acknowledgments borrowed from other sources and reproduced, with permission, in this textbook appear on appropriate page within text or on page C-1.

Pearson Education LTD.
Pearson Education Australia PTY, Limited
Pearson Education Singapore, Pte. Ltd
Pearson Education North Asia Ltd

Pearson Education, Canada, Ltd
Pearson Educación de Mexico, S.A. de C.V.
Pearson Education–Japan
Pearson Education Malaysia, Pte. Ltd

10 9 8 7 6 5 4 3 2 1

ISBN 0-13-221103-3

Visualizing The Past

PART 2

THE MIDDLE AGES   144

6

The High Middle Ages: The Rise of European Empires and States (1000–1300)   172

Medieval Society: Hierarchies, Towns, Universities, and Families (1000–1300)   194

Visualizing The Past

PART 3

EUROPE IN TRANSITION   216

The Late Middle Ages: Social and Political Breakdown (1300–1453)   218

Renaissance and Discovery   236

The Age of Reformation   262

12

The Age of Religious Wars   **290**

13

European State Consolidation in the Seventeenth and Eighteenth Centuries   312

14

New Directions in Thought and Culture in the Sixteenth and Seventeenth Centuries   340

Visualizing The Past

Science, Art, and the Printing Press in Early Modern Europe

15

Society and Economy Under the Old Regime in the Eighteenth Century

16

The Transatlantic Economy, Trade Wars, and Colonial Rebellion

PART 4

ENLIGHTMENT AND REVOLUTION   404

The Age of Enlightenment: Eighteenth-Century Thought   406

The French Revolution   432

20

The Conservative Order and the Challenges of Reform (1815–1832)   482

21

Economic Advance and Social Unrest (1830–1850)   506

Visualizing The Past

Imagining Women in the Eighteenth and Nineteenth Centuries

PART 5

TOWARD THE MODERN WORLD   534

22

The Age of Nation-States   536

23

The Building of European Supremacy: Society and Politics to World War I   562

Visualizing The Past

24

The Birth of Modern European Thought   590

25

Imperialism, Alliances, and War   614

26 ★

Political Experiments of the 1920s   646

27

Europe and the Great Depression of the 1930s   668

Visualizing The Past

PART 6

GLOBAL CONFLICT, COLD WAR, AND NEW DIRECTIONS   688

World War II   **690**

Visualizing The Past

History's Voices

Encountering the Past

Maps

SPECIAL FEATURES

Visualizing the Past

PREFACE

The heritage of Western civilization remains a major point of departure for understanding the twenty-first century. The unprecedented globalization of daily life that is a hallmark of our era has occurred largely through the spread of Western influences. From the sixteenth century onward, the West has exerted vast influences throughout the globe for both good and ill, and today's global citizens continue to live in the wake of that impact. It is the goal of this book to introduce its readers to the Western heritage, so that they may be better informed and more culturally sensitive citizens of the emerging global age.

The attacks upon the mainland of the United States on September 11, 2001, and the subsequent American invasions of Afghanistan and Iraq have concentrated the attention of teachers, students, and informed citizens upon the heritage and future of Western civilization as have no other events since the end of World War II. Whereas previously, commentary about global civilization involved analysis of the spread of Western economic, technological, and political influences, we now must explain how the West has defined itself over many centuries and think about how the West will articulate its core values as it confronts new and daunting challenges. The events of recent years and the hostility that has arisen in many parts of the world to the power and influence of the West require new efforts both to understand how the West sees itself and how other parts of the world see the West.

Twenty years ago, the West still defined itself mainly in terms of the East–West tensions associated with the Cold War. The West is now in the process of defining itself in terms of global rivalries arising from conflict with political groups that are not identical with nation-states, groups that define themselves in terms of opposition to what they understand the West to be. Whether or not we are witnessing a clash of civilizations, as Samuel Huntington, the distinguished Harvard political scientist, contends, we have certainly entered a new era in which citizens of the West need to understand how their culture, values, economy, and political outlooks have emerged. They cannot leave it to those who would attack the West to define Western civilization or to articulate its values.

Since *The Western Heritage* first appeared, we have sought to provide our readers with a work that does justice to the richness and variety of Western civilization and its many complexities. We hope that such an understanding of the West will foster lively debate about its character, values, institutions, and global influence. Indeed, we believe such a critical outlook on their own culture has characterized the peoples of the West since the dawn of history. Through such debates we define ourselves and the values of our culture. Consequently, we welcome the debate and hope that *The Western Heritage*, Teaching and Learning Classroom Edition, can help foster an informed discussion through its history of the West's strengths and weaknesses, and the controversies surrounding Western history.

Human beings make, experience, and record their history. In this edition as in past editions, our goal has been to present Western civilization fairly, accurately, and in a way that does justice to that great variety of human enterprise. History has many facets, no one of which alone can account for the others. Any attempt to tell the story of the West from a single overarching perspective, no matter how timely, is bound to neglect or suppress some important parts of that story. Like all authors of introductory texts, we have had to make choices, but we have attempted to provide the broadest possible introduction to Western civilization. To that end, we hope that the many documents included in this book will allow the widest possible spectrum of people to relate their personal experiences over the centuries and will enable our readers to share that experience.

We also believe that any book addressing the experience of the West must also look beyond its historical European borders. Students reading this book come from a wide variety of cultures and experiences. They live in a world of highly interconnected economies and instant communication between cultures. In this emerging multicultural society it seems both appropriate and necessary to recognize how Western civilization has throughout its history interacted with other cultures, both influencing and being influenced by them. Examples of this two-way interaction, such as that with Islam, appear throughout the text.

GOALS OF THE TEXT

Our primary goal has been to present a strong, clear, narrative account of the central developments in Western history. We have also sought to call attention to certain critical themes:

- The capacity of Western civilization from the time of the Greeks to the present to transform itself through self-criticism.
- The development in the West of political freedom, constitutional government, and concern for the rule of law and individual rights.
- The shifting relations among religion, society, and the state.
- The development of science and technology and their expanding impact on Western thought, social institutions, and everyday life.
- The major religious and intellectual currents that have shaped Western culture.

We believe that these themes have been fundamental in Western civilization, shaping the past and exerting a continuing influence on the present.

Flexible Presentation   *The Western Heritage*, Teaching and Learning Classroom Edition, is designed to accommodate a variety of approaches to a course in Western civilization, allowing teachers to stress what is most important to them. Some teachers will ask students to read all the chapters. Others will select among them to reinforce assigned readings and lectures.

Integrated Social, Cultural, and Political History   *The Western Heritage*, Teaching and Learning Classroom Edition provides one of the richest accounts of the social history of the West available today, with strong coverage of family life, the changing roles of women, and the place of the family in relation to broader economic, political, and social developments. This coverage reflects the explosive growth in social historical research in the past three decades, which has enriched virtually all areas of historical study.

While strongly believing in the study of the social experience of the West, we also share the conviction that internal and external political events have shaped the Western experience in fundamental and powerful ways. The experiences of Europeans in the twentieth century under fascism, national socialism, and communism demonstrate that influence, as has, more recently, the collapse of communism in the former Soviet Union and eastern Europe. We have also been told repeatedly by teachers that no matter what their own historical specialization, they believe that a political narrative gives students an effective tool to begin to understand the past. Consequently, we have sought to integrate the political with the social, cultural, and intellectual.

No other survey text presents so full an account of the religious and intellectual development of the West. People may be political and social beings, but they are also reasoning and spiritual beings. What they think and believe are among the most important things we can know about them. Their ideas about God, society, law, gender, human nature, and the physical world have changed over the centuries and continue to change. We cannot fully grasp our own approach to the world without understanding the intellectual currents of the past and how they influenced our thoughts and conceptual categories.

Clarity and Accessibility Good narrative history requires clear, vigorous prose. As in earlier editions, we have paid careful attention to our writing, subjecting every paragraph to critical scrutiny. Our goal was to make the history of the West accessible to students without compromising vocabulary or conceptual level. We hope this effort will benefit both teachers and students.

CHAPTER-BY-CHAPTER REVISIONS

Chapter 1 Increased coverage of Neolithic Europe, including an entire section on the "Ice man" found in the Alps. A major new section on the Persian Empire has also been added.

Chapter 6 Discussion of Late Antiquity now opens the chapter. Discussion of the Byzantine Empire has been expanded. Coverage of Islam and the early Islamic conquests has been increased.

Chapter 13 An entirely new chapter that examines European political history from the seventeenth to eighteenth centuries.

Chapter 18 Coverage of the French Revolution has been significantly revised and reorganized.

Chapter 25 Discussion of the New Imperialism has been significantly expanded, including a new section on the Scramble for Africa with case-study examinations of colonialism in Egypt, the Belgian Congo, and South Africa.

Chapter 27 New, fuller discussion of Keynesian economics.

Chapter 28 Revised and expanded section on the Holocaust and the destruction of Polish Jewry.

Chapter 29 Updated discussion of post–World War II European political history, especially as regards Russia, the European Union, and the invasions of Afghanistan and Iraq.

Chapter 30 Revised sections on immigration within Europe, Islam in Europe, and terrorism.

Recent Scholarship   As in previous editions, changes in this edition reflect our determination to incorporate the most recent developments in historical scholarship and the concerns of professional historians. Of particular interest are expanded discussions of cultural history, women's history, and the interaction between Islam and the West.

Maps and Illustrations   The entire map and photo program has been significantly revised. New maps include the Persian Empire, the slave trade, global migration in the nineteenth century, and the Holocaust. To help students understand the relationship between geography and history, approximately one-half of the maps include relief features. Up to two maps in each chapter feature interactive exercises on the Companion Website™ that accompanies the text. All maps have been carefully edited for accuracy. The text also contains abundant color and black and white illustrations, approximately one-third of which are new to this edition.

Pedagogical Features   This edition retains many of the pedagogical features of previous editions, while providing increased assessment opportunities.

- **NEW** • **Chapter Highlights** begin each chapter and provide a preview of the key developments and themes that are to follow.

- **Part Timelines** show the major events in social, political, and cultural history—side by side. Appropriate photographs enrich each timeline.

- **Chapter-Opening Questions**, organized by the main subtopics of each chapter, encourage careful consideration of important themes and developments. Each question is repeated at the appropriate place in the margin of the text.

- **Chronologies** within each chapter help students organize a time sequence for key events.

- **History's Voices**, including selections from sacred books, poems, philosophy, political manifestos, letters, and travel accounts, introduces students to the raw material of history, providing an intimate contact with the people of the past and their concerns. Questions accompanying the source documents direct students toward important, thought-provoking issues and help them relate the documents to the material in the text. They can be used to stimulate class discussion or as topics for essays and study groups.

- **Encountering the Past**   Each chapter includes an essay on a significant issue of everyday life or popular culture. These essays explore a variety of subjects including gladiatorial bouts and medieval games, midwivery, smoking in early modern Europe, and the politics of rock music in the late twentieth century. These thirty essays, each of which includes an illustration and study questions, expand *The Western Heritage* TLC Edition's rich coverage of social and cultural history. (See p. xxiii for a complete list of the "Encountering the Past" essays.)

- **Map Explorations** and **Critical-Thinking Questions** prompt students to engage with maps, often in an interactive fashion. Each Map Exploration is found on the Companion Website™ for the text.

- **Visualizing the Past** essays, found at the end of selected chapters, analyze important aspects of world history through photographs, fine art, sculpture, and woodcuts. Focus questions and a running narrative guide students though a careful examination of the historical issues raised by each topic in question. Two new "Visualizing the Past" essays have been added to this edition: "Imagining Women in the Eighteenth and Nineteenth Centuries," and "Identity and Nationalism in Contemporary Europe."

- **Chapter Review** questions help students focus on and interpret the broad themes of a chapter. These questions can be used for class discussion and essay topics.

- **Overview Tables** in each chapter summarize complex issues.

- **Quick Reviews,** found at key places in the margins of each chapter, encourage students to review important concepts.

- **Key Terms,** boldfaced in the text, are listed (with page reference) at the end of each chapter, and defined in the book's glossary.

 • Documents CD-ROM, containing over 200 documents in Western civilization, is bound with all new copies of the text. Relevant documents are listed at appropriate places in the margin of the text at the end of each chapter.

NEW • Study in Time, a laminated six-panel timeline of Western history, provides a succinct overview of key developments in social, political, and cultural history in Western civilization from earliest times to the present.

A Note on Dates and Transliterations   This edition of *The Western Heritage* TLC Edition continues the practice of using B.C.E. (before the common era) and C.E. (common era) instead of B.C. (before Christ) and A.D. (anno Domini, the year of the Lord) to designate dates. We also follow the most accurate currently accepted English transliterations of Arabic words. For example, today *Koran* is being replaced by the more accurate *Qur'an*; similarly *Muhammad* is preferable to *Mohammed* and *Muslim* to *Moslem.*

ANCILLARY INSTRUCTIONAL MATERIALS

The Western Heritage TLC Edition is available with an extensive package of ancillary materials.

For the Instructor

- **Instructor's Resource Binder** This innovative, all-in-one resource organizes the *Instructor's Manual,* the Test-Item File, and the transparency pack by each chapter of *The Western Heritage,* TLC Edition to facilitate class preparation. The *Instructor's Resource Binder* also includes an **Instructor's Resource CD-ROM,** which contains all of the maps, graphs, and many of the illustrations from the text in easily downloadable electronic files.

- The *Instructor's Resource CD-ROM,* compatible with both Windows and Macintosh environments, provides instructors with such essential teaching tools as hundreds of digitized images and maps for classroom presentations, PowerPoint™ lectures, and other instructional material. The assets on the IRCD-ROM can be easily exported into online courses, such as WebCT and Blackboard.

- *Test Manager* is a computerized test management program for Windows and Macintosh environments. The program allows instructors to select items from the Test-Item File to create tests. It also allows online testing.

- The *Transparency Package* provides instructors with full-color transparency acetates of all the maps, charts, and graphs in the text for use in the classroom.

For the Student

- *History Notes* (Volumes I and II) provides practice tests, essay questions, and map exercises to help reinforce key concepts.
- *Documents* in *Western Civilization* (Volumes I and II) is a collection of 200 primary source documents in global history. Questions accompanying the documents can be used for discussion or as writing assignments.
- Produced in collaboration with Dorling Kindersley, the world's most respected cartography publisher, *The Prentice Hall Atlas of Western Civilization* includes approximately 100 maps fundamental to the study of western civilization—from early hominids to the twenty-first century.
- *Reading Critically About History* is a brief guide to reading effectively that provides students with helpful strategies for reading a history textbook.
- *Understanding and Answering Essay Questions* suggests helpful analytical tools for understanding different types of essay questions, and provides precise guidelines for preparing well-crafted essay answers.
- Prentice Hall is pleased to provide adopters of *The Western Heritage*, TLC Edition with an opportunity to receive significant discounts when copies of the text are bundled with Penguin Classics titles in history. Contact your local Prentice Hall representative for details.

MEDIA RESOURCES

Prentice Hall's Online Resource, **OneKey** lets instructors and students in to the best teaching and learning resources—all in one place. This all-inclusive online resource is designed to help you minimize class preparation and maximize teaching time. Conveniently organized by chapter, OneKey for *The Western Heritage*, TLC Edition, reinforces what students have learned in class and from the text. Among the student resources available for each chapter are: a complete media-rich e-book version of *The Western Heritage*, TLC Edition; quizzes organized by the main subtopics of each chapter; over 200 primary-source documents; and interactive map quizzes.

For instructors, OneKey includes images and maps From *The Western Heritage*, TLC Edition, instructional material, hundreds of primary-source documents, and PowerPoint™ presentations.

Prentice Hall One Search with Research Navigator: History 2005 This brief guide focuses on developing critical-thinking skills necessary for evaluating and using online sources. It provides a brief introduction to navigating the Internet with specific references to history Websites. It also provides an access code and instruction on using Research Navigator, a powerful research tool that provides entry to three exclusive databases of reliable source material: ContentSelect Academic Journal Database, the *New York Times* Search by Subject Archive, and Link Library.

The Companion Website with Grade Tracker™ *(www.prenhall.com/kagan3)* works in tandem with the text and features objectives, study questions, Web links to related Internet resources, document exercises, interactive maps, online essays on technology and global history, and map labeling exercises.

Western Civilization Document CD-ROM Bound into every new copy of this textbook is a free Western civilization Documents CD-ROM. This is a powerful resource for research and additional reading that contains more than 200 primary source documents central to Western history. Each document provides essay questions that are linked directly to a Website where short-essay answers can be submitted online or printed out. A complete list of documents on the CD-ROM is found at the end of the text.

ACKNOWLEDGMENTS

We are grateful to the scholars and teachers whose thoughtful and often detailed comments helped shape this revision:

Jennifer Wynot, Metropolitan State College of Denver
William B. Whisenhunt, College of DuPage
Jonathan Perry, University of Central Florida
David Hudson, California State University, Fresno
Wanda L. Scarbro, Pellissippi State Technical Community College
Lynn Lubamersky, Boise State University
Paul J. L. Hughes, Sussex County Community College
Patti Harrold, Edmond Memorial High School
Miriam Pelikan-Pittenger, University of Illinois at Urbana-Champaign

Steven Ozment would like to acknowledge the help of Adam Beaver and Elizabeth Russell. Frank Turner would like to acknowledge the aid of Magnus T. Bernhardsson. We are grateful for the fine editorial work of George Kosar (Tufts University and Harvard University) in preparing this new TLC edition. Finally, we would like to thank the dedicated people who helped produce this revision. Our acquisitions editor, Charles Cavaliere; our production liaison, Louise Rothman; Laura Gardner, who created the beautiful new design of this edition; Benjamin D. Smith, our manufacturing buyer; Caterina Melara, production editor; and Teri Stratford, photo researcher.

D.K.
S.O.
F.M.T.

DONALD KAGAN is Sterling Professor of History and Classics at Yale University, where he has taught since 1969. He received the A.B. degree in history from Brooklyn College, the M.A. in classics from Brown University, and the Ph.D. in history from Ohio State University. During 1958–1959 he studied at the American School of Classical Studies as a Fulbright Scholar. He has received three awards for undergraduate teaching at Cornell and Yale. He is the author of a history of Greek political thought, *The Great Dialogue* (1965); a four-volume history of the Peloponnesian war, *The Origins of the Peloponnesian War* (1969); *The Archidamian War* (1974); *The Peace of Nicias and the Sicilian Expedition* (1981); *The Fall of the Athenian Empire* (1987); and a biography of Pericles, *Pericles of Athens and the Birth of Democracy* (1991); *On the Origins of War* (1995) and *The Peloponnesian War* (2003). He is coauthor with Frederick W. Kagan of *While America Sleeps* (2000). With Brian Tierney and L. Pearce Williams, he is the editor of *Great Issues in Western Civilization*, a collection of readings. He was awarded the National Humanities Medal for 2002.

STEVEN OZMENT is McLean Professor of Ancient and Modern History at Harvard University. He has taught Western Civilization at Yale, Stanford, and Harvard. He is the author of eleven books. *The Age of Reform, 1250–1550* (1980) won the Schaff Prize and was nominated for the 1981 National Book Award. Five of his books have been selections of the History Book Club: *Magdalena and Balthasar: An Intimate Portrait of Life in Sixteenth Century Europe* (1986), *Three Behaim Boys: Growing Up in Early Modern Germany* (1990), *Protestants: The Birth of A Revolution* (1992), *The Burgermeister's Daughter: Scandal in a Sixteenth Century German Town* (1996), and *Flesh and Spirit: Private Life in Early Modern Germany* (1999). His most recent publications are *Ancestors: The Loving Family of Old Europe* (2001), *A Mighty Fortress: A New History of the German People* (2004), and "Why We Study Western Civ," *The Public Interest* 158 (2005).

FRANK M. TURNER is John Hay Whitney Professor of History at Yale University and Director of the Beinecke Rare Book and Manuscript Library at Yale University, where he served as University Provost from 1988 to 1992. He received his B.A. degree at the College of William and Mary and his Ph.D. from Yale. He has received the Yale College Award for Distinguished Undergraduate Teaching. He has directed a National Endowment for the Humanities Summer Institute. His scholarly research has received the support of fellowships from the National Endowment for the Humanities and the Guggenheim Foundation and the Woodrow Wilson Center. He is the author of *Between Science and Religion: The Reaction to Scientific Naturalism in Late Victorian England* (1974); *The Greek Heritage in Victorian Britain* (1981), which received the British Council Prize of the Conference on British Studies and the Yale Press Governors Award; *Contesting Cultural Authority: Essays in Victorian Intellectual Life* (1993); and *John Henry Newman: The Challenge to Evangelical Religion* (2002). He has also contributed numerous articles to journals and has served on the editorial advisory boards of *The Journal of Modern History, Isis,* and *Victorian Studies.* He edited *The Idea of a University,* by John Henry Newman (1996) and *Reflections on the Revolution in France* by Edmund Burke (2003). Since 1996 he has served as a Trustee of Connecticut College. In 2003, Professor Turner was appointed Director of the Beinecke Rare Book and Manuscript Library at Yale University.

When writing history, historians use maps, tables, graphs, and visuals to help their readers understand the past. What follows is an explanation of how to use the historian's tools that are contained in this book.

TEXT

Whether it is a biography of Gandhi, an article on the Ottoman Empire, or a survey of Western civilization such as this one, the text is the historian's basic tool for discussing the past. Historians write about the past using narration and analysis. Narration is the story line of history. It describes what happened in the past, who did it, and where and when it occurred. Narration is also used to describe how people in the past lived, how they passed their daily lives and even, when the historical evidence makes it possible for us to know, what they thought, felt, feared, or desired. Using analysis, historians explain why they think events in the past happened the way they did and offer an explanation for the story of history. In this book, narration and analysis are interwoven in each chapter.

STUDY AIDS

A number of features in this book are designed to aid in the study of history. Each chapter begins with **Chapter Highlights**, mini-summaries that preview key themes and developments, and **Questions**, organized by the main subtopics of each chapter, which encourage careful consideration of important themes and developments. Each question is repeated at the appropriate place in the margin

EXPANSION OF EUROPEAN POWER AND THE NEW IMPERIALISM

WHAT WAS the New Imperialism?

Europe's power was based on the progress it made during the nineteenth century in science, technology, industry, agriculture, transportation, communications, and military weaponry. These advancements enabled Europeans (and Americans) to impose their wills on peoples many times their number. The growth of nation-states, a Western phenomenon, also gave Europeans the means to exploit their advantages to maximum effect. Confidence in the superiority of their civilization made them energetic, self-righteous expansionists.

MAPS

Maps are important historical tools. They show how geography has affected history and concisely summarize complex relationships and events. Knowing how to read and interpret a map is important to understanding history. Map 12–1 from Chapter 12 shows the religious divisions of Europe in 1600. It has three features to help you read it: a **caption**, a **legend**, and a **scale**. The caption explains the geographical distribution of Christian communities in Europe.

The legend is situated on the bottom-left corner of the map. The legend provides information for what each colored area of the map represents. The yellow color represents Lutherans; purple represents Calvinists; the areas in light orange are Anglican communities; and, the territories in green are Catholic. The letters "L," "C," "A," and "R" represent minorities.

The scale, located on the top of the map, informs us that three-quarters of an inch equals 1000 miles (or about 1600 kilometers). With this information, estimates of distance between points on the map are easily made.

Finally, a **critical-thinking question** asks for careful consideration of the relationship between geography and history.

MAP EXPLORATION

Interactive map: To explore this map further, go to **http://www.prenhall.com/kagan3/map12.1**

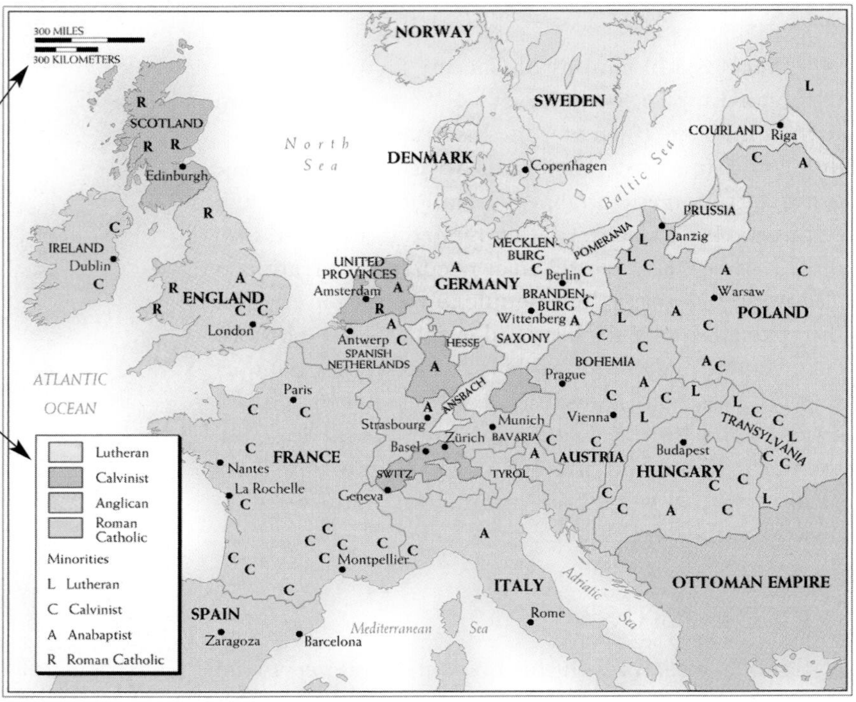

MAP 12–1

Religious Divisions about 1600 By 1600, few could seriously expect Christians to return to a uniform religious allegiance. In Spain and southern Italy, Catholicism remained relatively unchallenged, but note the existence elsewhere of large religious minorities, both Catholic and Protestant.

HOW WOULD you explain the division between Catholic and Protestant regions in Europe?

MAP EXPLORATIONS

Many of the maps in each chapter are provided in a useful interactive version on the text's Companion Website™. These maps are easily identified by a bar along the top (see example above) that reads **"Map Exploration."** An interactive version of Map 12–1 can be found at **www.prenhall.com/kagan3/map12.1.** The interactive version of this particular map provides an opportunity to move a timeline from left to right to see the spread of Muslim conquests.

The English artist Francis Hayman in 1760 portrayed the victory in 1757 of Robert Clive over the Siraj-ud-daulah, the Mughal Nawab of Bengal, at Plassey. The victory brought English domination of the Indian subcontinent for almost two centuries. Note the manner in which this English artist clearly makes the victory one of the West over the East by contrasting the English horse and the Indian elephant and the contrasting dress of the protagonists. Clive had won the battle largely through bribing many of the Nawab's troops and potential allies.

The Granger Collection, New York

ANALYZING VISUALS

Visual images embedded thoughout the text can provide as much insight into world history as can the written word. Within photographs and pieces of fine art lies emotional and historical meaning. Captions also provide valuable information, such as in the example on the left. When studying the image, consider questions such as: "Who are these people?"; "What are they doing?"; and "What can we learn from the way the people are dressed?" Such analysis allows for a fuller understanding of the way people lived in the past.

VISUALIZING THE PAST

These essays, found at the end of selected chapters, analyze important aspects of Western history through photographs, fine art, sculpture, and woodcuts. Focus questions and a running narrative guide students through a careful examination of the historical implications of each topic in question.

Visualizing The Past...
Imagining Women in the Eighteenth and Nineteenth Centuries

WHAT DOES the artistic depiction of women in the eighteenth and nineteenth centuries tell us about the ways in which Western artists have imagined the roles of women in modern society?

Although the roles of many women changed significantly in the eighteenth and nineteenth centuries, in part due to the new demands and opportunities brought about by industrialization, the themes of sexuality, docility, and maternal caring that characterized artists' imaginations of women in earlier eras also appear in the art of this period. Since most artists until the twentieth century were male, depictions of women and gender roles often derive from a male perspective on the *proper* roles of women in a society, and not necessarily on the reality of women's lives.

Thomas Gainsborough, *Robert Andrews and His Wife,* **1748.**
Portraits, such this one of the English landowner Robert Andrews and his wife, provide insights into the aristocratic and male dominance of landed society in the eighteenth century. The wife's seated posture next to her husband against the backdrop of his vast estate suggests the character of their legal relationship. Like the land, he controlled her property. She is as much one of his possessions as the rifle tucked beneath her arm and the dog at his feet.
Thomas Gainsborough, "Robert Andrews and His Wife". c. 1748-50. Oil on Canvas. 27 1/2" x 47" (69.7 x 119.3 cm). Photograph © Board of Trustees, National Gallery of Art, Washington, D.C.
▼

532

ENCOUNTERING THE PAST

Each of these short essays examines a fascinating aspect of social or cultural history from the past.

ENCOUNTERING THE PAST

MEDIEVAL COOKING

Medieval cooks served things that modern diners would recognize: roasts, pastas, meat pies, and custards. But where modern chefs are preoccupied primarily with the taste of their fare, medieval cooks worried about the effect of their dishes on diners' health. Medieval physicians traced illness to imbalances among the so-called four humors: blood, black bile, yellow bile, and phlegm. Because the humors were generated by food, recipes had to be planned like medicines. Health depended on maintaining a balance between the poles of the opposites that the humors nurtured: wet–dry, cold–warm. If not moderated by cool, wet seasonings, a spicy dish might produce an excess of hot, dry humors that made one ill.

Medieval people correctly intuited a link between diet and health, but from the modern point of view this did them little good. A fixation on meat as a prestige food meant vegetables were little appreciated. Most Europeans survived on a diet of mush or a porridge made by boiling bread in milk.

Medieval cooks were expected to be artists as well as scientists. Formal dining called for elaborately constructed dishes, such as castles executed in pastry or cooked birds stuffed back into their feathered skins. Dishes were sometimes tinted strange colors, modeled into odd shapes, or rendered otherwise amusing to the eye.

DID THE medieval understanding of the link between diet and health differ from the modern understanding—or was only the explanation different?

[Top] **The Lord of the Manor Dining.**
By permission of The British Library (10001020–021)
[Bottom] **Kitchen Scene; Chopping Meat.**
By permission of The British Library (1000278–001)

OVERVIEWS

The **Overview** tables in this text are a special feature designed to highlight and summarize important topics within a chapter. The Overview table shown here, for example, summarizes the developments in Science, Psychology, Sociology, and Fiction..

OVERVIEW	DEVELOPMENT IN SCIENCE, PSYCHOLOGY, SOCIOLOGY, AND FICTION	
Discipline	**Year**	**Development**
Science	1830s	Comte's positivism says all knowledge should be knowledge common to the physical sciences
	1859	Darwin's theory of evolution by natural selection disputes creationism
	1895	Roentgen announces the discovery of X-rays
Psychology	1900	Freud, the founder of psychoanalysis, publishes *The Interpretation of Dreams*
	early 1900s	Jung, student of Freud, theorizes that the subconscious is inherited from ancestors
	mid-1900s	Horney and Klein attempt to establish a psychoanalytic basis for feminism
Sociology	1850s	Gobineau presents first arguments that race is the major determinant of

QUICK REVIEWS

Quick reviews, placed at key locations in the margins of each chapter, provide pinpoint summaries of important concepts.

> **QUICK REVIEW**
>
> **Anti-Clericalism**
> - Corruption and incompetence marred church administration
> - City governments took steps to improve the situation by endowing preacherships
> - Fifteenth century witnessed a growing sense that clerical privileges were undeserved

Significant Dates from the Period of the Protestant Reformation

1517	Luther posts ninety-five theses against indulgences
1519	Charles V becomes Holy Roman Emperor
1521	Diet of Worms condemns Luther
1524–1525	Peasants' Revolt in Germany
1527	The Schleitheim Confession of the Anabaptists
1529	Marburg Colloquy between Luther and Zwingli

CHRONOLOGIES

Each chapter includes **Chronologies** that list, in chronological order, key events discussed in the chapter. The chronology, shown here from Chapter 11, lists the dates of key events in the history of the Protestant Reformation. Chronologies provide a review of important events and their relationship to one another.

WESTERN CIVILIZATION DOCUMENT CD-ROM

Bound into every new copy of this textbook is a Western Civilization Document CD-ROM. This is a powerful resource for research and additional reading that contains more than 200 primary source documents central to Western history. Each document provides essay questions that are linked directly to a website where short-essay answers can be submitted online or printed out. Particularly relevant or interesting documents are called out at appropriate places in the margin of each chapter (see example). A complete list of documents on the CD-ROM is found at the end of the text.

11.2
Luther's *Ninety-Five Theses*

PRIMARY SOURCE DOCUMENTS

Historians find most of their information in written records, original documents that have survived from the past. These include government publications, letters, diaries, newspapers—whatever people wrote or printed, including many private documents never intended for publication. Each chapter in the book contains a feature called **History's Voices**—a selection from a primary source document. The example shown here is a commentary on nationalism in the nineteenth century. Each **History's Voices** begins with a brief introduction followed by questions on what the document reveals.

HISTORY'S VOICES

LORD ACTON CONDEMNS NATIONALISM

 he English historian Lord Acton (1834–1902) was an important observer of contemporary events, and he was one of the first commentators to recognize the political dangers posed by nationalism.

WHAT THREATS did Acton believe that nationalism posed?

By making the State and the nation commensurate with each other in theory, it [nationalism] reduces practically to a subject condition all other nationalities that may be within the boundary. It cannot admit them to an equality with the ruling nation which constitutes the State, because the State would then cease to be national, which would be a contradiction of the principle of its existence. According, therefore, to the degree of humanity and civilization in that dominant body which claims all the rights of the community, the inferior races are exterminated, or reduced to servitude, or outlawed, or put in a condition of dependence. . . .

A State which is incompetent to satisfy different races condemns itself; a State which labors to neutralize, to absorb, or to expel them, destroys its own vitality; a State which does not include them is destitute of the chief basis of self-government. The theory of nationality, therefore, is a retrograde step in history. . . .

[N]ationality does not aim either at liberty or prosperity, both of which it sacrifices to the imperative necessity of making the nation the mold and measure of the State. Its course will be marked with material as well as moral ruin, in order that a new invention may prevail over the works of God and the interests of mankind.

From John Emerich Edward Dalbert-Acton, *First Baron Acton, Essays in the History of Liberty,* ed. by J. Rufus Fears (Indianapolis: Liberty Classics, 1985), pp. 431–433.

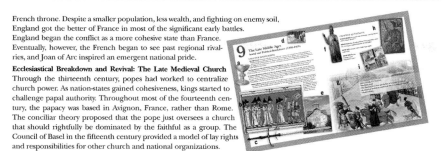

French throne. Despite a smaller population, less wealth, and fighting on enemy soil, England got the better of France in most of the significant early battles. England began the conflict as a more cohesive state than France. Eventually, however, the French began to see past regional rivalries, and Joan of Arc inspired an emergent national pride.

Ecclesiastical Breakdown and Revival: The Late Medieval Church Through the thirteenth century, popes had worked to centralize church power. As nation-states gained cohesiveness, kings started to challenge papal authority. Throughout most of the fourteenth century, the papacy was based in Avignon, France, rather than Rome. The conciliar theory proposed that the pope just oversees a church that should rightfully be dominated by the faithful as a group. The Council of Basel in the fifteenth century provided a model of lay rights and responsibilities for other church and national organizations.

Medieval Russia Kiev was the most important city in Russia around the turn of the millennium, so Prince Vladimir of Kiev's selection of Greek Orthodoxy as the state religion had ramifications that endure to the present. Starting in the eleventh century, Kiev lost its preeminence, and Russians split into three geographic and cultural groupings: the Great Russians, the White Russians, and the Little Russians or Ukrainians. In 1223, Ghengis Khan sent a Mongol (or Tatar) army into Russia. The Golden Horde brought much of Russia into the Mongol Empire. Mongol rule ended in 1480, by which time Moscow was the dominant city within Russia. In contrast to western Europe, where the nobility, the clergy, and the peasantry constituted distinct and easily identifiable groups in Russia the main social division was between freemen and slaves.

REVIEW QUESTIONS

1. What were the causes of the Black Death? Why did it spread so quickly? What were its effects on European society? How important do you think disease is in changing the course of history?

2. What were the causes of the Hundred Years' War? What advantages did each side have? Why were the French ultimately victorious?

3. What changes took place in the church and in its relationship to secular society between 1200 and 1450? How did it respond to political threats from increasingly powerful monarchs? How great an influence did the church have on secular events?

4. What is meant by the term "Avignon papacy"? What caused the Great Schism? How was it resolved? Why did kings in the late thirteenth and early fourteenth centuries have more power over the church than it had over them? What did kings hope to achieve through their struggles with the church?

5. How did the Kievan and medieval Russian states develop in terms of religion, politics, and social structure? What effect did Mongol rule have on Russian lands?

KEY TERMS

Avignon Papacy (p. 230)   **boyars** (p. 234)   Jacquerie (p. 226)
Black Death (p. 220)   **Estates General** (p. 226)

 For additional study resources for this chapter, go to:
www.prenhall.com/kagan3/chapter9

IMAGE KEY
for pages 218–219

a. Chalice, French, c.1325 (silver gilt)

b. Flagellants in the Netherlands town of Tournai (Doornik), 1349. Flagellants, known as the Brothers of the Cross, scourging themselves as they walk through the streets in order to free the world from the Black Death (Bubonic Plague)

c. Lugged Two-handed Sword, circa 1600

d. Detail from an illustrated manuscript of Boccaccio's "Decameron," physicians apply leeches to an emperor   Jean-Loup Charmet/Science Photo Library/Photo Researchers, Inc.

e. Exterior of a church, Novgorod, Russia

f. Statue of Pope Boniface VIII. Museo Civico, Bologna.   Scala/Art Resource. NY

g. Death of Wat Tyler (d. 1381) in front of Richard II, killed by Lord Mayor Walworth for wishing to abolish serfdom, by Jehan Froissart, (ca. 1460–80)

h. "Joan of Arc." Franco-Flemish miniature. Anonymous, 15h century. Archives Nationales, Paris, France. Photograph copyright Bridgeman-Giraudon/Art Resource, NY

i. A Caricature of physicians (early sixteenth century)

SUMMARIES, REVIEW QUESTIONS, AND ADDITIONAL STUDY RESOURCES

At the end of each chapter a **summary** and **review questions** reconsider the main topics. An **Image Key** provides information about the illustrations that appear at the beginning of the chapter. The URL for the Companion Website™ is also found at the end of each chapter; this is an excellent resource for additional study aids. In addition, a laminated "Study in Time" chart is found at the front of the text and provides a succinct timeline of Western history.

GLOSSARY/KEY TERMS

Significant historical terms are called out in heavy type throughout the text, defined in the margin, and listed at the end of each chapter with appropriate page numbers. These are listed alphabetically and defined in a glossary at the end of the book.

EXPLORE THE POWER OF ONEKEY

OneKey is Prentice Hall's premium exclusive online resource for instructors and students. **OneKey** gives you access to the best online teaching and learning tools—all available 24/7. Harnessing the power of WebCT, Blackboard, and Course Compass , OneKey puts all of your resources in one place for maximum convenience, simplicity, and success.

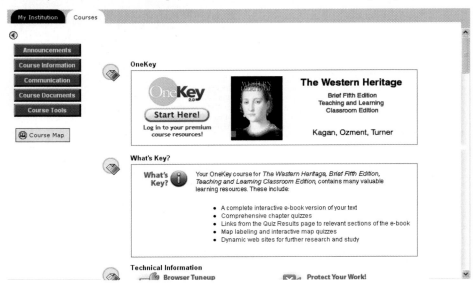

PRESENTATION RESOURCES FOR INSTRUCTORS

VISUALS

- Images
- Maps, Tables, Figures
- Map Outlines

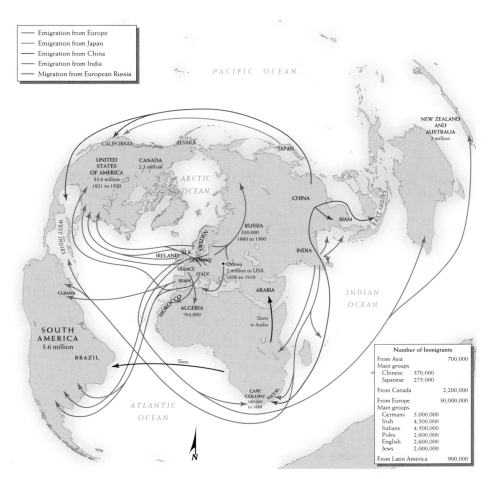

POWERPOINT™ PRESENTATIONS

- Lecture Aids—Visuals
- Lecture Aids—Text
- Lecture Aids—Lecture Outline

Changing Religious Life

✳ Religion in fifteenth-century life
  ◆ Clergy made up 6% to 8% of urban population
  ◆ Considerable political and religious power
  ◆ Monasteries were prominent and influential

✳ Religion in sixteenth-century life
  ◆ Numbers of clergy fell by 2/3
  ◆ Monasteries and nunneries nearly absent
  ◆ Worship conducted in the vernacular
  ◆ Clergy could marry, paid taxes

ANIMATIONS AND ACTIVITIES

- Interactive Maps

TEXT

- Instructor's Manual

ASSESSMENT RESOURCES FOR STUDENTS

HOMEWORK

- Review Questions
- e-book

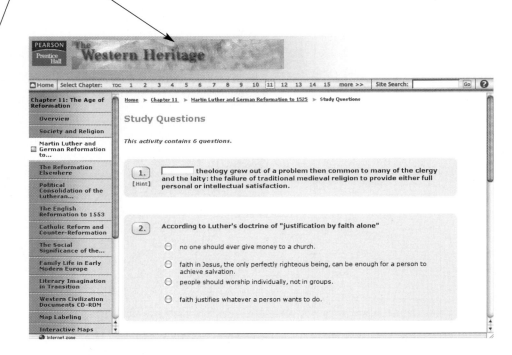

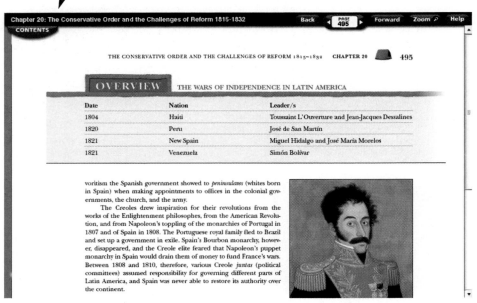

ADDITIONAL STUDENT RESOURCES

E-THEMES IN WORLD HISTORY

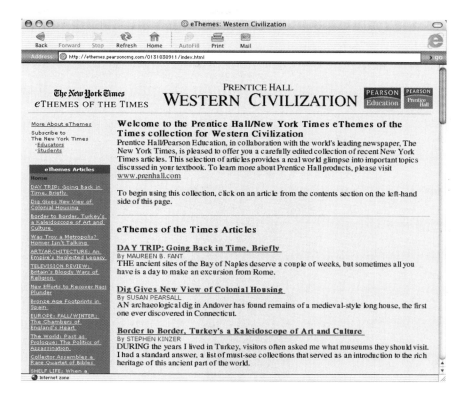

 RESEARCH NAVIGATOR

Take a tour at www.prenhall.com/onekey

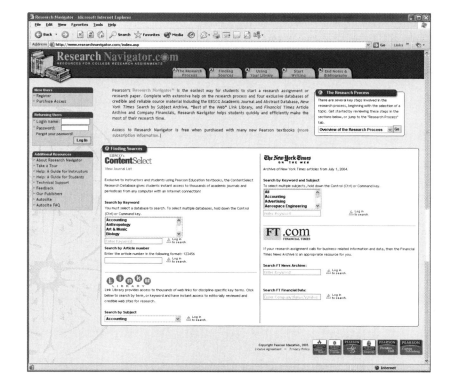

PART ONE　THE FOUNDATIONS OF WESTERN CIVILIZATION IN THE ANCIENT WORLD

POLITICS & GOVERNMENT

ca. 3100–2700 B.C.E.	Egyptian Early Dynastic Period; unification of Upper and Lower Egypt
ca. 2800–2340 B.C.E.	Sumerian city-states' Early Dynastic period
2700–2200 B.C.E.	Egyptian Old Kingdom
ca. 2370 B.C.E.	Sargon established Akkadian Empire

2200–2052 B.C.E.	Egyptian First Intermediate Period
2052–1786 B.C.E.	Egyptian Middle Kingdom
1792–1750 B.C.E.	Reign of Hammurabi; height of Old Babylonian Kingdom; publication of Code of Hammurabi
1786–1575 B.C.E.	Egyptian Second Intermediate Period
ca. 1700 B.C.E.	Hyksos' Invasion of Egypt

▲ Stele of Hammurabi

◄ Head of Sargon the Great

SOCIETY & ECONOMY

ca. 1,000,000–10,000 B.C.E.	Paleolithic Age
ca. 8,000 B.C.E.	Earliest Neolithic settlements
ca. 3500 B.C.E.	Earliest Sumerian settlements
ca. 3000 B.C.E.	First urban settlements in Egypt and Mesopotamia; Bronze Age begins in Mesopotamia and Egypt
ca. 2900–1150 B.C.E.	Bronze Age Minoan society on Crete; Helladic society on Greek mainland

ca. 2000 B.C.E.	Hittites arrive in Asia Minor
ca. 1900 B.C.E.	Amorites in Babylonia

◄ Venus of Willendorf

RELIGION & CULTURE

ca. 30,000–6000 B.C.E.	Paleolithic art
ca. 3000 B.C.E.	Invention of writing
ca. 3000 B.C.E.	Temples to gods in Mesopotamia; development of ziggurat temple architecture
2700–2200 B.C.E.	Building of pyramids for Egyptian god-kings, development of hieroglyphic writing in Egypt

2200–1786 B.C.E.	Rise of Amon-Re as chief Egyptian god
ca. 1900 B.C.E.	Traditional date for Hebrew patriarch Abraham

◄ Chauvet cave painting panel with horses

▲ Sumerian clay tablet

ca. 1600 B.C.E.	Fall of Old Babylonian Kingdom
1575–1087 B.C.E.	Egyptian New Kingdom (or Empire)
ca. 1400–1200 B.C.E.	Height of Hittite Empire
ca. 1400–1200 B.C.E.	Height of Mycenaean power
1367–1350 B.C.E.	Amunhotep IV (Akhenaten) in Egypt
ca. 1250 B.C.E.	Sack of Troy (?)
1087–1030 B.C.E.	Egyptian Post-Empire Period

Pharaoh Sety I ▶

◀ Queen Nefertiti

ca. 1000–961 B.C.E.	Reign of King David in Israel
ca. 961–922 B.C.E.	Reign of King Solomon in Israel
ca. 1100–615 B.C.E.	Assyrian Empire
ca. 800–400 B.C.E.	Height of Etruscan culture in Italy
ca. 650 B.C.E.	Spartan constitution formed
722 B.C.E.	Israel (northern kingdom) falls to Assyrians
ca. 700–500 B.C.E.	Rise and decline of tyranny in Greece
621 B.C.E.	First written law code in Athens
612–539 B.C.E.	Neo-Babylonian (Chaldean) Empire
594 B.C.E.	Solon's constitutional reforms, Athens
586 B.C.E.	Destruction of Jerusalem; fall of Judah (southern kingdom); Babylonian captivity
ca. 560–550 B.C.E.	Peloponnesian League begins
559–530 B.C.E.	Reign of Cyrus the Great in Persia
546 B.C.E.	Persia conquers Lydian Empire of Croesus, including Greek cities of Asia Minor
539 B.C.E.	Persia conquers Babylonia; temple at Jerusalem restored; exiles return from Babylonia
521–485 B.C.E.	Reign of Darius in Persia
509 B.C.E.	Kings expelled from Rome; Republic founded
508 B.C.E.	Clisthenes founds Athenian democracy

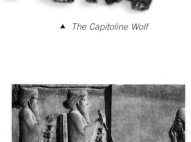

▲ The Capitoline Wolf

▲ Darius and Xerxes, detail, south wall of the treasury, Persepolis, Iran

ca. 1200 B.C.E.	Hebrews arrive in Palestine

Homer, detail of statue ▶

ca. 1100–750 B.C.E.	Greek "Dark Ages"
ca. 1000 B.C.E.	Italic peoples enter Italy
ca. 800 B.C.E.	Etruscans enter Italy
ca. 750–700 B.C.E.	Rise of *polis* in Greece
ca. 750–600 B.C.E.	Great age of Greek colonization
ca. 700 B.C.E.	Invention of *hoplite* phalanx
ca. 600–550 B.C.E.	Spartans adopt new communitarian social system
ca. 600–500 B.C.E.	Athens develops commerce and a mixed economy

Female athlete ▶ of Sparta

1367–1360 B.C.E.	Religious revolution led by Akhenaten makes Aton chief Egyptian god
1347–1339 B.C.E.	Tutankhamun restores worship of Amon-Re

◀ Tutankhamun and his queen

ca. 750 B.C.E.	Hebrew prophets teach monotheism
ca. 750 B.C.E.	Traditional date for Homer
ca. 750 B.C.E.	Greeks adapt Semitic script and invent the Greek alphabet
ca. 750–600 B.C.E.	Panhellenic shrines established at Olympia, Delphi, Corinth, and Nemea; athletic festivals attached to them
ca. 700 B.C.E.	Traditional date for Hesiod
ca. 675–500 B.C.E.	Development of Greek lyric and elegiac poetry
ca. 570 B.C.E.	Birth of Greek philosophy in Ionia
ca. 550 B.C.E.	Oracle of Apollo at Delphi grows to great influence
ca. 550 B.C.E.	Cult of Dionysus introduced to Athens
539 B.C.E.	Restoration of temple in Jerusalem; return of exiles

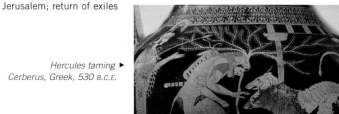

Hercules taming ▶ Cerberus, Greek, 530 B.C.E.

PART ONE   THE FOUNDATIONS OF WESTERN CIVILIZATION IN THE ANCIENT WORLD

POLITICS & GOVERNMENT

490 B.C.E.	Battle of Marathon
485–465 B.C.E.	Reign of Xerxes in Persia
480–479 B.C.E.	Xerxes invades Greece
478–477 B.C.E.	Delian League founded
ca. 460–445 B.C.E.	First Peloponnesian War
450–449 B.C.E.	Laws of the Twelve Tables, Rome
431–404 B.C.E.	Great Peloponnesian War
404–403 B.C.E.	Thirty Tyrants rule at Athens
400–387 B.C.E.	Spartan war against Persia
398–360 B.C.E.	Reign of Agesilaus at Sparta
395–387 B.C.E.	Corinthian War
392 B.C.E.	Romans defeat Etruscans
378 B.C.E.	Second Athenian Confederation
371 B.C.E.	Thebans end Spartan hegemony
362 B.C.E.	Battle of Mantinea; end of Theban hegemony
338 B.C.E.	Philip of Macedon conquers Greece

Ancient Greek Athenian coin ▶

336–323 B.C.E.	Reign of Alexander III (the Great)
334 B.C.E.	Alexander invades Asia
330 B.C.E.	Fall of Persepolis; end Achaemenid rule in Persia
323–301 B.C.E.	Ptolemaic Kingdom (Egypt), Seleucid Kingdom (Syria), and Antigonid Dynasty (Macedon) founded
287 B.C.E.	Laws passed by Plebeian Assembly made binding on all Romans; end of Struggle of the Orders
264–241 B.C.E.	First Punic War
218–202 B.C.E.	Second Punic War
215–168 B.C.E.	Rome establishes rule over Hellenistic world
154–133 B.C.E.	Roman wars in Spain
133 B.C.E.	Tribunate of Tiberius Gracchus
123–122 B.C.E.	Tribunate of Gaius Gracchus
82 B.C.E.	Sulla assumes dictatorship
60 B.C.E.	First Triumvirate
46–44 B.C.E.	Caesar's dictatorship
43 B.C.E.	Second Triumvirate

▲ Painted relief from Ptolemaic temple

SOCIETY & ECONOMY

ca. 500–350 B.C.E.	Spartan population shrinks
ca. 500–350 B.C.E.	Rapid growth in overseas trade
477–431 B.C.E.	Vast growth in Athenian wealth
431–400 B.C.E.	Peloponnesian War casualties cause decline in size of lower class in Athens, with relative increase in importance of upper and middle classes

◀ Alexander the Great and Darius III

ca. 300 B.C.E.–150 C.E.	Growth of international trade and development of large cities in Hellenistic/Roman world
ca. 218–135 B.C.E.	Decline of family farm in Italy; growth of tenant farming and cattle ranching
ca. 150 B.C.E.	Growth of slavery as basis of economy in Roman Republic

The Roman Forum ▶

RELIGION & CULTURE

ca. 500–400 B.C.E.	Great age of Athenian tragedy
469–399 B.C.E.	Life of Socrates
ca. 450–400 B.C.E.	Great influence of Sophists in Athens
ca. 450–385 B.C.E.	Great age of Athenian comedy
448–432 B.C.E.	Periclean building program on Athenian acropolis
429–347 B.C.E.	Life of Plato
ca. 425 B.C.E.	Herodotus' history of the Persian Wars
ca. 400 B.C.E.	Thucydides' history of the Peloponnesian War
ca. 400–325 B.C.E.	Life of Diogenes the Cynic
386 B.C.E.	Foundation of Plato's Academy
384–322 B.C.E.	Life of Aristotle
336 B.C.E.	Foundation of Aristotle's Lyceum

◀ Double bust of the Greek historians Herodotus and Thucydides

342–271 B.C.E.	Life of Epicurus
335–263 B.C.E.	Life of Zeno the Stoic
ca. 287–212 B.C.E.	Life of Archimedes of Syracuse
ca. 275 B.C.E.	Foundation of museum and library make Alexandria the center of Greek intellectual life
ca. 250 B.C.E.	Livius Andronicus translates the *Odyssey* into Latin
106–43 B.C.E.	Life of Cicero
ca. 99–55 B.C.E.	Life of Lucretius
86–35 B.C.E.	Life of Sallust
ca. 84–54 B.C.E.	Life of Catullus
70–19 B.C.E.	Life of Vergil
65–8 B.C.E.	Life of Horace
59 B.C.E.–17 C.E.	Life of Livy
43 B.C.E.–18 C.E.	Life of Ovid

Odysseus ▶ and Cyclops

31 B.C.E.	Octavian and Agrippa defeat Anthony at Actium
27 B.C.E.–14 C.E.	Reign of Augustus
14–68 C.E.	Reigns of Julio-Claudian Emperors
69–96 C.E.	Reigns of Flavian Emperors
96–180 C.E.	Reigns of "Good Emperors"
180–192 C.E.	Reign of Commodus
284–305 C.E.	Reign of Diocletian; reform and division of Roman Empire
306–337 C.E.	Reign of Constantine
330 C.E.	Constantinople new capital of Roman Empire
361–363 C.E.	Reign of Julian the Apostate
379–395 C.E.	Reign of Theodosius
376 C.E.	Visigoths enter Roman Empire

▲ *Roman fleet of Octavian*

Roman ▶
amphitheatre

ca. 150–400 C.E.	Decline of slavery and growth of tenant farming and serfdom in Roman Empire
ca. 250–400 C.E.	*Coloni* (Roman tenant farmers) increasingly tied to the land
301 C.E.	Edict of Maximum Prices at Rome

Caesar Augustus, ▶
Emperor of Rome

9 B.C.E.	Ara Pacis dedicated at Rome
ca. 4 B.C.E.	Birth of Jesus of Nazareth
ca. 30 C.E.	Crucifixion of Jesus
64 C.E.	Christians persecuted by Nero
66–135 C.E.	Romans suppress rebellions of Jews
ca. 70–100 C.E.	Gospels written
ca. 150 C.E.	Ptolemy of Alexandria establishes canonical geocentric model of the universe
ca. 250–260 C.E.	Severe persecutions by Decius and Valerian
303 C.E.	Persecution of Christians by Diocletian
311 C.E.	Galerius issues Edict of Toleration
312 C.E.	Constantine converts to Christianity
325 C.E.	Council of Nicaea
348–420 C.E.	Life of St. Jerome
354–430 C.E.	Life of St. Augustine
395 C.E.	Christianity becomes official religion of Roman Empire

▲ *Ara Pacis*

Columns of Hellenistic gymnasium ▶

1 The Birth of Civilization

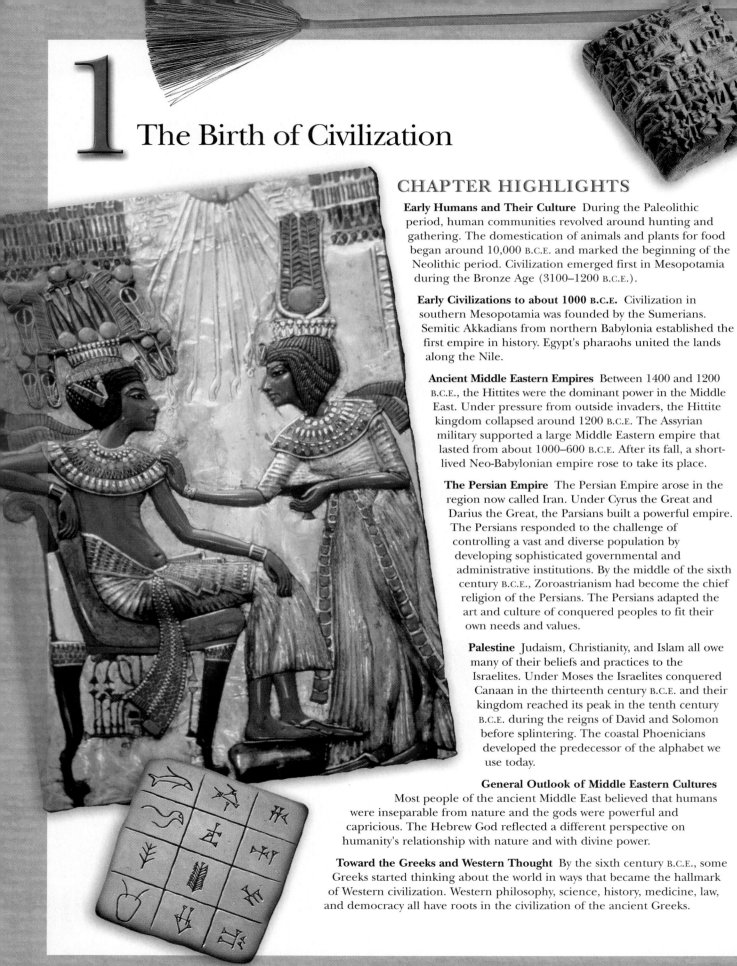

CHAPTER HIGHLIGHTS

Early Humans and Their Culture During the Paleolithic period, human communities revolved around hunting and gathering. The domestication of animals and plants for food began around 10,000 B.C.E. and marked the beginning of the Neolithic period. Civilization emerged first in Mesopotamia during the Bronze Age (3100–1200 B.C.E.).

Early Civilizations to about 1000 B.C.E. Civilization in southern Mesopotamia was founded by the Sumerians. Semitic Akkadians from northern Babylonia established the first empire in history. Egypt's pharaohs united the lands along the Nile.

Ancient Middle Eastern Empires Between 1400 and 1200 B.C.E., the Hittites were the dominant power in the Middle East. Under pressure from outside invaders, the Hittite kingdom collapsed around 1200 B.C.E. The Assyrian military supported a large Middle Eastern empire that lasted from about 1000–600 B.C.E. After its fall, a short-lived Neo-Babylonian empire rose to take its place.

The Persian Empire The Persian Empire arose in the region now called Iran. Under Cyrus the Great and Darius the Great, the Parsians built a powerful empire. The Persians responded to the challenge of controlling a vast and diverse population by developing sophisticated governmental and administrative institutions. By the middle of the sixth century B.C.E., Zoroastrianism had become the chief religion of the Persians. The Persians adapted the art and culture of conquered peoples to fit their own needs and values.

Palestine Judaism, Christianity, and Islam all owe many of their beliefs and practices to the Israelites. Under Moses the Israelites conquered Canaan in the thirteenth century B.C.E. and their kingdom reached its peak in the tenth century B.C.E. during the reigns of David and Solomon before splintering. The coastal Phoenicians developed the predecessor of the alphabet we use today.

General Outlook of Middle Eastern Cultures Most people of the ancient Middle East believed that humans were inseparable from nature and the gods were powerful and capricious. The Hebrew God reflected a different perspective on humanity's relationship with nature and with divine power.

Toward the Greeks and Western Thought By the sixth century B.C.E., some Greeks started thinking about the world in ways that became the hallmark of Western civilization. Western philosophy, science, history, medicine, law, and democracy all have roots in the civilization of the ancient Greeks.

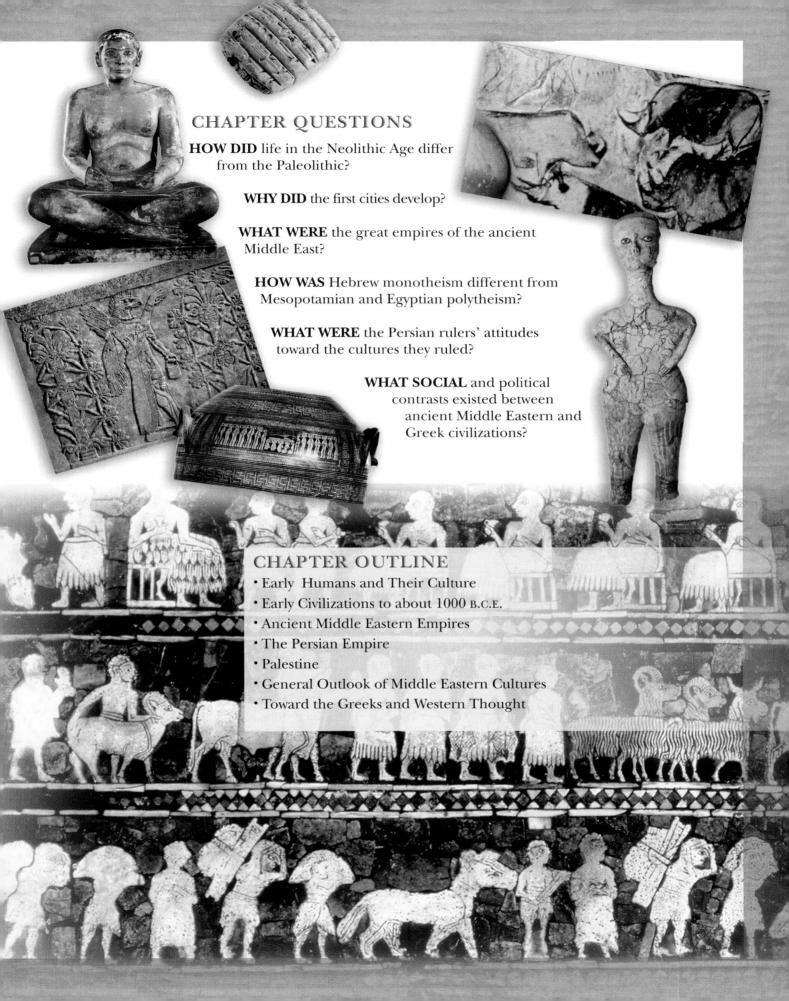

CHAPTER QUESTIONS

HOW DID life in the Neolithic Age differ from the Paleolithic?

WHY DID the first cities develop?

WHAT WERE the great empires of the ancient Middle East?

HOW WAS Hebrew monotheism different from Mesopotamian and Egyptian polytheism?

WHAT WERE the Persian rulers' attitudes toward the cultures they ruled?

WHAT SOCIAL and political contrasts existed between ancient Middle Eastern and Greek civilizations?

IMAGE KEY
for pages 4–5 is on page 30.

For hundreds of thousands of years, human beings lived by hunting and gathering what nature spontaneously provided. Only about 10,000 years ago did they begin to cultivate plants, domesticate animals, and settle in permanent communities. About 5,000 years ago, the Sumerians, who lived near the confluence of the Tigris and Euphrates Rivers (a region Greek geographers called "Mesopotamia," i.e., "between-rivers"), and the Egyptians, who dwelt in the Nile Valley, pioneered civilization. By the fourteenth century B.C.E.,[1] powerful empires had arisen and were struggling for dominance of the civilized world, but one of the region's smaller states probably had a greater influence on the course of Western civilization. The modern West's major religions (Judaism, Christianity, and Islam) are rooted in the traditions of ancient Israel.

HOW DID life in the Neolithic Age differ from the Paleolithic?

EARLY HUMANS AND THEIR CULTURE

Scientists estimate that Earth may be 6 billion years old and its human inhabitants have been developing for 3 to 5 million years. Some 1 to 2 million years ago, erect tool-using beings spread from their probable place of origin in Africa to Europe and Asia. Our own species, ***Homo sapiens***, is about 200,000 years old, and fully modern humans have existed for about 90,000 years.

Humans are distinguished by a unique capacity to construct cultures. A **culture** may be defined as a way of life invented by a group and passed on by teaching. It includes both material things (tools, clothing, and shelter) and ideas, institutions, and beliefs. Because cultural behaviors are guided by learning rather than instinct, they can be altered at will to enable human beings to adapt rapidly to different environments and changing conditions.

THE PALEOLITHIC AGE

Anthropologists identify prehistoric human cultures by the styles of their most durable and plentiful artifacts—stone tools. The earliest period in cultural development—the **Paleolithic** (Greek for "old stone") Age—began with the first use of stone tools about a million years ago and continued until about 10,000 B.C.E. Throughout this immensely long era, people were nomadic hunters and gatherers who depended for their food on what nature spontaneously offered. An uncertain food supply and the inability of human beings to understand or control the mysterious forces that threatened their existence persuaded them that they occupied a world governed by superhuman powers. Cave art, ritual burial practices, and other evidences of religious or magical beliefs appeared during the Paleolithic era, and they bear witness to a suspicion as old as humanity itself that there is more to the world than meets the eye.

Human society in the Paleolithic Age was probably based on a division of labor by sex. Males ranged far afield on the hunt. Females, whose mobility was limited by the burdens of childbearing and nursing, gathered edibles of various kinds in the vicinity of a base camp. The knowledge that people acquired as hunters and gatherers eventually equipped them to develop agriculture and herding, and these food-producing technologies drastically changed the human lifestyle.

Homo sapiens Our own species, which dates back roughly 200,000 years.

culture Way of life invented by a group and passed on by teaching.

Paleolithic Greek for "old stone"; the earliest period in cultural development that began with the first use of stone tools about a million years ago and continued until about 10,000 B.C.E.

---

[1]This book substitutes B.C.E. ("before the common era") and C.E. ("common era") for B.C. and A.D., and it uses the term "Middle East" in preference to "Near East."

THE NEOLITHIC AGE

About 10,000 years ago, people living in some parts of the Middle East made advances in the production of stone tools that marked the start of the **Neolithic** (i.e., "new stone") Age. But more significant than their tool-making technology was their shift from hunting and gathering to agriculture. They began to domesticate the wild species of sheep, goats, wheat, and barley that were native to the foothills of the region's mountains. Once domesticated, these species were transplanted to areas where they did not naturally occur.

Hunters and gatherers maintain their food supply by harvesting a district and then moving on, but farmers settle down next to the fields they cultivate. They establish villages, construct relatively permanent dwellings, and produce pottery in which to cook and store the grains they raise. The earliest Neolithic settlements featured small circular huts clustered around a central storehouse. Later Neolithic people built larger rectangular homes with private storage facilities and enclosures for livestock. The similarity in size and equipment of buildings suggests that a Neolithic village's residents differed little in wealth and social status. Although they engaged in some trade, their communities were largely self-sufficient.

The most exceptional of the known Neolithic settlements are Jericho (near the Dead Sea) and Çatal Hüyük (about 150 miles south of the capital of modern Turkey). Jericho was occupied as early as 12,000 B.C.E., and by 8000 B.C.E., it had a massive stone wall enclosing an area exceeding eight acres. (No other Neolithic site is known to have been fortified.) Çatal Hüyük was a somewhat later and larger community. It had a population well over 6,000. Its mud-brick dwellings were packed tightly together. There were no streets, and Çatal Hüyük's residents traveled across its buildings' roofs and used ladders to access their homes. Many interiors were elaborately decorated with sculptures and paintings that are assumed to have ritual significance.

Wherever agriculture and animal husbandry appeared, the relationship between human beings and nature changed forever. People began to try to control nature, not just respond to what it offered. This was a vital prerequisite for the development of civilization, but it was not without cost. Farmers had to work harder and longer than hunters and gatherers. They faced health threats from accumulating wastes. They had to figure out how to live together permanently in one place and cope with unprecedented population growth. The earliest Neolithic communities appeared in the Middle East about 8000 B.C.E., in China about 4000 B.C.E., and in India about 3600 B.C.E.

In 1991 a tourist discovered a frozen body in the Ötztal Tyrolean Alps on the Italian-Austrian border. The body turned out to be the oldest mummified human being yet discovered and sheds new light on the Neolithic period. Dated to 3300 B.C.E., it was the remains of a man between 25 and 35 years old, 5 feet 2 inches tall, weighing 110 pounds. He has been called Ötzi, the Ice Man from the place of his discovery. He had not led a peaceful life, for his nose was broken, several of his ribs were fractured, and an arrowhead in his shoulder suggests he bled to death in the ice and snow. Ötzi wore a fur robe of mountain animal skin, with a woven grass cape underneath and leather shoes stuffed with grass. He was heavily armed for his time, carrying a flint dagger and bow with arrows also tipped in flint. The blade of his axe was copper, indicating that metallurgy was already under way. His discovery vividly shows the beginning of the transition from the Stone Age to the Bronze Age.

At Ain Ghazal, a Neolithic site in Jordan, several pits contained male and female statues made of clay modeled over a reed framework. Similar figures have been found at Jericho and other sites, all from the same period, about 8500–7000 B.C.E. They were probably used in religious rituals, perhaps connected with ancestor worship, as were plastered skulls, masks, carved heads, and other artifacts.

Archaeological Museum, Amman, Jordan, kingdom. Photograph © Erich Lessing, Art Resource, NY

Neolithic "New stone" age, dating back 10,000 years to when people living in some parts of the Middle East made advances in the production of stone tools and shifted from hunting and gathering to agriculture.

THE BRONZE AGE AND THE BIRTH OF CIVILIZATION

As Neolithic villages and herding cultures were spreading over much of the world, another major shift in human life styles began on the plains near the Tigris and Euphrates Rivers and in the valley of the Nile River. Villages grew to become towns and cities that dominated large areas. These new urban centers usually had some monumental buildings whose construction required the sustained effort of hundreds or thousands of people over many years. There is evidence of social stratification—of the emergence of classes distiniguished by wealth, lineage, and religious and political authority. Writing was invented, probably to deal with the challenge of managing complex urban economies. Sophisticated works of art were created, and the first metal implements—made from bronze, an alloy of copper and tin—appeared. Although stone tools continued to be used, the increasing importance of metal ended the Stone Ages in the Middle East and inaugurated the **Bronze Age** (3100–1200 B.C.E.). The characteristics of Bronze Age cultures (i.e., urbanism; long-distance trade; writing systems; and accelerating technological, industrial, and social development) are regarded by historians as the hallmarks of **civilization**.

Ötzi is the nickname scientists have given to the remains of the oldest mummified human body yet discovered. This reconstruction shows his probable appearance and the clothing and weapons found on and with him.
Wieslav Smetek/Stern/Black Star

WHY DID the first cities develop?

Bronze Age   (3100–1200 B.C.E.) Began with the increasing importance of metal that also ended the Stone Ages.

civilization   Stage in the evolution of organized society that has among its characteristics urbanism, long-distance trade, writing systems, and accelerated technological and social development.

EARLY CIVILIZATIONS TO ABOUT 1000 B.C.E.

During the fourth millennium, populations of unprecedented density began to develop along Mesopotamia's Tigris and Euphrates Rivers and Egypt's Nile River. By about 3000 B.C.E., when the invention of writing began to produce the kinds of records that make the writing of history possible, urban life had spread throughout these regions and centralized states had begun to develop. Because city dwellers do not grow their own food, they need to establish some system to promote, collect, and disburse surpluses produced by rural farmers and herders. The arid climates of Mesopotamia and Egypt meant that farmers could meet the demands of urban populations for their products only with the help of extensive irrigation systems. Irrigation technology was more elaborate in Mesopotamia than in Egypt. In Egypt the Nile flooded at the right moment for cultivation, and irrigation simply involved channeling water to the fields. In Mesopotamia, however, the floods came at the wrong season. Dikes were needed to protect fields where crops were already growing and to store water for future use. The lifelines of Mesopotamian towns and villages were rivers, streams, and canals, and control of the water these channels supplied was a contentious issue that could lead to war. Mesopotamia was a flat plain. The terrain provided little protection from floods and allowed swollen rivers to carve

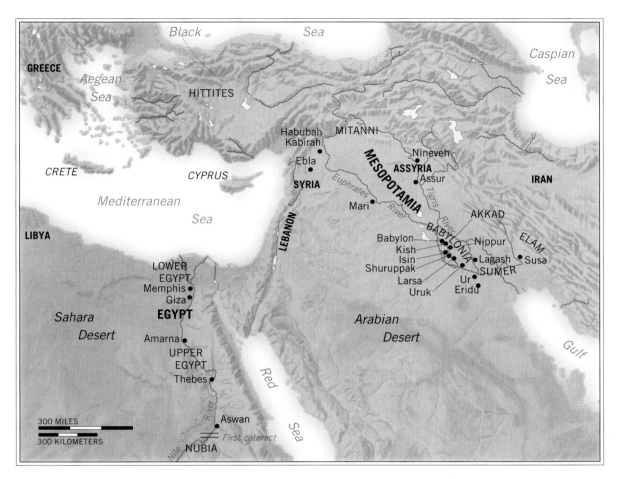

MAP 1–1

The Ancient Middle East   Two river valley civilizations thrived in the Ancient Middle East: Egypt, which was united into a single state, and Mesopotamia, which was long divided into a number of city-states.

BASED ON this map, what might explain why independent city-states were spread out in Mesopotamia while Egypt remained united in a single state?

new channels and change their courses. Cities were sometimes severely damaged or forced to relocate. At one time archaeologists assumed that the need to construct and manage irrigation systems caused the development of cities and centralized states, but they now know that large-scale irrigation appeared long after urban civilization was established. (See Map 1–1.)

MESOPOTAMIAN CIVILIZATION

Civilization seems to have made its first appearance in Babylonia, an arid portion of Mesopotamia that stretches from modern Baghdad to the Persian Gulf. The first cities appeared in Sumer, the southern half of Babylonia, during the fourth millennium B.C.E. The earliest urban center may have been at Uruk, a city that established outposts of its culture as far afield as Syria and southern Anatolia. During the Early Dynastic Period (i.e., 2800–2370 B.C.E.), Uruk was joined by a number of other city-states scattered along the banks of the Tigris and Euphrates. Competition for water and land led to wars among them.

QUICK REVIEW

The First Civilization

- Civilization first appeared in Babylonia

- First cities appeared in Sumer during fourth millenium B.C.E.

- Earliest urban center may have been at Uruk

The Victory Stele of Naram-Sin, the Akkadian ruler, commemorates the king's campaign (ca. 2230 B.C.E.) against the Lullubi, a people living in the northern Zagros Mountains, along the eastern frontier of Mesopotamia. Kings set up monuments like this one in the courtyards of temples to record their deeds. They were also left in remote corners of the empire to warn distant peoples of the death and enslavement awaiting the king's enemies (pink sandstone).

Louvre, Paris, France. The Bridgeman Art Library International Ltd.

1.5
Hammurabi's Law Code

Leagues and alliances were formed, and the weaker cities became subject to kingdoms built by the stronger. Legend seats history's first monarchs in the city of Kish.

The Sumerian language is not related to any known language, and most of the Sumerians' neighbors spoke Semitic tongues (i.e., languages belonging to the same family as Hebrew and Arabic). Many of the Semitic peoples were influenced by Sumerian civilization and adapted the Sumerian writing system for their own use. Among these were the Akkadians, a people whose first king, Sargon, established his seat at Akkade (near Baghdad). Sargon built history's first empire by conquering all the Sumerian city-states and extending his authority into southwestern Iran and northern Syria. Memory of the dynasty's splendor led later Mesopotamians to think of the reign of Naram-Sin, his grandson, as the high point of their history.

External attack and internal weakness eventually combined to destroy the Akkadian state, but about 2125 B.C.E., the kings of the Third Dynasty of the ancient Sumerian city of Ur restored unity to a part of the old empire. Under the leadership of the Third Dynasty of Ur, Sumerian civilization had its final flowering. Great monuments were built, epic poems were composed to celebrate the deeds of ancient heroes, and thousands of surviving documents witness to the existence of a highly centralized administrative system. Ur survived, however, for little more than a century. An extended period of agricultural failure may have produced a famine that undercut its ability to defend itself. The Elamites invaded Sumer from the east, and the Amorites invaded from the north. They brought an end to Sumerian rule and eventually absorbed the Sumerian peoples. The Sumerian language survived but only as a learned tongue studied by priests and scholars—much like Latin in the modern West.

New Amorite dynasties seated themselves at Isin and Larsa, but they were soon brought under the control of a powerful dynasty that founded the famous city of Babylon. Babylon extended its control over most of Mesopotamia and reached its peak during the reign of Hammurabi (r. ca. 1792–1750 B.C.E.), a ruler who is best remembered for the collection of laws issued during his reign. Earlier kings had compiled lists of laws, but the so-called Code of Hammurabi is the earliest major collection to survive. It provides intimate insights into the values and institutions of an early civilization.

Amorite society consisted of nobles, commoners, and slaves, and each of these classes was treated differently by the law. Crimes against highly ranked individuals were punished more severely than those against inferior persons, but even the poor and humble had some protection under the law. The principle of justice was retribution: "an eye for an eye, a tooth for a tooth." Professionally trained judges decided cases on the basis of evidence and the testimony of witnesses. When that was unavailable, accused persons might be compelled to prove their innocence by taking sacred oaths or undergoing physical ordeals.

The Royal Standard of Ur, a mosaic that dates from about 2750 B.C.E., shows officials from the Sumerian city of Ur celebrating a military victory as animals are brought in to be slaughtered for a feast.

British Museum, London, UK/Bridgeman Art Library

Government   Monarchy was already established in Mesopotamia by the time that historical records began to accumulate. But different kinds of monarchies appeared in different times and places. Early Sumerian art depicts kings leading armies, executing captives, and making offerings to gods. In the northern district of Assyria, kings were the chief priests, but in the south, in Babylonia, kings and priests held separate offices. Kings often appointed their sons and daughters to priesthoods. Enheduanna, daughter of the Akkadian emperor Sargon, was one of these. Some of the hymns she composed have survived—making her history's first identifiable author.

Royal and priestly households were supported by income from large estates. Some of their land was worked by low-ranking laborers in exchange for food rations, and some was leased to citizen entrepreneurs who paid rent or farmed for a share of the crop. The palace and temple establishments also maintained large herds of animals to support, among other things, the manufacture of textiles on a large scale. Wool cloth was exported to pay for metals, for Mesopotamia lacked ore deposits. Not all the land was controlled by kings and priests. Some belonged to private individuals and was bought and sold freely.

Writing and Mathematics   The challenge of administrating a Sumerian city prompted the invention of the world's first system of writing. Modern scholars have named it **cuneiform** (from Latin *cuneus*, "wedge") after the wedge-shaped marks that the Sumerian scribe made by pressing a reed stylus into the common writing material, a clay tablet. Writing began with a few simple signs intended to remind readers of something they already knew. Gradually the system evolved to the point where it was possible to record language and use writing to communicate whatever could be thought. Sumerian scribes had to learn several thousand characters, some of which stood for words and

cuneiform   Developed by the Sumerians as the very first writing system ever used, it used several thousand characters, some of which stood for words and some for sounds.

Code of Hammurabi

Photo: Ch. Larrieu. Reunion des Muses Nationaux et Ecoli du Louvre, Paris/ Art Resource, NY

polytheists Name given to those who worship many gods and/or goddesses.

others for sounds. Because it took considerable time and training to learn how to write, the skill was restricted to a tiny elite whose services were much in demand.

Before 3000 B.C.E., no one seems to have conceived of numbers in the abstract—that is, apart from their use in counting specific things. Different numerals were employed for different kinds of things, and the same sign might mean, for example, either 10 or 18 depending on what was being counted. However, once numbers began to be thought of as entities in themselves, development was rapid. Sumerian mathematicians employed a sexagesimal system (i.e., based on the number 60) that survives today in our conventional 60-minute hour and 360-degree circle. Mathematics enabled the Mesopotamians to make progress in the study of astronomy that led to the development of accurate calendars.

Religion The Mesopotamians produced a large body of sacred literature, some of which influenced the composition of the Hebrew Bible. They were **polytheists**. That is, they worshiped many gods and goddesses, most of whom represented phenomena of nature (e.g., the powers behind storms, earthquakes, and fecundity). They assumed the gods, although immortal and much greater in power than themselves, had the same needs as they did. They believed the gods had created humanity to fulfill those needs—to do the work of raising food and housekeeping that the gods would otherwise have had to do for themselves. A temple was literally a god's home. The image of the deity that it housed was provided with meals, draped in clothing, offered entertainment, and honored with ritual and ceremony. It was equipped with a garden for the god's pleasure and a bed for his or her nightly repose. Deities had universal authority, but each major god and goddess also laid claim to a specific city. The greater temples in the Sumerian cities were erected on the tops of huge terraced mounds of mud-brick called *ziggurats*. Poets sometimes described these structures as mountains linking earth with heaven, but their precise purpose and symbolism remain uncertain.

The gods were grouped into families, and heaven was assumed to be organized much like a human community. Each deity had his or her own area of responsibility. It might involve the processes of nature or human skills and crafts. The great gods who dominated heaven, like the kings who governed human affairs, were too remote to be approached by common people. Ordinary men and women took their concerns to minor deities whom they hoped would intercede for them with higher ranking members of heaven's court. Intercession was needed, for the Mesopotamians had a keen sense of the fragility of human life. Religion provided them with their primary tools for coping with crises and uncertainties. (See "Encountering the Past: Divination in Ancient Mesopotamia.")

The Mesopotamians did not hold out any hope for a better life after death. Death doomed spirits to a glum existence in a dusty, dark netherworld where they suffered hunger and thirst unless their living relatives continued to supply them with offerings. There was no reward in death for those who had led virtuous lives and no punishment for the wicked. Everyone was equally miserable. Because the desperate spirits of the dead might escape confinement to haunt the living, families took the precaution of burying their dead with offerings and holding ceremonies from time to time to placate departed kin. At the funerals of some of the early rulers, large numbers of their servants were sacrificed to provide them with retinues in the underworld.

ENCOUNTERING THE PAST

DIVINATION IN ANCIENT MESOPOTAMIA

Mesopotamians believed the world was full of omens—events that, if properly interpreted, would enable them to predict the future. They did not view the future as a predestined, unalterable fate, but they assumed that if they knew what was going to happen, appropriate rituals and planning would enable them to head off unfavorable developments. Divination is the practice of foretelling the future by magical or occult means, and the Mesopotamians were pioneers of the art. One of the earliest and most trusted divination methods involved the examination of the entrails of the animals offered at religious sacrifices. Deformities of organs were believed to be warnings from the gods. Clay models were made of these organs, and together with a report of the events they were believed to have predicted, these models were preserved in a kind of reference library for temple diviners.

Animal sacrifice was expensive and used most commonly by the state. Ordinary Mesopotamians relied on more economical methods to obtain the information they needed to plan for their futures. The seers who served them examined patterns made by the smoke of burning incense or oil poured onto water. Chance remarks of strangers, facial features, dreams, and birth defects were all considered significant. The movements of the heavenly bodies were believed to be extremely portentous for events on earth. Mesopotamian faith in astrology had the positive effect of gathering data that led to advances in astronomy. Any divergence from what were considered normal forms or patterns was considered a portent of disaster and called for prayers and magic to ward off suspected dangers.

HOW DID the Mesopotamians try to predict the future, and what did they do with the information they obtained?

Ancient Mesopotamians used astrology to predict the future. This calendar from the city of Uruk dates from the first millennium B.C.E. and is based on careful observation of the heavens.

Astrological calendar. From Uruk, Mesopotamia. Babylonian, 1st mill. B.C.E. Museum of Oriental Antiquities, Istanbul, Turkey. Photograph © Erich Lessing/Art Resource, NY

Society   Hundreds of thousands of cuneiform texts, dating from the early third millennium to the third century B.C.E., provide us with a detailed picture of life in ancient Mesopotamia. Evidence from the reign of Hammurabi is particularly abundant. In addition to his famous law code, there are numerous administrative documents and royal and private letters. The amount of space given to various topics in Hammurabi's code suggests the issues that were of chief concern to his subjects.

The code's third largest category of laws deals with commerce. Regulations governing debts, rates of interest, security, default, and the conduct of professionals (e.g., contractors, surgeons, etc.) testify to the complexity of Babylonian economic life. The second largest group of laws relates to land tenure and suggests that individual landholders feared that powerful officials would try to take

OVERVIEW — MESOPOTAMIAN AND EGYPTIAN CIVILIZATIONS

	Mesopotamia	Egypt
Government	Different kinds of monarchies appeared in different times and places. Sumerian kings led armies; northern Assyrian kings were the chief priests; and, in the south, Babylonian kings and priests held separate offices.	*Nomarchs*, regional governors whose districts were called *nomes*, handled important local issues such as water management. However, old kingdom pharaohs held much of the power and resources.
Language and Literature	Sumerians developed the world's first system of writing, *cuneiform*. Sumerian scribes had to learn several thousand characters; some stood for words, others for sounds.	Writing first appears in Egypt about 3000 B.C.E. The impetus most likely derived from Mesopotamian *cuneiform*. This writing system, *hieroglyphs*, was highly sophisticated, involving hundreds of picture signs.
Religion	The Mesopotamians were *polytheists*, worshipping many gods and goddesses, most of whom represented phenomena of nature (storms, earthquakes, etc.). The gods were grouped into families, heaven being organized like a community.	Egyptians had three different myths to explain the origin of the world, and each featured a different creator-god. Gods were represented in both human and animal form. Egyptians placed great trust in magic, oracles, and amulets to ward off evil.
Society	Parents usually arranged marriages. A marriage started out monogamous, but husbands could take a second wife. Women could own their own property and do business on their own.	Women's prime roles were connected with the management of the household. They could not hold office, go to scribal schools, or become artisans. Royal women often wielded considerable influence. In art, royal and nonroyal women are usually shown smaller than the male figures.
Slavery	The two main forms of slavery were chattel and debt slavery. Chattel slaves were bought and had no legal rights. Debt slaves, more common than chattel slaves, could not be sold, but they could redeem their freedom by paying off the loan.	Slaves did not become numerous in Egypt until the Middle Kingdom (about 2000 B.C.E.). Black Africans and Asians were captured in war and brought back as slaves. Slaves could be freed, but manumission was rare.

their property from them. The largest collection of laws is devoted to family issues (e.g., marriage, inheritance, and adoption). Parents arranged marriages for their children. Grooms made payments for their brides and a bride's family provided her with a dowry. A marriage was expected to be monogamous unless it failed to produce offspring. A man whose wife proved to be barren could take a second wife to provide the children needed to care for them in their old age. Husbands were permitted extramarital affairs with concubines, slaves, and prostitutes, but wives were not granted comparable license. A married woman's place was assumed to be in the home, but she could own property and run her own business so long as she did not neglect her duty to her husband and family. A woman could initiate divorce, and she could reclaim her dowry so long as her husband could not convict her of any wrongdoing. Single women sometimes supported themselves as tavern owners, moneylenders, midwives, nurses, priestesses, or temple servants.

Slavery: Chattel Slaves and Debt Slaves   There were two kinds of slavery in ancient Mesopotamia: chattel slavery and debt slavery. Chattel slaves were pieces of property. They had no legal rights, for they were usually foreigners—prisoners of war or aliens bought from slave merchants. They were expensive luxuries and used primarily as domestic servants. Debt slavery was more common. Individuals could pledge themselves or members of their families as security for loans. Because interest rates were high, debtors ran the risk of defaulting on their loans. If that happened, they were enslaved to work off what they owed. However, they could not be sold, and they regained their freedom when they repaid their loan. As slaves, they could have businesses and property of their own and marry free persons.

EGYPTIAN CIVILIZATION

While Mesopotamian civilization evolved along the banks of the Tigris and Euphrates Rivers, another great civilization developed in Egypt. It depended on the Nile, a river that flows from its source in central Africa some 4,000 miles north to the Mediterranean. The Nile divided Egypt into two geographically distinct districts: **Upper Egypt** (i.e., Egypt upstream), a narrow valley extending 650 miles from Aswan to the border of **Lower Egypt** (i.e., downstream Egypt), the Nile's 100-mile deep, triangularly shaped delta. Without the Nile, agriculture would have been impossible in Egypt's arid environment. Seasonal rains in central Africa caused the river to flood annually, saturating Egypt's fields and depositing a fresh layer of fertile silt just in time for the autumn planting season. As the waters retreated, farmers sowed their crops, and relatively simple irrigation techniques enabled them to maintain Egypt at a level of prosperity unmatched in the ancient world.

Egypt was a long, narrow country, but none of its people lived far from the Nile. The river tied them together, and by 3100 B.C.E., Upper and Lower Egypt were united under one government. While the Mesopotamian city-states warred among themselves and struggled with invaders, Egypt enjoyed remarkable stability and security. The cliffs and deserts that lined Egypt's borders protected it from invasion. The valley sheltered its people from the violent storms that swept the Mesopotamian plain, and the Nile's annual flooding was predictable and minimally destructive. The peace and order that characterized life in Egypt produced an optimistic outlook that contrasts markedly with the pessimistic tone of much Mesopotamian literature.

Ancient Greek historians grouped Egypt's rulers into thirty-one dynasties beginning with Menes, the king who united Upper and Lower Egypt, and ending with the death of Cleopatra (30 B.C.E.), the last member of a dynasty founded by one of Alexander the Great's Greek generals. Egypt was then absorbed into the Roman Empire and ruled by a Roman provincial governor. This 3,000-year-long era breaks down into three major periods of stability and creativity (the Old, Middle, and New Kingdoms) separated by relatively brief episodes of confusion (the Intermediate Periods).

The Old Kingdom (2700–2200 B.C.E.)   Egypt's first two dynasties (3100–2700 B.C.E., the Early Dynastic Period) unified the country and paved the way for the brilliant cultural achievements of the four dynasties that ruled the era called the Old Kingdom. The Old Kingdom produced many of the institutions, customs, and artistic styles that became the distinguishing features of ancient Egyptian civilization.

1.2
An Egyptian Hymn to the Nile

QUICK REVIEW

Egypt and the Nile
- Egyptian civilization developed along the Nile
- Predictable annual floods aided agriculture
- The Nile tied the people of Egypt together

Upper Egypt   Narrow valley extending 650 miles from Aswan to the border of Lower Egypt.

Lower Egypt   The Nile's 100-mile deep, triangularly shaped delta.

The Book of the Dead. The Egyptians believed in the possibility of life after death through the god Osiris. Aspects of each person's life had to be tested by forty-two assessor-gods before the person could be presented to Osiris. In the scene from a papyrus manuscript of the *Book of the Dead*, the deceased and his wife (on the left) watch the scales of justice weighing his heart (on the left side of the scales) against the feather of truth. The jackal-headed god Anubis also watches the scales, and the ibis-headed god Thoth keeps the record.

British Museum, London, UK/The Bridgeman Art Library International Ltd.

QUICK REVIEW

The Pyramids

- Reveal the power and resources of Old Kingdom pharaohs
- Built as tombs for pharaohs
- Pyramids were originally filled with offerings to support pharaohs in the afterlife

pharaoh The god-kings of ancient Egypt.

nomes Egyptian districts ruled by regional governors who were called nomarchs.

The land and people of Egypt were the property of an absolute ruler who came to be called a **pharaoh** (i.e., master of "the great house"). The pharaoh was one of the gods on whom the safety and prosperity of Egypt depended. By building temples and honoring fellow gods with rituals and offerings the pharaoh maintained *maat*, the equilibrium of the universe. Pharaoh's word was law, and an elaborate bureaucracy of officials helped him (or her—a few women held the office) administer Egypt. Pharaoh's central government controlled granaries, land surveys, tax collections, and disbursements from the royal treasury. Egypt also had *nomarchs*, regional governors whose districts were called **nomes**. They handled important local issues such as water management.

The power and resources of the Old Kingdom pharaohs are clearly revealed by their most imposing and famous monuments, the pyramids. Djoser, a pharaoh of the Third Dynasty, inaugurated the construction of pyramids in Egypt. The architect who designed his tomb erected the world's first major masonry building— a solid six-layered "stepped" pyramid surrounded by an elaborate funeral complex. Snefru, founder of the Fourth Dynasty, built the first smooth-sided pyramid, and his son Khufu (Cheops, in Greek sources) commissioned the largest pyramid ever constructed. It rose on the desert plateau of Giza opposite the Old Kingdom's capital, Memphis, a city on the border between Upper and Lower Egypt. Khufu's appropriately named "Great Pyramid" covers 13.1 acres, originally soared to a height of 481 feet, and is composed of approximately 2.3 million blocks of stone (averaging 2.5 tons each). It is as remarkable for its precise engineering as its size. Khufu's successors built additional pyramids at Giza, and the pharaoh Khafre added the famous Sphinx, a huge version of the enigmatic half-lion, half-human creature that was a common subject for Egyptian sculptors. The pyramids and their temples were originally provided with lavish offerings to support the pharaoh in the afterlife, but they were stripped of their contents by ancient grave robbers. The only major artifacts the thieves missed were two full-sized wooden boats buried near the Giza pyramids. These were intended to convey the pharaoh on his journeys in the next world.

The First Intermediate Period and the Middle Kingdom (2200–1630 B.C.E.)
The Old Kingdom came apart when mounting political and economic difficulties gave the nomarchs and other royal officials opportunities to break free from the pharaoh's control. Central government faded, and confusion reigned throughout the First Intermediate Period (2200–2025 B.C.E.). Finally, Amunemhet I, a *vizier* (i.e., chief minister) to a dynasty of petty pharaohs seated in the Upper-Egyptian city of Thebes, reunited Egypt and inaugurated the era of the Middle Kingdom.

The First Intermediate Period may have done some lasting damage to the traditions that supported the pharaoh's authority, for the rulers of the Middle Kingdom were regarded as less remote and godlike than their predecessors. The nomarchs who served them had more autonomy, and to secure an uncontested succession to the throne pharaohs found it wise to establish their heirs as co-regents during their lifetimes. The literature of the era stressed the pharaoh's role as the shepherd of his people and the defender of the weak.

Egypt began to emerge from its isolation during the Middle Kingdom and to pay more attention to foreign affairs. The pharaohs pushed up the Nile into Nubia and built fortresses to guard the trade routes that brought African goods to Egypt. Syria and Palestine became areas of concern, and the government fortified the delta's borders to staunch the flow of migrants from the east.

The Second Intermediate Period and the New Kingdom (1630–1075 B.C.E.)   For unknown reasons the crown passed rapidly from hand to hand during the thirteenth dynasty, and the weaker pharaohs were challenged by rivals from the western delta. In the eastern delta, Asiatic migration continued until the region passed into the hands of people the Egyptians called Hyksos (i.e., "foreign chiefs"). Archaeological remains suggest these newcomers were probably Amorites. They occupied the delta and dominated the valley for about a century until Ahmose, first king of the eighteenth dynasty, drove them out and founded the New Kingdom.

The pharaohs of the New Kingdom had imperialistic aspirations. Their armies reached the Euphrates in the east and drove deep into Africa—extending Egyptian influence 1,300 miles south from Memphis. The Egyptian empire provided the pharaohs with unprecedented wealth and subjected them to numerous foreign influences. The result was the establishment in Thebes of a cosmopolitan court of extraordinary splendor and sophistication and the launching of a spate of monumental building projects throughout Egypt. The pharaohs of this era, hoping perhaps to safeguard the vast treasures they accumulated for the afterlife, ceased to erect pyramids that advertised the sites of their

Major Periods in Mesopotamian and Egyptian History

Mesopotamia

ca. 3500 B.C.E.	Cities appear
ca. 2800–2370 B.C.E.	First Dynasties
2370–2205 B.C.E.	Sargon's empire
2125–2027 B.C.E.	III Dynasty of Ur
1792–1750 B.C.E.	Reign of Hammurabi
ca. 1600 B.C.E.	Fall of Amoritic Babylon

Egypt

ca. 3100–2700 B.C.E.	Early Dynastic Period (dynasties I–II)
ca. 2700–2200 B.C.E.	The Old Kingdom (dynasties III–VI)
2200–2025 B.C.E.	I Intermediate Period (dynasties VII–XI)
2025–1630 B.C.E.	The Middle Kingdom (dynasties XII–XIII)
1630–1550 B.C.E.	II Intermediate Period (dynasties XIV–XVII)
1550–1075 B.C.E.	The New Kingdom (dynasties XVIII–XX)

graves and chose to be buried in cavelike tombs cut into the walls of the desolate "Valley of the Kings" near Thebes. Despite elaborate precautions, however, they failed to secure their final resting places. Only one pharaonic tomb (that of a young eighteenth dynasty ruler named Tutankhamun) escaped looting by ancient grave robbers. He was a fairly minor king who died prematurely and was buried in haste. His grave was doubtless less lavishly equipped than those of the more prominent pharaohs, but its treasures are truly awe inspiring.

Tutankhamun was succeeded by a line of solider-pharaohs who erected some of Egypt's most imposing monuments. They fought the Hittites, a powerful empire based in Asia Minor, for control of Syria and Palestine and fended off attacks on the delta from the Libyans and from the Sea Peoples who sailed the Mediterranean. An increasingly volatile international situation slowly eroded their position until, by 1075, Egypt was no longer an imperial power. Weakened by internal divisions, it succumbed to a succession of foreign conquerors—Assyrian, Persian, Greek, and ultimately Roman.

Language and Literature   The Egyptians developed a writing system about 3000 B.C.E. They may have been inspired by Mesopotamia's example, but they invented their own techniques. The ancient Greeks called formal Egyptian writing **hieroglyphs** (i.e., "sacred carving"), for it was used to engrave holy texts on monuments. A cursive script that could be written much more rapidly and easily was used for ordinary everyday purposes. Egyptians wrote with pen and ink on sheets of paperlike material made from papyrus reeds. Texts were usually written on horizontal lines and read from right to left, but hieroglyphs were sometimes inscribed in horizontal columns. The hieroglyphic system was difficult to master, for its symbols could stand for syllables, words, or categories of speech.

The Egyptians produced a large and varied body of literature encompassing religious myths, entertaining stories, collections of proverbs, how-to advice for aspiring bureaucrats, love poems, personal letters, medical texts, astronomical observations, calendars, autobiographies, judicial records, and administrative documents. Curiously missing are any traces of epic poetry or of dramas, although the latter, at least, are known to have been performed as parts of cult rituals.

Religion: Gods, Temples, and the Afterlife   The Egyptians were apparently untroubled by a lack of consistency in their religious beliefs. They had three different myths to explain the origin of the world, and each featured a different creator-god. Some gods had overlapping functions, and some were known by a variety of names. Gods were represented in both human and animal form and as hybrids—human bodies with animal heads. As in Mesopotamia, gods were believed literally to inhabit their temples, some of which were of staggering size. The sacred complex at Karnak (near Thebes) was under construction for over 2,000 years. The gods were served by armies of priests and priestesses, who were sustained by lavish temple endowments. Ordinary people did not worship in the great temples but on occasions when the images of the gods were brought out from their sanctuaries and exposed to public view.

The fact that Egypt's religion was extremely ancient and deeply rooted in the traditions of its people did not deter a pharaoh of the eighteenth dynasty from attempting to overhaul it. Amunhotep IV swept aside all the gods and declared exclusive allegiance to the Aten, a god symbolized by the disk of the sun. The old temples were closed, and the pharaoh and his queen, Nefertiti, were proclaimed sole mediators between the new god and the Egyptian people. To honor the Aten, Amunhotep changed his name to Akhenaten (i.e., "the effective spirit of the Aten")

hieroglyphs   ("sacred carving") Greek name for Egyptian writing. The writing was often used to engrave holy texts on monuments.

and built a new capital called Akhetaten (i.e., "the horizon of the Aten") near Amarna north of Thebes. Akhenaten's religious reforms failed to take hold, and after his death the court returned to Thebes. Akhetaten was dismantled. The Aten cult was suppressed, and the worship of the former Theban sun-god, Amun, and Egypt's other deities was restored. The Aten was the only Egyptian god to be represented by an abstract symbol, not a human or animal image, and the art of the Amarna period also departed from the conventions of traditional Egyptian painting and sculpture. It was characterized by a unique expressionistic distortion of forms.

Most Egyptians worshiped at small local shrines, and many householders had private collections of sacred objects. Egyptians placed great trust in magic, oracles, and amulets to ward off evil and misfortune. Originally they assumed that only the pharaoh survived death to join the immortal gods, but gradually the belief spread that everyone who made the necessary preparations could enjoy this privilege. The spells needed to pass the various tests and fend off the

HISTORY'S VOICES

A HYMN OF ZOROASTER ABOUT THE TWO SPIRITS OF GOOD AND EVIL

Zoroaster's reform made Ahura Mazda (the "Wise Lord") the supreme deity in the Iranian pantheon. The hymns, or Gathas, depict him as the greatest of the ahuras, the divinities associated with the good. This faith views the world through a moral dualism of good and evil, in which one has the freedom to choose the Truth or the Lie. The "Very Holy [Spirit]" chose Truth ("Righteousness"), and the "Evil [Spirit]" (Angra Mainyu, or Ahriman), chose the evil of "the Lie." Humans similarly can choose good or evil.

WHAT LESSON or values does this passage teach?

(1) Then shall I speak, now give ear and hearken, both you who seek from near and you from far . . . (2) Then shall I speak of the two primal Spirits of existence, of whom the Very Holy thus spoke to the Evil One: "Neither our thoughts nor teachings nor wills, neither our choices nor words nor acts, not our inner selves nor our souls agree." (3) Then shall I speak of the foremost [doctrine] of this existence, which Mazda the Lord. He with knowledge, declared to me. Those of you who do not act upon this manthra, even as I shall think and speak it, for them there shall be woe at the end of life. (4) Then shall I speak of the best things of this existence. I know Mazda who created it in accord with truth to be the Father of active Good Purpose. And his daughter is Devotion of good action. The all-seeing Lord is not to be deceived. (5) Then shall I speak of what the Most Holy One told me, the word to be listened to as best for men. Those who shall give for me hearkening and heed to Him, shall attain wholeness and immortality. Mazda is Lord through acts of the Good Spirit . . . (8) Him shall I seek to turn to us by praises of reverence, for truly I have now seen with my eyes [the House] of Good Purpose, and of good act and deed, having known through Truth Him who is Lord Mazda. Then let us lay up supplications to Him in the House of Song. (9) Him shall I seek to requite for us with good purpose, Him who left to our will [the choice between] holy and unholy. May Lord Mazda by His power make us active for prospering our cattle and men, through the fair affinity of good purpose with truth. (10) Him shall I seek to glorify for us with sacrifices of devotion, Him who is known in the soul as Lord Mazda; for He has promised by His truth and good purpose that there shall be wholeness and immortality within His kingdom (khshathra), strength and perpetuity within His house.

From Mary Boyce, ed. and trans., *Textual Sources for the Study of Zoroastrianism* (Manchester, U.K.: Manchester University Press, 1984), p. 36.

monsters of the underworld were contained in the *Book of the Dead*, a text often inscribed on tombs. The dead were assumed to want and need the same things as the living, and persons who could afford to do so loaded their tombs with provisions and equipment for life after death. It was the duty of their descendants to make periodic offerings at their tombs to replenish their supplies.

Women in Egyptian Society The Egyptian woman's primary duty was the management of a household. She was not ordinarily admitted to scribal schools, artisan apprenticeships, or government offices, but she could own and manage property, sue for divorce, and claim the same legal protections as a man. Royal women were, of course, an exception. They often wielded considerable influence, and a few, such as Thutmosis I's daughter Hatshepsut, ruled Egypt either as regents for dependent males or in their own names. Women were common subjects for Egypt's artists, who depicted them making and receiving offerings and enjoying the pleasures of dining and hunting with their husbands.

Slaves Slaves were not common in Egypt until the foreign campaigns of the pharaohs of the Middle Kingdom began to produce Nubian and Asian prisoners of war. The imperialistic ventures of the New Kingdom vastly increased the number of captives taken in battle and sometimes led to the enslavement of entire peoples.

Slaves were assigned all kinds of tasks. Some worked in the fields alongside the native peasants. Some were domestic servants. Some were trained as artisans. A few even exercised authority as policemen or soldiers. They could be freed, but manumission was rare. There were, however, no racial or other features that set them apart from the free population.

ANCIENT MIDDLE EASTERN EMPIRES

WHAT WERE the great empires of the ancient Middle East?

During the era of Egypt's New Kingdom, the Middle East witnessed the rise and fall of many states. The most significant were the empires founded by the Hittites and the Assyrians, but it should be noted, if only in passing, that a horde of other peoples—the Hurrians, Mitanni, Kassites, Canaanites, Phoenicians, Chaldaeans, and Israelites—also jockeyed for position. (See Map 1–2.)

THE HITTITES

The Hittites, who migrated into the Middle East from Europe in the sixteenth century B.C.E., were Indo-Europeans. That is, they spoke a language that belongs to the same family as Greek, Latin, and Indian Sanskrit. This distinguished them from the older residents of the Middle East, most of whom spoke Semitic languages. The Hittites built a strong centralized kingdom with its seat at Hattusas, a site near modern Ankara. Between 1400 and 1200 B.C.E., the Hittites extended their territory until they became the dominant power in the Middle East. They destroyed their neighbors, the Mitannians, and contested control of Syria and Palestine with Egypt. An indecisive battle in 1285 B.C.E. culminated in a truce between these two superpowers. They enjoyed fairly amicable relations until about 1200 B.C.E., when they were both threatened by invaders whom the Egyptians called the Sea Peoples. Egypt retreated to the safety of its valley, but the Hittite kingdom collapsed.

The Hittites assimilated many aspects of Mesopotamian culture and adapted cuneiform to write their language. Their political institutions, however, were their own. Hittite kings did not claim to be divine or even to be agents of the gods. The king was advised by a council of nobles who limited his power, and an

Statue of Hatshepsut

"Statue of Hatshepsut". Red Granite. Dynasty 18, 1490-1480 B.C. (Egyptian). The Metropolitan Museum of Art, Rogers Fund and Edward S. Harkness Gift, 1929. (29.3.1)

MAP EXPLORATION

Interactive map: To explore this map further, go to **http://www.prenhall.com/kagan3/map1.2**

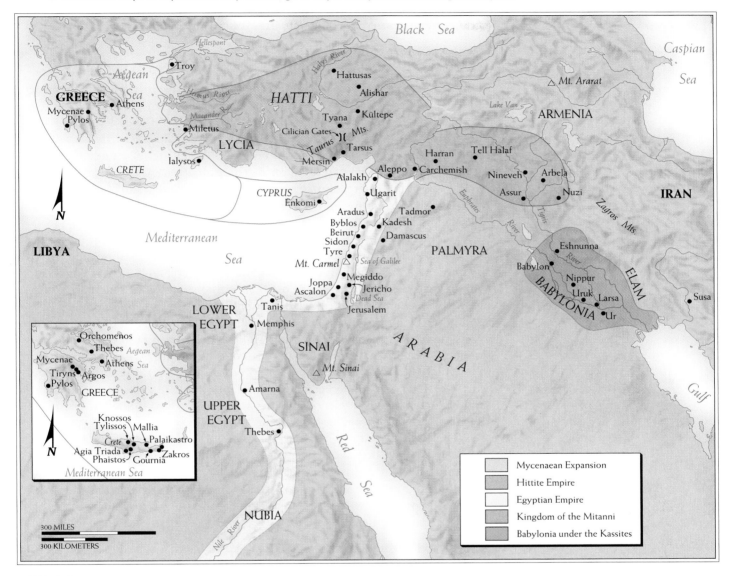

MAP 1–2

The Middle East and Greece CA. 1400 B.C.E.   About 1400 B.C.E., the Middle East was divided among four empires. Egypt extended south to Nubia and north through Palestine and Phoenicia. The Kassites ruled in Mesopotamia, the Hittites in Asia Minor, and the Mitanni in Assyrian lands. In the Aegean, the Mycenaean kingdoms were at their height.

BASED ON the locations of the various states that had risen by the fifteenth century B.C.E., what were these new states dependent on, geographically, to succeed?

heir's succession to the throne required ratification by the army. One thing that may have contributed to Hittite success was the invention in Asia Minor (prior to the rise of the Hittite kingdom) of techniques for smelting iron and forging it into weapons. Iron was more plentiful and, therefore, more economical than bronze, and its spreading use marked the beginning, about 1100 B.C.E., of a new era: the Iron Age. Clay tablets that survive from the Hittite archives have helped historians reconstruct the history of the Middle East, but they also contain the earliest information about the Greeks, the Hittites' western neighbors who were destined to play a major role in shaping Western civilization.

THE ASSYRIANS

The Assyrian homeland centered on Assur, a city on the Tigris River in northern Mesopotamia. The Assyrians had ancient trading ties with Babylonia, and they spoke a Semitic language related to Babylonian. During the fourteenth century B.C.E., Assyria expanded to the north and west. However, the general confusion that descended on the Middle East when Sumer collapsed at the end of the second millennium loosed an invasion by the Arameans that ended the first Assyrian attempt at building an empire. The Arameans spread throughout the Middle East from their point of origin in northern Syria, and their language, Aramaic, was spoken by some of the people who influenced the development of Judaism and Christianity.

About 1000 B.C.E., the Assyrians began to expand again, and by 665 B.C.E., they controlled Mesopotamia, southern Asia Minor, Syria, Palestine, and Egypt. They were famous for their innovative military technology and their willingness to commit atrocities to frighten their opponents into submission. The Assyrian empire was divided into provinces headed by military governors, and its subjects were kept in line by occupying armies. Pockets of potential resistance to Assyrian rule were sometimes broken up by evicting whole peoples from their homelands and resettling them in small groups scattered about the empire. Agricultural colonies were founded to bring unused land into production and provide supplies for the army. Great palaces were erected at Nineveh and Nimrud and ornamented with superb stone carvings in bas relief. They were designed to intimidate the vassal kings, who annually brought their tribute to the Assyrian capital.

The Assyrian empire may have become too large, given the communications available, to govern effectively, and squabbling among its leaders also set it up for disaster. The agents of its fall were the Medes, an Indo-European people settled in Iran, and the Babylonians (Chaldaeans). Overextended as it was, Assyria could not deal with both enemies at once, and the empire crumbled quickly. By 612 B.C.E., all the cities of the Assyrian homeland had been sacked.

THE NEO-BABYLONIANS

When the Medes failed to exploit the opportunity Assyria's fall gave them, the way was cleared for Babylon's king, Nebuchadnezzar, to build a Neo-Babylonian (or Chaldaean) empire. Babylon became the center of world trade, a city famous for its monuments and wonders. Nebuchadnezzar's empire was brilliant but unstable. Its throne passed rapidly through a number of hands, and its last heir so alienated his subjects that they failed to resist when Persia invaded Babylonia in 539 B.C.E. The city capitulated and survived to enjoy renewed prosperity within a new and more successful Persian Empire.

WHAT WERE the Persian rulers' attitudes toward the cultures they ruled?

THE PERSIAN EMPIRE

*T*he great Persian Empire arose in the region now called Iran. The ancestors of its rulers spoke a language from the Aryan branch of the family of Indo-European languages, related to Greek and Latin. The most important collections of tribes among them were the Medes and the Persians, peoples

MAP EXPLORATION

Interactive map: To explore this map further, go to **http://www.prenhall.com/kagan3/map1.3**

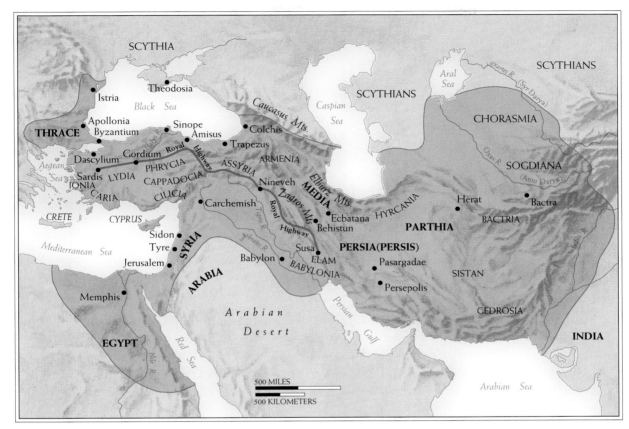

MAP 1–3

The Achaemenid Persian Empire   The empire created by Cyrus had reached its fullest extent under Darius when Persia attacked Greece in 490 B.C.E. It extended from India to the Aegean, and even into Europe, encompassing the lands formerly ruled by Egyptians, Hittites, Babylonians, and Assyrians.

so similar in language and customs that the Greeks used both names interchangeably. The Medes organized their tribes into a union and aggressively built a force that defeated the mighty Assyrian Empire in 612 B.C.E. The Persians were subordinate to the Medes until Cyrus II (called the Great) became King of the Persians (r. 559–530 B.C.E.), when the Persians began to dominate. About 550 B.C.E., Cyrus united the Medes and Persians under his own rule.

CYRUS THE GREAT

Cyrus quickly expanded his power, eventually extending it from the Aegean Sea to the Indus valley and modern Afghanistan. In the west, he decisively defeated King Croesus of Lydia in western Asia Minor, taking control of Croesus's capital city of Sardis and other Greek cities. At the same time Cyrus captured Babylon from an unpopular king, and was thus viewed as a liberator, not a conqueror. The cylinder that describes his version of events claims that the Babylonian god Marduk had "got him into his city Babylon without fighting or battle."

Unlike the harsh Babylonian and Assyrian conquerors who preceded him, Cyrus pursued a policy of toleration and restoration. He did not impose the

Darius. Persian nobles pay homage to King Darius in this relief from the treasury at the Persian capital of Persepolis. Darius is seated on the throne: his son and successor Xerxes stands behind him. Darius and Xerxes are carved in larger scale to indicate their royal status.

Courtesy of the Oriental Institute of the University of Chicago

Persian religion but claimed to rule by the favor of the Babylonian god. Instead of deporting defeated peoples and destroying cities, he allowed exiles to return and rebuilt cities. For example, upon his conquest of the Babylonian Empire, which included Palestine, Cyrus permitted the Hebrews, taken into captivity by King Nebuchadnezzar in 586 B.C.E., to return to their native land of Judah. Persian rule, however, was not entirely gentle; it demanded tribute and military service from its subjects, sometimes with brutal enforcement.

DARIUS THE GREAT

Cyrus's son Cambyses succeeded to the throne in 529 B.C.E. Cambyses conquered Egypt, establishing it as a satrapy (province) that extended to Lybia in the west and Ethiopia in the south. Civil war roiled much of the Persian Empire upon his death in 522 B.C.E. The following year Darius emerged as the new emperor. Found on a great rock hundreds of feet in the air near the mountains of Behistun, an inscription boasts of Darius's victories and the greatness of his rule. Discovered almost two thousand years later, it was carved in three languages, Babylonian, Old Persian, and Elamite, all in cuneiform script, thereby helping scholars to decipher all three languages. Darius's long and prosperous reign lasted until 486 B.C.E. and brought the Persian Empire to its greatest extent, with conquests in northern India, Scythian lands around the Black Sea, and Thrace and Macedonia on the fringes of the Greek mainland. In 499 B.C.E., the Ionian Greeks of western Asia Minor rebelled, launching wars between Greeks and Persians that would last for two decades.

GOVERNMENT AND ADMINISTRATION

Ahura Mazda The chief deity of Zoroastrianism, the native religion of Persia. Ahura Mazda is the creator of the world, the source of light, and the embodiment of good.

The Persian Empire was a hereditary monarchy that claimed divine sanction from the god **Ahura Mazda**. The ruler, known as *Shahanshah*, "king of kings," in theory owned all the land and peoples in the empire as absolute monarch, and demanded tribute and service for the use of his property. In practice he depended on the advice and administrative service of aristocratic courtiers, ministers, and satraps (provincial governors), and was expected to rule justly, as Ahura Mazda's chosen representative. Still, the king ruled as a semidivine autocrat with the power of life and death over his subjects. The Greeks would see him as the model of a despot or tyrant who regarded his people as slaves.

The empire was divided into twenty-nine satrapies, ruled by satraps with considerable autonomy over civil and military affairs. The king exercised a degree of control through appointed provincial secretaries and military commanders, as well as inspectors who, as the "eyes and ears of the king," traveled throughout the empire. A system of excellent royal roads made these travels swifter and easier, as did a royal postal system that was a kind of "pony express" with men mounted on fast horses at stations along the way. The royal postal service traveled the 1500 miles from Sardis in Lydia to the Persian capital at Susa in less than two weeks; normally such a trip took three months. The Persians adopted Aramaic, the most common language of Middle Eastern commerce, as the imperial tongue, thereby simplifying civil and military administration.

Medes and Persians made up the core of the army and supplied the empire with its officers and imperial administrators. When needed, the army drafted large numbers of subject armies. A large Persian army, such as the one that invaded Greece in 480 B.C.E., included hundreds of thousands of non-Iranian soldiers organized by ethnic group, each dressed in its own uniforms, taking orders from Iranian officers.

RELIGION

Persia's religion was different from that of its neighbors and subjects. It derived from the Indo-European traditions of the Vedic religion that Aryan peoples brought into India about 1500 B.C.E. Its practice included animal sacrifices and a reverence for fire and, although polytheistic, unusually emphasized its chief god Ahura Mazda, the "Wise Lord."

Zarathustra, a Mede whom the Greeks called Zoroaster, changed the traditional Aryan worship sometime between 1000 B.C.E. and 600 B.C.E. This religious prophet and teacher made Ahura Mazda the only god, dismissing the others as demons not to be worshipped but fought. Polytheism and sacrifices were forbidden, and the old sacrificial fire was converted into a symbol of goodness and light. Zarathustra portrayed life as an unending struggle between two great forces, Ahura Mazda, the creator and only god, representing goodness and light, and Ahriman, a demon, representing darkness and evil. The good would be rewarded with glory, while the evil would be punished with suffering. (See "History's Voices: A Hymn of Zoroaster about the Two Spirits of Good and Evil.") By the middle of the sixth century B.C.E., Zoroastrianism had become the chief religion of the Persians. On the great inscribed monument at Behistun, Darius the Great praised the god of Zarathustra and his teachings: "On this account Ahura Mazda brought me help . . . because I was not wicked, nor was I a liar, nor was I a tyrant, neither I nor any of my line. I have ruled according to righteousness."

ART AND CULTURE

The Persians learned from and adapted much from the peoples they conquered. They adapted the **Aramaic** alphabet of the Semites to create a Persian alphabet and used the cuneiform symbols of Babylon to write the Old Persian language they spoke. They borrowed their calendar from Egypt. Persian art

Aramaic   Semitic language spoken widely throughout the Middle East in antiquity.

and architecture also benefited from various talents and styles. Darius, for example, proudly described the varied sources of the construction of his palace at Susa:

> The cedar timber—a mountain by name Lebanon—from there it was brought . . . the yaka-timber was brought from Gandara and from Carmania. The gold was brought from Sardis and from Bactria . . . the precious stone lapis-lazuli and carnelian . . . was brought from Sogdiana. The . . . turquoise from Chorasmia. . . . The silver and ebony . . . from Egypt . . . the ornamentation from Ionia . . . the ivory . . . from Ethiopia and from Sind and from Arachosia. . . . The stone-cutters who wrought the stone, those were Ionians and Sardians. The goldsmiths . . . were Modes and Egyptians. The men who wrought the wood, those were Sardians and Egyptians. The men who wrought the baked brick, those were Babylonians. The men who adorned the wall, those were Medes and Egyptians.[1]

The Royal Palace at Persepolis, built by Darius and his successor Xerxes (r. 485–465 B.C.E.), is probably the most magnificent of Persian architectural remains. On a high foundation supported on all sides by a stone wall 20 or 30 feet high, the complex contained a Hall of a Hundred Columns where the kings carried out their official duties. The columns, grand stairway with carvings, and gateway with winged bulls reveal the grandeur of the ancient Persian Empire.

PALESTINE

HOW WAS Hebrew monotheism different from Mesopotamian and Egyptian polytheism?

*M*any large states flourished in the ancient Middle East, but none had as much influence on Western civilization as a tiny group of people who settled in Palestine about 1200 B.C.E. Three of the world's great religions (Judaism, Christianity, and Islam) trace their origins (at least in part) to this region and to the history of its inhabitants, the Israelites.

THE CANAANITES AND THE PHOENICIANS

Palestine's early settlers spoke Canaanite (a Semitic language), lived in walled cities, and earned their livings as farmers and seafarers. Their most influential cultural achievement was a highly simplified writing system. Instead of the hundreds of characters that were needed to write the cuneiform and hieroglyphic scripts, it used an alphabet of only twenty to thirty symbols. This made learning to read and write much easier, which promoted the spread of literacy.

The Israelite invaders who settled in Palestine about 1200 B.C.E. either forced the Canaanites of the interior region out or assimilated them. However, the Canaanites and Syrians who inhabited the northern coast hung on to their territory. They became the **Phoenicians**, a seafaring people who scattered trading colonies from one end of the Mediterranean to the other. The most famous of their colonial outposts was the city of Carthage (near modern Tunis in North Africa). Cultural influences accompanied the goods that flowed through the Phoenician trade network. The Phoenicians passed the alphabet to the Greeks, who handed it on to us.

Phoenicians   Seafaring people (Canaanites and Syrians) who scattered trading colonies from one end of the Mediterranean to the other.

[1] T. Cuyler Young, Jr., "Iran, ancient," *Encyclopedia Britannica Online.*

Exile of the Israelites. In 722 B.C.E. the northern part of Jewish Palestine, the kingdom of Israel, was conquered by the Assyrians. Its people were driven from their homeland and exiled all over the vast Assyrian Empire. This wall carving in low relief comes from the palace of the Assyrian king Sennacherib at Nineveh. It shows the Jews with their cattle and baggage going into exile.

Relief, Israel, 10th-6th Century: Judean exiles carrying provisions. Detail of the Assyrian conquest of the Jewish fortified town of Lachish (battle 701 BC). Part of a relief from the palace of Sennacherib at Niniveh, Mesopotamia (Iraq). British Museum

THE ISRAELITES

Our knowledge of the Israelites derives primarily from their chief literary monument, the Bible. The Bible contains some historical narratives (as well as collections of laws, ritual instructions, wisdom, literature, poetry, and prophecy), but it was not meant to be read simply as objective history. Scholars have developed many strategies for extracting historical data from it, but their findings are tentative.

According to tradition, the Israelites or Hebrews (i.e., "wanderers") were the descendants of Abraham, a Semitic nomad whose family came from the region of Ur. He and his successors (the patriarchs) led their tribe into Palestine in the early second millennium and eventually on to Egypt. They may have entered Egypt during the period when the Hyksos, fellow Semites, ruled the delta. In the thirteenth century B.C.E., a man named Moses led them out of Egypt. They resumed wandering in the Sinai desert, but eventually breached the frontiers of Canaan and settled in Palestine's mountainous interior. Their scattered tribes made little progress until they united under the leadership of a king named David. He won control of most of Canaan and founded the city of Jerusalem. The Hebrew monarchy reached its peak in the tenth century B.C.E., during the reign of his son and heir Solomon. Following Solomon's death, the kingdom split in two. The northern section, Israel, was the larger and more advanced, but the southern portion, Judah, retained control over Jerusalem, the site of the Israelites' first temple.

In 722 B.C.E., Assyria conquered Israel, dispersed its people, and Israel's **ten lost tribes** disappeared from history. Judah survived as an independent kingdom until 586 B.C.E., when it was conquered by the Neo-Babylonian ruler Nebuchadnezzar II. He destroyed Jerusalem and its temple and resettled many of the people of Judah (i.e., Jews) in foreign lands. This period, known as "the Exile" or "Babylonian Captivity," did not last long. Babylon fell to Persia in

ten lost tribes   Israelites who were scattered and lost to history when the northern kingdom of Israel fell to the Assyrians in 722 B.C.E.

539 B.C.E., and the new emperor permitted some Jews to return to rebuild Jerusalem and its temple. In 70 C.E., the Romans once again destroyed Jerusalem and scattered its people, but in 1948 C.E., Jewish leaders regained control of Jerusalem and reestablished the state of Israel.

THE JEWISH RELIGION

The tiny nation of Israel would be of little interest to historians were it not for its religious significance. The ancient Jews believed they had been chosen by God for a unique religious mission. Their ancestor Abraham had made a covenant (i.e., a contract) with God. It committed God to preserving them, and them to the task of revealing God by remaining exclusively loyal to him and living according to his law. Their history was to be sacred history, a revelation of God's will for humankind.

Hebrew **monotheism**—faith in a single God, an all-powerful creator who loves humankind but demands righteous conduct—may be as old as Moses and certainly dates back to the preaching of the great biblical prophets of the eighth century B.C.E. The Jews did not imagine God to be a force of nature or a superhuman being, but a reality so transcendent it cannot be pictured in any way. Transcendence did not, however, imply distance from God, for the Jews believed God was intimately involved in their history. Like the teachings of Zarathustra (Zoroaster) in Iran, they assumed there was a link between ethics and religion. God was not content with sacrifices and worship; God judged people according to how they treated one another. The Hebrew prophets, who spoke for God, assured their followers that God dealt mercifully with repentant sinners, and the prophets explained the misfortunes that befell the Jews as just punishments for their failure to honor the terms of Abraham's covenant. Centuries of oppression ultimately convinced the Jews that God would have to intervene in history on their behalf if the promises to Abraham were to be fulfilled. They began to look for a special leader, a messiah (i.e., "annointed one"), whom God would empower to lead them to complete their mission in history. Christianity diverges from Judaism in maintaining that Jesus of Nazareth was that messiah.

GENERAL OUTLOOK OF MIDDLE EASTERN CULTURES

*T*here were differences among the various cultures of the Middle East, but taken together they all diverge from the outlook of the Greeks, the ancient people who exerted the greatest influence on the Western tradition.

HUMANS AND NATURE

The peoples of the Middle East did not envision an absolute gulf between animate beings and inanimate objects. They believed all things are imbued with life and spirit and that the universe is an arena for a war of supernatural wills. Because nature seemed chaotic from the human perspective, it seemed to follow that the gods who governed the world must be capricious. The Babylonian creation myth claimed that the gods had created people for the sole purpose of serving them. Human life was, therefore, precarious, for the deities were interested only in themselves and paid scant attention to the wishes of their human servants. Even disasters, like wars, which might be explained as the products of human decisions, were assumed to be acts of the gods.

The helplessness of humankind in the face of irrational divine powers is the point of the story of a great primeval flood that is found in various forms in

WHAT SOCIAL and political contrasts existed between ancient Middle Eastern and Greek civilizations?

monotheism Having faith in a single God.

Babylonian, Egyptian, and Hebrew sources. In the Egyptian tale, the god Re, who created human beings, decides they are plotting against him, and Re sends the vicious goddess Sekhmet to destroy them. Humanity is saved only when Re has a last-minute, unexplained change of heart. In the Babylonian version of the story, it is the annoying noise made by an increasing human population that persuades the gods to destroy humanity. The species is saved when one man wins the favor of the god Enki, who helps him and his wife survive. In a world governed by such quixotic principles, human beings could not hope to understand and control events. At best, they might try to pit one mysterious force against another by means of magical spells.

HUMANS AND THE GODS, LAW, AND JUSTICE

Because the gods could destroy humankind—and might do so at any time for no apparent reason—people tried to win the gods' favor by offering prayer and sacrifice. There was, however, no guarantee of success, for gods were capricious beings who were not bound by reason or conscience.

In arenas that were more or less under human control, people attempted to establish more orderly and consistent principles to guide their lives. In the earliest civilized societies, rulers decreed laws to govern human relations, but effective laws are based on something more than a lawgiver's power to coerce obedience. The challenge for governments was to find justifications that would impart authority to laws. The Egyptians simply assumed that because the king was a god, he had the right to establish whatever rules seemed best to him at the moment. The Mesopotamians believed the gods commissioned their kings and gave them divine authority to keep order in the human herd. The Hebrews had a more subtle understanding of law. Their god was capable of destructive rages, but he was open to rational discussion and imposed certain moral standards on himself. In the biblical version of the flood story, God is wrathful but not arbitrary. His creatures deserve destruction as punishment for their sins. When God decides to save Noah, he does so because Noah is a good man who merits God's protection. The Hebrews believed God wanted human beings to live in just relationships with one another and that God was the leading advocate for human justice.

1.6
Laws of the
Hebrews

TOWARD THE GREEKS AND WESTERN THOUGHT

*M*any, if not most, Greeks in the ancient world must have thought about life in much the same way as their neighbors in the Middle East. Their gods resembled the arbitrary Mesopotamian deities; they trusted in magic and incantations to manage life's uncertainties; and they believed laws were to be obeyed simply because a power enforced them. The surprising thing is that some Greeks came to think differently about these things, and their strikingly original ideas charted a new path for the West.

In the sixth century B.C.E., thinkers who lived on the Aegean coast of Asia Minor began an intellectual revolution. Thales, the first Greek philosopher, urged his followers to try to explain natural events by referring them to other natural events and not to unknowable supernatural causes. His search for naturalistic explanations for phenomena launched Western science.

Rationalism of this kind characterized the approach major Greek thinkers took to exploring all kinds of issues. Xenophanes of Colophon, Thales's contemporary, pointed out that people had no grounds for imagining gods in human form. He argued that if oxen could draw pictures, they would sketch gods who looked like oxen. Comments like this might promote skepticism, but they also produced valuable insights. In the fifth century B.C.E., Thucydides of Athens wrote a history that made no reference to the gods and explained events as the result of human decisions and chance. Similarly, Hippocrates of Cos founded a school of medicine that diagnosed and treated disease without invoking the supernatural. The same lack of interest in divine causality characterized Greek attitudes toward law and justice.

IMAGE KEY

for pages 4–5

a. Cyprus papyrus

b. An administrative document in Sumerian cuneiform

c. King Tut's Throne shows Tutankhamen and Queen

d. Tablet covered with cuneiform writing

e. An Akkadian administrative document in cuneiform

f. "Seated Scribe" Dynasty 5, ca. 2510–2460 B.C.E. "Seated Scribe" from Saqqara, Egypt. 5th Dynasty, c. 2510-2460 B.C.E. Painted limestone, height 21' (53 cm). Musee du Louvre, Paris. Bridgeman-Giraudon/Art Resource, NY

g. Prehistorical grotto with many animal paintings, Vallon-pont-D'Arc, Ardeche, France

h. Detail. Relief: Eagle-headed winged being pollinating the sacred tree. From the Palace of Ashurnasirpal II (885–860 B.C.E.), King of Assyria The Metropolitan Museum of Art, Gift of John D. Rockefeller, Jr., 1932. (32.143.3) Photograph ©1983 The Metropolitan Museum of Art

i. Belly handled amphora, Kerameikos

j. Neolithic sculpture

k. The Royal Standard of Ur, a mosaic that dates from about 2750 B.C.E. British Museum, London, UK/Bridgeman Art Library

SUMMARY

Early Humans and Their Culture During the Paleolithic period, humans lived by hunting, fishing, and gathering food. They used tools, fire, and language; they believed in the supernatural. Around 10,000 B.C.E., humans started domesticating animals and plants for food. This Neolithic Revolution, which took place at different times in different parts of the world, was based on different crops in different environments. Civilization emerged, first in Mesopotamia, approximately during the Bronze Age, 3100 to 1200 B.C.E.

Early Civilizations to about 1000 B.C.E. Around 3000 B.C.E., civilizations along the Tigris and Euphrates Rivers in Mesopotamia, and the Nile River in Egypt, started to produce written records. Civilization in southern Mesopotamia was founded by Sumerians. Semitic Akkadians from northern Babylonia established the first empire in history; Sumerians returned to power in the Third Dynasty of Ur. Egypt's pharaohs united lands along the Nile. Hieroglyphs and tombs have left us an extensive record of life in ancient Egypt.

Ancient Middle Eastern Empires Between about 1400 B.C.E. and 500 B.C.E., new peoples and empires emerged in the Middle East. The Kassites and Mitannians were warrior peoples who ruled over the inhabitants of Babylonia and northern Syria/Mesopotamia, respectively. The Hittites based an empire in what is now Turkey. The Assyrian military supported a large Middle Eastern empire that lasted for almost half a millennium. Nebuchadnezzar overthrew the Assyrians and established a short-lived Neo-Babylonian dynasty.

The Persian Empire In the late sixth and early fifth centuries B.C.E., the Persian Empire reached the height of its power and geographical expansion under Cyrus the Great and Darius the Great. By assimilating cultures and peoples, the empire successfully combined a measure of autonomy among its twenty-nine satrapies (provinces) with a centralized authority based on the king's rule as a semidivine autocrat. Tolerance of other religions, use of the common language of Aramaic and existing writing systems, and an efficient communications system contributed to the Persians' imperial power. The Persian Empire was also built on the use of non-Persian soldiers and the art, architecture, and raw materials of its conquered lands.

Palestine Judaism, Christianity, and Islam all owe many of their beliefs and practices to the Israelites who settled in Palestine before 1200 B.C.E. Israelites under Moses conquered Canaan in the thirteenth century B.C.E., and their kingdom reached its peak in the tenth century B.C.E. in the reigns of David and Solomon before splintering. Polytheistic Canaanites had lived in Syria-Palestine and through the coastal Phoenicians gave the Greeks the predecessor of the alphabet we use today.

General Outlook of Middle Eastern Cultures Most people of the ancient Mideast believed humans were inseparable from nature, and the gods were powerful and capricious. The Hebrew God reflected a different perspective on humanity's relationship with nature and with divine power. All the ancient Middle Eastern attitudes toward religion, philosophy, science, and society in general differ markedly from what we will learn about the Greeks.

Toward the Greeks and Western Thought By the sixth century B.C.E., some Greeks started thinking about the world in ways that became the hallmark of Western civilization: They began to seek naturalistic, rational explanations for material phenomena and human behavior. Philosophy and science, as we understand them, could only develop once the Greeks had discarded supernatural explanations and reliance on divine intervention as ways of understanding the world. By the fifth century B.C.E., Greek thinkers had inaugurated the study of medicine and history, and by the fourth century B.C.E., Greek law and democracy had begun to evolve into forms recognizable to us.

REVIEW QUESTIONS

1. How was life during the Paleolithic Age different from life during the Neolithic Age? What advances account for the difference? Were these advances so significant that they warrant referring to the Neolithic as a revolutionary era?

2. What differences do you see in the political and intellectual outlooks of the Egyptian and Mesopotamian civilizations? How do their religious views compare? What influence did geography have on their religious outlooks?

3. What was significant about Cyrus the Great and Darius the Great? During their reigns, how did the Persians treat the cultures and peoples of subject lands?

4. What role did religious faith play in the political history of the Jews? Why did Middle Eastern civilizations regard the concept of Hebrew monotheism as a radical idea?

5. How did Greek thinkers diverge from the intellectual traditions of the Middle East? What new kinds of questions did Greeks ask?

KEY TERMS

Ahura Mazda (p. 24)
Aramaic (p. 25)
Bronze Age (p. 8)
civilization (p. 8)
culture (p. 6)
cuneiform (p. 11)

hieroglyphs (p. 18)
Homo sapiens (p. 6)
Lower Egypt (p. 15)
monotheism (p. 28)
Neolithic (p. 7)
nomes (p. 16)

Paleolithic (p. 6)
pharaoh (p. 16)
Phoenicians (p. 26)
polytheists (p. 12)
ten lost tribes (p. 27)
Upper Egypt (p. 15)

 For additional study resources for this chapter, go to:
www.prenhall.com/kagan3/chapter1

2 The Rise of Greek Civilization

CHAPTER HIGHLIGHTS

The Bronze Age on Crete and on the Mainland to about 1150 B.C.E. The Minoan civilization of Crete (2100–1150 B.C.E.) was built around the palaces of its kings. On the mainland, the Mycenaeans reached the height of their power between 1400 and 1200 B.C.E. Scholars have suggested a number of possible explanations for the fall of the Mycenaeans.

The Greek "Middle Ages" to about 750 B.C.E. The decline of the Mycenaeans led to a period of prolonged social and cultural decline and contributed to Greek migration around the Aegean. The *Iliad* and the *Odyssey* are our best sources of information about the Greek Dark Ages.

The *Polis* Greek social and political values are exemplified in the *polis*. *Polis* society was made possible by the *hoplite* phalanx. The power of kings and, later, the aristocrats was undermined by the emergence of these farmer-citizen-soldiers.

Expansion of the Greek World For about two centuries, starting around 750 B.C.E., the Greeks colonized widely throughout the Mediterranean world and trade became an increasingly important part of the Greek economy. By the end of the sixth century B.C.E., rule by tyrants had given way to new forms of government.

The Major States The two most powerful Greek *poleis* were Sparta and Athens. In the late sixth century B.C.E., Sparta was reorganized along military lines. By the fifth century B.C.E., democracy had taken root in Athens.

Life in Archaic Greece Social class shaped everyday life for the Ancient Greeks. The Greeks were polytheistic. Lyric poetry treated topics ranging from love to politics.

The Persian Wars In 490 B.C.E., the Persian emperor Darius launched an expedition to punish the Ionians for rebelling and the Athenians for supporting the rebels, an expedition that was defeated at Marathon. A Greek coalition turned back a much larger Persian invasion force between 481 and 479 B.C.E.

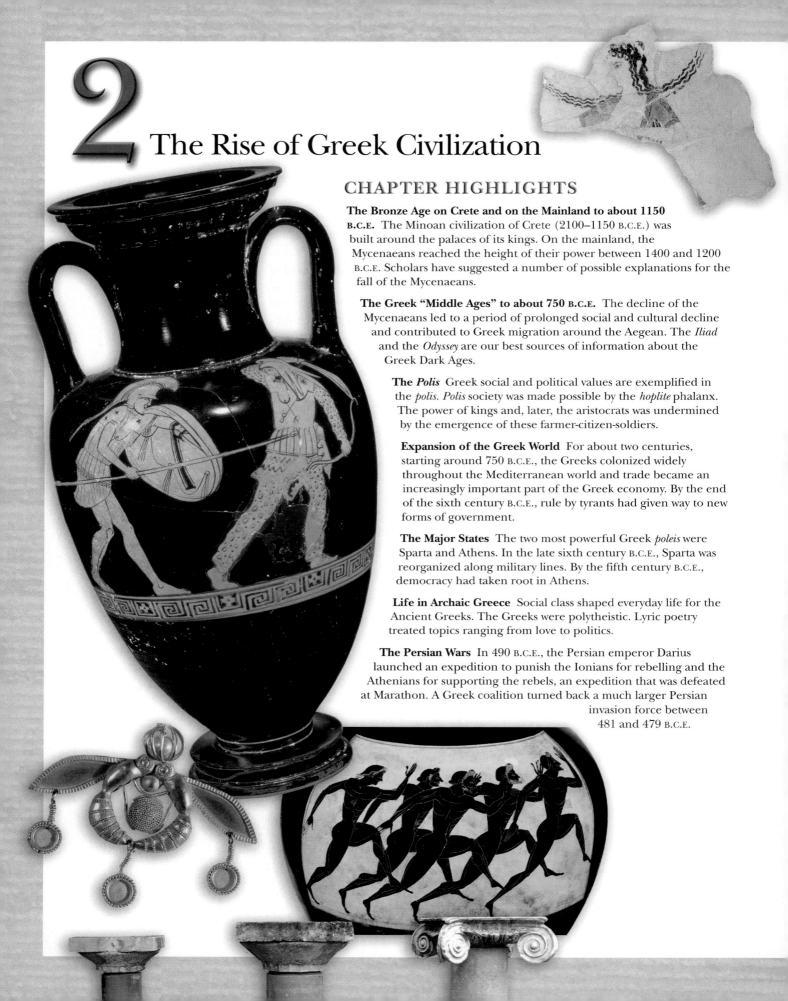

CHAPTER QUESTIONS

IN WHAT ways were the Minoan and Mycenaean civilizations different?

WHAT WERE the Greek Dark Ages?

DESCRIBE THE *polis* and how it affected society and government.

HOW and why did the Greeks colonize large parts of the Mediterranean?

HOW WERE the government and politics of Athens different from those of Sparta?

WHAT WAS the significance of the wars between the Greeks and t he Persians?

CHAPTER OUTLINE

- The Bronze Age on Crete and on the Mainland to about 1150 B.C.E.
- The Greek "Middle Ages" to about 750 B.C.E.
- The *Polis*
- Expansion of the Greek World
- The Major States
- Life in Archaic Greece
- The Persian Wars

IMAGE KEY
for pages 32–33 is on page 54.

About 2000 B.C.E., Greek-speaking peoples settled the lands surrounding the Aegean Sea and established communities that made major contributions to the Western heritage. The Greeks' location at the eastern end of the Mediterranean put them in touch, early in their history, with Mesopotamia, Egypt, Asia Minor, and Syria-Palestine. The Greeks acknowledged debts to the cultures of these regions but were conscious (and proud) of the ways in which their way of life was unique.

IN WHAT ways were the Minoan and Mycenaean civilizations different?

THE BRONZE AGE ON CRETE AND ON THE MAINLAND TO ABOUT 1150 B.C.E.

Bronze Age civilizations developed in three parts of the Aegean world: Crete, the smaller islands of the Aegean Sea, and the Greek mainland. Crete provided the bridge that linked these new cultural centers with the older civilizations of the Middle East.

THE MINOANS

Historians have named the Aegean's first civilization—the **Minoan** civilization of Crete—for Minos, a legendary king of the island. From 2100 to 1150 B.C.E. (the Middle and Late Minoan periods), Crete evolved a unique way of life. The palace sites that archaeologists have excavated at Phaestus, Haghia Triada, and especially Cnossus are its most striking remains. Cnossus was a labyrinth of rooms organized around great courtyards and rising in places to a height of four stories. The main and upper floors contained living quarters as well as workshops for making pottery and jewelry, and the cellars had elaborate storage facilities for oil and grain. There were richly decorated reception rooms and even bathrooms to which water was piped. Roofs were supported by columns of a unique design that tapered from broad capitals down to narrow bases. Murals depicting landscapes, seascapes, festivals, and sports in a unique style reflected Eastern influences.

Because Minoan palaces and settlements were wealthy, it is logical to assume they would have attracted raiders. It is surprising, therefore, that the great palace at Cnossos lacked defensive walls. Minoan command of the sea may have made the fortification of Crete unnecessary.

The Minoans wrote on clay tablets similar to those found in Mesopotamia. Many of the extant specimens were preserved accidentally when they were baked into tiles by a great fire that destroyed the palace at Cnossus. The Cnossus tablets are inscribed with three distinct kinds of writing: hieroglyphic (picture writing) and two different linear scripts (A and B). Only Linear B, which records an early form of Greek, has been deciphered.

The Linear B tablets found at Cnossus are pedestrian documents. Most are inventories, the working papers of the kind of elaborate bureaucracy that was characteristic of the ancient Middle Eastern monarchies. However, they raise an intriguing question. The Minoans were not Greeks, so why were records at Cnossus written in Greek?

THE MYCENAEANS

During the third millennium B.C.E. (the Early Helladic Period), the Greek mainland was occupied by people who, unlike the Greeks, were not Indo-Europeans. Some of the names they gave to places have survived, and these

This statuette of a female with a snake in each of her hands is thought to represent either the Minoan snake goddess herself or one of her priestesses performing a religious ritual. It was found on Crete and dates from around 1600 B.C.E.

Max Alexander/Dorling Kindersley © Archaeological Receipts Fund (TAP)

Minoan Civilization of Crete (2100–1150 B.C.E.), and the Aegean's first civilization, named for a legendary king on the island.

names do not fit the phonetic patterns of the Indo-European family of languages to which Greek belongs. Sometime after 2000 B.C.E., many of these Early Helladic sites were destroyed, abandoned, or occupied by a new people who were probably the Greeks. During the Late Helladic era (1580–1150 B.C.E.), the newcomers ruled the mainland and developed a civilization that historians have named **Mycenaean** for Mycenae, one of its cities. The Greek Linear B tablets found at Cnossus suggest that at the height of Mycenaean power (ca. 1400–1200 B.C.E.), the Mycenaeans conquered Crete. (See Map 2–1.)

The Mycenaean world contained a number of independent, powerful, and well-organized kingdoms. Their archaeological remains suggest a civilization that was influenced by, but very different from, that of Minoan Crete. The Mycenaeans appear to have been much more preoccupied with war than the Minoans were. The walls of Mycenaean palaces were decorated with scenes of battle and hunting, and Mycenaeans chose defensible sites for their cities. Military strife probably promoted the development of strong, centralized monarchies on the Greek mainland.

By 1500 B.C.E., Mycenaean kings were constructing monumental *tholos* tombs whose remains testify today to their wealth and power. Enormous blocks of dressed stones were used to construct great domed chambers that were buried beneath artificial mountains. The resources needed to finance such monuments probably came from raids and trade. Mycenaean ships visited the islands of the Aegean, the coast of Asia Minor, the cities of Syria, Egypt, and Crete, and ventured as far west as Italy and Sicily.

Chronology of the Rise of Greece

ca. 2900–1150 B.C.E.	Minoan period
ca. 1900 B.C.E.	Arrival of the Greeks on the mainland
ca. 1600–1150 B.C.E.	Mycenaean period
ca. 1250 B.C.E.	Sack of Troy
ca. 1200–1150 B.C.E.	Fall of the Mycenaean kingdoms
ca. 1150–750 B.C.E.	The Greek Dark Ages
ca. 750–500 B.C.E.	Greek colonial expansion
ca. 725 B.C.E.	Homer flourished
ca. 700 B.C.E.	Hesiod flourished
ca. 650 B.C.E.	Spartan constitution militarizes the state
546–510 B.C.E.	Athenian tyranny of Pisistratus and Hippias
508 B.C.E.	Clisthenes inaugurates Athenian democracy
499 B.C.E.	Miletus rebels against Persia
490 B.C.E.	Persian Wars: Darius
480–479 B.C.E.	Persian Wars: Xerxes

Mycenaean Civilization occupying mainland Greece during the Late Helladic era (1580–1150 B.C.E.).

The citadel of Mycenae, a major center of the Greek civilization of the Bronze Age, was built of enormously heavy stones. The lion gate at its entrance was built in the thirteenth century B.C.E.

Joe Cornish/Dorling Kindersley © Archaeological Receipts Fund (TAP)

MAP 2–1

The Aegean Area in the Bronze Age   The Bronze Age in the Aegean area lasted from about
1900 to about 1100 B.C.E. Its culture on Crete is called Minoan and was at its height about 1900–1400 B.C.E. Bronze Age Helladic culture on the mainland flourished from about 1600–1200 B.C.E.

WHAT SOCIETAL differences between the Mycenaean civilization on mainland Greece and the Minoan civilization of Crete might be a direct result of the geographic differences between the two civilizations?

The Mycenaeans reached the height of their power between 1400 and 1200 B.C.E. They expanded their trade, established commercial colonies in the Middle East, and the scribes who compiled the Hittite and Egyptian archives began to take note of them. About 1250 B.C.E., the Mycenaeans probably sacked the city of Troy on the coast of northwestern Asia Minor. This campaign may have been the Mycenaeans' last great adventure, for by 1200 B.C.E., their world was in trouble, and by 1100 B.C.E., it was gone. Some memory of them survived, however, to give rise to the earliest monuments of Greek literature: Homer's epics, the *Iliad* and the *Odyssey*.

The Dorian Invasion   Many Mycenaean towns fell about 1200 B.C.E., but some flourished for another century, and the lives of a few never were disrupted. Greek legends suggest that the Peloponnesus (the southern Greek peninsula) may have been invaded by Dorians, a rude people from the north whose Greek dialect was different from that of the Mycenaeans. This may have set in motion a chain of events that undermined Mycenaean civilization. The rigid bureaucracies of the highly centralized Mycenaean kingdoms may have been too inflexible to adjust to the crisis, but it is impossible to say with any certainty what caused the turmoil that characterized the late Aegean Bronze Age.

The Greek "Middle Ages"
to about 750 B.C.E.

WHAT WERE the Greek Dark Ages?

*T*he collapse of the Mycenaean kingdoms inaugurated a long period characterized by depopulation, impoverishment, and cultural decline in the Aegean region. Palaces and their staffs of literate bureaucrats were swept away, and the wealth and social order that made civilized life possible diminished.

Greek Migrations

The confusion that attended the Mycenaean decline caused many Greeks (including the Dorians who invaded the Peloponnesus) to relocate from the mainland to the Aegean islands and the coast of Asia Minor. Their resettlement turned the Aegean Sea into a Greek lake, but the disorder that attended the migrations hurt economic life and depressed cultures. Contacts among communities diminished, and people turned inward. No foreign power was poised to take advantage of the Aegean's situation, however, so the Greeks had a chance to recover and the freedom to evolve a new way of life. Little is known about this crucial era, for writing disappeared with the Mycenaean palaces and their scribes and was not reinvented until after 750 B.C.E. (when architecture, sculpture, and painting also resumed in the Greek world). For historians, therefore, this is a "dark age."

The Age of Homer

The *Iliad* and the *Odyssey* are our best sources of information about the Greek Dark Ages. They are the end products of a long tradition of oral poetry with roots in the Mycenaean era. For generations, bards passed on tales of the heroes who fought at Troy. They used rhythmic formulas to aid the accurate memorization of their verses, and this enabled some very old material to survive transmission over many generations. The poems were written down in the eighth century B.C.E. and attributed to an individual named Homer.

Although the poems narrate the adventures of Mycenaean heroes, the society they describe is not purely Mycenaean. Homer's warriors are not buried in *tholos* tombs but are cremated; they worship gods in temples, whereas no Mycenaean temples have been found; they have chariots but do not make much use of them in battle. These inconsistencies arise because Homer's epics combine memories of the ancient Mycenaeans with material drawn from the very different world in which the poets of the tenth and ninth centuries B.C.E. lived.

2.2
Homer, from the
Iliad

Iliad   Homer's poem narrates a dispute between Agamemnon the king and his warrior Achilles, whose honor is wounded and then avenged.

Odyssey   Homer's epic poem tells of the wanderings of the hero Odysseus.

This earliest depiction of the new method of warfare we call the hoplite phalanx appears on a wine jug known as the Chigi vase. It was made at Corinth in mainland Greece, around 650 B.C.E. It shows the two armies of heavily armed infantrymen in battle order ready to fight. The flute player set the beat for each army to keep in step and formation.

Hirmer Fotoarchiv, Munich, Germany

QUICK REVIEW

Homeric Kings

- Homeric kings had less power than their Mycenaean predecessors
- Homeric kings made decisions in consultation with nobles
- Right to speak at royal councils limited to noblemen, but common soldiers were not ignored

Black-Figure Hydria: Five Women Filling Hydriae in a Fountain House.

©2004 Museum of Fine Arts, Boston

arete   The highest virtue in Homeric society: the manliness, courage, and excellence that equipped a hero to acquire and defend honor.

Government and Society   The kings Homer describes had much less power than Mycenaean monarchs. Homeric kings had to arrive at decisions in consultation with their nobles, and these men felt free to debate vigorously and to oppose their king's wishes. In the *Iliad*, Achilles does not hesitate to accuse Agamemnon, the "most kingly" commander of the Trojan expedition, of having "a dog's face and a deer's heart." This was impolite but apparently it was not considered treasonous.

The right to speak before a royal council was limited to noblemen, but the common soldiers were not ignored. If a king planned a war or a major change of policy, he would call all his men together and explain his intentions. They could express approval or disapproval by shouting, but they could not debate or propose ideas of their own. The Greeks of the Dark Age seem, if only tentatively, to have experimented with popular government.

Homeric society was sharply divided into classes. A hereditary aristocracy presided over three kinds of commoners: *thetes*, landless laborers, and slaves. Individual *thetes* may have owned the land they worked, or their fields may have been the inalienable property of their family clans. The worst lot in life was that of the landless agricultural laborer. Slaves were attached to households that guaranteed them some protection and food, but free workers were desperately vulnerable. They were loners in a society in which the only safety lay in belonging to a group that looked out for its members. There were few slaves. Most were women who served as maids and concubines. Some male slaves worked as shepherds, but throughout Greek history most farmers were free men.

Homeric Values   The Homeric poems celebrated an aristocratic code that influenced all later Greek thinkers, for Greek education was based on Homer's works. The Greeks memorized Homer's texts and internalized respect for his values: physical prowess; courage; fierce protection of family, friends, and property; and, above all, defense of honor. The *Iliad* is the story of a dispute about honor. Agamemnon, the king who presides over the Greek army besieging Troy, wounds the honor of Achilles, his most important warrior. Achilles then refuses to fight and persuades the gods to avenge him by heaping defeat on the Greeks. When Achilles finally returns to the battlefield, he is brought back by a personal obligation to avenge the death of a friend, not by a sense of duty to his country.

The highest virtue in Homeric society was **arete**—the manliness, courage, and excellence that equipped a hero to acquire and defend honor. Men demonstrated this quality by engaging in contests with worthy opponents. Homeric battles were usually single combats between matched competitors, and most Homeric festivals (even the funeral of Achilles' friend Patroclos, which ends the *Iliad*) featured athletic competitions.

Homer's view of life is summed up by the advice Achilles' father gave him when he left for the Trojan war: "Always be the best and distinguished above others." The father of another Homeric hero added a codicil to this prescription: "Do not bring shame on the family of your fathers." These admonitions articulated the ultimate concerns of the Homeric aristocrat: to enhance the honor of one's family by a personal demonstration of *arete*.

Women in Homeric Society   The male-oriented warrior society that Homer describes relegated women to domestic roles. Their chief functions were to bear and raise children and to manage and safeguard their husbands' estates when the men were called away to battle. A husband might have sexual adventures, but a wife was expected to be unswervingly faithful. Homer's ideal woman was Penelope, Odysseus's wife. Her husband disappears for twenty years, but she does not give him up for dead. She refuses the many suitors who seek her hand (and his estate) and lives in chaste seclusion with her maids. She fills her days with the labor that Greeks associated with women of all classes: spinning and weaving. Penelope's opposite, the epitome of female evil, was Agamemnon's wife, Clytemnestra. While her husband leads the war at Troy, she takes a lover, and the two of them assassinate Agamemnon when he returns home. Homer's upper-class females were free to come and go as they wished. They attended banquets with their husbands and conversed with other men. No such privileges were enjoyed by their aristocratic sisters in later periods in Greek history. These women were expected to confine themselves to special women's quarters in their family homes and to be as invisible as possible.

THE *POLIS*

Classical Greek civilization is associated with the *polis* (plural *poleis*), a unique community that appeared during the Dark Ages. *Polis* is usually translated as "city-state," but that term implies too much and too little. All Greek *poleis* began as agricultural villages, and many never grew large enough to be considered cities. They were all states in the sense that they were self-governing, but a *polis* was more than a state—that is, more than a political institution. The citizens of a *polis* saw themselves as a kind of extended family—as descendants of a common legendary ancestor, people who shared religious cults and memberships in various hereditary subgroups, such as clans, tribes, and *phratries* (military fraternities).

In the fourth century B.C.E., hundreds of years after the *polis* became a fact of Greek life, the philosopher Aristotle devised a rationale for its existence. He said that the *polis* was simply a reflection of human nature. The human being is "an animal who lives in a *polis*," for the attributes that define humanity—the power of speech and the ability to distinguish right from wrong—emerge only when people live together.

THE DEVELOPMENT OF THE *POLIS*

Originally the word *polis* referred to a citadel, a defensible high ground to which the farmers of an area could retreat when attacked. (The most famous example is the **Acropolis** at the center of the city of Athens.) Unplanned towns tended to evolve spontaneously at such sites. Unlike the capitals of Mesopotamian city-states, the locations of Greek *poleis* were not determined by rivers and trade routes. Proximity to farmland and a natural fortress was the decisive factor. Spots well back from the coast were popular, for they minimized the danger of pirate raids. An *agora*—a place for markets and political assemblies—would be laid out in the shadow of the citadel to provide a center for community life.

Poleis probably appeared early in the eighth century B.C.E. and spread widely after 750 B.C.E. as the Greeks began to colonize the shores of the Mediterranean and Black Seas. Monarchy tended to disappear wherever *poleis* evolved. Sometimes vestigial kings survived to carry out ancient religious rites, but they had no

DESCRIBE THE *polis* and how it affected society and government.

Acropolis   At the center of the city of Athens, the most famous example of a citadel.

agora   Place for markets and political assemblies.

A large Spartan plate from the second quarter of the sixth century B.C.E.
Hirmer Fotoarchiv

political authority. A *polis* was often founded as a republic of aristocratic families, but over time political participation tended to be extended to commoners. About 750 B.C.E., coincident with the development of the *polis*, the Greeks reinvented writing. By adding symbols for vowels to the Phoenician writing system, they created the first complete alphabet. This made writing relatively easy to learn and empowered the ordinary man at a time when changes in military technology were also enhancing his importance.

THE *HOPLITE* PHALANX

Early Greek warfare was a disorganized free-for-all. Small troops of cavalry led by aristocratic "champions" cast spears at their enemies and then engaged individual opponents with swords at close quarters. Late in the eighth century B.C.E., a true infantry soldier called a **hoplite** began to dominate the battlefield. He was a heavily armed foot soldier, equipped with a spear and a large round shield (a *hoplon*). He fought in a tight formation called a **phalanx**, a company of men eight or more ranks deep. A phalanx that preserved its order on the field of battle could withstand cavalry charges and rout much larger armies consisting of less disciplined men. The phalanx reigned supreme in the ancient Mediterranean world until the more flexible Roman legion appeared.

A phalanx was effective only when all its members kept themselves in top physical condition, maintained their courage, and worked together as a team. *Hoplite* warfare favored brief violent battles that resolved disputes quickly with minimal risk to the property on which citizen families depended for their survival. Its goal was to kill or drive off an enemy, not enslave him or hold him for ransom.

Greeks had traditionally thought of war as an aristocratic profession, but in the era of the *hoplite* no *polis* could afford to limit recruitment to a small group of nobles. The strength of an infantry depended on numbers. Farmers working relatively small holdings had to join aristocrats in defending their cities, and because *hoplite* equipment was relatively inexpensive, they could afford to do so. Service in the army inevitably led to political enfranchisement, for a *polis* could not deny the men on whom it depended for protection the right to a share in its government.

EXPANSION OF THE GREEK WORLD

*A*bout the middle of the eighth century B.C.E., the Greeks launched a colonization movement that planted *poleis* from Spain to the Black Sea. The eastern end of the Mediterranean was already well populated, so they searched for sites in western regions that were still largely untouched by civilization. So many Greek colonies were established in southern Italy and Sicily that Italy's Latin-speaking Romans called this part of their world **Magna Graecia**—"Great Greece." (See Map 2–2.)

THE GREEK COLONY

The pressures of overpopulation probably explain why thousands of Greeks left the cities of their birth to found new *poleis*. Emigration was difficult, but potentially rewarding. Colonies were carefully planned, and most had excellent prospects as centers of trade. Many copied the constitutions and the religious rites of the cities that founded them, but they were not controlled or exploited by their homeland. Colonies governed themselves. Although they usually maintained friendly relations with their mother-cities and each might ask the other for help, a city that tried to dominate its colonies risked provoking war.

HOW AND why did the Greeks colonize large parts of the Mediterranean?

hoplite A true infantry soldier that began to dominate the battlefield in the late eighth century B.C.E.

phalanx Tight military formation of men eight or more ranks deep.

Magna Graecia ("Great Greece") The areas in southern Italy and Sicily where many Greek colonies were established.

MAP EXPLORATION

Interactive map: To explore this map further, go to **http://www.prenhall.com/kagan3/map2.2**

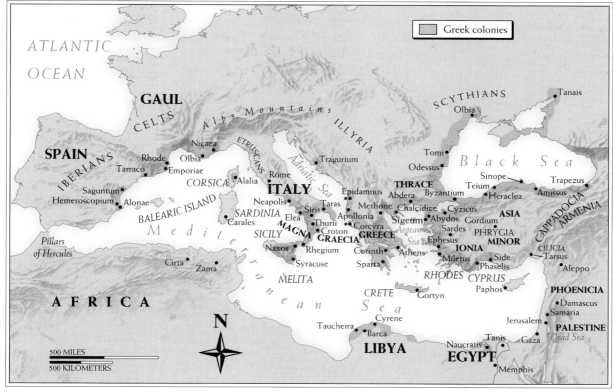

MAP 2–2

Greek Colonization   The height of Greek colonization was between about 750 and 550 B.C.E. Greek colonies stretched from the Mediterranean coasts of Spain and Gaul (modern France) in the west to the Black Sea and Asia Minor in the east.

NOTE THE area of penetration in the various colonized areas on this map. How is this indicative of a colonization achieved mainly by means of the sea?

Colonization added greatly to the material and cultural resources of Greek civilization. Over 1,000 *poleis* were established. This helped the Greeks of the mainland maintain peace among themselves by providing outlets for excess population. It also heightened the Greeks' sense of their unique identity by bringing them into contact with different cultures. *Poleis* throughout the Mediterranean sent competitors and spectators to festivals such as the Olympic Games to keep alive their memory of their common heritage. (See "Encountering the Past: Greek Athletics.")

As the network of Greek colonies spread, life in the Greek homeland was transformed. Mainland farmers began to concentrate less on local consumption and more on producing specialized crops (e.g., olives and wine) for export to colonial markets. Demand also increased for manufactured goods such as pottery, tools, weapons, and fine metalwork. Expanding commercial opportunities enlarged the class of independent commoners, and their increasing prosperity led them to resent the aristocrats' traditional political privileges. This produced turmoil that enabled tyrants to seize control of some *poleis*.

THE TYRANTS (CA. 700–500 B.C.E.)

A tyrant, in the ancient Greek sense, was a ruler who ignored legal niceties and simply took over. Often he enjoyed popular support. A typical tyrant was an aristocrat who broke with his class and took control of a city by appealing to the masses of its poor and politically disenfranchised. He usually expelled his aristocratic opponents, distributed their land among his followers, and instituted economic programs that benefited the masses.

A tyrant's authority was backed by a personal bodyguard and troops of mercenary soldiers, but his rule was not inevitably oppressive. Tyrants preferred to concentrate on domestic development that would keep the people happy. Because aggression against a neighboring state required fielding a citizen army that might turn on its tyrant, tyrants preferred to avoid wars. They financed popular public works projects that provided employment for the poor, and they sponsored festivals and commissioned works of art that fostered civic pride.

Despite the positive effect tyranny had on the development of some *poleis*, tyrannies faded away during the sixth century B.C.E. Something about tyranny was inconsistent with the forces that created the *polis*. The institutions of a *polis* were shaped by the responsibility all its citizens bore for its defense. Because they shared this traditional responsibility of the military aristocracy, they felt entitled also to share the customary aristocratic political prerogatives. The rule of a

Panhellenic (All Greek) Sense of cultural identity that all Greeks felt in common with one other.

ENCOUNTERING THE PAST

GREEK ATHLETICS

A thletic contests were an integral part of Greek civilization throughout its entire history. They were much more than entertainments. They were religious festivals in which the Greeks celebrated the virtues and attitudes that they considered central to their way of life. International or **Panhellenic ("all-Greek")** contests were scheduled in alternating annual cycles. The most prestigious of these were the games that began to be celebrated in honor of Zeus at the southern mainland city of Olympia in 776 B.C.E.

The Greeks' primary interest was not team sports, but contests in which individuals could prove their superiority. Races of various lengths were the heart of Olympic competition, but there were also field events such as discus and javelin throws and combat sports such as wrestling and boxing. Only male athletes were admitted to the games, and by the fifth century B.C.E., all contestants (except those in a race in full armor) competed nude. The official prizes were simple wreaths, but *poleis* lavishly rewarded the native sons who brought home these tokens of victory.

WHY DID the Greeks prefer individual contests to team sports? What motivated them to train and compete?

A foot race, probably a sprint, at the Panathenaic Games in Athens, ca. 530 B.C.E.

Panathenaic Prize Amphora (Foot Race), Euphiletos Painter. Greek, Attic, ca. 530 B.C. Terracotta, 62.23 cm (Ht.) The Metropolitan Museum of Art, Rogers Fund, 1914. (14.130.12)

tyrant, no matter how beneficent, was unacceptable, for it was arbitrary and could not be held accountable. Tyranny did, however, contribute to the growth of popular government by breaking the monopoly aristocracies had on political power.

THE MAJOR STATES

The many *poleis* were organized in many different ways. However, two cities were of such importance that they merit special attention: Sparta in the southern half of the Greek peninsula (the **Peloponnesus**) and Athens in the north.

SPARTA

A chain of events that began about 725 B.C.E. persuaded the Spartans to embrace a program of total military mobilization that created the most feared army in Greece. The Spartans conquered Messenia, their western neighbor. The acquisition of its land and enslavement of its people eased Sparta's economic problems but created a new threat to Spartan security. The Spartans found themselves outnumbered ten to one by **Helots**, their slaves. A slave revolt that nearly destroyed Sparta (ca. 650 B.C.E.) convinced the Spartans that they had to do everything possible to build up their army.

Spartan Society   The system the Spartans devised was designed to subordinate natural feelings of devotion to self and family to the needs of the state. The state required all its men to become superb soldiers. To this end, it persuaded them to sacrifice privacy and comfort and embrace a regimen of brutal physical conditioning and discipline. The Spartans allowed nothing to distract them from their goal of becoming the best warriors in the world. (See "History's Voices: Tyrtaeus on the Citizen Soldier.")

The Spartan *polis* controlled the life of each of its members from birth to death. Only infants whom officials of the state judged to be physically fit were allowed to live. At the age of seven boys left their mothers to begin training at military camps. They learned to fight, to endure privation, to bear physical pain, and to live off the land. At twenty they joined the army in the field, and they lived in barracks until the age of thirty. They were allowed to marry but not to enjoy the comforts of a home. Young Spartan husbands had to steal away from camp for conjugal visits with their wives. Only after a man acquired full citizen rights at the age of thirty could he set up a household. But even then he took his meals at a public mess with other members of his military unit. His sparse diet included little meat or wine, and he eschewed all luxuries. He was, however, financially secure, for he was supported by a grant from the state—a plot of land worked by Helots. He remained on active military duty until the age of sixty.

Females, like males, were trained to serve the Spartan state. Only fit female infants were raised, and young girls were given athletic training to strengthen them for childbearing. Because Spartan men were often absent from home or focused on military duties, Spartan women had much greater freedom and responsibility than other Greek females.

Spartan Government   The Spartan constitution mixed elements of monarchy, oligarchy, and democracy. Sparta had two royal families from which to choose its kings. The Spartan army was usually commanded by one of its kings

HOW WERE the government and politics of Athens different from those of Sparta?

2.4
Tyrtaeus, *The Spartan Code*

Peloponnesus   Southern half of the Greek peninsula.

Helots   Slaves to the Spartans that revolted and nearly destroyed Sparta in 650 B.C.E.

HISTORY'S VOICES

TYRTAEUS ON THE CITIZEN SOLDIER

T*he military organization of citizen soldiers for the defense of the* polis *and the idea of the* polis *itself that permeated Greek political thought found echoes in Greek poetry. A major example is this part of a poem by Tyrtaeus, who wrote in Sparta about 625 B.C.E.*

WHY, according to Tyrtaeus, is the Spartan soldier right and wise to risk his life by showing courage in battle?

I would not say anything for a man nor take account
    of him
for any speed of his feet or wrestling skill he might have,
not if he had the size of a Cyclops and strength to go
    with it,
not if he could outrun Bóreas, the North Wind of
    Thrace,
not if he were more handsome and gracefully
    formed than Tithónos,
or had more riches than Midas had, or Kinyras too, not
    if he were more of a king than Tantalid Pelops,
or had the power of speech and persuasion Adrastos
    had,
not if he had all splendors except for a fighting spirit.
For no man ever proves himself a good man in war
    unless he can endure to face the blood and the
    slaughter,
go close against the enemy and fight with his hands.
Here is courage, mankind's finest possession, here is
    the noblest prize that a young man can endeavor to
    win,
and it is a good thing his city and all the people
    share with him
when a man plants his feet and stands in the
    foremost spears
relentlessly, all thought of foul flight completely
    forgotten,
and has well trained his heart to be steadfast and to
    endure,
and with words encourages the man who is stationed
    beside him.
Here is a man who proves himself to be valiant in war.
With a sudden rush he turns to fight the rugged
    battalions

of the enemy, and sustains the beating waves of assault.
And he who so falls among the champions and loses
    his sweet life,
so blessing with honor his city, his father, and all his
    people,
with wounds in his chest, where the spear that he was
    facing has transfixed
that massive guard of his shield, and gave through
    his breastplate as well,
why, such a man is lamented alike by the young and
    the elders,
and all his city goes into mourning and grieves for
    his loss.
His tomb is pointed to with pride, and so are his
    children,
and his children's children, and afterward all the
    race that is his.
His shining glory is never forgotten, his name is
    remembered,
and he becomes an immortal, though he lies under
    the ground.
When one who was a brave man has been killed by
    the furious War God
standing his ground and fighting hard for his
    children and land.
But if he escapes the doom of death, the destroyer of
    bodies,
and wins his battle, and bright renown for the work
    of his spear,
all men give place to him alike, the youth and the
    elders,
and much joy comes his way before he goes down to
    the dead.
Aging he has reputation among his citizens. No one
tries to interfere with his honors or all he deserves,
all men withdraw before his presence, and yield their
    seats to him,
and youth, and the men of his age, and even those
    older than he.
Thus a man should endeavor to reach this high
    place of courage
with all his heart, and, so trying, never be backward
    in war.

Greek Lyrics, trans. by Richmond Lattimore (Chicago: University of Chicago Press. 1949, 1955, 1959), pp. 14–15.

when it was in the field, but kings did not govern Sparta. An oligarchic council of twenty-eight men (aged sixty or more and elected for life) devised policy and sat as a high court. All Spartan males over the age of thirty could take part in a democratic assembly that, in theory, had final authority. The assembly, however, could only consider proposals referred to it by the council. It was limited to ratifying decisions already taken or deciding between alternative proposals.

The administration of Sparta's government was the duty of a board of five *ephors*, executives elected annually by the assembly. They controlled foreign policy, oversaw the kings' management of campaigns, presided at the assembly, and policed the Helots.

The Peloponnesian League   Suppression of the Helots required all the energy Sparta had, and the Spartans did not want to overextend themselves by conquering and assimilating troublesome neighbors. They preferred to force these people into alliances that left them free internally but subservient to Sparta's foreign policy. Sparta eventually enrolled every southern Greek state except Argos in its Peloponnesian League and became the most powerful *polis* on the Greek mainland.

ATHENS

Athens evolved more slowly than Sparta. Because **Attica**, the region Athens dominated, was large by Greek standards (about 1,000 square miles), it was able to absorb a growing population without conquering its neighbors. But size slowed its consolidation as a *polis*, and its economic development was hampered by the fact that it was not situated on the trade routes most traveled during the eighth and seventh centuries B.C.E.

Political Tensions   In the seventh century B.C.E., aristocratic families held the most and the best land around Athens. They also dominated Attica by controlling the tribes, clans, and military fraternities that structured Athenian society. Athens's government was headed by the Council of the **Areopagus**, a group of nobles that annually chose the city's nine *archons*, the magistrates who administered the *polis*. There was no formal law, and leaders were guided primarily by custom and tradition.

Athens's political evolution was accelerated by an agrarian crisis that developed during the seventh century B.C.E. Many Athenians depended on small family farms that grew wheat, the staple of the ancient diet. Years of consistent cultivation diminished the fertility of their fields and the size of their harvests, but few could afford to shift to more profitable crops such as olives (pressed for oil) and grapes (for wine). A lot of capital was needed to bring a vineyard or olive grove into production. In bad years the poorer farmers were forced to borrow from their wealthier neighbors—mortgaging future crops and, therefore, their own labor (which was needed to raise these crops) as surety for their loans. This gradually reduced them to slavery, and some were even exported for sale outside Attica. The poor resented this and agitated for the abolition of debts and the redistribution of the land.

In 632 B.C.E., a nobleman named Cylon tried to exploit this situation to establish a tyranny. He failed, but his attempt frightened Athens's aristocratic leaders into taking steps to head off future coups. In 621 B.C.E., they commissioned a man named Draco to codify and publish Athens's laws. Draco decreed extremely hard punishments for crimes in hopes of deterring the blood feuds that resulted

Attica   Region (about 1,000 square miles) that Athens dominated.

Areopagus   Council heading Athens's government comprised of a group of nobles that annually chose the city's nine *archons*, the magistrates who administered the *polis*.

when victims sought revenge for wrongs done them. The establishment of a common standard of public justice for all Athenians was meant to dissuade individuals from taking things into their own hands.

In the year 594 B.C.E., the Athenians instituted a more radical reform. They empowered a single man, an *archon* named Solon, to reorganize the *polis* as he saw fit. Solon attacked agrarian problems by canceling debts and forbidding loans secured by the freedom of the borrower. He emancipated people who had been enslaved for debt and brought home many of the Athenians who had been sold abroad. Instead of alienating the rich by redistributing their land to the poor, however, he tried to expand Athens's economy to create different employment opportunities for the poor. He forbade the export of wheat (which might create shortages and drive up the price of the common person's food) but not olive oil (one of Attica's cash crops). He facilitated trade by conforming Athenian weights and measures to standards used by other commercial centers. And he developed industries by offering citizenship to foreign artisans who agreed to set up shop in Athens.

Solon also reformed Athenian political institutions. He divided Athens's citizens into four classes on the basis of wealth. Members of the two richest classes qualified for archonships and membership in the Council of the Areopagus. Men of the third class could serve as *hoplites* and be elected to a council of four hundred chosen by the citizens. Solon intended this council to serve as a check on the aristocratic Council of the Areopagus, and he gave it the power to decide the issues that were to be brought to the popular assembly, the political organization to which all adult male citizens belonged. The poorest class of Athenians, the *thetes*, voted in this assembly, participated in the election of *archons*, and sat on a new court that heard appeals from other jurisdictions. Women from citizen families were granted no role in the political process.

The Tyrannies   Because the beneficial effects of Solon's reforms were slow to be felt, tensions continued to mount in Athens. On several occasions rioting prevented the election of *archons*. A military hero named Pisistratus twice (in 560 B.C.E. and 556 B.C.E.) tried and failed to establish a tyranny, but his third attempt (in 546 B.C.E.) succeeded. Pisisitratus remained in power until his death in 527 B.C.E., and his son Hippias continued the tyranny until a competitor drove him from the city in 510 B.C.E.

Like the tyrants of other Greek cities, Pisistratus dominated his subjects by courting them. He sponsored public works programs, urban development, and civic festivals. He employed poets and artists to add luster to his court. And he secured his power by hiding it behind the facade of Solon's constitution. All the councils, assemblies, and courts continued to meet, and all the magistrates were elected. Pisistratus merely saw to it that his men won the key offices and dominated the important meetings. The constitutional cloak he spread over his tyranny won him a reputation as a popular, gentle ruler, but it also gave his subjects experience with (and a greater appetite for) self-government.

After Pisistratus's death, his elder son, Hippias, ruled Athens. Initially, he followed his father's example, but in 514 B.C.E., the murder of his brother, Hipparchus, led him to fear for his own safety and he began to impose harsh measures. His increasing unpopularity encouraged his enemies, and in 510 B.C.E., the Alcmaeonids, a noble family that had been exiled from Athens, persuaded the Spartans to overthrow Hippias. The Alcmaeonid leader, Clisthenes, then rallied the Athenians against the Spartans and established himself in control of Athens.

Democracy   Clisthenes weakened his aristocratic opponents by destroying the regional political machines that were the bases of their power. In 508 B.C.E., he divided Attica into small political units called *demes*. The *demes* were then grouped together to create the tribes that composed Athens's army and elected its government. Care was taken to make sure that each tribe was made up of *demes* from different parts of Attica. This prevented the wealthy aristocratic families, whose landed estates gave them control of large portions of the countryside, from dominating the new tribal organizations. Aristocrats now found themselves voting not with their economically dependent clients but with men who were strangers to them.

Clisthenes increased Solon's council from four hundred to five hundred members and gave it authority to receive foreign emissaries and manage some fiscal affairs. Its chief responsibility was to prepare legislative proposals for discussion by the popular assembly in which ultimate authority was vested. All adult male Athenians were members of this assembly and had the right to propose legislation and debate freely. Thanks to Solon, Pisistratus, and Clisthenes, Athens entered the fifth century B.C.E. well down the path to prosperity and democracy and prepared to claim a place among Greece's leading *poleis*.

QUICK REVIEW

Clisthene's Democracy
- Clisthenes sought to weaken his opponents by dividing Attica into *demes*
- Increased Solon's council from four to five hundred
- All adult male Athenians were members of the popular assembly

LIFE IN ARCHAIC GREECE

SOCIETY

Greek society's unique features began to become visible at the end of the Dark Ages. The vast majority of Greeks made their living from the land, but artisans and merchants acquired greater importance as contact with the non-Hellenic (non-Greek) world increased.

Farmers   Ordinary country folk rarely leave any record of their thoughts or activities, but the poet Hesiod (ca. 700 B.C.E.), who claimed in his *Works and Days* to be a small farmer, described what life was like for members of his class in ancient Greece. The crops farmers usually cultivated were barley, wheat, grapes for wine, olives for oil (for cooking, lighting, and lubrication), vegetables, beans, and fruit. Sheep and goats provided milk and cheese. Land that was fertile enough to grow fodder for cattle was needed to grow grain for human consumption, so supplies of meat were limited. Meat was most commonly eaten at religious festivals where worshipers shared the flesh of the animals sacrificed to the gods.

Hesiod had the help of oxen and mules and occasional hired laborers, but his life was one of continuous toil. The toughest season began with October's rains, the time for the first plowing. Plows were iron-tipped but light and fragile. Even with the aid of a team of animals it was difficult to break the sod. During autumn and winter, wood was cut and repairs were made to buildings and equipment. Vines needed attention in late winter. Grain was harvested in May. At the height of summer's heat there was time for a little rest, but in September grapes had to be harvested and pressed and the round of yearly tasks began again.

Hesiod says nothing about the pleasures and entertainments of ordinary people, but the fact that his poetry exists is witness to the presence in Greece of a more dynamic and confident rural population than we know of anywhere else in the ancient world.

Aristocrats Wealthy aristocrats worked their extensive lands with hired laborers, sharecroppers, and slaves. This gave them leisure for other kinds of activities. The centerpiece of aristocratic social life was the *symposium*, a men's drinking party. A *symposium* was sometimes only a pursuit of inebriation, but it could be more. It began with prayers and libations to the gods. There were usually games such as dice or *kottabos* (a contest in which wine was flicked from cups at a target). Sometimes dancing girls or flute girls offered entertainment. Guests also amused themselves by singing, reciting poetry, and engaging in philosophical discussions. These activities were often turned into contests, for aristocratic values put a premium on competition and the need to excel.

Athletics were fundamental to an aristocrat's education and lifestyle. Each *polis* maintained a *palaestra*, a place where the city's men gathered to train and compete. Races, wrestling, and field events were popular, but chariot races were the special preserve of the nobility. Only they could afford horses. Simple farmers led drab lives from the point of view of cultivated, leisured aristocrats.

RELIGION

Olympian Religion permeated every aspect of Greek life. The Greeks were polytheists whose official pantheon centered on twelve major deities, the residents of Mount Olympus. Zeus, a sky god, exercised patriarchal authority over the other gods. He had three sisters: Hera, who was also his wife; Hestia, goddess of the hearth; and Demeter, goddess of agriculture and marriage. Zeus's brother Poseidon was god of the seas and earthquakes. By various mates he had an assortment of children: Aphrodite, goddess of love and beauty; Apollo, god of the sun, music, poetry, and prophecy; Ares, god of strife; Artemis, goddess of the moon and the hunt; Athena, goddess of wisdom and the arts; Hephaestus, god of fire and metallurgy; and Hermes, a cunning messenger-god and patron of traders.

Gods were believed, apart from their superhuman strength and immortality, to resemble mortals. Zeus, the defender of justice, presided over the cosmos, but he and the other gods were not omnipotent. They operated within limits set by the Fates who personified the inviolable order of the universe. Olympian religion was shared by all the Greeks. Each *polis* honored one or more of the gods as its special guardian(s), but all of them supported shrines at Olympia (to Zeus), Delphi (to Apollo), Corinth (to Poseidon), and Nemea (also to Zeus). Each of these sanctuaries staged athletic festivals to which all Greeks were invited. Truces suspended wars so that everyone could safely participate.

In the sixth century B.C.E., the shrine of Apollo at Delphi became famous for its oracle, the most important of several that the Greeks looked to for guidance. Delphian Apollo endorsed the pursuit of self-knowledge and self-control. His mottos were "Know thyself" and "Nothing in excess!" *Hubris*, the arrogance produced by excessive wealth or good fortune, was believed to be the most dangerous of human failings. It caused moral blindness and tempted the gods to

symposium A men's drinking party at the center of aristocratic social life in archaic Greece.

hubris Arrogance produced by excessive wealth or good fortune.

take vengeance. The moral order the gods enforced was simple. Virtue consisted of paying one's debts, doing good to one's friends, and attacking one's enemies. Civic responsibility entailed honoring the state's deities, participating in political life, and serving in the army.

The Dionysian and Orphic Cults   The Olympian gods were the protectors of the state, not individuals. For their personal spiritual needs, Greeks turned to gods of a different kind. Countless lesser deities were associated with local shrines. Some of these gods were believed to have been men whose heroic deeds had won them divine status.

The worship of Dionysus, a fertility deity associated with the growing of grapes, was very popular—particularly with women. Dionysus was a god of drunkenness and sexual abandon. His female devotees (the *maenads*) cavorted by night and were reputed, when possessed by their god, to tear to pieces and devour any living creatures they encountered. The cult of Orpheus, a mythical poet, taught respect for life and offered the prospect of some kind of triumph over the grave—perhaps a transmigration of souls.

POETRY

A shift from epic to lyric poetry reflected the great changes that swept through the Greek world in the sixth century B.C.E. The poems of Sappho of Lesbos, Anacreon of Teos, and Simonides of Cos were intimately personal—often describing the pleasure and agony of love. Alcaeus of Mytilene, an aristocrat driven from his city by a tyrant, wrote bitter invectives. The most interesting poet of the century, at least from the political point of view, may be Theonis of Megara. He spoke for the aristocrats whose power over most *poleis* was waning. He insisted that only nobles could aspire to virtue, for only nobles possessed the crucial sense of honor. Honor, he claimed, could not be taught; it was innate, and noble families lost it if they debased their lines by marrying commoners. The political privileges of the nobility were reduced in most Greek states, but traditional assumptions of aristocratic superiority continued to influence important thinkers such as Plato.

This Attic cup from the fifth century B.C.E. shows the two great poets from the island of Lesbos, Sappho and Alcaeus.
Hirmer Fotoarchiv

THE PERSIAN WARS

The Greeks' era of freedom from interference from the outside world came to an end in the middle of the sixth century B.C.E. First, the Greek settlements that had flourished on the coast of Asia Minor since the eleventh century B.C.E. came under the control of Croesus (ca. 560–546 B.C.E.), king of the Anatolian nation of Lydia. Then in 546 B.C.E., Lydia and its dependencies passed into the hands of the Persians.

WHAT WAS the significance of the wars between the Greeks and the Persians?

THE PERSIAN EMPIRE

The Persian Empire was created in a single generation by Cyrus the Great, founder of the Achaemenid dynasty. When Cyrus ascended the Persian throne in 559 B.C.E., Persia was a small kingdom well to the east of southern Mesopotamia. He steadily expanded his domain in all directions, conquered Babylon, and ultimately reached Asia Minor where he defeated Croesus and occupied Lydia. Most of the Greek cities of Asia Minor resisted the Persians, but by 540 B.C.E., they had all been subdued. (See Chapter 1.)

THE IONIAN REBELLION

The Greeks of **Ionia** (the western coast of Asia Minor) had become accustomed to democratic governments, and they were restive under Persian rule. The Persians, however, were clever empire builders. They appointed Greek tyrants to govern Greek cities. Because these native leaders usually ruled benignly and Persian tribute was not excessive, many Greeks were soon reconciled to life in Persia's empire. Neither the death of Cyrus in 530 B.C.E., nor the suicide of his successor Cambyses, nor the civil war that followed that event in 522–521 B.C.E. prompted the Greeks to revolt. In 521 B.C.E. when Darius became Great King (the Persian royal title), Ionia submitted to him as it had to his predecessors.

Aristagoras, an ambitious tyrant of Miletus, ended the era of peaceful cooperation between Ionia and Persia. In 499 B.C.E., he sought to escape punishment for having committed the Persians to an unsuccessful campaign against the island of Naxos by persuading the Ionian cities to join him in a rebellion. He courted support by helping overthrow unpopular fellow tyrants and by endorsing democratic constitutions for some cities. He also sought help from the mainland states. The Spartans declined to become involved. They had no ties with the Ionians, no interests in the region, and could not risk weakening their hold over their slaves by sending their army abroad.

The Athenians were more sympathetic toward Aristagoras. They were related to the Ionians, and they had reasons of their own to fear the Persians. Hippias, the deposed tyrant of Athens, had found refuge at Darius's court, and the Great King was willing to help Hippias regain control of Athens. The Persians also held both shores of the Hellespont, the narrow waterway that connected the Aegean with the Black Sea—the region from which Athens imported much of its grain.

In 498 B.C.E., an army of Ionians and Athenians sacked Sardis, the capital of Lydia and the seat of the Persian *satrap* (governor). The fall of Sardis encouraged others to join the rebellion, but the Greeks did not follow up their victory. Athens withdrew, and the Persians gradually recovered the ground they had lost. In 495 B.C.E., they defeated the Ionian fleet at Lade, and a year later they leveled Miletus.

THE WAR IN GREECE

In 490 B.C.E., Darius launched an expedition to punish the rebels and add the Aegean to his empire. He leveled the island *polis* of Naxos and then took another of Miletus's allies, Athens's neighbor Eretria. Despite the failure of these cities to withstand Darius's assault, the Athenians refused to negotiate surrender. With Miltiades, an Athenian with a personal grudge against the Persians, at their head, they marched out to Marathon, a plain north of Athens where the Persians had made their landing. There some 10,000 Athenians and neighboring Plataeans defeated two or three times their number, killing thousands of the enemy while losing only 192 of their own men.

A Persian victory at Marathon would have destroyed Athenian freedom and led to the conquest of all the mainland Greeks. The greatest achievements of Greek culture, most of which lay in the future, would never have occurred. But the Athenians won a decisive victory, instilling them with a sense of confidence and pride in their *polis*, their unique form of government, and themselves.

Ionia   Western coast of Asia Minor.

560–546 B.C.E.	Greek cities of Asia Minor conquered by Croesus of Lydia
546 B.C.E.	Cyrus of Persia conquers Lydia and gains control of Greek cities
499–494 B.C.E.	Greek cities rebel (Ionian rebellion)
490 B.C.E.	Battle of Marathon
480–479 B.C.E.	Xerxes' invasion of Greece
480 B.C.E.	Battles of Thermopylae, Artemisium, and Salamis
479 B.C.E.	Battles of Plataea and Mycale

The Great Invasion   Problems elsewhere in the Persian Empire prevented Darius from taking swift revenge for his loss at Marathon, and almost ten years elapsed before his successor, Xerxes, turned his attention to the Greeks. In 481 B.C.E., Xerxes assembled an army of at least 150,000 men and a navy of about 600 ships and set out for the Aegean.

By then Athens had changed significantly. Themistocles, the city's leading politician, had begun to turn the *polis* into a naval power. During his *archonship* in 493 B.C.E., Athens (an inland city) had constructed a fortified port on the Attic coast at Piraeus, and a decade later the income from a rich vein of silver discovered in the state mines funded the construction of an Athenian navy. By the time Xerxes set out, Athens had over two hundred ships. They proved to be the salvation of Greece.

Of the hundreds of Greek states, only thirty-one (led by Sparta, Athens, Corinth, and Aegina) were willing to commit to fighting the great Persian army that gathered south of the Hellespont in the spring of 480 B.C.E. Xerxes' strategy was to overwhelm the Greeks with superior numbers, but Themistocles perceived a weakness in the emperor's plan. The Persian army depended on the Persian fleet for its supplies. If Xerxes' ships were destroyed, his army would have to retreat. Themistocles, therefore, argued that the Greeks should wage the war at sea. Athens's allies saw things differently. They chose the Spartans, Greece's premier soldiers, as their leaders, and Sparta, which had no navy, fought on land.

The Spartans and their allies made a stand at Thermopylae. The Persian army had to stay near the coast to maintain contact with its fleet, and at Thermopylae the coastal passage was extremely narrow because mountains lay near the sea. It was possible for a small force to stop the Persians here by blocking a strip of beach at the foot of the mountains. The Greek army with which the Spartan king, Leonidas, hoped to hold this spot numbered only about 9,000—of which 300 were Spartans.

The Greeks were encouraged when storms wrecked a number of Persian ships. For two days the Greeks stood their ground and butchered the troops Xerxes threw at them. On the third day, however, a Greek traitor showed the Persians a trail through the mountains, and a company of Persians outflanked the Greek army and attacked it from the rear. Leonidas realized the situation was hopeless. He dismissed his Greek allies while it was still possible for them to retreat, but he and his three hundred Spartans chose to stay and to die fighting. The Persians slaughtered them to the last man, marched into Attica, and

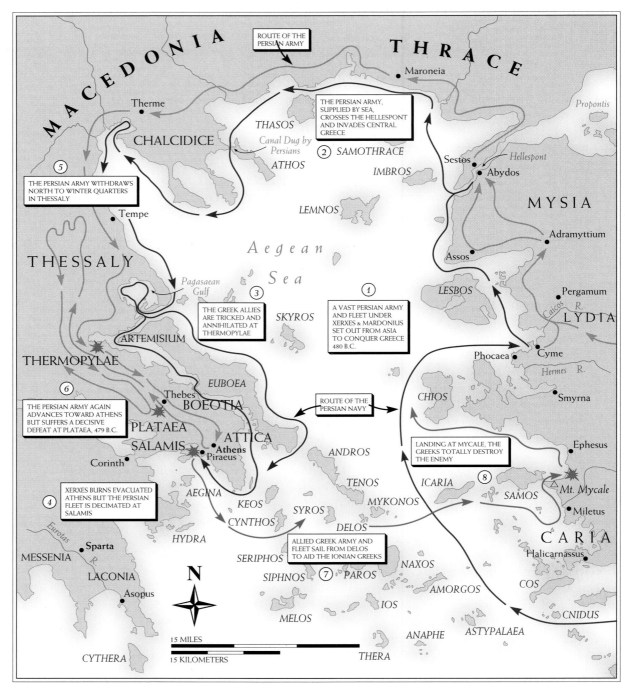

MAP 2–3

The Persian Invasion of Greece This map traces the route taken by the Persian king Xerxes in his invasion of Greece in 480 B.C.E. The gray arrows show movements of Xerxes' army, the purple arrows show movements of his navy, and the green arrows show movements of the Greek army and navy.

ALTHOUGH Xerxes' army had superior numbers, how did Greece's geography favor the Greek cities over the Persians?

burned Athens. If an inscription discovered in 1959 is authentic, Themistocles had foreseen this possibility and evacuated the city while the Greek army was still at Thermopylae.

The fate of Greece was decided, as Themistocles predicted, by a sea battle. It was fought in the narrow straits between Attica and the island of Salamis. The Spartans wanted the Athenian fleet to move south to guard the coast of the Peloponnese while they attempted another stand on the isthmus of Corinth, but Themistocles threatened to abandon the war and use the fleet to carry the Athenians to new homes in Italy. When the Persians sailed into the straits of Salamis, the Athenians sank more than half of Xerxes' ships. The emperor then chose to return to Persia, but he left an army behind to continue the war under the command of a general named Mardonius.

Mardonius went into winter camp in central Greece, and Pausanias, the new Spartan leader, used the time to amass the largest army the Greeks had ever fielded. In the summer of 479 B.C.E., it decisively defeated the Persians at a battle near Plataea in Boeotia. At the same time, the Ionian Greeks persuaded the Greek fleet to take the offensive against a key Persian naval base at Mycale on the coast of Asia Minor. When Mycale fell, the Persians retreated from the Aegean and Ionia. Greece was safe, but no one knew for how long.

SUMMARY

The Bronze Age on Crete and on the Mainland to about 1150 B.C.E. During the Bronze Age, the Minoan and Mycenaean civilizations ruled over the Greek mainland and Aegean islands. The Minoan civilization on Crete is renowned for its beautiful palaces. They were the organizational center of Minoan society, and Minoan kings employed a large bureaucracy. The lack of defensive walls is a notable feature of Minoan settlements. On the Greek mainland, starting around 1600 B.C.E., the Mycenaean culture was warlike and ruled by strong kings. Mycenaeans traded widely. Historians and archaeologists have suggested various explanations for the fact that, by 1100 B.C.E., the Mycenaean culture had disappeared.

Greek "Middle Ages" to about 750 B.C.E. The Dorian invasion destroyed the Mycenaean palace culture. The Greek peoples spread around the Aegean. Trade diminished; writing and other arts disappeared. Oral poetry flourished, and Homer's *Iliad* and *Odyssey* provide both great stories and insights into life in the Greek "Dark Ages." The aristocratic values of the tenth and ninth centuries B.C.E. idealized the individual hero.

The *Polis* Greek social and political values are exemplified in the Greeks' characteristic form of community, the *polis*. All citizens in a *polis* were, in theory, related; in practice, they all participated in building a commom culture. Early *poleis* developed around 800 B.C.E. in locations that featured fertile farmland and, nearby, natural defensive positions. Later *poleis* always included an *agora*, a marketplace and civic center. *Polis* society was made possible by a new military technology, the *hoplite* phalanx. Group loyalty and individual bravery were both essential to the *hoplite* phalanx's success. The power of the kings and, later, the aristocrats was undermined by the emergence of the farmer-soldier-citizen in the *polis*. Eighth-century B.C.E. Greeks created the first complete alphabet.

Expansion of the Greek World For about two centuries starting around 750 B.C.E., the Greeks colonized widely throughout the Mediterranean world. Trade became an increasingly important part of the Greek economy. Expo-

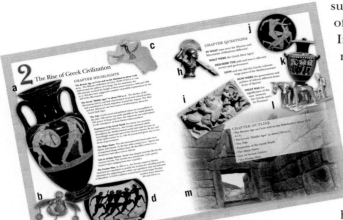

IMAGE KEY

for pages 32–33.

a. Greek vase, red-figured. Attic. ca. 480-470 B.C.E. Neck amphora, Nolan type. SIDE 1: "Greek warrior attacking a Persian." Said to be from Rhodes. Terracotta. H. 13-11/16 in. The Metropolitan Museum of Art, Rogers Fund, 1906. (06.1021.117) Photograph © The Metropolitan Museum of Art, Rogers Fund, 1903. (03.14.5) Photograph © 1986 The Metropolitan Museum of Art

b. Pendentive with Bees, ca. 1700-1400 B.C.E.

c. Dancing Lady, Palace of Knossos, Minoan, ca. 1500 B.C.E. (fresco painting)

d. Panathenaic Prize Amphora (Foot Race), Euphiletos Painter. Greek, Attic, ca. 530 B.C.E. Terracotta, 62.23 cm (Ht.) The Metropolitan Museum of Art, Rogers Fund, 1914. (14.130.12)

e., f., g. Three column capitals, two Doric and one Ionic, are displayed at the ancient site of Corinth

h. Warrior with spear and Beotian shield. Bronze statuette, ca. 500 B.C.E.

i. The "Alexander Sarcophagus" from the Phoenician royal necropolis at Sidon

j. Detail of Ancient Greek Cup with two athletes wrestling by Epictetos ca. 530 B.C.E.

k. Hydria (water jug). Greek, Archaic period, ca. 520 B.C.E. Athens, Attica, Greece, the Priam Painter. Ceramic, black-figure, H: 0.53 cm Diam (with handles): 0.37 cm. William Francis Warden Fund. © 2004 Museum of Fine Arts, Boston. Accession #61.195

l. Farmer plowing with oxen. First half 6th century B.C.E. Greek terracotta group from Thebes, Boetia. 11 x 22 cm. Inv.: CA 352. Photo: Herve Lewandownski. Louvre, Paris. Reunion des Musees Nationaux/Art Resource, NY

m. Lion Gate at Ancient Greek City of Mycenae

sure to other peoples and cultures fostered consciousness of Greek cultural identity and led to Panhellenic feelings. In some *poleis*, new social and economic conditions led to rule by tyrants. But by late in the sixth century B.C.E., tyrants had lost favor with the populace, and by the end of the century, they were gone.

The Major States The two most powerful Greek *poleis*, Sparta and Athens, developed differently. Starting around 725 B.C.E., Sparta gained land and power over the Messenians through warfare. Late in the sixth century B.C.E., Spartan society was reorganized along military lines to ensure that Sparta could continue its hold over Messenia. By 500 B.C.E., Sparta headed a Peloponnesian League, a mighty military alliance. In Athens, meanwhile, political and economic innovations included the publication of laws; by the fifth century B.C.E., prosperity and democracy had taken root in Athens.

Life in Archaic Greece Social class shaped everyday life for the ancient Greeks. Small farmers worked long, hard hours tending their crops. Members of the aristocracy enjoyed leisure activities that included attending *symposia*, sessions of drinking, conversation, entertainment, and games. Greeks were polytheistic, worshiping the Olympian gods and other deities through sacrifices and athletic contests. Lyric poetry treated topics ranging from love to politics.

The Persian Wars Cyrus the Great came to power in Persia in 559 B.C.E. and set about unifying and expanding his territory. For almost a century, starting around 550 B.C.E. and continuing into the mid–fifth century B.C.E., Greece faced intermittent military challenges from the Persian Empire. After Lydia came under Persian rule in 546 B.C.E., the Ionian Greeks sought military assistance from first the Spartans (who refused to get involved) and then the Athenians, who in 498 B.C.E. helped them in a short-lived revolt. Eventually the Persians withdrew from the Aegean Sea and Ionia.

REVIEW QUESTIONS

1. How were the Minoan and the Mycenaean civilizations similar? How were they different?

2. What was a *polis*? What role did geography play in its development? What contribution did it make to the development of Hellenic civilization?

3. How did the political, social, and economic institutions of Athens and Sparta compare around 500 B.C.E.? What explains Sparta's uniqueness? How did Athens make the transition from aristocracy to democracy?

4. Why did the Greeks and Persians go to war in 490 and 480 B.C.E.? Why were the Greeks victorious over the Persians?

KEY TERMS

Acropolis (p. 39)   *hoplite* (p. 40)   **Mycenaean** (p. 35)
agora (p. 39)   *hubris* (p. 48)   ***Odyssey*** (p. 37)
Areopagus (p. 45)   *Iliad* (p. 37)   **Panhellenic (All Greek)** (p. 42)
arete (p. 38)   **Ionia** (p. 50)   **Peloponnesus** (p. 43)
Attica (p. 45)   *Magna Graecia* (p. 40)   **phalanx** (p. 40)
Helots (p. 43)   **Minoan** (p. 34)   *symposium* (p. 48)

 For additional study resources for this chapter, go to:
www.prenhall.com/kagan3/chapter2

3 Classical and Hellenistic Greece

CHAPTER HIGHLIGHTS

Aftermath of Victory The unity the Greeks had shown while fighting against the Persians disintegrated. Athens and Sparta emerged as leaders of two spheres of influence.

The First Peloponnesian War: Athens Against Sparta The Peloponnesian Wars were the manifestation of conflict between Athens and Sparta. Initial Athenian victories gave way to Spartan advances and the first Peloponnesian War ended with the two sides agreeing to a thirty-year peace.

Classical Greece Athenian government was more democratic than any previous political system. All male citizens had important rights. The official status of women was severely circumscribed. Scholars debate the extent and importance of slavery to ancient Greek society.

The Great Peloponnesian War Between 435 and 404 B.C.E. Athens and Sparta fought for dominance in Greece. The war ended in 404 B.C.E. when Athens surrendered unconditionally to Sparta and its allies.

Competition for Leadership in the Fourth Century B.C.E. Missteps by Sparta led their allies, the Persians, to turn against them. Thebes and Athens enjoyed short-lived ascendancies, but in the second half of the century Greece descended into chaos.

The Culture of Classical Greece Classical Greece produced dramas, architecture, sculpture, and philosophical and historical works. Athenian culture was shaped by its religious and civic values and by sociopolitical changes brought about by the Peloponnesian War.

The Hellenistic World Greek culture mixed with Middle Eastern elements and spread throughout the eastern Mediterranean, Egypt, and far into Asia. This spread was facilitated by the conquests of Alexander the Great and by the kingdoms that were founded by his generals after his death.

Hellenistic Culture After the Macedonian conquest, Greeks turned from the political to the personal. In Athenian philosophy, the Epicureans and the Stoics gained prominence. Hellenistic styles in architecture and sculpture were diffused over a wide area. Mathematics and science blossomed.

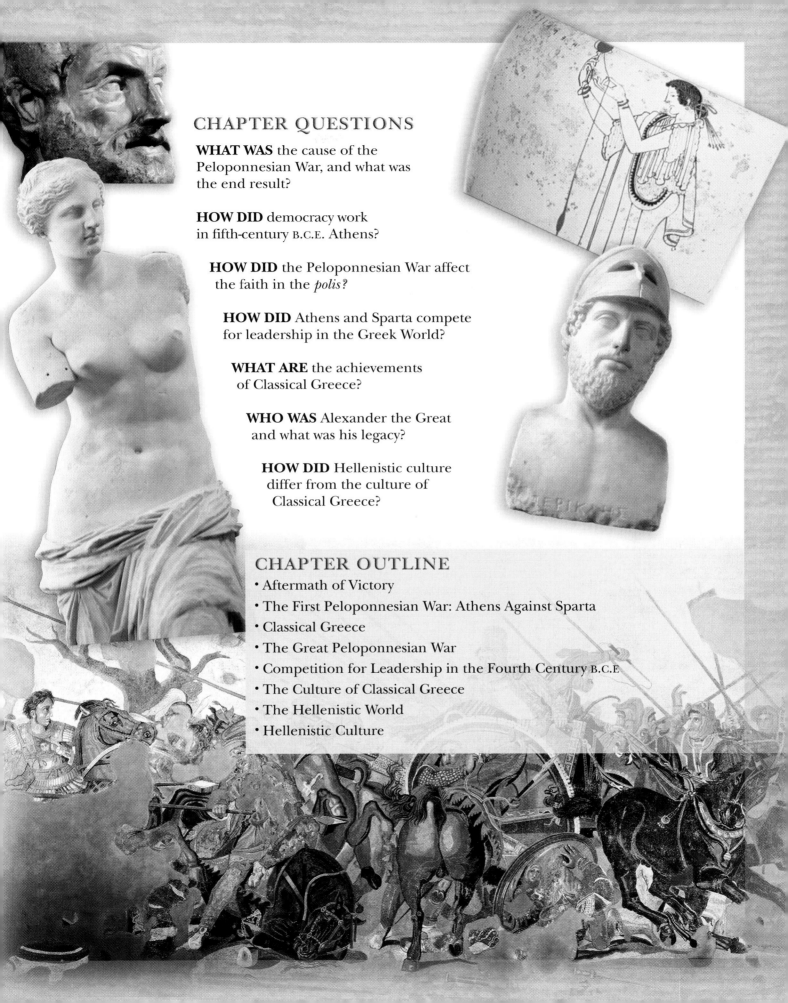

CHAPTER QUESTIONS

WHAT WAS the cause of the Peloponnesian War, and what was the end result?

HOW DID democracy work in fifth-century B.C.E. Athens?

HOW DID the Peloponnesian War affect the faith in the *polis*?

HOW DID Athens and Sparta compete for leadership in the Greek World?

WHAT ARE the achievements of Classical Greece?

WHO WAS Alexander the Great and what was his legacy?

HOW DID Hellenistic culture differ from the culture of Classical Greece?

CHAPTER OUTLINE

- Aftermath of Victory
- The First Peloponnesian War: Athens Against Sparta
- Classical Greece
- The Great Peloponnesian War
- Competition for Leadership in the Fourth Century B.C.E.
- The Culture of Classical Greece
- The Hellenistic World
- Hellenistic Culture

IMAGE KEY
for pages 56–57 is on page 83.

The Greeks' victory over the Persians (489–479 B.C.E.) marked the start of an era of great achievement. Fear of another Persian incursion into the Aegean led the Greeks to contemplate some kind of arrangement for their joint defense. The Spartans refused to make commitments that would take them away from their homeland, but the Athenians were eager for leadership opportunities. They negotiated a military alliance called the Delian League. It laid the foundation for an Athenian Empire, and fear of Athenian expansion led other states to ally with Sparta. The Greek world was polarized and finally erupted in a self-destructive civil war. In 338 B.C.E., Philip of Macedon intervened, took control, and ended the era of the independent polis.

AFTERMATH OF VICTORY

The Greek *poleis* found it hard to cooperate, even when faced with invasion by the Persian emperors. Only two years after their victory in the Persian Wars, divisions among the Greeks were again causing them to fight among themselves.

THE DELIAN LEAGUE

The Spartans, who led the Greeks to victory against the Persian invaders of the Greek mainland, were not prepared to assume responsibility for defending the Aegean against the return of the Persians. Sparta could not risk stationing its troops far from home for long periods lest its slaves rebel. A *polis* with a navy was also better equipped to defend the Aegean than the Spartan army.

Athens was Greece's leading naval power, and Athens was an Ionian state with ties to the Greeks whom the Persians still threatened on the Aegean islands and the coast of Asia Minor. In the winter of 478–477 B.C.E., at a meeting on the sacred island of Delos, the Athenians joined other Greeks in a pact to continue the war with Persia. The purpose of their **Delian League** was to free Greeks still under Persian rule, to defend against a Persian return, and to obtain compensation for the war by raiding Persian lands.

The league drove back the Persians and cleared the Aegean of pirates. In 467 B.C.E., when it won a great victory over the Persians at the Eurymedon River in Asia Minor, some cities decided the alliance had served its purpose and tried to withdraw. However, Athens refused to let them go, and what had begun as a voluntary association of free states began to become an empire dominated by Athens.

THE RISE OF CIMON

Themistocles fell from power at the end of the Persian Wars, and for two decades Athens was led by Cimon, son of Miltiades, the general who triumphed at Marathon. At home, Cimon preserved a limited version of Clisthenes' democratic constitution. Abroad, he maintained pressure on Persia and cultivated friendly relations with Sparta.

THE FIRST PELOPONNESIAN WAR: ATHENS AGAINST SPARTA

In 465 B.C.E., the island of Thasos rebelled against the Delian League. During the two years it took to put down the revolt, Cimon was absent from Athens. When he returned, his political opponents tried to bring him down by charging him with taking bribes. He was acquitted, but a radically democratic faction headed by a man named Ephialtes (and his protégé, Pericles) continued to attack Cimon for his pro-Spartan, proaristocratic policies.

WHAT WAS the cause of the Peloponnesian War, and what was the end result?

Delian League Pact joined in 478 B.C.E. by Athenians and other Greeks to continue the war with Persia.

THE BREACH WITH SPARTA

The people of Thasos asked Sparta to help them break free from the Delian League, and Sparta agreed to invade Attica. However, an earthquake sparked a Helot revolt, and instead of attacking Athens, Sparta asked the Athenians for help. Cimon's mistake was to talk his fellow Athenians into sending it. When the Spartans changed their minds about letting an Athenian army into their land and ordered Cimon to retreat, the humiliated Athenians exiled Cimon (461 B.C.E.) and allied with Argos, Sparta's enemy. With Cimon gone, the way was clear for the radical democrats and Pericles to dominate Athenian politics.

THE DIVISION OF GREECE

Because Sparta had been willing to help Thasos break up the Delian League, Pericles was able to persuade the Athenians to support the city of Megara when it withdrew from Sparta's Peloponnesian League. Megara was also strategically important to Athens, for it commanded the road that linked Attica with the Peloponnesus. Sparta's vigorous objection led to the outbreak of the first of the **Peloponnesian Wars**. The Athenians maintained the upper hand until about 455 B.C.E., when they lost a fleet they had sent to Egypt to harass the Persians. Some members of Athens's empire seized the opportunity this gave them to rebel, and Athens had to disentangle itself from war with Sparta. A truce was arranged, and in 449 B.C.E., Athens made peace with Persia.

In 446 B.C.E., war again broke out between Sparta and Athens, but it was ended by negotiation. Sparta recognized the Athenian Empire and Athens promised to cease efforts to take over more of the Greek mainland. The two *poleis* also pledged to keep the peace for thirty years. Hostilities stopped, but the Greeks were effectively divided between Sparta, which dominated the Greek mainland, and Athens, which ruled the Aegean Sea.

CLASSICAL GREECE

THE ATHENIAN EMPIRE

The Athenians used the failure of their Egyptian campaign as an excuse to move the league's treasury from the island of Delos to the greater security of Athens, and they began to keep one-sixtieth of its annual revenues for themselves. By 445 B.C.E., only Chios, Lesbos, and Samos maintained a semblance of equality with Athens by contributing their own ships to the league's navy. All the other states paid tribute, a mark of servitude that some resented. The fading

HOW DID democracy work in fifth-century B.C.E. Athens?

Peloponnesian Wars Series of wars between Athens and Sparta beginning in 460 B.C.E.

An Athenian silver four-drachma coin (tetradrachm) from the fifth century B.C.E. (440–430 B.C.E.). On the front (a) is the profile of Athena and on the back (b) is her symbol of wisdom, the owl. The silver from which the coins were struck came chiefly from the state mines at Sunium in southern Attica.
Hirmer Fotoarchive

(a)   (b)

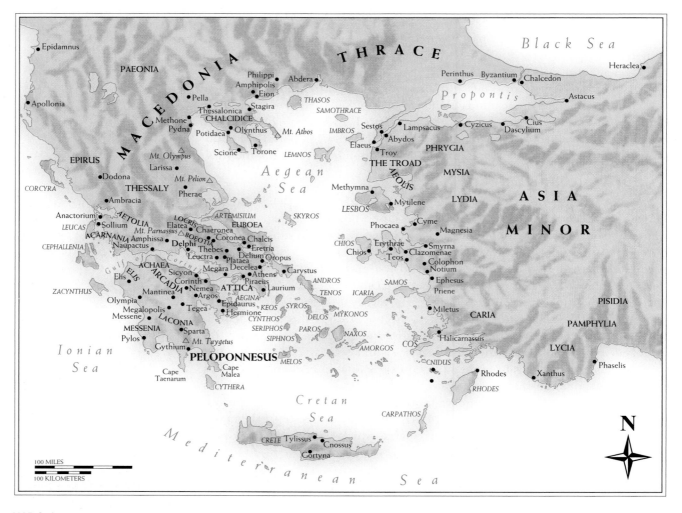

MAP 3–1

Classical Greece Greece in the Classical period (ca. 480–338 B.C.E.) centered on the Aegean Sea. Although there were important Greek settlements in Italy, Sicily, and all around the Black Sea, the area shown in this general reference map embraced the vast majority of Greek states

WHY WAS Athens not able to control its vast empire? What are some of the factors that led to its decline?

Persian threat had undercut the rationale for the league, but Athens profited too much from the Delian alliance to allow it to dissolve. Athenian dominance was also not universally unpopular. Athens supported democratic factions in its subject *poleis* and tried to behave more like a benevolent patron than an oppressor. (See Map 3–1.)

ATHENIAN DEMOCRACY

The people of Athens sensed no inconsistency in voting themselves more democratic privileges while they pursued an imperialistic foreign policy that diminished the freedoms of others. (See "Encountering the Past: The Panathenaic Festival.")

ENCOUNTERING THE PAST

THE PANATHENAIC FESTIVAL

G*reek religious festivals celebrated both the gods and the* poleis *that the gods protected. One of the most famous and joyous of these occasions was the* Panathenaia, *Athens's commemoration of the birth of Athena, the city's patron deity. The Panathenaia was of ancient origin, but the wealth Athenians derived from their empire enabled them to stage the event with unparalleled magnificence in the mid-fifth century* B.C.E. *The festival was observed annually, but every fourth year a Great Panathenaia was scheduled and celebrated with special splendor.*

The Panathenaia, like most Greek religious festivals, included athletic contests. The prizes were valuable, elaborately painted jars filled with olive oil (one of Athens's chief exports). There were competitions among *rhapsodes*, professional reciters of the *Iliad* and the *Odyssey*, and choruses of men and boys also sang and danced for prizes. The highlight of the occasion, however, was the procession that brought the gift of a brightly colored woolen robe to the image of the goddess in her temple on the Acropolis. This event is depicted by a frieze sculpted on the inner chamber of the Parthenon.

Although Athenian women usually avoided appearing in public, they played a major role in the Panathenaia. A group of priestesses and consecrated maidens spent a year weaving the goddess's robe, and they led the procession that conveyed it to her temple. The massive numbers of animals sacrificed to Athena provided a birthday feast for her worshipers. Because most Athenians rarely had an opportunity to eat fresh meat, the Panathenaia was an invitation to overindulgence. Several ancient sources refer to the (sometimes comical) consequences of crowds of people simultaneously gorging on meat.

HOW WERE religious and secular civic interests combined in the celebration of the Panathenaic festival?

Water-clock and Jury Ballots. Participants in an Athenian trial could speak for only a limited time. A water-clock (Clepsydra) like this kept the time. In front of it are two ballots used by the jurors to vote in favor of the plaintiff or the defendant.

Picture Desk/The Art Archive/Agora Museum Athens/Dagli Orti.

Democratic Legislation Under Pericles' leadership, the Athenians suspended the traditional property qualification that allowed only wealthy individuals to run for high office. Men who could afford to equip themselves for service as *hoplites* qualified for election as *archons*. Pay was provided for jurors to make it possible for the poor to take time off from their jobs to serve. Circuit judges were sent into the countryside so the rural poor would have access to Athenian justice.

As democracy made citizenship an increasingly valuable commodity, the electorate guarded its privileges by limiting the number of voters. Citizenship was granted only to men who could prove their mothers as well as their fathers descended from citizen families. Every Greek *polis* (including the most democratic) denied participation in government to large segments of its population—resident aliens, women, and slaves.

Pericles (ca. 495-429 B.C.E.) was the leading statesman of Athens for much of the fifth century. This is a Roman copy in marble of the Greek bronze bust that was probably cast in the last decade of Pericles' life.

Library of Congress

3.5
Pericles' Funeral Oration by Thucydides

How Did the Democracy Work? Athenian democracy gave citizens extensive powers. Every decision of the state had to be approved by the popular assembly—by the voters themselves and not by some small group of elected representatives. Every judicial decision was subject to appeal to a popular court composed of not fewer than 51 and possibly as many as 1,501 citizens selected from the Athenian population at large. Many officials were chosen by casting lots, which eliminated considerations of class. Successful candidates for the chief offices—the imperial treasurers and the city's ten generals (who had political as well as military functions)—were usually wealthy aristocrats. But the voters could, in theory, elect anyone. All public officials had to submit to examination before taking office. They could be removed from office, and they had to account at the end of their term for the uses they had made of their authority. Because there was no standing army or police force, leaders lacked instruments they might have used to coerce or intimidate voters.

Pericles was elected to the generalship fifteen years in a row and thirty times in all, not because he was a dictator but because he was a persuasive speaker and a respected leader. On the few occasions when he lost the people's confidence, they did not hesitate to remove him from office. At the start of his career, Pericles was an imperialist. But after the defeat of the fleet Athens sent to Egypt and the city's failure to expand its territory on the mainland, he decided it was better to preserve the empire Athens already had and pursue peace with Sparta.

ATHENIAN WOMEN: LEGAL STATUS AND EVERYDAY LIFE

Greek society, like most others throughout history, was dominated by men, and democratic Athens was no exception. Women from citizen families were excluded from most aspects of public life. They could not debate, vote, or hold office and were subject all their lives to the authority of a masculine guardian—a father, a husband, or other male relative. Women married young, usually between the ages of twelve and eighteen, but men often did not marry until they were in their thirties. This meant that most men probably took brides much younger than themselves whom they treated like dependent children. Marriages were arranged, often without consulting the bride. Brides were given dowries, but they had no control over them or any other property. It was difficult for a woman to initiate divorce, for she had to find a male relative who agreed to take responsibility for her after the dissolution of her marriage.

The chief function of an Athenian woman from a citizen family was the production of male heirs to perpetuate her husband's *oikos* ("household"). A woman whose father died without leaving a male heir became an *epikleros*, an heiress. If she was married at the time, she had to separate from her husband and wed one of her father's relatives to bear a son who would reestablish her father's male line.

Because citizenship was inherited, the legitimacy of children was important. Athenian males consorted freely with prostitutes and concubines, but citizen women had no contact with any men but close relatives. They were confined to special women's quarters in their homes and spent their time raising children, cooking, weaving, and managing their households. Occasionally they emerged in

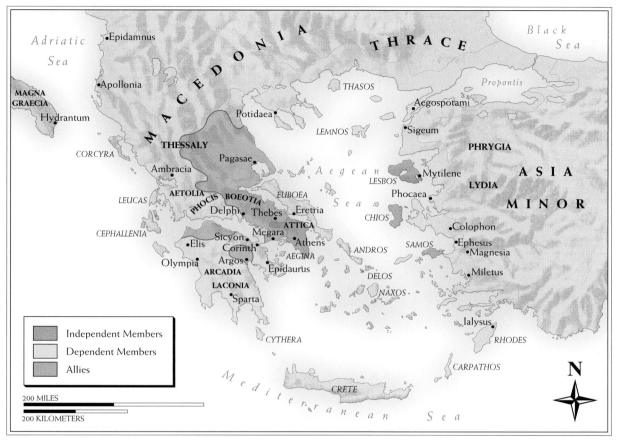

MAP 3–2

The Athenian Empire about 450 B.C.E.   The Athenian Empire at its fullest extent. We see Athens and the independent states that provided manned ships for the imperial fleet, but paid no tribute; dependent states that paid tribute; and states allied to, but not actually in, the empire.

WHY WOULD some of the weakest and most dependent Greek states be located in Asia Minor and Thrace?

public to take part in the state religion. But for the most part, they were expected to be invisible. In a frequently quoted speech, Pericles declared that "the greatest glory of women is to be least talked about by men, whether for good or bad."

Evidence from myths and from the works of the great Athenian dramatists (who often featured women in their plays) suggests that the roles played by Athenian women may have been more complex than their legal status implies. Only the rich could have afforded to lock their women up at home. The poor needed the labor of their women in fields and shops, and such women had to move about in public. Fetching water from the town wells and fountains was also women's work, and vase paintings and literature document the gathering of women at these places. Because historians disagree about the reliability of various sources, women's place in the Greek world remains a topic for debate.

An Exceptional Woman: Aspasia   Pericles' female companion, Aspasia, did not cultivate the invisibility that he said was "the greatest glory of women." She was a *hetaira*, an entertainer who came from Miletus (the city where Greek philosophy got its start). Highly intelligent and well educated, she could hold her own with thinkers such as Socrates. (Socrates' student, Plato, joked that she

QUICK REVIEW

Aspasia

• Pericles' female companion

• Highly intelligent and well educated

• Pericles discussed politics with her and respected her ideas

The Acropolis was both the religious and civic center of Athens. In its final form it is the work of Pericles and his successors in the late fifth century B.C.E. This photograph shows the Parthenon and to its left the Erechtheum.

Meredith Pillon, Greek National Tourism Organization

wrote Pericles' speeches.) Pericles clearly loved her. He divorced his wife, took her into his home, lavished affection on her, introduced her to his friends, discussed politics with her, and took her ideas seriously. Athens was scandalized—not because Pericles kept a woman, but because he treated one with such respect.

SLAVERY

Slavery always existed in Greece, but the earliest forms of bondage resembled serfdom more than chattel slavery. When the Spartans, for instance, conquered a people, they reduced them to the status of Helots, peasants who were bound to the land to work the farms that supported Sparta's citizen-soldiers. Until Solon put an end to the practice about 600 B.C.E., an Athenian citizen who defaulted on a debt was subject to temporary bondage or even sale into permanent slavery outside Attica.

Chattel slavery proper proliferated about 500 B.C.E. and remained important to Greek society thereafter. Most slaves of this kind were prisoners of war or persons abducted by pirates. The Greeks, like other ancient peoples, viewed foreigners as inferiors who were fit for slavery. Slaves were sometimes employed as shepherds, but Greek farms were often too small to afford more than one enslaved worker. As a rule, the landed estates of the upper classes were worked by free tenant farmers rather than slaves. Wealthy men usually invested in small scattered farms rather than the consolidated plantations associated with slave labor. Industries such as mining employed large numbers of slaves. Slaves also worked as craftsmen in almost every trade. Like slaves on small farms, these men and women labored alongside their masters. Householders used slaves for domestic help, and the state purchased slaves to serve as prison attendants, clerks, and secretaries.

Scholars debate the extent of slavery and its importance to ancient Greek society. Reliable statistics are hard to come by. Estimates of the number of slaves in Athens during the fifth and fourth centuries B.C.E. range from 20,000 to

100,000. If the truth is closer to the mean between these extremes, the city's 40,000 households owned about 60,000 slaves—or about two per family. Only a quarter to a third of free Athenians may have had slaves. This is comparable to the situation in the American South prior to the Civil War. Unlike the southern United States, however, the Athenian economy did not depend on a single cash crop produced by slave labor, and Greek slaves did not differ from their masters in skin color. (Slaves walked the streets of Athens with such ease as to offend class-conscious Athenians.) Americans also seldom emancipated slaves, but Greeks often did.

THE GREAT PELOPONNESIAN WAR

HOW DID the Peloponnesian War affect the faith in the *polis*?

*T*he thirty years of peace that Sparta and Athens pledged to maintain in 445 B.C.E. ended prematurely. About 435 B.C.E., a dispute in a remote part of the Greek world escalated to become a war that shook the foundations of Greek civilization.

CAUSES

The conflict began with a quarrel between Corinth and Corcyra, an island at the entrance to the Adriatic Sea. The Athenians decided to intervene to prevent Corinth, their commercial rival, from capturing Corcyra's large fleet. Corinth was understandably angered, and it appealed to Sparta, its ally, for help. At a meeting of the Peloponnesian League, which Sparta convened in the summer of 432 B.C.E., the Corinthians called for war with Athens, and the following spring (431 B.C.E.) the Spartans invaded Attica.

STRATEGIC STALEMATE

The Spartan strategy was traditional: invade the enemy's territory and by threatening the farms that supply their food, force them to accept battle with the Spartan infantry. Because the Spartans had the better army and outnumbered the Athenians by more than two to one, they were confident of victory.

Most *poleis* would probably have come to terms with Sparta, but Athens was in a unique position to resist. It had strong walls that Sparta could not breach, and it was connected to its port (the Piraeus) by the Long Walls, a kind of fortified highway. So long as the Athenians had their navy and their empire, they could ride out a siege by supplying themselves from the sea. By remaining secure behind their walls and ignoring the Spartan invasion, they could also show the world that Sparta's military might was useless against them. In the interim, the Athenian fleet could frighten Sparta's allies by raiding the Peloponnesian coast. Pericles believed this strategy would force the Peloponnesian League to recognize the hopelessness of the situation and sue for peace. The plan was brilliant but difficult to implement. The Athenians had to exercise great

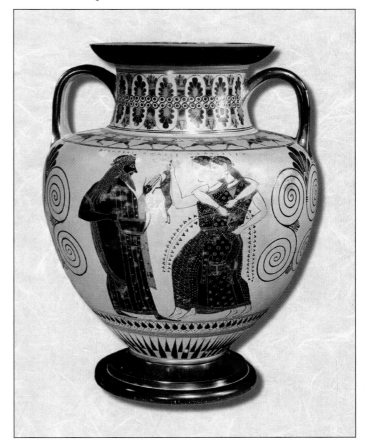

This storage jar (*amphora*), made about 540 B.C.E. is attributed to the anonymous Athenian master artist called the Amasis painter. It shows Dionysus, the god of wine, revelry, and fertility with two of his ecstatic female worshipers called maenads.

Cliché Bibliotheque Nationale de France—Paris

HISTORY'S VOICES

THUCYDIDES ON CIVIL WAR

I n 427 B.C.E., in the fifth year of the Pelopon-nesian War, a vicious and brutal civil war broke out on the island of Corcyra, an ally of Athens, between political factions—democrats who favored the Athenian alliance and oligarchs who preferred the Spartans. The historian Thucydides describes the affair and draws general conclusions from it about human behavior under extreme pressure.

ACCORDING TO Thucydides, how do the passions unleashed by such wars affect the behavior of individuals?

So bloody was the march of the revolution, and the impression which it made was the greater as it was one of the first to occur. Later on, one may say, the whole Hellenic world was convulsed; struggles being everywhere made by the popular chiefs to bring in the Athenians, and by the oligarchs to introduce the Lacedœmonians. In peace there would have been neither the pretext nor the wish to make such an invitation; but in war, with an alliance always at the command of either faction for the hurt of their adversaries and their own corresponding advantage, opportunities for bringing in the foreigner were never wanting to the revolutionary parties. The sufferings which revolution entailed upon the cities were many and terrible, such as have occurred and always will occur, as long as the nature of mankind remains the same; though in a severer or milder form, and varying in their symptoms, according to the variety of the particular cases. In peace and prosperity, states and individuals have better sentiments, because they do not find themselves suddenly confronted with imperious necessities; but war takes away the easy supply of daily wants, and so proves a rough master, that brings most men's characters to a level with their fortunes. Revolution thus ran its course from city to city, and the places which it arrived at last, from having heard what had been done before, carried to a still greater excess the refinement of their inventions, as manifested in the cunning of their enterprises and the atrocity of their reprisals. Words had to change their ordinary meaning and to take that which was now given them. Reckless audacity came to be considered the courage of a loyal ally; prudent hesitation, specious cowardice; moderation was held to be a cloak for unmanliness.

Thucydides, *The Peloponnesian War*, trans. by Richard Crawley (New York: Random House, 1951), p. 189.

self-control while Sparta destroyed their farms and taunted them. As citizens of a democracy, they could have changed their policies at any time, but Pericles' leadership helped them stay the course. In 429 B.C.E., however, plague swept the crowded city, Pericles died, and the politicians who succeeded him were less able men.

The Athenian electorate divided into two camps. One faction (led by a man named Nicias) wanted to continue Pericles' defensive strategy, but another (headed by a certain Cleon) proposed launching an offensive. In 425 B.C.E., when an Athenian naval expedition marooned and captured four hundred Spartans on an island on the coast of the Peloponnese, Athens passed up an opportunity to make peace. Sparta offered to end the war in exchange for the return of its men, but Cleon's party persuaded the Athenians to attempt some land battles.

The failure of two campaigns shook the Athenians' confidence in Cleon—particularly after the Spartan general, Brasidas, captured Amphipolis, an Aegean port that protected Athens's access to grain supplies. In 422 B.C.E., Cleon led an assault on Amphipolis in which he and Brasidas were killed, and the deaths of both leaders paved the way for a truce in the spring of 421 B.C.E. The struggle over Amphipolis had an additional outcome of a very different sort. An Athenian admiral named Thucydides was blamed for the loss of Amphipolis and punished with exile. He used his enforced leisure to write a masterful history of the war, which, as it turned out, was far from over.

THE FALL OF ATHENS

The Peace of Nicias, the agreement between Athens and Sparta, declared a truce that was supposed to last for fifty years, but neither side fulfilled all its treaty obligations. This meant that hostilities were likely break out again, but in 415 B.C.E. an ambitious young politician named Alcibiades persuaded the Athenians to squander their resources on a risky foreign adventure. Athens sent a huge expedition to Sicily and lost 200 ships and 4,500 men. When the subjects of the Athenian Empire seized the opportunity to rebel against a weakened Athens, Persia intervened to help the Greeks destroy themselves. It offered aid to Sparta.

The Athenians found the will to continue the fight, but their resources were no match for the support Spartans received from Persia. In 405 B.C.E., a Spartan fleet destroyed the Athenian ships that were guarding the city's grain-supply route. Lysander, the Spartan commander, cut off Athens's food supply and starved the city into submission (404 B.C.E.). Athens was stripped of its fleet and empire but allowed to survive.

COMPETITION FOR LEADERSHIP IN THE FOURTH CENTURY B.C.E.

Sparta tried to take Athens' place as leader of the Greek world, but its limited manpower, restive slaves, conservative traditions, and indebtedness to Persia doomed its efforts to maintain order in the Aegean. The Greeks soon reverted to fighting among themselves.

HOW DID Athens and Sparta compete for leadership in the Greek world?

THE HEGEMONY OF SPARTA

The Greeks grumbled when the Spartans repaid their debts to Persia by ceding Persia the cities of Ionia that the Greeks had liberated in the Persian Wars. Lysander made more enemies by trying to force the cities the Spartans had liberated from Athenian control into a new Spartan Empire. He overthrew democracies and installed oligarchies loyal to him in many Greek cities. He deployed Spartan garrisons to back up his puppet governments, and he exacted tributes that equaled those that Athens had demanded.

The oligarchs whom Lysander established in control of Athens following its surrender in 404 B.C.E. were so unpopular, they were called the Thirty Tyrants. Their oppression forced Athens's democratic leaders to flee to Thebes and begin to raise an army with which to retake the city. Sparta's cautious king, Pausanias, prevented an outbreak of fighting by recalling Lysander and allowing Athens to revert to democracy. So long as Athenian foreign policy remained under Spartan control, Sparta could afford to allow Athens to have any kind of government it wanted.

Persia might have been expected to take advantage of this confusion, but it was distracted by an internal power struggle. Following the death of the emperor Darius II in 405 B.C.E., a Persian prince named Cyrus tried to seize the Persian throne with the help of an army of Greek mercenaries. The Greeks routed the Persians. But when Cyrus died in battle in 401 B.C.E., they found themselves

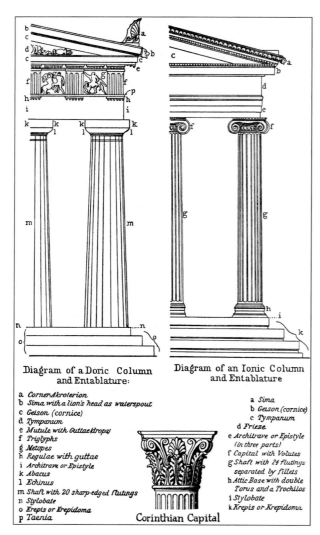

Diagram of a Doric Column
and Entablature:

a *Corner Akroterion*
b *Sima with a lion's head as waterspout*
c *Geison (cornice)*
d *Tympanum*
e *Mutule with Guttae (trops)*
f *Triglyphs*
g *Metopes*
h *Regulae with guttae*
i *Architrave or Epistyle*
k *Abacus*
l *Echinus*
m *Shaft with 20 sharp-edged flutings*
n *Stylobate*
o *Krepis or Krepidoma*
p *Taenia*

Diagram of an Ionic Column
and Entablature

a *Sima*
b *Geison (cornice)*
c *Tympanum*
d *Frieze*
e *Architrave or Epistyle
   (in three parts)*
f *Capital with Volutes*
g *Shaft with 24 flutings
   separated by fillets*
h *Attic Base with double
   Torus and a Trochilos*
i *Stylobate*
k *Krepis or Krepidoma*

Corinthian Capital

The three orders of Greek architecture, Doric, Ionic, and Corinthian, have had an enduring impact on Western architecture.

WHAT ARE the achievements of
Classical Greece?

stranded without a leader or a purpose deep in enemy territory. They fought their way home, but the cities of Asia Minor that had supported Cyrus now faced the threat of Persian revenge.

In 396 B.C.E., when the Spartan king, Agesilaus, led an army out to defend his interests in Asia Minor, the Persians countered by offering aid to any Greek state that rebelled against Sparta. Thebes, Athens's neighbor, accepted, and in 395 B.C.E., it enlisted the cooperation of Argos, Corinth, and a resurgent Athens. The war that resulted forced the Spartans to retreat from Asia Minor, and in 394 B.C.E., the Persian fleet destroyed Sparta's navy. The Athenians seized the opportunity that Sparta's difficulties gave them to refortify their city, rebuild their navy, and recover some of their foreign possessions.

The Persians, who believed Athens was potentially a greater threat than Sparta, then agreed to aid Sparta so long as it confined its ambitions to the Greek mainland. In 382 B.C.E., Agesilaus seized Thebes in a surprise attack. However, an attempt to take Athens failed, and by 379 B.C.E., the Thebans had regained their independence. In 371 B.C.E., the great Theban general, Epaminondas, crushed the Spartan army at the battle of Leuctra. He followed this up by freeing the Helots and helping them organize to fight the Spartans. Deprived of land and slaves, Sparta's days as a major power came to an end.

THE HEGEMONY OF THEBES: THE SECOND ATHENIAN EMPIRE

Epaminondas's humiliation of Sparta opened the way for Thebes to become the dominant power in Greece. Thebes did take control of the Greek states north of Athens and west along the shores of the Corinthian Gulf, but Athens organized resistance to Theban expansion. In 362 B.C.E., Epaminondas routed Athens and its allies at the Battle of Mantinea, but he died in the fighting. The loss of the leader struck a fatal blow to Theban ambition.

In 378 B.C.E. (sixteen years before the Battle of Mantinea), a Second Athenian Confederation had been organized to oppose Spartan aggression in the Aegean. Although its constitution was designed to prevent Athens from exploiting this alliance as it had the Delian League, it was difficult for the members of the confederation to trust Athens. The collapse of Sparta and Thebes and the fading of the Persian threat persuaded some of them that the alliance had outlived its purpose. They rebelled, and by 355 B.C.E., Athens once again had lost an empire. It was also clear that despite two centuries of almost continuous warfare, the Greek world was still unstable.

THE CULTURE OF CLASSICAL GREECE

The Greeks' victories in the Persian Wars gave them tremendous self-confidence and unleashed a flood of creative activity that was rarely, if ever, matched anywhere at any time. The result was what has come to be called Western civilization's Classical Period.

THE FIFTH CENTURY B.C.E.

Much Classical art and architecture is characterized by calm and serenity, but a common theme of tension runs through the thought, art, literature, and lives of the Greeks of the Classical Period. This reflected the difficulty of reconciling private ambition with the restraints imposed by *polis* citizenship and the conflict between the Greeks' competitive drives and their belief that excessive striving led to disaster. The Greeks' faith in themselves was ratified by their victory over Persia, but they knew that they, like Xerxes, risked punishment if they went too far. As Athens and Sparta teetered on the brink of self-destructive war, Athenian playwrights explored the problem of striking the right balance between human ambition and divine justice.

Attic Tragedy   Greek plays were staged in groups at festivals honoring the god Dionysus. Each of the three playwrights whose work was chosen for presentation by the *archons* wrote three tragedies (which might or might not have a common subject) and a satyr play (a concluding comic choral dialogue with Dionysus). Each play was performed by no more than three actors, who were paid by the state, and a chorus of singers and dancers that was sponsored by a wealthy citizen. Plays were presented in the temple of Dionysus, a 30,000-seat amphitheater on the south side of the Acropolis. A jury of Athenians, chosen by lot, awarded prizes for the best author, actor, and sponsor.

Athenian playwrights used the theater to encourage the *polis*'s citizens to think deeply about the use they made of their power as voters in a democracy. A play might dramatize a contemporary or historical event, but authors usually preferred to retell a myth in a way that would illuminate current affairs. Aeschylus and Sophocles, who wrote our earliest extant plays, dealt with abstract ideas (religion, politics, and ethics). Euripides, a somewhat later poet, was more interested in exploring human psychology.

Old Comedy   Comedies were added to the Dionysian festival early in the fifth century B.C.E. The only complete comic plays to survive are those of Aristophanes (ca. 450–385 B.C.E), who wrote humorously about serious issues. He employed scathing invective and satire to lampoon his contemporaries—even powerful politicians such as Pericles and Cleon.

Architecture and Sculpture   Like the plays that members of Pericles' generation witnessed, the buildings their city erected reflect the creative tension of the Classical era. In 448 B.C.E., Pericles began to rebuild the Acropolis (using income from the Delian League). His plan included new temples and an imposing gateway for the sacred precinct. Pericles' intent was to create an environment in which the power and intellectual genius of Athens would become tangible experiences—making Athens, in his words, "the school of Hellas."

Philosophy   The art of the fifth century B.C.E. aimed at defining the essence of humanity and illustrating its place in the natural order. Similar concerns had

The Competition for Leadership of Greece

479 B.C.E.	Battles of Plataea and Mycale
478–477 B.C.E.	Formation of the Delian League
465–463 B.C.E.	Thasos attempts to leave the league
462 B.C.E.	Pericles begins to lead Athens
460–445 B.C.E.	First Peloponnesian War
454 B.C.E.	Athens is defeated in Egypt
449 B.C.E.	Athens makes peace with Persia
435 B.C.E.	Corinth attacks Corcyra
432–404 B.C.E.	Great Peloponnesian War
421 B.C.E.	Peace of Nicias
415–413 B.C.E.	Athens's Sicilian campaign
404 B.C.E.	Sparta defeats Athens
404–403 B.C.E.	Thirty Tyrants govern Athens
382 B.C.E.	Sparta seizes Thebes
378 B.C.E.	Second Athenian Confederation
371 B.C.E.	Thebes defeats Sparta at Leuctra
362 B.C.E.	End of Theban hegemony
338 B.C.E.	Philip of Macedon dominates Greece
336–323 B.C.E.	Reign of Alexander the Great

QUICK REVIEW

Athenian Drama

- Plays were staged in groups of three at festivals honoring the gods
- Plays were presented in the temple of Dionysus
- Playwrights used the theater to encourage citizens to think about the issues of the day

3.4
Drama: *Antigone* by Sophocles

prompted the invention of philosophy in the sixth century B.C.E. Thales, the first philosopher, wondered how a world filled with changing phenomena could hang together as a stable, coherent whole. He suggested that the changes we see taking place in the things around us are only alterations in the state of a single universal substance from which all these things are made. He believed this substance was water, for water is found in nature as a solid, a liquid, and a gas. Later thinkers proposed other universal substances, but some claimed Thales was naive in assuming that change and permanence could both exist in the same system.

Heraclitus said that permanence is an illusion produced by our inability to perceive changes that are very slow. Parmenides of Elea and his pupil Zeno countered that the concept of change is a logical absurdity, for it implies that something can arise from nothing. Empedocles of Acragas suggested a compromise between these opposing points of view. He said the world is composed of permanent elements (fire, water, earth, and air) whose combinations change. Similarly, Leucippus of Miletus and Democritus of Abdera imagined the world to be made up of innumerable tiny, indivisible particles (*atomoi*) that clump together and spin apart in the void of space. These philosophies all embraced materialism. That is, they claimed that spirit is simply a refined form of matter and that, therefore, physical laws can be discovered to explain even intellectual phenomena. Anaxagoras of Clazomenae, however, disagreed. He believed the universe was indeed composed of tiny fundamental particles ("seeds"), but he claimed it was controlled by another kind of reality—a rational force he called *nous* ("mind"). The debate between materialism and idealism that Greek thinkers such as these began has yet to be resolved.

Most philosophical speculations were too abstract to interest ordinary Greeks. However, the Sophists, a group of professional teachers who flourished in the mid–fifth century B.C.E., attracted a popular following by teaching a practical skill: rhetoric. The arts of persuasion were highly valued in democratic Athens, where public debates decided most important issues. Sophists refrained from speculations about the physical universe and concentrated their attention on rational critiques of beliefs and institutions. They were particularly interested in the impact that nature and custom had on human social behavior. The more traditional among them argued that society's laws were of divine origin and based in nature, but others dismissed laws as mere conventions—arbitrary arrangements people make so they can live together. The most extreme Sophists maintained that law is contrary to nature, for the weak use the law to restrain the strong—a reversal of the order of nature. Critias, an Athenian oligarch, even claimed the gods were nothing but inventions designed to deter people from doing what they want. Speculations such as these undermined the concept of justice on which the *polis* was founded, and the later giants of philosophy, Plato and Aristotle, worked hard to refute them.

History Herodotus—"the father of history"—was born shortly before the outbreak of the Persian Wars. In writing an account of those wars, he far exceeded attempts by earlier prose writers to describe and explain human actions. Although his *History* was completed about 425 B.C.E. and shows a few traces of Sophist influence, it is reminiscent of an earlier age. Herodotus accepted legendary material as fact (although not uncritically), and he believed in oracles and divine intervention. However, his recognition of the crucial role human intelligence plays in determining the course of events was in sync with the rational, scientific spirit of his day. He also acknowledged the importance of institutions. He credited Greece's victory over Persia to the love of liberty the *polis* instilled in its citizens.

Thucydides was born about 460 B.C.E. and died a few years after the end of the Peloponnesian War, the conflict whose history he devoted his life to describing. His thought was influenced by the rational skepticism of the Sophists of the late fifth century B.C.E., and he shared the scientific attitudes that characterized the work of contemporaries such as the physician Hippocrates of Cos. Thucydides took great pains to achieve factual accuracy, and he searched his evidence for significant patterns of human behavior. He hoped that by discovering these patterns people would be able to foresee events. Because human nature was, he believed, essentially unchanging, people ought to respond to similar circumstances in similar ways. Thucydides admitted, however, that the lessons of history were not always enough to guarantee success in dealing with the challenges we face. He believed an element of randomness (chance) affects human destiny.

THE FOURTH CENTURY B.C.E.

The Peloponnesian War diminished faith in the *polis* as an effective form of government. The Greeks of the fourth century B.C.E. may not fully have grasped what was happening, but they did sense threats to their traditional institutions. Some tried to revive the *polis*. Others looked for alternatives to it. Still others gave up on public life altogether.

Drama   The poetry of the fourth century B.C.E. reveals the disillusionment some Greeks felt with the *polis*. Poets switched their attention from politics and public

The theater at Epidaurus was built in the fourth century B.C.E. The city contained the Sanctuary of Asclepius, a god of healing, and drew many visitors who packed the theater at religious festivals.

Hirmer Fotoarchiv

The striding god from Artemisium is a bronze statue dating from about 460 B.C.E. It was found in the sea near Artemisium, the northern tip of the large Greek island of Euboea, and is now on display in the Athens archaeological museum. Exactly whom he represents is not known. Some have thought him to be Poseidon holding a trident; others believe he is Zeus hurling a thunderbolt. In either case, he is a splendid representative of the early Classical period of Greek sculpture.

National Archaeological Museum, Athens

events to the private concerns of ordinary people—family and the interior lives of individuals. Old Comedy had focused on matters of public policy, but Middle and New Comedy humorously depicted daily life and satirized domestic situations and personal relationships. The role of the chorus, a kind of symbol for the *polis* community in earlier theater, was much diminished. Menander (342–291 B.C.E.), the pioneer of New Comedy, wrote domestic tragicomedy: gentle spoofs of the foibles of ordinary people and the trials of thwarted lovers—the material of modern situation comedies.

Tragedy, which drew its inspiration from the robust political life of the *polis*, declined during the fourth century B.C.E. No plays from the period have survived. Theatrical producers must have sensed a decline in quality, for they began to revive the plays of the previous century. Euripides' tragedies, which had rarely won top honors when first produced, finally found their audiences. More than the other great Athenian playwrights, Euripides had explored the interior lives of individuals, and some of his late plays are more like fairy tales, fantasy adventures, or love stories than tragedies.

Sculpture　The movement away from the grand, the ideal, and the general and toward the ordinary, the real, and the individual that we see in fourth-century B.C.E. literature is also apparent in sculpture. It explains the contrast between the work of Polycleitus (ca. 450–440 B.C.E.) and that of Praxiteles (ca. 340–330 B.C.E.) or Lysippus (ca. 330 B.C.E.).

PHILOSOPHY AND THE CRISIS OF THE *POLIS*

Socrates　Socrates (469–399 B.C.E.) was one of the first Greek intellectuals to recognize the shortcomings of the *polis*. He seldom involved himself in Athenian political life, but he did not entirely reject the *polis* ideal. He did his duty as a citizen—serving in the army to defend his city, obeying its laws, and seeking a rational justification for its values.

Because Socrates wrote nothing, our knowledge of him depends on the reports of his disciples, Plato and Xenophon, and later commentators. In his youth Socrates supposedly studied the early philosophers who sought explanations for the phenomena of nature, but his interests soon shifted to the interior world—to the processes that govern thought and decision making. Unlike some Sophists, he believed in the existence of truth and the power of reason to discover it.

Socrates said that he hoped to discover truths by cross-examining people who were reputed to have them—that is, those who were confident in their ideas. His conversations with them always ended in the same way: by demonstrating that, except for some technical information and practical skills, people had few beliefs they could rationally support. It is not surprising that the Athenians whose opinions were shaken by his rigorous critiques accused him of undermining their confidence in values fundamental to the *polis*. Socrates also made no attempt to conceal his contempt for Athenian democracy, a political system that he said empowered the ignorant to make decisions about things they did not understand.

In 399 B.C.E., an Athens that was struggling to come to terms with its loss of the Peloponnesian War decided it could no longer tolerate Socrates. He was tried, convicted, and sentenced to die for undercutting the Athenian way of life.

OVERVIEW   THE THREE GREAT GREEK INTELLECTUALS

Socrates (469–399 B.C.E.)	One of the first Greek intellectuals to recognize the shortcomings of the *polis*. He believed in the existence of truth and the power of reason to discover it. He made no attempt to conceal his contempt for Athenian democracy—a political system that he said empowered the ignorant to make decisions about things they did not understand. Socrates was eventually tried and executed for undercutting the Athenian way of life.
Plato (429–347 B.C.E.)	The most important of Socrates' followers, he was the first to formulate a consistent worldview and a method for exploring all of life's fundamental questions. Like Socrates, Plato believed in the *polis* and saw it as consistent with humanity's social nature. He established the "Academy" in 386 B.C.E., a school for training statesmen and citizens. Plato believed power should be entrusted to philosophers only and that the *polis* could only be redeemed by improving its ability to produce good citizens.
Aristotle (384–322 B.C.E.)	The most prominent of Plato's students, he founded the Lyceum (the school of the Peripatetics). Unlike Plato's students at the Academy, Aristotle's students gathered, ordered, and analyzed data from all fields of knowledge. He wrote on logic, physics, astronomy, biology, ethics, rhetoric, literary criticism, and politics. Aristotle believed human beings are social creatures and that the *polis* was necessary to realize their potential. He also stated that a moderate constitution was necessary to create a state dominated by the middle class, not by the rich or the poor.

Having made its point, the city had no need to execute Socrates, and it gave him a chance to escape. Plato says, however, that Socrates refused to do so out of respect for the law. By taking this stand, Socrates proved he was not a Sophist or a skeptic whose only purpose was to foster doubt. He said the authority of the laws of the *polis*, which had protected him all his life, could not be denied simply because he now found the law inconvenient. Although he claimed never to have found the truth, by dying he witnessed to his faith in the existence of truth that transcends human conventions.

Plato   Plato (429–347 B.C.E.), the most important of Socrates' followers, is the prime example of the pupil who becomes greater than his master. Plato was the first systematic philosopher—the first to formulate a consistent worldview and a method for exploring all of life's fundamental questions. He was also a brilliant writer. His twenty-six philosophical discussions—most cast in the form of dialogues—are artistic masterpieces that make the analysis of complicated philosophical ideas dramatic and entertaining.

Plato was an Athenian aristocrat who initially planned a career in politics, but Socrates' execution discouraged him. He left Athens and moved to Sicily to serve as tutor and adviser to two of the tyrants of Syracuse, Dionysius I and II. Having been disillusioned by democracy, he pinned his hopes for the creation of ideal states on rationally disciplined tyrants—philosopher kings. When his Sicilian experiment failed, he returned to Athens and established a school for training statesmen and citizens. The "**Academy**," which he founded in 386 B.C.E., survived until a Christian emperor closed it in the sixth century C.E.

Like Socrates and unlike the radical Sophists, Plato believed in the *polis*. He saw it as consistent with humanity's social nature and believed it could be made into an instrument for creating good people. Socrates' insistence that virtue is a

Academy   School founded by Plato in Athens to train statesmen and citizens.

kind of knowledge led Plato to reject democracy. The knowledge (*episteme*, "science") on which virtue is based was, he thought, beyond most people. Because only a few specially gifted and educated individuals could acquire it and because reason dictates that each person in society should do that to which he or she is best suited by nature, communities should entrust power only to philosophers. Only they are capable, in Plato's opinion, of subordinating private interests to those of the community. Only they could maintain harmony in a *polis* by eliminating the causes of strife: private property, family interests, and the personal ambitions that distract individuals from the public good.

Concern for the redemption of the *polis* was central to Plato's philosophy, and he believed the *polis* could only be redeemed and preserved by improving its ability to produce good citizens. That meant, of course, that he had to explore the nature of the kind of knowledge Socrates equated with goodness. Plato's attempt to work out a theory of knowledge led him into the realm of metaphysics and constituted what may be his most important contribution to the history of Western thought.

3.2
Aristotle,
Nichomachean Ethics

Aristotle   The most prominent of Plato's students was Aristotle (384–322 B.C.E.). He was born at Stagirus in the Chalcidice, the son of a physician to the court of Macedon. After Plato's death he moved from Athens to Assos and Mytilene in Asia Minor, where he conducted research in marine biology. In 342 B.C.E., he accepted an appointment as tutor to Alexander, son of King Philip of Macedon, and in 336 B.C.E., he returned to Athens to found the **Lyceum**, or the school of the Peripatetics (from *Peripatos*, a covered walkway on its grounds). Following Alexander's death in 323 B.C.E., anti-Macedonian feeling swept Greece, and Aristotle decided to leave Athens. He died at Chalcis in Euboea a year later.

The program of the Lyceum was different from that of the Academy. Plato's students concentrated on mathematics, but Aristotle's gathered, ordered, and analyzed data from all fields of knowledge. The range of Aristotle's interests is astonishing. He wrote on logic, physics, astronomy, biology, ethics, rhetoric, literary criticism, and politics. He began the study of every subject the same way— by collecting data (physical or anecdotal, depending on the field). Data were then rationally analyzed to see if they revealed any general principles. Like Plato, Aristotle viewed things teleologically; that is, he explained them in terms of their ultimate ends or purposes. Plato claimed that the things of this world were governed by universal ideas or forms—transcendent realities that people could not directly experience. Aristotle, however, inferred the purposes of most things from our experiences of them. He believed matter strove to realize the form (i.e., the idea) that made it intelligible (i.e., defined it) to the human mind— that the world around us is constantly evolving from potentiality to actuality.

This metaphysical model is at the heart of Aristotle's thinking about the *polis*. He rejected the Sophists' claim that social life is made up of conventions that frustrate human nature. He believed human beings are social creatures and the *polis* was, therefore, necessary for the realization of their potential. The most important function of the *polis* was not economic or military. It was moral. The *polis* was the means to human fulfillment and happiness.

Aristotle was less interested in theorizing about the perfect state than in designing the best achievable state. To determine what this was, he studied the constitutions of 158 functioning *poleis*. (Only the *Constitution of the Athenians* has survived.) He concluded that moderation was the key attribute of the most successful constitutions. A moderate constitution created a state that was dominated by the middle class, not by the rich or the poor. A large middle class was essential for political

Lyceum   School founded by Aristotle in Athens that focused on the gathering and analysis of data from all fields of knowledge.

stability, for the middle class, he claimed, is not tempted to the arrogance of the rich nor infected by the malice that resentment creates in the poor. Stable constitutions were also usually "mixed"—that is, they blended aspects of democracy and oligarchy.

All the political thinkers of the fourth century B.C.E. recognized the *polis* was in danger. Few, however, made such realistic proposals for its reform as Aristotle. It is ironic that his able defense of the *polis* ideal came on the eve of the *polis*'s demise.

THE HELLENISTIC WORLD

The term ***Hellenistic*** was coined in the nineteenth century to describe the period in Greek history that began when a Macedonian dynasty conquered both Greece and the Persian Empire. This blended aspects of Greek and Middle Eastern culture to create a new, cosmopolitan civilization.

THE MACEDONIAN CONQUEST

Macedon, the northernmost of the mainland Greek states, was a backward, semi-barbaric land by the standards of many Greeks. It had no *poleis* but was a kingdom ruled by a monarch who, like Homer's Agamemnon, had to contend with clans headed by powerful aristocratic families. Hampered by constant wars with raiders on its northern frontier, internal strife, weak institutions, and a poor economy, Macedon played no great part in Greek affairs until the fourth century B.C.E.

Philip of Macedon   Before Philip II (359–336 B.C.E.) inherited the Macedonian throne, he spent several years as a hostage in Thebes. This gave him an opportunity to study Greek politics and *hoplite* warfare under the tutelage of Epaminondas, the general who defeated Sparta. Philip's talent and training equipped him to forge Macedon into a true kingdom. He eliminated rivals to his power, pacified the tribes on Macedon's frontiers, and challenged Athenian dominance of the northern Aegean. The conquest of Amphipolis, the city Athens had lost to Sparta in the Peloponnesian War, gave him control of the gold and silver mines of nearby Mount Pangaeus, and he used this wealth to elevate the level of Macedonian culture. He founded cities and turned his army into the world's finest fighting force.

The Macedonian Army   Philip's army was more professional than the companies of amateur citizen-soldiers who defended most *poleis*. Philip recruited infantrymen from Macedon's sturdy farming class and feisty hill people and trained them in new combat techniques. He equipped them with pikes that were thirteen feet long. (The *hoplite*'s spear measured about nine feet.) This weapon allowed them to spread out and form a more open, flexible formation than the traditional phalanx. The Macedonian aristocrats who formed Philip's cavalry, the "Companions," lived with the king and were fiercely loyal to him. Philip also hired mercenaries who knew the latest tactics and were experienced with sophisticated siege machinery. Altogether, he could field an army of about 40,000 men.

The Invasion of Greece   Once Philip had Macedon firmly in hand, the Greeks gave Philip the excuse he needed to intervene in their affairs. The people of Thessaly asked Philip to assist them in a war with the Phocians. Philip won the war, occupied Thessaly, and marched on Thrace to take control of the Aegean's northern coast and the Hellespont.

These actions threatened the interests of Athens. Athens, however, was no longer the Athens of Pericles. It had a formidable fleet of three hundred ships, but its population was smaller than in the fifth century B.C.E. and it had no empire to help it fund a major war. The Athenians were, therefore, uncertain how to respond

WHO WAS Alexander the Great and what was his legacy?

Hermes and Dionysus.

Praxiteles (c. 400-300 B.C.E.), "Hermes and Dionysius", c. 350-330 B.C.E. National Archeological Museum, Olympia. Scala/ Art Resource, NY

Hellenistic   Term that describes the cosmopolitan civilization, established under the Macedonians, that combined aspects of Greek and Middle Eastern cultures.

to Philip. Eubulus, a financial official and conservative political leader, advocated a cautious policy of cooperation with Philip. He hoped that Philip's aims would prove to be limited and pose no real threat to Athens. Isocrates (436–338 B.C.E.), the head of an important rhetorical school, urged the Athenians to embrace Philip with enthusiasm. Isocrates believed that by uniting the Greeks and leading them into a war with Persia, Philip could solve the economic, social, and political problems that had mired the Greek world in poverty and civil strife ever since the Peloponnesian War. He was opposed by Demosthenes (384–322 B.C.E.), one of the greatest orators in Greek history. Demosthenes claimed Philip was a great danger to Greece, and he persuaded Athens to join Thebes in a war with Macedon. In 338 B.C.E., a cavalry charge led by Philip's eighteen-year-old son Alexander turned the tide in Macedon's favor at the Battle of Chaeronea and made Philip master of Greece.

The Macedonian Government of Greece   The Macedonian settlement of Greek affairs was not as harsh as many had feared. Macedonian garrisons were stationed throughout Greece to guard against rebellions, and Athens was spared on condition that it fall in with Philip's plans. In 338 B.C.E., Philip called representatives of the Greek states to Corinth where he announced the formation of the League of Corinth. The constitution of the new federation promised its members autonomy in local affairs, freedom from tribute and military occupation, and aid in suppressing piracy and civil war. It enabled the Greeks to submit to Macedonian dominance without loss of face. Their defeat at Chaeronea, however, effectively signaled the end of the independence of the *poleis*.

Philip had a reason for choosing Corinth as the site for the formation of a new panhellenic league. About 150 years earlier, the Greeks had gathered at Corinth to plan their strategy for the Persian Wars, and it was at Corinth, in 337 B.C.E., that Philip announced a new Persian War. He promised the Greeks that they could reclaim their past glory by joining him in invading the Persian Empire. They gathered in Macedon in the spring of 336 B.C.E., but on the eve of the campaign, Philip was assassinated.

ALEXANDER THE GREAT

The Conquest of the Persian Empire   Alexander III (356–323 B.C.E.), "the Great," was only twenty when he ascended his father's throne, but he had no hesitancy about implementing Philip's plan for invading Persia. The Persian Empire had enormous resources, but it was not an impossible target. Great size and the diversity of its population made it hard to control, and its rulers struggled with uprisings on their far-flung frontiers and intrigues within their courts. Like Macedon, Persia also had a new, untried king. But unlike Alexander, Darius III had a navy that controlled the sea, a huge army, and endless wealth.

In 334 B.C.E., Alexander crossed the Hellespont into Asia with an army of only about 30,000 infantry and 5,000 cavalry. He had little money and few ships. He could not risk heading inland until he had neutralized the Persian navy at his back, but he needed a quick victory to bolster the loyalty of his men and to obtain loot with which to pay them. Memnon, the commander of the Persian navy, proposed a plan that probably would have defeated Alexander. He urged his countrymen to retreat, avoid pitched battles, and scorch the earth to deprive the Greek invaders of supplies. The Persians, however, rejected his advice and gave Alexander exactly what he needed.

The Persians confronted Alexander at the Granicus River on the coast of Asia Minor. Alexander led a cavalry charge across the river and into the teeth of the enemy. He nearly lost his life, but his courage inspired his men to win a victory that opened all of Asia Minor to conquest by the Greeks. (See Map 3–3.)

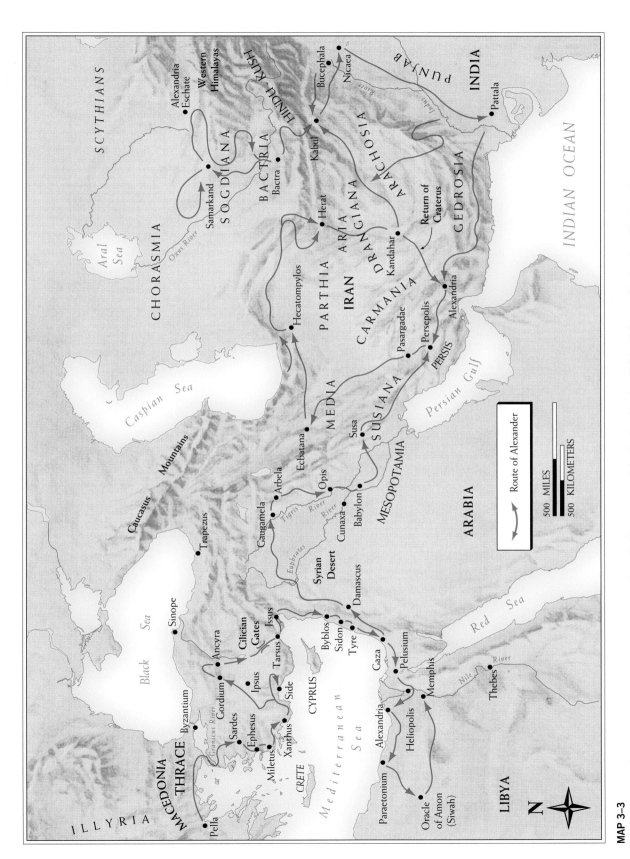

MAP 3–3

Alexander's Campaigns The route taken by Alexander the Great in his conquest of the Persian Empire, 334 to 323 B.C.E. Starting from the Macedonian capital at Pella, he reached the Indus Valley before being turned back by his own restive troops. He died of fever in Mesopotamia.

BEFORE CROSSING into Mesopotamia, what considerations determined Alexander's route? Was his aim merely to defeat the Persians?

In 333 B.C.E., Alexander crossed out of Asia Minor into Syria to meet the main Persian army and Darius. At Issus, Alexander led a cavalry charge that broke the Persian line, but instead of pursuing Darius as he retreated inland, Alexander continued south along the coast. He had to take all of Persia's ports to prevent the Persian navy from invading the Aegean and cutting him off from his homeland. When he arrived in Egypt, he was greeted as liberator and proclaimed pharaoh. Like all of Egypt's divine kings, he was declared a son of Re, the god who, as head of the Egyptian pantheon, the Greeks identified with Zeus.

In the spring of 331 B.C.E., Alexander marched into Mesopotamia to confront a huge army that Darius had amassed at Gaugamela (near the ancient Assyrian city of Nineveh). Once again the Persian line broke, and Darius fled. Alexander occupied Babylon, and in January 330 B.C.E., he entered Persepolis, the Persian capital. Acquisition of the Persian treasury ended Alexander's financial problems. The gold he showered on his troops put vast sums of money into circulation—an economic development whose effects were felt for centuries.

Alexander rested his men in Persepolis and then set out in pursuit of Darius. He failed to take the Persian king alive, however, for Darius's disillusioned men turned on him and killed him. Bessus, one of Darius's relatives, claimed the crown and retreated into the east. Alexander followed, routed what was left of the Persian army, and pushed on toward India.

Near Samarkand, in the land of the Scythians, Alexander founded Alexandria Eschate ("Farthest Alexandria"), one of many cities Alexander created as part of his plan for securing the future of his empire. Alexander planned to scatter Greeks throughout his new lands and encourage them to intermarry with its diverse peoples and accustom these people to the Greek way of life. To set an example, he took his first wife (a princess named Roxane, a native of a remote region called Bactria) and added 30,000 Persians to his army.

In 327 B.C.E., the Greeks crossed the Khyber Pass and entered the territory of modern Pakistan. Alexander forced Porus, its king, to submit, but by now it was clear to his men that the objectives of their campaign had changed. Alexander seemed intent on leading them literally to the ends of the earth, to the great river, Ocean, that Greek geographers believed encircled the world's landmass. Exhaustion drove them to mutiny and demand that he take them home for a rest. By the spring of 324 B.C.E., they were back in Babylon and celebrating, in true Macedonian style, with drunken sprees.

The Death of Alexander By now Alexander had reached the age of thirty-three, and he was filled with plans for his future. In June 323 B.C.E., however, he succumbed to a fever and died. He immediately became the subject of myths, legends, romances, and historical controversies. Some people have seen him as a man of grand and noble vision who transcended Greek and Macedonian ethnocentrism and imagined a world in which everyone was united on the basis of their common humanity. Others have described him as a calculating despot, who was given to drunken brawls, brutality, and murder. The truth probably lies in some mixture of the two points of view.

THE SUCCESSORS

Nobody was prepared for Alexander's sudden death. He had no obvious successor, and it is doubtful that even he, one of history's greatest generals and administrative geniuses, could have held together the huge empire he had so quickly conquered. His nearest adult male relative, a weak-minded half brother, could not fill his shoes. Roxane, his queen, bore him a son soon after his death, but an infant heir could not preserve Alexander's legacy. The Macedonian generals, therefore, divided up responsibility for ruling the empire—allegedly, only until Alexander's son came of age. They were, however, soon at each other's throats, and in the battles that followed, all the members of the Macedonian royal house were eliminated. After the deaths of Roxane and her son in 310 B.C.E., the surviving generals declared themselves kings of the portions of the empire they ruled, and three major Macedonian dynasties emerged. Ptolemy I (ca. 367–283 B.C.E.) claimed Egypt and founded its thirty-first dynasty of pharaohs. (Egypt's famous queen Cleopatra, who died in 30 B.C.E., was the last of the Ptolemies.) The Seleucid dynasty established by Seleucus I (ca. 358–280 B.C.E.) ruled Mesopotamia and Syria, and Asia Minor and the Macedonian homeland passed to Antigonus I (382–301 B.C.E.) and his Antigonid dynasty.

For about seventy-five years after Alexander's death, the world economy expanded. The money that Alexander had loosed to circulate promoted economic activity, and the opening of huge new territories to Greek trade increased demand for Greek products and supplies of all kinds of goods. Hellenistic kings pursued enlightened economic policies that encouraged the growth of commerce. Emigration to the cities they founded eased problems of overpopulation on the Greek mainland and provided people with all kinds of opportunities.

The prosperity that resulted was not evenly distributed. Urban Greeks, Macedonians, and Hellenized natives—the upper and middle classes—lived comfortable, even luxurious, lives, while the standard of living for rural laborers declined. The independent small farmers who had built the early *poleis* disappeared. Arable land was consolidated into large plantations, and free farmers were reduced to the status of dependent peasants. During prosperous times their lot was bearable, but the costs of continuing wars and the effects of the inflation produced by the influx of Persian gold steadily eroded their position. Kings bore down heavily on the middle class, which shifted the burden to the peasants and the other laborers. These people responded by slowing their work and staging strikes. In parts of Greece, there were demands for the abolition of debt and the redistribution of land, and civil war returned.

Internal tensions and the strain of endemic warfare rendered the Hellenistic kingdoms vulnerable, and by the middle of the second century B.C.E., all of them, except for Egypt, had succumbed to conquest by the Italian city of Rome. Rome itself, however, was soon overtaken by the powerful new Greek civilization that had arisen in the wake of Alexander's conquests.

HELLENISTIC CULTURE

*A*lexander the Great's life marked a turning point in the history of Greek literature, philosophy, religion, and art. His empire and its successor kingdoms ended the role the *polis* had played in shaping Greek culture. Hellenistic cities were not free sovereign states but municipal towns submerged within great centrally managed empires.

As the freedoms characteristic of life in a *polis* faded, Greeks lost interest in politics. They abandoned public affairs and turned to the private practice of religion, philosophy, and magic for help in dealing with life's challenges. The confident humanism of the fifth century B.C.E. gave way to a kind of resignation to fate, a recognition of helplessness before forces too great for humans to comprehend.

HOW DID Hellenistic culture differ from the culture of Classical Greece?

One of the masterpieces of Hellenistic sculpture, the *Laocoön*. This is a Roman copy. According to legend, Laocoön was a priest who warned the Trojans not to take the Greeks' wooden horse within their city. This sculpture depicts his punishment. Great serpents sent by the goddess Athena, who was on the side of the Greeks, devoured Laocoön and his sons before the horrified people of Troy.

Musei Vaticani

PHILOSOPHY

Athens survived as the center of philosophical studies during the Hellenistic era. Plato's Academy and Aristotle's Lyceum continued to operate and were joined by the new schools of the Cynics, Epicureans, and Stoics.

The Lyceum drifted away from the scientific interests of its founder and turned to literary and historical studies. The Academy was even more radically transformed. Its critique of the weaknesses of all schools of thought led some of its members to embrace a philosophy called Skepticism—the doctrine that nothing could be truly known. Skeptics urged their students, in lieu of better options, to accept conventional morality and not to try to change the world.

Other followers of Socrates and Plato drew a more radical conclusion from the elusive nature of truth and the inevitability of human ignorance. Socrates had urged his students to behave ethically, but disdain the pursuit of wealth and power and prefer contemplation to an active political life. Diogenes of Sinope (ca. 400–325 B.C.E.), whom Plato described as Socrates gone mad, pushed the Socratic retreat from the world to an extreme. He dismissed the rules of civilized behavior as baseless conventions and insisted that happiness lay in giving in to nature's cruder impulses. He begged for his bread, wore rags, lived in a tub, performed intimate acts of personal hygiene in public, and ridiculed religious observances. Although the Cynics claimed to follow Socrates, they contradicted some of his core beliefs. Where Socrates had criticized but ultimately defended the *polis*, the Cynics abandoned it altogether. When Diogenes was asked about his citizenship, he answered he was *kosmopolites*, "a citizen of the world."

These views held little appeal for most of the middle-class city dwellers of the third century B.C.E. They wanted help in finding the kind of dignity and meaning that the duties of *polis* citizenship had given to the lives of their ancestors.

The Epicureans   Like many thinkers of his day, Epicurus of Athens (342–271 B.C.E.) doubted that human beings could obtain certain knowledge. Like the atomists, Democritus and Leucippus, he believed the world was nothing more than a swirl of physical particles continually falling through a void. Thought was only the stream of impressions these atoms left on human sense organs, and because atoms swerved in arbitrary, unpredictable ways, there was no such thing as a fixed, eternal truth. Philosophers, he argued, should abandon the pursuit of knowledge of the world and teach people how to cope with its reality. Epicurus believed that philosophy could free people from things like the fear of death by helping them understand that death was merely the dispersal of the atoms that compose the body and soul. Because nothing of themselves survived death to suffer pain, loss, or punishment, there was no reason to fear death. The proper pursuit of humankind, Epicurus argued, was pleasure—in the sense of *ataraxia*, a state of being undisturbed by any extreme feeling, either good or bad. The happiest people were those who withdrew from the world and eschewed the duties of family and public life. Epicurus's ideal was the genteel, disciplined selfishness of intellectual men of means. It was a dream not calculated to be widely attractive.

The Stoics   Soon after Epicurus began teaching in Athens, Zeno of Citium (335–263 B.C.E.) established the Stoic school (named for the *stoa poikile*, the Painted Portico in the Athenian marketplace where Zeno taught his disciples). Like the Epicureans, the Stoics sought the happiness of the individual, but Stoics, unlike Epicureans, believed happiness is to be found by embracing and not fleeing responsibility. Stoics claimed happiness is the sense of fulfillment that comes from living in harmony with nature. Nature, they argued, is governed by a divine *logos*, an eternal rational principle. Every human being has a spark of this divine "fire," which returns at death to its source. Contentment lies in realizing the essential rationality of existence and accepting one's place in the natural order. To live in accordance with natural law, however, a person has to understand which things in life are good and evil and which are morally "indifferent." Things such as prudence, justice, courage, and temperance are rational goods. Things such as folly, injustice, and cowardice are irrational evils. Some things— such as life, health, pleasure, beauty, strength, and wealth—are morally neutral. By themselves they do not produce either happiness or misery, but misery results if the soul, through attachment to them, suffers painful passion. The goal of life is *apatheia*, freedom from passion.

For the Stoics the world was a great *polis* in which all people were equally subject to the power of *logos*. The wise lived in accordance with this divine force and fatalistically accepted their places in the scheme of things. They dispassionately played out the roles they were assigned—be they kings or slaves. The Stoic way of life made sense to the subjects of well-ordered Hellenistic empires— societies that valued docile submission more highly than initiative and innovation.

Epicureans   People who believed the proper pursuit of humankind is undisturbed withdrawal from the world.

Stoics   People who sought freedom from passion and harmony with nature.

The Archimedes Palimpsest: A page from *On Floating Bodies.*

© Christie's images Inc.

LITERATURE

Alexandria was the chief center of Hellenistic intellectual life in the third and second centuries B.C.E. Unlike the creative thinkers who participated in the government of the *poleis*, Alexandria's scholars were more preoccupied with the past than with current affairs. As subjects of great empires, they had little political influence. Alexandria owed its prominence to the "museum," a great research institute founded by the Ptolemies. Its library collected literature of all kinds and provided support for the specialists who edited and interpreted it. Much of their work was dry and petty, but they preserved the monuments of Classical literature.

ARCHITECTURE AND SCULPTURE

Hellenistic kings had great wealth and could afford to be lavish patrons of scholars, artists, and architects. They founded many cities and rebuilt old ones, usually on the efficient grid plan introduced in the fifth century B.C.E. by Hippodamus of Miletus. The famous artists who traveled the world, fulfilling royal commissions, created a kind of uniform international style. It abandoned the idealism that had been popular during the age of the *polis* in favor of a more emotional (sometimes sentimental) realism.

MATHEMATICS AND SCIENCE

Advances in mathematics and science were among the more original and significant achievements of the Hellenistic era. The scholars of Alexandria amassed the greater part of the scientific knowledge that was available to the West until the breakthroughs created by the scientific revolution of the sixteenth and seventeenth centuries C.E.

Euclid's *Elements* became the standard textbook for the study of plane and solid geometry in the third century B.C.E. and retained that post well into the modern era. Archimedes of Syracuse (ca. 287–212 B.C.E.) explained the principles of the lever in mechanics and invented hydrostatics. Heraclides of Pontus (ca. 390–310 B.C.E.) advanced a heliocentric theory of the universe that was fully developed by Aristarchus of Samos (ca. 310–230 B.C.E.). Unfortunately, however, because Hellenistic technology could not provide astronomical data to confirm their intuitions, their theories did not take hold. A geocentric model advanced by Hipparchus of Nicaea (born ca. 190 B.C.E.) and refined by a certain Ptolemy of Alexandria in the second century C.E. acquired currency and remained dominant until the work of Copernicus in the sixteenth century C.E. The scholars of the age knew the earth was round, and Eratosthenes of Cyrene (ca. 275–195 B.C.E.) calculated its circumference within about two hundred miles. His maps were more accurate than those available to Westerners during the Middle Ages.

Summary

Aftermath of Victory The tenuous unity the Greeks had shown while fighting against the Persians disintegrated. Sparta and Athens emerged as leaders of two spheres of influence. Sparta was uninterested in continued aggression against Persia. The Athenians and the Ionians shared an interest in driving the Persians out of the Aegean region; with others, they formed the Delian League under Athenian leadership.

The First Peloponnesian War: Athens Against Sparta Pericles led a democratic, but aggressive Athens. The Peloponnesian Wars were the manifestation of the conflict between Sparta and Athens. After an initial victory, Athens seemed almost invincible, but soon military defeat abroad and rebellion at home weakened Athens so much that Sparta invaded. Pericles agreed to a 30-year peace, abandoning all Athenian possessions on the Greek mainland outside of Attica, but gaining Spartan recognition of the Athenian Empire.

Classical Greece Athenian government had become more democratic than any previous political system. All male citizens gained important rights, regardless of their property class. The official status of women was severely circumscribed, both in public and in private. Greek art, drama, and mythology suggest that women may have had more freedom and power than a strict reading of the documentary evidence would allow. Before around 500 B.C.E. there was little chattel slavery in Greece—although serfdom and bond slavery were more or less common in various times and places—but later war captives and other foreigners were held as chattel slaves. Slaves worked in agriculture, industry, and households, and served as shepherds, policemen, and secretaries. Most Athenians did not own any slaves, and those that did generally owned only a few.

The Great Peloponnesian War The Thirty Years' Peace of 445 B.C.E. lasted just over ten years, until a conflict between Corcyra and Corinth drew in their allies, Athens and Sparta, respectively. Sparta violated a clause of the peace that required arbitration of all disagreements between Athens and Sparta, and instead, in 431 B.C.E., invaded Attica. The outnumbered Athenians followed a daring strategy and won an important victory in 425 B.C.E. After a mix of victo-

IMAGE KEY
for pages 56–57.

a. Assortment of silver coins from ancient Greece
b. The Nike of Samothrace, goddess of victory.   Marble figure (190 B.C.E.) from Rhodos, Greece. Height 328 cm, MA 2369, Louvre, Dpt. des Antiquites Grecques/Romaines, Paris, France. Photograph © Erich Lessing/Art Resource, NY
c. The Archimedes Palimpsest
d. Ancient Greek Athenian coin
e. The Acropolis. This photograph shows the Parthenon and to its left the Erechtheum   Meredith Pillon/Greek National Tourism Organization
f. Aristotle (384-322 B.C.E.), Greek philosopher
g. Venus D'Milo statue
h. Battle between Alexander the Great and King Darius   House of the Faun, Pompeii VI 12, 2 Inv. 10020. Museo Archelogico Nazionale, Naples, Italy. Photograph © Erich Lessing/Art Resource, NY
i. Daily life on Greek Vases, woman spinning thread. Wine-jug, made in Athens, ca. 500-480 B.C.E. Copyright The British Museum
j. Bust of Pericles, Statesman of Greece   (495-429 BC) copy of a Greek original, Roman, 2nd century AD (marble). British Museum, London, UK/Index/ Bridgeman Art Library

ries and defeats, both sides signed the Peace of Nicias in 421 B.C.E. This peace, too, was short lived; this time the Athenians were the aggressors, against Sicily, in a disastrous 415 B.C.E. expedition that brought the Persians into the war on Sparta's side. The Athenians fought on, however, until 404 B.C.E., when they surrendered unconditionally.

Competition for Leadership in the Fourth Century B.C.E. After defeating Athens, Sparta had a golden opportunity to claim leadership, but Spartan arrogance—among other problems—caused their allies the Persians to turn against them. Theban victory at Leuctra in 371 B.C.E. brought an end to Spartan hegemony. But Theban dominance was short lived, ending in 362 B.C.E. in a defeat at the hands of the Athenians. Athens, however, repeated many of the same mistakes that had cost it allies in the Delian League, and by 355 B.C.E., Athens again had to abandon most of its empire. Greece descended into chaos.

The Culture of Classical Greece Classical Greece produced dramas, architecture and sculpture, and philosophical and historical works. The Golden Age of Athens, between the Persian and Peloponnesian wars, is epitomized by Attic tragedy, including the works of Aeschylus, Sophocles, and Euripedes. The buildings of the Acropolis are the product of Athenian religious and civic sensibility, and individual artistry and achievement. Philosophy continued to explore questions about the natural world. Herodotus and Thucydides wrote histories that are models of the genre. Sociopolitical changes brought about by the Peloponnesian War were reflected in drama and sculpture, especially in the philosophical traditions of Socrates, Plato, and Aristotle.

The Hellenistic World Greek culture mixed with Middle Eastern elements and spread throughout the eastern Mediterranean, Egypt, and far into Asia. This Hellenistic world was largely the result of military conquests by a short-lived, father-and-son Macedonian dynasty. Philip of Macedon introduced tactical innovations into the Macedonian army, and he coupled military force with diplomacy to conquer Greece. In 336 B.C.E., Philip was assassinated and succeeded by his son Alexander. Alexander lead his troops to victory in Persia, Egypt, Mesopotamia, and as far as what is now Pakistan. After his death, three of Alexander's generals founded significant dynasties that helped spread Hellenism in Egypt, Mesopotamia, and Asia Minor. Within Greece, class conflict and other internal divisions were exacerbated by the new wealth Alexander's conquests had brought to the region.

Hellenistic Culture The true *polis* was destroyed by the Macedonian invasion. Greeks turned from the political to the personal. In Athenian philosophy, the Epicureans (whose goal was hedonistic human happiness) and Stoics (who sought happiness through harmony and freedom from passion) gained prominence. Hellenistic Alexandria fostered literature and humanistic scholarship. Hellenistic styles in architecture and sculpture diffused over a wide area. Mathematics and science—especially astronomy—blossomed.

REVIEW QUESTIONS

1. What caused the Great Peloponnesian War? What strategies did Athens and Sparta hope would bring them victory? Why did Sparta win?

2. What were the tensions that characterized Greek life in the Classical Period, and how were they reflected in its art, literature, and philosophy? How does Hellenistic art differ from art of the Classical Period?

3. How and why did Philip II conquer Greece? Why was Athens unable to stop him? Was his success due to Macedon's strength or to the weaknesses of the Greek city-states?

4. What were the consequences of Alexander the Great's early death? What were his lasting achievements? Did he consciously promote Greek civilization, or was he only an egomaniac devoted to endless conquest?

5. What were the most significant elements that made up Hellenistic civilization and culture?

KEY TERMS

Academy   (p. 73)
Delian League   (p. 58)
Epicureans   (p. 81)

Hellenistic   (p. 75)
Lyceum   (p. 74)

Peloponnesian Wars   (p. 59)
Stoics   (p. 81)

 For additional study resources for this chapter, go to:
www.prenhall.com/kagan3/chapter3

Visualizing The Past...

Goddesses and the Female Form in Ancient Art

ANCIENT ARTISTS created images of women as often as men in their art, but there were key differences in how they depicted the female versus the male form. What were these differences, why did they come about, and what did they signify?

Artists celebrated gods and human men alike for their roles in society, as priests, warriors, or commoners. By contrast, from ancient times to the present, sexuality has been central to artistic conceptualizations of women and the female role in the divine and human realms. Earthly women and goddesses alike were usually drawn or sculpted nude, at least from the waist up, and, given the link between female sexuality and fertility, with breasts and hips prominent or even exaggerated. Goddesses in the ancient world tended to have a dual nature, of death and regeneration, and to be linked to symbols of earth, love, death, and war, and often also to mastery of snakes, a prominent symbol in many cultures of male fertility.

Innana-Ishtar, ca. 2025–1763 B.C.E., Babylonian goddess of love and death.
Innana-Ishtar has a lovely feminine form but talons instead of feet, denoting her dual nature. She bears the tail of her symbol, the lion, and has the wings of an owl, symbol of her mastery over death. Her helmet signifies her martial and ruling power. Like many female goddesses, she is an ambiguous figure whose female form is linked both to sexual desire and to death.

H. Lewandowski/Art Resource, NY ©Reunion des Musees Nationaux/Art Resource, NY

Coatlicue, Aztec mother goddess. ▶
Although she was a goddess
from the New World, and
depicted in a radically different
artistic tradition, Coatlicue, the
"goddess of the serpent skirt,"
shares with goddesses of
the Old World an emphasis on
mastery of male sexual power (her
serpent skirt), fertility and
motherhood (she was the
mother of the powerful Aztec
god Huitzilopochtli), and death
(she craved human sacrifices).
Mexican National Tourist Council

"Snake Goddess," Minoan, ca. 1650 B.C.E.
Strong cultural and economic ties linked Mediter-
ranean and Near Eastern cultures, as can be seen
in the similarities between this small statuette of a
Minoan goddess and the preceding image of
Innana-Ishtar. As was typical in Minoan and Greek
art, this goddess is nude only from the waist up.
Like Innana-Ishtar, however, her arms are raised
and she holds symbols of power, in this case snakes.
Photograph © Erich Lessing/Art Resource, NY

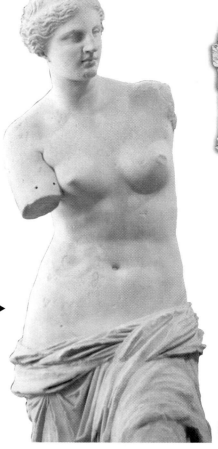

Venus D'Milo, statue, marble, 120–130 B.C.E. ▶
In this statue of Venus (Greek name: Aphrodite), the Roman goddess of love,
we again see the female figure nude to the waist and sexualized. Unlike the more
"masculine" Minerva (Greek name: Athena), goddess of wisdom born from the head
of the male god Jupiter (Greek name: Zeus), who was usually sculpted clothed
and helmeted, Venus personified love and sensuality. Like her counterparts
elsewhere in the world, she was also associated with strife and death, as her lover
was Mars (Greek name: Ares), god of war.
John Serafin/SBG.

4 Rome: From Republic to Empire

CHAPTER HIGHLIGHTS

Prehistoric Italy Bands of warring peoples speaking Italic languages invaded from across the Adriatic and along the northeastern coast starting around 1000 B.C.E. Their superior tools and craftsmanship helped them gain a dominant position in the lands they invaded.

The Etruscans Etruscan civilization emerged in Etruria around 800 B.C.E. Etruscan power peaked around 500 B.C.E. and declined rapidly under attack by the Gauls about 400 B.C.E.

Royal Rome During the sixth century B.C.E., under Etruscan rule, Rome developed political institutions that would endure for many centuries. The family was the center of Roman life. The two classes in royal Rome were the *patricians* and *plebeians*.

The Republic In 509 B.C.E., noble families revolted against the monarchy and created the Roman Republic. Plebeians chafed against the limits on their political participation, leading to the Struggle of the Orders. By the middle of the third century B.C.E., Rome controlled Italy. The Punic and Macedonian Wars contributed to Roman domination of the Mediterranean.

Civilization in the Early Roman Republic Greek thought and culture came to play an important role in Roman civilization. As Rome's conquests continued, slavery increased dramatically, leading to social, economic, and political problems.

Roman Imperialism: The Late Republic War, expansion, and the administration of the empire fundamentally altered Roman culture. Populist movements led by the Gracchi ended with their assassinations. Two ambitious generals, Marius and Sulla, competed for domination of the Republic.

The Fall of the Republic Crassus, Pompey, and Caesar formed the First Triumvirate to further their own private goals. Caesar's assassination led to civil war, ending with the defeat of his assassins and the ascendancy of Octavian.

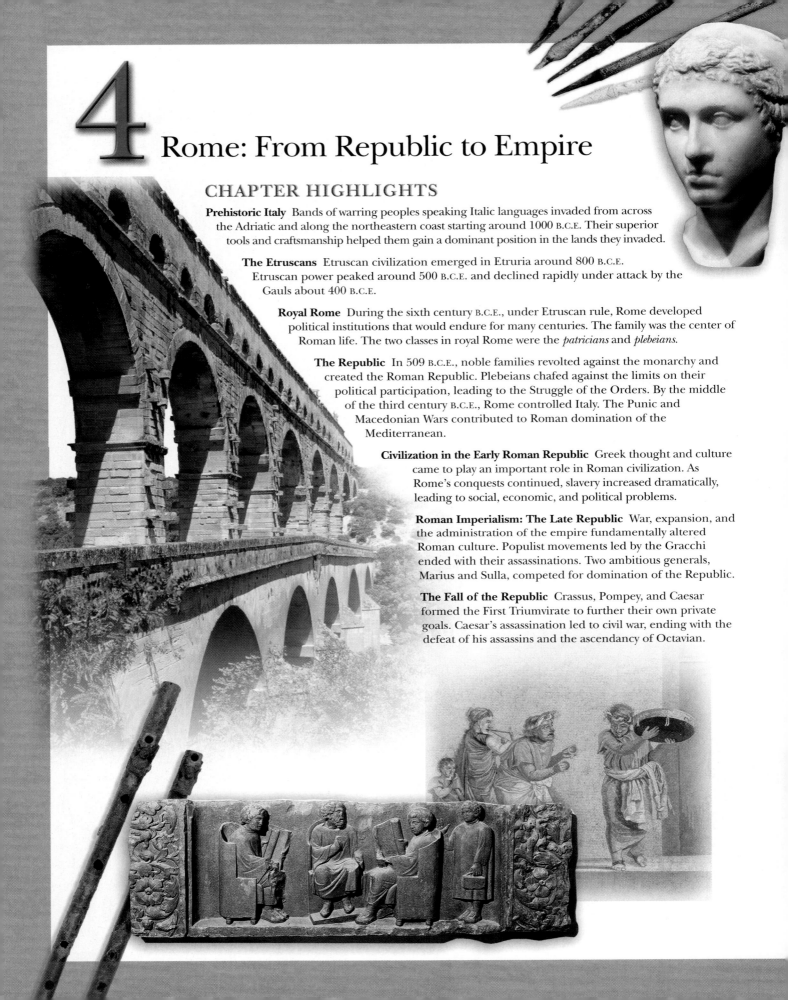

CHAPTER QUESTIONS

WHO WERE the Etruscans and how did they influence Rome?

WHAT ROLE did government, family, and women play in ancient Rome?

WHAT ROLE did consuls, the Senate, and the Assembly play in ancient Rome?

HOW DID contact with the Hellenistic world affect Rome?

HOW DID the expansion of Rome change the Republic?

WHAT EVENTS led to the fall of the Republic?

CHAPTER OUTLINE

- Prehistoric Italy
- The Etruscans
- Royal Rome
- The Republic
- Civilization in the Early Roman Republic
- Roman Imperialism: The Late Republic
- The Fall of the Republic

IMAGE KEY
for pages 88–89 is on page 111.

The Romans started with a small village in central Italy and went on to unite the peoples of the Western world and sustain the longest period of peace in Western history. By adapting Hellenistic culture and spreading it through their empire, they laid a universal Graeco-Roman foundation for Western civilization. The effects of their achievement are still being felt.

PREHISTORIC ITALY

Italy's cultural evolution began slowly. The Paleolithic era lingered in Italy until 2500 B.C.E., and Italy did not feel the effects of the Bronze Age until 1500 B.C.E. About 1000 B.C.E., the Umbrians, Sabines, Samnites, and Latins—immigrants from the east whose *Italic* languages gave the peninsula its name—pioneered Italy's Iron Age. By 800 B.C.E., they had occupied the highland pastures of the Apennines (the mountain range that runs the length of Italy) and had begun to challenge earlier settlers for control of the western coastal plains.

THE ETRUSCANS

WHO WERE the Etruscans and how did they influence Rome?

About 800 B.C.E., a mysterious people whose language was not Italic appeared in Etruria (modern Tuscany) on a plain west of the Apennines between the Arno and Tiber Rivers. Although the origin of these "Etruscans" is unknown, aspects of their civilization suggest connections with Asia Minor and the Middle East.

Much of what we know of the Etruscans comes from their funery art. This sculpture of an Etruscan couple is part of a sarcophagus.

© Erich Lessing/Art Resource, NY

DOMINION

Etruscan communities were independent, self-governing city-states loosely linked in a religious confederation. Early monarchies were replaced in most cities by aristocratic councils and annually elected magistrates. The Etruscans were a militarized ruling class that subjugated various Italic peoples and took to the sea as traders and pirates. They competed successfully with the other maritime powers of the western Mediterranean, the Carthaginians of North Africa and Italy's Greek colonists.

During the seventh and sixth centuries B.C.E., Etruscan domination spread from Tuscany north to Italy's Po Valley, overseas to the islands of Corsica and Elba, and south into **Latium** (a region that included the small town of Rome) and Campania (a plain the Greeks of Naples colonized). The expansion of Etruscan influence was the work of independent warrior-chieftains whose unwillingness to work together constituted a fatal weakness. By 400 B.C.E., Celts from **Gaul** (modern France) had driven the Etruscans from the Po Valley, an area the Romans later called Cisalpine Gaul ("Gaul-this-side-of-the-Alps"), and the cities of Etruria gradually lost their independence. Etruscan ceased to be a living tongue, but Etruscan culture was not forgotten. It had a profound effect on Rome.

CULTURAL INFLUENCES

Roman religion bore the stamp of powerful Etruscan influences. The Romans, like the Etruscans, believed that innumerable supernatural beings had the power to intervene in human affairs, and the Romans assumed human survival depended on understanding and placating these spirits—many of whom were evil.

Latium   Region located in present-day Italy that included the small town of Rome.

Gaul   Area that is now modern France.

To divine the wills of the mysterious forces that surrounded them, the Romans relied on Etruscan methods for interpreting omens.

A major contrast between Greek and Roman society was the greater freedom that Roman women enjoyed, and this, too, was probably a result of Etruscan influences. Greek women were expected to be virtually invisible. They were confined to their homes and given little education. Etruscan women, however, appeared in public and many could read and write. They witnessed and took part in athletic contests. They joined their husbands and other males as guests at banquets. A common subject in Etruscan art is a representation of a husband and wife reclining together on a dining couch, a pose that implies a loving relationship. Etruscan tomb inscriptions also suggest that women had significant status, for they often mention the mother as well as the father of the deceased.

ROYAL ROME

Rome evolved from a collection of villages established by Latins and others on the southern bank of the Tiber River in the mid-eighth century B.C.E. It was fifteen miles inland from the sea at the point where the Tiber emerges from the foothills of the Apennines. Many trails converged here, for just southwest of Rome's Capitoline Hill an island made it fairly easy to cross the Tiber. Rome was well situated to become the center for Italy's inland communication and trade. (See Map 4–1.)

GOVERNMENT

Rome's potential did not begin to be realized until the sixth century B.C.E., when Etruscan kings established themselves in Rome and subdued most of Latium. Although one family monopolized the royal office, Roman kingship was technically elective. The Roman Senate, an aristocratic council, had to approve a candidate for the throne, and only the assembly of the Roman people could bestow on him his unique power—the *imperium*, the right to enforce commands by fines, arrests, and corporal and capital punishment. The king was Rome's chief priest, high judge, and supreme military leader.

According to legend, Rome's Senate originated when Romulus, Rome's founder, chose one hundred of Rome's leading men to advise him. The early Senate had no formal executive or legislative authority. It met only when the king convened it to ask for advice. In practice, however, the Senate was very influential. It was composed of the most powerful men in the state, men a king could not safely ignore.

The curiate assembly, an organization to which all citizens belonged, was the third organ of government. It met only when summoned by the king, and he set its

imperium   Right held by a Roman king to enforce commands by fines, arrests, and corporal and capital punishment.

WHAT ROLE did government, family, and women play in ancient Rome?

MAP 4–1

Ancient Italy   This map of ancient Italy and its neighbors before the expansion of Rome shows major cities and towns as well as several geographical regions and the locations of some of the Italic and non-Italic Peoples.

WHY, GEOGRAPHICALLY, was Rome ideal to become the center for Italy's inland communication and trade?

Busts of a Roman couple, from the period of the Republic. Although some have identified the individuals as Cato the Younger and his daughter Porcia, no solid evidence confirms this claim.

Bust of Cato and Porcia. Roman sculpture. Vatican Museums, Vatican State. Photograph ©Scala/ Art Resources, NY

agenda and decided who could address it. Its job was to hear and ratify the king's decrees. Romans voted, not as individuals, but as members of groups. Citizens were registered in thirty *curiae*, and each *curia* had a single vote that was cast according to the will of its majority.

THE FAMILY

Family organizations were the basic units of Roman society. The head of a family was its "king" in the sense that he held *imperium* over all its members. Like the king who presided over the state cult, a father supervised his family's religious rites. Like the king, he had the power to execute his dependents or sell them into slavery—even his adult sons. The male head of a household had less authority over his wife, for she was protected by her birth family. A husband could not divorce his wife unless she was convicted of serious offenses by a court of her male blood relatives. A Roman wife had authority as the administrator of her husband's household. She controlled access to its storerooms, kept its accounts, supervised its slaves, and reared its children. She was also a respected adviser to her husband on all matters affecting her family.

WOMEN

Roman society was male dominated and hierarchical. All adult women had to have male guardians to handle their legal affairs. Women could own and dispose of property and enter into contracts but only with the aid of these guardians. Marriages of two kinds transferred a woman from the *manus* ("hand") of her father to that of her husband. A third kind of marriage left a bride under her father's *manus*. This gave her more freedom from her husband and more inheritance rights from her father. To preserve the arrangement, she had to spend at least three consecutive nights a year outside her husband's home.

CLIENTAGE

The head of a wealthy family could extend its influence by providing patronage to dependents called clients. Roman clientage was a formal, legally recognized institution. A patron provided a client with physical and legal protection and economic assistance. A client might receive a grant of land, become a tenant farmer, labor on his patron's estates, or simply subsist on daily handouts of food. In return, a client fought for his patron, voted as his patron ordered, and did any jobs requested of him. Even members of the upper classes, when it served their ambitions, became clients of families whose political connections could further their careers.

PATRICIANS AND PLEBEIANS

From the start of Rome's history, Roman families were divided into two hereditary classes. The **patricians**, the upper class, originally monopolized all political authority. Only they could serve as priests, senators, and magistrates. The **plebeians**, the commoner class, may have sprung from families of small farmers,

patricians Upper class of Roman families that originally monopolized all political authority. Only they could serve as priests, senators, and magistrates.

plebeians Commoner class of Roman families, usually families of small farmers, laborers, and artisans who were early clients of the patricians.

OVERVIEW   THE RISE OF THE PLEBEIANS TO EQUALITY IN ROME

509 B.C.E.	Kings expelled; republic founded
450–449 B.C.E.	Laws of the Twelve Tables published
445 B.C.E.	Plebeians gain right of marriage with patricians
367 B.C.E.	Licinian-Sextian Laws open consulship to plebeians
300 B.C.E.	Plebeians attain chief priesthoods
287 B.C.E.	Laws passed by Plebeian Assembly made binding on all Romans

laborers, and artisans who were early clients of the patricians. Wealth alone did not define the classes. Some plebeians were rich, and incompetence and bad luck sometimes impoverished patricians.

THE REPUBLIC

*A*ccording to Roman tradition, in 509 B.C.E., an atrocity committed by a king's son sparked a revolt that drove the last Etruscan ruler from the city. The patricians then decided not to appoint another king but to establish a republic.

CONSTITUTION

The Consuls   The Roman Republic had an unwritten constitution that enshrined conservative traditions. In the beginning, it simply transferred the duties and trappings of monarchy to elected magistrates. Two patricians were annually chosen as **consuls** and vested with *imperium*. Like the former kings, they led the army, oversaw the state religion, and sat as judges. They even used the traditional symbols of royalty—purple robes, ivory chairs, and *lictors* (guards who accompanied them bearing *fasces*, bundles of rods wrapped around an axe to signify the power to discipline and execute). A consul was, however, not a king, for he held office for only a year and had an equal, a colleague who could prevent him from taking independent action. Consular *imperium* was also limited. Consuls could execute citizens who were serving with the army outside the city, but in Rome citizens had the right to appeal all cases involving capital punishment to the popular assembly.

The checks on the consular office discouraged initiative, swift action, and change. This was what a conservative, aristocratic republic wanted. But because a divided command could create serious problems for an army in the field, the Romans usually sent only one consul into battle or assigned consuls sole command on alternate days. If this did not work, the consuls could, with the advice of the Senate, step aside to clear the way for the appointment of a *dictator*. A dictator's term of office was limited to six months, but his *imperium* was valid everywhere and unlimited by any right of appeal.

These devices worked well enough for a small city-state whose wars were short skirmishes fought near home. But as Rome's wars grew longer and were fought farther afield, adjustments had to be made. In 325 B.C.E., it was decided to create **proconsulships** to extend the terms of consuls who had important work to

WHAT ROLE did consuls, the Senate, and the Assembly play in ancient Rome?

consuls   Elected magistrates from patrician families chosen annually to lead the army, oversee the state religion, and sit as judges.

proconsulships   Extension of terms for consuls who had important work to finish.

Lictors were attendants of the Roman magistrates who held the power of *imperium*, the right to command. In republican times these magistrates were the consuls, praetors, and proconsuls. The lictors were men from the lower classes—some were even former slaves. They constantly attended the magistrates when the latter appeared in public. The lictors cleared a magistrate's way in crowds, and summoned, arrested, and punished offenders for him. They also served as their magistrate's house guard.

Alinari Art Resource, NY

QUICK REVIEW

The Struggle of the Orders

- Fueled by tensions between plebeians and patricians
- Plebeians used power of the army to gain concessions
- Plebeians made slow and incremental progress toward greater rights

censors Men of unimpeachable reputation, chosen to carry the responsibility for enrolling, keeping track of, and determining the status and tax liability of each citizen.

tribunes Officials elected by the plebeian tribal assembly given the power to protect plebeians from abuse by patrician magistrates.

---

finish. This maintained continuity of command during a long war, but it created a way for a man to perpetuate himself in power.

Consuls were assisted by financial officers called *quaestors*, and a need for more military commanders led to the introduction of other aides called *praetors*. A *praetor*'s primary function was judicial, but he could also be granted a general's *imperium* and have his term of service in the field extended beyond a year. In the second half of the fifth century B.C.E., the consuls' responsibility for enrolling and keeping track of citizens was delegated to new officials, two **censors**. Because they determined the status and the tax liability of each citizen, they had to be men of unimpeachable reputation. They were usually senior senators who viewed the office as the pinnacle of their careers. By the fourth century B.C.E., censors had the right to expel from the Senate members whose conduct disgraced senatorial dignity.

The Senate and the Assembly   The Senate was the only deliberative body continuously in session in the Roman Republic. Senators were prominent patricians, often leaders of clans and patrons with many clients. The Senate controlled the state's finances and foreign policy, and its advice was not lightly ignored by magistrates or the popular assemblies.

The *centuriate assembly*—the name for the Roman army when it was convened to deliberate rather than fight—was the early republic's most important popular assembly. It elected the consuls and several other magistrates, voted on bills the Senate put before it, made decisions of war and peace, and served as a court of appeal for citizens convicted of serious offenses. The centuriate assembly took its name from the *centuries*, the companies (theoretically of one hundred men) in which Roman men enrolled in the army and through which they voted. Because each soldier provided his own equipment, he was assigned to a century according to the kind of weapons and armor he could afford to buy. Each century cast a single vote, and votes were tallied beginning with the centuries that had the most expensive equipment, those of the cavalry and the first class of the infantry.

The Struggle of the Orders   Plebeians were barred from all political and religious offices in the early days of the republic. They could not serve as judges. They did not even know the law, for the law was an oral tradition passed down in patrician families. Whenever Rome conquered new land, patrician leaders were often able to claim it for themselves. They dominated the assemblies and the Senate, and they preserved their privileges by refusing to marry outside their caste. This was deeply resented by wealthy plebeian families.

Tensions between patricians and plebeians fueled the "struggle of the orders," a fight for political, legal, and social equality that lasted for two hundred years. Plebeians had a strong position from which to negotiate, for plebeians made up a large part of the republic's army. When danger threatened, they simply withdrew from the city and refused to fight until the patricians granted them concessions.

The plebeians made progress one step at a time. They formed a political organization of their own, the plebeian *tribal assembly*, and elected **tribunes**, officials with the power to protect plebeians from abuse by patrician magistrates. Tribunes could veto any action of a magistrate or any bill in a Roman assembly or the Senate. To protect their rights, the plebeians also demanded that Rome's laws be fixed and published. In 450 B.C.E., the Twelve Tables, which codified Rome's harsh methods of enforcing justice, appeared. In 445 B.C.E., plebeians won the right to marry patricians, but they were still barred from some public offices. The consulship remained closed to plebeians until 367 B.C.E., but gradually all offices—even the dictatorship, the censorship, and the priesthoods—were opened to them. In 287 B.C.E., the plebeians completed their triumph by securing passage of a law that made decisions of the plebeian tribal assembly binding on all Romans.

The struggle of the orders did not turn Rome into a democracy. It simply cleared the way for wealthy plebeian families to enter politics and share the privileges of the patrician aristocracy. The *nobiles*, a small group of rich and powerful families of both patrician and plebeian rank, dominated Rome. Because there was no secret ballot, the numerous clients of the wealthy *nobiles* could easily be intimidated into voting as their patrons ordered. This created a way for the great families to build political machines that maintained their holds on the republic's offices. From 233 to 133 B.C.E., twenty-six families produced 80 percent of the consuls, and ten of those families accounted for almost 50 percent of the successful candidates. Because the politically dominant families were all represented in the Senate, the Senate became the republic's chief deliberative body. The product of the struggle of the orders was, therefore, a republican constitution that empowered a senatorial aristocracy. Most Romans accepted it, for it led Rome well in the wars that won Rome an empire.

THE CONQUEST OF ITALY

Not long after the birth of the republic in 509 B.C.E., a coalition of Romans, Latins, and Greeks defeated the Etruscans and drove them out of Latium. Rome's neighbor, the Etruscan city of Veii, continued to be a problem, but in 392 B.C.E., Rome destroyed Veii and doubled its size by annexing Veii's territory.

The Romans preferred to use inducements and threats to come to terms with their foes—to turn enemies into allies who then joined Rome's army. When land was conquered, it was sometimes redistributed to the Roman poor so they could afford to equip themselves for military service. This gave the poor a stake in the republic's success and helped reconcile them to its aristocratic regime. The poor were also pleased when the long campaign that was needed to subdue Etruscan Veii forced the Romans to begin paying men for military service. Without such assistance, the soldiers, many of whom were self-supporting farmers, could not have stayed in the field.

Gallic Invasion of Italy and Roman Reaction   Rome was not always victorious. In 387 B.C.E., Gauls marched south from the Po Valley, routed the Roman army, and burned the city. The Romans fled their homeland and had to pay the Gauls a ransom to get it back. They quickly recovered from this humiliation, but in 340 B.C.E., Rome's neighbors formed the Latin League, an alliance dedicated to resisting Roman dominance. In 338 B.C.E., Rome defeated the league and offered the Latins terms that set precedents leading to the unification of Italy.

Roman Policy Toward the Conquered   The Romans did not destroy any of the Latin cities. Some were given Roman citizenship. Others were granted municipal privileges: the right to govern themselves, to intermarry and trade with Romans, and to move to Rome and apply for citizenship. The treaties by which other states became allies of Rome differed from city to city. Some were given Latin rights of intermarriage and commerce with Romans; some were not. Land was taken from some but not from others. Allies did not pay taxes to Rome, but they supplied troops to serve in Rome's army under Roman officers, and they were forbidden to make private agreements among themselves.

The Romans planted colonies of veteran soldiers on some of the land they annexed. These men staffed a permanent garrison that deterred rebellion. A network of military roads began to be built to link the colonies with Rome. This enabled a Roman army swiftly to reinforce any colony that faced an uprising.

The Roman settlement of Latium illustrates the strategies that resulted in Roman dominance of Italy. The Romans employed both diplomacy and force to divide their opponents. They cultivated a reputation for rapid and harsh punishment of their enemies, but they were also generous to those who submitted. Loyal allies could improve their prospects and even achieve Roman citizenship. Rome's allies saw themselves as colleagues more than subjects, and most of them remained loyal to Rome even when put to severe tests.

Defeat of the Samnites　After Rome settled its difficulties with the Latins, it faced a series of wars with the tough mountain people of the southern Apennines, the Samnites. Some of Rome's allies defected to the Samnites, and the Samnites were also aided by various Etruscans and Gauls. But most of the allies remained loyal, and by 280 B.C.E., Rome had subdued the Samnites and won mastery of central Italy.

At this point, Rome's expanding territory brought it into direct contact with the Greek cities of southern Italy, and Rome's intervention in a quarrel between two of these cities led to a war with a Greek mercenary, Pyrrhus, king of Epirus. Pyrrhus, who was probably the best general of the day, defeated the Romans on several occasions but suffered so many casualties that he decided he could not afford to continue his campaign. Having won victories that were not worth their cost (what are now called "Pyrrhic victories"), he withdrew from Italy and left his Greek employers no choice but to join the Roman confederation. By 265 B.C.E., Rome dominated all of Italy south of the Po River, an area of 47,200 square miles, and its defeat of Pyrrhus had brought it recognition as a major power in the Hellenistic world.

Rome became a naval power late in its history, to defeat Carthage in the First Punic War (264–241 B.C.E.). This sculpture in low relief shows a Roman ship, propelled by oars, with both ram and soldiers, ready for either to ram or board an enemy.

A Roman warship. Direzione Generale Musei Vaticani

ROME AND CARTHAGE

Late in the ninth century B.C.E., the Phoenician city of Tyre had planted a colony called Carthage ("New City") on the coast of northern Africa near modern Tunis. In the sixth century B.C.E., the conquest of Tyre by the Assyrians freed the Carthaginians to build an empire of their own. Carthage had a superb harbor and rich lands worked by slave labor.

During the sixth century B.C.E., Carthage's domain expanded west along the coast of North Africa past Gibraltar and east into Libya. Parts of southern Spain, Sardinia, Corsica, Malta, the Balearic Islands, and western Sicily also came under Carthaginian control. The inhabitants of these lands paid tribute to

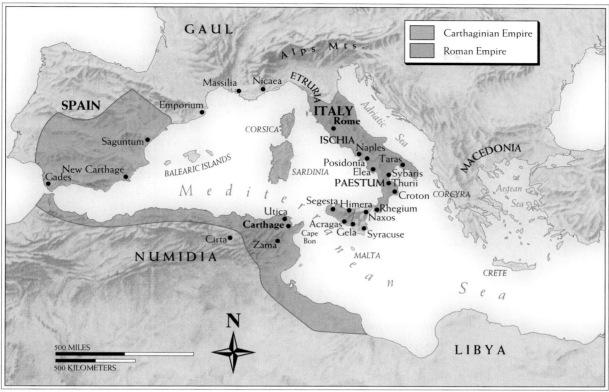

MAP 4–2

The Western Mediterranean Area During the Rise of Rome   This map illustrates the theater of conflict between the growing Roman dominions and those of Carthage in the third century B.C.E. The Carthaginian Empire stretched westward from the city (in modern Tunisia) along the North African coast and into southern Spain.

WHAT ECONOMIC and political effects did the Punic Wars have on Rome?

Carthage and were enlisted in the Carthaginian army and navy. Carthage claimed exclusive rights to trade in the western Mediterranean and warned other maritime powers to stay out of its waters. (See Map 4–2.)

Rome and Carthage became entangled when Hiero, tyrant of Syracuse, attacked the Sicilian city of Messana, a strategically important port that commanded the straits between Italy and Sicily. A band of Italian mercenaries, the Mamertines ("Sons of Mars"), had seized the city, and Hiero wanted to evict them. The Mamertines asked Carthage for help in fending him off, and Carthage agreed. But the Mamertines then tried to check Carthage by also inviting the Romans to send them aid. Rome realized that if it did not intervene, it was ceding control of the straits and possibly of Sicily to Carthage. Consequently, in 264 B.C.E., the assembly voted to send an army to Messana, a decision that led to three Punic Wars—conflicts that take their name from the Latin term for Carthaginian, *Puni* ("Phoenician").

The First Punic War (264–241 B.C.E.)   The Romans made no progress against Carthage until they built a fleet to blockade the Carthaginian ports at the western end of Sicily. Finally, in 241 B.C.E., the strain of what had become a war of attrition induced Carthage to capitulate. It surrendered Sicily and the islands between Italy and Sicily to Rome and agreed to pay a war indemnity. In 238 B.C.E., while Carthage struggled to put down a revolt of mercenary soldiers whom it had failed to pay, Rome seized Sardinia and Corsica and demanded an additional indemnity. This was a provocative action that was to cost Rome a second war with Carthage.

It is hard to understand why Rome sought more territory, for the administration of lands outside of Italy created serious problems. Because the Romans did not feel it was possible to treat distant foreigners like they had treated their neighbors in Italy, they turned Sicily, Sardinia, and Corsica into the first provinces of a Roman empire. Provinces were held by occupying armies and ruled by military governors. This was an arrangement open to horrific abuse, for Rome made no arrangements to oversee the conduct of the men who ran its provinces. Provincials were neither Roman citizens nor allies; they were subjects who paid tribute in lieu of serving in the army. Rome collected this tribute by selling the right to gather money in the provinces to "tax farmers," entrepreneurs who were free to take as much as they could get from the defenseless provincials. Provincial governments promoted corruption that undermined the machinery of the Roman Republic.

While Rome struggled to adjust to its new situation, Hamilcar Barca, the Carthaginian governor of Spain (237–229 B.C.E.), put Carthage on the road to recovery. His plan was to develop Spain to make up for the lands Carthage had lost to Rome. Hasdrubal, Hamilcar's son-in-law and successor, continued his policies with such success that the Romans were alarmed. They responded by imposing a treaty that obligated Carthage not to expand north of Spain's Ebro River. Hasdrubal doubtless assumed that if Carthage accepted the Ebro as its northern frontier, Rome would grant Carthage a free hand in the south. He was wrong. Within a few years the Romans had violated the Ebro treaty (at least in spirit) by allying with Saguntum, a town one hundred miles south of the Ebro.

The Second Punic War (218–202 B.C.E.) Hasdrubal was assassinated in 221 B.C.E., and the army chose Hannibal, the twenty-five-year-old son of Hamilcar Barca, to succeed him. Hannibal quickly consolidated his hold on Spain but avoided taking any action against Saguntum. However, when the Saguntines, encouraged by Rome's protection, began to stir up trouble for him, Hannibal captured the town. Rome then sent Carthage an ultimatum demanding Hannibal's surrender. Carthage refused, and Rome declared war (218 B.C.E.).

Although Rome had repeatedly provoked Carthage, it had taken no steps to prevent Carthage from rebuilding its empire and made no plans to defend itself against a Punic attack. Hannibal exacted a high price for these blunders. Rome expected to be able to fight Carthage on Carthaginian territory, but in the fall of 218 B.C.E., Hannibal crossed the Alps into Italy with an army the Gauls were eager to join. The Romans suffered the first of the many defeats he was to give them at the Ticinus River in the Po Valley. Not long thereafter he crushed the joint consular armies at the Trebia River, and in 217 B.C.E., he outmaneuvered and trapped another Roman army at Lake Trasimene. To take Rome, however, he had to persuade its allies to abandon it, and this most refused to do.

Sobered by their defeats, the Romans suspended consular government and chose a dictator, Quintus Fabius Maximus. Because time and supplies were on Rome's side, his plan was to avoid pitched battles and wear Hannibal's army down by harassing its flanks. In 216 B.C.E., Hannibal tempted the Romans to abandon this strategy by attacking a grain depot at Cannae in Apulia. They took the bait, met him on the field, and suffered the worst defeat in their history. Eighty thousand Roman soldiers were killed.

QUICK REVIEW

Hannibal on the Offensive
- 218 B.C.E.: crossed Alps and dealt Rome a series of defeats
- 216 B.C.E.: defeated Romans in Battle of Cannae, worst defeat in Roman history
- Victory at Cannae convinced some Roman allies to change sides

The disaster at Cannae shattered Rome's prestige, and many of the allies in southern Italy and the crucial port of Syracuse in Sicily went over to Hannibal. For the next decade, no Roman army dared confront Hannibal directly. Hannibal, however, had neither the numbers nor the supplies needed to besiege and starve walled cities into submission, and he did not have the equipment to storm them. So long as the Romans refused to fight, therefore, he could do little to bring the war to an end.

The Roman strategy for defeating Hannibal involved opening fronts outside of Italy. Publius Cornelius Scipio (237–183 B.C.E.), whose Carthaginian victories earned him the title "Africanus," undertook to conquer Spain to deprive Hannibal of reinforcements from that quarter. Scipio was not yet twenty-five, but he was almost as talented a general as Hannibal. Within a few years he had taken Spain and won the Senate's permission to invade Africa. In 204 B.C.E., Scipio bested the Carthaginian army in Africa, and this forced the city to order Hannibal to withdraw from Italy and come to the defense of his homeland. Hannibal had won every battle, but he had lost the war. His fatal error was to underestimate the determination of Rome and the loyalty of its allies. In 202 B.C.E., Hannibal and Scipio met at the Battle of Zama, and the day was decided by Scipio's generalship and the desertion of Hannibal's mercenaries. Carthage was allowed to survive, stripped of its lands and navy, and Rome emerged the undisputed ruler of the western Mediterranean.

THE REPUBLIC'S CONQUEST OF THE HELLENISTIC WORLD

The East   By the middle of the third century B.C.E., the three great Hellenistic kingdoms that dominated the eastern Mediterranean had achieved equilibrium. However, the balance of power among them was threatened by the plans that Philip V of Macedon (221–179 B.C.E.) and Antiochus III, the Seleucid ruler (223–187 B.C.E.), had to expand their domains. Philip had allied himself with Carthage during the Second Punic War, provoking Rome to stir up a conflict in Greece called the First Macedonian War (215–205 B.C.E.). Once the Second Punic War was over, Rome decided to make sure Macedon did not succeed Carthage as a threat to Italy. In 200 B.C.E., the Romans tried to intimidate Philip by ordering him to cease preying on the Greek cities, and two years later they demanded he withdraw from Greece entirely. Philip's refusal to comply provided Rome with justification for the Second Macedonian War. In 197 B.C.E., Flamininus, a gifted Roman general, defeated Philip at Cynoscephalae in Thessaly, and the following year (196 B.C.E.), Flamininus surprised the Greeks by restoring the autonomy of their city-states and pulling Rome's troops out of Greece.

Philip's retreat cleared the way for Antiochus to advance. On the pretext of freeing the Greeks from Roman domination, he invaded the Greek mainland. The Romans responded quickly, drove him from Greece, and, in 189 B.C.E., crushed his army at Magnesia in Asia Minor. Antiochus was forced to give up his war elephants and his navy and pay a huge indemnity. Although the Romans again annexed no territory, they treated Greece and Asia Minor as protectorates in whose affairs they could freely intervene.

In 179 B.C.E., Perseus succeeded Philip V as king of Macedon. His popularity with democratic, revolutionary

Significant Dates in Rome's Rise to Empire

509 B.C.E.	Republic founded
387 B.C.E.	Gauls sack Rome
338 B.C.E.	Rome defeats the Latin League
295 B.C.E.	Rome defeats the Samnites
287 B.C.E.	"Struggle of the Orders" ends
275 B.C.E.	Pyrrhus abandons Italy to Rome
264–241 B.C.E.	First Punic War
218–202 B.C.E.	Second Punic War
215–205 B.C.E.	First Macedonian War
200–197 B.C.E.	Second Macedonian War
189 B.C.E.	Rome defeats Antiochus
172–168 B.C.E.	Third Macedonian War
149–146 B.C.E.	Third Punic War
154–133 B.C.E.	Roman Wars in Spain

elements in the Greek cities convinced the Romans he was a threat to the stability of the Aegean. Following victory in a Third Macedonian War (172–168 B.C.E.), Rome dealt harshly with the Greeks. Macedon was divided into four separate republics. Their citizens were forbidden to intermarry or do business with each other, and leaders of anti-Roman factions in all the Greek cities were punished severely. Aemilius Paullus, the Roman general who defeated Perseus, brought so much booty home that Rome abolished some taxes. Romans were discovering that foreign campaigns could be profitable for the state, its soldiers, and its generals.

The West   Rome's worst abuses of power were directed not against the Greeks but against the people of the Iberian Peninsula whom the Romans considered barbarians. In 154 B.C.E., the natives of Iberia launched a fierce guerrilla campaign against their oppressors. By the time Scipio Aemilianus brought the war to a conclusion in 134 B.C.E. by taking the city of Numantia, Rome was having difficulty finding soldiers willing to go to Spain.

Although Carthage scrupulously observed the terms of its treaty with Rome and posed no threat to Rome, fear and hatred of Carthage were deeply ingrained in the Roman psyche. Cato, a prominent senator, is said to have ended all his speeches with a stern warning: "Besides, I think that Carthage must be destroyed." The Romans finally seized on a technical breach of the peace to declare war on Carthage, and in 146 B.C.E., Scipio Aemilianus destroyed the city. A province of Africa was then added to the five existing Roman provinces: Sicily, Sardinia-Corsica, Macedonia, Hither Spain, and Further Spain.

CIVILIZATION IN THE EARLY ROMAN REPUBLIC

HOW DID contact with the Hellenistic world affect Rome?

*T*he Roman attitude toward the Greeks ranged from admiration for their culture to contempt for their political squabbling and money grubbing. Conservatives such as Cato spoke contemptuously of the Greeks, but, as Roman life was transformed by association with the Greeks, even he learned Greek. The education of the Roman upper classes became bilingual, and young Roman nobles studied Greek rhetoric, literature, and philosophy. Greek refined the Latin language, and Greek literature provided the models that guided Latin authors.

RELIGION

The Romans equated their ancestral gods with similar Greek deities and worked Greek legends into their own mythology. But Roman religious traditions were little affected until the third century B.C.E., when new cults from the Middle East spread to Italy. In 205 B.C.E., the Senate endorsed worship of Cybele, the Great Mother goddess from Phrygia. Cybele's cult, however, involved rites that shocked and outraged conservative Romans, and the Senate soon reversed itself. For similar reasons, it banned the worship of Dionysus (Bacchus) in 186 B.C.E., and in 139 B.C.E., the Senate exiled Babylonian astrologers from Rome. (See "Encountering the Past: Roman Comedy.")

EDUCATION

In the early centuries of the Roman Republic, education was entirely the responsibility of the family. Fathers taught their sons vocational skills, moral rectitude, and respect for Roman tradition. (Daughters may not have been schooled in those days, but they were at a later period.) Boys learned to read, write, calculate, and farm. They memorized the laws of the Twelve Tables and legendary accounts of Rome's origin. They mastered the intricacies of religious rites, and they trained for military service.

ENCOUNTERING THE PAST

ROMAN COMEDY

I n Rome, as in Greece, religious festivals were public entertainments involving gladiatorial contests, chariot races, and dramas. Initially, Roman audiences sat on hillsides and watched performances staged on temporary wooden platforms. Toward the end of the republican period, however, wealthy Romans began to donate permanent amphitheaters to their communities, and theaters spread to all the lands Rome ruled.

Tragedies modeled on Greek examples were staged in Rome, but the works of the republic's best playwrights—Plautus (ca. 254–184 B.C.E.) and Terence (ca. 195–159 B.C.E.)—belong to the genre of Hellenistic New Comedy. The standard set for such plays was a city street where stock characters (clever slaves, dim-witted masters, young lovers, and shrewish women) enacted plots involving a tangle of mistaken identities, love affairs, and domestic disputes. The result was very similar to the situation comedies that are staples of modern television.

IS THERE any significance in the fact that the great plays that survive from the era of the Roman Republic are comedies, not tragedies?

This mosaic shows a scene from Roman comedy in which musicians played a significant role.

© Araldo de Luca/CORBIS

Hellenized Education   Contact with the Greeks of southern Italy in the third century B.C.E. produced momentous changes in Roman education. Greek teachers introduced the Romans to the study of language, literature, and philosophy—and to what the Romans called *humanitas*, the wide-ranging intellectual curiosity and habits of critical thinking that are the goals of liberal education.

Because Rome did not yet have much literature of its own, educated Romans learned Greek. Greek education centered on philosophy, but the practical Romans preferred rhetoric, the art of speaking and writing well. Rhetoric was of great use in political life and legal disputes. Some important Romans, such as Scipio Aemilianus (the destroyer of Carthage), enthusiastically advocated the study of Greek literature and philosophy. Scipio was the patron and friend of Polybius, a Greek who wrote a history of Rome's Punic wars. More conservative Romans, such as Cato the Elder, feared that Greek learning would weaken Roman moral fiber. The Senate occasionally expelled philosophers and teachers of rhetoric from Rome, but the Romans understood that if they were to deal with the Hellenistic Greeks, who were becoming their allies and subjects, they needed more sophisticated educations than those that had sufficed their simple agrarian ancestors.

humanitas   Wide-ranging intellectual curiosity and habits of critical thinking that are the goals of liberal education.

This carved relief from the second century C.E. shows a schoolmaster and his pupils. The pupil at the right is arriving late.

Rheinisches Landaesmuseum, Trier, Germany. Alinari/Art Resource, NY

In the late republic, Roman education, although still a family responsibility, became more formal and organized. Boys age seven to twelve attended elementary school in the care of a Greek slave called a *paedagogus* (pedagogue). He looked after them and helped them learn Greek by talking with them in his native language. They wrote on waxed tablets with styluses and learned to calculate using *calculi* (pebbles) and the abacus. From twelve to sixteen, they studied Greek and Latin literature with a *grammaticus*, who taught them dialectic, arithmetic, geometry, astronomy, music, and elements of rhetoric. Some young men sought advanced instruction in rhetoric, and a few, such as the great orator Cicero, traveled abroad to work with the great teachers of the Greek world.

Education for Women   Although evidence is limited, it suggests that upper-class girls received at least a basic education. They were probably taught at home by tutors and not sent out to school as was increasingly common for their brothers in the late republican period. Young women did not usually go on to study with philosophers and rhetoricians, for women were usually married by the age at which a man began this phase of his education. Still, some women did manage to continue their studies, and some became prose writers and poets. By the first century C.E., there were women in aristocratic circles who were famous or—as conservative males saw it—infamous for their learning.

SLAVERY

The Romans, like most ancient peoples, always had slaves. But the small farmers of early Rome owned few. Roman society only came to depend on slavery in the wake of Rome's conquests in the second century B.C.E. Between 264 B.C.E. and 133 B.C.E., the Romans enslaved some 250,000 prisoners of war. Children born to slaves further swelled the population of the unfree.

In Rome as in Greece, domestic slaves and those engaged in crafts and commerce could earn money of their own with which to purchase freedom. Emancipation was common, and it was not long before a considerable portion of the Roman population consisted of former slaves or their descendants. Some freedmen and their sons and grandsons earned fortunes and Roman citizenship. The importation of slaves from all over the Mediterranean world and their frequent emancipation made Rome an ethnically diverse place.

Rome's contribution to slavery was the invention of the plantation economy—huge commercial agricultural enterprises staffed by vast numbers of unfree workers. As the end of the republican era drew near, the number of slaves in Italy approached 2 to 3 million about 35 to 40 percent of the total population. Most labored on **latifundia**, great estates that produced capital-intensive cash crops (wool, wine, olive oil, cattle) for the international market. *Latifundia* were designed to produce maximum profits. Because slaves were simply a means to that end, they were

latifundia   Great estates that produced capital-intensive cash crops for the international market.

HISTORY'S VOICES

ROME'S TREATMENT OF CONQUERED ITALIAN CITIES

*T*itus Livius (59 *B.C.E.–17 C.E.*), called Livy in English-speaking countries, wrote a history of Rome from its origins until his own time. In the following excerpt from it he describes the kind of settlement they imposed on various Italian cities after crushing their revolt in the years 340–338 *B.C.E.*

WHAT PRINCIPLES and purposes underlay Rome's treatment of the different cities?

The principal members of the senate applauded the consul's statement on the business on the whole; but said that, as the states were differently circumstanced, their plan might be readily adjusted and determined according to the desert of each, if they should put the question regarding each state specifically. The question was therefore so put regarding each separately and a decree passed. To the people of Lanuvium the right of citizenship was granted, and the exercise of their religious rights was restored to them with this provision, that the temple and grove of Juno Sospita should be common between the Lanuvian burghers and the Roman people. The peoples of Aricia, Nomentum, and Pedum were admitted into the number of citizens on the same terms as the Lanuvians. To the Tusculans the rights of citizenship which they already possessed were continued; no public penalty was imposed and the crime of rebellion was visited on its few instigators. On the people of Velitrae, Roman citizens of long standing, measures of great severity were inflicted because they had so often rebelled; their walls were razed, and their senate deported and ordered to dwell on the other side of the Tiber; any individual who should be caught on the hither side of the river should be fined one thousand asses, and the person who had apprehended him should not discharge his prisoner from confinement until the money was paid down. Into the lands of the senators colonists were sent; by their addition Velitrae recovered its former populous appearance.

Livy, *History of Rome*, trans. by D. Spillan et al. (New York: American Book Company, n.d.), Vol. 1, p. 561.

ruthlessly exploited—fed poorly, worked relentlessly, and discarded when they were no longer productive.

Harsh treatment spawned slave rebellions of a kind unknown in other ancient societies. A rebellion in Sicily in 134 B.C.E. kept that island in turmoil for over two years. In 73 B.C.E., a gladiator named Spartacus raised an army of 70,000 fugitive slaves that defeated several legions and overran all of southern Italy before it was finally crushed.

Slavery began to decline in the second century C.E. As Rome's empire ceased to expand and its wars produced fewer captives, the cost of slaves rose. General economic decline also forced many of the free poor to become *coloni*, tenant farmers who were bound to the lands they worked. By the time the Roman Empire fell, slaves had largely been replaced by laborers of a different kind in the West.

ROMAN IMPERIALISM: THE LATE REPUBLIC

*R*ome had no plan for building an empire. Much of its land was acquired as a by-product of wars that were undertaken for defensive purposes. The primary objective of Rome's foreign policy was to provide security for Rome on Rome's terms. Because these terms were often unacceptable to other peoples, conflicts arose; and, intentionally or not, Rome's domain expanded. (See Map 4–3.)

HOW DID the expansion of Rome change the Republic?

coloni Tenant farmers who were bound to the lands they worked.

MAP EXPLORATION

Interactive map: To explore this map further, go to **http://www.prenhall.com/kagan3/map4.3**

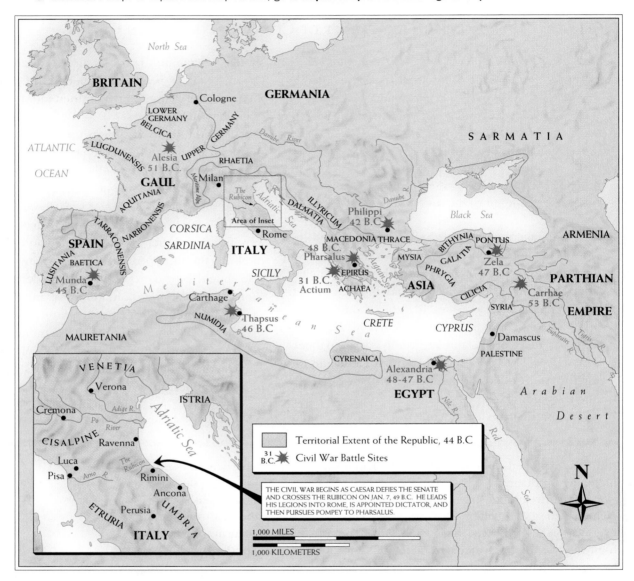

MAP 4–3

The Civil Wars of the Late Roman Republic   This map shows the extent of the territory controlled by Rome at the time of Caesar's death and the sites of the major battles of the civil wars of the late republic.

WHAT WAS the principal goal of Roman foreign policy during the period of the Roman Republic? How did this goal contribute to Roman expansion?

The burden of maintaining an empire undercut the republic the empire was built to protect. The republic was a government designed for a city-state. It could be adapted to rule Italy but not an empire that encircled the Mediterranean Sea.

THE AFTERMATH OF CONQUEST

Before the Punic Wars, most Italians owned their own farms and were largely self-sufficient. Some families had larger holdings than others, but they worked them with free laborers and, like their neighbors, grew grain for local consumption. The Punic Wars changed this. For fourteen years Hannibal marauded through Italy, doing terrible damage to its farms. Many veterans returned from the wars to find they did not have enough capital to get their devastated lands back into production. Some moved to Rome looking for work as day laborers. Others stayed in the country and became tenant farmers or hired hands. The farms they abandoned were taken over by the wealthy, who had the capital to convert them for the production of specialized crops for the world market. The upper classes had plenty of capital to invest in vineyards, olive orchards, and cattle ranches, for they monopolized political offices and, therefore, access to profitable provincial governorships. As the gap steadily widened between Rome's rich and poor, landed and landless, privileged and deprived, an increasingly tense situation developed that threatened to destabilize the republic.

THE GRACCHI

By the middle of the second century B.C.E., perceptive Roman nobles were aware that institutions fundamental to the republic were collapsing. The class of peasant farmers from which Rome recruited its soldiers was shrinking, and the patron-client organizations that ordered Roman society were weakening. Patrons found it hard to control rootless mobs of landless clients, and the introduction of the secret ballot in the 130s B.C.E. further diminished their declining ability to mobilize their political supporters.

Tiberius Gracchus   In 133 B.C.E., Tiberius Gracchus, a tribune, proposed land reform legislation that he claimed would solve these problems. He suggested reclaiming public land from the rich, who held it illegally, and redistributing it among the poor. Current occupants of this land were to be allowed to retain up to three hundred acres, but the state would take the rest and divide it up into plots for small-scale farmers. The men to whom these plots were given had to work them and were forbidden to sell them.

There was much opposition to Tiberius's proposal. Many wealthy senators would be hurt by its passage. Some worried about the precedent that would be set by interfering with property rights. Others feared the proposal would win Tiberius a popular following that would give him too much political power. When Tiberius put his land reform bill before the tribal assembly, he was not surprised, therefore, when one of his fellow tribunes, M. Octavius, vetoed it. Tiberius outmaneuvered Octavius by making a proposal that virtually eliminated the checks and balances of Rome's constitution. He urged the assembly to eliminate the veto that was blocking his popular legislation by voting Octavius out of office. This was an alarming development, for if the assembly could override the Senate and the veto of a tribune, Rome would cease to be an oligarchical republic and become a direct democracy like Athens.

This wall painting from the first century B.C.E. comes from the villa of Publius Fannius Synistor at Pompeii and shows a woman playing a cithera.

Fresco on lime plaster. H. 6 feet 1 1/2 inches W. 6 feet 1 1/2 inches (187 × 187 cm). The Metropolitan Museum of Art, Rogers Fund, 1903. (03.14.5) Photograph © 1986 The Metropolitan Museum of Art

4.4
Appian of Alexandria, *War, Slaves, and Land Reform: Tiberius Gracchus*

This statue of an unknown member of the Roman nobility from late in the first century illustrates a fundamental custom. He carries the images of two of his ancestors, probably his father and grandfather.

Marble. Musei Capitolini, Rome, Italy. Photograph ©Scala/Art Resource, NY

populares Politicians who followed Tiberius's example of politics and governing.

optimates ("the best men") Opponents of Tiberius and defenders of the traditional prerogatives of the Senate.

equestrians Men rich enough to qualify for cavalry service.

Having no hope of winning senatorial support, Tiberius drafted a second bill that was harsher than the first one he had proposed and, consequently, even more appealing to the masses. It contained a scheme for funding land redistribution. King Attalus of Pergamum had just died and left his kingdom to Rome, and Tiberius proposed using revenue from this source to finance implementation of land reform. This was a second assault on the constitution, for the Senate traditionally controlled Rome's finances and foreign affairs.

Tiberius knew he would be in personal danger once he lost the protection of his tribunal office, so he violated the republic's rules yet again by announcing he was going to run for reelection. By limiting its magistrates to single one- year terms, the republic prevented any individual from monopolizing a powerful office. If Tiberius changed the rules, he could conceivably have held the tribunate indefinitely and ruled Rome as a demagogue. Tiberius's enemies—seeing no legal recourse—resorted to illegal action. They killed Tiberius and some three hundred of his followers. The Senate beat back the threat to its rule but at the price of the first internal bloodshed in Rome's political history.

The tribunate of Tiberius Gracchus permanently changed the practice of politics in Rome. Heretofore, politics had been a struggle for honor and reputation among great families. Political rivalries rarely involved fundamental challenges to Rome's system of government. Tiberius, however, had shown how the tribunate could be used to evade senatorial dominance. Instead of courting a coalition of aristocratic supporters, he had cut out the aristocrats by appealing directly to the people with a popular issue. Politicians who followed his example came to be known as ***populares***, and their opponents, the defenders of the traditional prerogatives of the Senate, as ***optimates*** ("the best men"). These names did not signify the appearance of political parties with distinctive platforms. They only indicated alternative strategies for winning political power in Rome.

Gaius Gracchus In 123 B.C.E., ten years after Tiberius's death, Gaius Gracchus, his brother, became a tribune. Gaius kept himself in power by putting together packages of legislation that forced disparate groups of voters to support the whole in order to get the parts that benefited them. After Tiberius's murder, the Senate had placated the masses by allowing some land reform to begin, but without an enthusiastic backer the process had languished. Gaius renewed efforts to redistribute public land. He proposed new colonies, and he put through a law that stabilized the price of grain in Rome. Gaius undercut his opponents by pitting the republic's two wealthiest classes, the senators and the **equestrians** (men rich enough to qualify for cavalry service), against each other. In 129 B.C.E., Gaius won equestrian backing by passing a law that excluded senators from the juries that tried provincial governors. This prevented senators from sitting in judgment on themselves, but it did not improve the administration of the provinces. It meant that no senator could risk restraining the activities of the equestrian tax farmers in his province lest he find himself dragged before a court they controlled.

In 122 B.C.E., following reelection (which had become legal) to the tribunate, Gaius proposed legislation to right an injustice—and increase the number of his own supporters. He suggested extending citizenship to Rome's Italian allies. The allies had not received a fair share of the profits from the empire they had helped Rome win, and their resentment threatened to create serious problems for the republic. The Roman masses, however, did not want to dilute the power of their votes by creating more citizens. When they failed to support Gaius's bid for a third term in 121 B.C.E., the Senate seized its opportunity to murder him and some 3,000 of his followers. Force enabled the senatorial oligarchy to triumph once again over the *populares*, but the struggle was by no means over. Gaius's death simply convinced the *populares* that they had to find a way to match the Senate's violence, and a soldier named Marius showed them how.

MARIUS AND SULLA

In 111 B.C.E., a group of Italian businessmen in Numidia, a client kingdom in North Africa, were caught and killed in the crossfire of a dispute that had broken out over succession to the Numidian throne. The Roman electorate promptly declared war on Jugurtha, the Numidian prince whom it blamed for this insult to the republic's honor. The war dragged on longer than expected, and rumors circulated that Rome's generals were being bought off.

In 107 B.C.E., the assembly elected C. Marius (157–86 B.C.E.) to a consulship and (usurping the Senate's authority over foreign policy) commissioned him to end the Jugurthine War. Marius was not a member of the old Roman aristocracy, but a *novus homo*, a "new man" (the first in his family to hold a consulship). Marius quickly defeated Jugurtha, and the grateful Romans elected him to a second term to deal with another problem. In 105 B.C.E., two barbarian tribes, the Cimbri and the Teutones, had crushed a Roman army in the Rhone Valley. The long struggle needed to restore order in Gaul provided Marius with an excuse for holding five consecutive consulships.

Marius's military success owed much to the large armies he built, and the manpower for his armies was a product of his *populares* legislation. He persuaded the Romans to make it possible for poor men to have military careers by dropping the traditional property qualification for military service. Marius's army shifted the balance of power in Roman politics, for his soldiers were clients of their general. They were professionals paid by the state, and their continuing employment depended on his authority to use public money to reward them. Because a vote for him was a vote for themselves, they constituted a powerful political machine that kept him in office.

Marius's example inspired imitation. The most successful of his competitors was L. Cornelius Sulla (138–78 B.C.E.), an impoverished aristocrat who had served under Marius in the Jugurthine War. Sulla began his career by fighting in a war that Gaius Gracchus had tried to prevent. In 90 B.C.E. (about thirty years after Gaius Gracchus's death), Rome's Italian allies finally gave up hope of receiving fair treatment and formed an independent confederation of their own. Rome undercut their rebellion by offering citizenship to cities that remained loyal and to rebels who laid down their arms. Although all the allies eventually attained citizenship, hard fighting was still needed to put down the uprising.

Sulla's performance in the war brought him the consulship for 88 B.C.E. and command of a war against Mithridates, a native king who was threatening Roman interests in Asia Minor. Despite being seventy years old, Marius decided he wanted this assignment for himself and persuaded the assembly to rescind Sulla's commission. Sulla responded by marching on Rome with the army he had recruited for the Eastern campaign. Marius used the army to manipulate Rome politically, but Sulla was more direct. Sulla's command was restored, but after he left for the East, Marius and the consul Cinna occupied Rome with their armies.

Marius died soon after his election to a seventh consulship in 86 B.C.E., and Cinna inherited leadership of Marius's party. In 83 B.C.E., Sulla, who had forced Mithridates to retreat and agree to a truce, returned to Rome and drove Marius's followers from Italy.

Sulla claimed that to restore order he had to assume a dictatorship (a republican office). He wiped out his opponents by posting "proscription lists." Proscribed individuals were declared enemies of the state who were to be executed by anyone who found them. Their executioners were rewarded, and Sulla confiscated their property for redistribution among his followers. As many as 100,000 Romans may have died in Sulla's purge.

Sulla could have made himself the permanent ruler of Rome, but he opted to use his power to implement his conservative vision of the Roman Republic. He reaffirmed the Senate's political privileges and severely limited the tribunate, the office the Gracchi had used to undermine the Senate. In 79 B.C.E., Sulla declared his work complete and retired from public life. The political arrangements he had made proved much less durable than the lessons ambitious men drew from studying his rise to power.

THE FALL OF THE REPUBLIC

POMPEY, CRASSUS, CAESAR, AND CICERO

WHAT EVENTS led to the fall of the Republic?

Within a year of Sulla's death in 78 B.C.E., the Senate began to make exceptions to the very rules Sulla had designed to safeguard its power. It had no choice, for the only way to handle some crises was to create "special commands," which were special because they were free of the severe limitations imposed on constitutional magistracies. A general named Pompey (106–48 B.C.E.) built a remarkable career by advancing from one special command to another and largely ignoring elective offices.

Pompey emerged first in Roman politics as one of Sulla's supporters, and he made his reputation by helping track down and destroy the remnants of Marius's armies. In 73 B.C.E., the Senate commissioned him and Marcus Licinius Crassus, a wealthy senator, to put down the slave rebellion led by the gladiator, Spartacus. Crassus and Pompey then joined forces and used their influence to repeal most of Sulla's legislation. Ambitious generals understood how helpful demagogic tribunes could be in advancing their careers.

In 67 B.C.E., a special law aimed at the suppression of piracy gave Pompey *imperium* for three years over the entire Mediterranean and its coast inland for fifty miles. Pompey cleared the seas of pirates in a mere three months and then turned his attention to a second war that broke out with Mithridates. Pompey defeated Mithridates and then chose on his own initiative to push Rome's eastern frontier to the Euphrates River and the borders of Egypt.

Pompey returned to Rome in 62 B.C.E. By now he had more power than any Roman in history, and he could easily have emulated Sulla and established a dictatorship. Crassus was particularly worried, and he tried to protect himself by building alliances with leading politicians. The ablest of these was Gaius Julius Caesar (100–44 B.C.E.), a descendant of an old but obscure patrician family. Caesar was closely linked to the *populares*. Marius had married his aunt, and he had married Cinna's daughter. Both Crassus and Caesar knew that to survive in Roman politics, they had to build armies that could compete with Pompey's. To this end, Crassus funded the impoverished Caesar, and Caesar used his considerable rhetorical and political skills to advance their cause.

Cicero (106–43 B.C.E.), a "new man" from Marius's hometown of Arpinum, marshaled opposition to Crassus and Caesar. Although Cicero was an outsider to the senatorial aristocracy, he was a committed *optimates*. He thought he could engineer a "harmony of the orders" (the senators and the equestrians) that would consolidate the power of the propertied classes. The Senate backed him primarily to block the maneuvers of an extremist named Catiline. Cicero defeated Catiline for the consulship in 63 B.C.E., but Catiline refused to accept the verdict and made plans to seize control of Rome. Word leaked to Cicero, who exposed the plot in time for the Senate to rout Catiline and his men. This turn of events did not please Pompey.

4.6
Marcus Tullius Cicero:
The Laws

THE FIRST TRIUMVIRATE

Pompey landed at Brundisium in southern Italy near the end of 62 B.C.E. He had delayed coming home, hoping some crisis in Italy would justify returning with his army. Cicero's quick suppression of Catiline deprived him of a pretext, and Pompey had to disband his army to avoid the appearance of treason.

Pompey had achieved great things for Rome, and he expected the Senate to show its gratitude by deferring to him, ratifying the treaties he had negotiated in the East, and giving him land on which to retire his veterans. His requests were reasonable, and the Senate should have complied. However, it decided to delay in hopes of creating problems that would weaken Rome's strongman. The Senate's opposition drove Pompey into an alliance with his natural enemies, Crassus and Caesar. They formed the First Triumvirate, a private political arrangement that enabled them, by working together, to dominate the republic.

JULIUS CAESAR AND HIS GOVERNMENT OF ROME

With the aid of his colleagues, Caesar was elected to the consulship for 59 B.C.E., and he used the office to make sure each of the triumvirs got what he wanted. Pompey obtained land for his veterans and confirmation of his treaties. Crassus won tax concessions for the equestrians who were his chief backers. Caesar got a special military command that gave him a chance to rival Pompey. When Caesar's consulship ended, the triumvirs secured their gains by arranging for the election of friendly consuls and by forcing their leading opponents to leave Rome.

Caesar's special command gave him authority, for five years, over Cisalpine Gaul in the Po Valley and Narbonese Gaul on the far side of the Alps. With these provinces as his base, he set about conquering Gaul. He bought additional time in 56 B.C.E. by persuading Crassus and Pompey to renew the triumvirate, and by 50 B.C.E., Caesar had completed the work of pacifying Gaul as far north as the Lowlands and east to the Rhine River. In the process he had built a military machine that enabled him to rival Pompey.

As Caesar's term as governor of Gaul neared its end in 50 B.C.E., he searched for a way to retain an office that would allow him to keep his army. The triumvirate had dissolved in 53 B.C.E. when Crassus died leading an army into Parthia, the successor to the old Persian Empire, and the Senate had, in the intervening years, concluded that Pompey was a lesser threat than Caesar. It refused, therefore, to extend his term in Gaul and ordered him to lay down his command. Caesar knew this meant exile or death. Preferring treason, he ordered his legions to cross the Rubicon River, the boundary of his province, and march on Rome. This began a civil war from which Caesar emerged victorious in 45 B.C.E.

In theory, the Senate was to continue to play its traditional role in governing the republic, but Caesar's monopoly of military power made a sham of the

Senate's decrees. Caesar changed the character of the Senate by increasing its size and extending membership to Italians and Gauls as well as the sons of the old Roman families. In 46 B.C.E., the compliant Senate appointed Caesar dictator for ten years, and a year later it extended his term for life. Gaius Cassius Longinus and Marcus Junius Brutus concluded that Caesar was aiming at monarchy, and they persuaded about sixty of their fellow senators it was their patriotic duty to save the republic by murdering Caesar. The assassins struck during a meeting of the Senate on March 15, 44 B.C.E. They expected that once Caesar was dead the republic would automatically flourish, but they were wrong. Removing Caesar only cleared the way for renewed civil war—a thirteen-year conflict that ended the republican era and gave Rome an imperial form of government.

THE SECOND TRIUMVIRATE AND THE EMERGENCE OF OCTAVIAN

Caesar had adopted his grandnephew, an eighteen-year-old youth named Gaius Octavian (63 B.C.E.–14 C.E.). The Senate hoped to use the sickly, inexperienced young heir to block the rise of Rome's potential new strongman, Mark Antony. Mark Antony had been Caesar's second-in-command, and the troops automatically looked to him to lead them after Caesar's death. Mark Antony initially tried to steer a course between the Senate and Caesar's angry soldiers, but Octavian spoiled that plan. Despite his youth, Octavian won the consulship for 43 B.C.E., and then he called for war to avenge Caesar's death. Mark Antony and another of Caesar's officers, M. Aemilius Lepidus, knew this was what their armies expected Caesar's legitimate heirs to do, so they joined Octavian in establishing the Second Triumvirate. Unlike the first, this was a legal public arrangement, a joint dictatorship formed, ostensibly, for the purpose of restoring the republic.

In 42 B.C.E., the triumvirs defeated Brutus and Cassius at Philippi in Macedonia, and each of the victors rewarded himself with a command. The weakest member, Lepidus, was given Africa. Octavian took the West and its troubles: a war with one of Pompey's sons, the settlement of some 100,000 veterans, and the restoration of order in Italy. Antony received the most promising assignment: an Eastern command from which to launch an invasion of Parthia. A victorious Parthian campaign would have given Antony the resources and popularity he needed to sweep his fellow triumvirs aside.

The army Antony led into Parthia in 36 B.C.E. took heavy losses and was forced to retreat. This caused his soldiers to begin to doubt him, and it made him vulnerable to a propaganda campaign that Octavian had mounted. Octavian did a brilliant job of convincing the Romans that Antony was no longer responsible for himself—that passion had turned him into the helpless pawn of Egypt's queen, Cleopatra. By 32 B.C.E., all pretense of cooperation among the triumvirs had come to an end. Lepidus had already been shoved aside, and in 31 B.C.E., a minor naval skirmish at Actium off the western coast of Greece began Antony's precipitous fall from power.

Judging all to be lost, Antony and Cleopatra committed suicide. Their deaths ended the civil war and left Octavian, at the age of thirty-two, master of the Mediterranean world. His power was enormous, but so was the task before him. To restore peace and stability to Rome he needed to invent a form of government that could administer an empire without seeming to violate the republican traditions to which the Romans were still passionately devoted.

Portrait Head of Cleopatra VII.
©Sandro Vannini/CORBIS

SUMMARY

Prehistoric Italy The Neolithic era came late to Italy, around 2500 B.C.E., followed by the Bronze Age starting around 1500 B.C.E. Bands of warring peoples speaking Italic languages invaded from across the Adriatic and along the northeastern coast starting around 1000 B.C.E.; within two centuries they had occupied the Appenines and were challenging the earlier settlers on the western plains. Their tools and craftsmanship were better than those of Italy's earlier inhabitants. These peoples shaped Italy's history.

The Etruscans Etruscan civilization emerged in Etruria around 800 B.C.E. The Etruscans formed a military ruling class that held power over the native Italians. Etruscan religion exerted a strong influence throughout the region. Under Greek influence, the Etruscans started to worship human-shaped gods. Etruscan women had more visible roles than their Greek counterparts. Etruscans expanded their domains and controlled large holdings in Italy, Corsica, and Elba. Etruscan power had peaked by 500 B.C.E., then declined rapidly under attack by the Gauls around 400 B.C.E.

Royal Rome Rome's location on the Tiber River made it an important center for communication and trade. In the sixth century B.C.E., under the leadership of Etruscan kings, Rome developed political institutions that would endure through the Roman Republic, imperial Rome, and beyond. The kings of Rome held the power of *imperium*, but they were checked by the Senate and the curiate assembly. The family was the center of Roman life. Women and children had some protections. Upper-class women had positions of influence and respect greater than those available to Greek women. *Clientage* entailed mutual obligations between client and patron; the relationship was hereditary and sanctioned by religion. The two classes in royal Rome were *patricians*, a closed upper class that monopolized power, and the *plebeians*, who were originally poor but eventually came to include wealthy families unable to join the patrician class.

The Republic In 509 B.C.E., the noble families revolted successfully against the monarchy and created the Roman Republic. A limited form of the *imperium* was exercised by the consuls. Over the following centuries, the powers of the Senate increased substantially. Plebeians chafed against the limits on their political participation and other rights, leading to the Struggle of the Orders. By the middle of the third century B.C.E., Rome controlled the Italian peninsula. Conflict between Rome and Carthage in Sicily erupted in the First Punic War, through which Rome won control of Sicily. By mismanaging the peace, however, the Romans set the stage for the Second Punic War, in which Rome faced Hannibal. After winning every battle, Hannibal lost the war when the Roman general Scipio defeated the Carthaginians. Meanwhile, Rome had started meddling in Macedonian affairs, participating in the three Macedonian Wars. Rome's victory at the conclusion of the Third Macedonian War in 168 B.C.E. resulted in an uncharacteristically harsh peace.

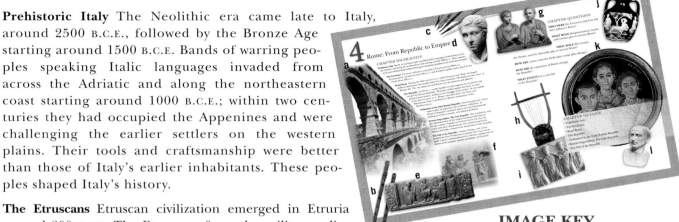

IMAGE KEY
for pages 88–89

a. Pont du Gard, Nimes, Provence, France

b. Bronze flutes

c. Reed and bronze pens as well as bronze, iron and ivory styli

d. Cleopatra VII

e. Roman relief from Noviomagn Rheinisches Landesmuseum, Trier, Germany. Alinari/Art Resource, NY

f. Mosaic showing a scene from a Roman comedy

g. Bust of Cato and Porcia. Roman sculpture.   Vatican Museums, Vatican State. Photograph © Scala/Art Resource, NY

h. Lyre musical instrument, with tortoise shell for amplification

i. Roman lictors. Marble relief from Concordia. Mostra Augustea, Rome

j. Portland Vase, 3rd C. B.C.E. Cameo-cut glass   British Museum, London

k. "Family Group," traditionally called the "Family of Vunnerius Keramus." C. 25 C.E. Engraved gold leaf sealed between glass. D: 2 3/8" (6 cm). Museo Civico dell'Eta Cristiana, Brescia; Fotostudio Rapuzzi

l. Bust of Julius Caesar, 100-44 B.C.E. Roman statesman   Museo Archeologico Nazionale, Naples, Italy. Photograph © Scala/Art Resource, NY

Civilization in the Early Roman Republic Educated Romans were bilingual, in Latin and Greek; Greek mythology was incorporated into Roman religion; education became Hellenized, and Greeks took on significant roles in the formal educational system. Girls did not attend school, but among the upper classes they were tutored at home. Slavery increased dramatically as the Romans enslaved prisoners of war. Manumission was common, and former slaves enjoyed social and economic mobility. The development of the *latifundia* system of agriculture—basically, cash-crop plantations that depended on slave labor—fueled the growth of a harsher and more oppressive form of slavery, with the result that significant slave rebellions occurred. Slavery declined gradually; in agriculture, tenant farmers called *coloni* slowly filled the economic niche of slavery.

Roman Imperialism: The Late Republic War, expansion, and the administration of an empire fundamentally altered Roman culture. The availability of cheap land and labor sharpened class differences throughout Italy. Tiberius Gracchus's unconstitutional tactics in attempting to pass land reform legislation in 133 B.C.E. led eventually to a riot in which Tiberius and three hundred of his supporters were killed. Roman politics was changed forever. Fundamental issues were now clearly at stake. Tiberius's brother Gaius Gracchus assumed the tribunate in 123 B.C.E. and passed some populist reforms, but he too was assassinated. Soon senatorial privilege was challenged from abroad, through the Jugurthine War that began in 111 B.C.E. Two ambitious generals, Marius and Sulla, gained power through their victories. Later, fighting barbarian tribes to the north, Marius introduced innovations into the army that made soldiers more loyal to their general than to the state. All Italians gained citizenship after a revolt. Between 88 and 83 B.C.E., Marius and Sulla dragged the Romans into civil war in their competition for power; Sulla won, assassinated his opponents, and attempted to reform the constitution and government institutions.

The Fall of the Republic Soon after Sulla's death, Crassus and Pompey intimidated the Senate into granting them extraordinary powers. By 60 B.C.E., when Crassus, Pompey, and Caesar all found their ambitions thwarted by the Senate, they formed the First Triumvirate, an informal political alliance to further their own private goals. Caesar was elected consul in 59 B.C.E. and enacted the triumvirs' program. Through impressive military conquest and intense diplomacy Caesar held on to power until his assassination fifteen years later. Mark Antony and Gaius Octavius vied to succeed Caesar, although they joined with M. Aemilius Lepidus to form the Second Triumvirate to fight against Caesar's assassins in a civil war. After the triumvirate won, Octavian patronized the Roman arts and fostered the impression that Antony was a stooge of Cleopatra. When the power struggle between Octavian and Antony degenerated into battle, at Actium in 31 B.C.E., Octavian's forces won.

REVIEW QUESTIONS

1. How did the institutions of family and clientage and the establishment of patrician and plebeian classes contribute to the stability of the early Roman Republic? What was "the struggle of the orders"? What methods did plebeians use to get what they wanted?

2. Until 265 B.C.E., how and why did Rome expand its territory? How was Rome able to conquer and to control Italy? Why did Romans and Carthaginians clash in the First and Second Punic Wars? Could the wars have been avoided? What problems did the victory create for Rome?

3. What social, economic, and political problems faced Italy in the second century B.C.E.? How did Tiberius and Gaius Gracchus propose to solve them? What were the political implications of the Gracchan reform program? Why did reform fail?

4. What were the problems that plagued the Roman Republic in the last century B.C.E.? What caused these problems, and how did the Romans try to solve them? To what extent were ambitious, power-hungry generals responsible for the destruction of the republic?

KEY TERMS

censors (p. 94)

coloni (p. 103)

consuls (p. 93)

equestrians (p. 106)

Gaul (p. 90)

humanitas (p. 101)

imperium (p. 91)

latifundia (p. 102)

Latium (p. 90)

optimates (p. 106)

patricians (p. 92)

plebeians (p. 92)

populares (p. 106)

proconsulships (p. 93)

tribunes (p. 94)

 For additional study resources for this chapter, go to:
www.prenhall.com/kagan3/chapter4

5
The Roman Empire

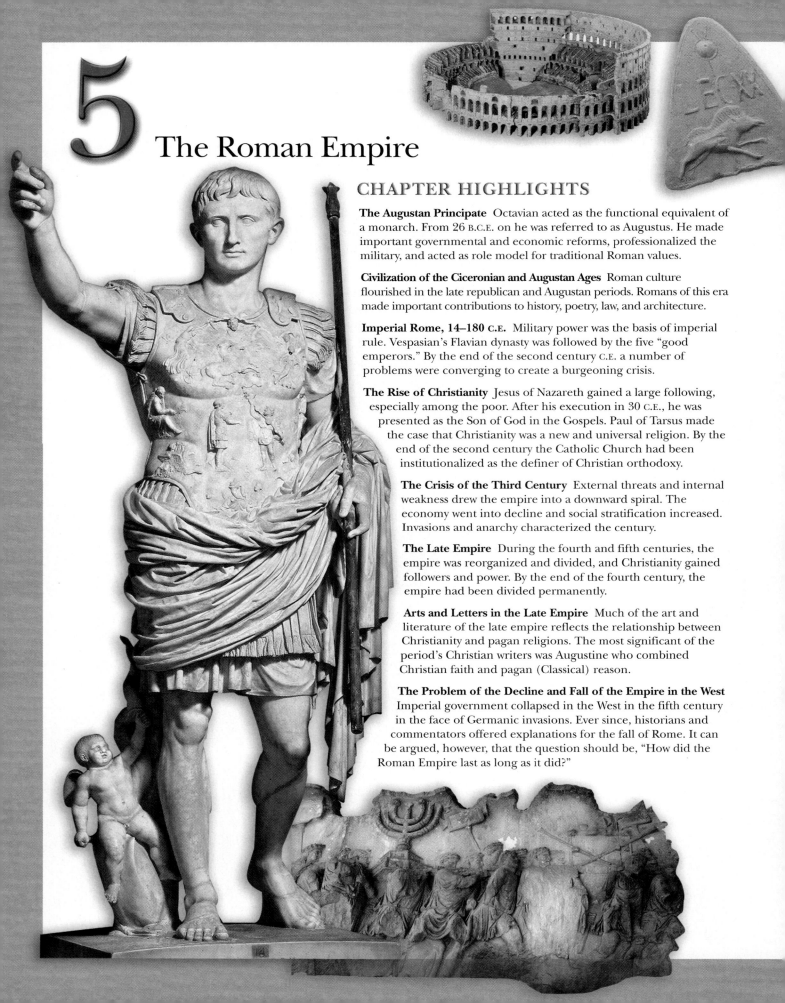

CHAPTER HIGHLIGHTS

The Augustan Principate Octavian acted as the functional equivalent of a monarch. From 26 B.C.E. on he was referred to as Augustus. He made important governmental and economic reforms, professionalized the military, and acted as role model for traditional Roman values.

Civilization of the Ciceronian and Augustan Ages Roman culture flourished in the late republican and Augustan periods. Romans of this era made important contributions to history, poetry, law, and architecture.

Imperial Rome, 14–180 C.E. Military power was the basis of imperial rule. Vespasian's Flavian dynasty was followed by the five "good emperors." By the end of the second century C.E. a number of problems were converging to create a burgeoning crisis.

The Rise of Christianity Jesus of Nazareth gained a large following, especially among the poor. After his execution in 30 C.E., he was presented as the Son of God in the Gospels. Paul of Tarsus made the case that Christianity was a new and universal religion. By the end of the second century the Catholic Church had been institutionalized as the definer of Christian orthodoxy.

The Crisis of the Third Century External threats and internal weakness drew the empire into a downward spiral. The economy went into decline and social stratification increased. Invasions and anarchy characterized the century.

The Late Empire During the fourth and fifth centuries, the empire was reorganized and divided, and Christianity gained followers and power. By the end of the fourth century, the empire had been divided permanently.

Arts and Letters in the Late Empire Much of the art and literature of the late empire reflects the relationship between Christianity and pagan religions. The most significant of the period's Christian writers was Augustine who combined Christian faith and pagan (Classical) reason.

The Problem of the Decline and Fall of the Empire in the West Imperial government collapsed in the West in the fifth century in the face of Germanic invasions. Ever since, historians and commentators offered explanations for the fall of Rome. It can be argued, however, that the question should be, "How did the Roman Empire last as long as it did?"

CHAPTER QUESTIONS

HOW DID Augustus transform Roman politics and government?

WHAT ROLE did literature play in the formation of imperial Rome?

HOW WAS imperial Rome governed and what was life like for its people?

WHO WAS Jesus of Nazareth?

WHAT FACTORS contributed to the decline and eventual fall of Rome?

CHAPTER OUTLINE

- The Augustan Principate
- Civilization of the Ciceronian and Augustan Ages
- Imperial Rome, 14–180 C.E.
- The Rise of Christianity
- The Crisis of the Third Century
- The Late Empire
- Arts and Letters in the Late Empire
- The Problem of the Decline and Fall of the Empire in the West

IMAGE KEY
for pages 114–115 is on page 141.

Octavian's victory over Mark Antony in 31 B.C.E. ended a century of civil strife that had begun with the murder of Tiberius Gracchus. Octavian (subsequently known as Augustus) stabilized Rome by establishing a monarchy hidden behind a republican facade. The unification of the Mediterranean world promoted peace and economic expansion. The spread of Latin and Greek as the empire's official languages promoted growth of a common Classical tradition that had a great influence on the development of a new religion that appeared in the first century C.E.: Christianity.

In the third century C.E., Rome's institutions began to fail, and its emperors resorted to drastic measures to try to maintain order. The result was growing centralization and militarization of an increasingly authoritarian government. A wave of invasions in the second half of the fifth century finally initiated the empire's collapse.

THE AUGUSTAN PRINCIPATE

HOW DID Augustus transform Roman politics and government?

*T*he memory of Julius Caesar's fate was fresh in Octavian's mind in 31 B.C.E. as he pondered what to do with the empire he had won. He controlled all of Rome's armies. He had loyal, capable assistants, and the confiscation of Egypt's treasury provided him with ample capital. He had the means to be a strong ruler, but Caesar's fate had taught him the dangers of appearing to threaten the republican traditions to which the Romans were so passionately devoted.

Slowly Octavian pieced together a government that was acceptable to the Romans and capable of running an empire. Despite its republican trappings and an apparent deference to the Senate, it was a monarchy. Octavian disguised this fact by referring to himself as *princeps* ("first citizen") or *imperator* ("commander in chief"), but these titles soon acquired connotations of royalty that accurately reflected the power of his office.

During the civil war, Octavian's legal authority derived from the triumvirate, a joint dictatorship set up to restore the republic. In the years immediately following the civil war, Octavian held consecutive consulships. This was inconsistent with Roman tradition and looked like a stepping-stone to monarchy, so Octavian gradually worked out a more acceptable arrangement. At a dramatic Senate meeting held on January 13, 27 B.C.E., he offered to resign all his offices. The Senate, however, prevailed on him to retain a consulship and a few provincial governorships. This was a less radical step than it seems, for Octavian retained control of the borderland provinces (Spain, Gaul, and Syria) where twenty of Rome's twenty-six legions were stationed. The Senate, however, declared that the return of some provinces to its control marked the restoration of the republic, and it thanked Octavian by hailing him as **Augustus** ("revered"). Historians refer to him by this title from this point on in his career to indicate his role in establishing Rome's first truly imperial government, the *Principate*. In 23 B.C.E. Augustus made another republican gesture. He resigned the consulship. Henceforth his authority rested on two special powers: proconsular *imperium maius* (supreme military command) and the political privileges of an honorary tribune.

ADMINISTRATION

The Romans were willing to go along with Augustus, for they benefited from his administration. He weeded out inefficient and corrupt magistrates. He blocked ambitious politicians and generals who might otherwise have disturbed the peace. He eased tension among classes and between Romans and provincials.

imperator "Commander in chief."

Augustus ("revered") Name by which the Senate hailed Octavian for his restoration of the republic.

This scene from Augustus' Ara Pacis, the altar of Peace, in Rome shows the general Marcus Agrippa (63–12 B.C.E.) in procession with the imperial family. Agrippa was a powerful deputy, close friend, and son-in-law of Augustus. He was chiefly responsible for the victory over Mark Antony at the Battle of Actium in 31 B.C.E.

Museum of the Ara Pacis, Rome, Italy

And he fostered economic development. With his reign, a long era of stability—the *pax Romana* ("Roman peace")—began.

The Senate took over most of the political functions of the assemblies, but it became a less parochial institution. Augustus manipulated elections and saw to it that promising young men, whatever their origin, had opportunities to serve the state. Those who did well were rewarded with appointments to the Senate. This allowed equestrians and Italians who had no connection with the old Roman aristocracy to earn Senate membership, and it ensured a Senate composed of talented, experienced statesmen.

Augustus was careful to court Rome's politically volatile residents. He founded the city's first public fire department and police force. He organized grain distribution for the poor and set up an office to oversee the municipal water supply. The empire's rapidly expanding economy enabled him to fund a popular program of public works.

The provinces, too, benefited from Augustus's union of political and military power. For the first time, Rome had a central government that was able to oversee the conduct of the men who administered its provinces. Good governors were appointed. Those who abused their power were disciplined, and the provincials themselves were granted a greater degree of political autonomy.

THE ARMY AND DEFENSE

Augustus professionalized the military and reduced its numbers to about 300,000 men, a force barely adequate to hold the frontiers. The army consisted of legions recruited from Italians with citizenship and auxiliary companies composed of provincials. Soldiers enlisted for twenty-year terms. Pay was good, with occasional bonuses and the promise of a pension on retirement. Military units were permanently based in the provinces where they were likely to be needed, and their presence helped acquaint native peoples with Roman culture. Soldiers married local women and settled new towns. These developments helped provincials identify with the empire and commit to its defense.

Augustus's chief military worry was the stability of the empire's northern frontier. On this front, only a narrow strip of Roman territory protected Italy from invasion by German barbarians. Augustus decided, therefore, to push into Germany to establish a more defensible border, but in 9 C.E., a German chief named Herrmann (Arminius, in Latin) staged an ambush that obliterated three Roman legions. Their loss forced the aging Augustus to abandon his plan.

RELIGION AND MORALITY

Augustus tried to repair the damage that a century of strife had done to Rome's fundamental institutions. He devised a program to restore traditional values of family and religion. He passed laws to curb adultery and divorce and encourage early marriage and large families. His own austere behavior set a personal example for his subjects. He even banished his only child, a woman named Julia, to punish her flagrant immorality.

Augustus restored the dignity of formal Roman religion by building temples, reviving old cults, invigorating the priestly colleges, and banning the worship of some foreign gods. He did not accept divine honors during his lifetime, but, like his adoptive-father, Julius Caesar, he was deified after his death.

5.1
Augustus's Moral Legislation: Family Values

WHAT ROLE did literature play in the formation of imperial Rome?

CIVILIZATION OF THE CICERONIAN AND AUGUSTAN AGES

*R*oman civilization reached its pinnacle in the last century of the republic and during the Augustan Principate. Hellenistic Greek influences were strong, but the spirit and sometimes the form of Roman art and literature were unique.

THE LATE REPUBLIC

Cicero   Cicero (106–43 B.C.E.), the most important literary figure of the late republic, wrote treatises on rhetoric, ethics, and politics, and he fostered Latin as a medium for philosophical disputation. The orations he delivered in Rome's law courts and the Senate and his private letters (many of which survive) are his most interesting works. They provide us with better insight into him than we have into any other figure from antiquity.

Cicero's thinking was pragmatic and conservative. He believed the world was governed by a divine natural law that human reason could comprehend and use to build civilized institutions. His respect for law, custom, and tradition as guarantors of stability and liberty led him to champion the Senate against *populares* leaders such as Mark Antony. When the Second Triumvirate seized power and began its purges, Antony marked Cicero for execution.

History   Much of the work of the historians who wrote during the last century of the republic has been lost. A few pamphlets on the Jugurthine War and the Catilinarian conspiracy of 63 B.C.E. are all that survive from the pen of Sallust (86–35 B.C.E.), who was reputed to be the greatest historian of his generation. Julius Caesar wrote treatises on the Gallic and civil wars—military narratives intended for use as political propaganda. Their direct, simple, and vigorous style still makes them persuasive reading.

OVERVIEW   THE GREAT AUGUSTAN POETS

Vergil (70–19 B.C.E.)	The most important of the Augustan poets, Vergil wrote somewhat artificial pastoral idylls. Virgil transformed the early Greek poet's praise of simple labor into a hymn to the human enterprise—the civilizing of the world of nature. His most important poem, the *Aeneid*, celebrated Italy's traditional religious cults and institutions.
Horace (65–8 B.C.E.)	The son of a freedman, Horace was a highly skillful lyric poet. He produced a collection of genial, sometimes humorous poems called *Satires* and a number of *Odes*, songs that glorify the Augustan order. He skillfully adapted Latin to the forms of Greek verse.
Propertius (50–16 B.C.E.)	Propertius joined Vergil and Horace as a member of the poetic circle favored by Augustus's wealthy friend Maecenas. He wrote elegies that were renowned for their grace and wit.
Ovid (43 B.C.E.–18 C.E.)	Ovid was the only one of the great poets to run spectacularly afoul of Augustus. His poetic celebrations of the loose sexual mores of sophisticated Roman aristocrats did not serve the *princeps's* purpose. When Ovid published a poetic textbook on the art of seduction, *Ars Amatoria*, Augustus exiled him to a remote region of the empire.

Law   Prior to the era of the Gracchi, Roman law evolved case by case from juridical decisions. However, contact with foreign peoples and the influence of Greek ideas forced a change. The edicts of *praetors* began to be added to the Roman legal code, and the decisions of the magistrates who dealt with foreigners spawned the idea of the ***jus gentium***—the law of all peoples as opposed to the law that reflected only Roman practice. In the first century B.C.E., Greek thought promoted the concept of the ***jus naturale***, a law of nature that enshrined the principles of divine reason that Cicero and the Stoics believed governed the universe.

Poetry   Two of Rome's greatest poets, Lucretius (ca. 99–ca. 55 B.C.E.) and Catullus (ca. 84–ca. 54 B.C.E.), were Cicero's contemporaries. Each represented a different aspect of Rome's poetic tradition. Hellenistic literary theory maintained that poets ought to educate as well as entertain, and this was the intent of Lucretius's epic poem, *De Rerum Natura* (*On the Nature of Things*). Lucretius hoped to rescue his readers from superstitious fears by persuading them of the truth of philosophical materialism. If they understood they were temporary agglomerations of lumps of matter that dissolved utterly at death, they would cease to be anxious about suffering punishment, regret, or a sense of loss in an afterlife.

Catullus's poems were personal, even autobiographical, descriptions of the joys and pains of love. He hurled invective at powerful contemporaries such as Julius Caesar. He amused himself by composing witty exchanges with his acquaintances, but he was not interested in moral instruction. He celebrated himself—affirming one of the characteristics of Hellenistic art: the importance of the individual.

THE AGE OF AUGUSTUS

Augustus's era was the golden age of Roman literature. The power of the *princeps* set limits to freedom of expression, but he and his friends provided patronage for some of Rome's greatest writers. Although they often served his political agenda, they were not mere propagandists. They were sincerely grateful for what he was doing for Rome.

jus gentium   Law of all peoples as opposed to the law that reflected only Roman practice.

jus naturale   Law of nature that enshrined the principles of divine reason that Cicero and the Stoics believed governed the universe.

This mosaic found in Tunisia shows the
poet Vergil reading from his *Aeneid* to
the Muses of Epic and Tragedy.

Roger Wood/CORBIS/Bettmann

Vergil The early works (*Eclogues* or *Bucolics*) of Vergil
(70–19 B.C.E.), the most important of the Augustan poets,
were somewhat artificial pastoral idylls. The subject for
Vergil's *Georgics*, a reworking of Hesiod's *Works and Days*, may
have been suggested to him by Maecenas, Augustus's chief
cultural adviser. Vergil transformed the early Greek poet's
praise of simple labor into a hymn to the heroic human enterprise—the civilizing of the world of nature.

Vergil's most important poem, the *Aeneid*, celebrated
Italy's traditional religious cults and institutions. Augustus
had rallied the Romans to his side during the civil war by
persuading them that Mark Antony had succumbed to alien
Eastern influences and only he, Augustus, could preserve
Italy's culture. As *princeps*, therefore, he was committed to
granting Italy special status within his empire, and in the
Aeneid Vergil explained why Italy deserved preference. Vergil
traced Roman ancestry to the basic myth of Hellenic civilization, the *Iliad's* account of the Trojan War. The *Aeneid's* hero,
the Trojan prince Aeneas, is not motivated by Homeric lust
for personal honor. He personifies Roman qualities: duty, responsibility, and
patriotism—the civic virtues of men such as Augustus who maintain the peace
and prosperity of the empire.

Horace Horace (65–8 B.C.E.), the son of a freedman, was a highly skillful lyric
poet. He produced a collection of genial, sometimes humorous poems called
Satires and a number of *Odes*, songs that glorify the Augustan order. He skillfully
adapted Latin to the forms of Greek verse.

Propertius Sextus Propertius joined Vergil and Horace as a member of the
poetic circle favored by Augustus's wealthy friend Maecenas. Propertius wrote
elegies that were renowned for their grace and wit.

Ovid Ovid (43 B.C.E.–18 C.E.) was the only one of the great poets to run spec-
tacularly afoul of Augustus. Augustus wanted to inspire the Romans to return to
the austere, family-centered values of their remote ancestors. Ovid's poetic celebrations of the loose sexual mores of sophisticated Roman aristocrats did not
serve the *princeps's* purposes. When Ovid published a poetic textbook on the art
of seduction, *Ars Amatoria*, Augustus exiled him to a remote region of the empire. Ovid tried, but failed, to recover favor by switching to less sensitive themes.
His *Fasti* was a poetic essay on Roman religious festivals, and his most popular
work, the *Metamorphoses*, was a charming survey of Greek mythology.

History Augustus's interest in inspiring reverence for Roman tradition encouraged the writing of history, and his contemporary, Livy (59 B.C.E.–17 C.E.),
devoted his life to writing a monumental survey of Roman history. Only a quarter
of it survives, but the extant portions treat the important period from the legendary origins of Rome until 9 B.C.E. Livy based his history on secondary accounts and did little original research, but he was a gifted narrator. His sketches
of historical figures have provided generations of teachers with materials for
memorable lessons in patriotism and virtuous conduct.

Architecture and Sculpture Augustus embarked on a building program designed to make Rome worthy of its history. He reconstructed the Campus Mar-
tius and the Roman Forum. He donated a new forum of his own to celebrate his

victory in the civil war and erected a splendid temple to his patron god, Apollo, on Rome's Palatine Hill. Most of his new building conformed to the Greek Classical style, which emphasized serenity and order, and the same attributes are visible in the best surviving sculpture of his era.

IMPERIAL ROME, 14–180 C.E.

THE EMPERORS

Because Augustus was ostensibly only the "first citizen" of a restored republic, he could not create a public process for choosing an heir to his power. He could only transfer it behind the scenes to his chief surviving male relative, his stepson Tiberius (r. 14–37 C.E.). Tiberius initially tried to follow Augustus's example and hide the monarchical nature of his authority. But as the Romans became accustomed to the new order, there was less reason to conceal its reality. The terms *imperator* and Caesar began to be used as titles for men whose connection with Julius Caesar's family positioned them to run the Roman world.

Tiberius was succeeded by his nephew, Gaius Caligula (r. 37–41 C.E.), who was widely thought to be insane. Vicious and cruel, Caligula spent large amounts of the state treasury and seized the property of wealthy Romans. In 41 C.E., the naked military basis of imperial rule was revealed when the Praetorian Guard, having assassinated Caligula, dragged his uncle, the lame, stammering, and frightened Claudius, from behind a curtain and made him emperor. Claudius left the throne to his stepson Nero (r. 54–68 C.E.), who so grossly mismanaged his affairs that he lost control of the army and committed suicide. Nero was the last member of the Julio-Claudian dynasty, the descendants of Augustus or Augustus's wife, Livia.

Following Nero's death power changed hands rapidly in 69 C.E., as a succession of Roman armies marched on Rome from the provinces. Vespasian (r. 69–79 C.E.), the fourth man to occupy the throne that year, restored order and founded the Flavian dynasty. Vespasian was the first emperor who had no connection with the old Roman nobility. He was a tough Italian soldier from the middle class. The sons who followed him to the throne, first Titus (r. 79–81 C.E.) and then Domitian (r. 81–96 C.E.), inherited his excellent administrative talents. Domitian, however, may have succumbed to paranoia, and his tyrannical behavior frightened his intimates into assassinating him.

Domitian had no close relative to succeed him, and those who killed him were not foolish enough to try to turn the clock back to the days of the republic. They appealed to the Senate to restore order by choosing a new emperor. The Senate elected one of its own, Nerva (r. 96–98 C.E.), the first of a line of dubbed "good emperors" that included Trajan (r. 98–117 C.E.), Hadrian (r. 117–138 C.E.), Antoninus Pius (r. 138–161 C.E.), and Marcus Aurelius (r. 161–180 C.E.). None of the first four men had a son to succeed him, so each followed Nerva's example and adopted an heir (who was usually an experienced adult). This system of succession was a fortunate historical accident, guaranteeing that worthy men were promoted to power. It provided a

HOW WAS imperial Rome governed and what was life like for its people?

Marcus Aurelius, Emperor of Rome from 161 to 180 C.E., was one of the five "good emperors" who brought a period of relative peace and prosperity to the empire. This is the only Roman bronze equestrian statue that has survived.

Capitoline Museums, Rome, Italy/Canali PhotoBank, Milan/Superstock

century of peace and competent government that ended when Marcus Aurelius's unworthy son, Commodus (r. 180–192 C.E.), followed him to the throne.

THE ADMINISTRATION OF THE EMPIRE

Although some of the emperors tried to enlist the help of the senatorial class (as counselors, judges, and administrators) in running the empire, the imperial government was largely staffed by professionals. These career bureaucrats were usually an improvement over the amateurs who had annually rotated through the offices of the republic.

The provinces especially benefited, for the emperor controlled their governors and promoted their economies by integrating them into the commercial exchange system of a huge empire. Rome's leaders tried to unify the empire while simultaneously respecting local customs and differences. The *Romanitas* ("Romanness") they spread across the empire was more than superficial. By 212 C.E., citizenship had been extended to almost every inhabitant of the empire, and members of provincial families were becoming senators and emperors. (See Map 5–1.)

Local Municipalities   Administratively, the empire resembled a federation of cities and towns. The typical city had about 20,000 inhabitants. Only three or four had populations of more than 75,000. Rome, however, certainly had more than 500,000 residents—perhaps more than a million. The central government dealt with city governments and had little contact with people who lived in the countryside. Municipal charters placed great responsibility in the hands of local councils and magistrates, and men who filled these positions earned Roman citizenship. This integrated the upper classes of the provinces into the Roman system, spread Roman law and culture, and nurtured the loyalty of influential provincial families. Rome's policy of encouraging assimilation did not succeed everywhere. Jews refused to compromise with Roman customs on religious grounds, and when they rebelled in 66–70, 115–117, and 132–135 C.E., they were savagely suppressed. Egypt's peasants, who were exploited with exceptional ruthlessness, were also not offered opportunities to integrate.

The emperors took a broad view of their responsibility for the welfare of their subjects. Nerva conceived and Trajan launched the *alimenta*, a program of public assistance for children of indigent parents. More and more the emperors intervened when municipalities got into difficulties, sending imperial troubleshooters to deal with problems that were usually financial. As the central administration took on more and more functions, the autonomy of the municipalities declined and the provincial aristocracy began to view public service as a burden rather than an opportunity. The price paid for increased efficiency was a loss of vitality by the empire's local governments.

Foreign Policy   For the most part, Augustus's successors continued his foreign policy and focused primarily on defending the lands they already held. Trajan, however, took

---

Significant Dates from the Imperial Period

The Julio-Claudian Dynasty

27 B.C.E.–14 C.E.	Augustus
[ca. 4 B.C.E.–30 C.E.	Jesus of Nazareth]
14–37 C.E.	Tiberius
37–41 C.E.	Gaius "Caligula"
41–54 C.E.	Claudius
54–68 C.E.	Nero
[69 C.E.	"Year of the Four Emperors"]

The Flavian Dynasty

69–79 C.E.	Vespasian
79–81 C.E.	Titus
81–96 C.E.	Domitian
[ca. 70–100 C.E.	Composition of the Gospels]

The "Good Emperors"

96–98 C.E.	Nerva
98–117 C.E.	Trajan
117–138 C.E.	Hadrian
138–161 C.E.	Antoninus Pius
161–180 C.E.	Marcus Aurelius

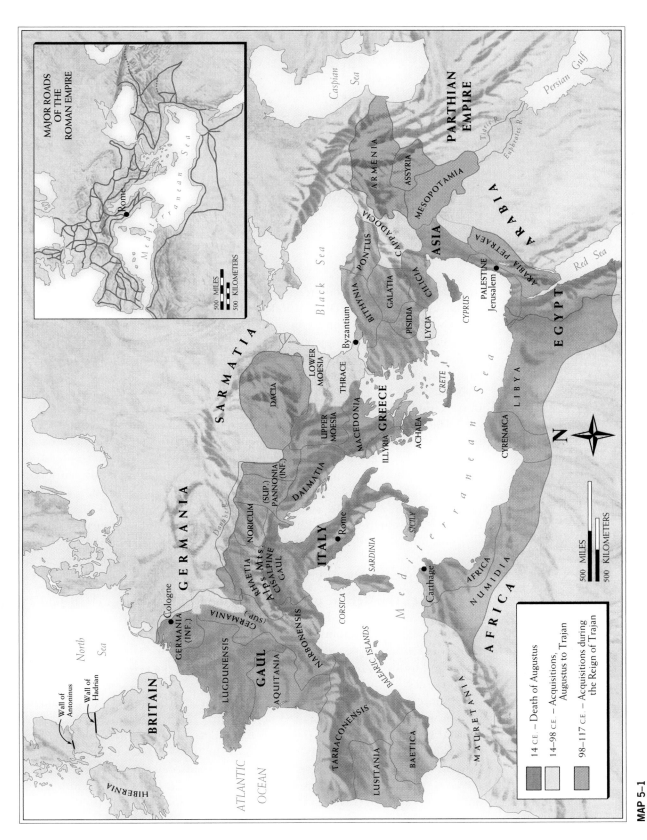

MAP 5–1

Provinces of the Roman Empire to 117 c.e. The growth of the empire to its greatest extent is here shown in three stages—at the death of Augustus in 14 c.e., at the death of Nerva in 98, and at the death of Trajan in 117. The division into provinces in 117. The insert shows the main roads that tied the far-flung empire together.

WHAT BOUNDARIES, both manmade and natural, did the Roman Empire have at each stage of its expansion?

123

Spoils from the temple in Jerusalem were carried in triumphal procession by Roman troops. This relief from Titus's arch of victory in the Roman Forum celebrates his capture of Jerusalem after a two-year siege. The Jews found it difficult to reconcile their religion with Roman rule and frequently rebelled.

Courtesy Davis Art Image

Imperial Roman cameo of Livia and Tiberius

©Burstein Collection/CORBIS

the offensive and added new territory to the empire. He crossed the Danube and added a province called Dacia (modern Romania) to the empire. His intent was probably to secure the frontier by occupying a wedge of territory between hostile barbarian tribes. Similar objectives may have motivated his invasion of the Parthian Empire (113–117 C.E.) and the creation of three additional eastern provinces: Armenia, Assyria, and Mesopotamia. It soon became apparent, however, that Trajan's conquests were overextending the empire, and Rome retreated from some of the land he had occupied.

Hadrian, Trajan's successor, concentrated on strengthening Rome's frontiers. Although the Romans rarely sought more territory, they often sent their armies beyond the borders of the empire to chastise and pacify troublesome neighbors. Hadrian diminished the need for such expeditions by hardening Rome's defenses. Where nature provided no protection, he built walls: a seventy-mile-long stone wall in the south of Scotland, and a wooden wall that spanned the space between the upper Rhine and Danube Rivers. Rome's retreat to defensive positions allowed the military initiative to pass to its barbarian neighbors. Marcus Aurelius had to spend most of his reign fending off their attacks in the east and on the Danube frontier.

Agriculture: The Decline of Slavery and the Rise of *Coloni*   The defense of the empire's frontiers made enormous demands on its resources, but the effect was slow to be felt. Economic growth continued well into the reigns of the "good emperors." Internal peace and efficient administration benefited agriculture, trade, and industry, by making it easier to market products to more people over greater areas.

Some small farms survived, but more and more large estates, managed by absentee owners, dominated agriculture. At first, these estates were worked by slaves, but by the first century C.E., that had begun to change. Economic pressures forced many members of the lower classes to become *coloni* (tenant farmers) and replace slaves as the mainstay of agricultural labor. *Coloni* were sharecroppers who paid rent in cash, in labor, or in kind. Their movements were restricted, and they were ultimately tied to the land they worked.

WOMEN OF THE UPPER CLASSES

Upper-class Roman women of the late republican era were rich, educated, and politically influential. They preferred the form of marriage that left a wife free of her husband's *manus*. Divorce became common, and some women conducted their sexual lives as freely as men. Privileged women were reluctant to have children, and they employed contraception and abortion to avoid offspring. Augustus worried about falling birthrates in Italy and issued decrees intended to encourage procreation and protect the integrity of the family. His laws had little effect. Women defended their freedoms, and in the fourth century C.E., the emperor Diocletian granted them the right to conduct their own legal affairs rather than work through a fictive male guardian.

Several of the women who belonged to the imperial family exercised great political influence, if only unofficially. Augustus's wife and adviser Livia was honored with the title "Augusta" and survived him to influence the reign of his heir and her son, Tiberius. Claudius's wife, Messalina, tried to overthrow him, and Nero may have owed his ascension to the throne to the maneuvers of his mother, Agrippina.

LIFE IN IMPERIAL ROME: THE APARTMENT HOUSE

Crowding, noise, and bustle were inescapable features of urban life in the Roman Empire. In the city of Rome the rich lived in large, elegantly decorated single-storied homes built around courtyards. These occupied about a third of the city's space. Because public buildings (temples, markets, baths, theaters, and forums) took up another quarter, this forced the vast majority of Romans to squeeze into less than half the city's territory. Ordinary folks found housing in *insulae*, apartment houses that soared to five, six, or more stories. Shortage of space kept rents high, even though these buildings were as uncomfortable as they were dangerous. They had neither central heating nor plumbing. Water had to be carried upstairs from public fountains and sewage toted down (or dumped out a window). Smoky stoves provided heat, and torches, candles, and oil lamps offered light. All these open fires created a great risk of conflagration,

The largest city of the ancient region of Tripolitania, Leptis Magna was located 62 miles southeast of Tripoli on the Mediterranean coast of Libya in North Africa. In its heyday, it was one of the richest cities in the Roman Empire, and it contains some of the finest remains of Roman architecture. The city was lavishly rebuilt by the Emperor Septimius Severus (r. 193–211 C.E.), who was born at Leptis in146 C.E.

Peter Wilson ©Dorling Kindersley

ENCOUNTERING THE PAST

CHARIOT RACING

Romans invested heavily in facilities for staging public entertainments, and among the earliest and most popular of these were race tracks. Romans were building race courses by the seventh and sixth centuries B.C.E. They called their tracks "circuses" ("circular") because of their curved layout. Rome's Circus Maximus ("Greatest Circus") was one of the earliest as well as the largest and most famous. It was used for a variety of events (riding exhibitions, wild animal hunts, etc.), but nothing rivaled the popularity of chariot racing.

The races staged in the Circus Maximus involved seven laps around the track, a distance of about 2.7 miles. As many as twelve chariots might compete at one time. Various numbers of horses could be used to pull a chariot, but the most common arrangement was the *quadriga*, the four-horse team. Short straightaways, sharp turns, and a crowded field made for a dangerous and, therefore, crowd-pleasing race. Raw speed was often less important than strength, courage, and endurance. Racing companies called *factiones* were formed to sponsor stables and professional riders. They were known by their colors.

The two first were the reds and the whites. They were eventually joined by the blues, greens, purples, and golds. Betting on the races was heavy, and factions went to extremes to win victories. Horses were drugged and drivers bribed—or murdered when they proved uncooperative.

WHY DID Roman politicians and emperors find it worth their while to spend lavishly on amusements like chariot races?

Romans bet heavily on the kind of chariot races shown on this low relief and were fanatically attached to their favorite riders and stables.
© Araldo de Luca/CORBIS

for *insulae* were cheaply built of flammable materials and kept in poor repair. Their collapse was not uncommon. Little wonder that the people of Rome spent most of their time out of doors.

THE CULTURE OF THE EARLY EMPIRE

Literature   The years between the death of Augustus and the reign of Marcus Aurelius (14–180 C.E.) are known as the Silver Age of Latin literature. The authors from this period are a bit more gloomy and pessimistic than the hopeful, optimistic Augustan poets. Their complaints and satirical comments reflect hostility to the power and excesses of the emperors, but to avoid irritating their rulers, they avoided commenting on contemporary affairs and events in recent history. Historical writing about remote periods was safe, as were scholarly studies, but the production of poetry declined. The third century C.E. saw a rise in demand for romances—entertaining, escapist literature that ignored reality.

Architecture   Advances in engineering enabled Rome's architects to design amazing buildings. The Flavian emperors commissioned Rome's immense free-standing amphitheater, the Colosseum, and the later emperors, Diocletian and Caracalla,

This mosaic shows a gladiator fighting a leopard. The Roman masses loved gladiatorial contests, which pitted man against man but also man against beast.

Scala/Art Resource, NY

funded construction of massive public baths. The Romans combined the post-and-lintel designs favored by the Greeks with the semicircular arch developed by the Etruscans, and they were the first to exploit the design potential of a Hellenistic invention: concrete. All these features appear in the Pantheon, which the emperor Hadrian erected in Rome (the only major Roman temple to survive intact into the modern era). They are also visible in multitudes of mundane but useful structures, such as bridges and aqueducts. (See "Encountering the Past: Chariot Racing.")

Society   The Roman Empire reached its peak during the first two centuries C.E., but the increasing power of its government correlated with a tendency of its citizens to retreat from the public sphere into a world of private pursuits and distractions. In the first century C.E., members of the upper classes vied with one another for election to magistracies and for the honor of serving their communities. By the second century C.E., emperors were having to force unwilling citizens to accept public office. Reluctance to serve was understandable, for the central government held municipal leaders personally responsible for raising the taxes due from their towns. Wealthy men sometimes moved to the countryside to avoid political office, for an official's private property could be confiscated to make up for any shortfall in the taxes he was charged with collecting.

The empire's declining economy explains why the central government put so much pressure on officials of local governments. The end of the civil war and the influx of wealth looted from the East had helped the empire's economy to grow during the first century C.E., but the impact of these factors faded in the first half of the second century C.E. Population declined, but the costs of government continued to rise. Emperors tried to meet these costs by increasing taxes and debasing coinage, but these policies created difficulties that mounted until they threatened to overwhelm the empire.

THE RISE OF CHRISTIANITY

*A*mong the significant developments of the early imperial centuries was the spread of the religion that was eventually to triumph over the West. There were significant odds against the success of Christianity. The faith originated among poor people in an unimportant, remote province of the empire. It had to compete with numerous cults and philosophies for converts, and it faced persecution by the imperial government.

JESUS OF NAZARETH

Christianity appeared in Judaea, a remote eastern province of the empire, in response to the life of an obscure Jew named Jesus from a village called Nazareth. Nothing is known about him apart from the information provided by the Christian scriptures (primarily the gospels of Matthew, Mark, Luke, and John). Mark's gospel, the earliest account of Jesus' ministry, was written about forty years after Jesus' death (ca. 70 C.E.), and it, like the other gospels, was not conceived as an objective historical narrative. Gospels are declarations of faith—proclamations of Jesus as the son of God who grants eternal life to those who believe in him.

Jesus was born during Augustus's reign, and his brief career as a preacher in the style of the Hebrew prophets came at about the midpoint of Tiberius's reign. Many of Jesus' Jewish contemporaries believed their prophets had predicted the coming of a **Messiah**, a redeemer who would vindicate their faith and establish the kingdom of God on earth. Jesus taught that the Messiah would not establish an earthly kingdom but would end the world as human beings know it at the Day of Judgment. God would then reward the righteous and punish the wicked. Jesus advised the faithful, who awaited the imminent apocalyptic event, to forget worldly ambitions and practice love, charity, and humility.

Jesus won a considerable following, but his criticism of the cultic practices associated with the temple in Jerusalem provoked the hostility of the Jewish religious authorities. The Roman governor of Judaea concluded that Jesus was a threat to peace and ordered his crucifixion (ca. 30 C.E.). Three days after his death, Jesus' followers claim he rose from the dead and that his resurrection revealed him to be the Messiah (or the equivalent Greek term, the *Christos*, the "anointed").

PAUL OF TARSUS

The most important missionary at work in the generation that founded the Christian church was a Jew named Paul (born Saul), a Roman citizen and native of the city of Tarsus in Asia Minor. Paul was originally a **Pharisee**, a member of a Jewish sect known for strict adherence to the Jewish law. He was an ardent opponent of Christianity who (ca. 35 C.E.) experienced a mysterious, precipitous conversion.

Jesus and his disciples were all Jews. Consequently, the early Christians had to consider the impact their new faith had on their relationship to Judaism. James, the brother of Jesus, led those who believed Christians should continue to adhere to Jewish law. The less conservative Hellenized Jews, who sided with Paul, saw Christianity as a new universal religion, and they argued that the imposition of the Jewish law—with its dietary prohibitions and painful rite of circumcision—would pose a needless obstacle to conversion.

Messiah Redeemer who would vindicate faith and establish the kingdom of God on earth.

Pharisee Member of a Jewish sect known for strict adherence to the Jewish law.

Paul's vigorous advocacy of a gentile mission made it possible for the Christian faith to spread beyond the confines of Judaism, and Paul, the church's first theologian, did much to define the content of that faith. Paul believed salvation could not be earned by affirming belief in doctrines and doing good deeds. True faith in Jesus as the Christ was a gift of God's grace, not an act of human will.

ORGANIZATION

The emphasis in Jesus' preaching on acts of love and charity focused the Christian community's attention on the needs of the weak, the sick, and the unprotected. Early Christianity was characterized by a warmth and a human appeal that contrasted markedly with the cold, impersonal pagan cults. The Christian message of salvation also confirmed the importance of each individual human soul to God, and this implied that all believers, no matter what their social class or gender, were spiritual equals. All these features of the faith helped it spread throughout the Roman Empire and beyond.

At first, Christianity appealed primarily to the urban poor, and its early rites were simple ceremonies congruent with the poverty of its people. Baptism by water brought converts into the community by cleansing them of original sin (the state of alienation from God into which they had been born). The central ritual of the church was a common meal, the ***agape***, or "love feast," followed by a **eucharist** ("thanksgiving"), a celebration of the Lord's Supper in which bread and wine were blessed and consumed. Prayers, hymns, and readings from the scriptures were also part of worship.

The church's unique organization contributed to its success. Christian communities initially had little formal structure, but the need to support missionary preachers and charitable work prompted churches to elect officers: presbyters ("elders") and deacons ("servers"). By the second century C.E., converts had increased to the point where a city was likely to have many churches. This necessitated the appointment of a bishop (*episkopos*, "overseer") to coordinate their activities. Gradually, bishops acquired authority over the countryside as well as urban centers, and by convening councils of their peers they could resolve disputes and promote unity within the church. The quasi-monarchical power of a bishop led to the doctrine of **apostolic succession**, the claim that Jesus gave his disciples (the first bishops) special powers passed down from one generation of bishops to another. It is unlikely that Christianity could have survived the travails of its early years without the strong government provided by its bishops.

THE PERSECUTION OF CHRISTIANS

The Roman authorities could not at first distinguish Christians from Jews and, therefore, they gave Christians the same tolerance they extended to Jews. However, worrisome differences between the two faiths gradually became clear. Christians and Jews both incurred suspicion by denying the existence of the pagan gods and refusing to take part in the state cult of emperor worship. The Romans accepted this from the Jews, a people with ancient traditions who kept to themselves. Christians, however, were ardent missionaries dedicated to spreading their belief that the Roman world was about to be destroyed. They had a network of communities spread throughout the empire, and they were secretive about the rituals they practiced.

The emperor Claudius expelled Christians from the city of Rome, and Nero made them scapegoats for the great fire that destroyed Rome in 64 C.E. Generally, however, the Roman authorities did not initiate attacks on Christians.

This second-century statue in the Lateran Museum in Rome shows Jesus as the biblical Good Shepherd.

"The Good Shepherd", marble, Height: as restored cm 99, as perserved cm 55, head cm 15.5. Late 3rd century A.D. Vatican Museums,Lateran Museums, Pio-Christian Museum, Inv. 28590. Courtesy of the Vatican Museums

5.5
The Letter of Paul to the Romans

agape Common meal, or "love feast," that was the central ritual of the church in early Christianity.

eucharist ("thanksgiving") Celebration of the Lord's Supper in which bread and wine were blessed and consumed.

apostolic succession Special powers that were passed down from one generation of bishops to another.

HISTORY'S VOICES

CHRISTIANS IN THE ROMAN EMPIRE

liny the Younger was governor of the Roman province of Bithynia in Asia Minor about 112 C.E. Confronted by problems caused by Christians, he wrote to the Emperor Trajan to report his policies and to ask for advice. The following exchange between governor and emperor provides evidence of the challenge Christianity posed to Rome and the Roman response.

WHAT PROCEDURES did Trajan recommend in dealing with the Christians?

To the Emperor Trajan

Having never been present at any trials of the Christians, I am unacquainted with the method and limits to be observed either in examining or punishing them.

In the meanwhile, the method I have observed towards those who have been denounced to me as Christians is this: I interrogated them whether they were Christians; if they confessed it, I repeated the question twice again, adding the threat of capital punishment; if they still persevered, I ordered them to be executed. For whatever the nature of their creed might be, I could at least feel no doubt that contumacy and inflexible obstinacy deserved chastisement. There were others also possessed with the same infatuation, but being citizens of Rome, I directed them to be carried thither. ...

Trajan to Pliny

The method you have pursued, my dear Pliny, in sifting the cases of those denounced to you as Christians is extremely proper. It is not possible to lay down any general rule which can be applied as the fixed standard in all cases of this nature. No search should be made for these people, when they are denounced and found guilty they must be punished; with the restriction, however, that when the party denies himself to be a Christian, and shall give proof that he is not (that is, by adoring our Gods he shall be pardoned on the ground of repentance even though he may have formerly incurred suspicion). Information without the accuser's name subscribed must not be admitted in evidence against anyone, as it is introducing a very dangerous precedent, and by no means agreeable to the spirit of the age.

Pliny the Younger, Letters, trans. by W. Melmoth, revised by W. M. Hutchinson (London: William Heinemann, Ltd, Cambridge, MA.: Harvard University Press, 1935), pp. 401, 403, 407.

QUICK REVIEW

Reasons for Persecution
- Christians were ardent missionaries
- Christians had a network of communities throughout the empire
- Christians were secretive about their beliefs and practices

orthodox ("correct") As in "correct" faith in Christianity.

catholic ("universal") As in "universal" majority of Christians.

heretics "Takers" of contrary positions, namely in Christianity.

(See "History's Voices: Christians in the Roman Empire.") Most of the persecutions during the church's first two centuries were the work of mobs, not governmental officials. Christians alarmed their pagan neighbors by ridiculing the ancient cults that protected the state. When misfortunes befell communities, it seemed logical that Christians were to blame for angering the gods. Persecution, however, strengthened the church by weeding out weaklings, uniting the faithful, and creating martyrs—the most persuasive witnesses to the power of Christian faith.

THE EMERGENCE OF CATHOLICISM

Internal disputes threatened the church as much as external persecution. The simple beliefs held by the great majority of Christians were open to a wide range of interpretations and left many questions unanswered. Consequently, arguments broke out about what constituted **orthodox** ("correct") faith, and minorities who disagreed with the **catholic** ("universal") majority were branded **heretics** ("takers" of contrary positions).

This porphyry sculpture on the corner of the church of San Marco in Venice shows Emperor Diocletian (r. 284–305 C.E.) and his three imperial colleagues. Dressed for battle, they clasp one another to express their mutual solidarity.

John Heseltine © Dorling Kindersley

To combat heresy, it was necessary to define orthodoxy. By the end of the second century C.E., the church had agreed on the core for the canon (the "standard"), the orthodox Christian scriptures: the Old Testament, the Gospels, and the Epistles of Paul. (Two more centuries passed before consensus was reached on the other items now found in the New Testament.) The church also drew up creeds, and bishops enforced conformity to these statements of faith. These measures ensured the clarity of doctrine, unity of purpose, and discipline needed for the church's survival.

ROME AS A CENTER OF THE EARLY CHURCH

At an early stage in the church's development, the bishops of the city of Rome began to lay claim to "primacy" (highest rank) among bishops. Rome was the capital of the empire, and it had the largest single Christian congregation of any city. Rome also claimed to be the place where Peter and Paul, the two most important leaders of the early church, were martyred. Peter, whom Rome claimed as its first bishop, was an especially significant figure, for a passage in the Gospel of Matthew (16:18) was interpreted as implying that Jesus had given Peter a unique commission. It quotes Jesus as responding to Peter's confession of faith by saying: "Thou art Peter [*Petros*, in Greek] and upon this rock [*petra*] I will build my church." The bishops of Rome claimed that this was Jesus' appointment of Peter as the head of the church, an office that passed to them as Peter's successors.

THE CRISIS OF THE THIRD CENTURY

Signs of serious trouble for the Roman Empire appeared during the reign of Commodus, the son and successor of Marcus Aurelius. Unlike the "good emperors," who were his predecessors, he was incompetent and autocratic.

BARBARIAN INVASIONS

The pressure on Rome's frontiers, which began to mount during the reign of Marcus Aurelius (d. 180 C.E.), reached massive proportions in the third century. In the East the empire was threatened by the Sassanians, an Iranian dynasty that replaced the Parthians in control of Persia in 224 C.E. The Sassanians raided deep into Roman provinces, and in 260 C.E. they captured and imprisoned the Roman emperor, Valerian.

On the empire's western and northern borders, an ever-increasing number of seminomadic German tribes posed a great danger. Although the Germans had been in contact with the Romans since the second century B.C.E., they had not been much affected by civilization. German males hunted, fought, and caroused. Their women and slaves did most of the farming and productive work. Tribes were led by the chiefs whom their warriors chose from a pool of candidates of royal lineage. A chief headed a *comitatus* ("fraternity"), a company of soldiers bound to him by personal oaths. These men were career raiders, and the wealthy Roman Empire was an irresistible target.

The Goths were the most aggressive of the Germans. By the third century C.E., they had wandered from the coast of the Baltic Sea, their original home, into southern Russia. They attacked Rome's Danube frontier, and about 250 C.E., they overran the empire's Balkan provinces. The threats posed by the Goths and the Sassanids forced the Romans to transfer men from their western to their eastern armies. This weakened the defenses of the West and made it easier for the tribes of the Franks and the Alemanni to cross the Rhine frontier.

Rome's internal weakness invited simultaneous attacks on multiple fronts. By the second century C.E., the Roman army was made up mostly of Romanized provincials, and the training, discipline, and professionalism of Rome's forces was declining. The situation was not improved when a manpower shortage that followed a devastating plague forced Marcus Aurelius to conscript slaves, gladiators, barbarians, and brigands.

Septimius Severus, who followed Marcus Aurelius's son Commodus to the throne (r. 193–211 C.E.), played a crucial role in transforming the character of the Roman army. Septimius was a usurper who owed his office to the support of his soldiers, many of whom were peasants from the less civilized provinces. He gave up all pretext of civilian authority and ruled as a military dictator.

ECONOMIC DIFFICULTIES

The role the army was coming to play in the empire was determined in part by Rome's financial difficulties (exacerbated by the barbarian attacks). To keep up with rising prices caused by inflation, Commodus had to raise the soldiers' pay and the Severan emperors had to double it. The cost to the imperial budget increased by as much as 25 percent, and emperors had to impose new taxes, debase their coinage, and even sell palace furniture to raise the funds they needed. Septimius also courted the soldiers by relaxing discipline and making military service the path to privileged social status.

As emperors devoted more of their attention and resources to the defense of the empire's frontiers, their ability to maintain internal order declined. Piracy, brigandage, and the neglect of roads and harbors hampered trade. Economic productivity diminished as taxation consumed the capital needed to fund economic activity. Efforts to stretch the money supply by debasing coinage produced inflation. The vitality of urban institutions declined as the upper classes fled the cities to escape taxation and the burdens of public office. Artisans began to close shops and peasants to abandon farms that were made unprofitable by excessive taxation. More and more the government had to force the civilian population to provide the supplies and labor needed to sustain the army.

THE SOCIAL ORDER

The new political and economic conditions transformed the social order. The senatorial and ruling classes were decimated by hostile emperors and economic losses. Their ranks were filled by men who came up through the army and increasingly militarized society. Social classes had been distinguished by dress in the republican era, but in the third and fourth centuries C.E. clothing became a kind of uniform that precisely identified status. Titles evolved for ranks in society as well as in the army. Septimius Severus drew a sharp line between the *honestiores* (senators, equestrians, municipal aristocrats, and all soldiers) and the *humiliores* (the inferior position occupied by everyone else). The *honestiores* enjoyed important legal privileges: lighter punishments for crimes, immunity from torture, and a right of appeal to the emperor. As these distinctions set in, it became steadily more difficult to move from the lower order to the higher. Peasants were tied to their lands, artisans to their crafts, soldiers to the army, and merchants and shipowners to state service. Freedom and private initiative faded as the state expanded its control over its citizens.

CIVIL DISORDER

In 235 C.E., the death of Alexander Severus, the last member of Septimius Severus's dynasty, inaugurated a half century of anarchy. The empire teetered on the brink of collapse as conspirators overthrew and replaced emperors in rapid succession. There were, however, a few able men among them. Claudius II Gothicus (r. 268–270 C.E.) and Aurelian (r. 270–275 C.E.) repulsed barbarian invasions and restored discipline within the military. But Aurelian's successors had to resort to strategies for defending the empire that acknowledged it was losing ground. They built walls around Rome, Athens, and other cities and drew their best troops back from the frontiers. The army became a kind of mobile imperial bodyguard poised to respond quickly to the crises that sprang up on all sides. Emperors recruited soldiers from the least civilized provinces and even from the German tribes. These soldiers became the empire's new aristocrats. They dominated its government and rose to occupy its throne. The Roman people succumbed to the army of foreign mercenaries they hired to protect them.

THE LATE EMPIRE

*A*s Roman emperors scrambled to find the resources they needed to meet the mounting problems of the empire, they instituted policies that smothered individuality, freedom, and initiative. The state became ever more autocratic, centralized, and intrusive.

THE FOURTH CENTURY AND IMPERIAL REORGANIZATION

At the start of the fourth century C.E., an emperor named Diocletian (r. 284–305 C.E.) extensively reorganized the empire in an attempt to save it. A native of the Balkan province of Illyria, he was a commoner who rose to power through the ranks of the army. Experience convinced him that the job of defending and governing the empire was too great for one man. Therefore, he established a **tetrarchy**—a coalition of four men, each of whom was responsible for a different part of the empire. Diocletian administered the provinces of Thrace, Asia, and Egypt. He assigned Italy, Africa, and Spain to his friend, Maximian. They were

WHAT FACTORS contributed to the decline and eventual fall of Rome?

tetrarchy Coalition of four men, each of whom was responsible for a different part of the empire, established by Diocletian.

the Augusti, the senior members of the tetrarchy, and each was assisted by a Caesar. Galerius governed the Danube-Balkan region for Diocletian, and Constantius, Britain and Gaul for Maximian. The tetrarchy stabilized the empire by giving four powerful men a stake in the status quo and by providing for an orderly process of succession to the throne. The Augusti chose and trained their Caesars to be their successors. The system built on the precedent set by the "good emperors," who adopted capable individuals to be their heirs.

Each tetrarch established a residence at a place convenient for frontier defense. No one chose Rome, for it was too remote from the centers of military activity. Maximian's base at Milan commanded the Alpine passes and functioned as the effective capital of Italy. Diocletian donated monumental baths to Rome, but he visited the city only once and resided at Nicomedia in Bithynia. (See Map 5–2.)

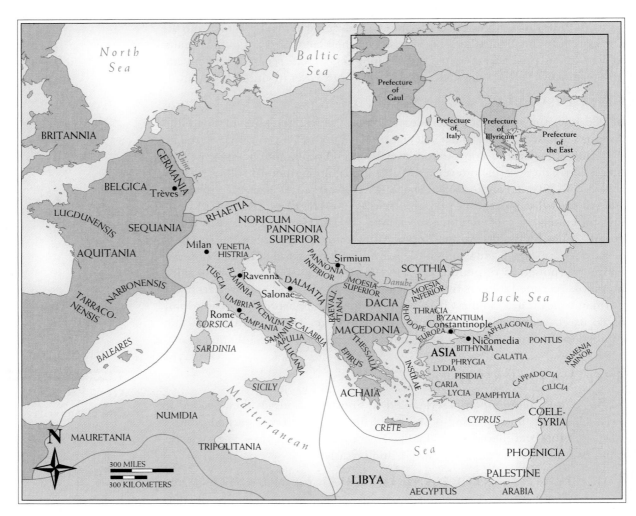

MAP 5–2

Divisions of the Roman Empire Under Diocletian Diocletian divided the sprawling empire into four prefectures for more effective government and defense. The inset map shows their boundaries, and the larger map gives some details of regions and provinces. The major division between the East and the West was along the line running south between Pannonia and Moesia.

DID DIOCLETIAN'S tetrarchy likely postpone or expedite the eventual fall of the Roman Empire?

In 305 C.E., Diocletian retired and compelled Maximian to do the same, but the hope for a smooth transition faded when Constantius died prematurely and his son, Constantine began a power struggle by claiming his father's throne. Constantine (r. 306–337 C.E.), who began the fight, ended it by defeating the last of five opponents in 324 C.E. He continued many of Diocletian's policies with two major exceptions. He ruled as sole emperor, and instead of trying to stamp out Christianity, as Diocletian had, Constantine became the church's patron.

Development of Autocracy The crises facing the government encouraged a drift toward total military mobilization. Traditions of popular government were suppressed in the name of improving efficiency. Emperors ruled by decree, consulting only a few high officials whom they themselves appointed. They protected themselves from assassination by distancing themselves from their people. They surrounded themselves with elaborate courts and appeared in crowns and robes that proclaimed their exalted status. People prostrated themselves before them, kissed the hems of their purple garments, and addressed them as *dominus* ("lord"), a title that implied their authority was divinely based.

Constantine built a superb new city to serve as the empire's capital. Constantinople (modern Istanbul) was situated midway between the eastern and Danubian frontiers on the Bosporus in a Greek district called Byzantium. The city's dedication in 330 C.E. marked the start of a new empire, one that repudiated Rome's pagan and republican traditions and embraced Christianity and autocracy.

Constantinople's rulers protected themselves by creating separate civil and military bureaucracies for their empire. This made it difficult for someone to combine both kinds of power and mount a coup. An elaborate administrative hierarchy divided responsibility and prevented anyone from having much power, and society was kept under surveillance by a network of spies and secret police. Unfortunately, these arrangements invited corruption and promoted inefficiency.

The costs of a 400,000-man army, a vast civilian bureaucracy, an imperial court, and the splendid buildings the emperors continued to commission were more than the Roman world's weak economy could sustain. The fiscal policies that Diocletian introduced and Constantine continued only made things worse. In 301 C.E., Diocletian tried to halt inflation by issuing the Edict of Maximum Prices, but rather than selling their goods and services at the legally mandated prices, people simply began to trade on an underground black market. Diocletian dealt with declining agricultural productivity by herding peasants onto state plantations. This drove poor farmers, who could not survive on their own and who faced enslavement by their government, into the arms of the wealthy few who owned large rural estates. They became *coloni* and worked the land for these new masters in exchange for protection from the emperor and his tax collectors.

Division of the Empire Constantine divided the empire among his three sons. Constantius II (r. 337–361 C.E.), the eldest, survived his brothers, reunited the empire, and bequeathed it to his cousin Julian (r. 361–363 C.E.). Julian "the Apostate" (as he was dubbed by Christian historians) is remembered primarily for attempting to revive Rome's pagan cults. His reign, however, was too short to permit his ideas to take root, and when he died in battle, the pagan renaissance died with him.

By the time a soldier named Valentinian (r. 364–375 C.E.) won the throne, there were so many trouble spots that the new emperor concluded he could not

QUICK REVIEW

Constantinople
- Dedicated by Constantine in 330 C.E.
- Situated on the Bosporus midway between eastern and Danube frontiers
- Marked the start of a new empire

defend his realm alone. He divided it and gave the eastern half to his brother Valens (r. 364–378 C.E.). Valentinian resided at Milan and spent his time defending the West against the German tribes of the Franks and Alemanni.

In the East, a group of Germans confronted Valens with a different kind of problem. In 376 C.E., the tribe of the Visigoths asked permission to enter the empire to escape the Huns, a fierce people who were migrating out of central Asia. Valens acquiesced but was unable to provide adequately for all the refugees who fled into the empire. When the desperate Goths began to plunder the Balkan provinces, Valens called out his army. He and his men confronted them near the city of Adrianople in 378 C.E. and were destroyed.

Control of the East then passed to an able general named Theodosius (r. 379–395 C.E.). He pacified the Goths and enlisted many of them in his army. After his western colleague died, Theodosius reunited the empire for what proved to be the last time.

The Rural West   The disintegration of the empire was encouraged not just by wars and politics, but by the diverging cultures of its eastern and western halves. The West, which had fewer and younger cities, was largely rural, and villas, fortified country estates, came to control much of its territory. As the rich abandoned urban life and moved to the country, they slipped from the control of the imperial authorities. The ability of the central government to provide essential services, such as the maintenance and policing of roads, declined. This handicapped commerce and made communications difficult. Standards of living fell, and regions became increasingly self-sufficient. By the fifth century C.E., the western empire had dissolved and been replaced by isolated estates. The rural aristocrats who owned the land dominated a population composed primarily of dependent laborers, and only the Christian church kept the memory of imperial unity alive.

The Byzantine East   The loss of the West strengthened the East by enabling Constantinople to concentrate on its own affairs. Constantinople diverted most of the barbarian invaders into the West and protected the ancient, thriving cities of the East. Central government continued to function, and a flourishing hybrid of Christian and Classical culture was born as the East entered the "Byzantine" phase in its civilization. For the next thousand years, Roman emperors reigned in Constantinople.

THE TRIUMPH OF CHRISTIANITY

Christianity's rise to become the Roman state religion was linked with political and cultural events that were transforming the empire in other ways. The traditional state cults were closely linked to the fading civic life of Rome's declining cities. Many people still adhered to the ancient rites, but the pagan deities seemed less and less effective as the problems of the fourth and fifth centuries C.E. mounted. Worshipers sought more powerful gods who offered them personal help in this world and immortality in the next. Many new religions appeared, and old ones were combined and reinterpreted. (See Map 5–3.)

Manichaeism, a religion founded by a Persian prophet in the third century C.E., offered early Christianity stiff competition. The Manichaeans interpreted human history as a war between forces of light and darkness, good and evil. They taught that the human body was a material prison for the element of light that was the human soul. To achieve salvation, individuals had to free the light by mastering the desires of the flesh. Manichaeans led ascetic lives, worshiped simply, and developed durable institutions. Their faith persisted into the Middle Ages.

Christianity drew much from the novel eastern cults with which it competed for converts. None, however, had its universal appeal, and none was as great a threat to it as the ancient philosophies and the state religion.

Imperial Persecution Rome's emperors largely ignored Christianity until the middle of the third century. As the empire's problems increased and Christians became more numerous and visible, this changed. A growing sense of insecurity made rulers less willing to tolerate dissent.

Serious trouble erupted for the church in 250 C.E., when an emperor named Decius (r. 249–251 C.E.), who was mired in a war with the Goths, ordered all citizens to sacrifice to the state gods. When Christians refused, Decius tried to purge them from the empire. Valerian (r. 253–260 C.E.) continued to persecute the church—partly out of desire to confiscate the wealth of rich Christians. Later emperors were, however, preoccupied by other more pressing matters, and persecution lapsed until the end of the century.

By Diocletian's day, both the numbers of Christians and hostility toward them had increased. Diocletian's plan for saving the empire demanded conformity to the imperial will, and in 303, he implemented the most serious and thorough of the attempts to obliterate the church. Persecution was, however, self-defeating. The government's extreme actions horrified many pagans, and the courageous demeanor of Christian martyrs aroused sympathy and made new converts.

In 311 C.E., Galerius, Diocletian's successor in the East and one of the most vigorous persecutors, was persuaded (perhaps by his wife) to issue an edict of toleration legitimating Christian worship. Constantine concurred, and a year later

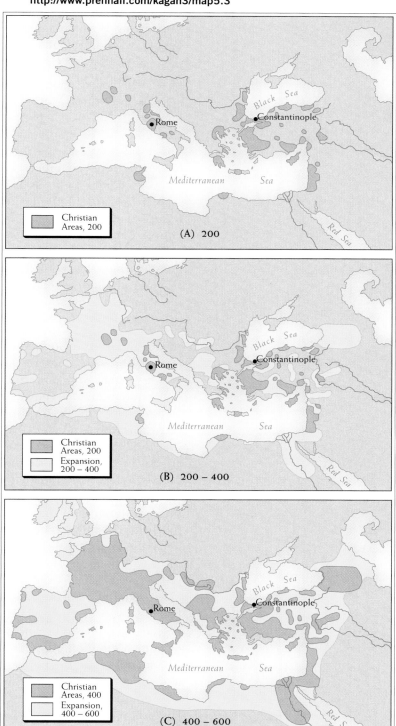

MAP 5–3
The Spread of Christianity   Christianity grew swiftly in the third, fourth, fifth, and sixth centuries—especially after the conversion of the emperors in the fourth century. By 600, on the eve of the birth of the new religion of Islam, Christianity was dominant throughout the Mediterranean world and most of western Europe.

HOW IMPORTANT was state acceptance of Christianity important to the religion's growth in the Roman Empire?

Constantine celebrated his conquest of the western empire by converting to Christianity. His patronage ensured the ultimate triumph of the church over its opponents and competitors.

Emergence of Christianity as the State Religion   Constantine's sons supported the new religion, but the succession of their cousin, Julian the Apostate, posed a brief threat. Julian was a Neoplatonist, a follower of the philosopher, Plotinus (205–270 C.E.). Neoplatonism combined rational speculation and mysticism and was contemptuous of Christianity's lack of intellectual sophistication. Julian did not persecute the church, but he withdrew its privileges, removed Christians from high offices, and introduced new forms of pagan worship. His reform lasted only as long as his brief reign.

In 394 C.E., Theodosius outlawed pagan rites and recognized Christianity as the sole legal religion of the empire. This solved some of the church's problems but created others. The church's growing prestige and influence threatened its spiritual fervor by attracting large numbers of people who converted for the wrong reasons. Dependence on state patronage also posed dangers. The strong eastern emperors subordinated the church to the state, and the collapse of the western empire deprived the church of its protector.

Arianism and the Council of Nicaea   Once the threat of persecution was removed, Christians were free to concentrate on their doctrinal disputes, and opposing factions were powerfully motivated to struggle for control of the wealthy state church. Their arguments spilled over into the streets, caused riots, and created serious problems for the state. Christians, as it turned out, could persecute Christians with as much zeal as pagan fanatics.

Arianism, the most disruptive of the doctrinal controversies, was sparked by an explanation that a priest named Arius of Alexandria (ca. 280–336 C.E.) proposed for the relationship between Christ, the Son, and God the Father. Arius insisted that Christ was the first of God the Father's creations and the being through whom the Father created all other things. For Arius, Jesus was neither fully man nor fully God but something in between. Arius was opposed by Christians who endorsed the doctrine of the Trinity, the belief that God is a unity of three equal persons (Father, Son, and Holy Spirit). Arius dismissed this as thinly veiled polytheism.

Arianism's simple, rational explanation of the central Christian mystery had great appeal. However, Athanasius (ca. 293–373 C.E.), bishop of Alexandria, objected that the Arian view of Christ destroyed Christ's effectiveness as an agent of human salvation. Athanasius noted that only a fully human and fully divine Christ could have the power to bridge the gap between humanity and divinity and reconcile sinners with God.

In 325 C.E., Constantine tried to resolve the issue by inviting all the Christian bishops to a meeting at Nicaea, a city near Constantinople. Athanasius's arguments prevailed and were enshrined in the council's Nicene Creed. This, however, did not stop the spread of Arianism. Some of the later emperors were Arians, and some of the most successful of the missionaries who worked among the Germans were Arians. Many of the German tribes embraced Arian Christianity before their entry into the empire. Christianity had the power to divide as well as to unite.

Arianism   Belief that Christ was the first of God the Father's creations and the being through whom the Father created all other things.

ARTS AND LETTERS IN THE LATE EMPIRE

Crucifixion, carving, c. 420 c.e. (ivory)
British Museum, London, UK/Bridgeman Art

*T*he art and literature of the late empire reflect the confluence of pagan and Christian ideas and the changing tastes of the Roman aristocracy, the ancient world's literary class. Much of the literature of the late empire is polemical, and much of its art is propagandist. The men who came to power as the empire declined were soldiers from the provinces whose roots were in the lower classes. By mastering and preserving Classical culture, these men hoped to stabilize their world and confirm their credentials as its rightful leaders.

THE PRESERVATION OF CLASSICAL CULTURE

Acquisition of Classical culture by the newly arrived ruling class was facilitated in several ways. Works by great authors were copied and circulated widely. Instead of being written on continuous rolls of papyrus or parchment, they were published in a more convenient new form as codices (bundles of pages stitched together like modern books). Scholars assisted novice readers by condensing long works and writing commentaries that explained difficult texts. Grammars for Greek and Latin also had to be created, for new languages were replacing the Classical tongues in many parts of the Roman world.

CHRISTIAN WRITERS

Original works by pagan writers of the late empire were neither numerous nor especially distinguished, but Christian literature abounded. Christian "apologists" used poetry and prose to explain Christian practices to pagans, and Christians wrote sermons, hymns, and biblical commentaries for their own use.

Several of Christianity's most influential scholars flourished during the waning years of the empire. Jerome (348–420 C.E.), who was thoroughly trained in Classical literature and rhetoric as well as Hebrew, created the **Vulgate**, the Latin translation of the Bible that became the standard text for the Catholic Church. Eusebius of Caesarea (ca. 260–ca. 340 C.E.) wrote an idealized biography of Constantine and an *Ecclesiastical History* that set forth a Christian view of history as a process whereby God's will is revealed. However, it is the work of Augustine (354–430 C.E.), bishop of Hippo in North Africa, that towers over all others and best illustrates the fruitfulness of the era's efforts to use the tools of Classical culture to explicate Christian faith.

Augustine was born at Carthage and trained as a teacher of rhetoric. His father was a pagan, but his mother was a Christian and hers was ultimately the stronger influence. He explored Manichaeism, skepticism, and Neoplatonism before he came to Christianity. But following his conversion, his Classical education in rhetoric and philosophy served him well. He became the most influential of the Latin theologians.

Augustine's belief that reason prepares people to accept what is revealed by faith helped him reconcile Christianity and Classical culture. His greatest works are *Confessions*, an autobiography that describes his journey to faith, and *The City of God*, a response to the pagan charge that a sack of Rome by the Visigoths in 410 C.E. took place because Rome abandoned its old gods. Augustine explained the course of history as a complex interaction of the secular, the "City of Man,"

Vulgate Latin translation of the Bible that became the standard text for the Catholic Church.

and the spiritual, the "City of God." The former was fated to be destroyed on the Day of Judgment, but Augustine saw no reason to assume that conditions would improve for human life before that. The fall of Rome was neither surprising nor all that significant, for all states, even a Christian Rome, were part of the City of Man. They were, therefore, corrupt and mortal. Only the City of God, the true church, was immortal, and it was untouched by earthly calamities.

THE PROBLEM OF THE DECLINE AND FALL OF THE EMPIRE IN THE WEST

Although Augustine doubted their transcendent significance, the events of the fifth century did change the course of Western civilization, and people have never ceased to speculate about reasons for the ancient world's collapse. Soil exhaustion, plague, climatic change, and even poisoning caused by lead water pipes have been proposed as contributing causes. Some scholars blame the institution of slavery for Rome's failure to make the advances in science and technology that might have solved its economic problems. Others claim that excessive governmental interference in the economic life of the empire was at fault—particularly insofar as this affected the fate of cities and the literate urban classes.

Although many of these things may have been contributing factors, there is a simpler explanation for Rome's failure. The growth of Rome's empire was fueled by conquests that fed on themselves. The resources from conquests funded additional conquests until the Romans overextended themselves. As pressure from outsiders grew, the Romans could not find the resources needed to fend off their enemies. To blame them for their failure to end slavery and bring on industrial and economic revolutions is fruitless, for we do not yet fully understand what caused those revolutions in the modern era. At the very least, the Romans deserve respect for their tenacity, for the real question we should ask about them may not be why their empire fell, but how it managed to last as long as it did.

SUMMARY

The Augustan Principate After defeating Mark Antony at Actium in 31 B.C.E., Octavian started transforming his rule into the functional equivalent of a monarchy. In 26 B.C.E., he made a show of giving up his powers, no doubt expecting the Senate to beg him to keep them, as it in fact did. From then on he was referred to as Augustus. He introduced administrative reforms, widened the talent pool from which senators were selected, and generally improved his subjects' standard of living. He professionalized the military and attempted to secure the northern frontier. He modeled austere morality and supported traditional Roman religion.

Civilization of the Ciceronian and Augustan Ages Roman culture flourished in the late republican period and in the Principate of Augustus. Hellenistic influences permeated the arts and literature, but the great works are clearly Roman in character. History, poetry, and law all found able practitioners in the late republic. Augustus simplified patronage for the arts. Augustan literature features some of the most recognizable names of the period: Vergil, Horace, Ovid, among others. Augustus also supported the visual arts; some of Rome's loveliest monuments were built under his reign.

Imperial Rome, 14–180 C.E. The monarchical, hereditary rule of Augustus's successors was based on undisguised military power. In 69 C.E., Vespasian, the first emperor who was not a descendant of Roman nobility, assumed the throne. His Flavian dynasty was followed by the five "good emperors." The provinces were generally peaceful during this period. Latin was spoken throughout the West; in the East, Greek was still the predominant language. Culturally, "Romanitas" spread throughout the cities and towns of the empire. The situation for Jews and for peasant farmers was not attractive. Border defenses, particularly in the north, were a recurring problem for the empire. Women's status improved. Many people lived in *insulae*, multistory apartment buildings that were cramped and uncomfortable. Latin literature experienced a "Silver Age" between 14 and 180 C.E., offering a more critical worldview than the works of the Augustan period. Architecture flourished. By the second century C.E., problems such as a decline in the vitality of local government, a stagnating economy, the expense of defense, and probably a mysterious decline in population were foreshadowing crises to come.

The Rise of Christianity Jesus of Nazareth was born in Judaea under the reign of Augustus. He gained a large following, particularly among the poor, with a message of a coming Day of Judgment and criticism of existing religious practices. Feared and misunderstood by the authorities, Jesus was crucified in Jerusalem, probably in 30 C.E. Written decades after his death, the Gospels present Jesus as the Son of God, a redeemer who was resurrected after death. The writings of Paul of Tarsus are especially important, since he makes the case that Christianity is a new and universal religion. The *agape* ("love feast") created a sense of solidarity across classes among early Christians, and it helped the religion spread throughout the Roman Empire and beyond. By the end of the second century C.E., the Catholic Church had been institutionalized as the definer of Christian orthodoxy.

The Crisis of the Third Century External military threats and internal social weakness interacted in a vicious circle. Commodus came to power in 180 C.E. When he was assassinated in 192 C.E., civil war again erupted and military strongman Septimius Severus emerged victorious. In the third century C.E., others invaded the outskirts of the empire. Repelling these challenges required more resources than the society could spare; labor shortages, inflation, and neglect of infrastructure such as roads weakened Rome's economy. Social stratification increased. Invasions and anarchy characterized the middle of the third century C.E.

The Late Empire During the fourth and fifth centuries, the empire was reorganized and divided, and Christianity gained followers and power. Diocletian introduced the tetrarchy, but it did not lead to a smooth succession when he

IMAGE KEY
for pages 114–115.

a. Augustus of Primaporta, c.20 B.C.E., Roman art

b. Model of Colosseum

c. Clay plaque for roof showing emblem of 20th Roman Legion, a charging boar

d. Arch of Titus, C.E. 81, Relief: Spoils from temple in Jerusalem

e. "The Good Shepherd", Late 3rd century C.E. Marble, Height: as restored cm 99, as perserved cm 55, head cm 15.5. Late 3rd century C.E. Vatican Musuems, Pio-Christian Museum, Inv. 28590. Courtesy of the Vatican Museums

f. The title of this mosaic in the Bardo Museum in Tunis, Tunisia is "Virgil writing the Aeniad, inspired by two muses," Cleo (left) is the muse of storytelling and Melpomene (right) is the muse of tragedy

g. Saturnia, Tellus, Goddess of Earth, Air and Water. Panel from the Ara Pacis. 13-9 B.C.E. Museum of the Ara Pacis, Rome. Nimathallah/Art Resource, NY

h. Imperial Roman Cameo of Livia and Tiberius

i. Head of the emperor Constantine from a colossal statue nearly forty feet high located in his monumental basilica

j. Crucifixion, carving, c. 420 C.E. (ivory). Bristish Museum, London, UK/Bridgeman Art Library

and his co-emperor retired in 305 C.E. Diocletian and Constantine both ruled autocratically from Eastern cities. Diocletian tried to suppress Christianity, whereas Constantine supported it. Constantine's death was followed by yet another struggle for power. By the end of the fourth century, the empire had been divided permanently. Christianity's continued viability depended on its ability to cope with political interference and doctrinal disputes.

Arts and Letters in the Late Empire   Much of the art and literature of the late empire reflects the relationship between Christianity and pagan religions. The empire's new rulers came from the lower classes of the provinces; in their efforts to restore classical culture, they inevitably reshaped it. Christian writings were numerous, the most significant among them the works of Augustine in which he combined Christian faith and pagan (Classical) reason.

The Problem of the Decline and Fall of the Empire in the West   Imperial government fell in the West in the fifth century, in the face of barbarian invasions. Ever since, historians and commentators have offered explanations, many of which seem specious. Like the early-twentieth-century historian Edward Gibbon, the authors believe the question should be more properly framed as, "How did the Roman Empire last as long as it did?" rather than, "Why did the Roman Empire decline and fall?" The Roman Empire could not expand forever; without the infusion of new people and new wealth that territorial conquest provided, the Roman Empire could not survive.

REVIEW QUESTIONS

1. How did Augustus alter Rome's constitution and government? How did his innovations solve the problems that had plagued the republic? Why were the Romans willing to accept him?

2. How did the literature of the "Golden Age" differ from that of the "Silver Age"? What did poets contribute to the success of Augustus's reforms?

3. Why were Christians persecuted by the Roman authorities? What enabled them to acquire such an enormous following by the fourth century C.E.?

4. What were the political, social, and economic problems that beset Rome in the third and fourth centuries C.E.? How did Diocletian and Constantine deal with them? Were these men able to halt Rome's decline? Were there problems they could not solve?

KEY TERMS

agape   (p. 129)

apostolic succession   (p. 129)

Arianism   (p. 138)

Augustus   (p. 116)

catholic   (p. 130)

eucharist   (p. 129)

heretics   (p. 130)

imperator   (p. 116)

jus gentium   (p. 119)

jus naturale   (p. 119)

Messiah   (p. 128)

orthodox   (p. 130)

Pharisee   (p. 128)

tetrarchy   (p. 133)

Vulgate   (p. 139)

 For additional study resources for this chapter, go to:
www.prenhall.com/kagan3/chapter5

PART TWO THE MIDDLE AGES

POLITICS & GOVERNMENT

330 Constantinople becomes new capital of Roman Empire

410 Visigoths sack Rome

451–453 Attila the Hun invades Italy

455 Vandals overrun Rome

476 Odovacer deposes the last Western emperor

489–493 Theodoric's Ostrogoth kingdom established in Italy

527–565 Reign of Justinian

568 Lombard invasion of Italy

Emperor Justinian ▶

SOCIETY & ECONOMY

400 Cities and trade begin to decline in the West; Germanic (barbarian) tribes settle in the West

533–534 *Corpus juris civilis* compiled by Justinian

◀ Interior of Hagia Sophia

RELIGION & CULTURE

312 Constantine embraces Christianity

325 Council of Nicaea

380 Christianity becomes the official religion of the Roman Empire

413–426 Saint Augustine writes *City of God*

451 Council of Chalcedon

496 The Franks embrace Christianity

Abbey of ▶ Monte Cassino

529 Saint Benedict founds monastery at Monte Cassino

537 Byzantine Church of Hagia Sophia completed

590–604 Pope Gregory the Great

622 Muhammad's flight from Mecca (Hegira)

◀ The Great Mosque in Mecca

632–733 Muslim expansion and conquests

732 Charles Martel defeats Muslims at Poitiers

768–814 Reign of Charlemagne

843 Treaty of Verdun partitions Carolingian empire

▲ *Charlemagne on horseback*

◄ *Bust of Charlemagne*

918 Saxon Henry I becomes first non-Frankish king, as Saxons succeed Carolingians in Germany

987 Capetians succeed Carolingians in France

1066 Battle of Hastings (Norman Conquest of England)

1071 Seljuk Turks defeat Byzantine armies at Manzikert

1099 Jerusalem falls to Crusaders

▲*Harold's crowning, The Bayeux Tapestry*

1152 Frederick I Barbarossa first Hohenstaufen emperor

1187 Saladin reconquers Jerusalem from West

1204 Fourth Crusade captures Constantinople

1214 Philip II Augustus defeats English and German armies at Bouvines

1215 Magna Carta

1240 Mongols dominate Russia

1250 Death of Frederick II (end of Hohenstaufen dynasty)

1257 German princes establish electoral college to elect emperor

▲ *Magna Carta*

632–733 Muslims disrupt western Mediterranean trade

700 Agrarian society centered around the manor predominates in the West

700–800 Moldboard plow and three field system in use

700 Islam enters its Golden Age

800 Byzantium enters its Golden Age

800 Introduction of collar harness

850 Muslims occupy parts of Spain

880s Vikings penetrate central Europe

900 Introduction of the horseshoe

900–1100 Rise of towns, guilds, and urban culture in West

1086 *Domesday Book*

◄ *11th or 12th century horseshoe*

Cathedral facade, ▶
Chartres, France

1130 Gothic architecture begins to displace Romanesque

1200 Shift from dues to rent tenancy on manors

725–787 Iconoclastic Controversy in East

ca. 775 *Donation of Constantine*

782 Alcuin of York runs Charlemagne's palace school

800 Pope Leo crowns Charlemagne emperor

◄ *Icon of the Virgin Episkepis*

910 Benedictine monastery of Cluny founded

◄ *Abbey at Cluny*

980s Orthodox Christianity penetrates Russia

1054 Schism between Eastern and Western churches

1075 Pope Gregory VII condemns lay investiture

1095 Pope Urban II preaches the First Crusade

1122 Concordat of Worms ends Investiture Controversy

1158 First European university founded in Bologna

1210 Franciscan order founded

1216 Dominican order founded

1265 Thomas Aquinas's *Summa Theologica* begun

ca. 1275 *Romance of the Rose*

St. Francis ▶

6 Late Antiquity and the Early Middle Ages
Creating a New European Society and Culture (476–1000)

CHAPTER HIGHLIGHTS

On the Eve of the Frankish Ascendancy Late antiquity, the centuries before and after the fall of Rome (476), was a vibrant period of self-discovery and self-definition for the peoples of the Mediterranean. The emergence of distinctive European, Byzantine, and Islamic civilizations took place against the backdrop of the collapse of the Roman Empire in the West.

The Byzantine Empire The eastern portion of the Roman Empire endured as the Byzantine Empire. It reached the peak of its power under Justinian in the mid–sixth century. Justinian codified Roman law and supported Orthodox Christianity. Constantinople was the economic, administrative, and cultural heart of the empire.

Islam and the Islamic World In the seventh century, Muhammad founded a new religion on the Arabian peninsula. By 750 the Islamic Empire stretched from Spain to India. The West profited from its contact with Islam.

Western Society and the Developing Christian Church As trade declined in the West, people migrated from cities to farmland. New social arrangements including serfdom, manorialism, and feudalism emerged. The Christian church played a key role in the emerging European civilization.

The Kingdom of the Franks Clovis founded the first Frankish dynasty, the Merovingians. The Carolingian dynasty made strategic alliances with the nobility and the Church. Under Charlemagne, the Franks built an impressive empire. The empire collapsed after his death in 814. During the ninth and tenth centuries, invasions by the Vikings and others ushered in a "dark age" for Europe.

Feudal Society The feudal system was built around the exchange of land, labor, and military protection. All participants in the feudal system constantly negotiated and competed for advantage. In time, feudalism contributed many of the political and legal institutions that developed into the modern nation-state.

CHAPTER QUESTIONS

HOW DID Germanic migrations contribute to the fall of the Roman Empire?

HOW DID the Byzantine Empire continue the legacy of Rome?

HOW DID Islamic culture influence the West?

HOW DID the developing Christian Church influence Western society during the early Middle Ages?

HOW DID the reign of Clovis differ from that of Charlemagne?

WHAT WERE the characteristics of a feudal society?

CHAPTER OUTLINE
- On the Eve of the Frankish Ascendancy
- The Byzantine Empire
- Islam and the Islamic World
- Western Society and the Developing Christian church
- The Kingdom of the Franks
- Feudal Society

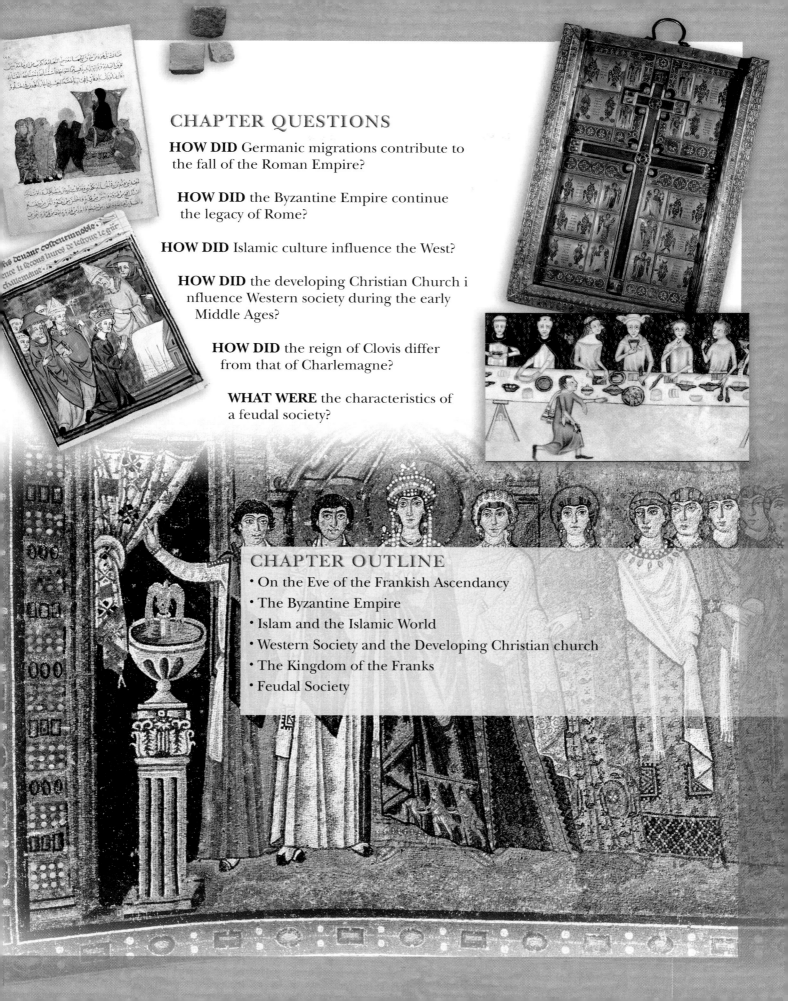

IMAGE KEY

for pages 146–147 is on page 170.

HOW DID Germanic migrations contribute to the fall of the Roman Empire?

Scholars increasingly view the period between 250 C.E. and 800 C.E.—called Late Antiquity— as a single world, both cohesive and moving apart, bounded by the Roman and Sassanian (Persian) empires. The western and eastern (Byzantine) empires of Rome never succumbed culturally to barbarian and Muslim invaders. In the east, the Sassanians created a power- ful empire and deeply penetrated Rome's provinces. By the mid–eighth century, Arab con- quests extended Muslim influence from the Middle East to North Africa and Spain. In western Europe, Germanic heritage, Judeo-Christian religion, Roman language and law, and Greco-Byzantine administration and culture gradually combined to create a uniquely European way of life.

ON THE EVE OF THE FRANKISH ASCENDANCY

The strategies devised to save the Roman Empire in the late third century succeeded only in influencing how it fell. Diocletian (r. 284–305) strengthened Rome's defenses by dividing his realm in half and appoint- ing a co-emperor. As this arrangement became permanent, the halves of the em- pire embarked on different courses. Imperial rule faded from the West and grew increasingly autocratic in the East.

The empire was briefly reunited by Constantine the Great (r. 306–337), and in 324, he moved its capital to Constantinople. This "new Rome" on the border between Europe and Asia Minor flourished as old Rome declined. Rome was even superceded as an administrative center in the West by the city of Milan, which had better communications with the Rhine and Danube fron- tiers. In 402, even Milan was judged too exposed to barbarian invasions, and the western court relocated to Ravenna on the Adriatic coast. By then, the west- ern empire's days were numbered, and Constantinople defended what was left of Roman prestige.

GERMANIC MIGRATIONS

The Germans who invaded the West were not strangers. Romans and Germans had traded and commingled for centuries, and some Germans even rose to command posts in the Roman army. However, in 376, the pace of German mi- gration began to accelerate until it overwhelmed the western half of the em- pire. The process began in 376, when the eastern emperor Valens (r. 364–378) admitted the Visigoths ("West Goths") into the empire. They were fleeing the approach of the notoriously violent Huns of Mongolia. The Huns were a po- tential threat to Rome as well, and by enlisting the Visigoths as *foederati* (allied aliens resident within the empire), Valens hoped to strengthen the East's de- fenses. (See Map 6–1.)

The Visigoths entered the empire as impoverished refugees. Exploitation of their misery by Roman profiteers caused them to rebel, and in 378, at the Bat- tle of Adrianople, they destroyed Valens and his army. Constantinople defended itself by persuading the Visigoths to invade Italy, and the western empire re- sponded by withdrawing troops from its frontiers to defend Italy. This allowed other German tribes to cross the Rhine unopposed and wander virtually through the western provinces.

Although the largest German tribe probably numbered no more than 100,000 people, the much larger Roman population offered little resistance to the German migration. The western empire was badly overextended and weak- ened by decades of famine, pestilence, and overtaxation. Its government was also handicapped by internal power struggles.

MAP EXPLORATION

Interactive map: To explore this map further, go to **http://www.prehnall.com/kagan3/map6.1**

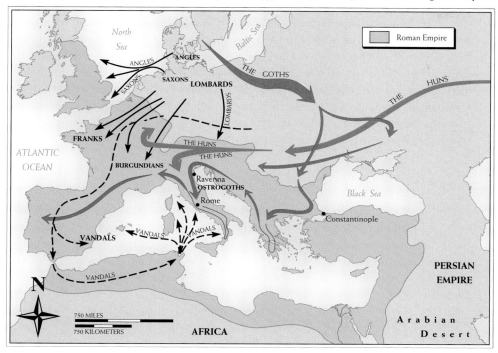

MAP 6–1

Barbarian Migrations into the West in the Fourth and Fifth Centuries   The forceful intrusion of Germanic and non-Germanic barbarians into the Roman Empire from the last quarter of the fourth century through the fifth century made for a constantly changing pattern of movement and relations. The map shows the major routes taken by the usually unwelcome newcomers and the areas most deeply affected by the main groups.

WHICH PART of the Empire was least affected by barbarian migrations?

NEW WESTERN MASTERS

In the early fifth century, Italy suffered a series of devastating blows. Led by a competent king named Alaric (ca. 370–410), the Visigoths sacked Rome in 410. In 452, the infamous Attila and the Huns invaded the peninsula, and in 455, the Vandals sacked Rome. By the mid–fifth century, barbarian chieftains had replaced Roman emperors throughout western Europe, and in 476 the barbarian general Odovacer (ca. 434–493) deposed the last of the West's figurehead emperors, Romulus Augustulus.

In 493, Constantinople's emperor Zeno (r. 474–491) sent the Ostrogoths ("East Goths") under their king Theodoric (ca. 454–526) west to reclaim Italy (nominally) for the eastern empire. By then, German tribes had thoroughly overrun the West. The Ostrogoths settled in Italy, the Franks in northern Gaul, the Burgundians in Provence, the Visigoths in southern Gaul and Spain, the Vandals in Africa and the western Mediterranean, and the Angles and Saxons in England.

The Germans did not reduce western Europe to savagery. They respected Roman culture and learned from their Roman subjects. Except in Britain and northern Gaul, vernacular Latin and Roman governmental institutions survived and blended with German customs. Only the Vandals and the Anglo-Saxons (and, after 466, the Visigoths) refused to keep the myth of the empire alive by professing titular obedience to Constantinople.

The Visigoths, the Ostrogoths, and the Vandals had converted to Christianity before entering the West, but the missionaries who worked among them were Arians (heretics who claimed Christ was a creature subordinate to God the Father). Their faith was an obstacle to relations with their orthodox Roman subjects. The leaders of the Franks wisely chose (about 500) to embrace the Catholic ("universal") version of Christianity endorsed by the bishops of Rome. This brought them popular support that helped them subdue rival tribes and become the dominant German power in western Europe.

THE BYZANTINE EMPIRE

HOW DID the Byzantine Empire continue the legacy of Rome?

As western Europe succumbed to the Germans, the eastern empire also changed. It became the medieval Byzantine Empire, a term that came into use first in the West after the empire's collapse in 1453. From the date of its founding in 324 to its conquest by the Ottoman Turks in 1453, Constantinople remained the seat of the "Roman" emperor whose subjects were Greek-speaking Christians.

THE REIGN OF JUSTINIAN

The Byzantine Empire reached a territorial and cultural peak during the reign of the emperor Justinian (r. 527–565). At a time when urban life was disappearing from the West, Justinian's domain boasted over 1,500 cities. Constantinople, with about 350,000 residents, was the largest, but the eastern empire had provincial cities with populations of about 50,000. They were bustling centers of economic and intellectual activity. At Justinian's command, fortifications, churches, monasteries, and palaces arose across

Empress Theodora and her attendants. The union of political and spiritual authority in the person of the empress is shown by the depiction on Theodora's mantle of three magi carrying gifts to the Virgin and Jesus.

Byzantine early christian mosaic. San Vitale, Ravenna, Italy. Photograph ©Scala/Art Resource, NY

the empire. Most famous and enduring is Constantinople's Church of Hagia Sophia (Holy Wisdom) completed in 537. Its key feature is a massive dome, 112 feet in diameter, and many windows and open spaces, which give the interior a remarkable airiness and luminosity.

Justinian's remarkable wife Theodora (d. 548) was his chief counselor. If the *Secret History* of Procopius, Justinian's court historian, is to be believed, Theodora was the daughter of a circus bear trainer and began her career as a prostitute. Her background may have given her a toughness that was useful to her husband. She was particularly helpful in dealing with the religious quarrels that threatened the unity of the empire. As emperor, Justinian professed orthodox Christianity, but Theodora's quiet support for the heretical **Monophysites** helped control a powerful popular movement. The Monophysites believed Jesus had a single nature (a composite of the human and divine), whereas the orthodox church claimed he had two distinct natures—one fully human and the other fully divine. The Monophysites were especially powerful in the eastern provinces of the empire. After Theodora's death, the imperial government tried to stamp them out. This was a mistake, for a few years later, when Persian and Arab armies invaded, the resentful Monophysites offered little resistance.

Law Byzantine policy emphasized centralized governmental control and social conformity ("one God, one empire, one religion"). To achieve this, Justinian commissioned scholars to codify Roman law. The *Corpus Juris Civilis* (*Body of Civil Law*), which resulted, was issued in four parts: the *Code* revised imperial edicts dating back to the reign of Hadrian (117–138), the *Novellae* (*New Things*) contained Justinian's decrees, the *Digest* summarized opinions of famous legal experts, and the *Institutes* provided a textbook for training lawyers. The medieval West was governed by what is called common law, but from the late medieval Renaissance on, Justinian's Roman law transformed the administration of justice and promoted the centralization of governments across Europe.

Reconquest in the West Justinian sought to reconquer the imperial provinces lost to the barbarians in the West. Beginning in 533, his armies overran the Vandal kingdom in North Africa and Sicily, the Ostrogothic kingdom in Italy, and part of Spain. The price of conquest was high: By Justinian's death, his empire was financially exhausted, and plague had ravaged Constantinople and must of the East. Byzantine rule survived in Sicily and parts of southern Italy until the eleventh century, but most of Justinian's Western and North African conquests were soon lost to Lombards and Muslim Arabs. (See Map 6–2.)

6.2
Corpus Juris Civilis: Prologue

Built during the reign of Justinian, Hagia Sophia (Church of the Holy Wisdom) is a masterpiece of Byzantine and world architecture. After the Turkish conquest of Costantinople in 1453, Hagia Sophia was transformed into a mosque with four minarets, still visible today.

Marvin Trachtenberg

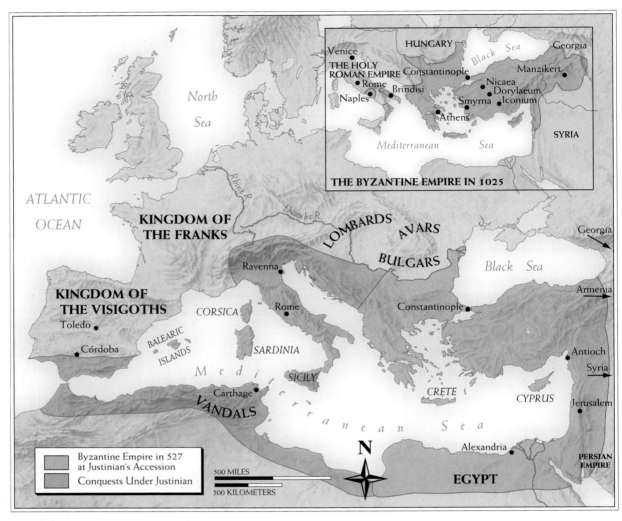

MAP 6–2

The Byzantine Empire at the Time of Justinian's Death Justinian reconquered lands in the West that once belonged to the Roman Empire. From 500 to 1100, the Byzantine Empire was the center of Christian civilization. The inset shows the empire in 1025, before its losses to the Seljuk Turks.

IN THE second half of the first millennium c.e., how did the power and influence of Rome and Constantinople compare?

THE SPREAD OF BYZANTINE CHRISTIANITY

In the late sixth and seventh centuries, nomadic, pagan tribes of Avars, Slavs, and Bulgars invaded and occupied the Balkan provinces of the eastern empire, more than once menacing Constantinople itself. Yet after almost two centuries of intermittent warfare, the Slavs and Bulgars eventually converted to Eastern Orthodoxy or Byzantine Christianity. In the ninth century the Slav Duke Rastislav of Moravia turned to Constantinople for help against Franks from the West, who had conquered the Avars and were attempting to convert his people to Roman Catholicism in Latin, a language they did not understand. In response, the emperor sent two learned missionaries to convert the Moravians: the priests, brothers, and future saints Constantine, later known as Cyril, and Methodius. They created a new, Greek-based alphabet, which permitted the Slavs to create their own written language, later known as Cyrillic after St. Cyril. That language gave the Christian gospels and Byzantine theology a lasting Slavic home. Known today as Old Church Slavonic, it was the international Slavic language through which Christianity penetrated eastern Europe.

PERSIANS AND MUSLIMS

During the reign of Emperor Heraclius (r. 610–641), the Byzantine Empire took a decidedly Eastern, as opposed to a Western Roman, direction. Heraclius spent his entire reign resisting Persian and Islamic invasions, the former successfully, the latter in vain. After 632, Islamic armies overran much of the empire, directly attacking Constantinople for the first time in the mid–670s. In the 700s the Byzantines repelled Arab armies and regained most of Asia Minor, having lost forever Syria, Egypt, and North Africa. This traumatic setback forced a change in provincial government, from governance by local elites to direct control by imperial generals, making possible a more disciplined and flexible use of military power. In the tenth century, the forces of Constantinople pushed back the Muslims in Armenia and northern Syria and conquered the Bulgar kingdom in the Balkans.

The empire's fortunes reversed in the eleventh century. After defeating the Byzantine army at Manzikert in Armenia in 1071, Muslim Seljuk Turks overran most of Asia Minor, from which the Byzantines had drawn most of their tax revenue and troops. The empire never fully recovered, although its end would not come until 1453, when the Seljuks' cousins, the Ottoman Turks, captured Constantinople. Threatened by the Turkish advance, the Byzantines called for Western aid, helping to spark the First Crusade. In 1204, the Fourth Crusade was diverted from Jerusalem to Constantinople, not to rescue the city, but rather to inflict more damage on it and the Byzantine Empire than all previous non-Christian invaders had done before. The Byzantines recovered their city in 1261, but their power and wealth were significantly reduced, tensions between Latin West and Greek East were even higher, and the Turks had become a constant threat.

ISLAM AND THE ISLAMIC WORLD

 new religion called **Islam** apeared in Arabia in the sixth century in response to the work of the Prophet Muhammad. It inspired a third medieval civilization and rapidly created one of history's greatest empires.

MUHAMMAD'S RELIGION

Muhammad (570–632) was orphaned at a young age and raised by various relatives. He had no fortune or powerful political connections. He worked on caravans as a merchant's assistant until, at the age of twenty-five, he married a wealthy widow. With her support, he became a kind of social activist fighting the increasing materialism of his contemporaries. When he was about forty, he had a religious experience, which he understood to be a visitation from the angel Gabriel. From time to time for the rest of his life, he was inspired to recite what his followers believed were literally God's words. Between 650 and 651, the revealed texts that God had chosen him to convey were collected in a sacred book, the **Qur'an** ("reciting"). At the heart of Muhammad's message was a call for all Arabs to submit to God's will as revealed through "the Prophet." The terms *Islam* and *Muslim* both imply submission or surrender.

Muhammad did not claim his message was new—only that it was final and definitive. What he taught was consistent with what the Jewish prophets, from Noah to Jesus, had taught. His unique mission was to be the last of the prophets. He claimed that after him God would send no more, but he also insisted "the Prophet" was only a

HOW DID Islamic culture influence the West?

    6.3
The Qur'an

Islam   New religion appearing in Arabia in the sixth century in response to the work of the Prophet Muhammad.

Qur'an   Sacred book comprised of a collection of the revealed texts that God had chosen Muhammad to convey.

man. Like Judaism, Islam was to be a strictly monotheistic, theocentric religion that rejected Christianity's trinitarian view of God and its claim that Jesus was God incarnate.

Muhammad's faith in a single transcendent God set him at odds with his people. Muhammad was a native of Mecca, the site of the **Ka'ba**, one of Arabia's holiest shrines. (The Ka'ba was a simple rectangular building built to contain a sacred black stone and numerous holy images.) When Muhammad began to preach against the idols of the Ka'ba, he not only assaulted traditional Arab religion, he threatened Mecca's economy. Respect for the Ka'ba helped make Mecca a center for Arab trade. In 622, the Meccan authorities forced Muhammad and his followers to flee to Medina, an oasis 240 miles north of Mecca. This event, the *Hegira*, provides the pivotal date for the Islamic calendar, for it marks the founding of the first Muslim community.

Muhammad and his followers prospered in Medina by raiding the caravans that served Mecca. Converts accumulated until, by 624, he was powerful enough to persuade Mecca to submit to his authority. He returned in triumph and cleansed the Ka'ba of its idols, but he preserved the building as a shrine. Islam, like Christianity, eased life for its converts by making compromises with the pagan traditions they cherished.

Muhammad stressed practice more than doctrine, and, as Islam matured, its characteristic disciplines emerged: (1) honesty and modesty in all conduct, (2) absolute loyalty to the Islamic community, (3) abstinence from pork and alcohol, (4) prayer toward Mecca five times a day, (5) giving alms to support the poor and needy, (6) fasting during daylight hours for one month each year, and (7) making a pilgrimage to Mecca at least once in a lifetime. Muslim men were allowed as many as four wives—provided they treated them all justly and equally. A man could divorce a wife with a simple declaration of his intent. A wife could also initiate divorce, but this was a more complicated process. A wife was expected to be totally devoted to her husband, and only he was to see her face.

Islam had no priesthood. It was led by the *ulema* ("persons with correct knowledge"), a scholarly elite. The *ulema*'s authority derived from the reputations of its members for piety and learning. Their opinions had the force of legislation in Muslim society, and they ensured that Muslim governments adhered to the law of the Qur'an.

ISLAMIC DIVERSITY

Islam succeeded in unifying Arab tribes and various pagan peoples by appealing to the pride of groups that had been marginalized in a world dominated by Judaism and Christianity. Islam declared Muhammad to be history's most important figure and Muhammad's followers to be the people whom God had chosen to receive his definitive revelation.

Passionate faith in Muhammad did not, however, prevent divisions from emerging within Islam. Factions contested who had the best claim to the **caliphate**, the office of the leader of the Muslim community. Doctrinal differences also spawned controversies just as they did among Christians.

The most radical Muslims were the Kharijites, who seceded from the camp of the fourth caliph, Ali (r. 656–661). They accused Ali of sacrificing important principles for political advantage, and in 661, a Kharijite assassinated him. The Kharijites were "Puritans" who wanted to purge Islam of persons who did not meet their rigorous moral standards.

More influential was the **Shi'a**, the "party" of Ali. The Shi'a believed Ali and his descendants (by virtue of their kinship with the Prophet and the Prophet's

Ka'ba One of Arabia's holiest shrines located in Mecca, the birthplace of Muhammad.

Hegira Forced flight of Muhammad and his followers to Medina, 240 miles north of Mecca. This event marks the beginning of the Islamic calendar.

ulema ("Persons with correct knowledge") Scholarly elite leading Islam.

caliphate Office of the leader of the Muslim community.

Shi'a The "party" of Ali. They believed Ali and his descendants were Muhammad's only rightful successors.

own will) were Muhammad's only rightful successors. For the Shi'a, Ali's assassination represented a basic truth of devout Muslim life: a true *imam* ("ruler") and his followers must expect persecution. A theology of martyrdom is the mark of Shi'a teaching, and the Shi'a is still an embattled minority within Islam.

A third group, which has dominated Islam for most of its history, is composed of the **Sunnis** (followers of *sunna*, "tradition"). Sunnis emphasize loyalty to the fundamental principles of Islam and have spurned the exclusivity and purism that cause the Kharijites and the Shi'a to separate from the wider Muslim community.

ISLAMIC EMPIRES

Under Muhammad's first three successors—the caliphs Abu Bakr (r. 632–634), Umar (r. 634–644), and Uthman (r. 644–656)—Muslim armies swept throughout the southern and eastern Mediterranean, acquiring lands still held by Muslim states. Islam's capital moved from Mecca to the more centrally located Damascus, and by the eighth century, the caliphs of the Umayyad dynasty ruled an empire that stretched from Spain to India. In 750, the Abbasid family overthrew the Umayyads and moved the seat of the caliphate to Baghdad. Shortly thereafter, their huge empire began to break up, and rival caliphs appeared to contest their authority. (See Map 6–3.)

The Muslim conquerors profited from the fact that their Byzantine and Persian opponents had exhausted themselves in a long war. The Arabs struck just as the Byzantine emperor Heraclius forced the Persians to evacuate Egypt, Palestine, Syria, and Asia Minor, but before Heraclius died in 641, the Arabs had taken all these lands (except Asia Minor) from him. By 643, they had overrun what remained of the Persian Empire, and by the end of the century, the last Byzantine outpost in North Africa had fallen to them. The Muslim advance was facilitated by the fact that many of the inhabitants of the Byzantine lands the Muslims occupied were Semitic peoples with ethnic ties to the Arabs. Constantinople's efforts to stamp out all forms of Christianity that it regarded as heretical also led many of the Christians of Egypt and Syria to welcome the Islamic invaders as liberators.

Islam swept across North Africa and Spain, but its thrust into the European heart of Christendom was rebuffed in 732 by Charles Martel, ruler of the Franks. His defeat of an Arab raiding party at Poitiers (in central France) marked the point at which the Muslim advance in the West was halted and slowly began to reverse.

THE WESTERN DEBT TO ISLAMIC CULTURE

Christian Europe was hostile to Islam, but it profited a great deal from contact with the Muslim world. The works of the great scientists and philosophers of the Classical era were largely forgotten by Europeans until Arabs reintroduced them. Latin translations of Arabic translations of and commentaries on Greek originals revolutionized intellectual life in medieval Europe. As late as the sixteenth century, the

Muslims are enjoined to live by the divine law, or Shari'a, and have a right to have disputes settled by an arbiter of the Shari'a. Here we see a husband complaining about his wife before the state-appointed judge, or qadi. The wife, backed up by two other women, points an accusing finger at the husband. In such cases, the first duty of the qadi, who should be a learned person of faith, is to try to effect a reconciliation before the husband divorces his wife, or the wife herself seeks a divorce.

Bibliothèque Nationale de France, Paris

Sunnis Followers of the *sunna*, "tradition." They emphasize loyalty to the fundamental principles of Islam.

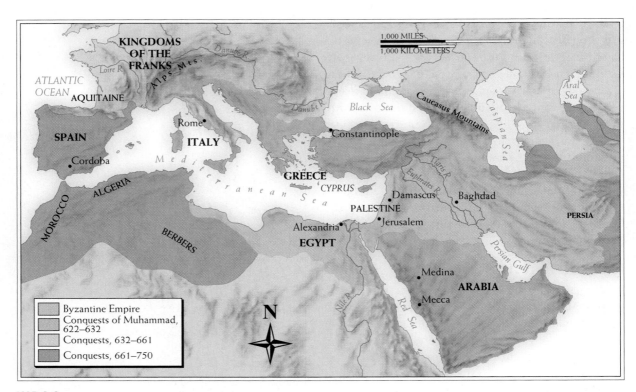

MAP 6–3

Muslim Conquests and Domination of the Mediterranean to about 750 C.E.   Within 125 years of Muhammad's rise, Muslims came to dominate Spain and all areas south and east of the Mediterranean.

HOW WERE Muslims able to dominate much of the area east and south of the Mediterranean within 125 years of Muhammad's rise?

study of medicine in Europe relied primarily on the works of the ancient physicians Hippocrates and Galen, the Baghdad physician Al-Razi, and the Muslim philosophers Avicenna (980–1037) and Averröes (1126–1198), Islam's greatest authorities on Aristotle. Multilingual Jewish scholars helped make the translations that bridged the gap between the Muslim and Christian worlds. The medieval Arabs also gave the West one of its most popular books: *The Arabian Nights*, poetic folk tales that are still read and imitated in the West.

WESTERN SOCIETY AND THE DEVELOPING CHRISTIAN CHURCH

HOW DID the developing Christian Church influence Western society during the early Middle Ages?

Facing barbarian invasions from the north and east and a strong Islamic presence in the Mediterranean, the West found itself in decline in the fifth and sixth centuries. In the seventh century, the Byzantine emperors, their hands full with the Islamic threat in the East, were unable to assert themselves in the West. Mediterranean shipping declined, compelling urban populations to seek employment and protection in the countryside on the estates of landholders. In short, western Europeans were developing a distinctive culture of their own.

Amidst these social changes, the Christian church remained firmly entrenched and became increasingly powerful. Like the imperial Roman administration, its governing structure was centralized and hierarchical. As Roman governors withdrew, bishops and cathedral chapters filled the vacuum of authority: The local cathedral became the center of urban life, the local bishop the highest local authority, and in Rome, the pope took control as the western emperors gradually departed and died out. The Christian church became the best repository of Roman administrative skills and classical culture, even as its deep involvement in secular affairs cost the church some of its spiritual integrity. It was a potent civilizing and unifying force, with a religious message of providential purpose and individual worth that could give solace and meaning to life at its worst. The church's ritual of baptism and its creed, or statement of belief, unified people across the traditional barriers of social class, education, and gender.

MONASTIC CULTURE

The early medieval church drew much of its strength from its monasteries. The first monks were Christians who fled the cities of the Roman Empire to live as hermits in the wilderness. They could not accept the fact that Christian life became safe and easy after Constantine endorsed the church, for they believed faith required them to witness against the world. Because martyrdom by the state was no longer a choice, they opted for harsh environments and ascetic disciplines that made their lives a kind of living martyrdom. The sufferings they embraced as a witness to faith made them the church's new heroes.

Medieval Christians viewed monastic life—governed, as it was, by the biblical "counsels of perfection" (the practice of chastity, poverty, and obedience)—as humanity's highest calling. Monks—and eventually the secular, or parish, clergy whom popular opinion forced to adopt some monastic disciplines—were expected to meet higher spiritual standards than ordinary Christians. Consequently, clergy came to be respected as superior to laity, a belief that served the papacy well in struggles with secular rulers.

The monastic movement was inspired by the lives of hermits, such as Anthony of Egypt (ca. 251–356), but monks soon abandoned solitude and formed communal institutions. Anthony's contemporary and fellow countryman, Pachomius (ca. 286–346), founded a highly regimented community in which hundreds of monks lived in accordance with a strict code. The form of monasticism that spread throughout the East, however, followed rules laid down by Basil the Great (329–379). It urged monks to focus less on personal asceticism and more on caring for the needy outside their communities.

The monastic practices evolving in the East were introduced to the West by Athanasius (ca. 293–373) and Martin of Tours (ca. 315–ca. 399), but it was a rule (constitution) written in 529 by Benedict of Nursia (ca. 480–547) for a monastery he established at Monte Cassino near Naples, Italy, that set the standard for the West. The Benedictine Rule discouraged the kind of flamboyant asceticism popular in the East. It decreed a daily schedule that governed a monk's every activity. It provided for adequate food, some wine, serviceable clothing, proper amounts of sleep, and opportunities for relaxation. Time was set aside each day for prayer, communal worship, study, and the manual labor by which monks supported themselves. The objective was to create autonomous religious communities that were economically, spiritually, and intellectually self-sufficient. Benedictine monks did not, however, turn their backs on the world. They were chiefly responsible for the missionary work that converted England and Germany to Christianity, and they kept civilization alive in Europe during the darkest of the Dark Ages. (See "History's Voices: The Benedicture Order Sets Its Requirements for Entrance.")

7.2
Benedict of Nursia: *The Rule of St. Benedict*

HISTORY'S VOICES

THE BENEDICTINE ORDER SETS ITS REQUIREMENTS FOR ENTRANCE

The religious life had great appeal in a time of political and social uncertainty. Entrance into a monastery was not, however, escapism. Much was demanded of the new monk, both during and after his probationary period, which is described here. Benedict's contribution was to prescribe a balanced blend of religious, physical, and intellectual activities within a well-structured community.

WHAT ARE Benedict's reasons for not allowing a monk to change his mind and leave the cloister, once vows have been taken?

When anyone is newly come for the reformation of his life, let him not be granted an easy entrance, but, as the Apostle says, "Test the spirits to see whether they are from God." If the newcomer, therefore, perseveres in his knocking, and if it is seen after four or five days that he bears patiently the harsh treatment offered him and the difficulty of admission, and that he persists in his petition, then let entrance be granted him, and let him stay in the guest house for a few days.

After that let him live in the novitiate, where the novices study, eat, and sleep. A senior shall be assigned to them who is skilled in winning souls, to watch over them with the utmost care. Let him exam-ine whether the novice is truly seeking God, and whether he is zealous for the Work of God, for obedience and for humiliations. Let the novice be told all the hard and rugged ways by which the journey to God is made.

If he promises stability and perseverance, then at the end of two months let this Rule be read through to him, and let him be addressed thus: "Here is the law under which you wish to fight. If you can observe it, enter; if you cannot, you are free to depart." If he still stands firm, let him be taken to the above-mentioned novitiate and again tested in all patience. And after the lapse of six months let the Rule be read to him, that he may know on what he is entering. And if he still remains firm, after four months let the same Rule be read to him again.

Then, having deliberated with himself, if he promises to keep it in its entirety and to observe everything that is commanded him, let him be received into the community. But let him understand that, according to the law of the Rule, from that day forward he may not leave the monastery nor withdraw his neck from under the yoke of the Rule which he was free to refuse or to accept during that prolonged deliberation.

St. Benedict's Rule for Monasteries, trans. by Leonard J. Doyle (Collegeville, MN.: Liturgical Press, 1948), pp. 79–80.

THE DOCTRINE OF PAPAL PRIMACY

The eastern emperors treated the church like a department of state. They intervened in its theological debates and chose its leaders. After the fifth century, however, the bishop of Rome had no emperor to contend with. He could assert "papal primacy" and claim leadership of a church that had a right to be totally independent of the state.

Papal primacy became an issue as early as 381, when the ecumenical Council of Constantinople declared the patriarch of Constantinople to be first in rank after the bishop of Rome. Pope Damasus I (366–384) objected and claimed that the Roman see's unique "apostolic" status meant its bishop had no peer. He was heir to the legacy of the Apostle Peter, the "rock" on which Jesus said the church was built (Matthew 16:18). In 451, the Council of Chalcedon ignored this and recognized the Byzantine patriarch as having the same primacy over the East that Rome traditionally had over the West. Pope Leo I (440–461) declared his belief that his office was superior to that of all other bishops by assuming the ancient Roman title *pontifex maximus* ("supreme priest"). At the end of the fifth century, Pope Gelasius I (492–496) made an even more extreme claim. He decreed that papal authority was "more weighty" than that of secular governments, for the church was responsible for the most serious human concern, salvation.

Constantinople's power to influence the papacy faded in proportion to its declining fortunes in Italy. The emperor Justinian had driven the Ostrogoths out and returned Italy to Byzantine control, but late in the sixth century, Lombard tribes crossed the Alps and forced the Byzantines to retreat. Having no alternative, Pope Gregory I, "the Great" (590–604), ignored the eastern emperor and negotiated an independent peace treaty with the Lombards.

THE RELIGIOUS DIVISION OF CHRISTENDOM

In both East and West, religious belief alternately served and undermined imperial political unity. In 391, Christianity became the official faith of the Eastern empire, while all other religions and sects were deemed "demented and insane." Since the fifth century, the patriarch of Constantinople had blessed Byzantine emperors, attesting to the close ties between rulers and the Eastern Church. Between the fourth and sixth centuries, the patriarchs of Constantinople, Alexandria, Antioch, and Jerusalem received generous endowments of land and gold from rich, pious donors, empowering the church to act as the state's welfare agency. However, from time to time rulers supported Christian heresies, and Christianity was compelled to absorb and adapt to certain local pagan practices and beliefs.

The empire was also home, albeit inhospitably, to large numbers of Jews. Pagan Romans viewed Jews as narrow, dogmatic, and intolerant but tolerated Judaism as an ancient and acceptable form of worship. When Rome adopted Christianity, Jews retained this legal protection as long as they did not attempt to convert Christians, build new synagogues, or try to hold certain positions or enter some professions. Neither persuasion, such as tax breaks, nor coercion succeeded in converting the empire's Jews.

The differences between Eastern and Western Christianity grew to be no less irreconcilable than those between Christians and Jews. One issue even divided Justinian and his wife Theodora. The former was strictly orthodox in belief, but Theodora supported a divisive teaching that the Council of Chalcedon in 451 had condemned as heresy, namely, that Christ had a single, immortal nature and was not both eternal God and mortal man in one and the same person. The **Monophysites**—believers in the single nature—became a separate church in eastern lands, from Armenia to Egypt.

A similar dispute appeared in Eastern debates over the relationship among the members of the Trinity, specifically whether the Holy Spirit proceeded only from the Father, as the Nicene–Constantinopolitan Creed taught, or from the Father and the Son (*filioque* in Latin), an idea that became increasingly popular in the West and was eventually adopted by the Western church and inserted into its creed. Eastern theologians argued that adding filioque to the creed weakened a core Christian belief—the divine unity and dignity of all three persons of the Trinity.

Another major rift between the Christian East and West took place over the veneration of images in worship. In 726, Emperor Leo III (r. 717–741) forbade the use of images and icons that portrayed Christ, the Virgin Mary, and the saints. Veneration had been commonplace for centuries, therefore the decree came as a shock. The change in policy, called **iconoclasm**, probably had several

Monophysites Believers in a single, immortal nature of Christ; not both eternal God and mortal man in one and the same person.

iconoclasm Opposition to the use of images in Christian worship.

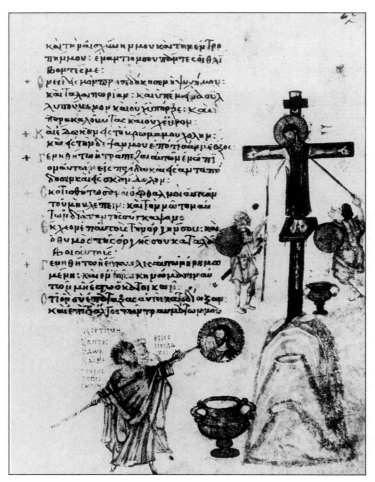

A ninth-century Byzantine manuscript shows an iconoclast whiting out an image of Christ. The Iconoclastic Controversy was an important factor in the division of Christendom into separate Latin and Greek branches.

State Historical Museum, Moscow

motivations, in particular the emperor's wish to accommodate Muslim sensitivities while at war with the Arabs (Islam strictly forbade making images, deeming it the exclusive preserve of Allah). Leo's decree drove the popes closer to the Franks to seek protection from iconoclasm. In the end, veneration of images was eventually restored in the Eastern churches.

A third difference between East and West was the Eastern emperors' pretension to absolute sovereignty, both secular and religious. Expressing their sense of sacred mission, the emperors presented themselves in the trappings of holiness and directly interfered in matters of church and religions, what is called **Caesaropapism**, or the emperor acting as if he were pope as well as caesar. To a degree unknown in the West, Eastern emperors appointed and manipulated the clergy, convening church councils and enforcing church decrees. By comparison, the West nurtured a distinction between church and state that became visible in the eleventh century.

The Eastern church also rejected several disputed requirements of Roman Christianity. It denied the existence of Purgatory, permitted lay divorce and remarriage, allowed priests, but not bishops, to marry, and conducted religious services in the languages that people in a given locality actually spoke (the so-called "vernacular" languages) instead of Greek and Latin. In these matters Eastern Christians gained opportunities and rights that Christians in the West would not enjoy, and then only in part, until the Protestant Reformation in the sixteenth century. (See Chapter 11.)

Over time, these differences ultimately resulted in a schism between the two churches in 1054, when a Western envoy of the pope visited the Patriarch of Constantinople, hoping to overcome the differences. The patriarch was not welcoming, and after mutual recriminations, before leaving the city, the papal envoy left a bull of excommunication on the altar of Hagia Sophia. In response, the patriarch proclaimed Western popes to be heretics. Attempts to heal the schism have since been made, including an ecumenical gesture in 1965, but such official pronouncements have not overcome the many religious and cultural differences between Eastern and Western Christianity.

THE KINGDOM OF THE FRANKS

MEROVINGIANS AND CAROLINGIANS: FROM CLOVIS TO CHARLEMAGNE

A chieftain named Clovis (ca. 466?–511), from the tribe of the Franks, founded the German dynasty that first attempted to pull Europe back together. Clovis united the Salian and Ripuarian Franks, subdued the Burgundians and Visigoths, won the support of the native Gallo-Romans by converting to orthodox Christianity, and turned the Roman province of Gaul into France ("land of the Franks").

HOW DID the reign of Clovis differ from that of Charlemagne?

Caesaropapism Emperor acting as if he were pope as well as caesar.

Governing the Franks   Clovis and his descendants, the Merovingian kings, struggled with the perennial problem of medieval politics: balancing the claims of the "one" against those of the "many." As kings worked to centralize governments, powerful local magnates fought to preserve their regional autonomy. The result was a battle between the forces of societal unification and fragmentation.

The Merovingian kings tried to pull their kingdom together by making pacts with the landed nobility and utilizing a new kind of royal official, the count. Counts were assigned authority over districts in which they held no personal land. This made them easier to control than the local aristocrats who commanded the loyalty of the people living on their estates. As time passed, however, counts established hereditary claims to their offices and effectively asserted their independence. The unification of the Frankish state was further impeded by Frankish inheritance customs, which gave all a king's legitimate male heirs a right to a share in his kingdom.

By the seventh century, the Merovingian king was king in title only. Real executive authority had devolved on his chief minister, the "mayor of the palace." The family of Pepin I of Austrasia (d. 639) monopolized this office until 751, when his descendant, Pepin III (with the pope's support), deposed the last Merovingian. Pepin's ascension to the Frankish throne inaugurated the Carolingian dynasty.

Pepin III's kingdom rested on a firm foundation laid by his predecessor, Charles "Martel" ("Hammer"; d. 741). Charles built a powerful cavalry by granting **fiefs** or benefices ("lands") to men to fund their equipment and service. His army proved its worth at Poitiers in 732, when it stopped the Muslim advance and secured the Pyrenees Mountains as Christendom's western frontier. Much of

fiefs   ("Lands") Granted to cavalry men to fund their equipment and service.

the land that Martel distributed to his soldiers came from the church. The church needed the protection of the Franks, and it could not prevent the confiscation of property used to fund its defense. Eventually, however, the church was partially compensated for its losses.

Where the Merovingians had tried to weaken the aristocrats by raising landless men to power, the Carolingians forged an alliance with the landed aristocracy and staffed their government almost entirely from its ranks. By playing to strength rather than challenging it, the Carolingians secured their position—at least in the short run.

The Frankish Church   The church played a major role in the Frankish government, for its monasteries were the intellectual centers of Carolingian society. The higher clergy were employed in tandem with counts as royal agents, and Christian missionaries helped pacify barbarian elements in new lands the Carolingians added to their domain. Conversion to orthodox Christianity was considered essential for the assimilation of new subjects.

The missions of the church and state tended to be confused when the king appointed Christian bishops to political offices, and the lines between the two institutions were also blurred by the arrangements that created the Carolingian dynasty. In 751, Pope Zacharias (741–752) sanctioned the deposition of the last of the Merovingian puppet kings and dispatched Boniface (ca. 680–754), an Anglo-Saxon missionary monk, to preside at Pepin III's coronation. As part of the ceremony, Boniface may have anointed Pepin, a ritual that gave the Carolingian monarchy a sacred character.

If the pope shared sacred authority with the Frankish king, the king returned the favor by bolstering the secular authority of the pope. In 753, Pepin took an army into Italy to help Zacharias's successor, Pope Stephen II (752–757), drive the Lombards back from Rome. In 755, the victorious Franks confirmed the pope as the secular ruler of central Italy, a region that came to be called the **Papal States**.

The Franks drew almost as slight a boundary between state and church as did the eastern emperors, and the papacy wanted to guard against domination of the church by its new German protector. About this time (750–800), a document called the *Donation of Constantine* appeared in the papal archives. It said that in gratitude for recovery from an illness Constantine had given the western half of his empire to the pope. This implied that the church had a certain precedence over the state in the West. The *Donation* was exposed as a forgery in the fifteenth century.

THE REIGN OF CHARLEMAGNE (768–814)

In 774, Charlemagne, the son of Pepin the Short, completed his father's work by conquering Italy's Lombards and assuming their crown. He devoted much of his reign to wars of conquest. The Saxons of northern Germany were brutally subdued. The Muslims were pushed a bit south of the Pyrenees, and the Avars (a tribe related to the Huns) were practically annihilated, bringing the Danubian plains into the Frankish orbit. By the time of Charlemagne's death (January 28, 814), he ruled modern France, Belgium, Holland, Switzerland, almost the whole of western Germany, much of Italy, a portion of Spain, and the island of Corsica. (See Map 6–4.)

The New Empire   Charlemagne believed his huge domain merited his assumption of the imperial title, and he did all he could to bolster the legitimacy of his claim. Because ancient Roman and contemporary Byzantine emperors ruled from fixed capitals, he constructed a palace city at Aachen (Aix-la-Chapelle), and like a Byzantine emperor, he intervened in the affairs of the church.

Papal States   Central part of Italy where Pope Stephen II became the secular ruler when confirmed by the Franks in 755.

MAP 6–4

The Empire of Charlemagne to 814   Building on the successes of his predecessors, Charlemagne greatly increased the Frankish domains. Such traditional enemies as the Saxons and the Lombards fell under his sway.

WHAT REASONS might Charlemagne have had for expanding the Frankish domains into the regions in which he did?

Charlemagne's imperial pretensions were confirmed on Christmas Day, 800, when Pope Leo III (795–816) crowned him emperor. The ceremony, which established a fateful link between Germany and Italy (the future **Holy Roman Empire**), was an attempt by the pope to gain some leverage over his powerful king. By arranging for the emperor to receive the crown from his hands, the pope set a precedent that was useful for the church in its future dealings with the state. At the time, however, Charlemagne's authority was in no way compromised. Even the eastern emperors reluctantly acknowledged his title.

Holy Roman Empire   The domain of the German monarchs who revived the use of the Roman imperial title during the Middle Ages.

6.7
The Book of Emperors and Kings: Charlemagne and Pope Leo III

The New Emperor   At a height of six feet three and one-half inches (his remains were exhumed and measured in 1861), Charlemagne literally towered over his contemporaries. His personality matched his physique. He was vigorous, restless, and gregarious—ever ready for a hunt or for a swim with his friends in Aachen's hot springs. He was known for his practical jokes, lusty humor, and hospitality. Foreign diplomats flocked to his festive court to do him honor. The most splendid of their gifts was probably the war elephant that the caliph of Baghdad, Harun-al-Rashid, sent him in 802.

Charlemagne had five official wives (in succession), many mistresses and concubines, and numerous children. This connubial variety caused some political problems. Pepin, his oldest son by his first marriage, grew jealous of the attention he showed the sons of his second wife and launched an ill-fated rebellion against his father. It was put down, and he was confined to a monastery for the rest of his life.

Problems of Government   Charlemagne employed about 250 counts in the administration of his empire. A count was usually a local magnate rich enough to support some soldiers of his own. Royal generosity persuaded him and his men to serve the king. A count defended territory, maintained order, collected dues, and administered justice in the king's name. The count's district law court (the *mallus*) delivered verdicts based less on evidence than on the reputations witnesses had for truthfulness. When witness testimony was insufficient, the court had recourse to duels or tests called *ordeals*. A defendant's hand might be immersed in boiling water and his innocence determined by the way his wounds healed. Or a suspect might be bound with ropes and thrown into a river or pond that had been blessed by a priest. If the water rejected him and he floated, he was assumed guilty. Once guilt was determined, the *mallus* ordered monetary compensation to be paid to injured parties. This settled grievances that otherwise might have sparked long bloody vendettas.

Charlemagne never solved the problem of adequately policing the men who served him. His counts, like their Merovingian predecessors, tended to become despots within their districts. Charlemagne issued *capitularies* (royal decrees) that defined the policies he wanted his administrators to follow. He sent envoys, the *missi dominici*, to check up on the counts and report back on their behavior. When the *missi*'s infrequent inspections had little effect, he appointed provincial governors (prefects, dukes, and margraves) to keep permanent watch over the counts. They, however, were no more trustworthy than the counts.

Charlemagne often appointed churchmen to government offices, for bishops were considered royal servants. This had little effect on the character of his administration, for the higher clergy shared the secular lifestyles and aspirations of the counts. They were generally indistinguishable from the lay nobility. To be a Christian at this difficult period in the history of Europe was largely a matter of submitting to rituals such as baptism and assenting to creeds. Both clergy and laity were too preoccupied with the struggle to survive to burden themselves with ethical scruples.

Alcuin and the Carolingian Renaissance   Charlemagne tried to improve the government of his empire by providing educations for the aristocratic boys who were destined for offices in the church and state. He attracted scholars from Spain, Ireland, and England as well as his own lands to staff his palace school. Alcuin of York (735–804), an Anglo-Saxon educator, supervised the development of a curriculum dedicated to giving students a grounding in grammar, logic, rhetoric, and simple mathematics—the tools of the career bureaucrat.

Although the aspirations of Charlemagne's scholars were modest, they constituted a true renaissance—a "rebirth" of intellectual activity. Alcuin and his colleagues halted the deterioration of Latin (the only written language). They improved communications by standardizing the use of a new legible style of handwriting called Carolingian "minuscule." They collected, restored, and copied ancient manuscripts. Alcuin worked on the text of the Bible and produced editions of the works of Gregory the Great and Benedict's rule. They reformed the church's liturgy, and they elevated standards for the clergy.

BREAKUP OF THE CAROLINGIAN KINGDOM

As Charlemagne aged and his vigilance diminished, his empire became progressively ungovernable. In feudal society the strength of a man's commitment to his lord depended on how near or how far away his lord was. People obeyed local leaders more readily than distant kings. Poor communications meant that Charlemagne had to grant a great deal of autonomous authority to the men who held the far-flung regions of his empire for him, and their power diminished his. The noble tail tended to wag the royal dog.

Louis the Pious   Charlemagne began the process of persuading the Germans that, as subjects of a unified empire, they were more than followers of regional and tribal leaders. However, his successor, his only surviving son, Louis the Pious (r. 814–840), was unable to maintain the unity of the empire. Louis had three sons by his first wife, and according to Salic law (the law of the Salian Franks), each was entitled to a share of his estate. Louis tried to break with tradition by recognizing his eldest son, Lothar (d. 855), as co-regent and sole imperial heir (817). In 823, however, Louis's second wife bore him a fourth son, Charles "the Bald" (d. 877). To secure an inheritance for this boy, she urged her stepsons, Pepin and Louis the German, to rebel and force their father to revise his will. The pope backed them, and they defeated their father in a battle near Colmar in 833.

The Treaty of Verdun and Its Aftermath   Pepin's death in 838 cleared one contender from the field, and in 843 the Treaty of Verdun divided the Carolingian empire among the three remaining princes. Lothar inherited the empty honor of the imperial title and a region called Lotharingia (roughly modern Holland, Belgium, Switzerland, Alsace-Lorraine, and Italy). France fell to Charles the Bald, and Germany to Louis the German.

The Treaty of Verdun was only the start of the division of the Carolingian lands. When Lothar died in 855, his "middle kingdom" was split up among his three sons. The much larger eastern and western Frankish kingdoms of France and Germany then seized portions of Lothar's legacy, and Carolingian power in Italy evaporated. The pope tried to fill the political vacuum this created, but developments were afoot that were about to turn popes and kings into petty figures and deliver Europe into the hands of the feudal nobility.

Carolingian cavalry, from a ninth-century Swiss manuscript.
Mansell Collection/Timepix/Getty Images, Inc.

Major Developments of the Early Middle Ages

313	Emperor Constantine legalizes Christianity
ca. 251–356	Anthony of Egypt inspires the monastic movement
410	Visigoths sack the city of Rome
476	Deposition of Romulus Augustulus, last western Roman emperor
ca. 466–511	Clovis founds the Franks' Merovingian dynasty
527–565	Reign of Byzantine emperor Justinian
622	Muhammad's *Hegira*, the foundation of Islam
732	Charles Martel stops the Muslim advance at Tours
751	Pepin III founds the Carolingian dynasty
768–814	Reign of Charlemagne
ca. 875–950	Invasions, feudal fragmentation, and the Dark Ages

This 75-foot-long Viking burial ship from the early ninth century is decorated with beastly figures. It bore a dead queen, her servant, and assorted sacrificed animals to the afterlife. The bodies of the passengers were confined within a burial cabin at mid-ship surrounded with a treasure trove of jewels and tapestries.
© Museum of CulturalHistory-University of Oslo, Norway

The last quarter of the ninth and the first half of the tenth centuries can accurately be characterized as Europe's Dark Ages. The gains that had been made in restoring political and religious institutions were lost as Europe confronted a second wave of invasions. Vikings (Normans, or North-men) descended from Scandinavia. Magyars (Hungarians from the plains of Russia) charged up the Danube Valley, and Muslims based in Sicily and Africa raided Italy and southern France. Kings and centralized governments could not move quickly enough to defend large territories that were simultaneously attacked from multiple directions. As their subjects turned to local strongmen for protection, political fragmentation spread.

The Vikings posed the most serious threat. They raided Europe's coasts, and their shallow-draft ships navigated its rivers to reach targets deep inland. They moved rapidly and struck randomly, making it hard to devise a strategy to defend against them. Leaders built forts and castles to which their people could flee when danger threatened. Sometimes they bribed raiders to withdraw. France's king created a duchy of Normandy for one group of Vikings in the hope they would fight off others.

VIKINGS, MAGYARS, AND MUSLIMS

At this point in European history—the late 800s and early 900s—one may speak with particular justification of a "dark age." These years saw successive waves of Normans (North-men), or Vikings, from Scandinavia; Magyars, or Hungarians, the great horsemen from the eastern plains; and Muslims from the south. The Vikings both traded and raided, and in the 880s even penetrated to Aachen and besieged Paris. They made York, England, a major trading post and traveled to Newfoundland and perhaps even to New England. The Magyars swept into Western Europe from the eastern plains, while Muslims made incursions across the Mediterranean from North Africa. In the resulting turmoil, local populations in Europe became more dependent than ever on local strongmen for life, limb, and livelihood—the essential precondition for the maturation of feudal society.

FEUDAL SOCIETY

*T*he inability of their formal governments to protect them meant medieval people had to make the private arrangements characteristic of feudalism. As the weaker submitted to the stronger, the medieval world fragmented and reorganized.

Feudal society was held together by personal oaths—by pledges to serve someone in exchange for protection or maintenance. Men who were tapped as soldiers took oaths of vassalage that bound them to warlords who granted them fiefs. They became members of a professional military fraternity governed by a code of knightly conduct. In the absence of any other authority, they assumed the right to govern the people who lived on their lands, and their personal relationships were the primary things that structured society.

ORIGINS

Beginning in the sixth and seventh centuries, the weakness of the West's governments forced freemen, who could not fend for themselves, to seek alliances with more powerful neighbors. Those who entered into contractual relations that

WHAT WERE the characteristics of a feudal society?

made them dependent on others were called **vassal**, collectively as *vassi* ("those who serve"). Owners of large estates (lords) acquired as many vassals as they could afford to equip as soldiers for their private armies. At first, they maintained their vassals in their households. But as numbers of vassals grew, this became impractical. The collapse of the economy caused money to disappear from circulation, so the only way to pay vassals was to grant them the right to use a piece of their lord's land to maintain themselves. This grant was called a *fief* or *benefice*. Vassals lived on their fiefs and were responsible for the peasants who farmed them.

VASSALAGE AND THE FIEF

A vassal swore fealty to his lord. That meant he promised to serve his lord and to refrain from actions contrary to his lord's interests. His chief function was that of a knight. Bargaining determined the specific terms of his military service, but custom limited the number of days his lord could keep him in the field. (In France in the eleventh century, forty days was standard.) A vassal was also expected to attend his lord's court when summoned and to render his lord financial assistance at times of special need: (1) to ransom him from his enemies, (2) to outfit him for a major military campaign, and (3) to defray the costs of the festivities at the marriage of a daughter or the knighting of a son.

Louis the Pious extended vassalage beyond the lay nobility to the higher clergy. He required bishops and abbots to swear fealty and to accept their appointments on the same terms as the fiefs given knights. He formally "invested" clerics with the rings and staffs that symbolized their spiritual offices. This practice was offensive to the church, for it implied the subservience of the church to the state. In the late tenth and eleventh centuries, reform-minded clergy refused to submit to "lay investiture," but they never considered surrendering the grants of land that were the rewards for oaths of homage.

A lord was obliged to protect his vassal from physical harm, to stand as his advocate in court, and to provide for his maintenance by giving him a fief. In Carolingian times a fief varied in size from a small villa to several *mansi* (a unit of 25 to 48 acres). Royal vassals might receive fiefs of 30 to 200 *mansi*. Prizes of this size made vassalage acceptable to the highest classes in Carolingian society. In the short run, oaths of vassalage marshaled the nobility behind the king. But in the long run, grants of fiefs undercut royal power, for kings found it difficult or impossible to reclaim land once it was granted to a vassal.

DAILY LIFE AND RELIGION

The Humble Carolingian Manor   Early medieval Europe's chief economic institution was a communal farm called a **manor**. Medieval farmers often preferred to cluster in villages rather than to live on individual farms. This provided security, but it also enabled them to share labor and the costs of expensive plows and oxen. The residents of a manor farmed communally, but they did not divide their harvests equally. Each family on a manor had specific fields assigned to it and lived from what grew on its land.

The status of peasants was determined by the nature of their holdings. A freeman had allodial property (land free from the claims of an overlord). A man who surrendered his land to a lord in exchange for protection became a **serf**. He received land back from his lord, but with a new set of rights and obligations. He had a right to stay on the land in exchange for working his lord's *demesne*, the

A seventh-century portrayal of a vassal, who kneels before his lord and inserts his hands between those of his lord in a gesture of mutual loyalty: the vassal promising to obey and serve his lord, the lord promising to support and protect his vassal.

Spanish School (7th century). Lord and vassal, decorated page (vellum). Archivo de la Corona de Aragon, Barcelona, Spain. Index/bridgeman Art Library

vassal   A person granted an estate or cash payments in return for rendering services to a lord.

manor   Communal farm considered to be early medieval Europe's chief economic institution.

serf   Peasant bound to the land he worked.

fields on the manor that produced the crops meant for the lord's table. Peasants who brought little property with them when they entered a lord's service became unfree serfs. They were more vulnerable to a lord's demands, often spending up to three days a week working his fields. Peasants who had nothing to offer but labor had the lowest status and were the least protected from exploitation.

A new type of plow came into use during the Carolingian era. It was heavy enough to break up the dense, waterlogged soils of northern Europe and work land that had defeated Roman farmers. Unlike the ancient "scratch" plow (a pointed stick), it cut deeply and had a moldboard that turned the earth over and utilized more of its fertility. Ancient farmers used a two-field system of cultivation to maintain the fertility of their fields. That is, they divided their land in half, and alternatively planted one half and left the other fallow. (A fallow field was plowed but not planted.) Medieval farmers developed a **three-field system** that was more productive. In the fall, one field was planted with winter crops of wheat or rye, which were harvested in early summer. In late spring, a second field was planted with summer crops of oats, barley, lentils, and legumes, which were harvested in August or September. The third field was left fallow. This arrangement limited the amount of nonproductive plowing, used crop rotation to restore soil fertility, and provided backup crops should one harvest fail. (See "Encountering the Past: Medieval Cooking.")

The Cure of Carolingian Souls   The masses of ordinary people who were burdened, fearful, and devoid of the hope of improving their lots this side of eternity sought comfort and consolation in religion. Privilege rendered the upper classes no less pious. Charlemagne frequented the Church of Saint Mary in Aachen several times a day, and his will decreed that most of his estate be used to fund masses and prayers for his soul.

The lower clergy, the parish priests who served the people, were poorly prepared to provide spiritual leadership. Lords owned the churches on their lands and staffed them with priests recruited from their serfs. The church expected a lord to liberate a serf who was ordained to the priesthood, but many such priests said mass on Sunday and toiled as peasants during the rest of the week.

Because priests on most manors were no better educated than their congregations, religious instruction barely existed. For most people religion was more a matter of practice than doctrine. They baptized their children, attended mass, tried to learn to recite the Lord's Prayer and the Apostles' Creed, and received the last rites when death approached. They were in awe of sacred relics and the saints who they hoped would intercede for them with their divine overlord in the court of heaven. Simple faith had little need for understanding.

FRAGMENTATION AND DIVIDED LOYALTY

A vassal who had sufficient land could portion out his fief and create vassals of his own. It was also possible for a vassal to accept fiefs from more than one lord. The concept of the "liege lord," the master to whom a vassal owed primary duty, evolved in the ninth century. This helped avoid confusion, but it did not halt progressive fragmentation of land and loyalty.

Kings were weakened by the fact that vassals tended to establish rights to the fiefs they were granted. Ownership of a fief technically remained with the lord who granted it, but it was hard for a lord to prevent a vassal's heir from inheriting that fief. In the ninth century, the hereditary rights of vassals were legally recognized. This confirmed the nobility's hold on their fiefs and led to their gradual appropriation of much of the royal domain.

three-field system   Developed by medieval farmers, a system in which three fields were utilized during different growing seasons to limit the amount of nonproductive plowing and to restore soil fertility through crop rotation.

ENCOUNTERING THE PAST

MEDIEVAL COOKING

Medieval cooks served things that modern diners would recognize: roasts, pastas, meat pies, and custards. But where modern chefs are preoccupied primarily with the taste of their fare, medieval cooks worried about the effect of their dishes on diners' health. Medieval physicians traced illness to imbalances among the so-called four humors: blood, black bile, yellow bile, and phlegm. Because the humors were generated by food, recipes had to be planned like medicines. Health depended on maintaining a balance between the poles of the opposites that the humors nurtured: wet–dry, cold–warm. If not moderated by cool, wet seasonings, a spicy dish might produce an excess of hot, dry humors that made one ill.

Medieval people correctly intuited a link between diet and health, but from the modern point of view this did them little good. A fixation on meat as a prestige food meant vegetables were little appreciated. Most Europeans survived on a diet of mush or a porridge made by boiling bread in milk.

Medieval cooks were expected to be artists as well as scientists. Formal dining called for elaborately constructed dishes, such as castles executed in pastry or cooked birds stuffed back into their feathered skins. Dishes were sometimes tinted strange colors, modeled into odd shapes, or rendered otherwise amusing to the eye.

DID THE medieval understanding of the link between diet and health differ from the modern understanding—or was only the explanation different?

[Top] **The Lord of the Manor Dining.**
By permission of The British Library (10001020–021)

[Bottom] **Kitchen Scene; Chopping Meat.**
By permission of The British Library (1000278–001)

Feudal ties were contractual relationships, but because few medieval laymen could read, contracts of vassalage had to be oral agreements. Specific ritual acts evolved to make the terms of what was being promised clear to everyone. A freeman became a vassal by an "act of commendation," by swearing an oath of fealty to a superior. In the mid–eighth century, the solemnity of the oath was enhanced by having the vassal swear with his hand on a sacred relic or a Bible. By the tenth and eleventh centuries, it had become customary for the vassal to take his oath with his hands cupped between those of his lord and for the two men to ratify their agreement with a kiss.

Despite feudalism's obvious vulnerability to abuse and confusion, the order it maintained made it possible for Europeans to rebuild their societies. The genius of feudal government lay in its adaptability. Contracts of different kinds could be made with almost anyone to serve almost any purpose. As lords and vassals fine-tuned their feudal arrangements, they reconstructed foundations for centralized government and for Europe's modern nation-states.

IMAGE KEY
for pages 146–147

a. Mohammed, Abu Bakr and Ali travel to the Ukaz Fair, from Siyar-i Nabi (Life of the Prophet) IV. 2, f. 132v.

b. Reproduction of St. Matthew and an Illuminated Initial Page from Codex 51, Latin Gospels, ca. 700–899

c. Reproduction of Crucifixion and Commencement of Penitentiale from Codex 1395, Latin Gospels 9th century

d., f., j. Tesserae—Brick tiles used to make mosaics found at Tockenham, UK

e. Saint Gregory the Great, shown here in a monastic scriptorium (an area devoted to copying and preserving books) Kunsthistorisches Museum, Wien oder KHM, Wien

g. A Qadi hears a case Bibliotheque Nationale de France, Paris

h. Coronation of Charlemagne at St. Peter's by Pope Leo III Grandes Chroniques de France, fol. 106r. Musee Goya, Castres, France. Giraudon/Art Resource, NY

i. The Court of Empress Theodora. Byzantine early christian mosaic. San Vitale, Ravenna, Italy, ca. 547

k. Byzantine (476–1453). The inner compartment of the reliquary of the True Cross. Constantinople, c.960 C.E. Treasury, Cathedral, Limburg an der Lahn, Germany

l. "The Lord of the Manor dining"

SUMMARY

On the Eve of the Frankish Ascendancy In the late fourth century, the western empire was weakening, and the Visigoths were being forced out of their own home territories by invading Huns. The Visigoths defeated the Romans in the ensuing conflict. Soon other barbarians had established territories within the Western empire. By the mid–fifth century, Rome had been sacked repeatedly, and by the end of the century the Western empire was history. Roman culture endured, although it was transformed through its contact with the Germanic peoples. Christianity, too, endured and changed through cultural contact.

The Byzantine Empire The eastern portion of the Roman Empire endured as the Byzantine Empire. Although the empire lasted until Constantinople (the capital) fell to the Turks in 1453, it peaked under Justinian, in the mid–sixth century. Although Justinian and his wife, the empress Theodora, were both Christians, she was a believer in Monophysitism, a heresy that influenced the later course of the empire's history. Justinian codified Roman law, which was to prove influential in the West for centuries. Justinian supported Orthodox Christianity, although some of his successors supported other forms of Christianity. Constantinople and smaller urban centers formed the economic, administrative, and cultural backbone of the empire. The empire's eastern orientation increased under Heraclius in the early seventh century. In the early eighth century, Leo's Caesaropapism led him to attempt to ban the use of images in churches.

Islam and the Islamic World In the seventh century, Muhammad founded a new religion on the Arabian peninsula. In 624, Muhammad's Medina-based army conquered Mecca, and in the following years the basic rules of Islamic life were articulated. Islam expanded substantially, until by 750 the Islamic Empire stretched from Spain through North Africa, the southern and eastern Mediterranean, and eastward into India. But this was the peak of Muslim territorial expansion, and Islam did not spread farther than Spain into the remnants of the Western Roman Empire. The West profited from its contact with Islam, since much of the Arab world's technology and scholarship was superior to Europe's in the early Middle Ages.

Western Society and the Developing Christian Church As trade declined throughout the West, people migrated from cities to farmlands. New types of relationships between landowners and peasants emerged, including serfdom, the manorial system, and the feudal system. The Christian church provided a strong element of continuity with the educational and administrative achievements of the Roman Empire. Monastic culture took shape. Christianity was a potent unifying and civilizing force within the West, although it was also the source of a fundamental rift with the Eastern Empire. By the middle of the eighth century, the papacy in Rome faced military threats from the north and doctrinal threats from the East; Pope Stephen boldly initiated an alliance with the Franks that influenced history for the next millennium or more.

The Kingdom of the Franks Clovis founded the first Frankish dynasty, the Merovingians. Then the Carolingian dynasty made strategic alliances with the landed nobility and with the church. The most illustrious Carolingian ruler, Charlemagne, conquered additional lands and, on Christmas Day in 800 had himself crowned Holy Roman Emperor by Pope Leo III. His capital, Aachen was a center of scholarship and intelligent administration. The social organization of the manor and innovations such as new plows improved agricultural productivity. Soon after Charlemagne's death in 814, his empire disintegrated as it was divided up, messily, among his grandsons. The late ninth and early tenth centuries were truly "dark ages" in Europe: Both secular and church-based organizations were weak, and at the same time invaders such as the Vikings were attacking. Peasants sought security at almost any price, so the institution of feudalism spread and matured.

Feudal Society   The feudal system was built around the exchange of land, labor, and military protection. Vassals would swear fealty to a more powerful individual, in return for the promise of protection. Kings and nobles built their military strength by acquiring increasing numbers of vassals; as the system developed, benefices replaced residence in the lord's household, scutage replaced direct military service, and other innovations formalized and institutionalized the relationships of feudal society. All participants in the feudal system constantly negotiated and competed for advantage. Loyalties could become divided as vassals swore fealty to multiple lords, to gain multiple land holdings. Eventually, vassals could claim hereditary possession of the lands they worked, reducing their sense of obligation to lords. Nonetheless, feudalism provided a first glimpse of many of the political and legal institutions that developed into the modern nation-state.

REVIEW QUESTIONS

1. What changes took place in the Frankish kingdom between its foundation and the end of Charlemagne's reign? What were the characteristics of Charlemagne's government? Why did Charlemagne encourage learning at his court? Why did his empire break apart?

2. How and why was the history of the eastern half of the former Roman Empire so different from that of its western half? Did Justinian strengthen or weaken the Byzantine Empire? How does his reign compare to Charlemagne's?

3. What were the tenets of Islam? How were the Muslims able to build an empire so quickly? What contributions did the Muslims make to the development of Western Europe?

4. How and why did feudal society begin? What were the essential features of feudalism? Do you think modern society could slip back into a feudal pattern?

KEY TERMS

Caesaropapism (p. 160)	**Islam** (p. 153)	**serf** (p. 167)
caliphate (p. 154)	**Ka'ba** (p. 154)	**Shi'a** (p. 154)
fiefs (p. 161)	**manor** (p. 167)	*Sunnis* (p. 155)
Hegira (p. 154)	**Monophysites** (p. 159)	**three-field system** (p. 168)
Holy Roman Empire (p. 163)	**Papal States** (p. 162)	*ulema* (p. 154)
iconoclasm (p. 159)	**Qur'an** (p. 153)	**vassal** (p. 167)

   For additional study resources for this chapter, go to:
www.prenhall.com/kagan3/chapter6

7

The High Middle Ages
The Rise of European Empires and States (1000–1300)

CHAPTER HIGHLIGHTS

Otto I and the Revival of the Empire Otto I continued the program of unification and expansion begun by his father, Henry I. The Ottonian dynasty faltered in the early eleventh century because Otto I's successors paid little attention to events in Germany, and the church established an independent base of power for itself.

The Reviving Catholic Church The Catholic Church shed the secular control of the ninth and tenth centuries to become a powerful independent institution. The reform movement that began in the monastery of Cluny was endorsed by the papacy, creating conflict between the church and secular authorities. The Crusades led to increased trade and exposure of the West to the civilizations of the East. Pope Innocent III made broad claims about the extent of papal authority.

England and France: Hastings (1066) to Bouvines (1214) William, duke of Normandy, won the Battle of Hastings (1066) and was crowned king of England. William's grandson Henry married Eleanor of Aquitaine, creating the Angevin Empire. English barons forced King John to accept the Magna Carta in 1215. The Capetian kings concentrated on securing their territory and controlling the nobility. The French defeated a combined English and German force at Bouvines (1214).

France in the Thirteenth Century: The Reign of Louis IX Louis IX enjoyed almost fifty years as the ruler of a unified and secure France. He focused on domestic reform and the cultivation of culture and religion. He was less successful in foreign affairs, allowing the English to maintain their claims on various French lands, setting the stage for the next century's Hundred Years' War.

The Hohenstaufen Empire (1152–1272) The leaders of the Holy Roman Empire failed to develop a sustainable political structure. Throughout the Hohenstaufen dynasty, conflicts with the popes and designs to control Italy distracted Frederick I and his successors from consolidating their control at home. By the late thirteenth century, the Hohenstaufen had little real power and Germany was fragmented.

CHAPTER QUESTIONS

HOW WAS Otto able to secure the power of his Saxon dynasty?

WHAT WAS the Cluniac reform movement?

HOW DID England and France develop strong monarchies?

IN WHAT ways were the leadership of Henry II of England and Louis IX of France similar?

WHY WAS Germany not as stable as the twelfth- and thirteenth-century governments of England and France?

2. CLUNY (NO).

CHAPTER OUTLINE

- Otto I and the Revival of the Empire
- The Reviving Catholic Church
- England and France: Hastings (1066) to Bouvines (1214)
- France in the Thirteenth Century: The Reign of Louis IX
- The Hohenstaufen Empire (1152–1272)

IMAGE KEY
for pages 172–173 is on page 192.

Europe in the High Middle Ages (1000–1300) was characterized by political expansion and consolidation and by intellectual flowering and synthesis. This may indeed have been a more creative era than the Italian Renaissance or the German Reformation.

The borders of western Europe were secured against invaders, and Europeans, who had long been the prey of foreign powers, mounted a military and economic offensive against the East. By adapting feudal traditions, the rulers of England and France established nuclei for centrally governed nation-states. The parliaments and popular assemblies that emerged in some places enabled the propertied classes to exert some political influence. Germany and Italy, however, resisted the general trend toward political consolidation and remained fragmented until the nineteenth century.

The distinctive Western belief in the separation of church and state was established during the High Middle Ages. The popes acquired monarchical authority over the church and prevented it from being absorbed into Europe's emerging nation-states. Their methods, however, led to accusations that the papacy was diverting the church from its spiritual mission into the murky world of politics.

HOW WAS Otto able to secure the power of his Saxon dynasty?

OTTO I AND THE REVIVAL OF THE EMPIRE

The fortunes of both the Holy Roman Empire and the papacy began to revive in the tenth century. Europe's Dark Age ended, and the most creative of the medieval eras began to unfold.

UNIFYING GERMANY

In 918, Henry I, "the Fowler," (d. 936) duke of Saxony, founded Germany's first non-Frankish dynasty and began to reverse the process of political fragmentation that had set in with the decline of the Carolingian Empire. He consolidated the duchies of Swabia, Bavaria, Saxony, Franconia, and Lotharingia and fended off invading Hungarians and Danes.

The state that Henry bequeathed to his son Otto I, "the Great," (r. 936–973) was the strongest kingdom in Europe, and Otto made it even greater. In 951, he invaded Italy and declared himself its king. In 955, he defeated the Hungarians at the Battle of Lechfeld and established secure frontiers for Germany and western Europe.

EMBRACING THE CHURCH

Otto secured the power of his Saxon dynasty by refusing to recognize the German duchies as independent hereditary states and treating them as subordinate parts of a unified kingdom. He curtailed the power of lay lords in his government by using bishops and abbots of monasteries as administrators of his lands. Clergy were more likely than laymen to favor strong royal government, and unlike laymen, they could not marry and produce sons with hereditary rights to the lands their fathers held from the king. The clergy were not concerned about potential conflicts between their spiritual and secular offices, and they eagerly embraced the wealth and power Otto offered them.

In 961, Otto helped Pope John XII (955–964) in a fight with an Italian nobleman, and on February 2, 962, the grateful pope revived the lapsed imperial title and bestowed it on Otto. The German king's intervention in Italian politics increased the power he was already exercising over the church. He appointed men to the major church offices and declared himself the protector of the Papal States. Pope John belatedly recognized the royal web in which he had become entangled. But when Otto discovered John was plotting against him, he ordered an ecclesiastical synod to depose the pope and to agree that no future pope take office without swearing allegiance to the emperor. Popes ruled at Otto's pleasure.

Otto's desire to found a Holy Roman Empire undercut the progress he had made toward the establishment of a German kingdom. Italy preoccupied his successors, Otto II (r. 973–983) and Otto III (r. 983–1002), and they allowed their German base to disintegrate. When the fledgling empire began to crumble in the first quarter of the eleventh century, the papacy seized the opportunity to reassert its independence.

The Reviving Catholic Church

While Otto was bringing the church under his control in Germany and Italy, a reform movement with a very different program was taking hold in France. Its goal was to liberate the clergy from the power of the feudal nobility.

WHAT WAS the Cluniac reform movement?

The Cluny Reform Movement

Since the last days of the Roman Empire, monks—the least worldly of the clergy—had been the church's most popular representatives. They were the best educated people in Europe. Their prayers and the sacred relics they guarded were believed to have a magical potency, and the religious ideals embodied in their way of life set the standard for all Christians.

In 910, William the Pious, duke of Aquitaine, endowed a new monastery at Cluny in south-central France. The church in William's day was in dire need of reform, and Cluny was intended as an experiment with a strategy for its renewal. The Cluniacs argued that so long as laymen had the power to use appointments to church offices to advance their personal political agendas and family interests, the church would suffer. It could realize its spiritual potential only if its leaders were chosen by the clergy themselves—by persons with genuine spiritual vocations. Cluny's patron granted its monks the right to choose their own leaders and manage their own affairs. As a result, Cluny quickly built a reputation for discipline and spiritual integrity.

The Cluniac movement spread from the monastery to all other parts of the church. The reformers argued that the **secular clergy** (those serving the *saeculum*, the "world") ought to imitate, insofar as possible, the ideal lifestyles of the **regular clergy** (those living under a *regula*, the rule of a monastic order). The higher clergy, who led the church, should also be free of feudal obligations and answerable only to an independent papacy.

The Cluniac reform spread to monasteries throughout France and Italy, until about 1,500 cloisters were affiliated with Cluny. Cluniacs pushed for changes that would benefit society at large as well as the church. In the late ninth and early tenth centuries, they tried to ease the suffering caused by the endemic warfare that plagued medieval society by promoting the "Peace of God" movement. Its decrees threatened soldiers who attacked noncombatants (women, peasants, merchants, and clergy) with excommunication. A subsequent "Truce of God" prohibited combat from Wednesday night to Monday morning and in all holy seasons.

Cluniac reformers advanced to high offices in the church, and Pope Leo IX (r. 1049–1054) appointed some to key administrative posts in Rome. They urged the pope to suppress *simony* (the sale of church offices) and to enforce celibacy among parish priests. The papacy itself, however, continued to be dominated by

secular clergy   Those clergy serving the *saeculum*, the "world."

regular clergy   Those clergy living under a *regula*, the rule of a monastic order.

powerful laymen. Emperor Henry III of Germany (r. 1039–1056) deposed three popes, who were pawns of the Roman aristocracy, and put Leo himself on the papal throne.

Henry's heir, Henry IV (r. 1056–1106), was a minor when he came to the throne. The weakness of the boy-king's regents gave the popes an opportunity to establish some important precedents. Pope Stephen IX (r. 1057–1058) reigned without seeking imperial confirmation of his title, and in 1059, Pope Nicholas II (r. 1059–1061) decreed that a group of high church officials (the College of Cardinals) would henceforth have the right to elect the popes. The procedures developed (and which are still followed) were intended to prevent Italian noble families and German kings from foisting their own candidates onto the papal throne, but laymen continued to exert considerable indirect influence on the process of choosing popes.

THE INVESTITURE STRUGGLE: GREGORY VII AND HENRY IV

7.1
Gregory VII's Letter to the Bishop of Metz, 1081

The German monarchy did not react to the papacy's new policies until the reign of Pope Gregory VII (r. 1073–1085), a fierce advocate of Cluny's reforms. In 1075, Gregory condemned "lay investiture," the appointment of someone to a church office by a layman. The pope's decree attacked the foundations of imperial government. Since the days of Otto I, German kings had preferred to use bishops rather than lay nobles to administer state lands. If the king lost the right to appoint men to ecclesiastical office, he lost the power to choose the men who administered much of his land. By prohibiting lay investiture, the pope emphasized the spiritual nature of the episcopacy, but he failed to recognize the church's religious offices had long since become entwined with the state's secular offices.

Henry opposed Gregory's action on the grounds it violated well-founded tradition, but the pope had important allies. The German nobles were eager for opportunities to increase their independence by diminishing the power of their king. Things came to a head in 1076. Bishops loyal to Henry assembled at Worms in January of that year and repudiated the pope's authority. Gregory responded by excommunicating Henry and absolving his subjects from their oaths of allegiance to him. The German magnates seized on this as an excuse and began to organize a rebellion against Henry.

Henry seized the initiative by crossing the Alps in midwinter to reach Canossa, Italy, where Gregory was waiting for the passes to clear so he could join the rebels in Germany. Henry compelled Gregory to grant him absolution by reportedly doing penance barefoot in the snow for three days. Henry's maneuver deprived his nobles of their excuse for rebelling and turned them against Gregory. The king regrouped his forces, and in March 1080, Gregory excommunicated Henry once again. The German nobles, however, refused to rise to the bait a second time. Four years later Henry drove Gregory into exile and placed his own man, Clement III, on the papal throne.

The investiture controversy ended in 1122 with a compromise spelled out by the Concordat of Worms. Emperor Henry V (r. 1106–1125) agreed to cease investing bishops with the ring and staff that symbolized spiritual office. In return, Pope Calixtus II (1119–1124) recognized the emperor's right to be present at episcopal consecrations and to preside at the ceremonies that bestowed fiefs on bishops. The old church-state "back scratching" continued, but now on a basis that made the church look more independent. The papacy's attempt to weaken Germany's kings did little to liberate the church. When the power of monarchs declined, the strength of the feudal nobles increased, enabling them to dominate the clergy.

QUICK REVIEW

Investiture Struggle

- Investiture struggle centered on authority to appoint and control clergy
- Pope Gregory excommunicated Henry IV when he proclaimed his independence from papacy
- Crisis settled in 1122 with Concordat of Worms

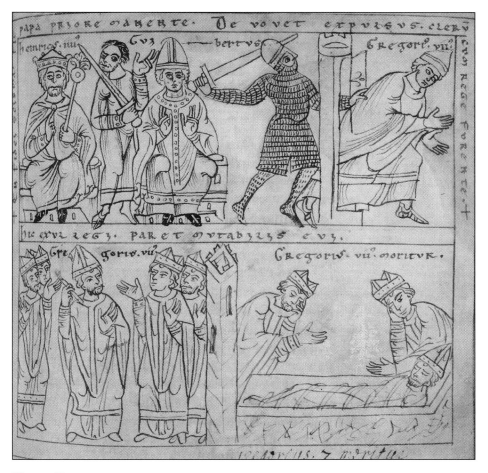

A twelfth-century German manuscript portrays the struggle between Emperor Henry IV and Pope Gregory VII. In the top panel, Henry installs the puppet pope Clement III and drives Gregory from Rome. Below, Gregory dies in exile. The artist was a monk; his sympathies were with Gregory, not Henry.

Thuringer Universitäts- und Landesbiblithek Jena

THE CRUSADES

What the Cluny reform was to the clergy, the **Crusades** to the Holy Land were to the laity—that is, an outlet for the religious zeal and self-confidence that characterized Europe in the High Middle Ages. Late in the eleventh century, Alexius I Comnenus, emperor of Constantinople, asked the pope to help him recruit soldiers for a war he hoped would win back lands his predecessors had lost to the Seljuk Turks. At the council of Clermont in 1095, Pope Urban II turned Alexius's request into a call for a Crusade. (See "History's Voices: Pope Urban II (r. 1088–1099) Preaches the First Crusade.")

The First Crusade appealed to different people for different reasons. The pope's successful launch of a Crusade confirmed his status as Europe's spiritual leader and won him leverage in dealing with the Byzantine church. The departure of large numbers of quarrelsome warriors pacified Europe, and hordes of restless young knights were enthralled by the opportunities the Crusade offered for adventure and personal profit. Many Crusaders were the younger sons of noblemen who had no inheritances to look forward to. Given limited land and soaring population, they had little hope of obtaining fiefs at home.

Although motives were mixed, the First Crusade was a less mercenary and more genuinely pious venture than some of the later Crusades. Popes recruited Crusaders by promising those who died in battle a plenary indulgence—a complete remission of punishment for their sins and from all suffering in purgatory. The Crusade was a true Holy War, a passionate struggle to rescue the most sacred Christian shrines from the clutches of hated infidels. It was also the ultimate

Crusades Campaigns authorized by the church to combat heresies and rival faiths.

HISTORY'S VOICES

POPE URBAN II (R. 1088–1099) PREACHES THE FIRST CRUSADE

When Pope Urban II summoned the First Crusade in a sermon at the Council of Clermont on November 26, 1095, he painted a savage picture of the Muslims who controlled Jerusalem. Urban also promised the Crusaders, who responded by the tens of thousands, remission of their unrepented sins and assurance of heaven. Robert the Monk is one of four witnesses who has left us a summary of the sermon.

WHAT ARE the images of the enemy he creates and how accurate and fair are they?

From the confines of Jerusalem and the city of Constantinople a horrible tale has gone forth and very frequently has been brought to our ears, namely, that a race from the kingdom of the Persians [that is, the Seljuk Turks], an accursed race, a race utterly alienated from God, a generation forsooth which has not directed its heart and has not entrusted its spirit to God, has invaded the lands of those Christians and has depopulated them by the sword, pillage and fire; it has led away a part of the captives into its own country, and a part it has destroyed by cruel tortures; it has either entirely destroyed the churches of God or appropriated them for the rites of its own religion. They destroy the altars, after having defiled them with their uncleanness. They circumcise the Christians, and the blood of the circumcision they either spread upon the altars or pour into the vases of the baptismal font. When they wish to torture people by a base death, they perforate their navels, and dragging forth the extremity of the intestines, bind it to a stake; then with flogging they lead the victim around until the viscera having gushed forth, the victim falls prostrate upon the ground. Others they bind to a post and pierce with arrows. Others they compel to extend their necks and then, attacking them with naked swords, attempt to cut through the neck with a single blow. What shall I say of the abominable rape of the women? The kingdom of the Greeks is now dismembered by them and deprived of territory so vast in extent that it can not be traversed in a march of two months. On whom therefore is the labor of avenging these wrongs and of recovering this territory incumbent, if not upon you? …

Jerusalem is the navel of the world; the land is fruitful above others, like another paradise of delights. This the Redeemer of the human race has made illustrious by His advent, has beautified by residence, has consecrated by suffering, has redeemed by death, has glorified by burial. This royal city, therefore, situated at the centre of the world, is now held captive by His enemies, and is in subjection to those who do not know God, to the worship of the heathens. She seeks therefore and desires to be liberated, and does not cease to implore you to come to her aid. From you especially she asks succor, because, as we have already said, God has conferred upon you above all nations great glory in arms.

Accordingly undertake this journey for the remission of your sins, with the assurance of the imperishable glory of the kingdom of heaven.

Translations and reprints from *Original Sources of European History*, Vol. I (Philadelphia: Department of History, University of Pennsylvania, 1910), pp. 5–7.

pilgrimage, and the desire to be part of it affected even those who did not leave home. They crusaded by massacring their Jewish neighbors.

The First Victory   Three great armies (perhaps 100,000 men) gathered in France, Germany, and Italy and converged on Constantinople in 1097 by different routes. They were not the disciplined, professional force Alexius had hoped to enlist. He was suspicious of their motives, and the common people whom they pillaged along the route of their march hardly considered them models of faith. Nonetheless, the Crusaders succeeded where earlier Byzantine armies had

MAP EXPLORATION

Interactive map: To explore this map further, go to **http://www.prenhall.com/kagan3/map7.1**

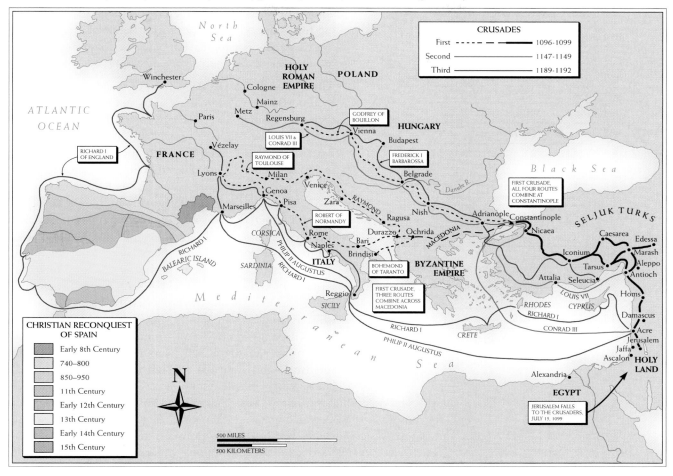

MAP 7–1

The Early Crusades   Routes and several leaders of the Crusades during the first century of the movement are shown. The names on this map do not exhaust the list of great nobles who went on the First Crusade. The even showier array of monarchs of the Second and Third Crusades still left the Crusades, on balance, ineffective in achieving their goals.

COMPARE AND contrast the scope and result of each of the first three Crusades. Overall, how successful were these Crusades?

failed. They defeated one Seljuk army after another, and, on July 15, 1099, they captured Jerusalem. They owed their success to the superior military technology Europeans had evolved and to the inability of the Muslim states to cooperate in mounting an effective resistance. (See Map 7–1.)

The Crusaders established feudal states (Edessa, Antioch, and Jerusalem) in the lands they conquered and proclaimed Godfrey of Bouillon first king of Jerusalem. Godfrey's realm was little more than a collection of European outposts in a hostile Muslim world. Its precarious situation became clear as the Muslims rallied to oppose the Christian "savages" who had invaded their lands. The Crusaders erected castles, hunkered down to live under conditions of perpetual

Significant Dates from the Period of the High Middle Ages

910	Cluniac reform begins
955	Otto I defeats Magyars
1059	College of Cardinals empowered to elect popes
1066	Norman conquest of England
1075–1122	Investiture Controversy
1095–1099	First Crusade
1144	Edessa falls; Second Crusade
1152	Hohenstaufen dynasty founded
1154	Plantagenet dynasty founded
1187	Jerusalem falls to Saladin
1189–1192	Third Crusade
1202	Fourth Crusade sacks Constantinople
1209	Albigensian Crusade
1210	Franciscan Order founded
1215	Fourth Lateran Council; Magna Carta
1250	Death of Fredrick II

siege, and became businessmen devoted to promoting trade between East and West. Orders of soldier-monks were established to protect and assist pilgrims to the Holy Lands, and the services they provided for travelers spawned banking and money-lending ventures. Some of the orders—most notably the Knights Templar—were among Europe's most powerful commercial organizations.

The Long-Term Results The Crusaders maintained their posts in the Middle East for about forty years, and then their grip began to loosen. Each setback prompted a call for a new Crusade. After Edessa fell to the Muslims in 1144, Bernard of Clairvaux (1091–1153), a prominent abbot and religious reformer, persuaded the king of France to lead a Second Crusade. It was an embarrassing failure. In October 1187, Saladin (r. 1138–1193), the Muslim ruler of Egypt and Syria, conquered Jerusalem, and Europe's most powerful monarchs enlisted in a Third Crusade (1189–1192). Germany's Emperor Frederick Barbarossa, England's King Richard "the Lion-Hearted," and France's King Philip Augustus all led armies to Jerusalem's rescue, but their campaign was a tragicomedy. Frederick Barbarossa drowned while fording a stream in Asia Minor. Richard and Philip Augustus drew near to Jerusalem. Intense personal rivalry, however, prevented them from working together, and Philip Augustus soon returned to France to prey on Richard's lands. When the deteriorating situation finally persuaded Richard (the most enthusiastic of the Crusaders) to head home, he was captured and held for ransom by the German emperor, Henry VI. England's bill for its king's Eastern adventure was greatly increased by the sum Germany demanded for his release.

The Crusades failed to achieve their political objectives, but their economic and cultural impact on Europe was significant. They stimulated trade between Europe and the Middle East, and the merchants of Venice, Pisa, and Genoa, who followed in the wake of the Crusaders, had more luck challenging Muslim domination at sea than the crusading armies did on land. As trade contacts proliferated, so did cultural exchanges.

THE PONTIFICATE OF INNOCENT III (R. 1198–1216)

The pope who inaugurated the Crusades hoped they would unite Europe behind the leader of its church. His successors shared the dream of winning some kind of authority over Europe's secular rulers, and none did more to make the dream a reality than Pope Innocent III.

The New Papal Monarchy Innocent greatly increased the flow of revenue to the church and used this wealth to create a papal monarchy that could compete with the power and organization of secular kingdoms. He collected an income tax of 2.5 percent from the clergy. Appointees to church offices paid *annates* (the equivalent of their first year's income). The pope demanded substantial fees for bestowing the *pallium*, the stole that symbolized an archbishop's authority. The papacy claimed the exclusive right to grant absolution for many kinds of sins (and to pocket the fees imposed as penances). Innocent also collected Peter's pence, a tax imposed on all but the poorest laymen.

Crusades in France and the East   The church's increasing wealth and secular influence was seen by some as a sign of its corruption and spiritual decline. Disillusionment with clerical greed prompted criticism that sometimes blossomed into heresy. When that happened, Innocent did not shrink from pitting Europeans against one another in Holy War.

In 1209, Innocent launched a Crusade to exterminate heretics called **Albigensians** (from the French town of Albi) or Cathars ("pure ones"). These people advocated a simple, pious way of life following the example set by Jesus and the Apostles, but they rejected key Christian doctrines. They denied that the wrathful god of the Old Testament, who created the sinful material world, was the same god as the heavenly Father to whom Jesus prayed. They saw history as a war between the god of flesh and the god of spirit, and their belief that the flesh was the source of the sins that imprisoned the spirit caused them to reject the Christian claim that God was incarnate in Jesus. The true church, they insisted, was a spiritual entity, not the materialistic institution headed by the pope. The more radical Cathars practiced strict asceticism and recommended celibacy, contraception, or abortion to prevent more immortal souls from being captured and imprisoned in sinful matter. Paradoxically, the Cathars' dualism could also lead to moral laxity. If flesh and spirit are totally separate realities, what the former does can have little impact on the latter.

The south of France, where the heresy spread, was a rich land, and knights from northern France seized on the pope's Crusade as an opportunity to dispossess their wealthy neighbors. Massacres and a campaign led by the French king, Louis VIII, in 1226 utterly devastated the prosperous Albigensian region. Pope Gregory IX (r. 1227–1241) followed up by sending the **Inquisition** to root out any heretics who remained. The Inquisition was a formal ecclesiastical court dedicated to discovering and punishing heresy. Bishops had used such courts in their dioceses since the mid–twelfth century, but Innocent III's Inquisition was a centralized organization that dispatched papal legates to preside at trials and executions throughout Europe.

In 1202, Innocent dispatched the Fourth Crusade. It was supposed to go to the Holy Lands, but it was diverted to an attack on Constantinople. Many of the approximately 30,000 Crusaders who gathered in Venice were poor soldiers of fortune who could not pay what the Venetians demanded for their transport. The Venetians persuaded them to work off their passage by conquering Zara, a Christian city that was one of Venice's commercial rivals. To the shock and anger of Pope Innocent III, the Crusaders obliged and then allowed Venice to lead them farther afield for an assault on Constantinople.

Once the Crusaders had taken Constantinople, the pope came to terms with them and shared the spoils. One of Innocent's confidants was appointed patriarch of Constantinople and charged with persuading the Greeks and the Slavs to submit to the authority of the pope. The Latins occupied Constantinople until 1261, when the Genoese, who envied Venice's coup, helped the exiled Byzantine emperor (Michael Paleologus) recapture the city. The Crusade and the subsequent half century of Latin mismanagement hardly helped reunite the church or strengthen the Christian position in the Middle East.

The Fourth Lateran Council   The culminating event of Innocent's papacy was the Fourth Lateran Council, which met in 1215 (a year before the pope's death). The doctrinal issues the meeting resolved and the disciplines it imposed were designed to enhance the authority of the church and its clergy. The council affirmed

Thirteenth-century statue of St. Maurice, patron saint of Magdeburg, Germany. An Egyptian Christian who commanded a Roman legion, St. Maurice was executed in 286 C.E. after refusing to worship the Roman gods. Portrayed as a white man for centuries, during the era of the Crusades, Maurice became a perfect talisman for Europeans venturing eastward.

Constantin Beyer

QUICK REVIEW

Suppression of the Albigensians

- 1209: Pope Innocent III launches Crusade against Albigensians
- 1226: Louis VIII's armies devastate Albigensian region
- Pope Gregory IX follows up by sending the Inquisition to the region

Albigensians   Heretical sect that advocated a simple, pious way of life following the example set by Jesus and the Apostles, but rejecting key Christian doctrines.

Inquisition   Formal ecclesiastical court dedicated to discovering and punishing heresy.

Dominicans (left), **and Franciscans** (right). Unlike the other religious orders, the Dominicans and Franciscans did not live in cloisters, but wandered about preaching and combating heresy. They depended for support on their own labor and the kindness of the laity.

Cliche Bibliothéque Nationale de France, Paris

the doctrine of **transubstantiation** as the explanation for the key Christian sacrament, the Eucharist. The doctrine states that at the moment of priestly consecration the bread and wine of the Lord's Supper become the body and blood of Christ. This was what many Christians had come to believe by the twelfth century, and it served the interests of the papacy. The power that clergy alone possessed to perform this miracle gave them precedence over the laity. The council further empowered the priesthood by formalizing the sacrament of penance and requiring every adult Christian to confess and commune at least annually (usually at Easter).

Franciscans and Dominicans   Piety and faith surged at the turn of the twelfth century, and new religious movements proliferated. Most advocated a life of poverty in imitation of Christ. Idealization of poverty was not heretical, but the criticism of the worldly clergy it implied caused groups such as the Waldensians, Beguines, and Beghards to be suspected of harboring heretical opinions.

Innocent created a safe outlet for the champions of poverty by licensing two new religious orders: the Franciscans and the Dominicans. These were orders of *friars* ("brothers"), who differed from traditional monks in that they refused to accept land and endowments and did not retreat into cloisters. They devoted themselves to preaching and caring for the poor and supported themselves by working and begging. The saintly behavior of these *mendicants* did much to restore respect for the church they served. The "Third orders" (tertiaries) they established allowed laypeople to affiliate with the movement and receive guidance that prevented their piety from drifting into heresy.

The Franciscan Order was founded in 1210 by Francis of Assisi (1182–1226), the son of a rich Italian cloth merchant. The Dominican Order (the Order of Preachers) was founded in 1216 by Dominic (1170–1221), a well-educated Spanish cleric. Both orders reported directly to the pope and not to the bishops of the dioceses in which they worked. They constituted a kind of army of dedicated servants that the central government of the church could dispatch on special missions.

Pope Gregory IX (1227–1241) canonized Francis only two years after Francis's death. However, the pope also diverted the Franciscans from the path Francis charted for them. He declared that absolute poverty was impractical and he announced the church would accept property and hold it in trust for the friars to fund their work. Most Franciscans accepted the pope's moderation of their lifestyle, but a radical branch, the Spiritual Franciscans, refused and were condemned by a pope in the fourteenth century.

transubstantiation   Christian doctrine which holds that, at the moment of priestly consecration, the bread and wine of the Lord's Supper become the body and blood of Christ.

The Dominicans specialized in combating heresy. They preached, staffed the offices of the Inquisition, taught at universities, and supervised convents of **Beguines** (sisterhoods of pious, self-supporting single women). They produced one of the greatest of medieval thinkers, Thomas Aquinas (d. 1274). His efforts to reconcile faith's revealed truths with human reason produced what the Catholic Church has acknowledged to be the definitive statement of its beliefs.

Beguines   Sisterhoods of pious, self-supporting single women.

England and France: Hastings (1066) to Bouvines (1214)

HOW DID England and France develop strong monarchies?

While struggles between popes and emperors were complicating the political development of Germany and Italy, England and France were evolving effective monarchies. There were, however, troublesome ties between these two kingdoms as between Germany and Italy.

The old Roman province of Britain became England ("Anglo-land") as Germans from the tribes of the Angles and Saxons took it over at the start of the Middle Ages. Edward the Confessor, the last of their kings, died childless in 1066, and a fight broke out for his throne. The Anglo-Saxons supported a native nobleman, Harold Godwinsson, but he was challenged by Edward's distant relative, Duke William of Normandy (d. 1087). The Normans invaded and obliterated the Anglo-Saxon army in a battle fought near Hastings on October 14, 1066. The victory made William king of England as well as duke of a major portion of northern France.

WILLIAM THE CONQUEROR

William constructed the most effective monarchy in Europe by judiciously combining continental feudalism and Anglo-Saxon custom. To discover precisely what he had won at Hastings, he carried out a county-by-county survey of its people, animals, and implements. The results were compiled as the *Domesday Book* (1080–1086), a virtually unique description of a medieval kingdom. William claimed all the land in England by right of conquest and compelled every landlord

QUICK REVIEW

William the Conqueror (d. 1087)

- October 14, 1066: Normans defeated Anglo-Saxons at the Battle of Hastings
- William's rule in England combined elements of continental feudalism and Anglo-Saxon tradition
- *Domesday Book* contained county-by-county survey of William's kingdom

The *Battle of Hastings*. Detail of the *Bayeux Tapestry*, c. 1073–83. Wool embroidery on linen, height 20" (50.7 cm).

Centre Guillaume le Conquérant. "Detail of the Bayeux Tapestry-XIth century" and "By special permission of City of Bayeux"

OVERVIEW   A COMPARISON OF LEADERS IN THE HIGH MIDDLE AGES

	England	France	Germany
Leader	Henry II	Louis IX	Frederick II
Reign	(1154–1189)	(1226–1270)	(1212–1250)
Accomplishments	Henry brought to the throne greatly expanded French holdings. The union with Eleanor created the Angevin (English–French) Empire. Henry conquered a part of Ireland and made the king of Scotland his vassal.	Louis IX embodied the medieval view of the perfect ruler. His greatest achievements lay at home. The French bureaucracy became an instrument of order and fair play in government under Louis. He abolished private wars and serfdom within his domain. Respected by the kings of Europe, Louis became an arbiter among the world's powers.	Within a year and a half of Frederick's crowing, the treacherous reign of Otto IV came to an end on the battlefields of Bouvines.
Failures	As Henry acquired new lands abroad, he became more autocratic at home. He tried to recapture the efficiency and stability of his grandfather's regime, but in the process steered the English monarchy toward an oppressive rule.	Had Louis ruthlessly confiscated English territories on the French coast, he might have lessened, if not averted altogether, the conflict underlying the Hundred Years' War.	During his reign, Frederick effectively turned dreams of a unified Germany into a nightmare of disunity. Living mostly outside of Germany during his rule, he did little to secure the rights of the emperor in Germany. Frederick's relations with the pope were equally disastrous, leading to his excommunication on four different occasions.

to take an oath of vassalage and to acknowledge his land was held as a fief from the king. Feudal nobles usually tried to weaken their kings, but the Norman nobles—having no support from their new Anglo-Saxon subjects—needed the help of a powerful leader. William's hand was further strengthened by the tax and court systems he found already in place in England, and he continued the Anglo-Saxon custom of parleying with the nobility before making major decisions. The tradition of consultation between the king and (at least some of) his subjects led ultimately to England's influential parliamentary system of government.

HENRY II

The strength of the English monarchy continued to grow under William's sons and heirs, William Rufus (r. 1087–1100) and Henry I (r. 1100–1135). But when Henry died leaving only a female heir, a civil war threatened near anarchy. In the end, the competing factions compromised and pledged their allegiance to

Henry II (r. 1154–1189), son of the duke of Anjou and Henry I's daughter Matilda. Henry's Plantagenet dynasty ruled England until the death of Richard III in 1485.

Henry, by inheritance and by marriage to Eleanor of Aquitaine (ca. 1122–1204), built the Angevin (from Anjou, his father's domain) Empire. In addition to England, he ruled much more of France than did the king of France, and he conquered part of Ireland and forced the king of Scotland to pledge homage. The French king did what he could to contain the English, but the French were not to evict the English from the Continent until the mid–fifteenth century.

ELEANOR OF AQUITAINE AND COURT CULTURE

Eleanor of Aquitaine had been married to King Louis VII of France before she wed Henry II of England, and she was a powerful influence on both their kingdoms. Women of Eleanor's generation began to venture into traditionally masculine fields, such as politics and business, and Eleanor led the way. She insisted on accompanying her first husband on the Second Crusade, and she stirred up so much trouble for her second husband that from 1179 until his death in 1189 he kept her under house arrest.

After her marriage to Henry, the court that Eleanor established in Angers (Anjou's chief town) became a major center of patronage for musicians and poets. Bernart de Ventadorn, one of the new troubadour poets, composed many of the popular love songs of the period in her honor. In 1170, Eleanor separated from Henry and moved to Poitiers to live with her daughter Marie, the countess of Champagne, another patroness of the arts. The court of Poitiers popularized an aristocratic entertainment to which modern scholars have given the name "courtly love." The troubadours who elaborated the rules of game contrasted carnal love with "courteous" love, a spiritual passion for a lady that ennobled her knightly lover. Chrétien de Troyes's stories of King Arthur and the Knights of the Round Table (and of Sir Lancelot's tragic, illicit love for Arthur's wife, Guinevere) are the most famous products of the movement.

POPULAR REBELLION AND MAGNA CARTA

Henry II believed the church should operate within parameters set by the state, and in 1164, his Constitutions of Clarendon spelled out new rules for the English clergy. Henry limited the right to appeal cases to the papal court, subjected clergy to the king's justice, and gave the king control over the election of bishops. Henry also bestowed the office of archbishop of Canterbury, the head of the English church, on his compliant chancellor Thomas à Becket (1118?–1170). Much to Henry's surprise, Becket opposed the Constitutions and mounted a furious campaign to force Henry to rescind them. In 1170, several of Henry's men assassinated the troublesome archbishop, and the church seized the opportunity to declare Becket a martyr and embarrass the king by canonizing him (1172). (See "Encountering the Past: Pilgrimage.")

Henry was followed on the throne by two of his sons: Richard the Lion-Hearted (r. 1189–1199) and John (r. 1199–1216). Neither was a success. Richard imposed ruinous taxation to fund the fruitless Third Crusade and died fighting to recover lands he lost to the French while he was in the Middle East. In 1209, Pope Innocent III excommunicated Richard's successor, John, in a dispute over the appointment of an archbishop for Canterbury. To extricate himself from a mess of his own making and to win support for a war with France, John surrendered to the pope and declared his kingdom a papal fief. John had lost most of England's territory on the continent, and the campaign he mounted in 1214 to win it back failed abysmally.

ENCOUNTERING THE PAST

PILGRIMAGE

Thomas à Becket's tomb at Canterbury quickly became one of the most frequented pilgrimage shrines in Europe. The perennially popular Canterbury Tales of Geoffrey Chaucer (ca. 1345–1400) provide a fictional account of one such trip. As Chaucer describes it, a medieval pilgrimage was both a spiritual and a social event. Because travel to distant shrines involved self-sacrifice (danger and expense), clergy often imposed pilgrimages as penances for sins. Pilgrims also set out on their own in the hope that contact with a saint's relics or the waters of a sacred well or spring would provide a miraculous cure for a bodily affliction. Parents even brought the corpses of dead infants to shrines to beg the saints to bring them back to life.

The most prestigious pilgrimages were those to the Holy Lands and to the graves of St. Peter in Rome and St. James at Compostela in northern Spain. Pilgrim traffic was so great that businesses sprang up along these routes to assist travelers. Transportation, shelter, emergency services, and even guidebooks were available. Pilgrims, particularly to distant locals, often traveled in groups, and an opportunity to share stories and adventures with others made for diverting entertainment. Travel then, as now, was highly educational.

WHY WERE pilgrimages so popular with medieval people?

A thirteenth-century stained glass window depicts pilgrims traveling to Canterbury Cathedral.
© Archivo Icongrafico, S.A./CORBIS

In 1215, John, facing rebellion by his disillusioned barons, agreed to limitations on his authority that were spelled out in a document called **Magna Carta** ("Great Charter"). Among the king's more significant concessions were promises not to arrest and hold people without giving reasons and not to impose new taxes without consulting representatives of the propertied classes. Magna Carta had little effect, for John repudiated it. But it kept alive traditions and precedents that came to undergird modern English law.

PHILIP II AUGUSTUS

In England during the High Middle Ages, the propertied classes struggled to prevent a strong monarchy from encroaching on their interests. The shoe was on the other foot in France, where kings confronted powerful subjects who opposed the growth of monarchy.

After the Carolingian line came to an end in France in 987, the nobles made the crown an elective office. They chose Hugh Capet, count of Paris, to be

Magna Carta ("Great Charter") Document spelling out limitations on royal authority agreed to by John in 1215. It created foundation for modern English law.

their king, and by repeatedly winning elections, his descendants created a Capetian dynasty. For the next two centuries, however, the great feudal princes were France's real rulers. The early Capetian kings were so weak that they were not even fully in control of their personal domain, the area around Paris and the region known as the Ile-de-France. By the time Philip II (r. 1180–1223) came to the throne, the Capetians had won recognition of their hereditary rights to the throne, and it was finally possible for them to assert their authority without the risk of being deposed. The Norman conquest of England in 1066 may actually have helped them, for it was in the self-interest of France's nobles to support them in their efforts to contain the far more powerful and threatening Plantagenet kings. The wealthy merchant class beginning to appear in France also favored a strong monarchy that could provide protection for commerce.

The king of England was, as duke of Normandy, a vassal of the French king. A skillful politician such as France's King Philip II Augustus (r. 1180–1223) was able to exploit the ambiguity of this relationship. Whenever his English rival failed to honor his obligations as a vassal, Philip could declare his fiefs forfeit and call on France's nobles for help in forcing the English king to give them up. Richard the Lion-Hearted and John both played into Philip's hands and allowed him to reclaim all the lands the English had occupied in France except for part of Aquitaine.

John of England tried to recover what he had lost by persuading the German emperor Otto IV (r. 1198–1215) to join him in invading France. A battle fought at Bouvines in Flanders on July 27, 1214, decided what was, in effect, Europe's first multinational war. Philip won, and his victory rallied his subjects in support of their monarchy. Otto IV fell from power, and John's subjects welcomed him home with the rebellion that culminated in Magna Carta.

FRANCE IN THE THIRTEENTH CENTURY: THE REIGN OF LOUIS IX

The legitimacy of the Capetians' growing power appeared to be confirmed by the achievements and reputation of Philip's grandson, Louis IX (r. 1226–1270). Louis so embodied the medieval ideal of a king that he was canonized shortly after his death. Louis had ascetic tastes, and his ethical standards were far superior to those of his royal and papal contemporaries. He was approachable and had compassion for the poor, but he was also a decisive leader and an enthusiastic soldier.

GENEROSITY ABROAD

Some of Louis's decisions suggest naiveté or an overly scrupulous conscience. He could, for instance, have driven the English off the Continent, but he refused to take advantage of the English king's weakness. In 1259, he negotiated the Treaty of Paris, a generous compromise that ended a long-simmering dispute between England and France. Had he been more ruthless and seized the last English outposts in France, he might have prevented subsequent wars and spared Europe a great deal of bloodshed.

Louis did not take the opportunity that a long struggle between the papacy and the German emperor Frederick II gave him to intervene in Italy. After Frederick's death, however, Louis's brother, Charles of Anjou, did enter the fray on the pope's side. In exchange for Charles's help in destroying Frederick's heirs, the pope confirmed Charles in possession of a royal title and Frederick's kingdom of Naples and Sicily.

IN WHAT ways were the leadership of Henry II of England and Louis IX of France similar?

Choir (c. 1060–75) and nave (1095–1115), St.-Savin-sur-Gartempe, France.

CORBIS/Bettmann

WHY WAS Germany not as stable as the twelfth- and thirteenth-century governments of England and France?

ORDER AND EXCELLENCE AT HOME

Louis's greatest achievements were the improvements he made in France's government. The bureaucratic machinery he inherited from his predecessors had been developed so the king might more efficiently exploit his subjects. Louis used it to secure order and improve the administration of justice. He sent out *enquêteurs* (auditors) to monitor the *baillis* and *prévôts* whom Philip Augustus had created to handle local administration. He abolished private warfare among the nobles and serfdom within the royal domain. He gave his subjects the judicial right of appeal from local to higher courts, and he made the tax system more equitable.

The French people's enthusiasm for monarchy grew in proportion to the services they received from their king, and his increasing significance in their lives helped them develop a sense of national identity. Other things contributed to this. Louis's reign was the golden age of Scholasticism, a time when scholars such as the Dominican, Thomas Aquinas, and the Franciscan, Bonaventure, made the University of Paris Europe's intellectual center. France led Europe in monastic reform, codes of chivalry, and the arts of courtly love. Suger, abbot of St. Denis and adviser to Louis IX's great-grandfather, Louis VII, pioneered the development of the Gothic style in art and architecture that spread throughout the medieval world. France's enduring reputation as the leader of European culture dates to the reign of St. Louis.

Louis's virtues were those of a medieval king. He was fanatical about religion. He supported the work of the Inquisition, and he personally led the last two major Crusades for the Holy Land. Both were failures, but Louis's death of a fever during the second of his holy wars only confirmed his reputation for saintliness. The Capetians' production of a king of Louis's stature confirmed many of their subjects in the belief that God had given them a divine right to France's throne.

THE HOHENSTAUFEN EMPIRE (1152–1272)

During the twelfth and thirteenth centuries, while stable governments were evolving in England and France, the Holy Roman Empire (Germany, Burgundy, and northern Italy) took quite a different course. Political fragmentation triumphed over monarchical centralization and created a troublesome legacy that endured into modern times.

FREDERICK I BARBAROSSA

The Investiture Controversy (the popes' assault on the right of kings to appoint the higher clergy) weakened Germany's monarchs but strengthened its feudal barons. The power the king lost to influence appointments to church offices simply passed to the German princes.

Imperial authority revived with the accession to the throne of Frederick I Barbarossa (r. 1152–1190), founder of the Hohenstaufen dynasty. Frederick had some help in laying a foundation for a new empire. Disaffection with the incessant squabbling of the feudal princes was widespread, and resentment of the theocratic pretensions of the papacy was growing. Irnerius (d. 1125), a scholar at the University of Bologna, had also revived the study of Roman law (Justinian's

Code). This was useful to Frederick, for Roman law promoted the centralization of states and provided a secular justification for imperial power that minimized the importance of papal coronation.

From a base of operation in Switzerland, Frederick waged a relatively successful campaign to assert his authority over the German nobility. The balance tipped in his favor in 1180, when his strongest rival, Henry the Lion (d. 1195), duke of Saxony, was exiled to Normandy. Frederick never grew strong enough to intervene in the internal affairs of Germany's greater duchies, but he vigilantly enforced his rights as their feudal overlord. This kept the memory of royal authority alive until a king was able to risk a showdown with Germany's powerful magnates.

Italy was both the means and the obstacle to the realization of Frederick's dreams of empire. In 1155, Frederick defeated Arnold of Brescia (d. 1155), a revolutionary who had wrested control of Rome from the papacy, and returned the city to Pope Adrian IV (1154–1159). Frederick's reward was an imperial coronation that implied he had some rights in Italy.

The imperial assembly sanctioned Frederick's claims, but the city of Milan organized fierce resistance to his exercise of royal authority. At this crucial juncture, Alexander III (1159–1181) was elected pope. As a cardinal, the new pope had previously negotiated an alliance between the papacy and the Norman kingdom of Sicily. As a result, Frederick soon found himself at war with Milan, the pope, and the kingdom of Sicily. In 1167, the combined forces of the northern Italian cities drove him back into Germany, and almost a decade later (1176) an Italian army soundly defeated him at Legnano. In 1183, Frederick agreed to a peace that recognized the Lombard cities' right to self-rule.

HENRY VI AND THE SICILIAN CONNECTION

Frederick ended his reign stalemated in Germany and defeated in Italy. In the last years of his life, however, he created an opportunity for his dynasty to renew its fight for dominance over Italy. The Norman ruler of the kingdom of Sicily, William II (r. 1166–1189), asked Frederick for help in a war with Constantinople. They sealed their alliance in 1186 by a marriage between Frederick's son, the future Henry VI (r. 1190–1197), and Constance, heiress to Sicily.

Sicily was a fatal acquisition for the Hohenstaufen kings. It tempted them to neglect Germany to pursue projects in Italy. It alarmed the Italians and increased their determination to resist. And by forecasting Hohenstaufen encirclement (and absorption) of Rome, it convinced the papacy that its survival hinged on the empire's destruction.

When Henry VI came to the throne in 1190, he faced a multitude of enemies: nervous Lombard cities, a hostile papacy, independent German princes, and even the king of England. (Henry the Lion, the exiled duke of Saxony, involved Richard the Lion-Hearted in plots against the Hohenstaufens.) In 1194, Constance bore her husband a son (the future Frederick II), and Henry campaigned vigorously for recognition of the boy's hereditary right to the imperial throne. The German princes were reluctant to compromise their right to elect their kings, and the encircled papacy was determined to prevent anything that might secure Hohenstaufen power.

OTTO IV AND THE WELF INTERREGNUM

Henry died prematurely in September 1197, and his widow tried to save at least the throne of Sicily for her infant son by arranging for him to become a ward of the papacy. The boy's uncle, Philip of Swabia, claimed the title of king in Germany,

QUICK REVIEW

Frederick I Barbarossa (r. 1152–1190)

- Founder of the Hohenstaufen dynasty
- From base in Switzerland waged war to control the German nobility
- Efforts to conquer Italy ended in defeat at Legnano in 1176

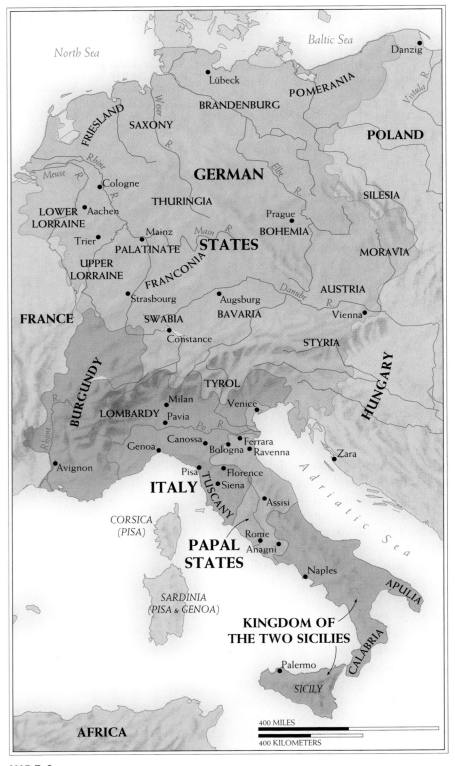

MAP 7–2

Germany and Italy in the Middle Ages Medieval Germany and Italy were divided lands. The Holy Roman Empire (Germany) embraced hundreds of independent territories that the emperor ruled only in name. The papacy controlled the Rome area and tried to enforce its will on Romagna. Under the Hohenstaufens (mid–twelfth to mid–thirteenth century), internal German divisions and papal conflict reached new heights; German rulers sought to extend their power to southern Italy and Sicily.

HOW DID Roman emperors, German rulers, and the papacy all vie for power in Germany and Italy in the Middle Ages?

but the Welf family, the Hohenstaufens' traditional German enemies, backed a rival—Otto of Brunswick, the son of the troublesome Henry the Lion. Richard of England supported Otto; the French supported the Hohenstaufens; and the papacy switched its allegiance back and forth to prevent anyone from becoming strong enough to threaten Rome. The result was anarchy and civil war.

After Philip's death in 1208, Otto's faction elected him king in Germany and Pope Innocent III (1198–1215) crowned him emperor. Four months after the coronation, the pope decided this had been a mistake. Otto attacked Sicily, a move that implied he had aspirations to conquer Italy and Rome. The pope excommunicated Otto and raised up Prince Frederick as a rival candidate for Germany's throne. (See Map 7–2.)

FREDERICK II

Pope Innocent's ward, the Hohenstaufen prince Frederick, was now of age, and unlike Otto he had a hereditary claim to the German crown. In December 1212, the pope, Philip Augustus of France, and Otto's German enemies arranged for Frederick II to be crowned king in the German city of Mainz. Philip Augustus's victory over Otto and John of England at the Battle of Bouvines in 1214 ended Otto's career and cleared the way for Frederick to mount the imperial throne in Charlemagne's city of Aachen (1215). The young ruler's allies probably expected him to be their puppet. If so, they were soon disabused of that notion.

Frederick had grown up in Sicily, and he had little interest in Germany. He spent only nine of the thirty-eight years of his reign there, and he wanted only one thing from the German princes: a secure hold on the imperial title for himself and his sons. To win this, he was willing to grant Germany's nobles virtual independence. Frederick's policy doomed hopes for the development of a centralized monarchy in Germany and condemned the country to six centuries of chaotic disunity.

Frederick's policy with respect to the papacy was equally disastrous. The popes excommunicated Frederick four times and came to view him as the Antichrist, the biblical beast of the Apocalypse whose persecution of the faithful will signal the end of the world. Frederick's chief political objective was to win control of Lombardy, unite it with his Sicilian kingdom, and surround Rome. The popes were desperate to prevent this.

Pope Innocent IV (1243–1254) organized and led the German princes against Frederick, and German and Italian resistance kept Frederick on the defensive throughout his last years. In the end, the popes won the fight, but their victory was Pyrrhic. The struggle forced Innocent to immerse the church ever more deeply in European politics. The wholesale secularization of the papacy increased criticism of the church by religious reformers and the patriotic champions of national monarchies.

Frederick died in 1250, and hopes for an effective German monarchy died with him. The German nobles repudiated the theory that succession to their throne was hereditary, and in 1257 they formed an electoral college that claimed the right to bestow the imperial title. This made it very likely they could control the kings they created.

Frederick's legitimate heir was a young grandson called Conradin, but the only adult defender of the Hohenstaufen legacy was an illegitimate son named Manfred. Manfred fought hard to save some of his father's lands, but he was defeated in 1266. In 1286, Charles of Anjou, the adventurous brother of the saintly Louis IX, killed Conradin and took possession of southern Italy and Sicily. Germany, at least for the moment, ceased to be a problem for Italy, but Italy was not free from the threat of external interference. The French and, to a lesser extent, the English saw Germany's retreat as an opportunity for them to meddle in Italy's affairs.

SUMMARY

Otto I and the Revival of the Empire In 918, Henry I became the first Saxon king of Germany; eighteen years later his son Otto I took power, continuing his program of unification and expansion. He invaded Italy in 951, and proclaimed himself king. By the end of his reign, Otto the Great had even established authority over the Papal States and the pope himself. The Ottonian dynasty faltered in the early eleventh century, however, because Otto I's successors did not pay enough attention to events in Germany, and the church established an independent base of power for itself. By contrast, during this same period the Capetian kings in France focused on their home turf and built the basis for enduring royal power.

The Reviving Catholic Church The Catholic Church shed the secular control of the ninth and tenth centuries to emerge as a powerful independent institution. The reform movement based at the French monastery in Cluny spread throughout Europe and was endorsed by the pope. In 1075, Pope Gregory VII outlawed lay investiture of the clergy; this led to a battle of wills between popes and emperors, until the 1122 Concordat of Worms formalized a new relationship between church and state. Meanwhile, the Crusades provided an outlet

IMAGE KEY
for pages 172–173

a. Virgin and Child wood sculpture from Auvergne region, France. Late 12th century.   Oak with Polycromy, H: 31: (78.7 cm). Gift of J. Pierpont Morgan, 1916 (16.32.194). The Metropolitan Museum of Art, New York

b. "The Battle of Hastings". Detail of the Bayeux Tapestry, ca. 1073-83

c. Round stained glass window

d. Medieval monk's habit

e. Emperor Otto receives the homage of the nations. Gospels of Emperor Otto (II or III), also called "Registrum Gregorii." Ottonian art, 10th   Photograph © Erich Lessing/Art Resource, NY

f. Friedrich I Barbarossa depicted as crusader. Miniature of 1188, engraved from the original in the Vatican Library, Rome

g. Capture of Antioch, 1098, Le Miroir Historical by Vincent de Beauvais; XV century   Musee Conde Chantilly. E. T. Archive, London

h. King Louis IX (1266–1270) giving justice   From "Justiniani in Fortiatum," fol. 34. France, 14th c. Biblioteca Real, El Escorial, Madrid, Spain. Photograph © Bridgeman-Giraudon / Art Resource, NY

i. A drawing of the Romanesque abbey church of Cluny, France, built between 1080 and 1225

j. Henry II of England

k. Romanesque Chapel at east end of Abbey in Conques, France

for popular religious zeal. Repeated Christian expeditions to the Holy Lands did not do much to encourage Muslim respect for Europeans, but the Crusades did stimulate trade and expose the West to the civilizations of the East. Around 1200, Pope Innocent III asserted increased papal power, suppressed internal dissent, clarified church doctrine, and sanctioned two new monastic orders: the Franciscans and the Dominicans.

England and France: Hastings (1066) to Bouvines (1214) William, the duke of Normandy, won the Battle of Hastings in 1066, and soon was crowned king of England. Building on Anglo-Saxon traditions, he created a strong monarchy that used parleying to channel communications between the king and other leaders. William's grandson Henry married Eleanor of Aquitaine, creating the Angevin Empire. Later kings of England became more oppressive, raised taxes, and caused other problems, until English barons revolted and forced King John to recognize the Magna Carta in 1215. In roughly this same period in France, the Capetian kings first concentrated on securing their territory, then on exercising authority over the nobility. By 1214, in the battle at Bouvines against a combined English and German force, the French were able to defeat their opponents.

France in the Thirteenth Century: The Reign of Louis IX In the middle of the thirteenth century, Louis IX enjoyed almost fifty years as the ruler of a unified and secure France. He was able to focus his energies on domestic reform and the cultivation of culture and religion. He improved the justice system and presided over the emergence of Paris as the intellectual capital of Europe. He was fiercely religious, sponsoring the French Inquisition and leading two Crusades. In his dealings with foreigners, especially the English, he might be accused of naiveté; he failed to press his advantage at the Treaty of Paris in 1259 and allowed the English to maintain their claims on various French lands, thereby setting the stage for the Hundred Years' War in the next century.

The Hohenstaufen Empire (1152–1272) While stable governments that balanced central authority with the local needs of the populace were developing in England and France, the leaders of the Holy Roman Empire were squandering their opportunities to develop a sustainable political structure, a failure that would have negative repercussions through centuries of German history. Throughout the Hohenstaufen dynasty, conflicts with the popes and imperial schemes to control Italian lands distracted Frederick I Barbarossa and his successors from the task of maintaining the allegiance of the nobility and keeping their territory unified. By the late thirteenth century, the Hohenstaufen dynasty had lost all meaningful power and Germany was fragmented.

REVIEW QUESTIONS

1. How did the Saxon king Otto I rebuild the German Empire and use the church to achieve his political goals? How did his program fit with the aspirations of the Cluny reform movement? What was at stake for each of the disputants in the Investiture Controversy? Who won?

2. What developments in western and eastern Europe led to the start of the crusading movement? How did the Crusades to the Holy Lands affect Europe and the Muslim world?

3. Why were France and England able to coalesce into reasonably strong states, but not Germany?

KEY TERMS

Albigensians   (p. 181)
Beguines   (p. 183)
Crusades   (p. 177)

Inquisition   (p. 181)
Magna Carta   (p. 186)
regular clergy   (p. 175)

secular clergy   (p. 175)
transubstantiation   (p. 182)

 For additional study resources for this chapter, go to:
www.prenhall.com/kagan3/chapter7

8 Medieval Society Hierarchies, Towns, Universities, and Families (1000–1300)

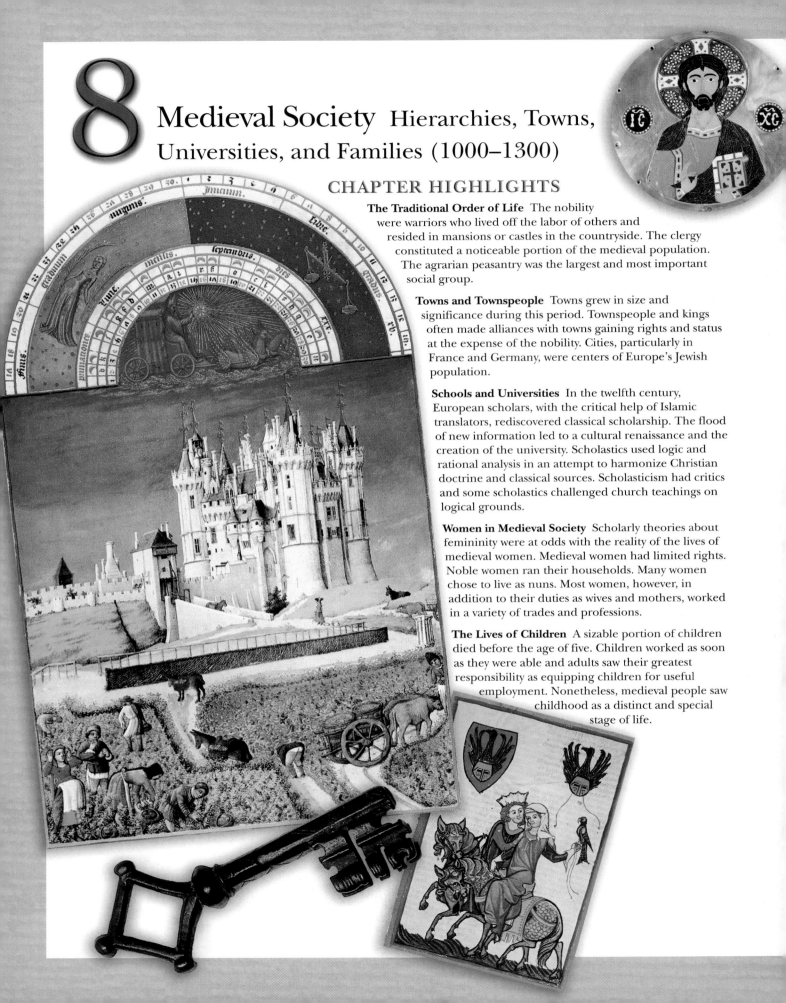

CHAPTER HIGHLIGHTS

The Traditional Order of Life The nobility were warriors who lived off the labor of others and resided in mansions or castles in the countryside. The clergy constituted a noticeable portion of the medieval population. The agrarian peasantry was the largest and most important social group.

Towns and Townspeople Towns grew in size and significance during this period. Townspeople and kings often made alliances with towns gaining rights and status at the expense of the nobility. Cities, particularly in France and Germany, were centers of Europe's Jewish population.

Schools and Universities In the twelfth century, European scholars, with the critical help of Islamic translators, rediscovered classical scholarship. The flood of new information led to a cultural renaissance and the creation of the university. Scholastics used logic and rational analysis in an attempt to harmonize Christian doctrine and classical sources. Scholasticism had critics and some scholastics challenged church teachings on logical grounds.

Women in Medieval Society Scholarly theories about femininity were at odds with the reality of the lives of medieval women. Medieval women had limited rights. Noble women ran their households. Many women chose to live as nuns. Most women, however, in addition to their duties as wives and mothers, worked in a variety of trades and professions.

The Lives of Children A sizable portion of children died before the age of five. Children worked as soon as they were able and adults saw their greatest responsibility as equipping children for useful employment. Nonetheless, medieval people saw childhood as a distinct and special stage of life.

CHAPTER QUESTIONS

WHAT WAS the life of a serf like during the Middle Ages?

WHAT PROCESSES led to the rise of towns and a merchant class?

WHAT WAS Scholasticism?

WHAT WAS life like for women during the Middle Ages?

WHAT WERE the characteristics of childhood in the Middle Ages?

CHAPTER OUTLINE
- The Traditional Order of Life
- Towns and Townspeople
- Schools and Universities
- Women in Medieval Society
- The Lives of Children

IMAGE KEY
Image Key for pages 194–195 is on page 212.

From the tenth to the twelfth centuries, increasing political stability helped Europe advance on multiple fronts. Agricultural production increased, population exploded, and trade and urban life revived. Crusades multiplied contacts with foreign lands that stimulated both economic and cultural development. A new merchant class, the ancestors of modern capitalists, appeared to serve the West's growing markets, and an urban proletariat developed.

Muslim intellectuals guided Europe's scholars in the rediscovery of Classical literature, and an explosion of information led to the rise of the university. Literacy increased among the laity and a renaissance in art and thought blossomed in the twelfth century. The creative vigor that surged through Europe in the High Middle Ages became tangible in the awesome Gothic churches that were the supreme products of medieval art and science.

WHAT WAS the life of a serf like during the Middle Ages?

THE TRADITIONAL ORDER OF LIFE

Medieval political theorists claimed that the maintenance of human communities required three essential services and God had made each one the responsibility of a separate class of people: knights provided protection, clergy interceded with prayer, and peasants and village artisans produced food and supplies. The revival of towns and trade in the eleventh century created a fourth class composed of merchants. Its members were thought of as a "middle class." They were economically productive like peasants, but they did not work the land. They had wealth like nobles and clergy, but they were not part of the political power structure. They did not fit neatly into the old social order, and the pressure they exerted ultimately caused it to collapse.

NOBLES

Nobles were distinguished by the fact that they owned significant amounts of land and exercised authority over other people. They did not farm or trade, but many had ancestors who had done these things. Late medieval society boasted both a higher and a lower nobility. The higher consisted of great landowners and territorial magnates, and the lower was populated by petty knights with fiefs, newly rich merchants who bought country estates, and prosperous farmers who rose from serfdom. Nobles were lords of manors who neither tilled the soil nor engaged in commerce—work that was beneath the dignity of an aristocrat.

Warriors European warfare had changed dramatically with the appearance of the stirrup in the eighth century. Stirrups gave riders secure seats on their mounts and thereby enabled them to strike blows at their enemies without lofting themselves off their horses. The stirrup gave cavalry the power to rout the infantry that had dominated battle in the ancient world. However, cavalry equipment and training were expensive, and lords who wanted to employ cavalrymen had to divide up their lands to create fiefs to support them. Thus the use of arms came to be associated with ownership of land and military service with nobility.

The code by which medieval nobles lived stressed the importance of physical strength, reputation, and aggressive behavior. Nobles welcomed war as an opportunity to increase their fortunes by plunder and to win respect by acts of courage. Peace threatened economic stagnation and boredom for nobles but held out the promise of prosperity for peasants and townspeople. Consequently, the interests of the medieval social classes conflicted, and the nobles dismissed the commoners' love of peace as cowardice.

The Joys and Pains of the Medieval Joust. This scene from a manuscript from c. 1300–1349 idealizes medieval noblewomen and the medieval joust. Revived in the late Middle Ages, jousts were frequently held in peacetime. They kept the warring skills of noblemen sharp and became popular entertainment. Only the nobility were legally allowed to joust, but over time, uncommon wealth enabled a persistent commoner to qualify.

University of Heidelberg

The quasi-sacramental ceremony that bestowed knighthood marked a man's entrance into the noble class. A candidate for knighthood first took a bath as a sign of ritual purification. He then confessed, communed, and stood a night-long prayer vigil. At his dubbing ("striking") ceremony, a priest blessed his standard, lance, and sword and girded him with the weapons he was to use in the defense of the church and the service of his lord. A senior knight then struck him on the shoulders with a sword and raised him to a status as sacred in its way as clerical ordination.

In the twelfth century, knighthood was legally restricted to men of high birth. The closing of the ranks of the nobility was a reaction to the growing wealth and power of the social-climbing commercial classes. Kings, however, reserved the right to bestow knighthood on anyone, and by selling titles to wealthy merchants (an important source of royal revenue) they kept an avenue of social mobility open.

Way of Life   Noblemen honed their military skills by hunting and taking part in tournaments. Their passion for hunting was so great that they forbade commoners to take game from the forests. Peasants resented being deprived of this source of free food, and anger at the nobility's hunting monopoly was one of many grievances that motivated peasant uprisings in the late medieval period.

Tournaments sowed seeds of social disruption of a different kind, for they tended to get out of hand. Serious bloodshed could lead to calls for vengeance and turned mock battles into real wars. The church opposed tournaments because of their promotion of violence and association with pagan revelry, and kings and princes finally agreed that tournaments were a threat to public order. Henry II of England proscribed tournaments in the twelfth century, but they continued in France until the mid–sixteenth century. (See "Encountering the Past: Warrior Games.")

During the twelfth century, distinctive standards for courtesy ("conduct at court") appeared to regulate the behavior of the nobility. Thanks to the influence of powerful women such as Henry II's queen, Eleanor of Aquitaine, knowledge of court etiquette became almost as important for a nobleman's advancement as battlefield expertise. The new codes required the knight to be both a courageous athlete and a cultivated gentleman. He was supposed to be strong in battle, but clean, well dressed, and sufficiently literate to compose lyric poems in honor of his lady. The woman who inspired his raptures was usually another man's wife. His songs might flirt with frank eroticism, but courtly love was supposed to be an ennobling experience that did not sink to the level of sexual seduction. Some poets warned that illicit carnal love led to suffering, and the courtly love movement may actually have been an attempt to curtail the notorious philandering of the noble classes.

Social Divisions   Medieval society was hierarchical, and status within the nobility was a function of how much authority one had over others. Lords with many vassals obviously outranked those with fewer, but shifts in wealth and power in the late Middle Ages drastically restructured the noble class. Climatic changes depressed the agricultural economy that was the source of the landed nobility's wealth, and famines and plagues caused massive demographic dislocations. Changing military tactics rendered noble cavalry nearly obsolete, and the influence of wealthy townsmen increased as they helped kings establish more effective control of the nobility. After the fourteenth century, a fortune counted more than a family tree as a qualification for social advancement.

ENCOUNTERING THE PAST

WARRIOR GAMES

The cultural environment surrounding the medieval nobility—poetry, songs, arts, and entertainments—glorified war. This was consistent with the interests of a warrior class whose men spent their lives fighting and training for battle. A young nobleman might receive his first horse and dagger at the age of two. By the time he turned fourteen, he was ready to handle adult weapons.

Tournaments (mock combats) provided him with both practical training and diversion. They proved so popular with all members of society that they survived as pastimes even after changes in warfare diminished the need for a knight's traditional skills.

The military preoccupations of the knights influenced the behavior of other members of medieval society. Aristocratic women hunted but were limited to the role of spectators at entertainments such as tournaments. Some clergy were famous sportsmen and warriors, but, like women, their taste for violence was usually satisfied vicariously by rooting for champions at tournaments and by playing chess, backgammon, and competitive games such as "Tick, Tack, Toe." Commoners attended tournaments and developed similar warlike games and sports of their own. The equivalent of a tournament for men and boys of the lower classes was a rough ball game—an early version of rugby, soccer, or football. Medieval people were ingenious at inventing diversions for their idle hours, as Pieter Breughel's painting, *Children's Games* (1560), documents. It depicts boys and girls engaged in seventy-eight different activities.

WHY DID the medieval nobility play warlike games? How did these influence the behavior of other members of society?

Breughel, *Children's Games.* Pieter the Elder Breughel (1525–1569), "Children's Games," 1560. Oil on oakwood, 118 × 161 cm. Kunsthistoriches Museum, Vienna, Austria.

Photo copyright Erich Lessing/Art Resource, NY

CLERGY

Clergy, unlike nobles and peasants, were ranked more by training and ordination than by birth. People of talent could climb the clerical hierarchy no matter what their origins. The church, therefore, offered gifted commoners their best opportunity for social mobility.

Secular and Regular Clerics There were two clerical vocations: secular and regular. The **secular clergy** lived and worked among the laity in the *saeculum* ("world"). The most prestigious of secular clergy were the wealthy cardinals, archbishops, and bishops (men often, but not always, of noble birth). Next in rank were the urban priests, the cathedral canons, and the court clerks. At the bottom of the clerical hierarchy was the humble parish priest, who was neither financially nor intellectually superior to the laypeople he served. Until the eleventh century, parish priests routinely lived with women in relationships akin to marriage and

secular clergy Clergy, such as bishops and priests, who lived and worked among the laity in the *saeculum* ("world").

stretched their meager incomes by working as teachers, artisans, and farmers. These customs were accepted and even defended by their parishioners.

Regular clergy were monks and nuns (although, strictly speaking, women were not accorded clerical status) who lived under the *regula* ("rule") of a cloister. They retreated from the world and adopted rigorous ascetic disciplines in the belief they were following the example set by Christ's life of poverty and self-sacrifice. Their devotion to what their contemporaries regarded as the ideal Christian way of life earned them respect and influence. The regular clergy were, however, never completely cut off from the secular world. They maintained contact with the laity as dispensers of charity, as instructors in schools, and as preachers and confessors who assisted in parish work. The intellectual gifts and educations of some monks fit them for service as secretaries and private confessors for kings and queens. Nunneries produced famous female scholars, and monasticism inspired many of the religious and social reform movements of the medieval era.

The Benedictine rule had been adopted by most Western monasteries by the end of the Carolingian era, but during the High Middle Ages many new orders appeared. The monastic rule devised by Saint Benedict emphasized the pursuit of economic self-sufficiency through hard physical labor more than rigorous ascetic discipline. Thanks, however, to generations of bequests and careful husbandry of resources, many Benedictine houses, like the famous Cluny, grew wealthy and self-preoccupied. Benedictine monks did little manual labor and spent their time chanting ever more elaborate liturgies in their ever more elegantly appointed sanctuaries. The new orders rejected this Benedictine "luxury" and sought to return to the ideals of Christlike poverty and simplicity that had characterized the monastic movement in the beginning.

The Carthusians, whose order was founded in 1084, were the strictest of the new monks. They lived apart from one another as hermits, fasted three days a week, observed long periods of silence, and disciplined their flesh by acts of self-flagellation.

The Cistercians, whose order was established in 1098 at Cîteaux in Burgundy, set out to restore what they believed was the original intent of the Benedictine rule. They condemned materialism and stressed cultivation of the inner life. To avoid contamination by the secular world and the temptations of wealth, they located their houses in remote wilderness areas where they faced a struggle to survive.

The monastic ideal was so popular in the eleventh century that many secular clergy (and some laypersons) tried to merge the spiritual disciplines of the cloister with traditional pastoral duties. The Canons Regular were groups of secular clergy who lived according to a rule credited to the fifth-century saint Augustine of Hippo, who stayed in the world to serve the laity. The mendicant friars (most notably, the Dominicans and Franciscans who appeared early in the thirteenth century) also combined the secular and regular clerical professions. During the late thirteenth and fourteenth centuries, satellite convents known as Beguine houses sprang up to accommodate unmarried women who for reasons of class or wealth were not admitted to traditional nunneries. (One hundred of these organizations appeared in the city of Cologne between 1250 and 1350.) The Franciscans and Dominicans often assumed responsibility for directing the Beguine houses and making sure their spiritual enthusiasm did not erupt into heresy.

Prominence of the Clergy   The clergy were far more numerous in the Middle Ages than they are today. By the fourteenth century, 1.5 percent of Europe's population may have been clergy. Like the nobility, they usually lived on the labor of

QUICK REVIEW

Clergy

• Secular clergy worked and lived among the laity

• Regular clergy were monks and nuns who lived under the rule of a cloister

• Regular clergy maintained contact with the secular world

Lovers playing chess on an ivory mirror back, ca. 1300.

The Bridgeman Art Library International

regular clergy   Monks and nuns who lived under the *regula* ("rule") of a cloister.

others. The church was a major landowner and had a huge income from rents and fees. The great fortunes claimed by monastic communities and high prelates brought them immense secular power.

Respect for clergy as members of society's "first estate" derived from their role as mediators between God and humankind. When the priest celebrated the Eucharist, he brought the very Son of God down to earth in tangible form. The priest alone had the power to extend God's forgiveness to sinners or to block their access to it by imposing excommunication (decrees that cut sinners off from the sacraments, the only means for their salvation).

Because a priest was the agent of a heavenly authority far superior to that of any earthly magistrate, it was considered inappropriate for him to be subservient to the laymen who governed the state. Clergy, therefore, had special privileges and immunities. They were not to be taxed by secular governments without approval from the church. Clerical crimes were under the jurisdiction of special ecclesiastical tribunals, not the secular courts. The churches and monasteries where clergy worked were also deemed to be outside the legal jurisdiction of the state. People who took refuge in them received asylum and could not be apprehended by officials of secular governments.

By the late Middle Ages, laypeople had come to resent the special privileges of the clergy, and the anticlerical sentiment that was mounting among them contributed to the success of the Protestant Reformation in the sixteenth century. Protestant theologians challenged medieval tradition by claiming that clergy and laity had equal spiritual standing before God.

PEASANTS

The largest and lowest class in medieval society was the one on whose labor the welfare of all the others depended: the agrarian peasantry. The fundamental institutions of medieval rural life are called *manors*. For the early Franks, manors were plots of twelve to seventy-five acres of land that were assigned a man by his tribe or clan. As others joined him on his land, he became the lord of the manor and assumed leadership of a self-sufficient community. A manor was not necessarily the same as a village, for a given village might be home to peasant workers who belonged to different manors.

The Duties of Tenancy The lord of a manor demanded a certain amount of produce and various services from the peasants who worked his land, but he left them free to divide the labor this entailed among themselves. Anything they produced above and beyond what they owed him they could keep. No set rules governed the size of a manor or the number of manors a lord could hold.

There were two kinds of manors: servile and free. The tenants (serfs) of free manors were descendants of Roman *coloni*, free persons who had traded their land and freedom for a guarantee of protection by their lord. Tenancy obligations on free manors were limited because the property their members brought to the manor gave them some leverage in negotiating the terms for their service on the manor. Tenants of servile manors were initially more vulnerable to the whims of their landlords, but time tended to obscure differences between the two types of manors. In many regions, self-governing communities of free peasants, who acknowledged no lord, could also be found.

The lord was the supreme authority on his manor. Serfs had to cultivate his *demesne* (the land producing his income) and reap his harvest before attending to their own fields. He could impress his tenants into labor gangs for special projects or lead them out as foot soldiers when he went to war. He could extort additional

8.1
Manorial Court Records

manor A self-sufficient rural community that was a fundamental institution of medieval life.

income from them in several ways. He owned and leased some of the instruments and facilities they needed to raise and process food, and he maintained profitable monopolies called **banalities** (e.g., the right to demand that his tenants pay to grind all their grain in his mill and bake all their bread in his oven). The lord also collected an inheritance tax from a serf's heir (usually the best animal from the deceased's estate). A serf who wished to travel or to marry outside his manor also had to obtain his lord's permission (and usually pay a fee).

The Life of a Serf   Burdened as a serf's life was, it was superior to chattel slavery. Serfs had their own dwellings and modest strips of land. They managed their own labor. They could sell any surpluses they produced for their own profit. They were free to choose their own spouses from the manor community. Their marriages were protected by the church. Their property passed to their children, and they could not be sold away from their land.

In this eleventh-century manuscript, peasants harvest grain, trim vines, and plow fields behind yoked oxen.

Giraudon/Art Resource, NY

Serfs seldom ventured far from the villages where they were born. The single village church that was available to them limited their religious options. However, the poverty of religious instruction meant that their beliefs and practices were by no means unambiguously Christian. There were social and economic distinctions among them, but the common struggle for survival forced them to work together. The ratio of seed to grain yield was poor throughout the Middle Ages. About two bushels of seed had to be sown to produce six to ten bushels of grain—in good years. There was rarely an abundance of bread and ale, the staple peasant foods. Europeans did not discover two of the crops on which the modern West depends, potatoes and corn (maize), until the sixteenth century. Pork was the major source of animal protein, for pigs, unlike cattle, could forage for themselves in the forests. As winter set in, excess plow animals were slaughtered and their meat dried or salted. Life hinged on grain crops. When they failed or fell short, there was no other resource that could be tapped to stave off famine.

Changes in the Manor   Technological advances such as the horse collar (ca. 800), the horseshoe (ca. 900), and the three-field system of crop rotation improved agricultural productivity. The stimulation of demand from the new markets that were created as towns proliferated during the High Middle Ages prompted peasant farmers to bring more land into production. These things produced surplus income that serfs used to buy their freedom from the obligation of feudal labor service. Once towns revived trade and restored a money-based economy, lords also found it more profitable to lease their lands to free entrepreneurial tenant farmers than to work them with unwilling serfs. As the medieval era waned, therefore, the manor and serfdom gave way to the independent single-family farm, but that did not mean peasants were not necessarily better off materially. In hard times serfs might expect assistance from their lords, for lords had to preserve the labor force that worked their manors. Free rent-paying farmers, however, had to take care of themselves.

The expanding economy and rising standards of living that characterized the High Middle Ages affected landed aristocrats as well as servile workers.

banalities Monopolies maintained by landowners giving them the right to demand that tenants pay to grind all their grain in the landowner's mill and bake all their bread in his oven.

The incomes that lords drew from their manors were fixed by tradition, but the costs of their lifestyle were not. It became progressively difficult for them to make ends meet, and in the mid–fourteenth century, nobles in England and France tried to increase taxes on peasants and to limit laborers' ability to bargain for higher wages. This prompted revolts that were brutally crushed, but which suggested that traditional medieval society was breaking up.

TOWNS AND TOWNSPEOPLE

WHAT PROCESSES led to the rise of towns and a merchant class?

In the eleventh and twelfth centuries, only about 5 percent of Europeans lived in towns, and most urban communities were small. Of Germany's 3,000 towns, 2,800 had populations under 1,000. Only 15 exceeded 10,000, and the largest (Cologne) had a mere 30,000. London was the only English city greater than 10,000. Paris was bigger than London, but not by much. Italy boasted Europe's greatest towns. Florence and Milan approached 100,000.

THE CHARTERING OF TOWNS

Despite their small size, towns were, in the Middle Ages as now, where the action was. The secular and ecclesiastical lords who dominated the medieval landscape often welcomed the growth of towns on their estates, for they wanted the products (and opportunities for levying taxes) that urban traders provided. New towns tended to be dominated by the feudal magnates who controlled the region in which they were built, but most won their independence by purchasing a charter from their lord. A charter spelled out privileges that granted the residents of a town much greater freedom than rural workers enjoyed. Freedom was a requirement of life for men and women who lived by invention and audacious commercial enterprise.

Towns hastened the disintegration of feudal society by providing serfs who wanted to escape manorial life with a place to go. It was tempting to flee, for the economy of a flourishing town offered individuals who mastered crafts and worked hard good prospects for improving their social standing. The mere possibility that a lord's serfs might migrate to a town, however, improved the lot of the peasants who stayed in the countryside as well as those who actually made the move. A lord who wanted to keep his labor force on his land had to offer them favorable terms.

THE RISE OF MERCHANTS

The first merchants were probably enterprising serfs or outcasts who found no place in the feudal system. Having no protector and no legal standing, they had to provide for themselves. They organized armed caravans, bought goods as cheaply as possible in one place, and then took them to another where they hoped to be able to sell them for a profit. Our modern urban lifestyle springs from the greed and daring of these rough-hewn men.

Merchants were considered an oddity, for they did not fit into the three classes (noble, clergy, and peasant) that theoretically constituted feudal society. As late as the fifteenth century, nobles still snubbed the urban patriciate (the hereditary ruling class that arose in some cities). Over time, however, the politically powerful grew to respect the merchants as much as the powerless aspired to imitate them, for wherever merchants were, wealth accumulated.

CHALLENGING THE OLD LORDS

As traders settled down and established towns, they grew in wealth and numbers and began to challenge the feudal authorities. In the eleventh century, they began to form merchant guilds (unions, protective associations) to oppose restrictions

MAP EXPLORATION

Interactive map: To explore this map further, go to **http://www.prenhall.com/kagan3/map8.1**

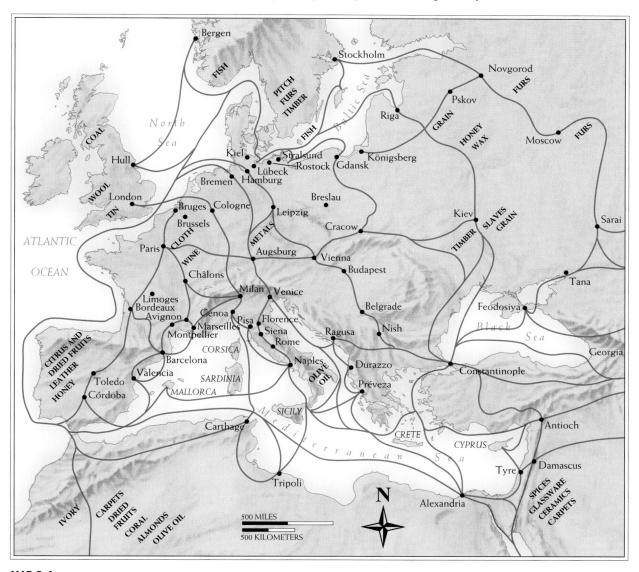

MAP 8–1

Some Medieval Trade Routes and Regional Products   The map shows some of the channels that came to be used in interregional commerce and what was traded in a particular region.

GIVEN THE KINDS of items traded, was international trade essential or peripheral to the lives of medieval people?

that hampered the flow of goods. Guilds of craftsmen appeared in the twelfth century, and all these organizations of commoners had as their objective the transformation of a social order that the feudal classes assumed to be natural and static.

Merchants opposed the fortress mentality that had prompted the division of the countryside into a plethora of tiny feudal jurisdictions. They wanted to end the myriad tolls and tariffs demanded by the petty lords through whose fiefs their caravans traveled. They favored governments that could enforce simple, uniform laws throughout large areas. City dwellers also wanted to wrest control of their communities away from the feudal nobility and improve security by reversing the political fragmentation that feudalism encouraged. For similar reasons, the church and Europe's kings were willing to join townspeople in efforts to bring the feudal nobility under control.

NEW MODELS OF GOVERNMENT

By 1100, the older noble families that had tried to dominate Europe's growing towns had merged with their communities' most prosperous commoner families. The rich began to work together to establish and control the town councils that became the chief organs of municipal government. Small artisans and craftsmen responded by forming associations and fighting for representation on these councils. The oppressed and economically exploited urban poor were generally left out of the power structure. This was dangerous because medieval townspeople were politically volatile. As citizens, not subjects, they believed they were entitled to certain rights. When necessary, they rioted to make this point. So long, however, as there was enough social mobility in urban communities to offer the poor hope, they had a stake in the system and were willing to support it.

Social Tensions   Despite democratic tendencies, townspeople were very conscious of class distinctions. The wealthiest urban groups aped the lifestyle of the old landed nobility. They acquired coats of arms, bought country estates, and built castles. Once the heads of great business enterprises had set up lines of communication and worked out banking procedures for transferring funds, they left traveling to underlings and settled down to run their companies from their rural mansions. The migration of these social-climbing entrepreneurs and capitalists to the countryside was an economic loss for the towns that had given them their starts.

A desire for social distinction was not confined to the rich. People at every level were tempted to imitate the dress and habits of their superiors. Towns tried to restrain costly competition of this kind by decreeing appropriate levels of dress and consumption for each social group and vocation. Conspicuous expenditure was regarded as a kind of indecent exposure, and it was punished by "sumptuary" laws (regulations that punished people who tried to live beyond what the community considered appropriate to their station). These rules were intended to maintain order by keeping each person in his or her proper place.

The need for laws to limit competition among classes hints at the tensions that strained medieval urban communities. Towns were collections of self-centered groups that had to live in close proximity to one another. Conflict among these factions particularly the haves and the have-nots was inevitable. The poorest workers in the export trades (usually the weavers and wool combers) were clearly inferior to independent artisans and small shopkeepers. In turn, the interests of these craftsmen differed from those of the great merchants. The latter imported foreign goods to compete with the things the former produced locally. Theoretically, poor men could work their way up this hierarchy, and some lucky ones

Skilled workers were an integral component of the commerce of medieval towns. This scene shows the manufacture of cannons in a foundry in Florence.

Scala/Art Resource, NY

actually did so. Until they reached a fairly high plateau, however, they were excluded from membership on the town council, and full citizenship came to be reserved for property-owning families of long standing. Urban self-government tended, therefore, to become progressively inbred and aristocratic.

Artisans assumed that by working together they could increase their political clout. The guilds they formed for this purpose benefited the "masters" who organized them but at a significant cost to others. Guilds used their power on town councils to establish monopolies—to win exclusive rights to deal in goods for the local market. They protected that market by ensuring that those who served it produced acceptable products at fair prices, but they discouraged improvements in techniques of production for fear this would give the inventors advantages over others. Once there were enough producers in town, a guild also avoided saturating its market by refusing to license new shops. This infuriated the journeymen who trained in guild shops, for it reduced the likelihood they would ever be able to set up in business for themselves. It condemned them to the status of politically disenfranchised workers who had no hope of advancement. The protectionism practiced by the guild-dominated urban governments of the Middle Ages created a true proletariat and ultimately depressed the economy for everyone.

TOWNS AND KINGS

A natural alliance developed between towns and the kings who were struggling to construct central governments for nation-states. Kings staffed their administrations with urban bureaucrats and lawyers familiar with Roman law, the tool for designing kingdoms. Towns provided the money that kings needed to hire professional agents and soldiers and free themselves from dependence on the feudal nobility. Towns, in short, had the human, financial, and technological resources to empower kings.

Towns wanted kings to establish effective monarchies, for royal governments that controlled large territories provided the best support for commerce. A strong king could control the local despots whose tolls and petty wars disrupted trade, and kings, unlike local magnates, tended to keep their distance and allow towns considerable autonomy. In addition to protection, monarchies also issued standardized currencies that made buying and selling much easier.

The relationship between kings and towns fluctuated with the fate of monarchical development in each part of Europe. In France, where the Capetian dynasty flourished, towns were integrated into royal government. In England, towns supported the barons against unpopular kings (such as John) but cooperated with the efforts of more effective monarchs to subdue the nobility. In Germany, where the feudal magnates triumphed over kings, towns came under the control of territorial princes. Italy, by comparison, offered towns quite different opportunities. Italy had no native royal family for towns to support against the nobility. Italy's townspeople also shared the nobility's opposition to the political ambitions of German kings and Roman popes. The two classes, therefore, worked together, and as their leaders intermarried, towns extended their authority into the countryside and began to resemble the ancient world's city-states.

Between the eleventh and fourteenth centuries, towns enjoyed considerable autonomy and once again became the centers of Western civilization. As centralized monarchies began to take hold in the fourteenth century, kings were able to assert increasing authority over towns and the church. By the seventeenth century, few towns had escaped integration into the larger purposes of the state.

QUICK REVIEW

Basis of the Alliance

- Towns were a source of human, financial, and technological resources for kings
- Effective royal government created the best environment for commerce
- Monarchies issued standardized currencies that facilitated buying and selling

JEWS IN CHRISTIAN SOCIETY

Medieval Europe's Jews could not take Christian oaths of homage. They were, therefore, excluded from feudal land tenure and forced to earn their livings from trade. They congregated in towns and (for both protection and the practice of their religion) formed tight separate communities. The church forbade them to employ Christians, and the lack of contacts between Christians and Jews promoted mutual suspicion. Ignorance of Jewish practices, resentment of the wealth acquired by some Jews, and a popular tendency to hold the Jews responsible for Christ's crucifixion fueled baseless rumors of Jewish schemes to undermine Christian society. These sparked periodic outbreaks of mob violence against Jews and the imposition of fines or sentences of exile on whole communities of Jews by governmental authorities.

WHAT WAS Scholasticism?

SCHOOLS AND UNIVERSITIES

*I*n the twelfth century, European scholars discovered Aristotle's treatises on logic, the writings of Euclid and Ptolemy, Roman law, and the basic works of Greek physicians and Arab mathematicians. Islamic scholars living in Spain were chiefly responsible for the translations and commentaries that made these ancient texts accessible to Europeans. The flood of new information created a cultural renaissance and a new kind of center for intellectual activity, the university.

UNIVERSITY OF BOLOGNA

All that the term *university* initially implied was a corporation of individuals working together for their mutual benefit. The new schools that sprang up in the twelfth century attracted students and teachers from great distances. Many were foreigners who had no civil rights in the towns where they worked. Their vulnerability to exploitation and abuse by landlords and civic authorities led them to organize (like members of an urban craft guild) to protect themselves. When their scholars' guild acquired legal recognition, a university was born.

The university in the Italian city of Bologna was the first of the great medieval schools to receive such recognition. Emperor Frederick Barbarossa issued it a charter in 1158, and it became a model for schools in Italy, Spain, and southern France. Bologna was a guild of students, who unionized to ensure that landlords and tavern owners charged them fair prices and teachers gave them excellent instruction. The students hired professors, set pay scales, and assigned lecture topics. Instructors who did not live up to their expectations were boycotted, and they countered price-gouging townspeople by threatening to move the university and the profitable business it generated to another town.

Bologna was Europe's premier center for advanced studies in law. In the late eleventh century, Europeans discovered the *Corpus Juris Civilis*, the collection of ancient Roman laws made by the Byzantine emperor Justinian in the sixth century. In the early twelfth century, Irnerius of Bologna began to show how Roman law could be used to create *glosses* (commentaries) that clarified existing European laws. Around 1140 in Bologna, a monk named Gratian wrote the text that became standard for studying the church's canon law: *Concordance of Discordant Canons*, or simply *Decretum*.

Students were not the only scholars to form guilds to protect their interests. Their teachers, or *masters*, did so as well, and faculty guilds dominated the uni-

OVERVIEW   TWO SCHOOLS OF THE HIGH MIDDLE AGES

University of Bologna	• Chartered in 1158
	• First of the great medieval schools to acquire recognition as a university
	• Students hired professors, set pay scales, and assigned lecture topics
	• Europe's premier center for advanced studies in law
University of Paris	• Chartered in 1200
	• Provided the model for the schools of northern Europe
	• Students given protections and privileges exceeding those of other citizens
	• Teachers were required to be examined thoroughly before being licensed
	• Twenty or more years were needed to earn a doctorate in theology

versities of northern Europe. Paris was preeminent among them. Masters' guilds held a monopoly on teaching, and tests for admission to these guilds set standards for certification of teachers. The licenses to teach that medieval guilds awarded were the predecessors of modern academic degrees.

CATHEDRAL SCHOOLS

Students usually entered the university between the ages of twelve and fifteen. Because all books and all instruction were in Latin, they were expected to arrive knowing how to read and speak that language. The first four years of their course of study were devoted to the *trivium* (grammar, rhetoric, and logic), which polished their Latin and earned them a bachelor's degree. A master's degree entailed an additional three or four years of work on the *quadrivium* (arithmetic, geometry, astronomy, and music). This was primarily the study of ancient texts dealing with mathematics, natural science, and philosophy. Doctoral degrees were available in a few fields such as law, medicine, and theology. Twenty or more years were needed to earn a doctorate in theology at the University of Paris.

The university's curriculum centered on the liberal arts programs that early medieval cathedral and monastery schools had created to train clergy. These were the only schools that existed during the early medieval centuries, and clergy were the only people whose vocations required literacy. But by the late eleventh century, students who wanted to become notaries or merchants—not clergy—began to frequent the church's schools. In 1179, a papal decree ordered cathedrals to provide teachers gratis for laity who wanted to learn. By the thirteenth century, the demand for literate men to staff the urban and territorial governments and merchant firms gave rise to schools offering secular vocational education. (See "History's Voices: Student Life at the University of Paris.")

Medieval school scene
German Information Center

UNIVERSITY OF PARIS

The University of Paris, which provided the model for the schools of northern Europe, evolved, in part, from the school maintained by Paris's Cathedral of Notre Dame. King Philip Augustus and Pope Innocent III chartered it in 1200 and gave its students protections and privileges exceeding those of ordinary citizens. Only in self-defense, for instance, was a citizen permitted to strike a student,

HISTORY'S VOICES

STUDENT LIFE AT THE UNIVERSITY OF PARIS

s the following account by Jacques de Vitry makes clear, not all students at the University of Paris in the thirteenth century were there to gain knowledge. Students fought constantly and subjected each other to ethnic insults and slurs.

WAS THE RIVALRY among faculty members as intense as that among students?

Almost all the students at Paris, foreigners and natives, did absolutely nothing except learn or hear something new. Some studied merely to acquire knowledge, which is curiosity; others to acquire fame, which is vanity; others still for the sake of gain, which is cupidity and the vice of simony. Very few studied for their own edification, or that of others. They wrangled and disputed not merely about the various sects or about some discussions; but the differences between the countries also caused dissensions, hatreds and virulent animosities among them, and they impudently uttered all kinds of affronts and insults against one another.

They affirmed that the English were drunkards and had tails; the sons of France proud, effeminate and carefully adorned like women. They said that the Germans were furious and obscene at their feasts; the Normans, vain and boastful; the Poitevins, traitors and always adventurers. The Burgundians they con-

sidered vulgar and stupid. The Bretons were reputed to be fickle and changeable, and were often reproached for the death of Arthur. The Lombards were called avaricious, vicious and cowardly; the Romans, seditious, turbulent and slanderous; the Sicilians, tyrannical and cruel; the inhabitants of Brabant, men of blood, incendiaries, brigands, and ravishers; the Flemish, fickle, prodigal, gluttonous, yielding as butter, and slothful. After such insults from words they often came to blows.

I will not speak of those logicians [professors of logic and dialectic] before whose eyes flitted constantly "the lice of Egypt," that is to say, all the sophistical subtleties, so that no one could comprehend their eloquent discourses in which, as says Isaiah, "there is no wisdom." As to the doctors of theology, "seated in Moses' seat." they were swollen with learning, but their charity was not edifying. Teaching and not practicing, they have "become as sounding brass or a tinkling cymbal," or like a canal of stone, always dry, which ought to carry water to "the bed of spices." They not only hated one another, but by their flatteries they enticed away the students of others; each one seeking his own glory, but caring not a whit about the welfare of souls.

Translations and reprints from the *Original Sources of European History*, Vol. 2 (Philadelphia: Department of History, University of Pennsylvania, 1902), pp. 19–20.

and all citizens were required to testify against anyone who was seen to abuse a student. University regulations required that teachers be examined thoroughly before being licensed to teach. French law, in short, recognized students as a valuable and vulnerable resource.

Paris originated the college or house system. The first colleges were charitable hospices set up to provide room and board for poor students who would not otherwise be able to afford to study. The university discovered these institutions were useful for maintaining discipline among its students, and it encouraged all its students to enroll in them. (Today, the University of Paris is popularly known by the name of its most famous college, the Sorbonne, founded about 1257 by a royal chaplain named Robert de Sorbon.) Endowed colleges changed the nature of the university. The first universities had no buildings of their own and relied on rented or borrowed space. They were mobile institutions that could easily relocate if need be. College buildings, however, rooted universities in place, and this reduced their leverage in negotiating with townspeople. The acquisition of physical facilities made it difficult for universities to threaten to move if the towns in which they were located failed to meet their demands.

THE CURRICULUM

The early cathedral and monastery schools provided a limited education consisting primarily of (Latin) grammar, rhetoric, and some elementary geometry and astronomy. The standard texts were the grammars of Donatus and Priscian, Augustine's *On Christian Doctrine*, Cassiodorus's *On Divine and Secular Learning*, Boethius's treatises on arithmetic and music, and a few of Aristotle's essays on logic. The books that Europeans obtained from the Muslim world in the early twelfth century vastly expanded Europe's libraries and provided materials for more elaborate programs of study at universities. The most revolutionary of the new texts were works by Aristotle that had previously been unknown in Europe. They had passed into general circulation by the mid–thirteenth century and inspired **Scholasticism**, the method of study associated with the medieval university.

In the High Middle Ages, scholars assumed truth was not something one had to discover for oneself. Truth was already enshrined in the works of the great authorities of the past—men such as Aristotle and the fathers of the church. Teachers did not prepare students to strive independently for new information, but only to comprehend and absorb what they found in ancient sources. They used logic and dialectic (rational analysis) to harmonize, not critique, the accepted truths of tradition. Dialectic, the art of discovering a truth by finding contradictions in arguments against it, reigned supreme in all disciplines. Medieval students did not observe phenomena for themselves. They read the authoritative texts in their fields, summarized them, disputed the pros and cons of various interpretations, and drew conclusions based on logical cogency.

All books were written out by hand, for printing with moveable type was not invented until the fifteenth century. Books were expensive, and few students could afford to purchase personal copies of the texts they studied. Most learned by listening to lectures and discussions and memorizing what they heard. The goal of an education was to equip a scholar with the rhetorical skills needed to construct subtle logical arguments and win debates. This required a person to become a walking encyclopedia filled with information that could be regurgitated as needed.

PHILOSOPHY AND THEOLOGY

Scholastics quarreled over the proper relationship between philosophy, by which they meant almost exclusively the writings of Aristotle, and theology, which they believed to be a "science" based on divine revelation. In Christian eyes, Aristotle's writings contained heresy; for example, Aristotle taught the eternality of the world, which called into question the Judeo-Christian teaching in the book of Genesis that God created the world in time. Church authorities wanted the works of Aristotle and other ancient authorities to be submissive handmaidens to Christian truth.

ABELARD

When philosophers and theologians applied the logic and metaphysics of Aristotle to the interpretation of Christian revelation, many believed it posed a mortal threat to biblical truth and church authority. Peter Abelard (1079–1142), the first European scholar to gain a large student audience, and possibly the brightest

In this engraving, a teacher at the University of Paris leads fellow scholars in a discussion. As shown here, all of the students wore the scholar's cap and gown.

CORBIS/Bettmann

8.4
St. Thomas Aquinas:
The Summa Against the Gentiles (Summa Contra Gentiles, 1259–1264)

Scholasticism Method of study associated with the medieval university.

logician and dialectician of the high Middle Ages, gained great notoriety for such wrongful interpretation of the Scriptures. He boldly subjected church teaching to Aristotelian logic and dialectic, making him many powerful enemies at a time when there was no tenure to protect genius and free speech in schools and universities. Accused of multiple transgressions of church doctrine, he ended his life in a monastery and wrote an autobiography about the calamitous results of his teachings and behavior.

Abelard's critics especially condemned him for his subjective interpretations of Scripture. His ethical teachings questioned vital theological issues like the nature of the Holy Trinity and Christ's crucifixion. He stressed Christians' intent over their deeds, asserting that the motives of the doer made an act good or evil, not the act itself. Inner feelings were thus more important for receiving divine forgiveness than the church's sacrament of penance administered by a priest.

In Paris, Abelard gave his powerful enemies an opportunity to strike him down when he seduced Heloise, a bright, seventeen-year-old niece of a powerful canon (cathedral priest) who had hired him to be her tutor in his home. Their passionate affair ended in scandal, with Heloise pregnant and Abelard, being a university teacher, required to be single and celibate. They wed secretly and placed their illegitimate child with Abelard's sister to raise. The enraged uncle exposed their secret marriage and hired men to castrate Abelard. Heloise entered a convent, where she lived another twenty years and gained renown for positive efforts to reform cloister rules. Abelard became a self-condemning recluse, with his works officially condemned. Their story powerfully reveals both public and private life in the Middle Ages.

WOMEN IN MEDIEVAL SOCIETY

WHAT WAS life like for women during the Middle Ages?

Scholarly theories about femininity were at odds with the reality of the lives of medieval women. Studies of the Bible and Graeco-Roman medical, philosophical, and legal texts convinced medieval theologians that women were physically, mentally, and morally inferior to men. The Bible clearly taught that a female is a "weaker vessel" who requires protection and guidance from a male. It ordered wives to submit to their husbands—even, medieval authorities assumed, to the point of accepting beatings for conduct that displeased their husbands. As celibates, Christian clergy viewed marriage as a debased condition and honored virgins and chaste widows more highly than wives.

Contrary forces shaped roles for women in medieval society. The church reinforced traditional negative assumptions about women, but insisted on the female's spiritual equality with the male. The learned churchman Peter Lombard argued, for instance, that the fact that God took Eve from Adam's side meant woman was neither to rule nor be ruled but to be a partner with her husband in a marriage characterized by mutual aid and trust. In chivalric romances, in courtly love literature, and in the cult of the Virgin Mary that swept Europe in the twelfth and thirteenth centuries, female traits of gentleness, compassion, and grace were seen as essential correctives for the rougher male virtues. Women were put on pedestals and worshiped as men's superiors in the arts of self-control and civilized conduct.

Women in German tribes had been treated better than those in civilized Rome, and this helped create some rights for medieval women. In ancient Rome, women had married in their early teens and usually wed men who were much older than themselves. German women, however, married later in life and took husbands of their same age. German grooms endowed their brides with property

of their own to support them if they were widowed, and the Germanic law codes recognized the right of women to inherit, administer, dispose of, and bequeath family property and personal possessions. German women could also prosecute men in court for bodily injury and rape.

Polygyny, concubinage, and casual divorce were all part of German tradition, but in the ninth century, the church persuaded the Carolingian rulers that monogamous marriage should be official policy. This was both a gain and a loss for women. On the one hand, the choice of a wife became a very serious matter, and wives gained greater dignity and legal security. But on the other hand, a woman's burden as household manager and bearer of children greatly increased. Where previously several women shared responsibility for running a nobleman's estate and providing heirs to continue his line, all these duties now came to rest on the shoulders of one woman. Mortality rates for Frankish women rose following the ninth century, and their average life spans decreased.

A fourteenth-century English manuscript shows women at their daily tasks: carrying jugs of milk from the sheep pen, feeding the chickens, carding and spinning wool.

Life Choices   The demands medieval society placed on wives explain why the cloister had so much appeal for women. Few women, however, had the option of choosing the celibate life. Nuns were required to make sizable donations to their cloisters, and only a few upper-class women could afford the price of admission. There may have been no more than 3,500 nuns in all of England at the end of the Middle Ages. Monasteries did, however, offer women unique opportunities to obtain educations and exercise political influence and leadership.

Most medieval women were neither administrators of aristocratic households nor nuns. They were women who, in addition to their duties as wives and mothers, were members of a community's work force. They could not attend the universities and were, therefore, excluded from the learned professions of scholarship, medicine, and law. They were, however, admitted to craft and trade guilds. Between the ages of ten and fifteen, middle-class girls, like boys, served apprenticeships. When they married, they might become assistants and partners in their husband's line of work, or operate a bakery, brewery, or other business of their own. Medieval women worked in virtually every field from butcher to goldsmith. They were especially prominent in the food and clothing industries and domestic service. Some earned the rank of master in guilds, but employment opportunities for women were more restricted than those for men. Women were paid about 25 percent less than men for comparable work. Some urban women had opportunities to attend school and learn to read and write their vernacular tongues. Peasant women, however, labored beside their men in the fields and had no opportunities for self-improvement.

WHAT WERE the characteristics of childhood in the Middle Ages?

THE LIVES OF CHILDREN

With children, as with women, image and reality diverged in medieval society. The Romans regulated family size by exposing unwanted children, but they showered affection on the offspring they chose to raise. The Germans, by contrast, had large families but paid little attention to their children. In German law, the *wergild*—the compensatory fine paid as recompense for an injury—was much lower for a child's loss than an adult's.

Although the church condemned infanticide, it continued throughout the Middle Ages. This might suggest children were held in low esteem, and the fact that medieval artists depicted children as small adults has suggested to some historians that medieval people did not regard childhood as a distinct period of life requiring special treatment. Given that 30 to 50 percent of children died before the age of five, these historians speculate that medieval parents minimized emotional trauma by not becoming attached to their offspring. However, high rates of infant and child mortality may just as well have made children all the more precious to their parents. The many kinds of children's toys and pieces of child-rearing equipment (e.g., walkers and potty chairs) that existed in the Middle Ages suggest people paid a great deal of attention to children. Medieval medical texts also offered advice on postnatal care and treatments for childhood diseases. They cautioned against abuse and recommended moderation in discipline. The church urged parents to love their children as Mary loved Jesus, and in medieval art and literature parents are depicted as grieving as much over the loss of a child as families would today.

Childhood was brief in the Middle Ages, and young children were introduced early to adult responsibilities. Peasant children joined their parents in the fields as soon as they could physically manage some labor. The urban working class sent children as young as eight away from home to begin apprenticeships. The church allowed boys to marry at fourteen and girls at twelve. The pressure put on children to mature and learn may have been a sign of concern for them, for no parental responsibility was deemed greater than that of equipping a child for useful employment.

SUMMARY

The Traditional Order of Life The nobility were warriors who lived off the labor of others and resided in mansions or castles in the countryside. The clergy constituted a noticeable portion of the medieval population. The "regular" clergy, who lived separately from the world, and the "secular" clergy, who lived among the laity, had their own hierarchies and responsibilities. The agrarian peasantry were the largest and most significant group. During the Middle Ages, families were the basic socioeconomic unit.

Towns and Townspeople Towns grew in size and significance. The nobility and upper clergy's newfound taste for fancy manufactured goods was an early impetus for the growth of towns. Ironically, as towns grew and artisans and traders gained status, it was generally the nobility that suffered. Throughout Europe, it was common for townspeople and kings to form alliances that impinged on the traditional powers of the nobility. Especially in France and Germany, cities also attracted large numbers of Jews.

Schools and Universities Starting in Bologna in 1158, Western universities taught the *trivium* (language arts) and the *quadrivium* (math). Scholasticism, the favored method of study, relied on logic, memorization, argumentation, and recitation. Most of the content of the instruction came from Latin translations of Greek and Arabic texts. Because education had been limited previously to mostly theological instruction for clerical students, and given the pervasiveness of religion in everyday life, it is not surprising that some of the writings of the ancient philosophers studied by university students—especially the writings of Aristotle—were controversial.

Women in Medieval Society The male Christian clergy portrayed women in the Middle Ages as having two options: subjugated housewife or confined nun. The vast majority of them, in fact, worked in a range of trades, although they were concentrated in the food and clothing industries. Nuns avoided the problems associated with pregnancy and could attain some power. Aristocratic women could manage large households.

The Lives of Children Most historians have probably misunderstood the lives of children in the Middle Ages. Children had a 30 to 50 percent chance of dying before they turned five, so some historians have suggested that parents would not risk making a big emotional investment in young children. Children worked as soon as they were able and are depicted in medieval art as "little adults," so some historians have wondered whether people in the Middle Ages had an understanding of childhood as a distinct phase of life, with its own needs. But medieval medical and clerical authorities did, in fact, write about childhood as a special stage in life, and evidence indicates that parents and society at large cherished their babies and children.

REVIEW QUESTIONS

1. How did the responsibilities of the nobility differ from those of the clergy and peasantry during the High Middle Ages? What led to the revival of trade and the growth of towns in the twelfth century? How did towns change medieval society?

2. What were the strengths and weaknesses of the educations provided by medieval universities? How would you evaluate the standard curriculum?

3. How would you define Scholasticism? What was the Scholastic program and method of study? Who were the main critics of Scholasticism, and what were their complaints?

4. Do Germanic law and Roman law reflect different understandings of the position of women in society? How did options and responsibilities differ for women in each of the social classes? What are the theories concerning the concept of childhood in the Middle Ages?

KEY TERMS

banalities   (p. 201)   regular clergy   (p. 199)   Scholasticism   (p. 209)
manor   (p. 200)   secular clergy   (p. 198)

 For additional study resources for this chapter, go to:
www.prenhall.com/kagan3/chapter8

Visualizing The Past...
The Divine in the Middle Ages

HOW DID artists of different religions depict the divine? How did their differing conceptions of the divine, and rules within religions about how, and whether, the divine should be depicted, shape religious art?

The Middle Ages witnessed the creation of a new world religion, Islam, and the expansion and consolidation of others, including, in the West, Christianity and Judaism. Each of these religions fostered forms of religious art suited to its conception of the divine. Religious and secular leaders alike commissioned the art as objects or focuses of worship, teaching tools, and decorations. Secular leaders enhanced their status by associating themselves with the divine through patronage of religious art.

Jonah Eaten by the Whale, from a Hebrew Bible, 1299 (Vellum) by Joseph Asarfati (fl. 1299)
Although Jewish tradition prohibits creating any sort of image of God, European Jewish illuminated manuscripts did depict the human form, and thus like the Christian illuminated manuscripts they closely resembled, were filled with images of scenes from the Torah and Jewish history. Hebrew writing also developed into an elaborately beautiful calligraphy. Many of these Jewish medieval illuminated manuscripts were, like their Christian counterparts, commissioned by wealthy and influential leaders of Jewish communities in Europe.

Instituto da Biblioteca Nacional, Lisbon, Portugal/Bridgeman Art Library

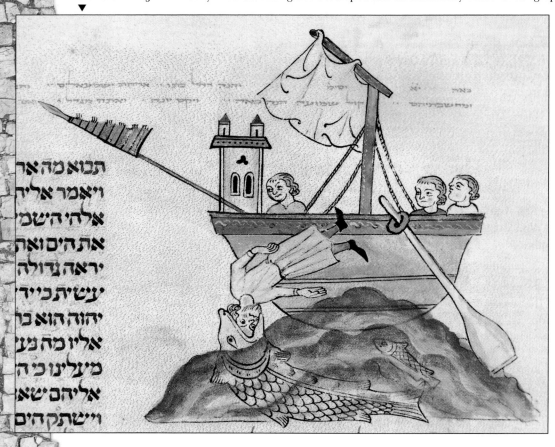

This is a page from a vellum medieval Qur'an with a rosette in the margin, by the medieval Islamic school. Islam follows the Jewish tradition in prohibiting images of God (Allah). Because Islam also prohibits depicting the human form (although some Islamic artists did produce images of people and animals), as this picture shows, Islamic art tended to be highly abstract, and Islamic writing itself became an art form of great beauty and refinement.

The Bridgeman Art Library International Ltd. Musee Conde, Chantilly, France/Bridgeman Art Library

"The Virgin of Paris," Anonymous Early fourteenth century, Notre Dame, Paris. This sculpture communicates another important way in which medieval Christians envisioned God, as the infant Jesus in the arms of his mother, Mary, to whom Catholics prayed to intercede for them with her son. In this image, an excellent example of northern Gothic sculpture, Mary also personifies the Catholic Church, "mother" of the faithful, and Our Lady of France.

Art Resource, NY ©Giraudon/Art Resource, NY

This cloisonné and gold medallion crafted by Georgian artists for a Byzantine icon frame, ca. 1100 C.E., shows Jesus Christ. His divinity is communicated by his halo, and his wisdom as a human teacher by the book he carries. By the Middle Ages, the Byzantine world had produced many icons, and the defeat in the ninth century of the iconoclasts, who opposed the creation of religious images for fear that ordinary people would worship them, ensured that religious art replete with images of God, Jesus, and the saints would dominate medieval Christian art throughout Europe.

Art Resource, NY ©Giraudon/Art Resource, NY

215

POLITICS & GOVERNMENT

1309–1377	Pope resides in Avignon
1337–1453	Hundred Years' War
1356	*Golden Bull* creates German electoral college

1415–1433	Hussite revolt in Bohemia
1428–1519	Aztecs expand in central Mexico
1429	Joan of Arc leads French to victory in Orléans
1434	Medici rule begins in Florence
1455–1485	Wars of the Roses in England
1469	Marriage of Ferdinand and Isabella
1487	Henry Tudor creates Court of Star Chamber

▲ *Palace of Popes*

SOCIETY & ECONOMY

▲ *Joan of Arc*

1315–1317	Greatest famine of the Middle Ages
1347–1350	Black Death peaks
1358	*Jacquerie* shakes France
1378	Ciompi Revolt in Florence
1381	English peasants' revolt

1450	Johann Gutenberg invents printing with movable type
1492	Christopher Columbus encounters the Americas
1498	Vasco da Gama reaches India

RELIGION & CULTURE

◄ *Two scenes from English peasant revolt of 1381*

1414–1417	The Council of Constance
1425–1450	Lorenzo Valla exposes the *Donation of Constantine*
1450	Thomas à Kempis, *Imitation of Christ*
1492	Expulsion of Jews from Spain

1300–1325	Dante Alighieri writes *Divine Comedy*
1302	Boniface VIII issues bull *Unam Sanctam*
1350	Boccaccio, *Decameron*
1375–1527	The Renaissance in Italy
1378–1417	The Great Schism
1380–1395	Chaucer writes *Canterbury Tales*
1390–1430	Christine de Pisan writes in defense of women

Canterbury Cathedral ▶

1519	Charles V crowned Holy Roman Emperor
1530	*Augsburg Confession* defines Lutheranism
1547	Ivan the Terrible becomes tsar of Russia
1555	*Peace of Augsburg* recognizes the legal principle, *cuius regio, eius religio*
1558–1603	Reign of Elizabeth I of England
1572	Saint Bartholomew's Day Massacre
1588	English defeat of Spanish Armada
1598	Edict of Nantes gives Huguenots religious and civil rights

1624–1642	Era of Richelieu in France
1629–1640	Charles I's years of personal rule
1640	Long Parliament convenes
1642	Outbreak of civil war in England
1643–1661	Cardinal Mazarin regent for Louis XIV
1648	Peace of Westphalia
1649–1652	The *Fronde* in France
1649	Charles I executed
1660	Charles II restored to the English throne
1661–1715	Louis XIV's years of personal rule
1682–1725	Reign of Peter the Great
1685	James II becomes king of England Louis XIV revokes Edict of Nantes
1688	"Glorious Revolution" in Britain

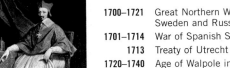

▲ *Cardinal Richelieu*

1700–1721	Great Northern War between Sweden and Russia
1701–1714	War of Spanish Succession
1713	Treaty of Utrecht
1720–1740	Age of Walpole in England and Fleury in France
1740	Maria Theresa succeeds to the Habsburg throne
1740–1748	War of the Austrian Succession
1756–1763	Seven Years' War
1767	Legislative Commission in Russia
1772	First Partition of Poland
1776	American Declaration of Independence
1778	France aids the American colonies

Declaration of Independence ▶

▲ *Ferdinand Magellan's ship, Vittoria*

1519	Hernan Cortes lands in Mexico
1519–1522	Ferdinand Magellan circumnavigates the Earth
1525	German Peasants' Revolt
1532–1533	Francisco Pizarro conquers the Incas
1540	Spanish open silver mines in Peru, Bolivia, and Mexico
1550–1600	The great witch panics

1600–1700	Period of greatest Dutch economic prosperity
1600–early 1700s	Spain maintains commercial monopoly in Latin America
1607	English settle Jamestown, Virginia
1608	French settle Quebec
1618–1648	Thirty Years' War devastates German economy
1619	African slaves first bought at Jamestown, Virginia
1650s–1670s	Commercial rivalry between Dutch and English
1661–1683	Colbert seeks to stimulate French economic growth
1690	Paris Foundling Hospital established

1715–1763	Era of major colonial rivalry in the Caribbean
1719	Mississippi Bubble in France
1733	James Kay's flying shuttle
1750s	Agricultural Revolution in Britain
1750–1840	Growth of new cities
1763	Britain becomes dominant in India
1763–1789	Enlightened absolutist rulers seek to spur economic growth
1765	James Hargreaves's spinning jenny
1769	Richard Arkwright's waterframe
1773–1775	Pugachev's Rebellion

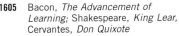

Jamestown, Virginia ▶

◀ *Elizabeth I, The Armada Portrait*

1513	Niccolo Machiavelli, *The Prince*
1516	Erasmus compiles a Greek New Testament
1516	Thomas More, *Utopia*
1517	Martin Luther's Ninety-five theses
1534	Henry VIII declared head of English Church
1540	Jesuit order founded
1541	John Calvin becomes Geneva's reformer
1543	Copernicus, *On the Revolutions of the Heavenly Spheres*
1545–1563	Council of Trent
1549	English *Book of Common Prayer*

1605	Bacon, *The Advancement of Learning*; Shakespeare, *King Lear*, Cervantes, *Don Quixote*
1609	Kepler, *The New Astronomy*
1611	King James Version of the English Bible
1632	Galileo, *Dialogue on the Two Chief Systems of the World*
1637	Descartes, *Discourse on Method*
1651	Hobbes, *Leviathan*
1687	Newton, *Principia Mathematica*
1689	English Toleration Act
1690	Locke, *Essay Concerning Human Understanding*

▲ *First page of Hobbes' Leviathan, 1651*

1739	Wesley begins field preaching
1748	Montesquieu, *Spirit of the Laws*
1750	Rousseau, *Discourse on the Moral Effects of the Arts and Sciences*
1751	First volume Diderot's *Encyclopedia*
1762	Rousseau, *Social Contract* and *Émile*
1763	Voltaire, *Treatise on Tolerance*
1774	Goethe, *Sorrow of Young Werther*
1776	Smith, *Wealth of Nations*
1781	Kant, *Critique of Pure Reason* Joseph II adopts policy of toleration in Austria

Portraits of ▶ *Encyclopedists*

9 The Late Middle Ages
Social and Political Breakdown (1300–1453)

CHAPTER HIGHLIGHTS

The Black Death Between 1348 and the early fifteenth century, close to 40 percent of the population of Western Europe was killed by the Black Death. The fear inspired by the disease, and by the responses to it, influenced European attitudes and religious beliefs for centuries. The sharp drop in population caused by the plague had profound social, economic, and political consequences, creating new challenges and opportunities for Europeans.

The Hundred Years' War and the Rise of National Sentiment The direct cause of the Hundred Years' War was the controversy over the succession to the French throne. England began the conflict as a more cohesive state than France. However, over the course of the conflict, the French developed an emerging sense of national unity.

Ecclesiastical Breakdown and Revival: The Late Medieval Church Throughout the thirteenth century, popes had worked to centralize church power. As nation-states gained cohesiveness, kings began to challenge papal authority. For most of the fourteenth century, the papacy was based in Avignon. Discontent with the clergy was expressed in popular movements like those led by John Wycliffe and John Huss. Opposition to the Avignon papacy led to the Great Schism (1378–1417) and the Conciliar Movement.

Medieval Russia Starting in the eleventh century, Kiev began to lose its prominence as Russia's most important city. As Kiev declined, Russia split into three geographic and cultural groupings: the Great Russians, the White Russians, and the Little Russians or Ukrainians. In 1223 Ghengis Khan led the Mongol conquest of Russia. Mongol rule came to an end in 1480, by which time Moscow had become Russia's political and religious capital. In Russia the main social division was between freemen and slaves.

CHAPTER QUESTIONS

WHAT WERE the social and economic consequences of the "Black Death"?

WHAT WAS the Hundred Years' War, and what were the strengths and weaknesses of each side?

HOW DID secular rulers challenge papal authority?

HOW DID Russia emerge as an important state?

CHAPTER OUTLINE
• The Black Death
• The Hundred Years' War and the Rise of National Sentiment
• Ecclesiastical Breakdown and Revival: The Late Medieval Church
• Medieval Russia

IMAGE KEY

Image Key for pages 218–219 is on page 235.

The West endured so many calamities as the Middle Ages drew to a close that European civilization seemed in imminent danger of collapse. From 1337 to 1453, France and England were locked in a bloody conflict called the Hundred Years' War. Between 1347 and 1350, a devastating plague swept through Europe and carried off a third of its population. In 1378, a quarrel between competing candidates for the papacy began a schism that kept the church divided for thirty-nine years. In 1453, the Turks overran Constantinople and charged up the Danube valley toward the heart of Europe.

These crises were accompanied by intellectual developments that undercut many of the assumptions about faith, life, and the social order that had comforted earlier generations. Some philosophers concluded that human reason is much more limited in scope than the Scholastics had realized. Feudal institutions, which had been assumed to be divinely ordained, were assaulted by kings who aspired to absolute monarchy. Competing claims to authority were made by kings and popes, and both of these leaders were challenged by political theorists who argued that subjects had the right to hold rulers accountable for how they used their power.

WHAT WERE the social and economic consequences of the "Black Death"?

9.1
The Flagellants

THE BLACK DEATH

PRECONDITIONS AND CAUSES

European society in the late Middle Ages was still thoroughly agrarian. Nine-tenths of the population worked the land. The three-field system of seasonal planting and crop rotation had increased food production, but population growth kept pace with the food supply. The number of people living in Europe doubled between 1000 and 1300, until the point was reached where there were more mouths than could be fed. At least once during the average European life span of thirty-five years, an individual could expect to suffer extreme hunger.

Between 1315 and 1317, crop failures produced the worst famines of the Middle Ages. Starvation undermined health and increased vulnerability to a virulent plague that struck in 1347. This **Black Death** (so called because of the way it discolored the bodies of its victims) followed the trade routes from Asia into Europe. Appearing first in Sicily, it entered Europe through the ports of Venice, Genoa, and Pisa. Some places, such as Bohemia, where there were no major trade routes, were little affected, but by the early fifteenth century, the plague may have reduced the population of western Europe by two-fifths.

Flea bites injected the plague bacilli into an individual's bloodstream, and a victim's sneezes could also spread the contagion. Medieval physicians had no understanding of these processes and could offer no explanation, defense, or cure. (See "Encountering the Past: Medieval Medicine.") Consequently, the plague inspired deep pessimism, panicky superstition, and an obsession with death and dying. Amulets and folk remedies abounded. Some people put their trust in a temperate, disciplined regimen. Others, fearing that death was near, threw themselves into the pursuit of pleasure. Troops of flagellants, religious fanatics who did penance by whipping themselves, paraded through the countryside stirring up mass panic. Groundless rumors that unpopular minorities (particularly the Jews) were spreading the disease sparked bloody purges.

SOCIAL AND ECONOMIC CONSEQUENCES

Farms Decline   The plague was most virulent in places where people lived close together. Whole villages and urban districts were sometimes wiped out. This reduced the labor force and created a demand for workers that drove up wages. Agricultural profits diminished because consumers were fewer, and prices rose for luxury and manufactured goods (the products of skilled artisans who had become scarce).

Black Death   Virulent plague that struck in Sicily in 1347 and spread through Europe. It discolored the bodies of its victims. By the early fifteenth century, the plague may have reduced the population of western Europe by two-fifths.

MAP EXPLORATION

Interactive map: To explore this map further, go to **http://www.prenhall.com/kagan3/map9.1**

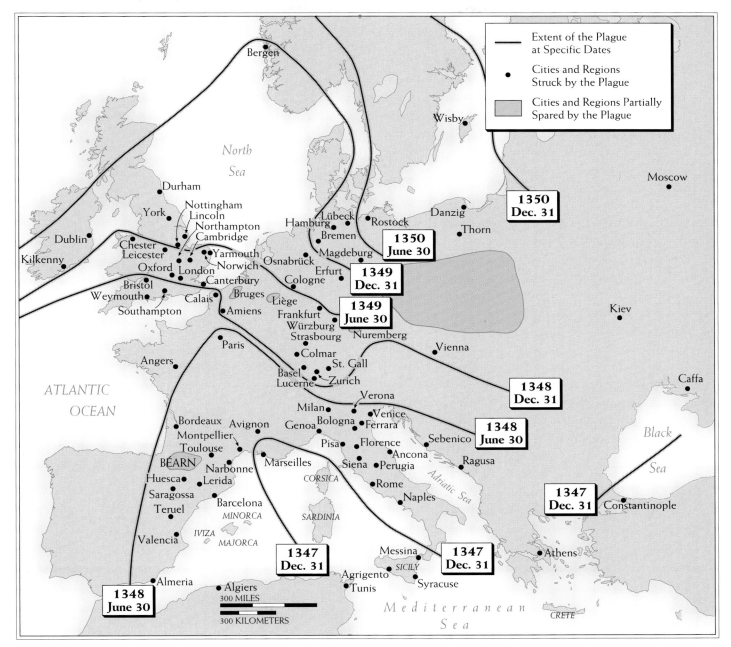

MAP 9–1

Spread of the Black Death   Apparently introduced by seaborne rats from Black Sea areas where plague-infested rodents had long been known, the Black Death brought huge human, social, and economic consequences. One of the lower estimates of Europeans dying is 25 million. The map charts the plague's spread in the mid–fourteenth century. Generally following trade routes, the plague reached Scandinavia by 1350, and some believe it then went on to Iceland and even Greenland. Areas off the main trade routes were largely spared.

WHAT DOES the spread of the plague indicate about the networks of trade routes and economic development in Europe in the mid-fourteenth century?

ENCOUNTERING THE PAST

MEDIEVAL MEDICINE

Medieval medicine was a mix of practices ranging from diet, exercise regimens, and medicines to prayer, magical amulets, and incantations. Celestial forces (the stars and planets) were assumed to influence human physical and mental states, and physicians turned to astrology for help in explaining illnesses and devising treatments. In a world where lives tended to be short and suffering difficult to ease, people were desperate for cures and willing to take advice from any source. The wealthy sought help from university-trained physicians. These men were the most prestigious, if not inevitably the most effective, healers. They relied on diet and medication to treat internal illnesses. Apothecaries supplied their patients with medicinal herbs, and surgeons performed any physical operations they prescribed. Some surgeons had university educations, but many were humble barbers who learned their trade as apprentices.

Bloodletting was prescribed as a treatment for illness and a preservative of health, for medical theory held that illness was a result of an imbalance of humors (fluids) in the body. Greek science maintained there were four elements (earth, air, fire, and water), each associated with a quality (hot, cold, moist, and dry). The mix of these in the body determined its condition, and treatment called for draining off excesses or shifting humors to different locations in the body. Physicians commonly diagnosed problems by examining urine and blood and checking pulses.

The urine flask was the medieval equivalent of the stethoscope—the badge of the physician.

WHAT KIND of medical help was available to medieval people?

A caricature of physicians (early sixteenth century). A physician carries a uroscope (for collecting and examining urine); discolored urine signaled an immediate need for bleeding. The physician/surgeon wears surgical shoes and his assistant carries a flail—a comment on the risks of medical services.

Hacker Art Books Inc.

Serfs began to abandon farming for more lucrative jobs in towns. All of these economic developments hurt the privileged classes, whose incomes derived in large part from landed estates. To keep workers on their manors, landowners had to offer them better deals and lower the rents their peasants paid. The clergy were insulated from some of the problems that afflicted the secular nobility. As a great landholder, the church suffered economic losses, but these were offset by an increased demand for masses for the dead and by a flood of gifts and bequests.

Some landowners tried to recoup their losses by converting arable land to sheep pasture. Herding required far fewer expensive laborers than did grain cultivation. Nobles also used their monopoly of political power to reverse their declining fortunes. They passed laws freezing wages at low levels and ordering peasants to stay on the land. Resentment of this legislation fueled France's Jacquerie and England's Peasants' Revolt.

OVERVIEW   EFFECTS OF THE BLACK DEATH

Social	Rumors abounded that unpopular minorities were spreading the disease. Serfs began to abandon farming for more lucrative jobs in towns.
Economic	Agricultural profits diminished because consumers were fewer. Prices rose for luxury and manufactured goods as artisans became scarce.
Cultural	Churches saw increased demand for masses for the dead. Deep pessimism, superstition, and obsession with death were inspired.
Political	Nobles used their monopoly of political power to reverse declining fortunes. Laws passed freezing low wages and ordering peasants to stay on the land.

Cities Rebound Although the plague hit urban populations especially hard, cities ultimately profited from its effects. The omnipresence of death whetted the appetite for pleasure and for the luxuries produced by cities. Initially the demand for manufactured goods could not be met, for the first wave of plague drastically diminished a supply of artisans that the guilds had purposefully kept low. This caused the prices of manufactured and luxury items to rise to new heights. As wealth poured into cities, the shrunken population reduced demand for agricultural products. Falling prices made food cheaper and lowered the cost of living for urban dwellers. The forces that enriched townspeople impoverished the landed nobility. City dwellers began to buy up manors whose value had diminished. This extended the power of the town into the countryside and began to blend the rural gentry with the urban patriciate.

The rapidly changing economic conditions the plague created were not an unmixed blessing for towns, for they increased tensions that had long seethed within urban communities. The merchant classes found it difficult to maintain their traditional dominance over the prospering artisans' guilds. The guilds used their growing political clout to enact restrictive legislation that protected local industries. Master artisans kept demand for their products high by limiting the number of shops licensed to share their market. This frustrated many journeymen who were eager to set up in business for themselves, and it created strife within the guilds.

This Burgundian manuscript, c. 1470, depicts a bath said to be fit for a cardinal or king, seen standing at the door. The couple on the left, behind a closable curtain, suggests a house of prostitution, while on the right the men and their younger, good-looking, bejeweled partners appear not to be husbands and wives.

AGK London Ltd.

THE HUNDRED YEARS' WAR AND THE RISE OF NATIONAL SENTIMENT

Late medieval rulers headed what were still feudal governments but grander in scale and more sophisticated than those of their predecessors. The Norman kings of England and the Capetian kings of France centralized royal power by fine-tuning feudal relationships. They stressed the duties of lesser magnates to greater ones and insisted on the unquestioning loyalty of all vassals to the king. They struck up alliances with powerful factions (among the nobles, clergy, and townspeople) within their domains. This fostered a sense of "national" consciousness that equipped both kingdoms for war on an unprecedented scale.

WHAT WAS the Hundred Years' War, and what were the strengths and weaknesses of each side?

CAUSES OF THE WAR

A disputed claim to the French throne provided justification for the events that led to the outbreak of the Hundred Years' War in May 1337. In 1328, the death of Charles IV of France extinguished the senior branch of the Capetian royal house. Edward III (r. 1327–1377), king of England, claimed France's throne by right of his mother, Charles IV's sister. The French barons, however, had no intention of turning themselves over to England's king. They pledged their allegiance to a cadet branch of the Capetian house, to Charles IV's cousin, Philip VI, duke of Valois (r. 1328–1350). (This began the Valois dynasty that ruled France into the sixteenth century.)

England and France had long been on a collision course, and the English king's claim to the French throne provided an excuse for war that had multiple causes. Since the days of the Norman conquest, the king of England had held fiefs on the Continent as a vassal of the king of France. English possession of French land hampered attempts by the French kings to centralize the government of their nation. England and France also had competing economic interests in Flanders and on the high seas. The Hundred Years' War was a struggle for national identity and sovereignty as much as for territory.

French Weakness   France should have had no difficulty in winning the war. It had three times the population of England, far greater resources, and the advantage of fighting on its own soil. Yet, until 1415, all the major battles were stunning victories for the English.

Internal disunity prevented France from marshaling all its forces against the English, and powerful feudal traditions slowed France's adaptation to novel military strategies that the English employed. England's infantry was more disciplined than France's, and English archers wielded a formidable weapon, the longbow. A longbowman could fire six arrows a minute and pierce the armor of a knight at two hundred yards.

PROGRESS OF THE WAR

The war unfolded in three stages.

The Conflict During the Reign of Edward III   The first steps toward war were taken when Edward forbade shipment of the English wool that fed the Flemish cloth-making industry. His intent was to encourage Flanders to repudiate its feudal ties with Philip VI. In 1340, the Flemish cities decided their economic interests lay with England, and they acknowledged Edward's claim to be king of France and overlord of Flanders. On June 23 of that year, Edward defeated the French fleet in the Bay of Sluys, the first great battle of the war. (See Map 9–2.)

In 1346, Edward invaded Normandy. A series of easy raids was capped by a major battle at Crécy. England's bowmen tipped the balance in Edward's favor at Crécy, but Edward lacked the manpower to exploit his victory. He seized the port of Calais and returned to England. Exhaustion and the onset of plague forced a truce. There was no further action until 1356, when the English won their greatest victory. Near Poitiers, they routed France's feudal levies and captured the French king, John II "the Good", r. 1350–1364. The loss of king and vassals caused a breakdown of government in France.

Power shifted momentarily to the **Estates General**, an assembly of representatives from France's propertied classes. The powerful merchants of Paris, led by Etienne Marcel, demanded rights similar to those that Magna Carta had promised to the English privileged classes. The Estates General was, however, too divided to provide effective government. Leaders of the far-flung regions of a large nation such as France were strangers to one another, and they found it difficult to communicate and agree on plans of action.

MAP 9–2

The Hundred Years' War   The Hundred Years' War went on intermittently from the late 1330s until 1453. These maps show the remarkable English territorial gains up to the sudden and decisive turning of the tide of battle in favor of the French by the forces of Joan of Arc in 1429.

USING THE map as a reference, what were the major English victories or French weaknesses that led to England's significant influence in France by 1429?

MAP EXPLORATION

Interactive map: To explore this map further, go to **http://www.prenhall.com/kagan3/map9.2**

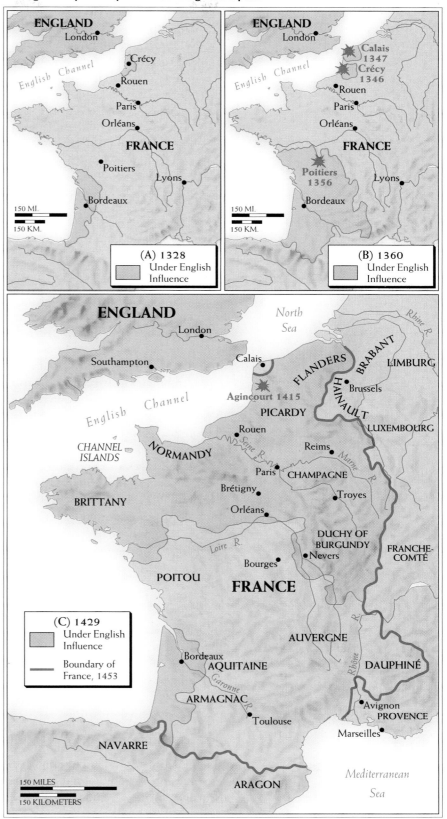

The French privileged classes avoided taxation and foisted the costs of the war with England onto the backs of peasants. Beginning in 1358, the desperate peasants waged a series of bloody rebellions called the **Jacquerie** (from "Jacques Bon-homme," a peasant caricature). The nobles restored order by matching the rebels atrocity for atrocity.

On May 9, 1360, England compelled France to accept terms spelled out in the Peace of Brétigny. Edward renounced his claim to the French throne, but he demanded an end to his vassalage to the king of France and confirmation of his sovereignty over the lands he held in France (Gascony, Guyenne, Poitou, and Calais). France was also required to pay a ransom of 3 million gold crowns for King John's return. The treaty was unrealistic, and sober observers on both sides knew the peace it brought could not last. Within a few years France had re-opened hostilities, and by the time of Edward's death in 1377, the English occupied only a few coastal enclaves and the territory around Bordeaux.

French Defeat and the Treaty of Troyes   Late in Edward's reign, England began to have problems at home that caused it to lose interest in its war with France. Edward's grandson and successor, Richard II (r. 1377–1399), faced a popular uprising similar to the Jacquerie. In June 1381, John Ball, a priest, and Wat Tyler, a journeyman, led a mob in an assault on London. The "Peasants' Revolt" was put down, but it left scars that took decades to heal.

Richard's autocratic behavior turned his nobles against him, and he was forced to abdicate the throne in favor of his cousin, Henry IV. Henry's son and heir, Henry V (r. 1413–1422), revived the war with France as a strategy for rallying his people to support the new royal line. His moment was well chosen, for the French nobility had split into warring factions that refused to cooperate in defending their country. At the Battle of Agincourt in Normandy (1415), Henry defeated the army of the Armagnacs. This shocked their opponents, the party of the duke of Burgundy, and led to efforts to heal the breach that had divided France's forces. Hope for cooperation was shattered, however, in September 1419, when the duke of Burgundy was assassinated by an Armagnac. Burgundy's son and heir then avenged his father's death by helping the English invade Armagnac territory. Henry took Paris, captured the French king, Charles VI, and married Charles's daughter. In 1420, the Treaty of Troyes disinherited the French king's son and proclaimed Henry V heir to the French throne. When Henry and Charles died within months of one another in 1422, Henry's infant son, Henry VI, was declared king of both France and England.

Joan of Arc and the War's Conclusion   Charles VI's son, the future Charles VII, escaped the English and asserted his right to his father's throne. His eventual victory owed much to a remarkable young peasant woman from Domrémy, Joan of Arc (1412–1431). In March 1429, Joan appeared at Charles's court-in-exile and informed him God had commissioned her to rescue the city of Orléans from the English armies that were besieging it. The king was skeptical, but he was willing to try anything to reverse France's fortunes.

Circumstances worked to Joan's advantage. By the time she arrived, the siege of Orléans had gone on for six months. The exhausted English troops were already contemplating withdrawal when Joan arrived with a fresh French army. The English retreat from Orléans was followed by a succession of victories popularly attributed to Joan. She deserved credit—if not for military genius, for an ability to inspire her men

Estates General   Assembly of representatives from France's propertied classes.

Jacquerie   (From "Jacques Bon-homme," a peasant caricature) Name given to the series of bloody rebellions that desperate French peasants waged beginning in 1358.

A contemporary portrait of Joan of Arc (1412–1431) in the National Archives in Paris.

HISTORY'S VOICES

JOAN OF ARC REFUSES TO RECANT HER BELIEFS

*J*oan of Arc, threatened with torture, refused to recant her beliefs and instead defended the instructions she had received from the voices that spoke to her. Here is a part of her self-defense from the contemporary trial record.

WHY WAS Joan deemed "heretical" and not "insane" when she acknowleged hearing voices?

On Wednesday, May 9th of the same year [1431], Joan was brought into the great tower of the castle of Rouen before us the said judges and in the presence of the reverend father, lord abbot of St. Cormeille de Compiegne, of masters Jean de Châtillon and Guillaume Erart, doctors of sacred theology, of André Margucric and Nicolas de Venderos, archdeacons of the church of Rouen, of William Haiton, bachelor of theology, Aubert Morel, licentiate in canon law, Nicolas Loiscleur, canon of the cathedral of Rouen, and master Jean Massieu.

And Joan was required and admonished to speak the truth on many different points contained in her trial which she had denied or to which she had given false replies, whereas we possessed certain information, proofs, and vehement presumptions upon them. Many of the points were read and explained to her,

and she was told that if she did not confess them truthfully she would be put to the torture, the instruments of which were shown to her all ready in the tower. There were also present by our instruction men ready to put her to the torture in order to restore her to the way and knowledge of truth, and by this means to procure the salvation of her body and soul which by her lying inventions she exposed to such grave perils.

To which the said Joan answered in this manner: "Truly if you were to tear me limb from limb and separate my soul from my body, I would not tell you anything more and if I did say anything, I should afterwards declare that you had compelled me to say it by force." Then she said that on Holy Cross Day last she received comfort from St. Gabriel, she firmly believes it was St. Gabriel. She knew by her voices whether she should submit to the Church, since the clergy were pressing her hard to submit. Her voices told her that if she desired Our Lord to aid her, she must wait upon Him in all her doings. She said that Our Lord has always been the master of her doings, and the Enemy never had power over them. She asked her voices if she would be burned and they answered that she must wait upon God, and He would aid her.

The Trial of Jeanne D'Arc, trans. by W. P. Barrett (New York: Gotham House, 1932), pp. 303, 304.

with self-confidence and enthusiasm for a common cause. Within a few months of the liberation of Orléans, Charles VII had recovered the city of Rheims and been anointed king in its cathedral (the traditional place for French coronations).

Charles showed little gratitude to his unconventional female ally and abandoned her after the Burgundians captured her in May 1430. The Burgundians and the English tried to demoralize their opponents by discrediting Joan. They accused her of heresy and turned her over to the Inquisition for trial. After ten weeks of brutal interrogation, the "Maid of Orléans" was executed as a relapsed heretic (May 30, 1431). Twenty-five years later (1456), Charles reopened her case and had her cleared of all charges, but she was not canonized as Saint Joan until 1920.

Once France was united behind Charles VII, the English had no hope of clinging to their continental possessions. In 1435, the duke of Burgundy recognized the inevitable, abandoned the English, and came to terms with Charles. By the time the war ended in 1453, England held only a little territory around the port of Calais.

QUICK REVIEW

Joan of Arc (1412–1431)

- March 1429: Joan appears at Charles' court-in-exile
- Joan inspires French to a string of victories starting with Orléans
- Captured by the Burgundians in May 1430 and executed by the English as a heretic in May 1431

The long struggle that ended in England's decisive separation from France determined the destiny of both countries. The Hundred Years' War awakened French nationalism and hastened France's transition from a feudal monarchy to a powerfully centralized state. In England, however, the loss of the war and continental empire diminished faith in the government and led to domestic upheaval.

ECCLESIASTICAL BREAKDOWN AND REVIVAL: THE LATE MEDIEVAL CHURCH

HOW DID secular rulers challenge papal authority?

*K*ings seized the opportunities that the rising power of the towns and the declining status of the feudal nobility gave them to centralize governments and economies. The church might have vigorously opposed their promotion of national sentiments, but it faltered just as the new monarchies began to flex their muscles. The plague had weakened the church by killing large numbers of clergy, but the church's major problems were of its own creation.

THE THIRTEENTH-CENTURY PAPACY

In the latter half of the thirteenth century, the papacy appeared to be in a strong position. Frederick II had been vanquished. Imperial pressure on Rome had been removed. The saintly French king, Louis IX, enthusiastically supported the church. In 1274, the Eastern orthodox clergy even accepted reunion with Rome in a bid to persuade the Latin West to aid Constantinople against the Turks.

Papal power reached its medieval pinnacle during the reign of Pope Innocent III (r. 1198–1216), but even then there were signs of trouble. Innocent's creation of a centralized papal monarchy with a clearly defined political mission had increased the church's secular power but diminished its spiritual authority. The thirteenth-century papacy created laws to govern the conduct of Europe's Christians and enforced its legislation in its own courts. It employed a highly efficient bureaucracy and was preoccupied with finances and the pursuit of secular power. The papacy grew strong by focusing more on its own needs than on those of the church at large.

Many contemporary observers noted how far the papacy had drifted from the simplicity and otherworldliness of the Christian leaders described in the New Testament. Some even began to make a distinction between the papal monarchy and the "true" church.

Political Fragmentation The papacy's position in Italy was paradoxically undermined by the success of its campaign against the Hohenstaufen emperors. As external threats from Germany retreated, political intrigues swept the Italian states. In the turmoil that resulted, the papacy became just another prize up for grabs.

Pope Gregory X (r. 1271–1276) had tried to ensure free papal elections by ordering sequestration for the cardinals whenever they were faced with choosing a successor to the papal throne. Physical isolation was supposed to prevent outsiders from promoting candidates

Significant Dates from the Period of the Late Middle Ages

1309–1377	Avignon Papacy
1340	Sluys, first major battle of Hundred Years' War
1346	Battle of Crécy and seizure of Calais
1347	Black Death strikes
1356	Battle of Poitiers
1358	Jacquerie disrupts France
1360	Peace of Brétigny
1378–1417	Great Schism
1381	English Peasants' Revolt
1414–1417	Council of Constance
1415	Battle of Agincourt
1420	Treaty of Troyes
1431	Joan of Arc executed as a heretic
1431–1449	Council of Basel
1453	End of Hundred Years' War

simply to advance political agendas, but this was a weak safeguard for the highly politicized College of Cardinals. Infighting was so great that from 1292 to 1294 the college was unable to elect a pope. In frustration, the cardinals finally chose a compromise candidate, a saintly but inept Calabrian hermit who took the name Celestine V. Celestine shocked Europe by abdicating after only a few weeks in office, and his death, which soon followed, led to rumors he had been murdered to clear his successor's title. The worldly wisdom of the new pope, Boniface VIII (r. 1294–1303), contrasted vividly with Celestine's naive innocence.

BONIFACE VIII AND PHILIP THE FAIR

Germany had been defeated, but in England and France, Boniface faced rising monarchies. France's Philip IV "the Fair" (r. 1285–1314), was a ruthless politician who taught Boniface that the power the pope had presumably inherited from Innocent III was more illusion than reality.

The Royal Challenge to Papal Authority   If Edward I (r. 1272–1307) of England had been able to resolve his problems with Scotland, the Hundred Years' War might have been underway by the time Boniface ascended the papal throne. France and England were both mobilizing resources for a war they considered inevitable, and their preparations created a problem for Boniface. Despite the fact that Pope Innocent III had decreed in 1215 that rulers had no right to tax the clergy without papal approval, both kings were levying extraordinary taxes on their clergy. This forced Boniface to take a stand, and on February 5, 1296, he issued the bull *Clericis Laicos* to caution the kings they had no jurisdiction over the church.

Edward retaliated by denying the clergy and their property the protection of the state's courts. Philip deprived the papacy of the bulk of its income by forbidding the export of money from France to Rome. Boniface had no choice but to come to terms, and he issued a second bull that conceded the right of a king to tax clergy "during an emergency." He also courted Philip by agreeing to canonize Philip's grandfather, Louis IX.

For much of his reign, Boniface was besieged by powerful enemies in Italy. The Colonnas (rivals of Boniface's family, the Gaetani) joined the radical Spiritual Franciscans in a campaign to invalidate Boniface's election. They alleged that Boniface had forced his predecessor from office, murdered him, and won the papacy by bribing the cardinals. Boniface defended himself effectively, and he was greatly encouraged by the response to his proclamation of 1300 as a "Jubilee year." Tens of thousands of pilgrims flocked to Rome to take advantage of the special opportunity this created to be absolved of their sins, and the pope interpreted the crowds as a show of popular support for his administration.

The Jubilee emboldened Boniface to imitate Innocent III and exercise a leadership role in international politics. The support he offered the Scots infuriated Edward, but his most serious difficulties were with Philip. Philip arrested Boniface's Parisian legate, Bishop Bernard Saisset of Pamiers, and convicted him in the royal courts of heresy and treason. The king then demanded that Boniface recognize the legitimacy of the proceedings. To do so, however, would have been to relinquish the pope's jurisdiction over the French clergy. Boniface, therefore, demanded Saisset's unconditional release and revoked his previous concessions on the matter of clerical taxation. In December 1301, Boniface sent Philip the bull *Ausculta Fili* (*Listen, My Son*), which baldly stated the papacy's claim that "God has set popes over kings and kingdoms."

Philip responded with a ruthless attack on the papacy's claim to temporal authority, and on November 18, 1302, Boniface released another bull, *Unam*

Pope Boniface VIII (r. 1294–1303), depicted here, opposed the taxation of the clergy by the kings of France and England and issued one of the strongest declarations of papal authority over rulers, the bull *Unam Sanctam*. This statue is in the Museo Civico, Bologna, Italy.

Statue of Pope Boniface VIII. Museo Civico, Bologna. Scala/Art Resource, NY

Sanctam. It insisted that the temporal authority of kings was "subject" to the spiritual power of the church. Philip announced this was a declaration of war. His chief minister, Guillaume de Nogaret, informed the French clergy that the pope was a criminal and common heretic, and the French army invaded Italy and captured the pope in residence in Anagni. Boniface was nearly killed before the people of Anagni rescued him. The French retreated, and the aged pontiff returned to Rome, where he died two months later.

Boniface's successor, Benedict XI (r. 1303–1304), excommunicated Nogaret. He was, however, in no position to retaliate against the French king, and his successor, Clement V (r. 1305–1314), himself a Frenchman, utterly capitulated. He lifted Nogaret's excommunication and declared that *Unam Sanctam* was not intended to diminish royal authority in any way. He also cleared the way for Philip to confiscate the wealth of the Knights Templar by yielding to the king's demand that the Crusading order be condemned for heresy and dissolved. France's victory was crowned in 1309 by Clement's decision to move the papal court to Avignon—supposedly for safety and convenience. Avignon was an independent town on land that belonged to the pope, but it was in the southeast corner of territory that was culturally French. The papacy remained in Avignon for almost seventy years.

THE AVIGNON PAPACY (1309–1377)

During Clement V's pontificate, Frenchmen flooded into the College of Cardinals, and he and successive Avignon popes appeared—even when they were not—to be dominated by the French king. Cut off in Avignon from their Roman estates, the popes had to find new sources of income, and their ingenuity and success earned them unfortunate reputations for greed and materialism. Clement V increased papal taxation of the clergy. Clement VI (r. 1342–1352) began selling indulgences (releases from penance for sin). The doctrine of purgatory (a place where souls ultimately destined for heaven atoned for venial sins) developed as part of this campaign. By the fifteenth century, the church was urging the living to buy reduced sentences in purgatory for deceased loved ones.

Pope John XXII By the time Pope John XXII (r. 1316–1334) ascended the throne, the popes were well enough established in Avignon to reenter the field of international politics. A quarrel that erupted between the pope and the German emperor, Louis IV, launched an important debate about the nature of legitimate authority.

John had backed a candidate who lost the imperial election to Louis, and the pope obstinately and without legal justification refused to confirm Louis's title. Louis retaliated by accusing John of heresy and declaring him deposed in favor of an antipope. Two outstanding pamphleteers made the case for the king: William of Ockham (d. 1349), whom John excommunicated in 1328, and Marsilius of Padua (ca. 1290–1342), whose teaching John declared heretical in 1327.

William of Ockham was a brilliant logician and critic of philosophical realism, the theory that abstract terms (*church,* for instance) refer to transcendent entities that have some sort of real existence. Ockham was a nominalist who believed such words are only names the human mind invented for its own convenience. Ockham argued that the real church is the historical human community, not some supernatural entity and the pope is only one of its members. As such, he has no special powers of infallibility. The church is best guided, Ockham argued, not by popes but by scripture and by councils representing all the Christian faithful.

Avignon Papacy Period from 1309 to 1377 when the papal court was situated in Avignon, France, and gained a reputation for greed and worldly corruption.

In *Defender of Peace* (1324), Marsilius of Padua argued that the jurisdiction of the clergy was limited to the spiritual realm and that—the punishment for spiritual transgressions being a matter for the next life and not this one—the clergy had no legitimate coercive authority over the laity. An exception might be made only if a secular ruler declared a divine law a law of the state, for it was the state's exclusive, God-given right to use force to maintain social order. A true pope would, like the Apostles in the New Testament, eschew all earthly pomp and power and lead only by spiritual example.

National Opposition to the Avignon Papacy   John's successor, Benedict XII (r. 1334–1342), began construction of a lavish palace at Avignon, and his high-living French successor, Clement VI (r. 1342–1352), presided over a splendid, worldly court. His cardinals grew rich serving as lobbyists for various secular patrons, and the papacy's fiscal tentacles spread farther and farther afield.

Secular governments reacted to these developments by passing laws that restricted papal jurisdiction and taxation. The English had no intention of supporting a papacy they believed was the puppet of their French enemy. The French insisted on their "Gallican liberties," a well-founded tradition that granted the king extensive authority over ecclesiastical appointments and taxation. German and Swiss cities also took steps to limit and even revoke well-established clerical privileges and immunities.

John Wycliffe and John Huss   Mass discontent with the worldly clergy and the politicized papacy generated lay popular movements that were highly critical of the church and traditional religious practices. The Lollards in England and the Hussites in Bohemia were the most significant. The Lollards drew their inspiration from John Wycliffe (d. 1384)—as did John Huss (d. 1415), the martyr whose death launched the successful Hussite revolt against papal authority.

9.2
Propositions of Wycliffe Condemned at London, 1382, and the Council of Constance, 1415

Wycliffe, an Oxford theologian, was a major defender of the rights of kings against the secular pretensions of popes. Wycliffe strongly supported the steps that the English monarchy took (beginning about 1350) to curtail the power of the Avignon papacy over the church in England. Like the original Franciscans, he believed clergy ought to embrace poverty and be content with basic food and clothing. His arguments were popular with secular governments, for they justified the state's confiscation of ecclesiastical property.

Wycliffe maintained that because all authority comes from God, only leaders who live pious lives (as God requires) can claim legitimacy. He believed faithful laypeople have the right to pass judgment on corrupt ecclesiastics and take the lead in reforming the church. Wycliffe anticipated some positions that Protestants would eventually take. He challenged papal infallibility, the doctrine of transubstantiation that gave the priesthood power over the laity, and church policies that restricted the laity's access to the Scriptures. Opposition to the Avignon papacy persuaded the English king to protect him, even though the argument he made for repudiating corrupt clergy could just as easily be used to justify rebellion against a secular ruler. The subjects of any leader who behaved badly could argue he had forfeited his mandate from God.

The Lollards who embraced Wycliffe's ideas preached in the vernacular, disseminated translations of the Scriptures, and championed clerical poverty. So long as they restricted themselves to religion, the English authorities tolerated them. But after the Peasants' Revolt of 1381, the government became suspicious of the egalitarian implications of Wycliffe's works. In 1401, Lollardy was declared a capital offense.

Heresy was not so easily suppressed in Bohemia, for government was weaker there than in England. The University of Prague, founded in 1348, became a center

A portrayal of John Huss as he was led to the stake at Constance. After his execution, his bones and ashes were scattered in the Rhine River to prevent his followers from claiming them as relics. This pen-and-ink drawing is from Ulrich von Richenthal's *Chronicle of the Council of Constance* (ca. 1450).

CORBIS/Bettmann

for Czech nationalists who opposed the increasing prominence of Germans in Bohemia. In 1403, John Huss, a student of Wycliffe's thought, became rector of the university and began a religious reform movement that was also a defense of Czech identity. The reformers used vernacular translations of the Bible and rejected practices (particularly some associated with the Eucharist) that smacked of superstition. Like the Lollards, they believed a sinful priest had no power to perform a valid sacrament, and they denied that clergy were spiritually superior to laity. Medieval Catholic custom reserved the cup at communion to the priest. The Hussites, however, thought this smacked of clerical privilege, and they gave the people the consecrated wine as well as the bread. Opposition to priestly claims to special powers also led the Hussites to reject the doctrine of transubstantiation.

Huss was excommunicated in 1410, and in 1414, he successfully petitioned for a hearing before an international church council convening in Constance, Switzerland. Although the Holy Roman Emperor Sigismund guaranteed Huss safe conduct, he was imprisoned, tried, and burned at the stake for heresy in 1415. The reaction in Bohemia to his execution and that of his colleague, Jerome of Prague, a few months later was fierce. The Taborites, a militant branch of the Hussites, took up arms under John Ziska and declared their intention to turn Bohemia into a state that incorporated Huss's religious and social ideals. Within a decade, they had won control of the Bohemian church.

THE GREAT SCHISM (1378–1417) AND THE CONCILIAR MOVEMENT TO 1449

In January 1377, Pope Gregory XI (r. 1370–1378) yielded to international pressure and announced the papacy would leave Avignon and return to Rome. Europe rejoiced—prematurely, as it turned out—at the end of the church's "Babylonian Captivity" (the exile of the ancient Israelites from their homeland).

Urban VI and Clement VII Gregory died soon after returning to Rome, and the cardinals elected an Italian archbishop, Pope Urban VI (r. 1378–1389). When Urban announced his intention to reform the Curia (the church's central administration), the cardinals, most of whom were French, sensed a challenge to their power and insisted on returning the papacy to their base of operation in Avignon. Five months after Urban's enthronement, a group of thirteen cardinals declared Urban's election invalid. It had, they said, been forced on them by the Roman mob. They then proceeded to elect a "true" pope, Clement VII (r. 1378–1397), a cousin of the French king. Urban denied their allegations and appointed new cardinals to replace them in his college.

Europe, confronted with two papal courts, distributed its support along political lines: England and its allies (the Holy Roman Empire, Hungary, Bohemia, and Poland) acknowledged Urban VI, whereas France and those in its orbit (Naples, Scotland, Castile, and Aragon) supported Clement VII. (Today, the Roman Catholic Church accepts the Roman line of popes as the legitimate one.)

The schism threatened the survival of the church in its traditional form, and there were many reasons to end it as quickly as possible. The easiest solution would have been for one or both of the popes to resign, but neither was willing to sacrifice himself for the common good.

Conciliar Theory of Church Government Europe's leaders, seeing no other option, finally decided an ecumenical church council had to be convened to end the schism. Only a pope, however, could call a legitimate council, and

John Huss

- 1403: Huss becomes rector of the University of Prague and begins religious reform movement
- Reformers used vernacular translations of the Bible and rejected practices they saw as superstitious
- Huss was burned at the stake as a heretic in 1415

none of the popes wanted to summon a council that intended to depose him. Because a pope's authority derived directly from God and not from his people, it was also uncertain that a council had authority to depose a pope.

Scholars called *conciliarists* developed the arguments needed to legitimate the council. In the process, they radically altered medieval assumptions about the nature of authority and created a rationale for popular government. The conciliarists defined the church as the community of all Christian peoples. Because the papacy had been established by God to care for the people's church, a pope was, the conciliarists argued, ultimately accountable to the people whose well-being it was his job to protect. If he failed in his mission, his people had a natural right to depose him to save their church.

The Council of Pisa (1409–1410)   In 1409, thirty-one years after the schism began, cardinals from both Rome and Avignon tried to resolve the schism themselves. They met in Pisa, deposed their respective popes, and united in support of a new one. To their consternation, the popes in Rome and Avignon ignored them and appointed new colleges of cardinals. The attempt to end the schism had succeeded only in creating a third pope.

The Council of Constance (1414–1417)   Emperor Sigismund finally prevailed on John XXIII, the Pisan pope, to summon a council to meet in the Swiss city of Constance in 1414. Europe's kings agreed to cooperate, which deprived the competing popes of the support they needed to continue their fight. The three popes either resigned or were deposed, and the cardinals at the council chose a new pope whom everyone agreed to accept, Martin V (r. 1417–1431). The council also issued a decree (*Sacrosancta*) stating that councils, not popes, were the ultimate source of authority in the church, and it established a schedule for convening future councils at regular intervals.

The Council of Basel (r. 1431–1449)   Conciliar power peaked when a council meeting at Basel entered into negotiations with Bohemia's Hussites, whom the pope regarded as heretics. In November 1433, it granted the Bohemians jurisdiction over their church similar to that held by the French and English. The Hussites also won the right to a unique liturgy and disciplinary system that put clergy and laity on the same footing.

In 1438, the pope upstaged the council and restored the prestige of his office by negotiating a reunion with the Eastern church. The agreement signed in Florence in 1439 was short lived, but it marked the point at which support for conciliarism began to fade. The council of Basel disbanded in 1449, and a decade later the papal bull *Execrabilis* (1460) condemned conciliarism. The movement had, however, achieved several things. By giving secular governments greater authority over religious matters, it helped establish national or territorial churches. It also popularized the tenet that the role of the leader of an institution is to care for the well-being of its members. This idea had wide-ranging ramifications for the governments of states as well as the church.

MEDIEVAL RUSSIA

*P*rince Vladimir (r. 980–1015) received delegations at his court in Kiev representing the Muslim, Roman Catholic, Hebrew, and Greek Orthodox faiths. He then reviewed what each camp had to offer and chose the Greek option. His decision determined Russia's religion and strengthened commercial ties between Russia and the Byzantine Empire.

QUICK REVIEW

Church Councils

- Council of Pisa (1409–1410): Attempt to resolve schism ended in creating a third pope
- Council of Constance (1414–1417): Three popes resigned or were deposed and Martin V was chosen as new pope
- Council of Basel (1431–1449): Entered into negotiations with the Hussites

Justice in the late Middle Ages. Depicted are the most common forms of corporal and capital punishment in Europe in the late Middle Ages and the Renaissance. At top: burning, hanging, drowning. At center: blinding, quartering, the wheel, cutting of hair (a mark of great shame for a freeman). At bottom: thrashing, decapitation, amputation of hand (for thieves).

Herzog August Bibliothek

HOW DID Russia emerge as an important state?

POLITICS AND SOCIETY

Vladimir's successor, Yaroslav the Wise (r. 1016–1054), turned Kiev into a magnificent political and cultural center that rivaled Constantinople. After his death, however, rival princes split the Russian people into three groups (the Great Russians, the White Russians, and the Little Russians or Ukrainians), and a diminished Kiev became simply one principality among many.

The governments of the Russian states combined monarchy (a prince), aristocracy (a council of noblemen), and democracy (a popular assembly composed of all adult males). The broadest social division was between freemen and slaves. Freemen included clergy, army officers, **boyars** (wealthy landowners), townsmen, and peasants. Slaves were mostly prisoners of war, and debtors working off their debts formed a large semifree group.

MONGOL RULE (1243–1480)

In the thirteenth century, Mongols (or Tatars) swept over China, much of the Islamic world, and Russia. The armies of Ghengis Khan (1155–1227) invaded Russia in 1223, and Kiev fell to the Mongol general Batu Khan in 1240. A division of the Mongol Empire, the *Golden Horde* (a name derived from the Tatar words for the color of Batu Khan's tent), established a capital on the lower Volga River and exacted tribute from the Russian cities. The Mongols converted to Islam, and their Eastern culture pulled the Russians away from the European West. Some Russian women began to wear veils and to seclude themselves, but the Mongols interfered little with the political institutions and religion of their Russian subjects. The order they maintained and the trade links they established improved economic prospects for most Russians. The princes of Moscow grew wealthy by assisting their Mongol masters with the collection of tribute. As Mongol rule weakened, Moscow's power increased, and its rulers embarked on a project called "the gathering of the Russian Land." It aimed at expanding the territory under Moscow's control by all possible means: purchase, colonization, and conquest.

In 1380, Grand Duke Dimitri of Moscow (r. 1350–1389) gave the Tatar forces a defeat that precipitated the decline of Mongol hegemony. Another century passed before Ivan III, "the Great" (d. 1505) brought all of northern Russia under Moscow's control and ended Mongol rule (1480). By the last quarter of the fourteenth century, Moscow had become Russia's political and religious capital, and after Constantinople fell to the Turks in 1453, it declared itself the "third Rome" and the guardian of Orthodox civilization.

SUMMARY

The Black Death Between 1347 and the early fifteenth century, close to 40 percent of the population of western Europe was killed by the Black Death. People had no idea what the bubonic plague was, how it was transmitted, or how to treat the sick. The fear inspired by the disease itself, and by the responses to it, influenced European attitudes and religious beliefs for centuries. The sharp reduction in population changed fundamental social, economic, and political patterns. Increased demand and reduced supply of luxury goods brought more power and wealth to cities and to skilled artisans; the landed nobility suffered economically as demand for food diminished.

The Hundred Years' War and the Rise of National Sentiment The so-called Hundred Years' War between England and France actually lasted for more than a century, from 1337 to 1453, although there were long intervals of peace during this period. The direct cause of the war was controversy over the succession to the

boyars Wealthy landowners among the freemen in late medieval Russia.

French throne. Despite a smaller population, less wealth, and fighting on enemy soil, England got the better of France in most of the significant early battles. England began the conflict as a more cohesive state than France. Eventually, however, the French began to see past regional rivalries, and Joan of Arc inspired an emergent national pride.

Ecclesiastical Breakdown and Revival: The Late Medieval Church

Through the thirteenth century, popes had worked to centralize church power. As nation-states gained cohesiveness, kings started to challenge papal authority. Throughout most of the fourteenth century, the papacy was based in Avignon, France, rather than Rome. The conciliar theory proposed that the pope just oversees a church that should rightfully be dominated by the faithful as a group. The Council of Basel in the fifteenth century provided a model of lay rights and responsibilities for other church and national organizations.

Medieval Russia Kiev was the most important city in Russia around the turn of the millennium, so Prince Vladimir of Kiev's selection of Greek Orthodoxy as the state religion had ramifications that endure to the present. Starting in the eleventh century, Kiev lost its preeminence, and Russians split into three geographic and cultural groupings: the Great Russians, the White Russians, and the Little Russians or Ukrainians. In 1223, Ghengis Khan sent a Mongol (or Tatar) army into Russia. The Golden Horde brought much of Russia into the Mongol Empire. Mongol rule ended in 1480, by which time Moscow was the dominant city within Russia. In contrast to western Europe, where the nobility, the clergy, and the peasantry constituted distinct and easily identifiable groups in Russia the main social division was between freemen and slaves.

REVIEW QUESTIONS

1. What were the causes of the Black Death? Why did it spread so quickly? What were its effects on European society? How important do you think disease is in changing the course of history?

2. What were the causes of the Hundred Years' War? What advantages did each side have? Why were the French ultimately victorious?

3. What changes took place in the church and in its relationship to secular society between 1200 and 1450? How did it respond to political threats from increasingly powerful monarchs? How great an influence did the church have on secular events?

4. What is meant by the term "Avignon papacy"? What caused the Great Schism? How was it resolved? Why did kings in the late thirteenth and early fourteenth centuries have more power over the church than it had over them? What did kings hope to achieve through their struggles with the church?

5. How did the Kievan and medieval Russian states develop in terms of religion, politics, and social structure? What effect did Mongol rule have on Russian lands?

IMAGE KEY
for pages 218–219

a. Chalice, French, c.1325 (silver gilt)

b. Flagellants in the Netherlands town of Tournai (Doornik), 1349. Flagellants, known as the Brothers of the Cross, scourging themselves as they walk through the streets in order to free the world from the Black Death (Bubonic Plague)

c. Lugged Two-handed Sword, circa 1600

d. Detail from an illustrated manuscript of Boccaccio's "Decameron," physicians apply leeches to an emperor   Jean-Loup Charmet/Science Photo Library/Photo Researchers, Inc.

e. Exterior of a church, Novgorod, Russia

f. Statue of Pope Boniface VIII. Museo Civico, Bologna.   Scala/Art Resource, NY

g. Death of Wat Tyler (d. 1381) in front of Richard II, killed by Lord Mayor Walworth for wishing to abolish serfdom, by Jehan Froissart, (ca. 1460–80)

h. "Joan of Arc." Franco-Flemish miniature. Anonymous, 15h century. Archives Nationales, Paris, France. Photograph copyright Bridgeman-Giraudon/Art Resource, NY

i. A Caricature of physicians (early sixteenth century)

KEY TERMS

Avignon Papacy (p. 230)   **boyars** (p. 234)   **Jacquerie** (p. 226)

Black Death (p. 220)   **Estates General** (p. 226)

 For additional study resources for this chapter, go to:
www.prenhall.com/kagan3/chapter9

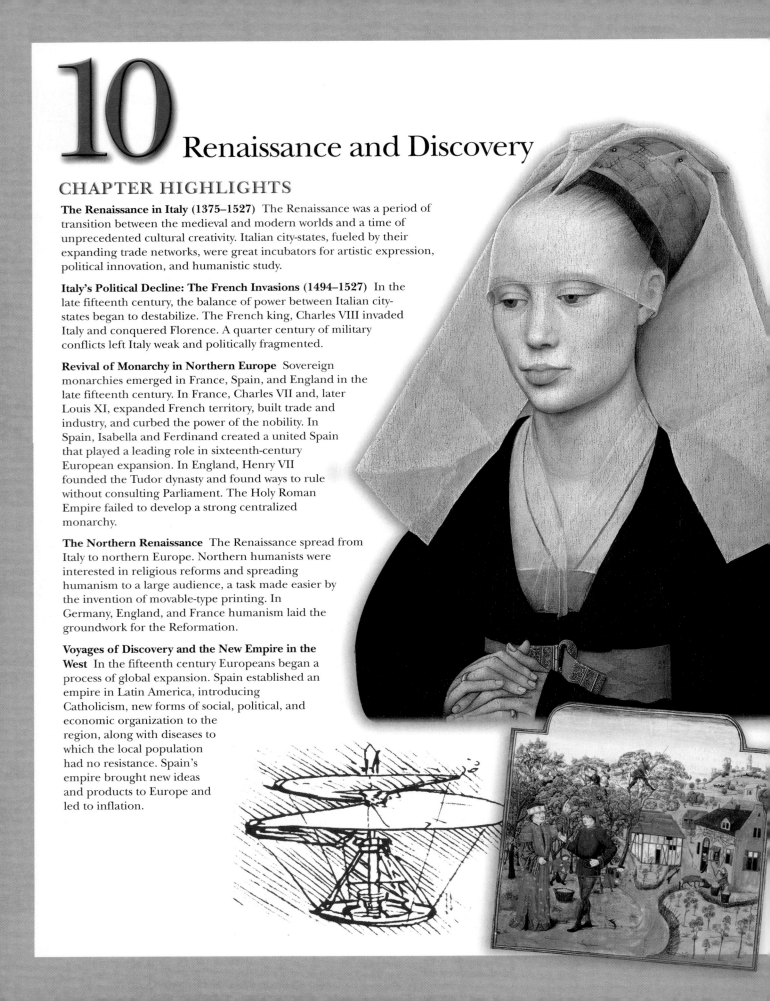

10 Renaissance and Discovery

CHAPTER HIGHLIGHTS

The Renaissance in Italy (1375–1527) The Renaissance was a period of transition between the medieval and modern worlds and a time of unprecedented cultural creativity. Italian city-states, fueled by their expanding trade networks, were great incubators for artistic expression, political innovation, and humanistic study.

Italy's Political Decline: The French Invasions (1494–1527) In the late fifteenth century, the balance of power between Italian city-states began to destabilize. The French king, Charles VIII invaded Italy and conquered Florence. A quarter century of military conflicts left Italy weak and politically fragmented.

Revival of Monarchy in Northern Europe Sovereign monarchies emerged in France, Spain, and England in the late fifteenth century. In France, Charles VII and, later Louis XI, expanded French territory, built trade and industry, and curbed the power of the nobility. In Spain, Isabella and Ferdinand created a united Spain that played a leading role in sixteenth-century European expansion. In England, Henry VII founded the Tudor dynasty and found ways to rule without consulting Parliament. The Holy Roman Empire failed to develop a strong centralized monarchy.

The Northern Renaissance The Renaissance spread from Italy to northern Europe. Northern humanists were interested in religious reforms and spreading humanism to a large audience, a task made easier by the invention of movable-type printing. In Germany, England, and France humanism laid the groundwork for the Reformation.

Voyages of Discovery and the New Empire in the West In the fifteenth century Europeans began a process of global expansion. Spain established an empire in Latin America, introducing Catholicism, new forms of social, political, and economic organization to the region, along with diseases to which the local population had no resistance. Spain's empire brought new ideas and products to Europe and led to inflation.

CHAPTER QUESTIONS

HOW DID humanism affect culture and the arts in fourteenth- and fifteenth-century Italy?

WHAT WERE the causes of Italy's political decline?

HOW WERE the powerful monarchies of northern Europe different from their predecessors?

HOW DID the northern Renaissance affect culture in Germany, England, France, and Spain?

WHAT WERE the motives for European voyages of discovery, and what were the consequences?

CHAPTER OUTLINE

- The Renaissance in Italy (1375–1527)
- Italy's Political Decline: The French Invasions (1494–1527)
- Revival of Monarchy in Northern Europe
- The Northern Renaissance
- Voyages of Discovery and the New Empires in the West

IMAGE KEY
Image Key for pages 236–237 is on page 260.

The late medieval period was an era of creative disruption. The social order that had persisted in Europe for a thousand years failed, but Europe did not decline. It merely changed direction. By the late fifteenth century, its population had nearly recovered from the losses inflicted by the plagues, famines, and wars of the fourteenth century. Able rulers were establishing stable, centralized governments, and Italy's city-states were doing especially well. Italy's strategic location enabled it to dominate world trade, which still centered on the Mediterranean. Italy's commercial wealth gave its leaders means to provide patronage for education and the arts and fund the famous Italian Renaissance.

Renaissance scholars, the humanists, revived the study of classical Greek and Latin languages and literature. They reformed education and, thanks to the invention of the printing press, became the first scholars able to reach out to the general public. In their eagerness to educate ordinary men and women, they championed the use of vernacular languages as vehicles for art and serious thought.

During the late fifteenth and the sixteenth centuries, powerful nations arose in western Europe and sponsored voyages of exploration that spread Europe's influence around the globe. The colonies they planted and empires they built yielded a flood of gold, information, and new materials that transformed the Western way of life.

HOW DID humanism affect culture and the arts in fourteenth- and fifteenth-century Italy?

THE RENAISSANCE IN ITALY (1375–1527)

The Renaissance began the transition from the medieval to the modern worlds. Medieval Europe was a fragmented feudal society with a marginal agrarian economy. Intellectually, it was dominated by the church. Renaissance Europe, after the fourteenth century, was characterized by political centralization, awareness of national identities, capitalistic urban economies, and an increasingly secular culture. These changes appeared first in Italy.

THE ITALIAN CITY-STATE

Italy's location had always given it cultural and commercial advantages over the rest of Europe. Italy dominated the Mediterranean Sea, the center of international trade, and the wealth and stimulating foreign influences that flowed through Italy promoted the growth of a unique urban culture. During the thirteenth and fourteenth centuries, Italy's towns extended their authority over the countryside and became city-states. (See Map 10–1.)

Florentine women doing needlework, spinning, and weaving. These activities took up much of a woman's time and contributed to the elegance of dress for which Florentine men and women were famed.

Palazzo Schifanoia, Ferrara/Alinari Art Resource, NY

Growth of City-States The destiny of Italy's cities was shaped by endemic warfare between Guelf (pro-papal) and Ghibelline (pro-imperial) factions. If either the pope or the emperor had enjoyed a free hand in Italy, he might have brought its cities under control. Instead, each man tried to undercut the other, and the cities were the winners. They escaped dominance by kings and popes, took charge of the regions in which they were located, and became self-governing city-states. The five greatest were the duchy of Milan, the republics of Florence and Venice, the Papal States, and the kingdom of Naples.

Social Class and Conflict Competition among leaders, political factions, and social classes contributed to instability in Italy's city-states and led, by the fifteenth century, to despots assuming power in most of them. Venice was a notable exception; it remained an oligarchic republic governed by a small group of merchant families.

Florence offers a more typical example of the evolution of a Renaissance city. Four groups jockeyed for advantage in Florence: the old rich (the *grandi*, the noble and established families that traditionally led); an emerging merchant class (wealthy capitalists and bankers—the *popolo grosso*, "fat people"); the middle-burgher ranks (guild masters, shop owners, and professionals); and the *popolo minuto* (the "little people"). In 1457, about one-third of the residents of Florence were listed as paupers—as having no wealth.

Despotism and Diplomacy In 1378, the economic dislocation caused by the Black Death prompted the Ciompi Revolt, a great uprising of the Florentine poor. Stability was not fully restored until Cosimo de' Medici (1389–1464), the richest man in Florence, took charge in 1434. Cosimo de' Medici was an astute statesman. He controlled the city from behind the scenes by skillfully manipulating its constitution and influencing elections. Florence was governed by the *Signoria*, a council of six (later, eight) men elected from the most powerful guilds. Cosimo's influence with the electoral committee ensured that his men dominated the *Signoria*, and his grandson, Lorenzo the Magnificent (1449–1492; r. 1478–1492), established a virtually totalitarian government. He was, however, careful to court popular support.

Despotism was less subtle elsewhere. Whenever internal fighting and foreign intrigue threatened to paralyze a city's government, its warring factions would agree to appoint a *podestà*. He was a neutral outsider, a hired strongman charged to do whatever was necessary to maintain law and order and foster a good climate for business. Because a despot could not depend on everyone's cooperation, he policed and protected his town with a mercenary army hired from military brokers called ***condottieri***. The *podestà*'s job was hazardous. He might be dismissed by the oligarchy that hired him or assassinated by factions he offended. The potential spoils of his career were, however, worth the risk because a *podestà* might establish a dynasty. The Visconti family that ruled Milan after 1278 and the Sforza family that followed them in 1450 both had *podestà* founders.

The kind of government that maintained discipline in an Italian city seemed to have little effect on the climate it offered for intellectual and artistic activity. Despots promoted Renaissance culture as enthusiastically as republicans, and spiritually minded popes were no less generous than worldly vicars of Christ.

MAP EXPLORATION

Interactive map: To explore this map further, go to
http://www.prenhall.com/kagan3/map10.1

MAP 10–1

Renaissance Italy The city-states of Renaissance Italy were self-contained principalities whose internal strife was monitored by their despots and whose external aggression was long successfully controlled by treaty.

HOW DID city-states help shape the political climate of Renaissance Italy?

condottieri Military brokers from whom one could hire a mercenary army.

HUMANISM

Leonardo Bruni (1374–1444), a Florentine, was the first to describe the scholarship of the Renaissance as *studia humanitas* or **humanism**. Modern authorities do not agree on how to define humanism. Some claim it is an un-Christian philosophy emphasizing human dignity, individualism, and secular values. There were, however, Christian humanists who defended faith from attack by extreme rationalists. Humanism, for many of its Renaissance proponents, may have been less a philosophical position than an educational program. It championed the study of Latin and Greek classics and Christian church fathers as an end in itself and as a guide to reforming society. The first humanists were orators and poets, specialists in rhetoric. Some taught at universities, but many worked as secretaries, speech writers, and diplomats at princely and papal courts.

Italy's humanists were not the first Europeans to take an interest in the study of classical and Christian antiquities. There had been a Carolingian renaissance in the ninth century, and another was led by the cathedral school of Chartres in the twelfth century. The University of Paris was transformed by the study of Aristotle in the thirteenth century, and the works of Augustine of Hippo reinvigorated intellectual life in the fourteenth century. These scholarly revivals pale, however, in comparison with Italy's Renaissance.

The medieval Scholastics were governed by an evolving tradition that was created as they summarized and reconciled the views of respected commentators on the subjects they studied. Renaissance humanists swept aside layers of interpretation and went directly to original sources. They avidly searched out forgotten manuscripts to recover all that remained of ancient Greek and Latin literature, edited what they found, and made it generally available. They so assimilated the classics and so identified with the ancients that they came to think of the immediate past as a hiatus, a "dark middle age" during which civilization languished awaiting its rebirth in their own day.

Petrarch, Dante, and Boccaccio Francesco Petrarch (1304–1374), "the father of humanism," modeled his writing on the works of the giants of Roman literature. His *Letters to the Ancient Dead* was an imagined correspondence with Cicero, Livy, Vergil, and Horace. His epic poem *Africa* (a tribute to the Roman general Scipio Africanus) was conceived as a continuation of Vergil's *Aeneid*, and his biographies of famous Romans, *Lives of Illustrious Men*, were modeled on Plutarch's essays. Petrarch's most popular work, however, was not an imitation of the classics. It was a collection of highly introspective Italian love sonnets, which he addressed to a married woman named Laura. Like a medieval courtly lover, he worshiped her from afar.

Classical and Christian values coexist in Petrarch's work. He dismissed Scholasticism as sterile and useless, but he wrote tracts refuting Aristotelian arguments that undercut faith in personal immortality. His acceptance of many traditional medieval Christian beliefs is also apparent in the set of imaginary dialogues with the fifth-century saint, Augustine of Hippo, which he composed.

Petrarch's point of view was, however, more secular than that of his famous near contemporary, Dante Alighieri (1265–1321). Dante's *Vita Nuova* and *Divine Comedy* rank with Petrarch's sonnets as cornerstones of the new vernacular literature associated with the Renaissance, but they are also expressions of medieval piety. Petrarch's student, Giovanni Boccaccio (1313–1375), created bridges of another kind between medieval literature and humanism. His best known work, *Decameron*, is a collection of one hundred tales (many re-

10.1
Petrarch: Rules for
the Ruler

***studia humanitas* (humanism)**
Scholarship of the Renaissance that championed the study of Latin and Greek classics and Christian church fathers as an end in itself and as a guide to reforming society. Some claim it is an un-Christian philosophy emphasizing human dignity, individualism, and secular values.

told from medieval sources), but he was famous in his own day for an encyclopedia of Greek and Roman mythology.

Educational Reforms and Goals   Humanists were activists. They believed the intensive study of the ancients would cure the ills that plagued contemporary society by teaching the practice of virtue. Humanist learning was intended to ennoble people by promoting the free use of their gifts of mind and body.

Traditional methods of education had to be reformed to nurture the kind of well-rounded people the humanists wanted to produce. The rediscovery in 1416 of the complete text of Quintilian's *Education of the Orator* provided them with a classical guide for the revision of curricula. Vittorino da Feltre (d. 1446) described the goals and methods of the reform. He advised students to master difficult works by Pliny, Ptolemy, Terence, Plautus, Livy, and Plutarch, but also to undergo vigorous physical training. Humanist learning was not confined to the classroom. Baldassare Castiglione's (1478–1529) influential *Book of the Courtier*, a practical guide for conduct at the court of Urbino, urged its readers to combine the study of ancient languages and history with the practice of athletic, military, and musical skills. Castiglione also warned that a true courtier needed more than good manners and accomplishments. He required exemplary moral character.

Women, most notably Christine de Pisan (1363?–1434), profited from educational reform and helped guide it. Christine's father was physician and astrologer to the court of King Charles V of France. At the French court she received as fine an education as any man and became an expert in classical, French, and Italian languages and literature. Married at fifteen and widowed with three children at twenty-seven, she turned to writing lyric poetry to support herself. Her works were soon being read at all the European courts. Her most famous book, *The Treasure of the City of Ladies*, chronicles the accomplishments of the great women of history.

The Florentine "Academy" and the Revival of Platonism   Italy's Renaissance differed from earlier revivals of interest in the past in its passionate devotion to Greek literature, particularly the works of Plato. In 1397, Florence invited a Byzantine scholar, Manuel Chrysoloras, to come to Italy and open a school offering training in Greek. More Greek scholars (bringing more manuscripts) arrived in 1439 to attend the Council of Ferrara-Florence and negotiate a reunion of the Greek and Latin churches. More Greeks arrived in 1453 as refugees following the Turkish conquest of Constantinople.

The Scholastics' enthusiasm for Aristotle led to a preoccupation with logic and science. The humanists' love of Plato promoted an interest in poetry and mysticism. Platonism's appeal lay in its flattering view of human nature and the fact that it could be more easily reconciled with Christianity than Aristotelianism. Platonism posited the existence of a realm of eternal ideas that were the prototypes for the imperfect, perishable things of this world. Plato claimed that human beings had an innate knowledge of mathematical truths and moral standards that proved they were rooted in the eternal.

Cosimo de' Medici (1389–1464) encouraged the study of Plato and the Neoplatonic philosophers by founding the Platonic Academy, a gathering of influential Florentine humanists headed first by Marsilio Ficino (1433–1499) and

Christine de Pisan, who has the modern reputation of being the first European feminist, presents her internationally famous book, *The Treasure of the City of Ladies*, also known as *The Book of Three Virtues*, to Isabella of Bavaria amid her ladies in waiting.

Historical Picture Archive/CORBIS/Bettmann

later by Pico della Mirandola (1463–1494). The Platonism to which the Florentine scholars introduced Europe was more confident about the potential of human nature than medieval Christianity. Pico's *Oration on the Dignity of Man* boldly articulated the Renaissance's humanistic faith. Published in Rome in December 1486, the *Oration* was a preface to a collection of nine hundred theses that Pico proposed for a public debate. It lauded human beings as the only creatures endowed with the freedom to create themselves—to become angels or pigs.

Critical Work of the Humanists: Lorenzo Valla   The humanists' careful study of classical languages sometimes had unexpected consequences. Lorenzo Valla (1406–1457), a papal secretary who wrote the era's standard text on Latin philology (*Elegances of the Latin Language*), published a devastating critique of *The Donation of Constantine*. Since the eighth century, popes had used the *Donation* to bolster their claim to authority over emperors, but Valla proved on linguistic grounds the document was a forgery that could not have dated from the era of the emperor Constantine. He also pointed out errors in the Vulgate, the church's authorized Latin Bible.

Civic Humanism   Although some humanists were clubbish snobs whose narrow, antiquarian interests appealed only to an intellectual elite, others advocated a "civil humanism," an educational program designed to foster virtue and equip people for public service. They entered politics, employed their artistic and literary skills to promote their cities, urged scholars to use the vernacular so ordinary people could profit from their work, and wrote histories of contemporary events.

RENAISSANCE ART

The Renaissance (like the later religious movement, the Reformation) reversed the medieval tendency to value the clerical lifestyle more highly than that of the laity. Its affirmation of secular values and purely human pursuits led to significant adjustments in medieval Christian attitudes. Europe's increasing "this-worldliness" also owed something to the crises within the papacy that diminished the medieval church's power and prestige. The new attitudes were consistent, as well, with the rise of patriotic nationalism, the increasing prominence of laypersons in governmental bureaucracies, and the rapid growth of educational opportunities for the laity in the late medieval period.

The new perspective on life can be perceived in the painting and sculpture of the "high," or mature, Renaissance (the late fifteenth and early sixteenth centuries). Whereas medieval art was abstract and formulaic, Renaissance art described the natural world and expressed human emotions. Its rational (mathematical) organization and its focus on symmetry and proportionality reflect the humanistic faith in a harmonious, intelligible universe.

Artists developed techniques during the fifteenth century that allowed them to do new things. Slow-drying oil-based paints, new methods of drafting, the use of *chiaroscuro* (shading to enhance naturalness), linear perspective, the adjustment of the size of figures to create the illusion of depth—all promoted greater realism. Whereas two-dimensional Byzantine and Gothic paintings were intended to be read like pages in a book, Renaissance paintings were windows on a three-dimensional world filled with life. (See "Encountering the Past: The Garden.")

Giotto (1266–1336), the father of Renaissance painting, was the first to intuit what could be done with the new techniques. He dealt with serious religious themes, but his work was less abstract and more naturalistic than that of a medieval painter. The Black Death of 1340 slowed the development of art, but Giotto's ideas were taken up in the fifteenth century by the painter Masaccio (1401–1428)

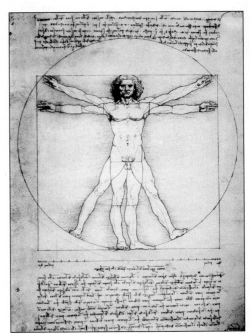

Vitruvian Man, by Leonardo da Vinci, c. 1490. Like most Ranaissance artists, Leonardo sought to portray human beauty and perfection. This sketch is named after the first-century c.e. Roman architect Marcus Pollio Vitruvius, who used squares and circles to demonstrate the human body's symmetry and proportionality.

CORBIS/Bettmann

ENCOUNTERING THE PAST

THE GARDEN

Gardens were sources of both necessities and pleasures for the people of the Middle Ages and the Renaissance, and every household from the grandest to the humblest had one. In addition to their practical functions, gardens had religious and social associations. They were enclosed behind walls, fences, or hedges to protect their contents, and they served as private retreats in a world that offered little shelter for privacy. They called to mind the Garden of Eden and the more sensuous pleasures of the garden described in the Bible's Song of Songs (4:12). They were symbols of paradise and reminders of the temptations that led to Adam's fall.

Wealthy people had gardens (adorned with grottoes and fountains) that were designed primarily for pleasure. They provided ideal settings for the romantic trysts of courtly lovers. Even great houses, however, like the cottages of the poor, also had gardens devoted to much more utilitarian purposes. A medieval/Renaissance household depended on its garden for much of its food and medicine. The fruit it produced was mainly used to concoct sweet drinks, and it was the source of the limited range of vegetables medieval people consumed: cabbage, lentils, peas, beans, onions, leeks, beets, and parsnips. The herbs and flowers from gardens were highly prized as flavorings for a diet heavy on bland, starchy foods. They were also the era's most effective medicines.

A wealthy man oversees apple picking at harvest time in a fifteenth-century French orchard. In the town below, individual house gardens can be seen. Protective fences, made of woven sticks, keep out predatory animals.

By permission of The British Library

and the sculptor Donatello (1386–1466). The heights were reached by the great masters of the High Renaissance: Leonardo da Vinci (1452–1519), Raphael (1483–1520), and Michelangelo Buonarroti (1475–1564).

Leonardo da Vinci   Leonardo came closer than anyone to achieving the Renaissance ideal of universal competence. He was one of the greatest painters of all time—as his famous portrait, the *Mona Lisa*, demonstrates. He also had one of the great scientific minds of his age. He was in demand as a military engineer. He did significant descriptive work in botany. He defied the church by dissecting corpses to study human anatomy, and he filled sketch books with designs for such modern machines as airplanes and submarines. He had so many ideas it was difficult for him to concentrate long on any one of them.

Raphael   Raphael, an unusually sensitive man, was loved for both his work and his kindly personality. He is best known for his tender depictions of madonnas. Art historians consider his fresco *The School of Athens*, a group portrait of the great Western philosophers, a perfect example of Renaissance technique.

Combining the painterly qualities of all the Renaissance masters, Raphael created scenes of tender beauty and subjects sublime in both flesh and spirit.

Musee du Louvre, Paris/Giraudon, Paris/SuperStock

mannerism Reaction against the simplicity, symmetry, and idealism of High Renaissance art. It made room for the strange, even the abnormal, and gave free reign to the subjectivity of the artist. The name reflects a tendency by artists to employ "mannered" ("affected") techniques—distortions that expressed individual perceptions and feelings.

WHAT WERE the causes of

Italy's political decline?

Michelangelo Michelangelo, like Leonardo, excelled in several fields. His *David*, an eighteen-foot-high sculpture of a biblical hero in the guise of a Greek god, splendidly illustrates the Renaissance artist's devotion to harmony, symmetry, and proportion—and to the glorification of the human form. Four different popes commissioned works from Michelangelo. The most famous are the frescoes that Pope Julius II (r. 1503–1513) ordered for the Vatican's Sistine Chapel. They originally covered 10,000 square feet and featured 343 figures—most of which Michelangelo executed himself with minimal help from his assistants. It took him four years to complete the extraordinarily original images, some of which have become the best known icons of the Christian faith.

Michelangelo lived to be nearly ninety, and his later works illustrate the passing of the High Renaissance and the advent of a new style called **mannerism**. Mannerism was a reaction against the simplicity, symmetry, and idealism of High Renaissance art. It made room for the strange, even the abnormal, and gave free reign to the subjectivity of the artist. The name reflects a tendency by artists to employ "mannered" ("affected") techniques—distortions that expressed individual perceptions and feelings. The Venetian Tintoretto (d. 1594) and the Spanish El Greco (d. 1614) represent mannerism at its best.

SLAVERY IN THE RENAISSANCE

The vision of innate human nobility that inspired the Renaissance's artists and thinkers was marred by what modern observers would consider a major inconsistency. Slavery flourished in Italy as extravagantly as art and culture. Spaniards began to sell Muslim war captives to wealthy Italians as early as the twelfth century. Slaves were usually employed as domestic servants, but the slave-based sugarcane plantations that the Venetians established on Cyprus and Crete during the High Middle Ages provided the model for later New World slavery.

The demand for slaves soared after the Black Death (1348–1350) reduced the supply of laborers throughout western Europe. A strong young slave cost the equivalent of the wages paid a free servant over several years. Given the prospect of a lifetime of free service, however, slaves were a good bargain. If need be, their owners could also recover their capital by reselling them, for legally they were private property. Most well-to-do Italian households had slaves, and even the clergy owned them.

Slavery was not based on any concept of race, and peoples from Africa, the Balkans, Constantinople, Cyprus, Crete, and the lands surrounding the Black Sea were enslaved. As in ancient Greece and Rome, slaves of the Renaissance era were often integrated into households like family members. Some female slaves became mothers of their masters' children, and quite a few of these children were adopted and raised as legitimate heirs. It was in owners' self-interest to protect their investments by keeping their slaves healthy and happy, but slaves were uprooted, resentful people who posed a threat to social stability.

ITALY'S POLITICAL DECLINE: THE FRENCH INVASIONS (1494–1527)

*I*taly's ability to defend itself from foreign invasion depended on the ability of its independent city-states to work together. During the last half of the fifteenth century, the Treaty of Lodi (1454–1455) allied Milan and Naples (traditional enemies) with Florence against Venice and the Papal States and created a balance of power that helped stabilize Italy internally. The peace established by the Treaty of Lodi ended in 1494 when Naples, Florence, and Pope Alexander VI joined forces to oppose Milan. The despot who ruled Milan, Ludovico il Moro, appealed to France for help. France had ruled Naples from 1266 to 1435, and its young king, Charles VIII (r. 1483–1498), was eager to win it back.

CHARLES VIII's MARCH THROUGH ITALY

Charles responded to Ludovico's call with lightning speed. It took him only five months to cross the Alps (August 1494) and drive through the territory of Florence and the Papal States to Naples. When Piero de' Medici, Florence's ruler, tried to placate the French king by ceding him the city of Pisa and other Florentine possessions, the radical preacher Girolamo Savonarola (1452–1498) rallied the angry Florentines, and they drove Piero into exile. Savonarola claimed that France's invasion was God's punishment for Florence's sins, and he persuaded the Florentines to do penance by submitting to Charles and paying him a ransom to spare their city. Savonarola dominated Florence for four years, but the Florentines eventually tired of his puritanical tyranny and executed him (May 1498).

Charles's advance into Italy alarmed Spain's Ferdinand of Aragon. He viewed an axis of Franco-Italian states as a threat to his homeland, and he proposed an alliance of Aragon, Venice, the Papal States, and the Emperor Maximilian I against the French. When Milan, which had come to regret inviting the French into Italy, joined Ferdinand's League of Venice, Charles was forced to retreat.

POPE ALEXANDER VI AND THE BORGIA FAMILY

An alliance between Louis XII (r. 1498–1515), Charles's successor, and Pope Alexander VI (r. 1492–1503) allowed the French to return to Italy. Alexander, a member of the infamous Borgia family, may have been the church's most corrupt pope. His intent was to create a hereditary duchy for his son Cesare by using the power of the papacy to recover Romagna, a district on the Adriatic coast northeast of Rome that had broken free from the Papal States while the papacy was headquartered in Avignon. Venice's opposition to this scheme caused the pope to break with the League of Venice and side with France.

France, with papal assistance, conquered Milan, and the pope's reward was the hand of the sister of the king of Navarre for his son and the promise of French military aid in Romagna. In 1500, Louis and Ferdinand of Aragon agreed on a division of the Kingdom of Naples, and the pope and Cesare completed the conquest of Romagna.

POPE JULIUS II

Julius II (r. 1503–1513), the "warrior pope," suppressed the Borgias and reclaimed Romagna for the papacy. Julius's reign marked the pinnacle of the Renaissance papacy's military prowess and convoluted diplomatic maneuvers. Once he had established firm control over Romagna (1509) and the Papal States, he set about ridding Italy of his former allies, the French. To this end, he formed a second Holy League with Ferdinand of Aragon and Venice in October 1511. Emperor Maximilian I and the Swiss also signed on, and by 1512, the alliance had forced the French to retreat.

Significant Dates from the Italian Renaissance (1375–1527)

1434	Medici rule established in Florence
1454–1455	Treaty of Lodi
1494	Charles VIII of France invades Italy
1495	League of Venice
1499	Louis XII invades Italy
1500	The Borgias conquer Romagna
1512–1513	The Holy League defeats the French
1515	Francis I invades Italy
1527	Sack of Rome by imperial soldiers

QUICK REVIEW

The Warrior Pope

- Julius II's (r. 1503–1513) reign marked the pinnacle of the papacy's military prowess
- After securing Romagna and the Papal States, he set about pushing the French out of Italy
- Julius formed a Holy League with Ferdinand of Aragon and Venice in 1511 for this purpose

The French were, however, nothing if not persistent. Louis's successor, Francis I (r. 1515–1547), invaded Italy yet again and dealt a severe blow to the Holy League by defeating the Swiss at Marignano in September 1515. The Habsburg emperor then stepped into the breach and launched the first of four Habsburg-Valois wars—none of which France won.

Francis had better luck in dealing with the pope. In August 1516, the pope agreed to the Concordat of Bologna. He ceded Francis control over the French clergy in exchange for the right to continue to collect certain fees from the French clergy and France's support for the pope's campaign to repudiate conciliarism. By virtually nationalizing the French Catholic church, the Concordat ensured that France's kings would have nothing to gain by embracing the Reformation that was soon to sweep Germany and Switzerland.

NICCOLÒ MACHIAVELLI

10.2
Machiavelli: From the *Discourses*

As the armies of France, Spain, and Germany made a shambles of Italy, Niccolò Machiavelli (1469–1527), a Florentine scholar, struggled to make sense of the tragedies befalling his homeland. Italy's experience persuaded him that political ends—the maintenance of peace and order—are justified by any means.

Machiavelli's humanist education had included a close, if somewhat romanticized, study of the history of ancient Rome. He was impressed by the apparent ability of the Romans to act decisively and heroically for the good of their country, and he lamented the absence of such traits among his compatriots. He believed that if Italians ceased their feuding and worked together, they could defend their country from invaders. Machiavelli was devoted to republican ideals, but political realities convinced him that only a strongman could rescue the Italians from the consequences of their shortsighted behavior. The salvation of Italy required, he believed, a cunning dictator who was willing to use "Machiavellian" techniques to manipulate his people.

Machiavelli may have intended *The Prince*, which he wrote in 1513, to be a satire on politics, not a serious justification for despotism. However, he seems to have been in earnest when he defended fraud and brutality as necessary means to the higher end of unifying Italy. Machiavelli hoped the Medici family might produce the leader Italy needed. In 1513, its members controlled both the papacy (Leo X, r. 1513–1521) and Florence. *The Prince* was dedicated to Lorenzo de' Medici, duke of Urbino and grandson of Lorenzo the Magnificent. The Medicis, however, failed to rise to the challenge Machiavelli set them, and in the year he died (1527), a second Medici pope, Clement VII (r. 1523–1534), watched helplessly as the army of Emperor Charles V sacked Rome—an event that some scholars see as marking the end of the Renaissance. (See "History's Voices: Machiavelli Discusses the Most Important Trait for a Ruler.")

Santi di Tito's portrait of Machiavelli, perhaps the most famous Italian political theorist, who advised Renaissance princes to practice artful deception and inspire fear in their subjects if they wished to be successful.

Scala/Art Resource, NY

HOW WERE the powerful monarchies of northern Europe different from their predecessors?

REVIVAL OF MONARCHY IN NORTHERN EUROPE

Medieval monarchies tended to be weak, for various factions jockeyed for advantage within them. Vassals sought maximum independence from their lords, and nobles, clergy, and townsmen joined forces in representative assemblies (such as the English Parliament, the French Estates General, the German Diet, and the Spanish *Cortés*) to moderate royal authority. By 1450, however, kings had won the upper hand in many parts of Europe and true sovereigns were establishing themselves in control of national monarchies.

HISTORY'S VOICES

MACHIAVELLI DISCUSSES THE MOST IMPORTANT TRAIT FOR A RULER

achiavelli believed that the most important personality trait of a successful ruler was the ability to instill fear in his subjects.

HOW WOULD you describe Machiavelli's views about the nature and characteristics of man?

Here the question arises: whether it is better to be loved than feared or feared than loved. The answer is that it would be desirable to be both but, since that is difficult, it is much safer to be feared than to be loved, if one must choose. For on men in general this observation may be made: they are ungrateful, fickle, and deceitful, eager to avoid dangers, and avid for gain, and while you are useful to them they are all with you, offering you their blood, their property, their lives, and their sons so long as danger is remote, as we noted above, but when it approaches, they turn on you. Any prince, trusting only in their words and having no other preparations made, will fall to his rain, for friendships that are bought at a price and not by greatness and nobility of soul are paid for indeed, but they are not owned and cannot be called upon in time of need. Men have less hesitation in offending a man who is loved than one who is feared, for love is held by a bond of obligation which, as men are wicked, is broken whenever personal advantage suggests it, but fear is accompanied by the dread of punishment which never relaxes.

Niccolò Machiavelli, *The Prince* (1513), trans. and ed. by Thomas G. Bergin (New York: Appleton-Century- Crofts. NY. 1947). p. 48.

Towns were crucial in effecting this political transition. Townspeople made feudalism anachronistic by taking over many of the functions of the feudal nobility. They helped kings reclaim the powers of taxation, war making, and law enforcement that feudalism had delegated to semiautonomous vassals. As these vassals ceded these functions to centralized governments, the people who lived on their fiefs began to look beyond them to their monarch and to develop "national" consciousness. The hereditary nobility cultivated a local power base, but the loyalty of a monarch's professional civil servants (such as the Spanish *corregidores*, the English justices of the peace, and the French bailiffs) was to the state.

The machinery of bureaucratic government gave kings the instruments they needed to enforce their decrees directly and to bypass feudal councils and representative assemblies. Ferdinand and Isabella, who ruled Spain at the end of the fifteenth century, rarely called the *Cortés* into session. The French Estates General did not meet from 1484 to 1560. And after 1485, when England's Parliament granted Henry VII (r. 1485–1509) the right to collect the customs revenues he needed to cover the costs of government, the king summoned no more parliaments.

By the fifteenth century, monarchs had also begun to create standing armies that ended the feudal nobility's traditional military monopoly. Professional soldiers who fought for pay and booty were more efficient than feudal vassals who fought for honor's sake. Changing weaponry and tactics (artillery, for instance) also shifted the emphasis on the battlefield away from the noble cavalry and to the common man's infantry. The strength of infantry derives from numbers, and monarchs wanted large armies. Professional soldiers tend to mutiny, however, if payrolls are not met. Royal governments had, therefore, to find sources of income to meet the rising costs of warfare in the fifteenth and sixteenth centuries. Efforts to expand royal revenues were hampered by the upper classes' attitude toward taxation.

Feudal tradition held that the king should meet the costs of his government, as his vassals did, from the income of his personal estates. Nobles considered taxation demeaning, and their fierce resistance tempted kings to take the easier route of shifting the tax burden to their less powerful and far less wealthy subjects.

Monarchs had several sources of income. They collected rents from the royal domain. They levied national taxes on basic food and clothing. France, for instance, had a tax on salt, and Spain had a 10 percent sales tax. Rulers could also, with the approval of parliamentary bodies (in which the lower classes had no representation), levy direct taxes on the peasantry. The French monarch collected such a tax, the *taille*, and set new rates for it annually. Governments sometimes sold public offices, issued high-interest bonds, and leaned heavily on bankers for loans. A king's most powerful subjects were often also his creditors.

FRANCE

Charles VII (r. 1422–1461) was a king made great by those who served him. His ministers created a permanent professional army, which Joan of Arc inspired to drive the English out of France. An enterprising merchant banker, Jacques Coeur, served the king as a kind of finance minister and strengthened France's economy, diplomatic corps, and central administration. These tools helped Charles's son, the ruthless Louis XI (r. 1461–1483), turn France into a great power.

The rise of France in the fifteenth century followed the defeat of two opponents: the king of England and the duke of Burgundy. The Hundred Years' War ended the threat England posed to France, but at the war's end the duchy of Burgundy, England's sometime ally, was Europe's strongest state. Its ruler, Charles the Bold, intended to use his considerable military might to link up his scattered possessions and form a "middle kingdom" between France and Germany. A coalition of continental powers formed to block him, and after his death in battle in 1477, the dream of a Burgundian empire faded.

Louis XI and the Habsburg emperor, Maximilian I, divided up Burgundy's lands. The Habsburgs got the better parts, but Burgundy's fall left Louis XI free to concentrate on France's internal affairs. He fostered trade and industry, disciplined the feudal nobility, and ended his reign with a kingdom almost twice the size of the one with which he had started.

The dream of conquering Italy distracted Louis's successors from focusing, as he had, on the consolidation of royal power in France. The long series of losing wars they fought with the Habsburgs left their country, by the mid–sixteenth century, almost as divided internally as it had been during the Hundred Years' War.

SPAIN

In 1469, the marriage of Isabella, queen of Castile (r. 1474–1504), and Ferdinand, king of Aragon (r. 1479–1516), laid a foundation for a monarchy ruling most of the Iberian peninsula. Castile was the richer and more populous of the two kingdoms, having about 5 million inhabitants to Aragon's 1 million. Castile also had a lucrative, centrally managed sheep-farming industry run by a state-backed agency called the *Mesta*.

The two Spanish kingdoms were united by the royal marriage, but each retained its own government agencies, laws, armies, coinage, taxation, and cultural traditions. Ferdinand and Isabella were, however, able to do together what neither could do alone: bring the nobility under control, secure the borders of their realms, launch wars of conquest, and enforce a common Christian faith among all their subjects. In 1492, they conquered Granada, the last Muslim state on the

Iberian peninsula. Naples became a Spanish possession in 1504, and by 1512, Ferdinand had completed the conquest of Aragon's northern neighbor, the kingdom of Navarre.

Ferdinand and Isabella relied on the *Hermandad*, a league of cities and towns, for help in subduing the powerful landowners who dominated the countryside. Townspeople replaced nobles within the royal administration, and the monarchy circumscribed the power of the nobility by exerting its authority over wealthy chivalric orders.

Spain had long been remarkable among European lands as a place where Islam, Judaism, and Christianity managed to coexist—and sometimes cooperate. Ferdinand and Isabella, however, sought to unify their country by imposing a state-controlled Christian church on all their subjects, and they greatly strengthened the Inquisition (the ecclesiastical court that tried cases of heresy) to enforce religious conformity in Spain. In 1479, the Inquisition's director, Isabella's confessor, Tomás de Torquemada (d. 1498), assumed responsibility for policing the activities of the forced converts—the *conversos* (former Jews) and the *Moriscos* (Muslims). In 1492, the Jews who refused to convert were exiled and their properties confiscated by the crown. In 1502, the same fate befell the Moors of Granada. Rigorous enforcement of orthodoxy kept Spain a loyal Catholic country and made it a base of operations for the Counter-Reformation, the Catholic Church's program for regaining ground lost to the Protestant Reformation in the sixteenth century.

The marriages arranged for Ferdinand and Isabella's children were part of a grand plan to surround and contain France, and they shaped Europe's political destiny for a century. In 1496, Ferdinand and Isabella's eldest daughter and heir, Joanna ("the Mad") wed Archduke Philip, the son of the Habsburg emperor, Maximilian I. Charles V, the child of this union, inherited Spain, Flanders-Burgundy, and the Habsburgs' central European domain. His election as Holy Roman Emperor in 1519 gave him some authority over Germany and Italy as well—creating an empire almost as large as Charlemagne's. Ferdinand and Isabella's second daughter, Catherine of Aragon, wed Arthur, heir to England's king, Henry VII. Following Arthur's early death, she married his brother and became the first of King Henry VIII's six wives. The Spanish portion of Charles's legacy also included the lands in the Western Hemisphere that the Genoese explorer, Christopher Columbus (1451–1506), had claimed for his sponsors, Ferdinand and Isabella. Mexico and Peru yielded a flood of gold and silver that helped Spain dominate Europe during the sixteenth century.

ENGLAND

The last half of the fifteenth century was an especially difficult period for the English. In the wake of England's loss of the Hundred Years' War, a fight broke out between two branches of its royal family, the House of York and the House of Lancaster. This began a thirty-year-long dynastic struggle called the Wars of the Roses. (York's heraldic emblem was a white rose and Lancaster's a red rose.) From 1455 to 1485, England was in a state of turmoil.

The war began when Henry VI (r. 1422–1461), a weak king from the Lancastrian house, was challenged by his more competent cousin, the duke of York. In 1461, the duke of York's son seized power as Edward IV (r. 1461–1483). Although his reign was interrupted (1470–1471) by a short-lived restoration of Henry VI, Edward recovered the throne and did much to restore the power and wealth of the monarchy. Edward's brother, Richard III (r. 1483–1485), usurped

QUICK REVIEW

Unification of Spain
- Aragon and Castile unified by marriage of Ferdinand and Isabella
- 1492: The last Muslim state in the Iberian peninsula, Granada, falls
- Ferdinand and Isabella sought to create religious uniformity in their lands by force

the throne from Edward's young heirs, and he was, in turn, overthrown by Henry Tudor, a distant relation who had inherited the leadership of the Lancastrian faction. Henry's victory terminated the medieval Plantagenet line and launched the Tudor dynasty. Shakespeare's powerful play *Richard III*, which depicts Richard as an unprincipled villain, reflects the influence of Tudor propaganda.

Henry VII (Henry Tudor, r. 1485–1509) wed Edward IV's daughter, Elizabeth of York, and her bloodline provided added legitimacy for the Tudor dynasty. In 1487, Henry further secured the monarchy, winning Parliament's sanction for the establishment of the Court of Star Chamber. This court had jurisdiction over cases involving noblemen, and the king found it a useful instrument for intimidating the English nobles and forcing them to submit to his control. Henry construed legal precedents to the advantage of the crown, and he found excuses for confiscating so much property that he did not have to convene Parliament to raise the money he needed to govern. Thanks in part to Henry, Queen Elizabeth I, his granddaughter, was among early modern Europe's most effective rulers.

THE HOLY ROMAN EMPIRE

Germany and Italy were exceptions to the general trend toward political centralization that swept Europe during the last half of the fifteenth century. Germany's rulers often reverted to the ancient practice of partitioning their lands among all their male heirs, and by the end of the Middle Ages, Germany was divided into some three hundred autonomous entities. The powerlessness of its fragmented governments helps explain the success of the revolution that produced the Protestant Reformation.

In 1356, the Holy Roman Emperor and the major German territorial rulers agreed on arrangements that helped stabilize Germany. The emperor's **Golden Bull** limited participation in the election of emperors to a college of seven "electors": the archbishops of Mainz, Trier, and Cologne, the duke of Saxony, the margrave of Brandenburg, the count of Palatine, and the king of Bohemia. It acknowledged that the emperor reigned more than ruled. (The extent of his powers, especially over the seven electors, was to be renegotiated with each imperial election.) In the fifteenth century, a national convention (the imperial diet, or *Reichstag*) began to meet on a regular basis. It provided opportunities for the seven electors, the nonelectoral princes, and Germany's sixty-five imperial free cities to debate and agree on common policies.

In 1495, the diet won concessions from Maximilian I (r. 1493–1519) that brought more order to a disorderly country. It banned private warfare, established a court (the *Reichskammergericht*) to enforce peace, and appointed an imperial Council of Regency (the *Reichsregiment*) to coordinate the development of policy. Although these reforms were helpful, they fell far short of the creation of a centralized state. The territorial princes were virtually sovereign rulers in their domains throughout the sixteenth and seventeenth centuries.

Golden Bull Arrangements agreed to by the Holy Roman Emperor and the major German territorial rulers in 1356 that helped stabilize Germany.

HOW DID the northern Renaissance affect culture in Germany, England, France, and Spain?

THE NORTHERN RENAISSANCE

Renaissance humanism nourished interest in religious and educational reforms, and an environment favorable to change evolved as knowledge of the works of Italy's humanists spread throughout Europe. The Brothers of the Common Life, an influential lay religious movement in the Netherlands, founded schools that became important centers of humanist scholarship in northern Europe.

The northern humanists developed an identity of their own. They tended to come from more diverse social backgrounds and to be more interested in religious reform than their Italian colleagues. They were also more willing to write for lay audiences. This was to have significant consequences, for a printing press with movable type appeared in the mid–fifteenth century. For the first time in history, the press enabled intellectual elites to argue their cases before the public and spark mass movements.

THE PRINTING PRESS

Since the days of Charlemagne, Europe's rulers had understood the importance of schools and literacy. Effective government required a staff of officials who could read, think critically, keep records, and write accurate reports. During the late Middle Ages, the number of universities in Europe tripled from twenty to sixty, and these schools spread literacy far beyond the ranks of the clergy.

However, it was not only schools that made literacy a more common skill. Late medieval inventions made writing materials more affordable. In the early Middle Ages, scribes copied out books longhand on expensive sheets of leather called *vellum*. Books were extremely costly. A complete text of the Bible, for instance, required 170 calfskins or 300 sheepskins. A block of wood was sometimes carved and inked to produce a single-sheet woodcut print—a kind of medieval poster.

In the mid–fifteenth century, the growing demand for books prompted Johann Gutenberg (d. 1468) of Mainz to invent printing with movable type. This and the development of a process for manufacturing inexpensive paper dramatically reduced costs of production and vastly multiplied the number of books. Booksellers were soon making books and pamphlets (on subjects ranging from theology to farming and child rearing) available to the public in all price ranges. The new technology generated a great demand, and the number of presses exploded. By 1500 (about fifty years after Gutenberg opened his shop), printers were operating in over two hundred of Europe's cities.

Spreading literacy equipped more and more people with an enhanced sense of self-esteem and a critical frame of mind. The print revolution gave everyone access to standardized texts, and access to a common fund of information made anyone who could read an authority. Ordinary men and women became less credulous and docile than their ancestors, but print also gave their rulers a powerful tool for manipulating them.

Albrecht Dürer. Portrait of the Moorish Woman Katharina.

Photograph ©Foto Marburg/Art Resource, NY

ERASMUS

The career of Desiderius Erasmus (ca. 1466–1536), the most famous of the northern humanists, illustrates the impact of the printing press. Erasmus was both an educational and a religious reformer—one of many loyal Catholics who advocated religious reform before the Protestant Reformation erupted.

Erasmus was a prolific writer who supplemented his income as a tutor. For his students he wrote a popular collection of short Latin dialogues called *Colloquies*. They provided people with inspiring examples of how to live as well as models of how to speak, and thus they promoted both reform and literacy. Erasmus's interest in religious reform prompted him to expand their subsequent editions to include anticlerical dialogues and satires of religious superstitions. He offered more helpful, practical advice in a popular collection of proverbs entitled *Adages*. It went through many editions and expanded from 800 examples to over 5,000. It is the source of common expressions such as "Leave no stone unturned," and "Where there is smoke, there is fire."

The printing press made possible the diffusion of Renaissance learning. No book stimulated more at this time than did the Bible. With Gutenberg's publication of a printed Bible in 1454, scholars gained access to a dependable, standardized text, so Scripture could be discussed and debated as never before.

This item is reproduced by permission of The Huntington Library, San Marino, California

Erasmus advocated a life that combined the classical ideals of humanity and civic virtue with the Christian virtues of love and piety. He believed disciplined study of the classics and the Bible would reform individuals and society, and he opposed anyone, Catholic or Protestant, who let doctrine and disputation take precedence over pious humility and the practice of Christian principles. He characterized his position as the *philosophia Christi* (philosophy of Christ): simple, ethical piety modeled on Christ's life.

Erasmus used his knowledge of classical languages to produce an improved text of the Bible based on the best manuscript sources available to him. His Greek edition of the New Testament in 1516 became the basis for the publication of a more accurate Latin Vulgate in 1519. He believed that a pure, unadulterated scriptural text was the best guide for reforming contemporary society, but church authorities were unsettled by the so-called improvements he made to their traditional Bible (and by his popular satires of the clergy). At one point in the mid–sixteenth century, the church placed all of Erasmus's works on a list of books that Catholics were not supposed to read. Luther, the Protestant leader, also condemned some of Erasmus's views. Both his friends and foes, however, used the scholarly tools he forged to promote reform.

HUMANISM AND REFORM

Humanism encouraged educational and religious reforms, but with different results in different parts of Europe.

Germany Italian learning was introduced to German intellectual circles by Rudolf Agricola (1443–1485). Conrad Celtis (d. 1508), the first German poet laureate, and Ulrich von Hutten (1488–1523), a knight, gave German humanism a nationalistic tinge that promoted hostility to non-German (especially Roman) cultures. Hutten attacked indulgences, published an edition of Valla's exposé of the *Donation of Constantine*, and was killed taking part in a revolt of the German knights against their princes.

The so-called Reuchlin affair helped create common ground for reform-minded German humanists. About 1506, the Dominican friars of Cologne and a man named Pfefferkorn—a convert to Christianity from Judaism—inaugurated a campaign to suppress Jewish literature. Pfefferkorn attacked Johann Reuchlin (1455–1522), a respected scholar who was Europe's foremost Christian authority on Judaism. Reuchlin was the first Christian to compile a reliable Hebrew grammar, and he was personally attracted to Jewish mysticism. Concern for academic freedom (not Judaism) prompted many German humanists to come to Reuchlin's defense, and the controversy produced one of the great books of the period, the *Letters of Obscure Men* (1515), a merciless satire of monks and Scholastics. It also predisposed humanists to support Martin Luther in 1517, when some of the same people who attacked Reuchlin attacked Luther.

England English scholars and merchants and touring Italian prelates introduced humanism to England. Erasmus lectured at Cambridge and made a close friend of Thomas More (1478–1535), the most famous of the English humanists. More's *Utopia* (1516), a critique of contemporary values, ranks with the plays of Shakespeare as one of the most read pieces of English literature from the sixteenth century. *Utopia* described an imaginary society that overcame social and political injustice by holding all property and goods in common and requiring all persons to earn their bread by their own labor.

OVERVIEW HUMANISM AND REFORM

Germany	• Rudolf Agricola, the father of German humanism, brought Italian learning to Germany.
	• German humanism was given a nationalist coloring hostile to non-German cultures.
	• The Reuchlin affair caused the unification of reform-minded German humanists.
	• When Martin Luther came under attack in 1517, many German humanists rushed to his side.
England	• Thomas More is the best known English humanist.
	• More's *Utopia* depicted a tolerant, just society that held property and goods in common.
	• Humanism in England played a key role in preparing the way for the English Reformation.
France	• Guillaume Budé and Jacques Lefèvre d'Etaples were the leaders of French humanism.
	• Lefèvre's works exemplified the new critical scholarship and influenced Martin Luther.
	• A new generation was cultivated by Marguerite d'Angoulême.
	• The future Protestant reformer John Calvin was a product of this native reform circle.
Spain	• Unlike the other countries, in Spain humanism entered the service of the Catholic Church.
	• Francisco Jiménez de Cisneros was the key figure in Spanish humanism.
	• In Jiménez's *Complutensian Polygot Bible*, Hebrew, Greek, and Latin appeared together.
	• This with church reform helped keep Spain strictly Catholic in the Age of Reformation.

Humanism in England, as in Germany, paved the way for the Protestant Reformation, but some humanists, such as More and Erasmus, remained steadfastly loyal to the Roman Catholic Church. More, one of Henry VIII's chief councillors, resigned his office and was executed in July 1535 for refusing to accept the king's decision to divorce Catherine of Aragon and break with the papacy.

France France's invasions of Italy led to Italy's humanism invading France. Guillaume Budé (1468–1540), an accomplished Greek scholar, and Jacques Lefévre d'Etaples (1454–1536), a biblical authority, led the movement. Lefévre's work exemplified the kind of critical scholarship that stimulated Martin Luther's thinking and brought on the Reformation. Marguerite d'Angoulême (1492–1549), sister of King Francis I, queen of Navarre, and a noted spiritual writer, provided patronage for a generation of young reform-minded French humanists. The Protestant reformer, John Calvin, was among them.

Spain In Spain, humanism served to strengthen the Catholic faith more than challenge it. The country's leading humanist was Francisco Jiménez de Cisneros (1437–1517), confessor to Queen Isabella and, after 1508, the Grand Inquisitor and Spain's chief defender of orthodoxy. In 1509, he founded the University of Alcalé near Madrid. He sponsored printing of a Greek edition of the New Testament, and he translated religious tracts that were used to reform clerical life and train the clergy to guide the pious practices of the laity. His greatest achievement was the *Complutensian Polyglot Bible*, a six-volume edition of the Hebrew, Greek, and Latin texts of the Bible in parallel columns.

WHAT WERE the motives for
European voyages of discovery,
and what were the consequences?

VOYAGES OF DISCOVERY AND THE NEW EMPIRE IN THE WEST

*T*he discovery of the Americas dramatically expanded the geographical and intellectual horizons of Europeans. Commercial supremacy progressively shifted from the Mediterranean and Baltic Seas to the Atlantic seaboard, while knowledge of the New World's inhabitants and the exploitation of its mineral and human wealth set new cultural and economic forces in motion throughout western Europe.

THE PORTUGUESE CHART THE COURSE

In 1415 Prince Henry "the Navigator" (1394–1460), brother of the king of Portugal, captured the North African Muslim city of Ceuta, thus beginning the Portuguese exploration of the African coast. His and subsequent quests had aims that were religious—converting Muslims and pagans to Christianity—and mercenary—trading in gold, spices, and slaves. By the century's end, the Portuguese had found a sea route around Africa to Asia's spice markets. The pepper and cloves obtained from this trade preserved and enhanced the dull European diet, and in the fifty years before 1500, Portuguese ships delivered 150,000 slaves to Europe.

Prior to this sea route, Europeans could only get spices through the Venetians, who traded with Muslim merchants in Egypt and the Ottoman Empire. By sailing directly to Asia, the Portuguese beat this powerful monopoly, but the first voyages were slow and tentative: with each attempt to round the next cape, sailors feared that winds would not return them to land. Each navigational step down the African coast became a victory and a lesson, giving the crews the skills they needed to cross the oceans to the Americas and East Asia.

In addition to mercantile advantage, the explorations raised hope of Christian victories against the Muslims, along with mass conversions. In 1455, a self-interested pope granted the Portuguese voyagers all the spoils of war—land, goods, and slaves—from the West African coast to the Indies in East Asia.

Bartholomew Dias (ca. 1450–1500) pioneered the eastern Portuguese Empire in 1487 after safely rounding the Cape of Good Hope at the tip of Africa. In 1498, Vasco da Gama (1469–1525) reached India, returning to Portugal with a cargo of spices worth sixty times the cost of the voyage. The Portuguese would later establish Indian colonies, directly challenging the Arab and Venetian spice trade.

The Spanish aimed to find a shorter route to the East Indies by sailing westward across the Atlantic. Instead, Christopher Columbus (1451–1506) discovered the Americas.

THE SPANISH VOYAGES OF COLUMBUS

Thirty-three days after departing the Canary Islands on October 12, 1492, Columbus landed in San Salvador (Watlings Island) in the eastern Bahamas. He mistook his first landfall as an island of Japan—understandable, since Columbus had been relying in part on Martin Behaim's map of the presumed world, in which only ocean and Cipangu (Japan) divided the Europe's west coast and Asia's east coast. Only in 1498, while on his third voyage to the Caribbean, did Columbus realize he had not reached Japan and China.

Naked, friendly natives—Taino Indians—met Columbus and his crew. They amazed him with their generosity, as they freely gave his men all the corn, yams,

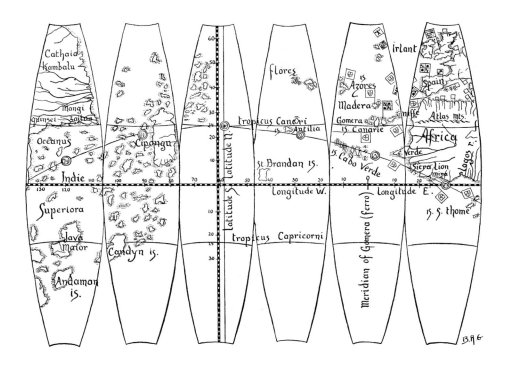

What Columbus knew of the world in 1492 was contained in this map by the Nuremberg geographer Martin Behaim, creator of the first spherical globe of the earth. The ocean section of Behaim's globe is reproduced here. Departing the Canary Islands (in the second section from the right), Columbus expected his first major landfall to be Japan (Cipangu, in the second section from the left). When he landed at San Salvador, he thought he was on the outer island of Japan. Thus, when he arrived in Cuba, he thought he was in Japan.

From "Admiral of the Ocean Sea" by Samuel Eliot Morison. Copyright ©1942 by Samuel Eliot Morison; Copyright ©renewed 1970 by Samuel Eliot Morison. By permission of Little, Brown and Company, (Inc.)

and sexual favors they desired. He also observed how easily the Spanish could enslave them. Believing he had landed in the East Indies, Columbus called these people Indians, a name that stuck with Europeans.

Subsequently, Amerigo Vespucci (1451–1512), after whom America is named, and Ferdinand Magellan (1480–1521) explored the South American coastline, confirming that Columbus had indeed discovered an entirely unknown continent. Magellan was continuing the search for a westward route to the Indies, and sailed around South America to the Philippines. Although killed there in a skirmish, his squadron sailed on to Spain and became the first sailors to circumnavigate the globe.

INTENDED AND UNINTENDED CONSEQUENCES

Columbus's first voyage marked the beginning of more than three centuries of a vast Spanish empire in the Americas. The Christian wars of Aragon and Castile against Islamic Moors in Spain had ended in 1492, yet the zeal for conquering and converting non-Christians persisted, helping to turn voyages of discovery into expeditions of conquest.

The voyages created Europe's largest and longest-surviving trading bloc and spurred colonial ventures from other European countries. Wealth from America financed Spain's religious and political wars in Europe and fueled a Europe-wide economic expansion. Europeans introduced many new fruits, vegetables, and animals into the Americas, and brought American species back home. Diseases were exchanged, too: Vast numbers of Native Americans died from measles and smallpox epidemics, while Europeans died from a form of syphilis that may have come from America. For the Native Americans, the voyages of discovery began a long history of conquest, disease, and slave labor. Spanish rule left a lasting imprint of Roman Catholicism, economic dependency, and hierarchical social structure, all still visible today. (See Map 10–2.)

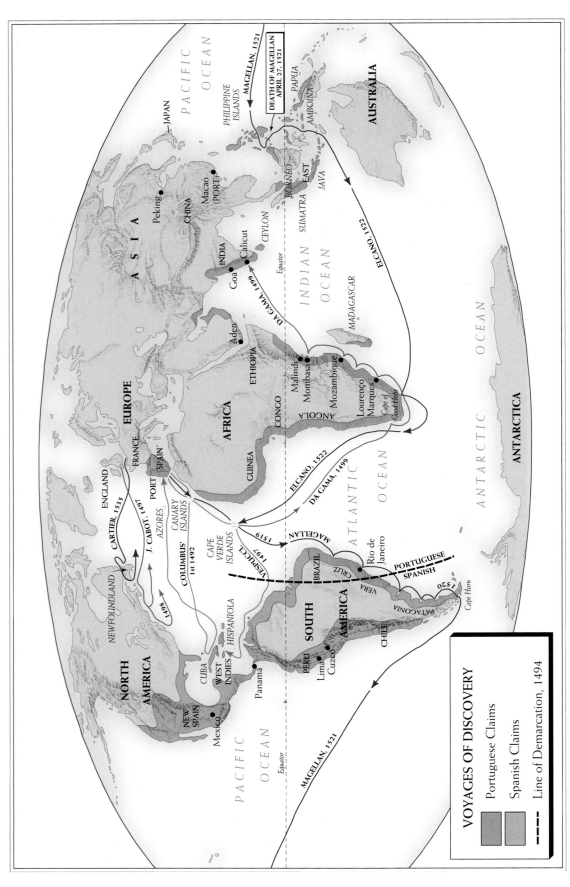

MAP 10–2

European Voyages of Discovery and the Colonial Claims of Spain and Portugal in the Fifteenth and Sixteenth Centuries

The map depicts Europe's global expansion in the fifteenth and sixteenth centuries.

WHAT REASONS did European explorers have for their many voyages of discovery?

VOYAGES OF DISCOVERY

Portuguese Claims

Spanish Claims

- - - Line of Demarcation, 1494

THE SPANISH EMPIRE IN THE NEW WORLD

The Aztecs   When the first Spanish explorers arrived, Mesoamerica was dominated by the Aztecs and Andean America by the Incas. The forebears of the Aztecs settled the Valley of Mexico early in the twelfth century, and in 1428, one of their chiefs, Itzcoatl, inaugurated an era of rapid conquest that built an Aztec Empire ruled from the city of Tenochtitlán (Mexico City). The Aztecs extorted heavy tribute from the peoples they subjugated, for their religion held that their gods must literally be fed on human blood. The thousands of captives they claimed for sacrifice each year spread fear and resentment among their subject peoples.

In 1519, Hernán Cortés landed on the coast of Mexico with a mere five hundred men. Montezuma, the Aztec ruler, may initially have believed Cortés was the Aztec god Quetzalcoatl, who had departed centuries earlier but promised to return. Montezuma tried to appease Cortés with gold, but this only stimulated the Spaniards' appetites. Cortés's forces marched on Tenochtitlán and captured Montezuma, who died under unexplained circumstances. The Aztecs rose up and nearly wiped the Spaniards out, but Cortés returned, and in 1521, he defeated the last Aztec ruler, Cuauhtemoc (ca. 1495–1525). He razed Tenochtitlán and built a new capital on its site to govern a territory he called "New Spain."

The Incas   The Incas of the highlands of Peru rapidly expanded the territory under their control in the fifteenth century, and by the time the Spaniards arrived, the Incas ruled an empire that rivaled that of the Chinese and the Ottoman Turks. Instead of tribute, they exacted military service and labor on public works projects from their subjects.

In 1531, Cortés's example prompted Francisco Pizarro to land on the western coast of South America and invade the Inca Empire. He had only two hundred men, but guns, swords, and horses gave them a great advantage over the Incas. Pizarro lured the Inca chief Atahualpa to a conference where he seized him and killed hundreds of his followers. Atahualpa paid a huge ransom in gold, but in 1533, Pizarro executed him. Insurrections by the natives and squabbles among the Spaniards prolonged the struggle to impose royal control over the sprawling Inca territories until the late 1560s.

The conquests of Mexico and Peru are among the most brutal episodes in modern world history. Small numbers of European invaders subdued large strong empires in a remarkably brief period of time. They owed much of their success to the diseases they inadvertently spread to the Americas. Illnesses to which Europeans had evolved defenses devastated Native Americans, who had quite different immune systems. In addition to the wholesale loss of life, whole civilizations and much of the evidence of their histories and achievements were also destroyed. Native American cultures endured, but they had to change to accommodate European dominance. The Spanish conquest began the process that turned South America into Latin America.

THE CHURCH IN SPANISH AMERICA

Many of the priests who accompanied Spain's invading armies were imbued with the social and religious ideals of humanism. They were eager to convert the Native Americans to the "philosophy of Christ" and to civilization as Europeans knew it. Conquest created opportunities for missionary work, but some priests objected to the treatment given subjugated native peoples. Bartolomé de Las

10.4
Bartholomé de La Casas: *"Amerindians and The Garden of Eden"*

Casas (1474–1566), a Dominican friar, wrote an exposé of the situation that prompted the Spanish government to issue some reforming regulations. Las Casas's work also become the source of the "Black Legend," a tradition that has exaggerated Spanish cruelty and soft-pedaled such things as Aztec human sacrifice.

The church in Spanish America quickly became one of the chief props for colonialism. It prospered, like the Spanish laity, by exploiting the resources and peoples of the New World. As a great landowner, it ceased to voice objections to any but the most extreme modes of Spanish economic dominance, and by the time the colonial era came to an end in the late eighteenth century, the church had become one of the most conservative forces in Latin America.

THE ECONOMY OF EXPLOITATION

The Americas were quickly drawn into the Atlantic economy and the world of competitive European commercialism. For the native peoples of Latin America—and later the blacks of Africa—that meant various forms of forced labor. The colonial economy of Latin America had three components: mining, agriculture, and shipping.

Mining   The early **conquistadores** ("conquerors") were primarily interested in finding gold, but by the middle of the sixteenth century, silver mining had become the major source of metallic wealth. The chief mining centers were Potosí in Peru and various smaller sites in northern Mexico. The Spanish crown received one-fifth (the *quinto*) of all mining revenues and held a monopoly on the production and sale of the mercury used to process silver. Mining by forced native labor for the benefit of Spaniards epitomized the extractive economy that was fundamental to colonial life.

Agriculture   Slavery and the importation of black Africans was introduced to the Americas on sugar plantations in the West Indies (Cuba, Hispaniola, Puerto Rico, and other islands). It was an extension of a system of forced labor that the Spanish and the Portuguese had previously used in Europe.

The agricultural institution that characterized most Spanish colonies was not a slave-based plantation but a large landed estate called a **hacienda**. Its owners were either *peninsulares*, individuals born in Spain, or *creoles*, persons of Spanish descent born in America. Some kind of formal servitude bound the people who worked a hacienda to its owners, and they were usually bound to the land and prevented from moving from the service of one master to another.

Labor Servitude   The Spaniards developed several strategies for exploiting the labor of the native Indians. The earliest was the *encomienda*, a legal grant of the right to the labor of a specific number of Indians for a particular period of time. Spain's monarchs were suspicious of this arrangement, for they feared the holders of *encomienda* might establish a powerful, independent aristocracy in the New World. The *encomienda* was gradually phased out in favor of the *repartimiento*, a kind of tax paid in labor. It required all adult male Indians to devote a certain number of working days annually to Spanish economic enterprises. *Repartimiento* duty was often extremely harsh. The temptation was to work men who were obligated only for a limited term of service literally to death, for they were due to be replaced anyway. Eventually a shortage of workers and the crown's opposition to extreme kinds of forced labor led to employment of free laborers. The freedom of Indian workers was, however, more apparent than real. They had to purchase

conquistadores
"Conquerors"

hacienda   Large landed estate that characterized most Spanish colonies.

encomienda   Legal grant of the right to the labor of a specific number of Indians for a particular period of time. This was used as a Spanish strategy for exploiting the labor of the natives.

the goods they needed from the land and mine owners who employed them, and this led to debt *peonage*—a lifetime struggle to pay off an ever-mounting obligation.

Deaths in combat, by forced labor, and from European diseases had devastating demographic consequences for Indian communities. Within a generation of the conquest, the Indian population of New Spain (Mexico) shrank from 25 million to 2 million.

THE IMPACT ON EUROPE

The loss of life and destruction of cultures in the New World was a mixed blessing for the Old World. The bullion that flowed into Europe through Spain vastly increased the amount of money in circulation and fueled an inflation rate of 2 percent a year. In Spain prices doubled by 1550 and quadrupled by 1600. In Luther's Wittenberg, the cost of basic food and clothing increased almost 100 percent between 1519 and 1540. Wages and rents, in contrast, lagged well behind the rise in prices.

The new money enabled governments and private entrepreneurs to sponsor basic research and industrial expansion. The economic thinking of the age favored the creation of monopolies, the charging of high interest for loans, and the free and efficient accumulation of wealth. The late fifteenth and the sixteenth centuries saw the maturation of this type of capitalism and its attendant social problems. Owners of the means of production were ever more clearly separated from the workers who produced. The new wealth raised expectations among the poor and encouraged reactionary behavior by the rich.

The revolutionary passions that found expression in the Reformation were fed by resentment of the social distinctions that were becoming increasingly visible and even by the discoveries of explorers like Columbus. Europeans learned there was much more to the world than their ancestors had imagined. This emboldened them to criticize traditional institutions and sparked their appetite for innovations—especially those that promised freedom and a chance at a better life.

Armored Spanish soldiers, under the command of Pedro de Alvarado (d. 1541) and bearing crossbows, engage unprotected and crudely armed Aztecs, who are nonetheless portrayed as larger than life by Spanish artist Diego Duran (sixteenth century).

Codex Duran: Pedro de Alvarado (c. 1485–1541), companion-at-arms of Hernando Cortés (1845–1547) besieged by Aztec warriors (vellum) by Diego Duran (16th Century), Codex Duran, Historia De Las Indias (16th century). Biblioteca Nacional, Madrid, Spain

SUMMARY

The Renaissance in Italy (1375–1527) The Renaissance first appeared in Italy and thrived from 1375 to 1527. This period, a transition between the medieval and modern worlds, was a time of unprecedented cultural creativity. Italian city-states, with their extensive trade networks and their competition with one another, were great incubators for artistic expression, political innovation, and humanistic studies. The significance of "humanism" is debated by scholars today, but for Renaissance Italians humanism implied studies of Classical languages and arts that offered moral preparation for a life of virtuous action. Authors and artists, including Petrarch, Dante, Boccaccio, Leonardo da Vinci, Raphael, and Michelangelo, exemplify the values of Renaissance humanism.

IMAGE KEY
for pages 236–237

a. Rogier van der Weyden (Netherlandish, 1399.1400-1464), "Portrait of a Lady". 1460. 370 x .270 (14 1/16 x 10 5/8); framed: .609 x .533 x .114 (24 x 21 x 4 1/2). Photo: Bob Grove. Andrew W. Mellon Collection. Photograph © Board of Trustees, National Gallery of Art, Washington, D.C.

b. Plan by Leonardo da Vinci for a flying machine

c. 15th century French orchard

d. Santi di Tito (1536-1603), "Portrait of Niccolo Machiavelli (1469–1527)." Italian philosopher and writer. Palazzo Vecchio, Firenze

e. Cosimo de' Medici (1389–1464) Jacopo Pontormo (1494–1556), "Cosimo de' Medici the Elder, Pater Patriae," (1389–1464). Oil on wood, 87 x 65 cm. Inv. 3574. Uffize, Florence. Photograph © Erich Lessing/Art Resource, NY

f. School of Athens, from the Stanza della Segnatura, 1510–11 (fresco) by Raphael (Raffaello Sanzio of Urbino) (1483–1520)

g. Ferdinandes Magalanes Lusitanus (Magellan)

h. Bible. 1450–55

i. Donatello (1386–1466), "David" (Frontal view) Museo Nazionale del Bargello, Florence. Nimatallah/Art Resource, NY

j. Albrecht Dürer (1471–1528), "Self-portrait at age 28 with fur coat" 1500. Oil on wood, 67 x 49 cm. Alte Pinakothek, Munich, Germany. Photograph ©Scala/Art Resource, NY

Italy's Political Decline: The French Invasions (1494–1527) In the late fifteenth century, the balance of power among Italian city-states that had been enforced by the Treaty of Lodi started to unravel. In 1495, at the invitation of the Milanese leader Ludovico il Moro, French king Charles VIII invaded Italy and conquered Florence. This invasion triggered several rounds of diplomacy, alliance making, and strategic marriages involving families of popes, the leaders of Italian city-states, French kings, and the rulers of Aragon and Brittany, among others. A quarter century of military conflicts led to political fragmentation and military weakness in Italy. In 1513, Niccolò Machiavelli wrote *The Prince*, in which he argued that only a strong and cunning dictator could unify Italy.

Revival of Monarchy in Northern Europe Sovereign monarchies, in which kings and their appointed agents—usually townspeople, not nobility—control national policies on taxation, warfare, and law enforcement, emerged in France, Spain, and England in the late fifteenth century. In France, Charles VII and, later, Louis XI were able to capitalize on the French victories over England and Burgundy, to expand French territory, build trade and industry, and suspend the Estates General. In Spain, Isabella of Castile and Ferdinand of Aragon married in 1469, and they proceeded to impose state control on religion, arrange marriages for their children that would shape future European history, and sponsor global exploration. In England, Henry VII founded the Tudor dynasty and found ways to govern without consulting Parliament. The Holy Roman Empire (Germany) was northern Europe's chief example of a country that failed to develop a strong centralized monarchy.

The Northern Renaissance The Renaissance spread from Italy to northern Europe through traders and merchants, students, religious practitioners, and others. Northern humanists, however, were more interested in religious reforms and in spreading humanism to a broad audience than Italian humanists had been. Gutenberg's invention of the moveable-type printing press facilitated the wide dissemination of texts. Erasmus exemplified northern humanists' interest in reform of the Catholic Church. In Germany, England, and France, humanism laid the groundwork for the Reformation, but in Spain, the humanist movement, like most other aspects of culture, was controlled by Ferdinand and Isabella, and therefore did not challenge the church.

Voyages of Discovery and the New Empire in the West In the fifteenth century, Europeans began the process of expansion that eventually led to European control over huge regions of the globe. Searching for gold, spices, and later, slaves, the Portuguese, Spanish, and others established maritime trade routes to the coasts of Africa, India, and the Americas. Spain established an empire in what became Latin America, introducing Catholicism, new forms of social, political, and economic organization—including servitude—and diseases to which the indigenous peoples had no resistance. Mexico lost approximately 92 percent of its population within a generation after the Spanish conquest. Spain's empire brought new ideas and products to Europe and led to inflation.

REVIEW QUESTIONS

1. How would you define Renaissance humanism? In what ways was the Renaissance a break with the Middle Ages? Who were the leading literary and artistic figures of the Italian Renaissance? What defined them as people of the Renaissance?

2. What was the purpose and outcome of the French invasion of Italy in 1494? Given the cultural productivity of Renaissance Italy, is it a valid assumption that creative work thrives best in periods of calm and peace?

3. How did the northern Renaissance differ from the Italian Renaissance? In what ways was Erasmus the embodiment of the northern Renaissance?

4. What prompted the voyages of discovery? How did the Spanish establish their empire in the Americas? What did native peoples experience during and after the conquest?

KEY TERMS

condottieri (p. 239)
conquistadores (p. 258)
encomienda (p. 258)

Golden Bull (p. 250)
hacienda (p. 258)
mannerism (p. 244)

studia humanitas **(humanism)** (p. 240)

 For additional study resources for this chapter, go to:
www.prenhall.com/kagan3/chapter10

11 The Age of Reformation

CHAPTER HIGHLIGHTS

Society and Religion The Protestant Reformation had roots in political, social, and economic concerns. The increased cultural authority of the laity, combined with the declining credibility of the church, created circumstances in which calls for reform could turn into a full-blown Reformation.

Martin Luther and the German Reformation to 1525 Martin Luther was concerned about the church's sale of indulgences and other questionable financial and political arrangements. He believed in the notion of justification by faith alone. His ninety-five theses sparked the Reformation.

The Reformation Elsewhere In much of Europe, variations of Protestantism developed. Ulrich Zwingli orchestrated the Swiss Reformation. More radical groups emerged, notably the Anabaptists. John Calvin and his followers turned Geneva into a theocracy.

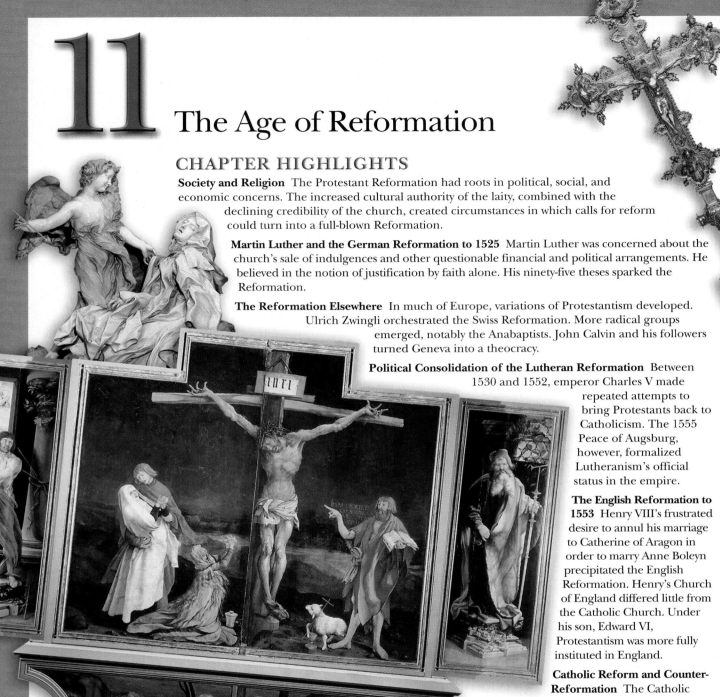

Political Consolidation of the Lutheran Reformation Between 1530 and 1552, emperor Charles V made repeated attempts to bring Protestants back to Catholicism. The 1555 Peace of Augsburg, however, formalized Lutheranism's official status in the empire.

The English Reformation to 1553 Henry VIII's frustrated desire to annul his marriage to Catherine of Aragon in order to marry Anne Boleyn precipitated the English Reformation. Henry's Church of England differed little from the Catholic Church. Under his son, Edward VI, Protestantism was more fully instituted in England.

Catholic Reform and Counter-Reformation The Catholic Church mounted a vigorous response to the Reformation, including the creation of many new reform-minded orders. The Council of Trent instituted important reforms and reasserted Catholic doctrine.

The Social Significance of the Reformation in Western Europe The Reformation revolutionized religious practice and institutions in the areas where it took strongest root. Protestant reformers helped disseminate humanism along with new visions of the nature of marriage and family.

Family Life in Early Modern Europe Marriage occurred later in life in the early modern period. Parents were involved in arranging their children's marriages. A nuclear family with two to four children was the norm. Parents demonstrated their love of their children and marriage partners in ways that reflected the realities of early modern life.

Literary Imagination in Transition Cervantes lived and worked in Catholic Spain. Shakespeare was a product of Protestant England. Their writings reflect the different conditions and concerns of their respective countries.

CHAPTER QUESTIONS

WHAT WAS the social and religious background of the Reformation?

WHY DID Martin Luther challenge the church?

WHERE DID other reform movements develop and how were they different from Luther's?

WHAT WERE the political ramifications of the Reformation?

HOW WAS the English Reformation more political than theological?

WHAT WAS the Counter-Reformation?

WHAT WAS the social significance of the Reformation and how did it affect family life?

WHAT WAS family life like in early modern Europe?

HOW WAS the transformation from medieval to modern reflected in the works of the great literary figures of the era?

CHAPTER OUTLINE

IMAGE KEY

Image Key for pages 262–263 is on page 288.

WHAT WAS the social and religious background of the Reformation?

In the second decade of the sixteenth century, a powerful religious movement began in northern Germany. Reformers, attacking what they believed to be superstitions and abuses of authority, rebelled against the medieval church. The Protestant Reformation that resulted from their efforts opposed aspects of the Renaissance—especially the optimistic view of human nature that humanist scholars derived from classical literature. The reformers did, however, embrace some Renaissance ideas, particularly educational reforms and training in ancient languages that equipped scholars to go to the original sources of important texts. Protestant challenges to Catholic practices were based on appeals to the Hebrew and Greek Scriptures.

SOCIETY AND RELIGION

A struggle between the rulers who were centralizing governments of nation-states and the towns and regions that were fighting to preserve their autonomy set the stage for the Reformation. During the fourteenth century, the king's law began (almost everywhere) to supersede local law and custom. Many townspeople and village folk saw rebellion against the church as a part of a wider fight to limit encroachment on their liberties.

The Reformation began in the free cities of Germany and Switzerland. There were about sixty-five of these, and most developed Protestant movements even if they did not ultimately become Protestant towns. In their efforts to defend themselves against intervention in their affairs by princes, cities were hampered by deep internal social and political divisions. Some factions favored the Reformation more than others. Guilds whose members were prospering and rising in social status were often in the forefront of the Reformation, but less distinguished groups were also attracted to the Protestant revolt. People who felt pushed around by either local or distant authorities tended, at least initially, to develop Protestant sympathies. The peasants on the land responded as much as the townsfolk, for their freedoms, too, were eroded by princely governments.

Many converts to Protestantism saw religion and politics as two sides of the same coin. When Protestant preachers scorned the authority of ecclesiastical landlords and ridiculed papal laws as arbitrary human inventions, they touched political as well as religious nerves. An attack on the legitimacy of the one kind of authority translated easily into a critique of the other.

POPULAR RELIGIOUS MOVEMENTS AND CRITICISM OF THE CHURCH

The Protestant Reformation was partially a response to the crises in leadership that the church suffered in the late Middle Ages: the papacy's "exile" in Avignon, the Great Schism, the conciliar movement, and the flagrant worldliness of the Renaissance popes. These troubling developments prompted many clergy and laity to become increasingly critical of traditional teachings and spiritual practices. They prompted calls for reform and widespread religious experimentation.

The laity were less subservient to the clergy in the late medieval period than in earlier eras. Urban residents had opportunities for travel (as merchants, pilgrims, soldiers, and explorers) that increased their understanding of the wider world and politics. The establishment of postal systems and printing presses made more information available to them. Easier access to books and libraries improved their literacy rates, and humanist educational reforms encouraged them to take more responsibility for themselves.

The lay religious movements that preceded the Reformation were all inspired by an ideal of apostolic poverty. They urged all Christians (and especially clergy) to model their lives on the example Jesus and his disciples set in the Gospels. They wanted a more egalitarian church that gave a voice to its members, and they wanted a more spiritual church that emulated the simplicity of the church described in the New Testament.

The Modern Devotion   One of the most constructive lay religious movements of the period was led by the Brothers of the Common Life. They exemplified the "Modern Devotion," a religious discipline inaugurated by Gerard Groote (1340–1384), that spread through northern Europe from its base in the Netherlands. The brothers brought clergy and laity together in quasi-monastic communities. Lay members did not take formal vows, wear religious dress, or abandon their secular vocations, but they shared a common life that stressed individual piety and practical religion. Thomas à Kempis (d. 1471) captured the spirit of the movement in a perennially popular devotional tract, the *Imitation of Christ*. This guide to the inner life was intended for monks and nuns, but it spoke to laity who sought spiritual growth through the practice of ascetic disciplines.

The Brothers of the Common Life flourished at a time when the laity's appetite for good preaching and religious instruction was increasing. The brothers helped meet this need by running schools, working as copyists, sponsoring publications, and running hospices for poor students. The noted humanists Erasmus and Reuchlin began their training with the brothers.

The Modern Devotion has been credited with inspiring humanist, Protestant, and Catholic reformers, but it was actually a very conservative movement. By integrating traditional clerical doctrines and values with an active common life, the brothers met the need of late medieval people for a more personal religion and a better informed faith. The Modern Devotion helped ordinary men and women develop fuller religious lives without turning their backs on the world.

Lay Control over Religious Life   The medieval papacy's successful campaign to wrest control of appointments to church offices from the laity did not improve the church's administration. Popes sold ecclesiastical posts to the highest bidders. The purchasers collected the income from the offices they bought, but they did not personally have to carry out the duties attached to those offices. They hired inexpensive (often poorly trained and motivated) substitutes to do their work while they resided elsewhere. Rare was the late medieval German town that did not complain about clerical malfeasance or dereliction of duty.

City governments sometimes took the initiative and tried to improve religious life in their communities by endowing preacherships. These positions supported well-educated spiritual leaders whose preaching and pastoral care were far superior to the perfunctory services offered by other clergy. These prominent urban pulpits became platforms for Protestant reformers.

As holy places, medieval churches and monasteries were exempted from secular taxes and laws. Holy persons (clergy) were also not expected to do "dirty jobs" (such as military service, compulsory labor, standing watch at city gates, and other obligations of citizenship). Nor was it thought right that any of the laity should sit in judgment over God's priestly intermediaries. On the eve of the Reformation, however, a growing sense that clerical privileges were undeserved was leading secular governments to curtail them.

Long before 1520, when Luther published a famous summary of economic grievances (*Address to the Christian Nobility of the German Nation*), communities

Martin Schongauer (c. 1430-1491), a German engraver, portrays the devil's temptation of St. Anthony in the wilderness as a robust physical attack by demons rather than the traditional melancholic introspection.

National Gallery of Art, Washington D.C.

11.1
Erasmus: A Diatribe Against the Pope

QUICK REVIEW

Anti-Clericalism

- Corruption and incompetence marred church administration
- City governments took steps to improve the situation by endowing preacherships
- Fifteenth century witnessed a growing sense that clerical privileges were undeserved

were protesting the financial abuses of the medieval church—particularly the sale of indulgences (papal letters that released sinners from time in purgatory). Rulers and magistrates who received a share of the profits usually did not object, but it was a different matter when local revenues were siphoned off for projects far from home. The state did not join the campaign against the church's financial exactions until its rulers recognized how they might profit from religion. The appeal of Protestantism for some rulers was the rationale it provided for disbanding monasteries and confiscating church property.

WHY DID Martin Luther challenge the church?

MARTIN LUTHER AND THE GERMAN REFORMATION TO 1525

The kings of France and England were strong enough to limit papal taxation and jurisdiction within their homelands, but Germany lacked the political unity needed to enforce "national" religious policies. The restraints that England and France imposed on the church on a universal level were enacted locally and piecemeal in Germany whenever popular resentment of ecclesiastical abuses boiled over. By 1517, mass discontent was pervasive enough to win Martin Luther a widespread, sympathetic audience.

Luther (1483–1546) was the son of a successful Thüringian miner. He received his early education in a school run by the Brothers of the Common Life, and in 1501, he attended the University of Erfurt. After receiving his master of arts degree in 1505, Luther did what his parents wished and registered with the law faculty, but he never began the study of law. On July 17, 1505, he disappointed his family by entering a monastery in Erfurt (the Order of the Hermits of Saint Augustine). A terrifying lightning storm had prompted him to promise Saint Anne, the patron of travelers in distress, that he would enter a cloister if she saved his life. There was, however, more to his decision than this. Behind it lay many years of personal spiritual struggle.

Luther led a conventional monastic life and was ordained to the priesthood in 1507. In 1510, he went to Rome on business for his order and saw firsthand some of the abuses that were discrediting the church. In 1511, he moved to the Augustinian monastery in Wittenberg. A year later, he earned his doctorate in theology from Wittenberg's university and joined its faculty.

JUSTIFICATION BY FAITH ALONE

Reformation theology was a response to the fact that many of the laity and clergy were ceasing to find traditional medieval religious beliefs and practices personally satisfying. Luther was especially plagued by his inability to achieve the righteousness that medieval theology taught that God required for salvation. The sacrament of penance failed to console Luther and give him hope, for the church seemed to demand of him a perfection he knew neither he nor any other human being could achieve.

The study of St. Paul's letters finally brought Luther an insight into the process of salvation that quieted his fears. Luther concluded from his reading of the Scriptures that the righteousness that God demanded did not consist of good works and participation in rituals. It was a gift God gives to those who believe and trust in Jesus Christ—who alone is perfectly righteous. Believers in Christ, Luther claimed, stood before God clothed in Christ's righteousness. They were justified solely by faith in him and not by their own actions.

THE ATTACK ON INDULGENCES

Luther's doctrine of justification by faith was incompatible with the church's practice of issuing indulgences, for an **indulgence** was a remission of the obligation to perform a "work of satisfaction" for a sin. The medieval church taught that after priests absolved penitents of guilt, penitents still had to pay penalties for their sins. They could discharge their penalties in this life by prayers, fasting, almsgiving, retreats, and pilgrimages. If their works of satisfaction were insufficient at the time of their deaths, they would continue to suffer for them in purgatory.

Indulgences had originally been devised for Crusaders whose deaths in battle with the enemies of the church deprived them of an opportunity to do penance for their sins. Gradually, the church extended indulgences to others who were anxious about the consequences of neglected penances and unrepented sins. In 1343, Pope Clement VI (r. 1342–1352) declared the existence of a "treasury of merit," an infinite reservoir of credit that the saints and Christ had earned that the pope could appropriate for use by lesser Christians. Papal "letters of indulgence" were drafts on this treasury to cover the works of satisfaction owed by penitents. In 1476, Pope Sixtus IV (r. 1471–1484) greatly expanded the market for these letters by proclaiming the church's power to grant indulgences not only to the living but also to souls in purgatory.

Originally, indulgences had been granted only for major services to the church, but by Luther's day their price had been significantly discounted to encourage mass marketing. In 1517, Pope Leo X (r. 1513–1521) revived a special Jubilee indulgence for sale to raise funds for rebuilding Saint Peter's in Rome. Archbishop Albrecht of Mainz welcomed the opportunity it provided him. He was in debt to the Fugger bank of Augsburg for a loan he had taken out to pay the pope for permission to ignore church law and simultaneously occupy the archbishoprics of Mainz and Magdeburg and the bishopric of Halberstadt. Albrecht agreed to promote the sale of the Jubilee indulgence in Germany for a share of the proceeds, and John Tetzel (d. 1519), a popular preacher, was given the job of drumming up business in Luther's neighborhood.

According to tradition, Luther posted his ninety-five theses opposing the sale of indulgences on the door of Castle Church in Wittenberg on October 31, 1517. Luther was especially disturbed by Tetzel's insinuation that indulgences remitted sins and released the dead from punishment in purgatory. Luther believed Tetzel's claims went far beyond traditional practice and made salvation something that could be bought and sold.

ELECTION OF CHARLES V

The ninety-five theses made Luther famous overnight and prompted official proceedings against him. In April 1518, he was summoned to appear before the general chapter of his order in Heidelberg, and the following October he was called to Augsburg to be examined by the papal legate and general of the Dominican Order, Cardinal Cajetan. At that point the Holy Roman Emperor, Maximilian I, died (January 12, 1519), and attention was diverted from Luther to the election of a new emperor.

Maximilian's nineteen-year-old grandson, Charles V, was chosen to succeed him, but the electors exacted a price for their votes. They forced Charles to agree

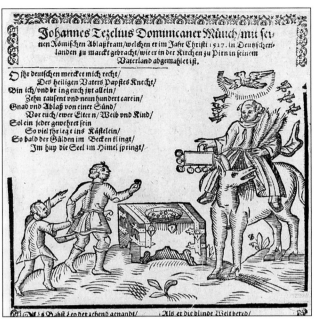

A contemporary caricature depicts John Tetzel, the famous indulgence preacher. The last lines of the jingle read: "As soon as gold in the basin rings, right then the soul to Heaven springs." It was Tetzel's preaching that spurred Luther to publish his ninety-five theses.

Courtesy Stiftung Luthergedenkstaten in Sachsen-Anhalt/Lutherhalle, Wittenberg

11.2
Luther's *Ninety-Five Theses*

indulgence Remission of the obligation to perform a "work of satisfaction" for a sin.

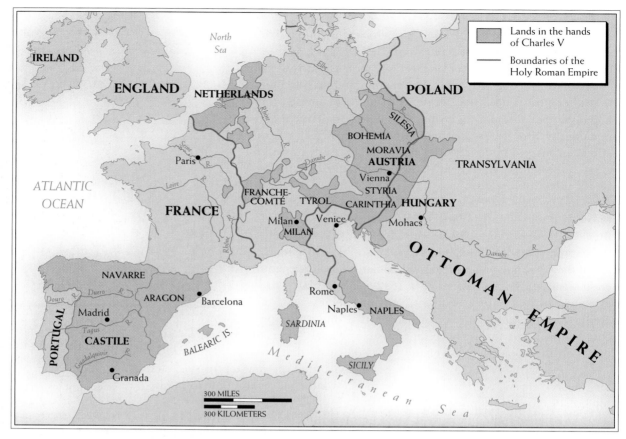

MAP 11-1

The Empire of Charles V Dynastic marriages and simple chance concentrated into Charles's hands rule over the lands shown here, plus Spain's overseas possessions. Crowns and titles rained down on him; his election in 1519 as emperor gave him new distractions and responsibilities.

WERE THE acquisitions of large portions of Europe more of a burden than a privilege for Charles V?

to consult with the imperial diet on all major domestic and foreign issues. This prevented Charles from taking unilateral action in Germany—something for which Luther was soon to be thankful. (See Map 11-1.)

LUTHER'S EXCOMMUNICATION AND THE DIET OF WORMS

While the imperial election was being held, Luther went to Leipzig to debate John Eck, a professor from Ingolstadt (June 27, 1519). Luther used the occasion to question the infallibility of the pope and the inerrancy of church councils and, for the first time, to suggest the Scriptures should be regarded as the sole authority governing faith.

In 1520, Luther explained his position in three famous pamphlets. *Address to the Christian Nobility of the German Nation* urged the German princes forcefully to reform the Roman Catholic Church and curtail its political and economic power. *The Babylonian Captivity of the Church* examined the sacraments and concluded that only two of the church's seven (baptism and the Eucharist) were authentic. The pamphlet also claimed that the Scriptures, decrees of church councils, and decisions of secular princes were superior to the authority of a pope. *Freedom of a Christian* eloquently argued the case for Luther's key theological insight, that salvation came from faith not works.

On June 15, 1520, a papal bull, *Exsurge Domine*, condemned Luther for heresy and gave him sixty days to retract his opinions. The final bull of excommunication, *Decet Pontificem Romanum*, was issued on January 3, 1521. In April of that year, Luther appeared before the imperial diet and the newly elected Charles V in the city of Worms. Luther refused the diet's order to recant, for such an act, he claimed, would violate Scripture, reason, and conscience. On May 26, 1521, Luther was placed under the imperial ban, which made his heresy a crime punishable by the state. Friends protected him and hid him in Wartburg Castle. He spent about a year (April 1521 to March 1522) in seclusion and devoted his time to the creation of one of the essential tools of the Reformation: a German translation of Erasmus's Greek text of the New Testament.

IMPERIAL DISTRACTIONS: FRANCE AND THE TURKS

Charles V was too preoccupied with military ventures to pay much attention to the Reformation that erupted in Wittenberg in the wake of Luther's trial. France was invading Italy to drive a wedge between parts of this empire, and the Ottoman Turks were threatening it in the East. Charles needed friendly relations with the German princes in order to recruit German troops for his armies.

In 1526, the Turks overran Hungary at the Battle of Mohacs, and in western Europe the French organized the League of Cognac to prepare for the second of the four Habsburg-Valois wars (1521–1559). Busy as Charles was meeting these challenges, he had little time for Germany. At the Diet of Speyer in 1526, he granted each German prince the right to deal as he saw fit with the situation Luther was creating. This cleared the way for the Reformation to put down roots in places where princes sympathized with it, and it established a tradition of princely control over religion that was enshrined in law by the Peace of Augsburg in 1555.

HOW THE REFORMATION SPREAD

In the 1520s and 1530s, leadership of the Reformation passed from theologians and pamphleteers to magistrates and princes. City governments acted on the proposals of Protestant preachers and their growing flocks, and as they mandated reforms, religious practices ceased to be a matter of slogans and became laws binding on all of a town's residents. Like urban magistrates, some regional princes (notably, the elector of Saxony and the prince of Hesse) implemented the reform in large states. They saw political and economic advantages in overthrowing the Roman Catholic Church and urged their colleagues in other states to join them. Powerful alliances were negotiated, and Protestant leaders prepared for war with their Catholic emperor.

THE PEASANTS' REVOLT

In its first decade, the Protestant movement suffered more from internal division than from imperial resistance. By 1525, Luther had become as controversial a figure in Germany as the pope, and

AETERNA IPSE SVAE MENTIS SIMVLACHRA LVTHERVS EXPRIMIT·AT VVLTVS CERA LVCAE OCCIDVOS·
·M·D·X·X·

In 1520, Luther's first portrait, shown here, depicted him as a tough, steely eyed monk. Afraid that this portrayal might convey defiance rather than reform to Emperor Charles V, Elector Frederick the Wise of Saxony, Luther's protector, ordered court painter Lucas Cranach to soften the image. The result was a Luther placed within a traditional monk's niche reading an open Bible, a reformer, unlike the one depicted here, who was prepared to listen as well as to instruct.

Martin Luther as a monk, 1521. © Foto Marburg/Art Resource, NY

A handwritten manuscript depicts the Execution of Jaklein Rohrbach. The sixteenth-century German radical burns at a stake inside a ring of fire.

Courtesy of the Library of Congress

many of his early supporters had broken with him. Germany's peasants, who had welcomed Luther as an ally, had a particular reason for losing faith in him. Since the late fifteenth century, their leaders had been struggling to prevent the territorial princes from ignoring traditional limits and imposing oppressive regulations and taxes. Many peasants assumed Luther's defense of Christian freedom and criticism of monastic landowners implied his support for their cause. Luther and his followers sympathized with the peasants, but Lutherans were not social revolutionaries. Luther's freedom of the Christian individual was an inner experience of release from guilt and anxiety for one's soul. It did not entail restructuring society by violent revolution. When the peasants rebelled against their masters in 1524, Luther condemned them in the strongest possible terms and urged the princes to crush the revolt. Possibly as many as 100,000 peasants died in the struggle. Had Luther supported the Peasants' Revolt, he would not only have misrepresented his own teaching, he would probably have ended any chance for his reform to survive beyond the 1520s.

THE REFORMATION ELSEWHERE

uther's revolt against the church was the first, but similar reform movements soon developed independently in France and Switzerland.

WHERE DID other reform movements develop and how were they different from Luther's?

ZWINGLI AND THE SWISS REFORMATION

Switzerland, like Germany, offered the kind of politically diverse environment in which rebellion had a good chance to succeed. It was a loose confederacy of thirteen autonomous cantons (states). Some (particularly, Zurich, Bern, Basel, and Schaffhausen) became Protestant. Some (especially in the heartland around Lucerne) remained Catholic, and a few sought a compromise.

Two developments prepared the ground for the Swiss Reformation. The first was the growth of national feeling that sprang from opposition to the practice of impressing Swiss soldiers into mercenary service outside their homeland. The second was the interest in church reform that was stimulated by the famous church councils that met in the Swiss cities of Constance (1414–1417) and Basel (1431–1449).

The Reformation in Zurich   Ulrich Zwingli (1484–1531), the leader of the Swiss Reformation, credited Erasmus and humanism for sparking his interest in reform. He also served as chaplain to Swiss soldiers in Italy in 1515, an experience that made him an ardent opponent of mercenary service. By 1518, he was publicly objecting to the sale of indulgences and denouncing some traditional religious practices as superstitions.

In 1519, Zwingli applied for the post of people's priest in Zurich's main church. His fitness was questioned because he acknowledged having had an affair with a barber's daughter. Many of his contemporaries, however, sympathized with clergy who found celibacy more than they could bear, and Zwingli defended himself forthrightly. Later he led a fight to abolish clerical celibacy and grant clergy the right to marry.

Zwingli's post as the people's priest in Zurich gave him a pulpit from which to campaign for reform, and on January 29, 1523, the Zurich town government decided to implement his ideas. The standard Zwingli proposed for judging religious practice was simple. Whatever lacked literal support in Scripture was to be neither believed nor done. This conviction caused him, like Luther, to question many aspects of medieval Catholicism: fasting, transubstantiation, the worship of

HISTORY'S VOICES

ZWINGLI LISTS THE ERRORS OF THE ROMAN CHURCH

P rior to the first Zurich Disputation (1523), which effectually introduced the Protestant Reformation in Zurich, the reformer Zwingli wrote the Sixty-Seven Articles, which summarized for public disputation his criticisms of the Roman Church. Here are some of them.

TO ZWINGLI, what is the source of divine authority and who in the church has power?

All who consider other teachings equal to or higher than the Gospel err, and they do not know what the Gospel is.

In the faith rests our salvation, and in unbelief our damnation; for all truth is clear in Christ.

In the Gospel one learns that human doctrines and decrees do not aid in salvation.

That Christ, having sacrificed himself once, is to eternity a certain and valid sacrifice for the sins of all faithful, wherfrom it follows that the Mass is not a sacrifice, but is a remembrance of the sacrifice and assurance of the salvation which Christ has given us.

That God desires to give us all things in his name, whence it follows that outside of this life we need no [intercession of the saints or any] mediator except himself.

That no Christian is bound to do those things which God has not decreed, therefore one may eat at all times all food, where from one learns that the decree about cheese and butter is a Roman swindle.

That no special person can impose the ban upon anyone, but the Church, that is, the congregation of those among whom the one to be banned dwells, together with their watchman, i.e. the pastor.

All that the spiritual so-called state [i.e., the papal church] claims to have of power and protection belongs to the lay [i.e., the secular magistracy], if they wish to be Christians.

Greater offence I know not than that one does not allow priests to have wives, but permits them to hire prostitutes.

Christ has borne all our pains and labor. Hence whoever assigns to works of penance what belongs to Christ errs and slanders God.

The true divine Scriptures know naught about purgatory after this life.

The Scriptures know no priests except those who proclaim the word of God.

Ulrich Zwingli (1484–1531): Selected Works, ed. by Samuel M. Jackson (Philadelphia: University of Pennsylvania Press, 1972), pp. 111–117.

saints, pilgrimages, purgatory, clerical celibacy, and some of the sacraments. The rigor with which the Swiss purged their church of these practices led eventually to the so-called puritan element in Protestantism. (See "History's Voices: Zwingli Lists the Errors of the Roman Church.")

The Marburg Colloquy   Landgrave Philip of Hesse (1504–1567) believed Protestants had to cooperate if they hoped to fend off attacks from Catholics, and he tried to unite the Swiss and German reformations. He arranged for Luther and Zwingli to meet in his castle at Marburg in early October 1529, but theological disagreements over the nature of Christ's presence in the Eucharist drove a permanent wedge between the two leaders. Luther dismissed Zwingli as a dangerous fanatic, and Zwingli charged that Luther was irrationally in thrall to medieval ideas. The disagreement at Marburg splintered the Protestant movement. Cooperation between the two sides did not cease entirely, but the followers of Luther and Zwingli published separate creeds and formed separate defense leagues.

Swiss Civil Wars   Protestants and Catholics divided up the Swiss cantons and wars erupted among them. There were two major battles—both at Kappel (one in June 1529, the other in October 1531). The first was a Protestant victory that forced the Catholic cantons to repudiate their foreign alliances and recognize the rights of Protestants. The second battle cost Zwingli his life, but the treaty that ended the fighting confirmed the right of each canton to determine its own religion. Heinrich Bullinger (1504–1575), Zwingli's protégé, assumed leadership of the Swiss Reformation, and under his direction, Protestantism came to be accepted as an established religion in Switzerland.

ANABAPTISTS AND RADICAL PROTESTANTS

Some people were discontented by what they regarded as the failure of the Lutheran and Zwinglian reformations to elevate standards of ethical conduct and by the slow pace of change the two factions effected in society's institutions. Protestants who wanted a more rapid and thorough restoration of the "primitive Christianity" described in the New Testament accused the leading reformers of going only halfway. They struck out on their own and formed more radical Protestant organizations. The most important of these were called **Anabaptists** ("rebaptizers") by their enemies. The name derived from their rejection of infant baptism and their insistence on baptizing adult converts who had been baptized as infants.

Conrad Grebel (1498–1526) inaugurated the Anabaptist movement by performing the first baptism of a previously baptized adult in Zurich in January 1525. A few years earlier (in October 1523), Grebel's passion for biblical literalism had caused him to break with Zwingli, his mentor. He opposed Zwingli's decision to respect the town government's plea to proceed slowly in altering religious practices. In 1527, Grebel's followers, the Swiss Brethren, published a statement of their beliefs, the *Schleitheim Confession*. They endorsed adult baptism, opposed the swearing of oaths, pledged themselves to pacifism, and refused to recognize the authority of secular governments. Anabaptists literally withdrew from society to be free to live as they believed the first Christians had lived. States interpreted this as an attack on society's fundamental bonds.

The Anabaptist Reign in Münster   Lutherans and Zwinglians joined Catholics in persecuting the Anabaptists. In 1529, rebaptism became a capital offense throughout the Holy Roman Empire, and from 1525 to 1618 between 1,000 and 5,000 people were executed for undergoing rebaptism.

Brutal punishments for nonconformists increased after a group of Anabaptist extremists took over the German city of Münster in 1534. Anabaptist converts won control of Münster's town government and used their authority to compel Lutherans and Catholics to convert or emigrate. They turned Münster into an Old Testament theocracy run by charismatic prophets who shocked their contemporaries by reviving the ancient Hebrew practice of polygamy. Outraged Protestants and Catholics fought side by side to reconquer Münster, and the bodies of its Anabaptist leaders were hung up in public as a warning to others who might be tempted to push religious reform beyond socially acceptable limits.

After this bloody episode, the Anabaptists reasserted their commitment to pacifism and attempted to maintain low profiles. Their movement found more moderate leaders and survived largely in rural districts. It is represented today by the Mennonites (followers of Menno Simons, 1496–1561) and the Amish.

Anabaptists   ("rebaptizers") The most important of several groups of Protestants forming more radical organizations that sought a more rapid and thorough restoration of the "primitive Christianity" described in the New Testament.

Other Nonconformists   The Anabaptists were not the only Protestant radicals. The Reformation also produced the Spiritualists—extreme individualists who believed the only religious authority was the guidance of God's spirit in each person's heart. Thomas Müntzer (d. 1525), an early convert to Lutheranism and a leader of a peasants' revolt, belonged to this camp, as did Sebastian Franck (d. 1541), a freelance critic of all dogmatic religion, and Caspar Schwenckfeld (d. 1561), a prolific author for whom the tiny Schwenckfeldian denomination is named.

At the other extreme, the Reformation's critique of religious superstition turned some Protestants into rationalists. They preached a commonsense, rational religion that focused primarily on ethics. Some, like the Spanish reformer Michael Servetus (1511–1553), were Antitrinitarians. Servetus sought refuge from Catholic persecution in Geneva, but its Protestant government executed him for his rejection of the doctrine of the Trinity. In Italy, the reformers Lelio (d. 1562) and Faustus Sozzini (d. 1604) founded a humanistic faith called Socinianism. It opposed all the emerging Protestant orthodoxies and advocated religious toleration.

JOHN CALVIN AND THE GENEVAN REFORMATION

In the second half of the sixteenth century, Calvinism replaced Lutheranism as the dominant Protestant force in Europe. Calvinists believed strongly in predestination, but they also believed Christians were called to reorder society in accordance with God's plan. They were zealous reformers who used the machinery of government to compel men and women to live according to codes of conduct they believed were set forth in the Scriptures.

Calvinism's founder, John Calvin (1509–1564), was the son of a well-to-do secretary to the bishop of Noyon in Picardy. The church benefices the boy was given at age twelve paid for the excellent education he received at Parisian colleges and the law school in Orléans. Young Calvin was drawn to the writings of Catholic humanists such as Jacques Lefèvre d'Etaples and Marguerite d'Angoulême, the queen of Navarre. Calvin eventually concluded that these people were ineffectual agents for reform, but they helped awaken his interest in reform movements.

Calvin described his conversion to Protestantism (which probably occurred in the spring of 1534) as God's making his "long stubborn heart … teachable." In May 1534, he took the decisive step of surrendering the church benefices that provided his income and declared his support for the Reformation.

Political Revolt and Religious Reform in Geneva   In Luther's Saxony, religious reform paved the way for political revolution. In Calvin's Geneva, political revolution awakened the appetite for religious reform.

In 1527, the city-states of Fribourg and Bern helped the Genevans drive out their resident prince-bishop and win their independence from the House of Savoy. Late in 1533, Bern sent the Protestant reformers Guillaume Farel (1489–1565) and Antoine Froment (1508–1581) to Geneva to advise the city's new governing councils. In the summer of 1535—and following much internal turmoil—the Genevans discontinued the Catholic mass and various other religious practices.

On May 21, 1536, Geneva officially endorsed the Reformation, and in July of that year Calvin came to Geneva. He fled France to avoid persecution for his religious beliefs and had intended to seek refuge in Strasbourg. The third Habsburg-Valois war forced him to detour to Geneva, where Farel persuaded him to stay. Before a year had passed, Calvin had drawn up articles for the governance of Geneva's new church as well as a catechism to guide its people. Both were presented for approval to the city councils in early 1537. The strong measures they proposed for policing the moral conduct of the Genevans led to accusations that the reformers wanted to establish a "new papacy." Opponents within Geneva and elsewhere objected to any attempt to impose a new orthodoxy, and Bern, which had adopted a more moderate Protestant reform, persuaded the Genevans to retain some of the ceremonies and holidays that Calvin and Farel wanted to eliminate. In February 1538, the four syndics (the leading city magistrates) turned against the reformers and drove them out.

Calvin went to Strasbourg to became pastor to a group of French exiles. While in Strasbourg, he wrote a second edition of his masterful *Institutes of the Christian Religion*. Many scholars consider this the definitive theological explication of Protestant faith. Calvin also married, took part in ecumenical discussions, and learned important lessons in practical politics from the Strasbourg reformer Martin Bucer.

Calvin's Geneva   In 1540, Geneva elected syndics who wanted to establish their city's independence from Bern. They believed Calvin would be a valuable ally and invited him to return. Within months of his arrival in September 1540, the city implemented new ecclesiastical ordinances, and its civil magistrates promised to work with its clergy to maintain a high standard of discipline among its residents.

Calvin created four kinds of officials to oversee the practice of religion in Geneva: (1) five presiding pastors; (2) teachers and doctors charged with religious instruction; (3) twelve elders, laymen chosen by and from the Genevan councils to "oversee the life of everybody"; and (4) deacons, laymen who managed the church's charitable disbursements. Calvin believed a Christian city could not tolerate any conduct that was displeasing to God. A strong church government was needed, therefore, to maintain the highest moral standards in the community. This responsibility was assigned to the consistory, a committee composed of the elders and the pastors of the church and chaired by one of the four syndics. It meted out punishments for a broad range of moral and religious transgressions—everything from missing church services (a fine of 3 sous) to fornication (six days on bread and water and a fine of 60 sous). The making of statements critical of Calvin and the consistory was listed among the sins meriting punishment. Calvin branded his opponents wanton "Libertines" and showed them little mercy. His most prominent victim was Michael Servetus, the Antitrinitarian he burned at the stake.

By 1555, the city's syndics were all solidly behind Calvin, and he began to attract disciples from across Europe. Geneva welcomed the thousands of Protestants who were driven out of France, England, and Scotland, and at one point more than a third of the population of the city consisted of refugees (over 5,000 of them). They were utterly loyal to Calvin, for in their experience Geneva was Europe's only "free" city. Whenever they were allowed to return to their homes, they took their ardent Calvinism with them.

QUICK REVIEW

Theocracy in Geneva

- Four kinds of officials created to oversee religion in Geneva
- Consistory handed out punishments for moral and religious transgressions
- Calvin and his followers showed little mercy to their opponents

WHAT WERE the political ramifications of the Reformation?

POLITICAL CONSOLIDATION OF THE LUTHERAN REFORMATION

y 1530, the Reformation had become irreversible, but it took several decades for that fact to be accepted throughout Europe.

THE EXPANSION OF THE REFORMATION

Emperor Charles V spent most of his reign in Spain and Italy, but in 1530, he came to Germany to preside over a diet at Augsburg. The purpose of the meeting was to resolve the religious conflicts begun by Luther's break with the papacy in 1520. Charles ended the meeting by bluntly ordering all Lutherans to return to the Catholic faith. The Reformation was, however, too far advanced by then to be halted by such a peremptory gesture. The emperor's mandate served only to bring the Lutherans together in a defensive alliance, the Schmalkaldic League. The league endorsed the **Augsburg Confession**, a moderate Protestant creed that Charles had rejected at the diet, and in 1538, Luther issued a more strongly worded declaration of theological principles, the *Schmalkaldic Articles*. Lutheran states replaced the bishops who had previously administered their churches with regional consistories (courts staffed by theologians and lawyers). The outbreak of new hostilities with the French and the Turks prevented Charles from doing much about these developments, and the league's leaders, Landgrave Philip of Hesse and Elector John Frederick of Saxony, were able to hold him at bay while Lutheranism spread.

Christian II (r. 1513–1523) introduced Lutheranism to Denmark, where it became the state religion. In 1527, Sweden's king Gustavus Vasa (r. 1523–1560) and his nobles embraced the reform and the opportunity it gave them to confiscate the church's property. Poland, having no centralized government to enforce conformity, became a model of religious pluralism and toleration. In the second half of the sixteenth century, it provided refuge for Lutherans, Anabaptists, Calvinists, and even Antitrinitarians.

REACTION AND RESOLUTION: THE PEACE OF AUGSBURG

In 1547, the armies of Charles V crushed the Schmalkaldic League, and the emperor issued the Augsburg Interim. It ordered Protestants to return to Catholic beliefs and practices but made a few concessions to Protestant tastes. Clerical marriage was permitted in individual cases that received papal approval, and laity were allowed to receive both the bread and the wine at communion. Many Protestant leaders chose exile rather than comply with the terms of the Interim, and the Reformation was too entrenched by 1547 to be ended by brute force and imperial fiat.

Maurice of Saxony, whom Charles V hand-picked to replace Elector John Frederick as ruler of Saxony, recognized the inevitable and shifted his allegiance to the Protestants. Charles, wearied by three decades of war, also gave up the struggle to restore Europe's religious unity. In 1552, he reinstated John Frederick and Philip of Hesse and issued the Peace of Passau, which granted Lutherans religious freedom. The Peace of Augsburg in September 1555 made the religious division of Christendom permanent by endorsing the principle of *cuius regio, eius religio*—the right of a ruler to choose the religion for his people. Subjects who disagreed with their ruler's choice were expected to move to a place where their faith was legal, for it was assumed a state would not be politically stable unless all its citizens conformed to the same religion.

THE ENGLISH REFORMATION TO 1553

*T*he king of England was the only major European monarch to break with the papacy, but England's Reformation owed more to politics than theology.

THE PRECONDITIONS OF REFORM

England had a long history of asserting the crown's right to limit papal intervention in English affairs. Edward I (d. 1307) successfully opposed Pope Boniface VIII's attempt to deny kings the right to tax their clergy. In the mid–fourteenth

HOW WAS the English Reformation more political than theological?

Augsburg Confession
Moderate Protestant creed endorsed by the Schmalkaldic League (a defensive alliance of Lutherans).

Hans Holbein the Younger (1497–1543) was the most famous portrait painter of the Reformation. Here he portrays a seemingly almighty Henry VIII.

National Gallery of Ancient Art, Rome, Italy/Canali PhotoBank, Milan/SuperStock

century, the English Parliament passed the first Statutes of Provisors and Praemunire. These curtailed the right of the pope to appoint candidates to church offices in England, limited the amount of money that could be sent out of England to Rome, and restricted the number of court cases that could be appealed to Rome from English jurisdictions.

In the late Middle Ages, the critiques of papal and priestly authority by Wycliffe and the Lollards spread proto-Protestant ideas at every level in English society. In the early 1520s, advocates of reform began to smuggle Lutheran writings into England. An English-language New Testament, translated by William Tyndale (ca. 1492–1536) and printed in Cologne and Worms, was circulating by 1526. Access to a Bible in the language of the people became the centerpiece of the English Reformation.

THE KING'S AFFAIR

Henry VIII (r. 1509–1547), the king who severed England's ties with the papacy, initially opposed the Reformation. When Luther's ideas first began to circulate, Henry's advisers, Cardinal Thomas Wolsey (ca. 1475–1530) and Sir Thomas More (1478–1535), urged him to rush to the pope's defense. Henry declared his Catholic convictions by publishing a treatise justifying the seven sacraments. It earned him a contemptuous response from Luther and the grant of a title ("Defender of the Faith") from Pope Leo X.

It was the king's unhappy marriage, not his theology, that allowed the Reformation to take root in English soil. In 1509, Henry had preserved an alliance with Spain by wedding his brother's widow, Catherine of Aragon (d. 1536), daughter of Ferdinand and Isabella and aunt of Emperor Charles V. The marriage had required a papal dispensation, for a biblical passage (Leviticus 18:16, 20:21) implied it was incestuous. By 1527, the union had produced miscarriages and stillbirths and only one surviving child, a daughter named Mary. Henry feared that civil war would erupt if he left his throne to a daughter (as it had on the one other occasion in England's history when this was tried). Eagerness for a younger wife who might bear him a son convinced the king his marriage had been cursed for violating God's law. Catherine, however, staunchly refused to cooperate in dissolving their bond.

By 1527, Henry's affections had been captured by Anne Boleyn, one of the aging Catherine's youthful ladies in waiting. To wed her he needed a papal annulment of his marriage to Catherine. It would have been difficult for the pope to justify the annulment of a marriage that had been approved by a papal dispensation, and the political situation made it impossible. The soldiers of the Holy Roman Empire had recently mutinied and sacked Rome, and Pope Clement VII was a virtual prisoner of Catherine's nephew, Charles V.

Henry assigned the task of negotiating the annulment to Cardinal Wolsey, his Lord Chancellor. After two years of profitless diplomatic maneuvering, Henry concluded that Wolsey had failed and dismissed him in disgrace (1529). Two men with Lutheran sympathies, Thomas Cranmer (1489–1556) and Thomas Cromwell (1485–1540), succeeded Wolsey as the king's advisers, and they proposed a different course. Why not, they asked, free England from the interference of foreigners in its affairs and simply declare its king supreme over its church as he was over its state?

THE "REFORMATION PARLIAMENT"

In 1529, a Parliament that was to sit for seven years began to chip away at the power of the pope over the English church. In January 1531, Convocation (a legislative assembly representing the English clergy) recognized Henry as head of the church in England "as far as the law of Christ allows." In 1532, Parliament passed a decree (the Submission of the Clergy) that gave the king jurisdiction over the clergy and canon law. Another act (the Conditional Restraint of Annates) recognized the king's power to withhold the payment of dues traditionally owed the pope.

In January 1533, Thomas Cranmer secretly wed Henry to the pregnant Anne Boleyn. In February 1533, Parliament's Act for the Restraint of Appeals forbade appeals from the king's courts to those of the pope. In March 1533, Cranmer became archbishop of Canterbury and used his authority as England's primate (highest ranking clergyman) to declare the king had never been validly married to Catherine. In 1534, Parliament ended all payments by the English clergy and laity to Rome and gave Henry jurisdiction over ecclesiastical appointments. The Act of Succession in the same year declared Anne Boleyn's children legitimate heirs to the throne, and the **Act of Supremacy** proclaimed Henry "the only supreme head on earth of the Church of England." In 1536, the first Act for Dissolution of Monasteries closed the smaller houses, and three years later all English monasteries were disbanded and their endowments confiscated by the king.

Not all of Henry's subjects approved of the nationalization of their church, but Henry encouraged compliance by making examples of two of his most prominent critics. He executed Thomas More, his former chancellor, and John Fisher, bishop of Rochester, for refusing to accept the Act of Succession and the Act of Supremacy.

WIVES OF HENRY VIII

Henry was a more successful politician than husband. In 1536, he charged Anne Boleyn, who had disappointed him by bearing him a second daughter (Elizabeth), with treason and adultery and beheaded her. Henry married four more times. His third wife, Jane Seymour, died in 1537, shortly after giving birth to the long-desired male heir, Edward VI. Henry then wed Anne of Cleves as part of a plan that Cromwell promoted to forge an alliance among Protestant princes. Neither the alliance nor Anne—whom Henry thought bore a remarkable resemblance to a horse—proved worth the trouble. The marriage was annulled by Parliament, and Cromwell was executed. Catherine Howard, Henry's fifth wife, was beheaded for adultery in 1542. His last wife, Catherine Parr, was a patron of humanists and reformers. Henry was her third husband, and she survived him to marry a fourth time.

THE KING'S RELIGIOUS CONSERVATISM

Henry was far bolder in politics than in piety. Except for breaking with Rome and using an English Bible, Henry did not want the English church to depart from its traditional faith and practice. The Ten Articles he issued in 1536 to summarize his position made only slight concessions to Protestant tenets. In 1539, the king tried to stem a rising tide of support for Protestantism by publishing the Six Articles. They reaffirmed transubstantiation, denied the Eucharistic cup to the laity, preserved mandatory celibacy for the clergy, authorized private masses, and ordered the continuation of auricular confession. England had to wait for Henry to die before it could become a genuinely Protestant country.

Act of Supremacy   Act of 1534 proclaiming Henry VIII "the only supreme head on earth of the Church of England."

THE PROTESTANT REFORMATION UNDER EDWARD VI

Henry's son, Edward VI (r. 1547–1553), was only ten years old at the time of his succession. The regents chosen to educate him imbued him with Protestant ideas, and he even corresponded with John Calvin. Edward's pro-Protestant government repealed Henry's Six Articles and laws against heresy, and it sanctioned clerical marriage and lay communion with both cup and bread. In 1547, the *chantries*, endowments supporting priests who said masses for the dead, were dissolved. In 1549, the Act of Uniformity imposed Thomas Cranmer's *Book of Common Prayer* on all English churches, and a year later images and altars were ordered removed from those churches.

In 1552, the Second Act of Uniformity revised the *Book of Common Prayer*. Thomas Cranmer wrote a forty-two-article creed that endorsed the Protestant doctrines of justification by faith and supremacy of Holy Scripture. It recognized only two sacraments and rejected the doctrine of transubstantiation (while still affirming the real presence of Christ in the Eucharistic elements).

The turn toward Protestantism that took place during Edward's reign was reversed by his heir, Catherine of Aragon's fervently Catholic daughter, Mary. In 1553, Mary succeeded her teenaged half brother and made it her mission, as queen, to restore England to the Catholic community. Despite a bloody persecution of Protestants, she failed to undo the work her father and brother had begun. When she died childless in 1558, her half sister, Anne Boleyn's daughter Elizabeth (d. 1603), inherited her throne. Elizabeth's policy favored compromise and the establishment of a nationalized, but only moderately Protestant, church in England.

CATHOLIC REFORM AND COUNTER-REFORMATION

WHAT WAS the Counter-Reformation?

*B*efore Luther spoke out, some Catholics were already calling for the reform of their church. Popes, however, were suspicious of proposals for change, for they remembered how the councils of Constance and Basel had attacked the traditions on which papal authority rested.

SOURCES OF CATHOLIC REFORM

In 1517, the Oratory of Divine Love was founded in Rome. Consistent with the principles of the New Devotion, the Oratory brought together learned laity and clergy who were deeply committed to the cultivation of inner piety, Christian living, and reform.

There was no lack of fervor among Catholics in the sixteenth century, and it produced recruits for many new religious orders. The Theatines (founded in 1524) groomed devout, reform-minded leaders for the higher levels of the church hierarchy. The Capuchins (established in 1528) returned to the ideals of Francis of Assisi and ministered to the poor. The Somaschi (in the mid-1520s) and the Barnabites (in 1530) dedicated themselves to caring for the residents of war-torn areas of Italy. The Ursulines (founded in 1535) provided education for girls from all social classes. The Oratorians (established in 1575) produced religious literature and church music. The great hymnist and musician Giovanni Palestrina (1526–1594) was one of them. In addition to new orders, older ones were renewed by the inspiration of the Spanish mystics, Teresa of Avila (1515–1582) and John of the Cross (1542–1591).

IGNATIUS OF LOYOLA AND THE JESUITS

The most influential of the new orders, the Society of Jesus, was organized in the 1530s by Ignatius of Loyola (1491–1556). Ignatius, a dashing courtier and *caballero*, began his spiritual pilgrimage in 1521 when he was seriously wounded in battle. He passed a lengthy and painful convalescence reading Christian classics and studying the techniques the church's saints used for overcoming mental anguish and pain. A dramatic conversion experience determined him to do whatever was necessary to become a "soldier of Christ." Ignatius's personal spiritual struggle convinced him that, through study and discipline, a person could create a new self, and he wrote a devotional guide (*Spiritual Exercises*) to teach others what he had learned about the quest for spiritual self-mastery.

The Protestant reformers of Ignatius's day made a virtue of challenging the authority of the traditional church. Ignatius, however, urged his followers to humble themselves and submit to the church. They were to cultivate self-control, enthusiasm for traditional spirituality, mysticism, and a willingness to subordinate personal goals to those of their church. Within a century, Ignatius's original ten "Jesuits" had become an order numbering 15,000. As soldiers of the papacy, they assumed responsibility for the church's most difficult jobs. They won back Austria, Bavaria, and the Rhineland from the Protestants and staffed the missions that followed Europe's explorers to India, Japan, and the Americas.

THE COUNCIL OF TRENT (1545–1563)

11.6
The Catholic Response:
The Council of Trent

Pope Paul III (r. 1534–1549) ultimately yielded to pressure from Emperor Charles V and called a council to address the crisis created by the Reformation. The pope appointed Caspar Contarini (1483–1542), a member of the Oratory of Divine Love, chair of the commission that prepared for the council. Contarini was such an enthusiastic reformer that he was branded a "semi-Lutheran," and the report he presented to the pope in February 1537 was so blunt an indictment of the papal curia that Protestants circulated it to justify their break with the papacy.

The opening of the council, which met in Trent in northern Italy, was delayed until 1545, and it continued for eighteen years (1545–1563). War, plague, and politics caused long gaps between sessions. Unlike the late medieval councils, Trent was strictly under papal control and dominated by Italian clergy. Only high-ranking churchmen could vote. Theologians from the universities, the lower clergy, and the laity had no voice in the council's decisions.

The council focused on the restoration of internal church discipline. It curtailed the selling of church offices and other religious goods. It ordered bishops who resided outside their dioceses to go home and to work to elevate the conduct of their priests. Bishops were enjoined to preach and to conduct frequent tours of inspection of the clergy. Trent also tried to increase respect for the parish priest by requiring him to be neatly dressed, better educated, strictly celibate, and active among his parishioners. Trent called for the construction of a seminary in each diocese to provide educational opportunities for priests.

Trent made no doctrinal concessions to Protestantism. On the contrary, it ringingly affirmed most of the things to which Protestants objected: scholastic education; the importance of good works for salvation; the authority of tradition; the seven sacraments; transubstantiation; the withholding of the Eucharistic cup from the laity; clerical celibacy; purgatory; indulgences; and the veneration of saints, relics, and sacred images.

Trent did not set out to heal the rifts that had developed within Christendom but to strengthen the Roman Catholic Church in opposition to Protestantism.

MAP EXPLORATION

Interactive map: To explore this map further, go to **http://www.prenhall.com/kagan3/map11.2**

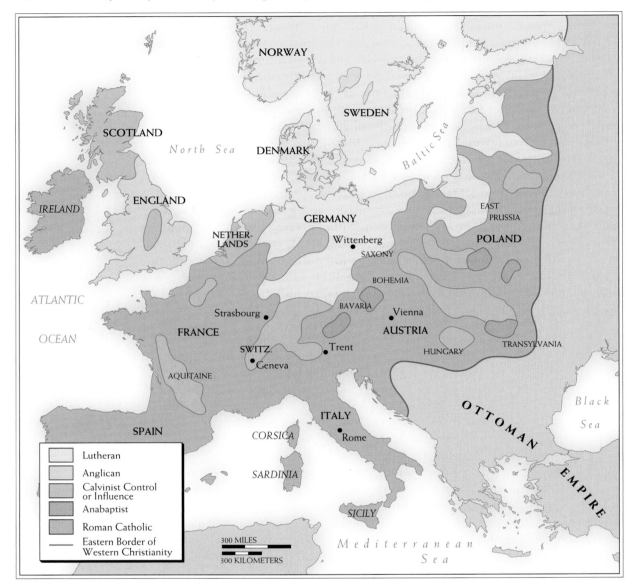

MAP 11-2

The Religious Situation about 1560 By 1560, Luther, Zwingli, and Loyola were dead, Calvin was near the end of his life, the English break from Rome was complete, and the last session of the Council of Trent was about to assemble. This map shows the "religious geography" of western Europe at the time.

HOW WOULD you characterize Christianity in western Europe at this time? Which reform movements seem to have had the most success?

Some secular rulers were initially leery of Trent's assertion of papal authority, but they were reassured as the new legislation took hold and parish life revived under the guidance of a devout and better trained clergy. The religious polarization of Europe that Trent encouraged was, however, a source for worry. (See Map 11–2.)

THE SOCIAL SIGNIFICANCE OF THE REFORMATION IN WESTERN EUROPE

*L*uther, Zwingli, and Calvin believed Christians should not separate themselves from the world but take up their duties as citizens of the state. They have been called "magisterial reformers," meaning not only that they were leaders of major movements but that they were willing to use the magistrate's sword to advance their causes.

Some modern observers condemn this as a compromise of religious principles, but the reformers did not see it that way. They knew their reform programs had to deal with the realities of their world. They were so sensitive to what they believed was politically and socially possible that some scholars claim they fought to preserve the status quo. Despite their innate political conservatism, however, they effected radical changes in traditional religious practices and some social institutions.

THE REVOLUTION IN RELIGIOUS PRACTICES AND INSTITUTIONS

Religion in Fifteenth-Century Life   On the eve of the Reformation, the clergy and other religious accounted for 6 to 8 percent of the inhabitants of the central European cities that were about to become Protestant. They exercised both spiritual authority and considerable political power. They legislated, taxed, tried cases in special church courts, and enforced discipline with threats of excommunication. About one-third of the year was given over to religious observances, and the church calendar regulated daily life. Monasteries had great influence. They educated the children of prominent citizens and enjoyed the patronage of powerful aristocratic families. Business boomed at religious shrines, where pilgrims gathered by the hundreds or thousands. Begging friars constantly worked the streets, and several times each year special preachers appeared to sell letters of indulgence.

The conduct of the religious professionals was a source of concern. Clergy were sworn to celibacy, but many had concubines and children. Society's reaction to this situation was mixed, and the church tolerated it—if appropriate fines were paid as penances. There were complaints about the clergy's exemption from taxation and immunity from prosecution in civil courts, and people grumbled when nonresidents collected the income from church offices and either neglected or assigned the work of those offices to others.

Religion in Sixteenth-Century Life   The Reformation made few changes in the politics or class structures of cities. The same aristocratic families continued to govern, and the same people were rich and poor. The Reformation did, however, profoundly alter the lives of clergy.

WHAT WAS the social significance of the Reformation and how did it affect family life?

Significant Dates from the Period of the Protestant Reformation

1517	Luther posts ninety-five theses against indulgences
1519	Charles V becomes Holy Roman Emperor
1521	Diet of Worms condemns Luther
1524–1525	Peasants' Revolt in Germany
1527	The Schleitheim Confession of the Anabaptists
1529	Marburg Colloquy between Luther and Zwingli
1529	England's Reformation Parliament convenes
1531	Formation of Protestant Schmalkaldic League
1533	Henry VIII weds Anne Boleyn
1534	England's Act of Supremacy
1534–1535	Anabaptists take over Münster
1536	Calvin arrives in Geneva
1540	Jesuits, founded by Ignatius of Loyola, recognized as order by pope
1546	Luther dies
1547	Armies of Charles V crush Schmalkaldic League
1547–1553	Edward VI, king of England
1555	Peace of Augsburg
1553–1558	Mary Tudor, queen of England
1545–1563	Council of Trent
1558–1603	Elizabeth I, queen of England; the Anglican settlement

Their numbers fell by two-thirds. One-third of parish churches and of religious holidays disappeared. Monasteries and nunneries were closed or turned into hospices and schools. Worship services were conducted in the vernacular, not Latin. Sometimes the walls of sanctuaries were stripped bare and whitewashed.

The Reformation also had an impact on the lives of the laity. They were no longer obliged to observe any fasts. Local shrines honoring saints, relics, and images were closed down, and punishments were decreed for venerating such things. Copies of Luther's translation of the New Testament or excerpts from it proliferated in private hands. Instead of controlling access to the Bible, Protestant clergy urged the laity to study it. Protestant clergy married, paid taxes, and could be prosecuted in civil courts. Laity as well as clergy served on the committees that supervised the morals of Protestant communities, and secular magistrates had the last word whenever there were disputes.

Not all Protestant clergy were happy about sharing power with the laity, and some laity complained about "new papists"—Protestant preachers who tried to exercise the same authority over their lives that the Catholic clergy had claimed. Some laity could be just as reactionary as some clergy. Over half of the initial converts to Protestantism returned to the Catholic fold before the end of the sixteenth century.

THE REFORMATION AND EDUCATION

The humanist curriculum emphasized language skills and the importance of consulting original sources. This was an ideal program of study for Protestants, who acknowledged no authority higher than that of Scripture. Reformers' views on doctrine and human nature often differed from those of the humanists, but they shared with the humanists a belief in the unity of wisdom and the importance of rhetorical eloquence and the active life. The Reformation's endorsement of humanist education had significant cultural impact.

In 1518, Philip Melanchthon (1497–1560), a young professor of Greek, joined Luther at the University of Wittenberg and delivered an inaugural address (*On Improving the Studies of the Young*) attacking scholasticism and defending classical studies. Melanchthon and Luther completely restructured Wittenberg's curriculum. New chairs of Greek and Hebrew were created. Canon law and commentaries on Lombard's *Sentences* were dropped. Straightforward historical and textual analysis replaced lectures consisting of scholastic glosses and commentaries on Aristotle's works. Candidates for theological degrees defended their theses by exegetical analyses of biblical passages and not by citations from the "authorities." Luther and Melanchthon also pressed for universal compulsory education so that both boys and girls could at least learn to read the Bible in vernacular translation.

The university that developed in Geneva from an academy founded by John Calvin and his successor, Theodore Beza, developed a program similar to Wittenberg's. The many refugees who flocked to Geneva came under its influence and spread its educational reforms when they returned to France, Scotland, and England, or established homes in the New World.

The focus of humanist education may have narrowed as Protestants took it over, but humanist culture and learning profited from the Reformation. By the seventeenth century, a working knowledge of Greek and Hebrew was commonplace in educated circles, and Protestant schools preserved many of the pedagogical achievements of humanism and transmitted them to the modern world. (See "Encountering the Past: Table Manners.")

ENCOUNTERING THE PAST

TABLE MANNERS

Humanists believed that education ought to mix pleasure with discipline. The family meal was, therefore, a suitable occasion for instructing the young in the lessons of life. Learning required neatness, order, respect, and attentiveness—traits that Hans Sachs, a sixteenth-century father, wanted his children to learn at his table.

HOW DO table manners prepare a child for life?

Listen you children who are going to table.

Wash your hands and cut your nails.

Do not sit at the head of the table;

This is reserved for the father of the house.

Do not commence eating until a blessing has been said.

...permit the eldest to begin first.

Proceed in a disciplined manner.

Do not snort or smack like a pig.

Do not reach violently for bread....

Do not stir food around on your plate or linger over it....

Rushing through your meal is bad manners.

Do not reach for more food while your mouth is still full,

Nor talk with your mouth full....

Chew your food with your mouth closed.

Do not lick the corners of your mouth like a dog....

Do not belch or cry out....

Do not stare at a person as if you were watching him eat.

Do not elbow the person sitting next to you....

Do not rock back and forth on the bench, lest you let loose a stink....

If sexual play occurs at table, pretend you do not see it....

Do not pick your nose....

Let no one wipe his mouth on the table cloth....

Silently praise and thank God for the food he has graciously provided.

Translation by S. Ozment from S. Ozment, *When Fathers Ruled: Family Life in Reformation Europe* (Cambridge, MA: Harvard University Press, 1983), 142–143.

A Family Meal. In Max Geisberg, *The German Single-Leaf Woodcuts*, ill: *1500–1550*, rev. and ed. by W. L. Strauss (New York, Hacker Art Books, 1974).

Used by permission of Hacker Art Books

THE REFORMATION AND THE CHANGING ROLE OF WOMEN

The Protestant reformers rejected ascetic disciplines as vain attempts to earn salvation. They urged clergy to marry to dispel the belief that the lives of clergy were spiritually more meritorious than those of laity. This created a more positive attitude toward sexuality that improved views of women.

Medieval thinkers tended to look down on sexually active women (as following the path of Eve) and exalt virgins (imitators of Jesus' mother, Mary). Protestants, however, saw women as worthy in their own right and honored their roles as wives and mothers as biblical vocations. Reformers acknowledged the contributions their wives made to their ministries. They viewed husband and wife as co-workers in the family, and they regarded the family as a sacred, God-ordained institution. Protestant marriage was, however, not a sacrament. Divorce was possible, and women had the right to leave husbands who flagrantly violated marriage contracts. From a modern perspective, Protestant women were still subservient to men, but they were accorded new respect and given greater legal protection.

Protestants promoted literacy among women, for they expected women to study the Bible to learn how to function as pious housewives. Female authors contributed to the literature of the Reformation, and some of them made much of the biblical passages that suggested women were equal to men before God. This encouraged serious thought about women's roles that inched society marginally closer to female emancipation.

FAMILY LIFE IN EARLY MODERN EUROPE

WHAT WAS family life like in early modern Europe?

uring the sixteenth and seventeenth centuries, customs associated with marriage and family life changed in many ways, but this was only partially due to the Reformation.

LATER MARRIAGES

Men and women of the Reformation era tended to wait longer before marrying than their medieval ancestors had. The church-sanctioned minimum age for marriage remained fourteen for men and twelve for women, and betrothal could occur at these young ages if parents approved. Grooms, however, were usually in their mid-to-late twenties rather than their late teens and early twenties. Brides wed in their early-to-mid twenties rather than their teens. These later marriages reflected the difficulty couples had in amassing enough capital to establish independent households. Increasing family size and population during the fifteenth and early sixteenth centuries led to property being divided among more heirs. Smaller shares meant couples had to work longer to prepare materially for marriage. Up to 20 percent of sixteenth-century women may not have married. Their lot was often to suffer increasing impoverishment as they aged without the support of husband or children.

ARRANGED MARRIAGES

Marriages tended to be arranged in the sense that the male heads of the families to which the potential bride and groom belonged usually met to consider the prospect of marriage before admitting their children to the discussion. It was rare, however, for the man and woman involved not to know each other or have no prior relationship. Children had a legal right to resist an unwanted marriage, and a forced marriage was, by definition, invalid. The best marriage was one desired by both parties and approved by their families.

The custom of marrying later in life meant the average length of marriages decreased and the rate of remarriage increased. Older women were more likely to die bearing children, and as the rapid growth of orphanages and foundling homes between 1600 and 1800 testifies, delayed marriage exposed more of them to the problems created by out-of-wedlock pregnancies.

FAMILY SIZE

The early modern family was conjugal or nuclear. It consisted of a father and a mother and an average of two to four surviving children. Pregnancies might occur about every two years. About one-third of the children born died by age five, and one-half were dead by age twenty. Rare was the family at any social level

OVERVIEW   THE REFORMATION AND THE CHANGING ROLE OF WOMEN

Education	• Encouraged female literacy in the vernacular
	• Women found biblical passages that suggested they were equal to men
	• Women became independent authors
Later Marriages	• Men and women tended to wait until their mid-to-late twenties to marry
	• Later marriages meant marriages of shorter duration
	• Remarriage was now more common for men who lost wives in childbearing
Arranged Marriages	• Bride and groom often knew each other in advance of marriage
	• Emotional feeling for one another was increasingly respected by parents
	• Forced marriages were, by definition, invalid and often failed
Family Size	• Large households consisted of in-laws, servants, laborers, and boarders
	• The average husband and wife had seven or eight children but most families experienced infant mortality and child death
Wet Nursing	• Church and physicians condemned the use of wet nurses
	• Upper-class women viewed the use of wet nurses as a symbol of high rank
	• The practice increased the rate of infant mortality

that did not suffer the loss of children. Martin Luther fathered six children, two of whom died—one at eight months and another at thirteen years.

BIRTH CONTROL

Birth control methods of limited effectiveness (acidic ointments, sponges, and coitus interruptus, for example) have been available since antiquity. The church's growing condemnation of contraception in the thirteenth and fourteenth centuries suggests its use was increasing. Thomas Aquinas justified the church's position by arguing that a natural act, such as sex, was moral only when it served the end for which it was created—in this case, the production of children.

WET NURSING

Theologians and physicians both condemned the widespread custom of turning newborn infants over to wet nurses. A wet nurse was usually a poor woman who was paid to suckle a wealthier woman's child. Wet nursing often exposed infants to greater risks from disease and neglect, but nursing a child was a chore many upper-class women found distasteful. Husbands also disliked it, for the church forbade sexual intercourse while a woman was lactating on the theory that sexual activity spoiled a woman's milk. Nursing also depresses a woman's ovulation cycles, and some women may have prolonged nursing to fend off another pregnancy. For wealthy burghers and noblemen who wanted an abundance of male heirs, the time their wives spent nursing was time wasted.

LOVING FAMILIES?

In addition to wet nursing, other practices of early modern families seem cold and unloving from our perspective. A child who spent the first year of life living away from home with a wet nurse might, between the ages of nine and fourteen, find herself or himself sent away from home again for an apprenticeship or employment. Husbands were often much older than wives. This may have hampered their intellectual intimacy. Widowed individuals sometimes remarried very quickly.

Expressions of love and affection are, however, as relative to time and culture as other behaviors. Given the context, a kindness in one historical period can seem a cruelty in another. Conditions made single life difficult in the sixteenth century and necessitated rapid remarriage. Children who began their apprenticeships at an early age had an advantage in a competitive economic environment that offered limited educational opportunities. No persuasive evidence indicates that people of the Reformation era were less capable of loving one another than modern people are.

LITERARY IMAGINATION IN TRANSITION

*A*s Europe approached the seventeenth century, it was no longer medieval but neither was it yet modern. The great literary figures of the era produced transitional works that combined traditional values and fresh perspectives on human life.

HOW WAS the transition from medieval to modern reflected in the works of the great literary figures of the era?

MIGUEL DE CERVANTES SAAVEDRA: REJECTION OF IDEALISM

There was religious reform in Spain but no Protestant Reformation. The state used the Inquisition to enforce religious conformity in Spain, and the religion of which the state approved was the mystical, ascetic Christianity of the early Middle Ages. For centuries, Spain had been a nation of crusaders, and the union of Catholic piety and secular power, characteristic of crusades, imbued Spain's culture with tinges of medieval chivalry. The novels and plays of the period are almost all devoted to stories in which the virtues of honor and loyalty are tested.

Miguel de Cervantes Saavedra (1547–1616), generally described as Spain's greatest writer, was fascinated by the strengths and weaknesses of religious idealism. Cervantes was self-educated. He read widely and immersed himself in the "school of life." As a youth, he lived for a while in Rome working for a Spanish cardinal. He entered the army and was decorated for gallantry in the Battle of Lepanto (1571). He was later captured by pirates and spent five years as a slave in Algiers. Back in Spain, his work as a tax collector inadvertently set him on the path to literary repute. In prison in 1603 for padding his accounts, he began to write his great book, *Don Quixote.*

Cervantes set out to satirize the chivalric romances popular in Spain in his day, but he developed an affection for Don Quixote, the deluded knight whose story his novel tells. *Don Quixote* is superficially satirical. It asks serious questions about what gives meaning to human lives. Don Quixote is a none-too-stable, middle-aged man driven mad by reading too many chivalric romances. He aspires to become the knight of his own imagination and sets out on a quest for opportunities to prove himself. As a courtly lover, he dedicates himself to the service of Dulcinea, a quite unworthy peasant girl whom he mistakes for a refined, noble lady. Sancho Panza, a clever, worldly wise peasant, accompanies him as his squire and watches with bemused skepticism as the Don repeatedly makes a fool of himself. The story ends tragically when a well-meaning friend restores Don Quixote's reason by defeating him in battle and forcing him to renounce his quest for knighthood. Stripped of the delusion that gave meaning to his life, the Don returns to his village to die a shamed and brokenhearted old man. *Don Quixote* places the modern realism of Sancho Panza beside the old-fashioned religious idealism of the Don and comes to the conclusion that both are essential elements in fully developed humanity.

WILLIAM SHAKESPEARE: DRAMATIST OF THE AGE

Little is known about William Shakespeare (1564–1616), the greatest playwright in the English language. He married young (at age eighteen), and by 1585, he and his wife, Anne Hathaway, had three children. He may have worked for a time as a schoolteacher. The wide but erratic knowledge of history and classical literature that informs his plays suggests he was not schooled as a professional scholar.

Once he could afford it, Shakespeare chose to live the life of a country gentleman. He entered eagerly into the commercialism and the bawdy pleasures of the Elizabethan Age, and his work shows no trace of Puritan anxiety about worldliness. He was radical in neither politics nor religion, and his few allusions to Puritans are more critical than complimentary. By modern standards he was a political conservative, accepting the social rankings and the power structure of his day and demonstrating unquestioned patriotism.

Shakespeare knew every aspect of life in the theater. He was playwright, actor, and owner-producer. He wrote and performed for an important company of actors, the King's Men, and, between 1590 and 1610, many of his plays were staged at Elizabeth's court. French drama in Shakespeare's day closely imitated classical models, but the Elizabethan audience that Shakespeare strove to please welcomed a mixture of styles. Shakespeare drew inspiration from the past and from his contemporaries, and his work combined aspects of classical drama, medieval morality plays, and current Italian short stories.

Shakespeare's most original tragedy may be *Romeo and Juliet* (1597). His four greatest were written in close succession: *Hamlet* (1603), *Othello* (1604), *King Lear* (1605), and *Macbeth* (1606). He also wrote comedies and plays based on historical events. The latter reflect propaganda that served the interests of the Tudor monarchy, but almost all of Shakespeare's plays have demonstrated a remarkable ability to transcend the limits of the world for which they were written. Their keen analyses of motivation, stirring evocation of emotion, and stunning language keep them alive and still filling theaters.

SUMMARY

Society and Religion   The Protestant Reformation had roots in political, social, and economic concerns. The emergence of centralizing national governments was challenging local custom and authority through much of Europe; in Germany and Switzerland, the free imperial cities were important early hotbeds of Protestantism. Often, groups (such as guilds) or regions in which people felt controlled by authority figures were particularly receptive to Protestantism. Laypeople were gaining power to criticize, and attempt to reform, the church, both because they were gaining cultural authority in general and because the church's crises had cost it so much credibility.

Martin Luther and the German Reformation to 1525   Martin Luther, like many other Germans, was concerned about the church's sale of indulgences and other financial and political arrangements. An ordained priest with a doctorate in theology, he developed the doctrine of justification by faith alone, which

IMAGE KEY

for pages 262–263

a. The Ecstasy of Saint Teresa de Avila by Gianlorenzo Bernini

b. Isenheim altarpiece, c. 1513-1515. Mathias Grunewald, 1470/80–1528, German

c. 15th Century Italian Silver Cross

d. Gemalde von Lucas Cranach d. A., 1529, "Dr. Martin Luther und seine Ehefrau Katharina von Bora." (Martin Luther and his wife Katharina von Bora)

e. Henry VIII, 16th century, Hans the younger Holbein—C.1497–1543, German

f. Painting, Flemish, 17th century Peter Paul Rubens (1577-1640) "The Miracle of Saint Ignace Loyola"

g. A portrait of the young John Calvin Bibliotheque Publique et Universitaire, Geneva

h. "The Subservient Husband" by Hans Schaufelein

offers salvation to believers in Christ. In 1517, Luther posted ninety-five theses against indulgence on the door of a church in Wittenberg. This sparked the Reformation. In the following years, Luther developed and publicized his theology; he was excommunicated in 1521. German humanists, peasants, and others supported Luther and his ideas, although Luther urged princes to suppress the peasants' revolt of 1524–1525.

The Reformation Elsewhere In Switzerland, France, and elsewhere in Europe, variations of Protestantism developed. In the 1520s, Ulrich Zwingli orchestrated the Swiss Reformation, from his post as the people's priest in the main church of Zurich. Zwingli believed a literal reading of Scripture should guide Christian beliefs and practices. More radical groups emerged, including Anabaptists, who believed baptism should only be performed on adults, who were capable of choosing their religion. John Calvin and his followers wanted to transform society morally, starting in Geneva in 1540. In the second half of the sixteenth century, Calvinism displaced Lutheranism as Europe's dominant form of Protestantism.

Political Consolidation of the Lutheran Reformation Between 1530 and 1552, the emperor Charles V made repeated attempts to persuade or force Protestants to revert to Catholicism. The 1555 Peace of Augsburg formalized Lutheranism's official status in the empire. Lutheranism also became the official state religion in Denmark and Sweden. Calvinists and Anabaptists, among others, were still excluded from official recognition throughout Europe.

The English Reformation to 1553 King Henry VIII's marital history had dramatic consequences for England's religion: because Henry wanted to marry Anne Boleyn, and because Pope Clement VII would not annul Henry's marriage to Catherine of Aragon, Parliament decreed that the king, not the pope, was the "supreme head on earth of the Church of England." But, by the 1530s, many of Henry's subjects were far more sympathetic to Protestantism than the king himself was; Henry's Church of England differed little from the Catholic Church. Only under the reign of his son, Edward VI, was Protestantism really instituted in England.

Catholic Reform and Counter-Reformation Protestants were not the only critics of the Catholic Church. Although the popes resisted reform, many new reform-oriented orders were established in the sixteenth century. Ignatius of Loyola founded what became one of the most significant of these orders, the Jesuits, who stressed a powerful combination of discipline and traditional spirituality. Between 1545 and 1563, a council of the church met at Trent to reassert Catholic doctrine. As a result of the Council of Trent, internal church discipline was reformed, but doctrine became even more strongly traditional and scholastic in orientation. Improvements in the education and behavior of local clergy helped revive parish life.

The Social Significance of the Reformation in Western Europe Although the Reformation was politically conservative, it revolutionized religious practice and institutions in part of Europe. In cities that became Protestant, many aspects of life were transformed. The numbers of clergy in these cities declined by two-thirds, one-third of all churches were closed, there were one-third fewer religious holidays, and most cloisters were closed. Some changes did not endure: more than half the original converts to Protestantism returned to the Catholic Church by the end of the sixteenth century. Protestant reformers helped disseminate humanist learning and culture. The ideal of the companionate marriage and other Protestant views helped improve the status of women.

Family Life in Early Modern Europe   Marriage occurred at a later age in the sixteenth through eighteenth centuries than it had previously in Europe and England. One reason for this shift was that, in a time of population growth, it took couples longer to accumulate the capital needed to raise a family. Parents were involved in arranging their children's marriages, although the couple's own wishes also carried significant weight. Generally, two to four children survived to adulthood in the European nuclear family. Birth control was not very effective; wet nursing was controversial. Although they sometimes exhibited it in ways that may seem strange to us, early modern parents almost certainly loved their children, and probably also each other.

Literary Imagination in Transition   Miguel de Cervantes Saavedra and William Shakespeare are among the most renowned authors of this period. Cervantes lived and worked in Catholic Spain; Shakespeare was a product of Protestant England. Their writings reflect their very different situations and interests. Cervantes's most famous work, *Don Quixote*, pays homage to the tradition of chivalric romance. Shakespeare's dramas cover a wide range of topics, including history; his universal themes and brilliant technique explain his enduring popularity.

REVIEW QUESTIONS

1. What were the main problems of the church that contributed to the Protestant Reformation? On what did Luther and Zwingli agree? On what did they disagree? What about Luther and Calvin?

2. What was the Catholic Reformation? What were the major reforms instituted by the Council of Trent? Did the Protestant Reformation have a healthy effect on the Catholic Church?

3. Why did Henry VIII break with the Catholic Church? Did he establish a truly Protestant religion in England? What problems did his successors face as a result of his religious policies?

4. What impact did the Reformation have on women in the sixteenth and seventeenth centuries? What new factors and pressures affected relations between men and women, family size, and child care during this period?

KEY TERMS

Act of Supremacy   (p. 277)   **Augsburg Confession**   (p. 275)   **indulgence**   (p. 267)
Anabaptists   (p. 272)

   For additional study resources for this chapter, go to:
www.prenhall.com/kagan3/chapter11

12 The Age of Religious Wars

CHAPTER HIGHLIGHTS

Renewed Religious Struggle After the 1555 Peace of Augsburg, religious strife in Europe centered on the conflict between Calvinism and Catholicism. In time, some intellectuals, and a very few political leaders, came to support religious toleration.

The French Wars of Religion (1562–1598) The rulers of France tried to suppress the France's Huguenots. Conflict between Catholic and Protestant elites led to bloodshed and civil war. In 1593 Henry IV renounced Protestantism and, in 1598, issued the Edict of Nantes.

Imperial Spain and the Reign of Philip II (r. 1556–1598) Philip II controlled vast territories, many people, and much wealth. During the first half of his reign, Philip focused his attention on the demographic and economic changes within his realm, conflict with the Turks, and the annexation of Portugal. The second half of his reign was dominated by the failed effort to hold on to control of the Netherlands.

England and Spain (1553–1603) Under Mary I, England returned to Catholicism and Protestants were persecuted. Over the course of her long reign, Mary's successor, Elizabeth I, steered a middle course in all areas, most notably religion, where she created a moderate Anglican church.

The Thirty Years' War (1618–1648) Germany's political fragmentation set the stage for the Thirty Years' War. The war had four distinct periods: the Bohemian period (1618–1625), the Danish period (1625–1629), the Swedish period (1630–1635), and the French period (1635–1648). The war was brought to an end by the 1648 Treaty of Westphalia.

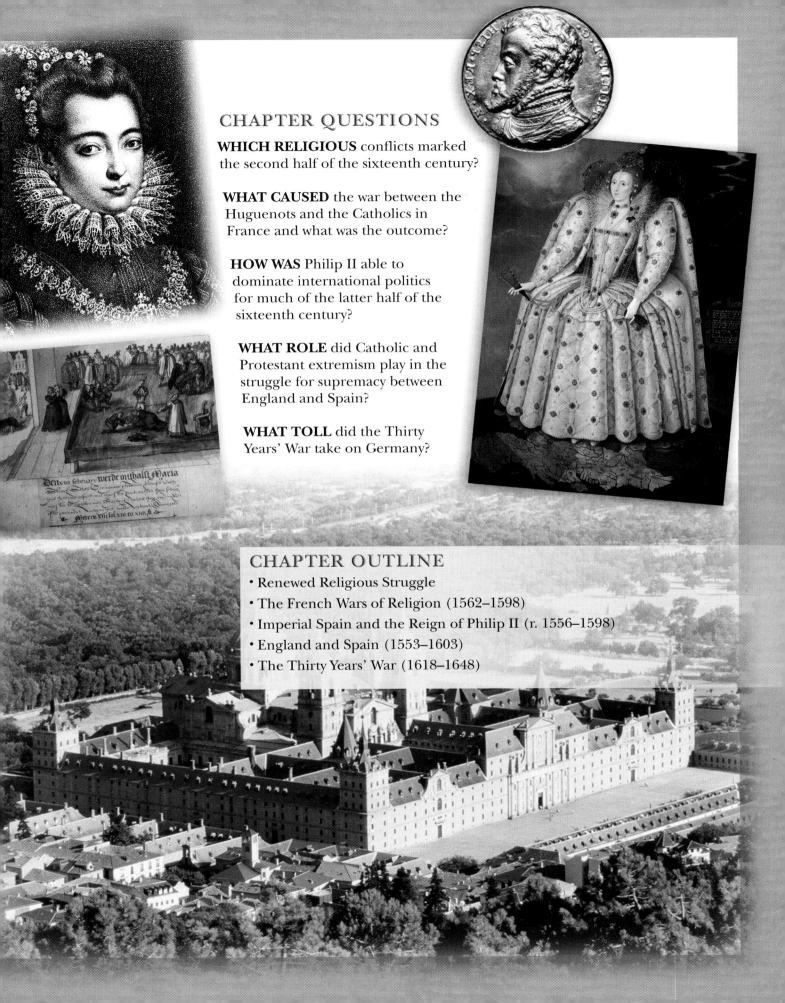

CHAPTER QUESTIONS

WHICH RELIGIOUS conflicts marked
the second half of the sixteenth century?

WHAT CAUSED the war between the
Huguenots and the Catholics in
France and what was the outcome?

HOW WAS Philip II able to
dominate international politics
for much of the latter half of the
sixteenth century?

WHAT ROLE did Catholic and
Protestant extremism play in the
struggle for supremacy between
England and Spain?

WHAT TOLL did the Thirty
Years' War take on Germany?

CHAPTER OUTLINE

IMAGE KEY
Image Key for pages 290–291 is on page 310.

WHICH RELIGIOUS conflicts marked the second half of the sixteenth century?

Counter-Reformation   A reorganization of the Catholic Church that equipped it to meet the challenges posed by the Protestant Reformation.

Contrast between an eighteenth-century Catholic baroque church in Ottobeuren, Bavaria and a seventeenth-century Calvinist plain church in the Palatinate. The ornamental Catholic church inspires worshipers to self-transcendence, while the undecorated Protestant church focuses attention on God's word.

(Left) Art Resource, NY (Right) German National Museum, Nuremberg, Germany

Political rivalries and religious conflicts combined to make the late sixteenth and the early seventeenth centuries an "age of religious wars." The era was plagued by civil conflicts within nations and by battles among nations. Catholic and Protestant factions contended within France, the Netherlands, and England. The Catholic monarchies of France and Spain attacked the Protestant regimes in England and the Netherlands. Ultimately, every major nation in Europe was drawn into a conflict that devastated Germany: the Thirty Years' War (1618–1648).

RENEWED RELIGIOUS STRUGGLE

During the first half of the sixteenth century, religious war was confined to parts of central Europe where Lutherans fought for recognition. In the second half of the sixteenth century, the primary arena for hostilities shifted to western Europe (France, the Netherlands, England, and Scotland) where Calvinists struggled for their cause.

The Peace of Augsburg (1555) ended the first phase of the war in central Europe by granting each ruler of a region within the Holy Roman Empire the right to determine the religion of his subjects. The only kind of Protestantism that Augsburg recognized, however, was Lutheranism. Lutherans and Catholics joined forces to suppress Anabaptists and other sectarians, and Calvinists were not yet numerous enough to attract attention.

By the time the Council of Trent adjourned in 1563, the **Counter-Reformation** had reinvigorated the Roman Catholic Church, and the Jesuits were spearheading an offensive to recover regions lost to Protestantism. John Calvin, who died in 1564, made Geneva both a refuge for Protestants fleeing persecution and a school to train them to meet the Catholic challenge.

Genevan Calvinism and post-Trent Catholicism were equally dogmatic and aggressive and mutually incompatible. Calvinism mandated a presbyterian organization that distributed authority over the church among local boards of lay and clerical *presbyters* (elders) representing individual congregations. The administration of the Roman Catholic Church was, by contrast, a centralized hierarchy under the absolute control of the pope. The pope and bishops ruled supreme without the necessity of consulting the laity. Calvinism attracted people who favored the decentralization and distribution of political power and who opposed authoritarian rule, whereas Catholicism was preferred by advocates of absolute monarchy—by those who favored "one king, one law, one faith."

As religious wars engulfed Europe, intellectuals perceived the wisdom of religious pluralism and toleration. Skepticism, relativism, and individualism in matters of faith increasingly came to be seen as virtues. Valentin Weigel (1533–1588), a Lutheran who surveyed a half century of religious strife in Germany, spoke for many when he advised people to look within themselves for religious truth and not to churches and creeds.

Politicians were slower than intellectuals to embrace principles of toleration, but the ones who did succeeded best at keeping religious tension under control. These so-called *politiques* (pragmatic monarchs such as Elizabeth I of England) preserved order by endorsing moderation and compromise. Rulers who took religion with utmost seriousness (Mary I of England, Philip II of Spain, and England's Oliver Cromwell, for example) failed to maintain stability.

THE FRENCH WARS OF RELIGION (1562–1598)

In the 1520s, Lutheran ideas began to circulate in Paris and to excite the suspicions of the French government. French Protestants were dubbed **Huguenots** after Besançon Hugues, the leader of the revolt that won Geneva its freedom at that time.

In 1525, Emperor Charles V captured King Francis I of France at the Battle of Pavia in Italy. The French authorities then began to persecute Protestants in the hope that by cooperating with Charles's anti-Protestant campaign they might win favorable terms for the king's release. A second crackdown followed a decade later in reaction to Protestant groups that (on October 18, 1534) plastered Paris and other cities with anti-Catholic placards. The government's actions persuaded some French reformers (John Calvin among them) to flee their homeland.

The Habsburg-Valois wars between France and the Holy Roman Empire ended with the Treaty of Cateau-Cambrésis in 1559. The treaty marked a shift in the European balance of power that favored Habsburg Spain, and it was followed by the outbreak of civil war in France.

In 1559, France's king Henry II (r. 1547–1559) was mortally wounded in a tournament, and his sickly fifteen-year-old son, Francis II, ascended the throne.

WHAT CAUSED the war between the Huguenots and the Catholics in France and what was the outcome?

politique   Ruler or person in a position of power who puts the success and well-being of his or her state above all else.

Huguenots   French Protestants, named after Besançon Hugues, the leader of the revolt that won Geneva its freedom at that time.

Catherine de Médicis (1519–1589) exercised power in France during the reigns of her three sons Francis II (r. 1559–1560), Charles IX (r. 1560–1574), and Henry III (r. 1574–1589).

Liaison Agency, Inc.

The queen mother, Catherine de Médicis (1519–1589), headed a regency government for her son, and its weakness tempted three powerful families to make bids for power. The Bourbons dominated southern and western portions of France. The Montmorency-Chatillons were strong in the center, and the base for the Guises was in the east.

The Guises initially enjoyed most influence with the young king. Duke Francis of Guise had commanded Henry II's army. His brothers, Charles and Louis, were both cardinals, and King Francis married their niece, Mary Stuart, Queen of Scotland. The Guises were militant, reactionary Catholics. France's Protestants rallied in support of their opponents, the Bourbon prince of Condé, Louis I (d. 1569), and the Montmorency-Chatillons admiral, Gaspard de Coligny (1519–1572).

APPEAL OF CALVINISM

French Calvinism drew its recruits primarily from ambitious aristocrats and discontented townspeople. By 1561, there were more than 2,000 Huguenot congregations in France, but Huguenots accounted for only about one-fifteenth of France's population. They were in the majority in only two regions (Dauphiné and Languedoc). However, they controlled important districts and were heavily represented among the more powerful classes in French society. Over two-fifths of the country's aristocrats became Huguenots. Many saw Protestantism as a route to greater authority over their domains. They hoped it would lead to France endorsing a principle of territorial sovereignty for magnates akin to the arrangements the imperial diet negotiated in the Peace of Augsburg.

The military forces led by Condé and Coligny gradually merged with the Huguenot churches, for they had much to gain from one another. Calvinism provided both a theological justification and a practical motive for opposing the Catholic monarchy. Calvinism needed military support if it hoped to become a viable religion in France, but the confluence of secular and sacred motives raised doubts about the religious sincerity of some Huguenot leaders. Religious conviction was neither the only nor always the main reason for their conversion to Protestantism.

CATHERINE DE MÉDICIS AND THE GUISES

Francis II died in 1560, but his mother, Catherine de Médicis, continued to rule France as regent for his heir, her second son, Charles IX (r. 1560–1574). Catherine's overriding concern was to preserve the prerogatives of the monarchy. To balance the power of the Guises, she sought allies among the Protestants. In 1562, she issued the January Edict, a decree that granted Protestants the right to hold public worship services in the countryside and private meetings in towns. Royal efforts to encourage toleration ended abruptly, however, when in March 1562, the duke of Guise massacred a Protestant congregation at Vassy. Had Condé and the Huguenot armies rushed immediately to the queen's side after this attack, they might have secured an alliance with Catherine, who feared the powerful Guises. But the Protestant leaders hesitated, and the Guises won control of the young king and his mother.

The Peace of Saint-Germain-en-Laye The duke of Guise was assassinated during the initial phase of the French religious wars (April 1562 to March 1563). Hostilities flared up again in 1567–1568, and the bloodiest phase in the conflict raged from September 1568 to August 1570. Huguenot leadership passed to Coligny, a fine military strategist, and in 1570, he negotiated the Peace of Saint-Germain-en-Laye. The crown acknowledged the power of the Protestant nobles by granting them religious freedom within their territories and the right to fortify their cities.

Queen Catherine tried to protect the throne by balancing the fanatical Huguenot and Guise extremes. She, however, favored Catholicism and tolerated Protestants only to counter Guise domination of the monarchy. After the Peace of Saint-Germain-en-Laye strengthened the Huguenots, Catherine switched sides and began to plot with the Guises to prevent the Protestants from winning over her son. Catherine had reason to fear Coligny, for he was on the verge of persuading the young king to invade the Netherlands to help the Dutch Protestants against their Catholic Habsburg ruler. This would have set France on a collision course with Spain, Europe's strongest state, and likely disaster.

The Saint Bartholomew's Day Massacre   On August 18, 1572, the French nobility gathered in Paris for the wedding of the king's sister, Marguerite of Valois, to Henry of Navarre, a Huguenot leader. Four days later, an attempt was made on Coligny's life. Catherine had apparently been party to a plot by the Guises to eliminate Coligny, and when it failed, she panicked. She feared both the king's reaction to her complicity with the Guises and what the Huguenots and Coligny might do in seeking revenge. In desperation, she convinced Charles that a Huguenot coup was afoot and only the swift execution of the Protestant leaders could save the crown.

On Saint Bartholomew's Day, August 24, 1572, Coligny and 3,000 fellow Huguenots were ambushed in Paris and butchered. Within three days, an estimated 20,000 Huguenots died, the victims of coordinated attacks throughout France. Protestants everywhere were horrified, whereas Pope Gregory XIII and Philip II of Spain greeted the news with special religious celebrations.

Catholics came to regret the slaughter of the Huguenots, for Saint Bartholomew's Day changed the nature of all the struggles between Protestants and Catholics. The disastrous outcome of France's religious squabbling convinced Protestants in many lands that they were engaged in an international fight to the death with an adversary whose cruelty justified any means of resistance.

Protestant Resistance Theory   At the start of the Reformation, Protestants tried to honor the Scripture that admonishes subjects to obey the rulers God gives them (Romans 13:1). Only after Charles V ordered Protestants to return to the Catholic faith (1530) did Luther grudgingly approve opposition to the emperor. Calvin, secure in his control of Geneva, condemned rebellion against lawfully constituted governments. He, however, also taught that the lower magistrates of those governments had the duty to oppose higher officials if these officials abused their authority. John Knox, a Scot driven into exile by the Catholic regent for Scotland, Mary of Guise, was strongly motivated by his personal experiences to develop a Calvinist rationale for revolution. Knox's *First Blast of the Trumpet Against the Terrible Regiment of Women* (1558) declared that the removal of a heathen (Catholic) tyrant was not only permissible but a Christian duty. The Saint Bartholomew's Day Massacre brought other Calvinists around to his point of view. François Hotman's *Franco-Gallia* (1573) argued that the Estates General, France's representative assembly, was the country's highest authority and empowered to authorize resistance to the crown. Theodore Beza's *On the Right of Magistrates over Their Subjects* (1574) justified the overthrow of tyrants by lower authorities, and Philippe du Plessis Mornay's *Defense of Liberty Against*

QUICK REVIEW

Saint Bartholomew's Day Massacre

- August 24, 1572: 3,000 Huguenots ambushed in Paris and killed
- Within three days, some 20,000 Huguenots were killed throughout France
- Massacre changed the nature of the conflict between Protestants and Catholics throughout Europe

HISTORY'S VOICES

THEODORE BEZA DEFENDS THE RIGHT TO RESIST TYRANNY

Luther and other Protestants, although accused by Catholics of fomenting social division and revolution, had defended strict obedience to established political authority. After the 1572 St. Bartholomew's Day Massacre however, many Protestants urged resistance to tyranny. In 1574, Theodore Beza pointed out the duties of rulers to their subjects and explained circumstances that justified resistance to authority.

TO BEZA, what are the obligations of rulers? What are the rights of subjects?

It is apparent that there is a mutual obligation between the king and the officers of a kingdom; that the government of the kingdom is not in the hands of the king in its entirety, but only the sovereign degree; that each of the officers has a share in accord with his degree; and that there are definite conditions on either side. If these conditions are not observed by the inferior officers, it is the part of the sovereign to dismiss and punish them. . . . If the king, hereditary or elective, clearly goes back on the conditions without which he would not have been recognized and acknowledged, can there be any doubt that the lesser magistrates of the kingdom, of the cities, and of the provinces, the administration of which they have received from the sovereignty itself, are free of their oath, at least to the extent that they are entitled to resist flagrant oppression of the realm which they swore to defend and protect according to their office and their particular jurisdiction? . . .

We must now speak of the third class of subjects, which though admittedly subject to the sovereign in a certain respect, is, in another respect, and in cases of necessity the protector of the rights of the sovereignty itself, and is established to hold the sovereign to his duty, and even, if need be, to constrain and punish him. . . . The people is prior to all the magistrates, and does not exist for them, but they for it. . . . Whenever law and equity prevailed, nations neither created nor accepted kings except upon definite conditions. From this it follows that when kings flagrantly violate these terms, these who have the power to give them their authority have no less power to deprive them of it.

Constitutionalism and Resistance in the Sixteenth Century: Three Treatises by Hotman, Beza, and Mornay, trans, and ed. by Julian H. Franklin (New York: Pegasus, 1969), pp. 111–114.

Tyrants (1579) urged princes, nobles, and magistrates to cooperate in rooting out tyranny wherever it appeared. (See "History's Voices: Theodore Beza Defends the Right to Resist Tyranny.")

THE RISE TO POWER OF HENRY OF NAVARRE

Henry III (r. 1574–1589), the last of Henry II's sons to wear the French crown, was caught between the vengeful Huguenots and the Catholic League, an alliance of radicals that Henry of Guise formed in 1576. Like his mother Catherine, Henry sought a middle course and appealed to the moderate Catholics and Huguenots, who valued political stability more than religious unity. The terms Henry offered in the Peace of Beaulieu (May 1576) promised the Huguenots almost complete religious and civil freedom, but the Catholic League (which had Spain's backing) was able to force Henry to reverse himself. In October 1577, the Edict of Poitiers again restricted Huguenot worship to specifically designated areas.

By the mid–1580s, Henry II was desperate to escape domination by the Catholic League, and in 1588 (on the "Day of the Barricades"), he launched a surprise attack to try to rout the league. It failed, and the king fled. But the timely arrival of the news that the English had given Spain a major defeat emboldened him to order the assassinations of both the duke and the cardinal of Guise. These murders enraged the Catholic League, which was led by another Guise brother, Duke Charles of Mayenne. In April 1589, the king was driven to seek an alliance with the Protestant leader, Henry of Navarre, the Bourbon heir to the throne. As the two Henrys prepared to attack the Guise stronghold in Paris, a fanatical Jacobin friar assassinated Henry III, the Valois king, and cleared the way for Henry of Navarre to become Henry IV (r. 1589–1610), France's first Bourbon monarch. Pope Sixtus V and King Philip II of Spain were aghast at the prospect of France suddenly becoming a Protestant nation. Philip sent troops to support the Catholic League and to claim the throne of France for his daughter, Isabella, Henry II's granddaughter.

Henry IV of France (r. 1589–1610) on horseback, painted in 1594.

Art Resource, NY

Spain's intervention rallied the people of France to Henry IV's side and strengthened his hold on the crown. Henry was a popular man who had the wit and charm to neutralize any enemy in a face-to-face meeting. He was also a *politique*, a leader who considered religion less important than peace. Henry reasoned that because most of his subjects were Catholics, he could best rule (and protect Protestants) as a Catholic. Consequently, on July 25, 1593, he converted to Catholicism—allegedly quipping, "Paris is worth a mass." The Huguenots were horrified. Pope Clement VIII was skeptical, but most of the French were relieved. They had had enough of war.

THE EDICT OF NANTES

On April 13, 1598, Henry's Edict of Nantes ended the civil wars of religion, and on May 2, 1598, the Treaty of Vervins made peace between France and Spain. The Edict of Nantes confirmed a promise of toleration that Henry IV had made the Huguenots (who now numbered well over a million) at the start of his reign. It designated certain towns and territories within France as places where Huguenots could openly worship, hold public offices, enter universities, and maintain forts. Nantes, however, was more a truce than a peace. It came close to creating states within the state, and it turned a hot war into a cold one that claimed Henry as a victim. In May 1610, he was assassinated by a Catholic fanatic.

DOCUMENT CD-ROM

11.5
The Edict of Nantes

IMPERIAL SPAIN AND THE REIGN OF PHILIP II (R. 1556–1598)

PILLARS OF SPANISH POWER

Philip II of Spain dominated international politics for much of the latter half of the sixteenth century. Bitter experience had led his father, Charles V, to conclude that the Habsburg family lands were too extensive to be governed by one man. He, therefore, divided them between his son and his brother. Philip inherited the intensely Catholic and militarily supreme western half. The eastern portion (Austria, Bohemia, and Hungary) and the imperial title went to Philip's uncle, Ferdinand I.

HOW WAS Philip II able to dominate international politics for much of the latter half of the sixteenth century?

Philip was a reclusive man who preferred to rule as the remote executive manager of a great national bureaucracy. His character is reflected in the unique residence he built outside Madrid, the Escorial. A combination palace, church, tomb, and monastery, it was a home for a monkish king. Philip was a learned and pious Catholic, a regal ascetic with a powerful sense of duty. He may even have arranged the death of his son Don Carlos (1568), when he concluded the prince was too mad and treacherous to be entrusted with the power of the crown.

New World Riches Philip's home base, Castile, was populous and prosperous, and the wealth of the New World that flowed through the port of Seville gave him ample funds to finance wars and international intrigues. Despite the floods of bullion, however, Philip's expenses exceeded his income. Near the end of his reign he destroyed one of Europe's great banking families, the Fuggers of Augsburg, by defaulting on his loans.

The American wealth that flowed through Spain had a dramatic impact on Europe. Increased prosperity supported population growth. By the early seventeenth century, the towns of France, England, and the Netherlands had tripled and quadrupled in size, and Europe's population had reached about 100 million. More people with more currency to spend meant more competition for food and jobs, which caused prices to double and triple. Inflation proceeded steadily at the rate of 2 percent per year while wages stagnated. This was especially true in Spain, where the new wealth was concentrated in the hands of a few. Nowhere did the underprivileged suffer more than in Castile. Philip's peasants, the backbone of his empire, were the most heavily taxed people in Europe.

Supremacy in the Mediterranean At the start of Philip's reign, a struggle with the Turks demanded all his attention. During the 1560s, the Turks had advanced deep into Austria, and their fleets had spread out across the Mediterranean. Between 1568 and 1570, armies under Philip's half brother, Don John of Austria, the illegitimate son of Charles V, suppressed and dispersed the Moors in Granada. In May 1571, Spain, Venice, and the pope formed the Holy League and dispatched Don John to counter Turkish maneuvers in the Mediterranean. On October 7, 1571, Don John's fleet engaged the Ottoman navy off Lepanto in the Gulf of Corinth and won the greatest naval battle of the sixteenth century. Thirty thousand Turks died, and over one-third of the Turkish fleet was sunk or captured. Spain dominated the Mediterranean—at least for the moment.

In 1580, Philip further improved his position by annexing Portugal. The Portuguese fleet augmented Philip's navy, and he added the Portuguese colonies in Africa, India, and the Americas to his empire.

THE REVOLT IN THE NETHERLANDS

Philip had far less success in northern Europe than in the Mediterranean. A rebellion in the Netherlands, the richest district in Europe, set in motion a chain of events that ended Spain's dream of world dominion. The Netherlands was governed for Philip by his half sister, Margaret of Parma, and a council headed by Cardinal Granvelle (1517–1586). Granvelle hoped to check the spread of Protestantism in the Netherlands by promoting church reform. He also wanted to limit the liberties of the seventeen Netherlands provinces and establish a centralized royal government directed from Madrid. The merchant towns of the Netherlands were, however, accustomed to considerable independence, and many, such as magnificent Antwerp, had become Calvinist strongholds. Two members of the governing council opposed their Spanish overlords: the Count of Egmont (1522–1568) and the Prince of Orange, William of Nassau (1533–1584), or "William the Silent" (so called because of his small circle of confidants).

William of Orange was a *politique* who considered the political autonomy and well-being of the Netherlands to be more important than allegiance to religious creeds. In 1561, he, a Catholic, married Anne of Saxony, the daughter of the Lutheran elector Maurice and the granddaughter of the late landgrave Philip of Hesse. He converted to Lutheranism six years later, and he became a Calvinist following the Saint Bartholomew's Day Massacre in 1572.

In 1561, Cardinal Granvelle began an ecclesiastical reorganization of the Netherlands that was intended to tighten the Catholic hierarchy's control over the country and to accelerate its assimilation as a Spanish dependency. Orange and Egmont, with the support of the Dutch nobility, engineered Granvelle's removal from office in 1564. The aristocrats who took Granvelle's place were, however, inept governors, and popular unrest mounted.

In 1564, Philip unwisely insisted the decrees of the Council of Trent be enforced throughout the Netherlands. Opposition materialized under the leadership of William of Orange's younger brother, Louis of Nassau, who had been raised a Lutheran. The Calvinist-inclined lesser nobility and townspeople joined him in drawing up the *Compromise*, a solemn pledge to oppose Trent and the Inquisition. In 1566 (after Margaret's government spurned the protesters as "beggars"), the Calvinists rioted, and Louis appealed to France's Huguenots and Germany's Lutherans for aid. Rebellion against the Spanish regency seemed about to erupt.

The Duke of Alba   A revolt failed to materialize, for the Netherlands' higher nobility were repelled by the behavior of Calvinist extremists and refused to support them. Philip sent an army of 10,000 men under the command of the duke of Alba to restore order and make an example of the would-be revolutionaries. Power to govern the Netherlands was delegated to a special tribunal, the Council of Troubles (as Spain called it) or the Council of Blood (as it was known among the Netherlanders). The new government inaugurated a reign of terror. It executed the counts of Egmont and Horn and several thousand suspected heretics, and it imposed high taxes to force the Netherlanders to pay the cost of Spain's occupation of their country. Tens of thousands of refugees fled the Netherlands during Alba's cruel six-year rule, and the duke came to be more hated than Granvelle or the radical Calvinists.

Resistance and Unification   William of Orange, who spent these turbulent years as an exile in Germany, emerged as the leader of an independence movement. Orange was the *stadholder* (governor) of Holland, Zeeland, and Utrecht, and these northern, Calvinist-inclined provinces provided his base. In the Netherlands, as elsewhere, the fight for political independence was linked with the struggle for religious liberty.

The uprising in the Netherlands was a true popular revolt that enlisted all kinds of people. William even backed the raids of the "Sea Beggars," an international group of anti-Spanish exiles and criminals who were brazen pirates. In 1572, the Beggars captured Brill and other seaports in Zeeland and Holland and incited the native population to join the rebellion. Resistance spread steadily southward. In 1574, the people of Leiden heroically withstood a long Spanish siege, and the Dutch opened the dikes and flooded their country to repulse the hated Spanish. The faltering Alba had by then ceded power to Don Luis de Requesens.

NOT LONGE TIME SINCE I SAWE A COWE. DID FLAVNDERS REPRESENTE VPON WHOSE BACKE KINGE PHILLIP RODE AS BEING MALECONTNT.

THE QVEENE OF ENGLAND GIVING HAY WHEARE ON THE COW DID FEEDE. AS ONE THAT WAS HER GREATEST HELPE IN HER DISTRESSE AND NEEDE.

THE PRINCE OF ORANGE MILKT THE CO AND MADE HIS PVRSE THE PAYLE THE COW DID SHYT IN MONSIEVRS HAN WHILE HE DID HOLD HER TAYLE.

The Milch Cow, a sixteenth-century satirical painting depicting the Netherlands as a cow in whom all the great powers of Europe have an interest. Elizabeth of England is feeding her (England had long-standing commercial ties with Flanders); Philip II of Spain is attempting to ride her (Spain was trying to reassert its control over the entire area); William of Orange is trying to milk her (he was the leader of the anti-Spanish rebellion); and the king of France holds her tail (France hoped to profit from the rebellion at Spain's expense).

Rijksmuseum, Amsterdam

The greatest atrocity of the war followed Requesens's death in 1576. Leaderless and unpaid, Spanish mercenaries ran amok in Antwerp on November 4, 1576. By the time order was restored, 7,000 people lay dead in the streets. This spate of violence (the so-called Spanish Fury) did more to unify the Netherlanders than all previous appeals to religion and patriotism. The ten predominantly Catholic southern provinces (roughly modern Belgium) joined the seven largely Protestant northern provinces (the modern Netherlands) in opposing Spain.

The Netherlanders resolved religious differences by agreeing to territorial arrangements similar to those that the Peace of Augsburg mandated for the Holy Roman Empire in 1555, and the Pacification of Ghent declared the Netherlands unified on November 8, 1576. In January 1577, the last four provinces joined the Union of Brussels, and for the next two years the Spanish faced a united, determined Netherlands.

In November 1576, Don John, the victor over the Turks at Lepanto, took command of Spain's land forces and promptly suffered his first defeat. In February 1577, he signed the Perpetual Edict, a humiliating treaty that required him to withdraw all Spanish troops from the Netherlands within twenty days. The Spanish were, however, nothing if not persistent. The nobility's fear of Calvinist extremism undermined the Union of Brussels, and Don John and Alessandro Farnese of Parma, the regent Margaret's son, reestablished Spanish control in the southern provinces. In January 1579, these provinces formed the Union of Arras and made peace with Spain. The northern provinces responded by organizing the Union of Utrecht.

Netherlands' Independence   Philip tried to break the back of the Netherlands' resistance by declaring William of Orange an outlaw and placing a bounty of 25,000 crowns on his head. This, however, only stiffened the resistance of the northern provinces, and Orange, in the *Apology,* a famous speech he delivered before the Estates General of Holland in December 1580, denounced Philip as a heathen tyrant who had no claim on the Netherlands.

On July 22, 1581, most of the northern provinces belonging to the Union of Utrecht formally repudiated Philip's authority and pledged allegiance to the duke of Alençon, Catherine de Médicis's youngest son. Alençon was seen as a compromise between the extremes of Spanish Catholicism and Calvinism, and he was expected to aspire to nothing more than titular authority over the provinces. In 1583, however, when it became clear that he aspired to much more than that, he was deposed and sent back to France.

William of Orange was assassinated in July 1584, and his son, Maurice (1567–1625), succeeded him as leader of the Dutch resistance. Fortunately for him and his cause, Philip II was by then overextending himself. By meddling in the affairs of France and England, he stretched his resources, and after England defeated his great Armada in 1588, his empire began to fray. By 1593, the northern provinces had driven all of Spain's soldiers out, and in 1596, France and England formally recognized the independence of these provinces. They concluded peace with Spain in 1609 and received international recognition in the Peace of Westphalia in 1648.

ENGLAND AND SPAIN (1553–1603)

MARY I

As it became clear that Henry VIII's son, Edward VI (d. 1553), would not live to sire children of his own, he tried to protect the Reformation in England by disinheriting his Catholic half sister, Mary Tudor (r. 1553–1558). His Protestant cousin, Lady Jane Grey, was named as his heir, but the people of England rallied to Mary, and Jane lost her head as well as the crown.

Queen Mary exceeded the worst fears of the Protestants. Her Parliaments repealed Edward's Protestant statutes, and she restored many Catholic practices. She executed the Protestant leaders who had served her brother (John Hooper, Hugh Latimer, and Thomas Cranmer), and she convicted 287 individuals of heresy and burned them at the stake. Many Protestants avoided martyrdom by fleeing to the Continent. These "Marian exiles" settled in Germany and Switzerland, where they established communities, wrote tracts urging armed resistance, and waited for the time when a Protestant counteroffensive could be launched in their homeland. Many returned to England more radical than when they had left.

In 1554, Mary displeased her subjects by marrying Prince Philip—later to become King Philip II—of Spain. She favored him because Spain headed the militant Catholic offensive against Protestantism, and Mary wanted to return England to the Catholic fold. Many of Mary's subjects feared the marriage would produce a child who, as heir to both England and Spain, would absorb England into Spain's great empire. The marriage was, however, unproductive, and Mary died knowing that her half sister, Elizabeth, the daughter of her father's first Protestant marriage, would claim the throne.

ELIZABETH I

Elizabeth I (r. 1558–1603), the daughter of Henry VIII and Anne Boleyn, was perhaps the most astute politician of the sixteenth century, and with the help of a shrewd adviser, Sir William Cecil (1520–1598), she built a strong monarchy. Between 1559 and 1563, she and Cecil guided a religious settlement through Parliament. It merged a centralized episcopal system of administration for the church (which the queen controlled) with broadly defined Protestant doctrine and traditional Catholic ritual. The Anglican church it created avoided inflexible religious extremes and spared England (at least for the time being) the religious conflicts that were bloodying continental nations. (See "Encountering the Past: Going to the Theater.")

Catholic and Protestant Extremists Religious compromises were unacceptable to zealots of both persuasions, and subversive groups worked to undermine Elizabeth. At the time of her coronation, most of her subjects were Catholics, and the radicals among them (aided by the Jesuits) plotted to replace her with

Portrait of Mary I (r. 1553–1558), Queen of England. By Sir Anthony Mor (Antonio Moro) (1517/20–1576/7), Prado, Madrid. 1554 (panel).

The Bridgeman Art Library International

ENCOUNTERING THE PAST

GOING TO THE THEATER

The Elizabethan era was a Golden Age for English theater. During the late Middle Ages, troupes of players had toured the countryside performing morality plays. *The church often sponsored these companies, for plays offered religious education and moral instruction as well as entertainment. The rural theater was nothing more than a circular field ringed with mounds of earth on which spectators sat. Four tents were pitched at the points of the compass to give actors opportunities to enter and exit the action as the plot required.*

During the fifteenth century, players began to stage their productions in the courtyards of urban inns. Inns were renovated to provide permanent stages and more complex sets. The enclosed space also made it possible to limit the audience to paying customers and to turn theater into a profitable business enterprise. The urban setting altered the content as well as the staging of plays. The allegorical moralizing of the medieval country theater was replaced by a more ribald, worldly entertainment, and the inn setting provided the workmen and young women who comprised much of the audience with rooms to which to retreat for performances of their own.

London's theater world matured in the late sixteenth and early seventeenth centuries in the work of Shakespeare and his contemporaries. Special theaters (notably The Rose and The Globe, for which Shakespeare wrote) were built in the 1590s on the south bank of the river Thames. Plays were hugely popular with Londoners. Women were excluded from the stage, so all parts were acted by men and boys. Audiences (particularly in "the pit," the ground floor) were rowdy. They responded to the witty repartee

and bawdy action on stage and overindulged in the food and drink sold during the performance.

HOW DID medieval theater differ from the theater of Elizabeth's era?

A seventeenth-century sketch of the Swan Theatre, which stood near Shakespeare's Globe Theatre on the south bank of the Thames.
The Bridgeman Art Library

Scotland's Catholic queen, Mary Stuart. Unlike Elizabeth, whose father had declared her illegitimate, Mary Stuart had an unblemished claim to the throne inherited from her grandmother, Henry VIII's sister. Elizabeth responded swiftly to Catholic assassination plots but rarely let emotion override her political instincts. Despite proven cases of Catholic treason and even attempted regicide, she executed fewer Catholics during her forty-five years on the throne than Mary Tudor had executed Protestants during her brief five-year reign.

Elizabeth dealt cautiously with England's "Puritans," Protestants who wanted to "purify" the church of every vestige of "popery." The Puritans had two major grievances. They despised the Church of England's retention of Catholic ceremony and vestments, for these things made it appear that no Reformation had taken place. They also wanted to end the system of episcopal government, which gave the queen a kind of papal authority over the church.

The more extreme Puritans, the **Congregationalists**, believed every congregation ought to be autonomous, a law unto itself controlled by neither bishops nor presbyterian assemblies. Most sixteenth-century Puritans, however, were **Presbyterians**. That is, they favored a national church of semiautonomous congregations governed by representative presbyteries (the model Calvin had established in Geneva). Neither of these options was acceptable to the queen, for the episcopal hierarchy was the instrument through which she controlled the church. The Conventicle Act of 1593 gave Puritan "separatists" the option of either conforming to the practices of the Church of England or facing exile or death.

Deterioration of Relations with Spain Despite the sincere desire of both Philip II and Elizabeth I to avoid direct confrontation, events led inexorably to war between England and Spain. In 1567, when the Spanish duke of Alba marched his army into the Netherlands, many in England assumed that Spain intended to use the Netherlands as a base for an invasion of England. In 1570, Pope Pius V (r. 1566–1572) confirmed their fears by branding Elizabeth a heretic and proposing a military expedition to recover England for Catholicism.

In 1571, Don John's demonstration of Spain's awesome sea power at the Battle of Lepanto prompted England and France to sign a mutual defense pact. England also took to the sea. Throughout the 1570s, Elizabeth's privateers, John Hawkins (1532–1595) and Sir Francis Drake (1545–1596), preyed on Spanish shipping in the Americas, and Drake's circumnavigation of the globe (1577–1580) forecast England's ascendancy on the high seas.

The Saint Bartholomew's Day Massacre forced Elizabeth to change her foreign policy. Protestants in France and the Netherlands appealed to her for protection, and in 1585, she sent English soldiers to the Netherlands. Funds she had previously funneled covertly to Henry of Navarre, the Protestant leader in France, now flowed openly. These developments strained relations between England and Spain, but the event that precipitated war was Elizabeth's decision to execute Mary, Queen of Scots (1542–1587).

Mary, Queen of Scots Mary Stuart, the daughter of King James V of Scotland and Mary of Guise, had left Scotland for France at the age of six. She was raised in France to prepare her for the role as the wife of its king, Francis II. The death of her young husband in 1561 sent Mary back to Scotland to rule a land she barely knew.

A year before Mary returned to Scotland, the Scots had embraced a fervent Protestant Reformation. Mary had grown up at France's Catholic court, and she had no sympathy with Scotland's new religion—especially its dour morality. She wanted her Scottish court to mirror the gaiety and sophistication of Paris. John Knox, the leader of Scotland's Reformation, objected strenuously to the queen's

An idealized likeness of Elizabeth Tudor when she was a princess, attributed to Flemish court painter L. B. Teerling, ca. 1551. The painting shows her blazing red hair and alludes to her learning by the addition of books.

Unknown, formerly attributed to William Scrots. Elizabeth I, when Princess (1533–1603). The Royal Collection © 2002, Her Majesty Queen Elizabeth II.

12.2
Elizabeth's Act of Uniformity

Congregationalists The more extreme Puritans who believed every congregation ought to be autonomous, a law unto itself controlled by neither bishops nor presbyterian assemblies.

Presbyterians Puritans who favored a national church of semiautonomous congregations governed by representative presbyteries.

continuing to practice her Catholic faith even in private, for Scottish law made this a capital offense. Queen Elizabeth personally despised Knox, but she encouraged his defense of Protestantism. It served her foreign policy by making it difficult for Mary to persuade the Scots to cooperate with France against England.

In 1568, a scandal cost Mary her throne. Mary had married Lord Darnley, a youth with connections to the royal houses of both England and Scotland. She had a son by him (the James who was eventually to inherit the crowns of both Scotland and England). Darnley, however, proved an impossible husband, and Mary reputedly took the earl of Bothwell as her lover. He, in turn, allegedly murdered Darnley, abducted Mary, and married her. This amounted to usurpation of the throne, and the outraged Scots forced Mary to abdicate in favor of her infant son.

Mary fled Scotland and unwisely sought refuge from her cousin Elizabeth in England. Mary was a threat to Elizabeth, for Catholics considered Mary the rightful heir to the English throne. Elizabeth placed Mary under house arrest and held her captive for nineteen years. In 1583, Elizabeth's vigilant secretary, Sir Francis Walsingham, discovered that the Spanish ambassador, Bernardino de Mendoza, was scheming to unseat Elizabeth. In 1586, Walsingham exposed still another Spanish plot, and this time he had proof of Mary's involvement. Elizabeth was loath to execute Mary. She feared that such an act would diminish the aura of divine right that was one of the props of monarchy, and she knew it would raise a storm of protest among Catholics. In the end, however, she concluded she had no choice, and Mary was beheaded on February 18, 1587. Mary's death dashed Catholic hopes for a bloodless reconversion of England and persuaded Philip II that the time had come for a military assault on the Protestant nation.

The Armada   Spain's preparations for war were interrupted in the spring of 1587 by raids Sir Francis Drake led on the port city of Cádiz and the coast of Portugal. These attacks forced Philip to postpone his invasion of England, but on May 30, 1588, the Armada (130 ships and 25,000 men) set sail. The expedition's commander, the duke of Medina-Sidonia, soon found himself in trouble. The barges that were to transport his soldiers from their galleons onto England's shores were late in leaving Calais and Dunkirk for their rendezvous with the fleet. While the Spanish vessels waited, an "English wind" sprang up and helped the swifter English and Dutch ships scatter the Spanish forces.

Spain never fully recovered from the Armada's loss, and by the time of Philip's death (September 13, 1598), it was experiencing reversals on multiple fronts. Philip's successors, Philip III (r. 1598–1621), Philip IV (r. 1621–1665), and Charles II (r. 1665–1700), were all inadequate men. Spain's decline allowed France to emerge as the leading continental power, while the Dutch and English nibbled away at Spain's empire.

When Elizabeth died on March 23, 1603, she left behind a strong nation poised on the brink of acquiring a global empire. Because she had never married (choosing instead to use the hope of winning her hand as a tool for English diplomacy), her death ended the Tudor dynasty. Ironically, her heir was Mary's son, James VI of Scotland (James I of England).

THE THIRTY YEARS' WAR (1618–1648)

The Thirty Years' War in the Holy Roman Empire was the last and the most destructive of the wars of religion. The passions it raised escalated to the point where the combatants seemed willing to sacrifice everything in pursuit of victories that were increasingly less worth winning. Virtually every major European

---

QUICK REVIEW

The Spanish Armada
- Assembled for invasion of Protestant England
- Attacks by Sir Francis Drake in 1587 forced Philip to postpone invasion
- Failure of Armada in May 1588 dealt a severe blow to Spain's military power

WHAT TOLL did the Thirty Years' War take on Germany?

state was drawn into the conflict. When the hostilities ended in 1648, the agreements among the victors drew the map of northern Europe much as it appears today.

PRECONDITIONS FOR WAR

Fragmented Germany   In the second half of the sixteenth century, Germany was a collection of about 360 autonomous political entities: secular principalities (duchies, landgraviates, and marches), ecclesiastical principalities (archbishoprics, bishoprics, and abbeys), free cities, and regions dominated by knights with castles. The Peace of Augsburg (1555) had granted each a degree of sovereignty within its borders. This made trade and travel difficult, for each levied its own tolls and tariffs and coined its own money. Many little states also had pretensions that exceeded their powers.

During the Thirty Years' War, Germany—Europe's crossroads—became Europe's stomping ground. The great conflict had many causes, but chief among them was the threat that the unification of Germany posed to the balance of power in Europe. Protestants suspected a conspiracy by the papacy and the Holy Roman Empire to work together to reimpose Catholic dominance first in Germany and then in the rest of Europe. The imperial diet, which was controlled by Germany's territorial leaders, was leery of any attempt to consolidate the empire, for this threatened its members' liberties. Some urged allies outside of Germany to help them fend off attempts by the emperor to strengthen his authority over them. Many governments had a variety of reasons for being alarmed at the prospect of a united Germany controlled by a Catholic emperor.

Religious Division   By 1600, there may have been slightly more Protestants than Catholics in the Holy Roman Empire. The territorial principle proclaimed by the Peace of Augsburg in 1555 was intended to freeze Lutherans and Catholics in place by forcing each territory to declare its faith, but as time passed, there were unsettling shifts of jurisdiction. As Lutherans gained ground in some Catholic areas and Catholics in a few places designated as Lutheran, tensions increased. Catholic rulers, who were in a weakened position after the Reformation, resented the concessions they had had to make to Protestants, and they insisted the ecclesiastical property administered by clergy who converted be returned to Catholic control. Protestants, however, were often unwilling to comply. The situation was further complicated by divisions within the Protestant camp between liberal and conservative Lutherans and between Lutherans and Calvinists. (See Map 12–1.)

Calvinism was not recognized as a legal religious option by the Peace of Augsburg, but it won a foothold in the empire when Frederick III (r. 1559–1576), elector Palatine, declared it the official religion of his domain. Heidelberg, his capital, became the German "Geneva"—the staging area for Calvinist penetration of the empire. Lutherans came to fear Calvinists almost as much as they did Catholics, for the bold missionary forays of the Palatine Calvinists threatened the stability that the Peace of Augsburg had brought the empire. Lutherans were also offended by blunt Calvinist criticism of Lutheran doctrines (particularly the Lutheran belief in Christ's real presence in the Eucharist).

The Jesuits joined the Calvinists in undermining the Peace of Augsburg. Catholic Bavaria, led by Duke Maximilian and supported by Spain, did for the Counter-Reformation what the Palatinate did for Calvinism. Jesuit missionaries, operating from Bavaria, returned major cities (notably, Strasbourg and Osnabrück) to the Catholic fold. In 1609, Maximilian organized a Catholic League to counter a Protestant alliance formed in the same year by the Calvinist elector Palatine, Frederick IV (r. 1583–1610). The army the league assembled under the command of Count Johann von Tilly tipped Germany into war.

QUICK REVIEW

Religious Divisions in the Holy Roman Empire

- By 1600 slightly more Protestants than Catholics in Holy Roman Empire
- Peace of Augsburg (1555) did not succeed in freezing religion of territories
- Divisions within Protestant camp complicated situation

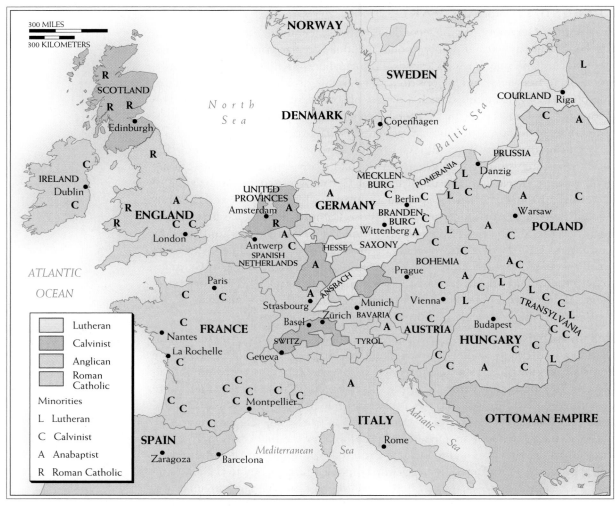 MAP EXPLORATION

Interactive map: To explore this map further, go to **http://www.prenhall.com/kagan3/map12.1**

MAP 12–1

Religious Divisions about 1600 By 1600, few could seriously expect Christians to return to a uniform religious allegiance. In Spain and southern Italy, Catholicism remained relatively unchallenged, but note the existence elsewhere of large religious minorities, both Catholic and Protestant.

HOW WOULD you explain the division between Catholic and Protestant regions in Europe?

FOUR PERIODS OF WAR

The Bohemian Period (1618–1625) The war broke out in Bohemia following the ascent to the Bohemian throne in 1618 of Ferdinand, the Habsburg archduke of Styria and heir to the empire. Ferdinand, who had been educated by Jesuits, was determined to restore Catholicism to the Habsburg lands. No sooner had he become king of Bohemia than he revoked the religious liberties that had been granted to Bohemia's Protestants. The Protestant nobility responded in May 1618 by literally throwing his regents out a window (the "defenestration of Prague"). A year later, when Ferdinand (II) became Holy Roman Emperor, the Bohemians repudiated him in favor of the Calvinist elector Palatine, Frederick V (r. 1616–1623).

The Bohemian revolt triggered an international war. Ferdinand was supported by Spain, Maximilian of Bavaria, and the Lutheran elector of Saxony, John George I (r. 1611–1656). He saw the war as an opportunity to expand his domains at the expense of his fellow Protestant, the Calvinist elector Palatine. Johann von Tilly, who commanded Ferdinand's armies, routed Frederick V's troops in 1620, and by 1622, Ferdinand had subdued Bohemia and conquered the Palatinate. As the remnants of Frederick's army retreated north, Duke Maximilian of Bavaria followed, claiming land as he went.

Bohemian protesters throw three of Emperor Ferdinand II's agents out of windows at Hradschin Castle in Prague to protest his revocation of Protestant freedoms.

Art Resource, NY

The Danish Period (1625–1629)
Maximilian's successful forays into northwestern Germany raised the alarming prospect of German unification. This prompted England, France, and the Netherlands to urge Christian IV (r. 1588–1648), the Lutheran king of Denmark and duke of the German duchy of Holstein, to go to the rescue of Germany's Protestants. Duke Maximilian, however, quickly forced him to retreat.

Emperor Ferdinand, who felt threatened by Maximilian's growing power, turned the conduct of the war over to Albrecht of Wallenstein (1583–1634), a mercenary he had employed against the Bohemians. Wallenstein was a brilliant military strategist, ruthless, and a law unto himself, but by 1629, he had so effectively broken the back of Protestant resistance that Ferdinand issued the Edict of Restitution. It outlawed Calvinism and ordered the Lutherans to return to Catholic ownership all the church lands they had acquired since 1552. This entailed the surrender of sixteen bishoprics and twenty-eight cities and towns, and it had the unintended effect of reigniting resistance to the Habsburgs.

The Swedish Period (1630–1635) Gustavus Adolphus of Sweden (r. 1611–1632), a pious Lutheran monarch and a military genius, took up the gauntlet for Protestantism. He was handsomely bankrolled by two very interested bystanders—the Dutch (long-standing opponents of the Habsburgs) and the French. Cardinal Richelieu, chief adviser to the Catholic king of France, was eager to prevent a powerful Habsburg Empire from materializing on France's border.

The Swedish king suddenly reversed the course of the war by winning a stunning victory at Breitenfeld in 1630. The battle was significant, but far from decisive, and the Protestant cause faltered when Gustavus Adolphus died battling Wallenstein's forces at Lützen in November 1632. Two years later, Ferdinand arranged for Wallenstein, who was outliving his usefulness, to be assassinated, and he negotiated a truce with the German Protestants (the Peace of Prague, 1635). The Swedes, however, refused to compromise with the Catholic emperor, and support from France and the Netherlands helped them renew hostilities.

The Swedish-French Period (1635–1648) The French openly entered the war in 1635 and prolonged it for thirteen more years. French, Swedish, and Spanish soldiers looted the length and breadth of Germany while the Germans, too disunited to put up much resistance, simply looked on and suffered. By the

MAP EXPLORATION

Interactive map: To explore this map further, go to **http://www.prenhall.com/kagan3/map12.2**

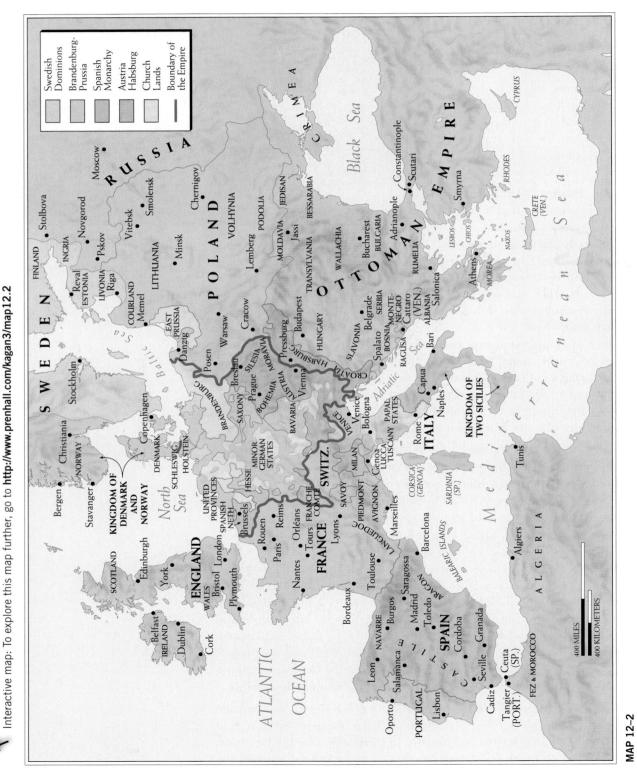

MAP 12–2

Europe in 1648 At the end of the Thirty Years' War, Spain still had extensive possessions. Austria and Brandenburg-Prussia were rising powers, the independence of the United Provinces and Switzerland was recognized, and Sweden had footholds in northern Germany.

WHAT DOES this map indicate about the German lands and the Holy Roman Empire in 1648?

time peace talks began in the Westphalian cities of Münster and Osnabrück in 1644, Germany's population may have been reduced by a third. It was the worst catastrophe suffered by a European state since the Black Death of the fourteenth century.

THE TREATY OF WESTPHALIA

The Treaty of Westphalia ended hostilities in 1648 by ensuring the continued fragmentation of Germany. The territorial principle proclaimed by the Peace of Augsburg in 1555 was reasserted, and rulers were confirmed in their right to determine the religions of their subjects. Calvinism was added to the list of legal religious options, and the German princes won recognition of their independence. Bavaria was elevated to the rank of an elector state, and Brandenburg-Prussia emerged as the most powerful north German principality. The Swiss Confederacy and the United Provinces of Holland were recognized as sovereign states, and France acquired considerable territory. (See Map 12–2.)

12.4
The Peace of Westphalia, 1648

War between France and Spain continued outside the empire until 1659, when the French forced the Spanish to accept the humiliating Treaty of the Pyrenees. Germany's fragmentation and Spain's humbling left France the dominant power in Europe. The roots of the competitive nationalisms that have loomed so large in the history of the modern world are to be found in the religious conflicts of the seventeenth century.

SUMMARY

Renewed Religious Struggle The Peace of Augsburg recognized Lutheranism as a legal religion in the Holy Roman Empire in 1555. For the remainder of the sixteenth century, religious strife centered on the conflict between Calvinism and Catholicism. Calvinism and Catholicism both were dogmatic, aggressive, and irreconcilable. Even the art and architecture of the Catholic Counter-Reformation, with its baroque energy, stands in marked contrast to Protestant restraint. Slowly some intellectuals—and a very few political leaders—came to adopt a more skeptical, tolerant view of religion, but in the meantime the Thirty Years' War between 1618 and 1648 drew every nation of Europe into some degree of religious conflict.

The French Wars of Religion (1562–1598) The rulers of France repeatedly cracked down on France's Protestant Huguenots. After the death of King Henry II, the French monarchy was weak. Although Calvinists made up only a small part of the population, France's Calvinists included much of the aristocracy. Catherine de Médicis attempted with some success to play Catholics and Huguenots off against each other. In 1593, a few years after the Bourbon Huguenot Henry of Navarre took the French throne, Henry renounced his Protestantism in favor of Catholicism; his 1598 Edict of Nantes sanctioned minority religious rights within Catholic France.

Imperial Spain and the Reign of Philip II (r. 1556–1598) Philip II, who ruled Spain through most of the second half of the sixteenth century, controlled vast territories, many people, and much wealth. For the first twenty-five years or so of Philip's reign, his attention was focused on the demographic and economic changes within his kingdom, defense against the Turks in the Mediterranean,

and the annexation of Portugal (which led to control over Portugal's wealthy colonies). The second half of his reign was overshadowed by unrest and, eventually, defeat in the Netherlands.

England and Spain (1553–1603) Catholic Mary I ruled England for five bloody years. Many Protestants were martyred or exiled during her reign. She married Spain's Prince Philip. Her half sister, Elizabeth I, succeeded her and ruled for most of the second half of the sixteenth century (r. 1558–1603). Elizabeth was probably the most successful European leader of her time. She steered a middle course between extremes in all areas, most notably religion, where she created the moderate Anglican church. She took firm measures against extremist Puritans (with the Conventicle Act), against would-be assassins (she executed Mary Queen of Scots for plotting against her), and Spain (the English navy defeated Spain's Armada in 1588).

The Thirty Years' War (1618–1648) Germany's political fragmentation, and conflict throughout Europe among Lutherans, Catholics, and Calvinists, set the stage for the Thirty Years' War. This devastating conflict drew in all the major lands of Europe before it was over; it has shaped the map of Europe up to the present. There were four distinct phases to the war, named after the region that was most actively involved in fighting at that time: the Bohemian period (1618–1625), the Danish period (1625–1629), the Swedish period (1630–1635), and the Swedish-French period (1635–1648). Finally, the 1648 Treaty of Westphalia put an end to hostilities and, among other provisions, reasserted the right of each ruler to determine the religion in his or her land.

IMAGE KEY

for pages 290–291

a. Artwork of a 17th century musket made of wood and metal finishing

b. The massacre of Protestants at Vassy, France, by order of Francois de Lorraine, Duc de Guise, on 1 March 1562; colored engraving, French, 17th century

c. French closed helmet, 1575

d. A 16th century sword

e. A 16th century sword hilt

f. Catherine de Médicis (1519–1589)

g. A portrayal of the execution of Mary, Queen of Scots. Unknown Dutch Artist

h. Spain, Madrid, San Lorenzo del Escorial, high view over monastery

i. Gold medal of King Philip II of Spain and Queen Mary I of England, 1554

j. Elizabeth I (1558-1603) of England in 1592   By courtesy of the national Portrait Gallery, London

REVIEW QUESTIONS

1. What part did politics play in the religious positions adopted by France's leaders? How did the French monarchy decide which side to favor? What led to the infamous Saint Bartholomew's Day Massacre? What resulted from it?

2. How did Spain acquire the dominant position in Europe in the sixteenth century? What were its strengths and weaknesses as a nation? What were Philip II's goals? Which did he fail to achieve? Why?

3. What changes occurred in the religious policies of England's government in the process of establishing the Anglican church? What were Mary I's political objectives? What was Elizabeth I's "settlement"? How was it imposed on England? Who were her opponents? What were their criticisms of her?

4. Why was the Thirty Years' War fought? Could matters have been resolved without war? To what extent did politics determine the outcome of the war? What were the terms and objectives of the Treaty of Westphalia?

KEY TERMS

Congregationalists (p. 303)   **Huguenots** (p. 293)   **Presbyterians** (p. 303)
Counter-Reformation (p. 292)   *politique* (p. 293)

 For additional study resources for this chapter, go to:
www.prenhall.com/kagan3/chapter12

13 European State Consolidation in the Seventeenth and Eighteenth Centuries

CHAPTER HIGHLIGHTS

The Netherlands: Golden Age to Decline The United Netherlands enjoyed a Golden Age in the seventeenth century and was more urbanized than any other area in Europe. Dutch agriculture and financial systems were the models for the rest of Europe. After the death of William of Orange in 1702, the Netherlands entered a period of stagnation and decline.

Two Models of European Political Development England and France developed forms of government that served as models for other European nations. In England, elites forced the monarch to defer to the wishes of Parliament. In France, elites tied their own interests to the power and person of the monarch.

Constitutional Crisis and Settlement in Stuart England Conflict between the king and Parliament led to civil war and the execution of Charles I. From 1649 until the restoration of Charles II in 1660, England was officially ruled by Parliament. In 1688, James II was deposed and replaced with William and Mary in the "Glorious Revolution." Under the leadership of Sir Robert Walpole (1676–1745), Britain enjoyed increased stability and power.

Rise of Absolute Monarchy in France: The World of Louis XIV Louis XIII and his chief advisor Cardinal Richelieu concentrated on centralizing power in the hands of the monarch. Louis XIV's attitudes were shaped by his experience of the *Fronde*. Louis XIV believed he ruled by divine right. His palace at Versailles contributed to the subjugation of the nobility. His near constant wars placed France in grave fiscal danger.

Central and Eastern Europe A weak, elective monarchy and an ineffectual legislative body undermined effective government in Poland. The expansion of the Habsburg Empire was not matched by increased political unity and the empire grew increasingly fragile. In Prussia, militaristic monarchs reformed the state in ways that increased the power and prestige of Prussia's military.

Russia Enters the European Political Arena Under the Romanovs, Russia took its place as a major European power in the seventeenth century. The Russian nobility retained considerable power until Peter the Great assumed personal rule in 1689. Peter was determined to westernize Russia and increase the nation's military strength. When he died in 1725, however, he had failed to appoint a successor and power reverted to nobles and soldiers.

The Ottoman Empire The Ottoman Empire dominated the Muslim world after 1516. However, social and political hurdles blocked innovation and seventeenth-century military defeats marked the beginning of the end for the Empire.

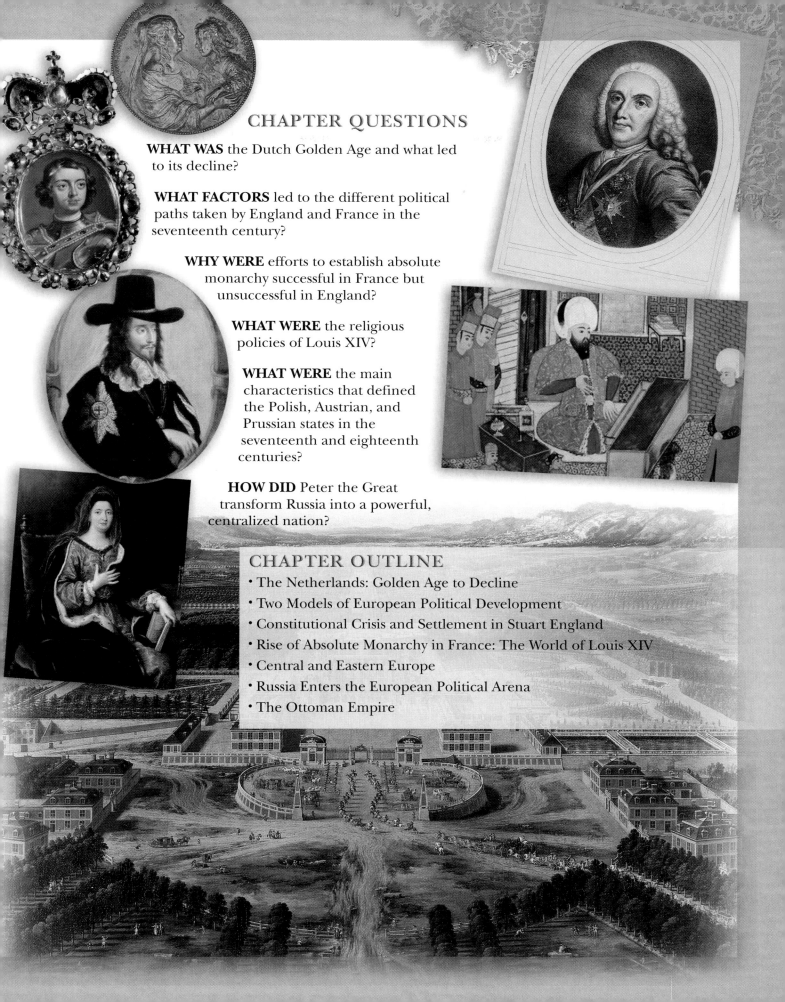

CHAPTER QUESTIONS

WHAT WAS the Dutch Golden Age and what led to its decline?

WHAT FACTORS led to the different political paths taken by England and France in the seventeenth century?

WHY WERE efforts to establish absolute monarchy successful in France but unsuccessful in England?

WHAT WERE the religious policies of Louis XIV?

WHAT WERE the main characteristics that defined the Polish, Austrian, and Prussian states in the seventeenth and eighteenth centuries?

HOW DID Peter the Great transform Russia into a powerful, centralized nation?

CHAPTER OUTLINE

- The Netherlands: Golden Age to Decline
- Two Models of European Political Development
- Constitutional Crisis and Settlement in Stuart England
- Rise of Absolute Monarchy in France: The World of Louis XIV
- Central and Eastern Europe
- Russia Enters the European Political Arena
- The Ottoman Empire

IMAGE KEY

Image Key for pages 312–313 is on page 337.

WHAT WAS the Dutch Golden Age and what led to its decline?

Between the early seventeenth and mid–twentieth centuries, no region so dominated other parts of the world politically, militarily, and economically as Europe. Such had not been the case before this period, nor would it be so after World War II. This era of European dominance coincided with a shift of power with Europe itself from the Mediterranean—in particular, Spain and Portugal—to the states of northern Europe.

By the mid–1700s, five states—Great Britain, France, Austria, Prussia, and Russia—organized themselves politically and came to dominate Europe, and later, large areas of the world through military might and economic strength. These states arose at the expense of Spain, Portugal, the United Provinces of the Netherlands, Poland, Sweden, the Ottoman Empire, and the Holy Roman Empire.

THE NETHERLANDS: GOLDEN AGE TO DECLINE

The United Provinces of the Netherlands was the only genuinely new state to appear in Europe during the early modern period. Resistance to Spanish domination brought its seven component districts together in 1572, and its sovereignty as an independent state was internationally recognized in 1648.

The Netherlands was a republic governed by the States General, an assembly representing its provinces. Whenever a situation demanded a powerful executive, the Dutch would choose a leader from the noble House of Orange. The threat posed by Louis XIV of France brought William III, the *stadtholder* of Holland, to power. William, with his wife Mary, also ascended England's throne. After his death in 1702 and the conclusion of peace with France in 1714, the Dutch republic was restored.

The Netherlands officially embraced the (Calvinist) Reform faith, but allegiance to a state church was not enforced. The Dutch enjoyed a reputation for tolerance, and the Netherlands provided a refuge for Jews driven out of other countries. Religious tolerance spared the Netherlands the internal strife that plagued so many other European states.

URBAN PROSPERITY

The technologically advanced fleet of the Dutch East India Company, shown here at anchor in Amsterdam, linked the Netherlands' economy with that of southeast Asia.

Andries van Eertvelt (1590–1652), "The Return to Amsterdam of the Fleet of the Dutch East India Company in 1599." Oil on copper. Johnny van Haeften Gallery, London, UK. The Bridgeman Art Library

The Dutch were regarded as remarkable by their contemporaries as much for their prosperity as their spirit of tolerance. While other states squandered resources on religious wars, the Dutch invested theirs in economic development. They transformed agriculture, promoted trade and finance, and built an overseas empire. The Netherlands became the most urbanized region in Europe, and the percentage of its population that lived in cities was not equaled by other countries until the industrial era.

The concentration of the Dutch in cities was made possible by agricultural innovations copied throughout Europe. During the seventeenth century, Dutch farmers reclaimed a great deal of land from the sea. The cheap grain that Dutch traders imported from the Baltic to feed their people freed Dutch farmers to devote their land to profitable cash crops (dairy products, meat, and tulip bulbs). Dutch fishing fleets supplied much of the herring (the major source of inexpensive protein) consumed on the Continent, and Dutch mills provided textiles to many parts of Europe. Dutch ships moved much of the trade of Europe, and shipbuilding itself was a highly lucrative industry for the Netherlands. Profits from all these enterprises provided capital for banks, and the Dutch created the most advanced financial system of their day. Shareholders funded ventures such as the Dutch East Indies Company, which took control of the East Asian spice trade away from the Portuguese. The Netherlands retained colonies in Indonesia until World War II.

ECONOMIC DECLINE

For a variety of reasons, the Dutch economy began to weaken in the eighteenth century. After William III's death in 1702, the provinces blocked the rise of another *stadtholder*, and their government suffered from the lack of a strong executive. The fishing industry declined. Dutch manufacturing began to stagnate, and the Dutch lost the technological lead in shipbuilding. As countries began to construct their own vessels rather than relying on Dutch ships to carry their goods, naval supremacy began to pass to England. Weak political leadership handicapped efforts to confront these challenges, but the Netherlands retained considerable influence thanks to its banks and stock exchange.

TWO MODELS OF EUROPEAN POLITICAL DEVELOPMENT

*I*n the second half of the sixteenth century, changing military technology sharply increased the cost of warfare and forced governments to look for new sources of revenue. Monarchs who, like France's kings, found sources of income that were not controlled by nobles or by assemblies representing their wealthy subjects achieved absolute power. In places such as England, where rulers had insufficient funds and limited powers of taxation, kings had to negotiate political policies with the groups on which they depended for financial support, and royal authority was compromised.

The contrast between the French and English political systems (between royal **absolutism** and **parliamentary monarchy**) was visible by the end of the seventeenth century, but not in 1603 when England's Elizabeth I died. The much revered queen had broad support, and Parliaments met during her reign only to approve taxes. The Stuart kings who succeeded to her throne had a different experience. Their fiscal and religious policies alienated their nation's propertied classes and united them against the crown.

Elizabeth's contemporary, Henry IV (r. 1589–1610) of France, presided over a divided nation that was only beginning to emerge from the turmoil of religious war. His successor, Louis XIII (r. 1610–1643), asserted more of the crown's authority, and in the second half of the seventeenth century, Louis XIV brought the French nobles under control. The aristocratic *Parlement* of Paris won the right to register royal decrees before they officially became law, and the king allowed regional *parlements* considerable latitude to deal with local issues. However, the nobles lost interest in turning the Estates General into something comparable to England's Parliament, for they saw a strong monarchy as a source of rich patronage and a guardian of their privileged place in society. Once the king won control over taxation, there was little reason for the Estates General to meet, and no sessions were called between 1614 and 1789 (the eve of the French Revolution).

WHAT FACTORS led to the different political paths taken by England and France in the seventeenth century?

absolutism　Government by a ruler with absolute authority.

parliamentary monarchy English rule by a monarch with some parliamentary guidance or input.

parlements　Regional courts allowed considerable latitude by Louis XIV to deal with local issues.

WHAT WERE the conflicts between Parliament and the monarchy over taxation and religion in early Stuart England?

CONSTITUTIONAL CRISIS AND SETTLEMENT IN STUART ENGLAND

JAMES I

When the childless Elizabeth died in 1603, the heir to her throne was James VI of Scotland, the son of Mary Stuart, Queen of Scots, and the grandnephew of Henry VIII. No one disputed his coronation as James I of England, but his prospects for a successful reign were not good. As a Scot, he was an outsider who had no native constituency to help him deal with England's religious factions or raise the funds needed to pay his kingdom's substantial debts. James was also an advocate of the divine right of kings. He had even written a book on the subject: *A Trew Law of Free Monarchies* (1598). His understanding of monarchy set him on a collision course with English tradition.

England's Parliament, the country's chief check on royal power, met only when the monarch summoned it to authorize tax levies. James figured out ways to fund his government without calling Parliament. Relying on the authority of ill-defined privileges that he alleged were royal prerogatives, he created new customs duties called *impositions*. Members of Parliament resented these, but they preferred to wrangle and negotiate behind the scenes rather than risk serious confrontation.

Religious problems added to the political tensions of James's reign. **Puritans** within the Church of England had hoped James's upbringing as a Scottish Presbyterian would dispose him to support their program for reforming the English church. They wanted to eliminate elaborate priestly rituals and end government of the church by bishops. They favored simple services of worship and congregations run by presbyters elected by the people. James, however, had no intention of turning his national church into a model of representative government—a political system he rejected as an infringement on the divine right of kings. In January 1604, James responded to a list of Puritan grievances (the Millenary Petition) by pledging to maintain and even strengthen the Anglican episcopacy. As he explained, "A Scottish presbytery agreeth as well with monarchy as God and the devil. No bishops, no king." James did, however, yield to the Protestant demand for the use of vernacular Scriptures, and he established a commission to make a new translation. In 1611, the eloquent Authorized (King James) Version of the Bible appeared.

James had no sympathy with English Puritanism's implicit moral agenda. He viewed recreations and sports, which the Puritans condemned, as innocent activities that were good for people. He also believed Puritan rigidity about such things discouraged Roman Catholics from converting to the Church of England. Consequently, in 1618, James tried to force a change by ordering the clergy to read his *Book of Sports*—a royal decree legalizing the playing of games on Sunday—from their pulpits. They refused, and he backed down. Religion even touched on issues of sports and smoking. (See "Encountering the Past: Early Controversy over Tobacco and Smoking.")

James's lifestyle was as offensive to Puritans as his policies, for scandal and corruption made the royal court infamous. The king was powerfully influenced by a few court favorites. One of these, the duke of Buckingham, was rumored to be James's homosexual lover. Buckingham controlled access to the king and openly sold peerages and titles to the highest bidders.

Disappointment and disgust with James led some Puritans voluntarily to leave England for the New World. In 1620, Puritan separatists founded Plymouth

Puritans English Protestants who wanted simpler forms of church ceremony and strictness and gravity in personal behavior.

ENCOUNTERING THE PAST

EARLY CONTROVERSY OVER TOBACCO AND SMOKING

King James defended sports from the Puritan charge that all amusements were sinful when enjoyed on the Sabbath, but the king did not favor all popular pleasures. He was ardently opposed to tobacco, one of the novelties that Europeans discovered in the Americas. Tobacco smoking excited opposition almost from the start. Spanish missionaries associated it with pagan religious practices. Sir Francis Bacon (1561–1626) noted it was addictive, and it was condemned by both Christian and Muslim clerics. None of this, however, impeded the spreading use of the pipe.

In 1604, James published a work that left smokers in no doubt as to his opinion of them and their practice. In *A Counterblast to Tobacco* he wrote, "Have you not reason then to be ashamed, and to forbear this filthy novelty…? In your abuse thereof sinning against God, harming yourselves in person … [with a] custom loathsome to the eye, hateful to the nose, harmful to the brain, dangerous to the lungs, and the black stinking fume thereof, nearest resembling the horrible Stygian smoke of the pit that is bottomless." [*A Counterblast to Tobacco* (1604), reprinted by the Rodale Press, London, 1954, p. 36.] James tried to stem the use of tobacco by heavily taxing it. When this had the result of encouraging smugglers, James lowered the tax. That, however, produced a stream of revenue that became increasingly important to his government. In 1614, he made the importation of tobacco a royal monopoly, and by 1619, Virginia was shipping 40,000 pounds of tobacco to England annually. James's government, like modern ones, put itself in the odd position of depending on taxes imposed to stop the practice that produced those taxes.

Practically from the moment of its introduction into Europe tobacco smoking was controversial. Here a court jester is portrayed as exhaling rabbits from a pipe as three pipe-smoking gentlemen look on.

© Christel Gerstenberg/CORBIS

Colony in Cape Cod Bay. Later in the same decade another larger and better financed group founded the Massachusetts Bay Colony.

James's conduct of foreign affairs roused as much opposition as his domestic policies. James preferred peace to war, for he knew wars would generate debts and debts would make him dependent on Parliament. In 1604, he negotiated a peace with Spain that was long overdue, but some of his subjects saw it as an indication of their king's pro-Catholic sentiments. Their suspicions increased when James tried (unsuccessfully) to relax the penal laws against Catholics. His reasonable hesitation to send English troops to aid German Protestants at the start of the Thirty Years' War offered further confirmation of their fears—as did his plan to wed his heir to the Infanta, the daughter of the king of Spain.

As James aged and his health failed, the reins of his government passed to his son Charles (and to Buckingham). Parliamentary opposition and Protestant sentiment combined to defeat his pro-Spanish foreign policy. The marriage alliance was rejected, and in 1624, shortly before James's death, Parliament pushed England into a war with Spain.

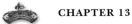

OVERVIEW TWO MODELS OF GOVERNMENT

	France's Absolutism	England's Parliamentary Monarchy
religious factors	Louis XIV, with the support of Catholics, crushed Protestantism for religious uniformity.	A strong Protestant religious movement known as Puritanism limited the monarchy.
institutional differences	Opposition to the monarchy lacked a tradition of liberties, representation, or bargaining tools.	Parliament was to be consulted, and it appealed to concepts of liberty when conflicts arose.
economic policies	Louis XIV made French nobility dependent on his good will by supporting their status.	Political groups invoked traditional liberties to resist the monarchy's economic intrusions.
the role of personalities	Louis XIV had guidance from Cardinals Mazarin and Richelieu, training him to be hardworking.	The four Stuart monarchs, acting on whims, had trouble simply making people trust them.

QUICK REVIEW

Charles I (r. 1625 – 1649)

- 1629: Charles dissolves Parliament in face of criticism of his policies
- Unable to wage foreign wars without funds granted by Parliament
- 1640: Efforts to enforce religious conformity within England and Scotland force Charles to reconvene Parliament

CHARLES I

Parliament favored war with Spain, but distrust of Buckingham undercut its willingness to finance the venture. This forced Charles I (r. 1625–1649), with the help of the unpopular Buckingham, to find novel ways to raise the money he needed. He imposed tariffs and import duties without consulting Parliament, restored discontinued taxes, and subjected people of property (under threat of imprisonment) to the "forced loan" (a levy that the government was, in theory, supposed to refund someday). Soldiers in transit to war zones were also quartered in English homes.

By the time Parliament met in 1628, its members were furious. They refused to acquiesce to the king's request for funds unless he agreed to abide by terms they set forth in a Petition of Right. They demanded that he cease to force loans and collect taxes Parliament had not ratified. They insisted he not imprison citizens without due cause, and they wanted an end to the billeting of troops in private homes. Charles acquiesced to these demands, but Parliament did not trust him to keep his word. The next year after further disputes, Charles dissolved Parliament and did not recall it until 1640.

Without funds from Parliament, Charles could not wage foreign wars. When he made peace with France in 1629 and Spain in 1630, however, some of his subjects accused him of wanting to strengthen his ties with Roman Catholic nations. To allow Charles to rule without having to negotiate with Parliament for money, the king's minister, Thomas Wentworth, earl of Strafford (after 1640), imposed strict efficiency and administrative centralization in the government and exploited every fund-raising device, enforcing previously neglected laws and extending existing taxes into new areas.

Charles might have avoided calling another Parliament if he had maintained the tolerant religious policies of his father. Instead, he made the mistake of trying to impose religious conformity within England and Scotland. Charles favored Anglo-Catholicism, a state church with a powerful episcopacy and plenty of pomp and ceremony. In 1637, William Laud (1573–1645), his religious adviser and archbishop of Canterbury (after 1633), supported his decision to impose the English episcopal system and prayer book on Scotland. This drove the Scots to rebel and forced Charles to convene Parliament.

The members of Parliament were in the peculiar position of wanting to oppose their king's policies while crushing the rebellion against him. Led by John Pym (1584–1643), they refused to discuss funding for the war until Charles agreed to redress their grievances. The angry king responded by dissolving what came, for obvious reasons, to be known as the Short Parliament (April–May 1640). A few months later, the Presbyterian Scots invaded England, defeated an English army at Newburn, and left Charles no choice but to recall Parliament for what proved to be a long, fateful session.

The Long Parliament and Civil War   The aptly named Long Parliament met from 1640 to 1660. It enjoyed support from many important factions. It represented the landowners and the merchant classes who resented the king's financial exactions and paternalistic rule, and many of its members were Puritans who disliked Charles's religious policies.

The House of Commons began by impeaching the king's chief advisers, the earl of Strafford and Archbishop Laud. (Strafford was executed for treason in 1641 and Laud in 1645.) Parliament then abolished the courts that had enforced royal policy and prohibited the levying of new taxes without its consent. It announced it could not be dissolved without its own consent and that no more than three years could elapse between its meetings.

Parliament, however, was sharply divided over religion. All the Puritans—the Presbyterian moderates and the extremist Independents—wanted to abolish the episcopal system and end use of the *Book of Common Prayer.* Many conservatives in both houses of Parliament did not want any changes in England's church at all. These divisions intensified in October 1641, when a rebellion in Ireland compelled the king to ask Parliament for more money for his army. Pym and his followers argued that Charles could not be trusted and that Parliament itself should take command of England's military.

On December 1, 1641, Parliament presented Charles with the Grand Remonstrance, a summary of over two hundred grievances against the crown. In January 1642, Charles responded by invading Parliament to arrest Pym and other leaders, but they escaped. The House of Commons authorized Parliament to raise its own army. The king withdrew from London, and for the next four years (1642–1646) civil war engulfed England, with the King's supporters known as Cavaliers and the parliamentary opposition as Roundheads.

OLIVER CROMWELL AND THE PURITAN REPUBLIC

Two things contributed to Parliament's victory. The first was an alliance with Scotland in 1643 that committed Parliament to a presbyterian system of church government. The second was the reorganization of the parliamentary army under Oliver Cromwell (1599–1658), a middle-aged country squire who favored the Independents. He and his "godly men" wanted neither the king's episcopal system nor Scotland's presbyterian organization. The only state church they supported was one that granted freedom of worship to Protestant dissenters.

Defeated by June 1645, for the next several years Charles tried to exploit the divisions within Parliament, but members who might have been sympathetic to the monarch were expelled from Parliament in December 1648. On January 30, 1649, after trial by a special court, Parliament executed the king and abolished the monarchy, the House of Lords, and the Anglican church. The civil war had become a political revolution that turned England into a Puritan Republic.

From 1649 to 1660, England was officially governed by Parliament, but Cromwell was in firm control. The military achievements of the Republic were

King CHARLES *the* FIRST *in the* HOUSE *of* COMMONS, *demanding the* FIVE *impeached* MEMBERS *to be delivered up to his* AUTHORITY.

One of the key moments in the conflict between Charles I and Parliament occurred in January 1642 when Charles personally arrived at the House of Commons intent on arresting five members who had been responsible for for opposing him. They had already escaped. Thereafter Charles departed London to raise his army. The event was subsequently often portrayed in English art. The present illustration is from an eighteenth-century engraving.

The Granger Collection, New York

QUICK REVIEW

The Long Parliament (1640–1660)
- Enjoyed wide support
- Members united in desire to curb power of monarchy but divided on issue of religious reform
- Request by king for more money in October 1641 intensified divisions

Oliver Cromwell's New Model Army defeated the royalists in the English Civil War. After the execution of Charles I in 1649, Cromwell dominated the short-lived English republic, conquered Ireland and Scotland, and ruled as Lord Protector from 1653 until his death in 1658.

Stock Montage, Inc./Historical Pictures Collection

impressive. Cromwell conquered Ireland and Scotland and united the countries that now compose Great Britain. Cromwell was, however, a better general than a politician. In 1653, when the House of Commons entertained a motion to disband his expensive army of 50,000 men, he disbanded Parliament.

Thereafter Cromwell ruled as Lord Protector according to a written constitution (the Instrument of Government) that created a military dictatorship. It had minimal popular support. Commerce suffered, and people chafed under Cromwell's rigorous enforcement of Puritan codes of conduct. The Lord Protector was as intolerant of Anglicans as the king had been of Puritans. (See "History's Voices: John Milton Defends Freedom to Print Books.") By the time he died in 1658, a majority of the English were ready to end experimentation and return to traditional institutions of government. In 1660, the exiled Charles II (r. 1660–1685), son of Charles I, was invited home to restore the Stuart monarchy.

CHARLES II AND THE RESTORATION OF THE MONARCHY

Charles II, a man of considerable charm and political skill, ascended the throne amid great rejoicing, and England returned to the institutions it had rejected in 1642: a hereditary monarchy that was not required to consult with Parliament, and an Anglican church with bishops and an official prayer book. Charles's secret Catholic sympathies led him to favor religious toleration, which offered Catholics as much safety as they could hope for in England. Few in Parliament, however, believed the state could risk giving free rein to religious diversity. Between 1661 and 1665, Parliament enacted the Clarendon Code, which excluded Roman Catholics, Presbyterians, and Independents from religious and political offices. Penalties were imposed for attending non-Anglican worship services.

Charles's foreign policy centered on a series of naval wars with Holland. In 1670, Charles allied with the French, who were also at war with Holland, and received French aid to underwrite the cost of his campaign. In exchange for a substantial subsidy from France's King Louis XIV, Charles secretly pledged to announce, at some propitious moment, his conversion to Catholicism. The time to fulfill that promise never came.

In 1672, Charles tried to rally his English subjects in support of the war with Holland (and to show good faith with Louis XIV) by issuing the Declaration of Indulgence, which suspended the laws against Roman Catholics and Protestant nonconformists. Parliament, however, opposed the king's efforts to promote religious tolerance, and it forced Charles to rescind the declaration by refusing to grant him money for the war. Parliament also passed the Test Act, which barred Roman Catholics from office by requiring royal officials to swear oaths repudiating the doctrine of transubstantiation. The Test Act was aimed in large measure at the king's brother, James, duke of York, heir to Charles's throne and a devout convert to Catholicism.

In 1678, a notorious liar, Titus Oates, accused Charles's Catholic wife of plotting with Jesuits and Irishmen to kill her husband and bring his Catholic brother to the throne. Oates's alleged "Popish Plot" whipped Parliament into a state of hysteria. Several people were executed, and a faction in Parliament, the Whigs, nearly won passage for a bill excluding James from the succession.

HISTORY'S VOICES

JOHN MILTON DEFENDS FREEDOM TO PRINT BOOKS

Some Puritans worried that Parliaments might govern as tyrannically as kings. Parliament's imposition of strict censorship during the English Civil War prompted John Milton, the poet who wrote Paradise Lost, to compose an essay ("Areopagitica," 1644) in defense of freedom of the press.

WHY DOES Milton think it may be more harmful to attack a book than to attack a person? Is he right?

I deny not but that it is of greatest concern in the Church and Commonwealth to have a vigilant eye how books demean themselves as well as men; and thereafter to confine, imprison, and do sharpest justice on them as [if they were criminals]; for books are not absolutely dead things, but do contain a progeny of life in them to be as active as that soul was whose progeny they are; nay, they do preserve as in a vial the purest efficacy and extraction of that living intellect that bred them. ... He who kills a man kills a reasonable creature, God's Image; but he who destroys a good book, kills reason itself, kills the Image of God, as it were. ... Many a man lives [as] a burden to the Earth; but a good book is the precious life-blood of a master spirit, embalmed and treasured up on purpose to a life beyond life. It is true, no age can restore a life, whereof, perhaps there is no great loss; and revolutions of ages do not oft recover the loss of a rejected truth, for the want of which whole nations fare the worse. We should be wary, therefore, what persecution we raise against the living labours of public men, how we spill that seasoned life of man preserved and stored up in books; since we see a kind of homicide may be thus committed, sometimes a martyrdom, and if it extends to the whole impression, a kind of massacre, whereof the execution ends not in the slaying of an elemental life, but strikes at that ethereal ... essence, the breath of reason itself; slays an immortality rather than a life.

From J. A. St. John, ed., *The Prose Works of John Milton* (London: H. G. Bohn, 1843–1853), 2:8–9.

Chronically short of money and having little hope of persuading Parliament to grant him what he wanted, Charles increased customs duties, extracted more financial aid from Louis XIV, and avoided convening a Parliament after 1681. By the time he died in 1685 (after making a deathbed conversion to Catholicism), he had cowed his opponents and positioned James II, his successor, to call a Parliament filled with royal friends.

THE "GLORIOUS REVOLUTION"

James II (r. 1685–1688) did not know how to use his opportunities. He alienated Parliament by insisting on the repeal of the Test Act. When Parliament balked, he dissolved it and flaunted the Test Act by openly appointing known Catholics to high offices. In 1687, he issued a Declaration of Indulgence that suspended religious tests and permitted free worship.

A birth galvanized James's enemies into action. They had hoped he would die without a male heir and the throne would pass to Mary, his eldest daughter. She was a Protestant and the wife of William III of Orange, *stadtholder* of the Protestant Netherlands, great-grandson of William the Silent, and the leader of the European states that were threatened by Louis XIV's military ventures. On June 20, 1688, James's second wife alarmed England's Protestants by giving birth to a son, a Catholic heir to their throne. Within days of the boy's birth, Whig and

QUICK REVIEW

James II (r. 1685–1688)
- Policy of toleration of Catholicism alienated Parliament
- June 20, 1688: Birth of son alarms opponents
- James forced to leave England and William and Mary of Orange invited to become new monarchs

Tory members of Parliament had agreed to invite William and Mary to invade England and establish a monarchy that would preserve "traditional liberties."

William of Orange's army landed in England in November 1688, and James, receiving no support from his subjects, was forced to flee to France. Parliament then carried out a bloodless **"Glorious Revolution"** by declaring the throne vacant and proclaiming William and Mary its heirs. The new monarchs, in their turn, issued a Bill of Rights that limited their power and protected the civil liberties of England's privileged classes. Henceforth, England's rulers would be subject to law and would govern with the consent of a Parliament that convened in regular sessions and not only when summoned by the crown. The Bill of Rights prohibited Roman Catholics from occupying the English throne, but the Toleration Act of 1689 legalized all forms of Protestantism (except those that denied the Trinity). Roman Catholicism was outlawed.

In 1701, the Act of Settlement closed the "century of strife" (as the seventeenth century came to be known in England) by decreeing that the English crown would pass to the Protestant House of Hanover in Germany if none of the children of Queen Anne (r. 1702–1714), the last of the Stuart monarchs, survived her. Anne did outlive her children, and in 1714, the elector of Hanover became King George I of England—the third foreigner to occupy England's throne in just over a century.

THE AGE OF WALPOLE

Despite surviving a challenge to the throne in 1715, George I's reign remained politically unstable until Sir Robert Walpole (1676–1745) took over the helm of government. Walpole, regarded as the first prime minister of Great Britain, owed his power to royal support, his ability to handle the House of Commons, and his control of government patronage. He maintained peace abroad, promoted the status quo at home, and presided over an expansion of foreign trade. The central government did not interfere with the local power of nobles and other landowners, who consequently cooperated by serving as administrators, judges, and military commanders, and also collected and paid taxes.

The power of British monarchs and their ministers had real limits. Members of Parliament maintained independent views, and Britain enjoyed freedom of speech, freedom of association, and religious toleration. British political life became the model for all progressive Europeans who questioned the development of absolutism on the Continent.

15.1
Richelieu: Controlling the Nobility

WHY WERE efforts to establish absolute monarchy successful in France but unsuccessful in England?

"Glorious Revolution"
Parliament's bloodless 1688 declaration of a vacant throne and proclamation that William and Mary were its heirs.

RISE OF ABSOLUTE MONARCHY IN FRANCE: THE WORLD OF LOUIS XIV

Historians once portrayed Louis XIV's reign (r. 1643–1715) as a time when the French monarchy exerted far-reaching, direct control of the nation at all levels. A somewhat different picture has now emerged.

The French monarchy only gradually achieved the firm authority for which it became renowned in the late seventeenth century. Two powerful chief ministers, Cardinal Richelieu (1585–1642), under Louis XIII (r. 1610–1643), and then Cardinal Mazarin (1602–1661), laid the groundwork for Louis XIV's absolutism. They attempted to impose direct royal administration on France, and Richelieu circumscribed many of the political privileges that French Protestants had gained under the Edict of Nantes (1598). These policies provoked widespread rebellions among French nobles between 1649 and 1652. Though unsuccessful, these rebellions, known as the ***Fronde*** (after the slingshots used by street boys) convinced Louis XIV and his advisors that, even as they concentrated unprecedented authority in the monarchy, they needed to assure nobles and other wealthy groups of their social standing and influence on the local level.

YEARS OF PERSONAL RULE

Upon Mazarin's death in 1661, Louis XIV assumed personal control of the government at the age of twenty-three. With no chief minister to resist, rebellious nobles would now be challenging the king directly. Devoting enormous personal energy to his political tasks, Louis ruled through councils that controlled foreign affairs, the army, domestic administration, and economic regulations. He depended on families with long histories in royal service, and also promoted figures just rising in the social structure, thus ensuring their loyalty to the crown, not to local power bases.

Louis made sure that the nobility and other social groups benefited from the growth of his own authority. He limited the national, but not local influence of noble institutions, and never tried to abolish them. He conferred with regional judicial bodies, called *parlements*, before making rulings that would affect them. Although he curtailed the power of the Parlement of Paris in 1673, even this act had the support of many regional *parlements* and other authorities that had long resented its power.

VERSAILLES

Louis and his advisors became masters of propaganda and political image creation. By manipulating symbols, Louis never missed an opportunity to impress the grandeur of his crown on the French people, most especially on the French nobility. For example, when the *dauphin* (the heir to the French throne) was born in 1662, Louis appeared for the celebration dressed as a Roman emperor.

Gold fleur-de-lis with gold crown.

Neil Lukas ©Dorling Kindersley, Courtesy of l'Etablissement Public du Musee et du Domaine National de Versailles

Fronde Widespread rebellions in France between 1649 and 1652 (named after a slingshot used by street ruffians) aimed at reversing the drift toward absolute monarchy and preserving local autonomy.

Versailles, as painted in 1668 by Pierre Patel the Elder (1605–1676). The central building is the hunting lodge built by Louis XIII earlier in the century. Louis XIV added the wings, the gardens, and the forecourt.

Pierre Patel, *Perspective View of Versailles*, Chateau de Versailles et de Trianon, Versailles, France. Copyright Giraudon/Art Resource, NY

The palace of Versailles was the central element of the monarchy's image. Built between 1676 and 1708 on the outskirts of Paris, Versailles became Louis's permanent residence after 1682. Designed and decorated to proclaim the glory of the Sun King, as Louis was known, it had magnificent fountains and gardens, housed thousands of the more important nobles and officials, and had stables that could hold 12,000 horses.

By ruling personally, Louis became the chief source of favors and patronage in France. Court life was organized around every aspect of his own daily routine. Moments near the king—such as the chance to hold Louis's night candle as he went to bed—were important to most court nobles because they were effectively excluded from the real business of government. Many bobles depleted their resources to remain in residence at Versailles, or depended on royal patronage to reside there. Some nobles, of course, avoided Versailles, managing their own estates. Yet even here Louis's support of France's traditional social structure and noble privileges strengthened his reign.

KING BY DIVINE RIGHT

An important source for Louis's concept of royal authority was his devout tutor, the political theorist Bishop Jacques-Bénigne Bossuet (1627–1704). Bossuet defended what he called the "**divine right of kings**" and cited examples of Old Testament rulers divinely appointed by and answerable only to God. Medieval popes had insisted that only God could judge a pope; so Bossuet argued that only God—not mere nobles, nor parliaments—could judge a king. Such assumptions lay behind Louis XIV's alleged declaration: "*L'etat, c' ést moi*" ("I am the state").

Despite these claims, Louis's rule did not exert the oppressive control over the daily lives of his subjects that police states would do in the nineteenth and twentieth centuries. His absolutism functioned in the making of war and peace, the regulation of religion, and the oversight of economic activity. Local institutions and elites retained their social and financial privileges. Unlike the Stuart kings of England, Louis prevented noble interference to his authority on the national level.

LOUIS'S EARLY WARS

By the late 1660s, France was superior to any other European nation in population, administrative bureaucracy, army, and national unity. Because of the economic policies of his minister Jean-Baptiste Colbert (1619–1683), Louis could afford to raise and maintain a large, powerful army. His enemies claimed that Louis wished to dominate all of Europe, but it would appear that his chief military and foreign policy goal was to secure France's international boundaries—especially along the Spanish Netherlands, the Franche-Comté, Alsace, and Lorraine, traditional areas from which foreign armies had invaded France. Nevertheless, Louis's pursuit of French interests threatened and terrified neighboring states and led them to form coalitions against France.

Louis's early wars included conflicts with Spain and the United Netherlands. The first was the War of the Devolution, in which Louis contended that inheritance of the Spanish Netherlands should have "devolved" upon his first wife, Marie Thérèse. In 1667, Louis's armies invaded Flanders and the Franche-Comté, but was repulsed by England, Sweden, and the United Provinces. The next year, under the Treaty of Aix-la-Chapelle, Louis gained control of some towns on the Netherlands border. Louis invaded the Netherlands again in 1672, but was met by an alliance that included the Prince of Orange, the future

"divine right of kings" The belief that God appoints kings and that kings are accountable only to God for how they use their power.

William III of England, the Holy Roman Emperor, Spain, Lorraine, and Brandenburg. The Peace of Nijmwegen in 1678 and 1679 ended the war inconclusively, but France gained more territory, including the Franche-Comté.

LOUIS'S REPRESSIVE RELIGIOUS POLICIES

Louis believed that political unity and stability required religious conformity. To that end he repressed both Roman Catholics and Protestants.

Suppression of the Jansenists   The French had long guarded their ecclesiastical independence or "Gallican Liberties" from papal authority in Rome, but after King Henry IV converted to Roman Catholicism in 1593, Jesuit influence in France grew. The Jesuit religious order, fiercely loyal to Papal authority, monopolized the education of French upper-class men, even serving as confessors to Henry IV, Louis XIII, and Louis XIV.

In the 1630s, a Roman Catholic religious movement known as **Jansenism**, named after the Flemish theologian and bishop of Ypres Cornelius Jansen (d. 1638), arose in opposition to Jesuit theology and political influence. Influenced by the teachings of St. Augustine (354–430), the serious and uncompromising Jansenists opposed Jesuit teachings about grace and salvation. They believed that original sin had so corrupted humankind that individuals could do nothing good nor secure their own salvation without divine grace.

The Jansenists, whose theology resembled Calvinism, were known to live extremely pious and morally austere lives. Though firm Roman Catholics, they resembled English Puritans. Jansenism spread among prominent families in Paris and became associated with opposition to royal authority. Some Jansenist families had been involved in the Fronde.

In 1653, Pope Innocent X declared heretical five Jansenist theological propositions on grace and salvation and banned a book by Jansen that attacked Jesuit teachings. In 1713, Pope Clement XI issued another official condemnation of Jansenism. Louis XIV supported these papal decisions, but in so doing, turned his back on the long tradition of protecting **Gallican Liberties** of the French Church. This had long-term political significance, for it fostered a core of opposition to royal authority. During the eighteenth century, French judicial bodies, such as the Parlement of Paris, reasserted their authority and held in common with Jansenists resistance to the Monarchy's power and what eighteenth-century public opinion saw as the corruption of the French royal court.

Revocation of the Edict of Nantes   After the Edict of Nantes in 1598, relations between the Catholic majority and Protestant minority remained hostile. French Huguenots numbered about 1.75 million out of a total population of approximately 18 million, but their numbers were declining. The French Catholic church had long supported their persecution as both pious and patriotic. After the Peace of Nijmwegen, persecution of Protestants intensified. Influenced by his mistress and eventually second wife Madame de Maintenon (1635–1719), a deeply pious Catholic who drew Louis toward a much more devout religious observance, the king launched a methodical campaign against

Pierre Mignard "Portrait of Françoise d'Aubigne marquise de Maíntenon (1635–1719), mistress and second wife of Louis XIV," by Pierre Mignard (1612–1695)

Oil on canvas, 128 x 97 cm. Inv.: MV 3637. Chateaux de Versailles et de Trianon, Versailles. Bridgeman-Giraudon/Art Resource, NY

Jansenism   Appearing in the 1630s, it followed the teachings of St. Augustine, who stressed the role divine grace played in human salvation.

Gallican Liberties   The French Roman Catholic Church's ecclesiastical independence of papal authority in Rome.

the Huguenots. Intending to unify France religiously, Louis hounded Huguenots out of public life, banning them from government office and certain professions. In October 1685, Louis revoked the Edict of Nantes. Under the religious repression that followed. Protestant churches and schools were closed, nonconverting laity were forced to be galley slaves, and Protestant children were baptized by Catholic priests.

The revocation was a major blunder. Henceforth, Protestants across Europe considered Louis a fanatic who must be resisted at all costs. More than a quarter million people, many highly skilled, left France and formed new communities in England, Germany, Holland, and the New World. France became a symbol of religious repression in contrast to England's reputation for moderate, if not complete, religious toleration.

LOUIS'S LATER WARS

The League of Augsburg and the Nine Years' War   After the Treaty of Nijmwegen in 1678–1679, Louis maintained his army at full strength and restlessly probed beyond his borders. New defensive coalitions formed against him, one of which, the League of Augsburg, supported by Habsburg emperor Leopold I (r. 1658–1705), included England, Spain, Sweden, the United Provinces, and the major German states. The League and France battled each other for nine years, while England and France struggled to control North America. The Peace of Ryswick ended the war in 1697, securing Holland's borders and thwarting Louis's expansion into Germany.

War of the Spanish Succession   The last Habsburg king of Spain, Charles II (r. 1665–1700), died in 1700 without direct heirs. He left his entire inheritance to Louis's grandson Philip of Anjou, who became Philip V of Spain (r. 1700–1746). Spain and the trade with its American empire appeared to have fallen to France, prompting England, Holland, and the Holy Roman Empire to form the Grand Alliance in 1701 to preserve the existing balance of power. The Alliance also wanted to secure Flanders permanently as a barrier between Holland and France and gain a fair share of the Spanish inheritance for the emperor (who was a Habsburg). Louis increased the stakes by recognizing the Stuart claim to the English throne.

The War of the Spanish Succession, which lasted from 1701 to 1714, enveloped western Europe, and marked the first time Louis went to war with inadequate finances, a poorly equipped army, and mediocre generals. The English, in contrast, had advanced weaponry (flintlock rifles, paper cartridges, and ring bayonets) and superior, more maneuverable tactics. John Churchill, the Duke of Marlborough (1650–1722) scored successes in every major engagement, although French arms triumphed in Spain. By 1714, Philip V remained king of Spain, England had become a Mediterranean power by securing Gibraltar and the island of Minorca, and Louis had recognized the right of the House of Hanover to the English throne.

FRANCE AFTER LOUIS XIV

Despite France's military reverses, it remained a great power. Although less strong in 1715 than in 1680, it still had the largest European population, an advanced, if troubled, economy, and Louis's administrative structure. Moreover, all the major states of Europe were drained by war. Louis XIV was succeeded by his five-year-old great-grandson Louis XV (r. 1715–1774). The boy's uncle, the duke of Orléans,

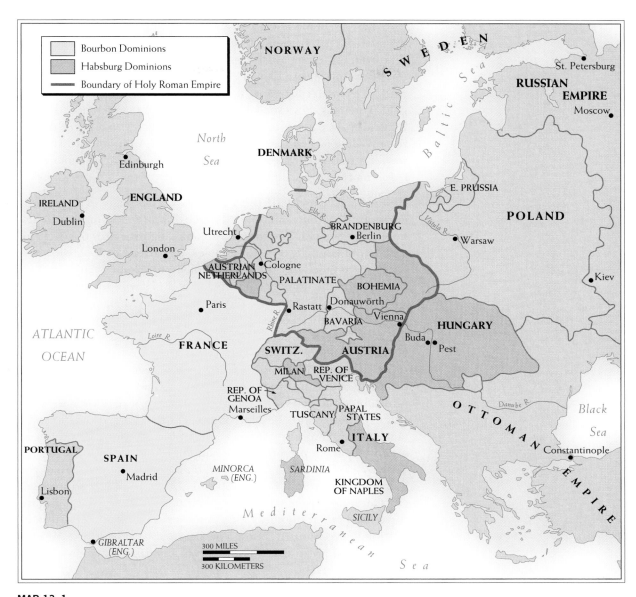

MAP 13–1
Europe in 1714   The War of the Spanish Succession ended a year before the death of Louis XIV. The Bourbons had secured the Spanish throne, but Spain had forfeited its possessions in Flanders and Italy.

HOW DID the territorial makeup of Europe change during the long reign of Louis XIV?

presided over a regency that lasted until 1720 and that was marked by financial and moral scandals, which further undermined the monarchy's faltering prestige.

John Law and the Mississippi Bubble   The duke of Orléans was a gambler, and for a time he entrusted the kingdom's financial management to John Law (1671–1729), a Scottish mathematician and fellow gambler. With the regent's permission, Law established a bank in Paris that, by issuing paper money, Law believed would stimulate France's economic recovery. Law then organized the Mississippi Company, which had a monopoly on trading privileges with the French colony of Louisiana in North America, and which took over management of the French national debt.

Law's scheme backfired, harming France economically and bringing disgrace on the government. In exchange for government bonds, which had fallen sharply in value, the Mississippi Company issued shares of its own stock. In 1719 the stock's price rose handsomely. Smart investors netted profits by selling their stock in exchange for paper money at Law's bank, and then sought to trade it for gold. The bank, however, lacked enough gold to redeem all the paper money. By 1720, all gold payments in France were halted. The burst of the so-called Mississippi Bubble forced Law to flee the country. Although the Mississippi Company was later reorganized and functioned profitably, fear of paper money and speculation marked French life for decades.

Renewed Authority of the *Parlements*   The duke of Orléans made a second decision that diminished the monarchy's power. Attempting to draw the French nobility once again into the decision-making processes of government, he set up a system of councils on which nobles were to serve along with bureaucrats. The experiment failed, for the years of idle noble domestication at Versailles had removed from the nobility both the talent and desire to govern.

The nobles, however, did not surrender their ancient ambition to assert their rights, privileges, and local influence over those of the monarchy. Their most effective instrument was the *parlements,* or courts dominated by the nobility. Different from the English Parliament, these French courts did not legislate; instead they had power to recognize or not to recognize the legality of an act or law promulgated by the monarch. Reversing Louis XIV's policy, the duke of Orléans reinstituted the *parlements'* full power to allow or disallow laws. In the eighteenth century, these courts became natural centers for aristocratic and popular resistance to royal authority. Thus, they—not the monarch—would come to be seen as more nearly representing the nation.

By 1726, the general political direction of the nation had come under the authority of Cardinal Fleury (1653–1743), who sought to maintain the monarchy's authority (for example, by continuing repression of Jansenists) and to preserve the French nobility's local interests. Like Walpole in Britain, he pursued economic prosperity at home and peace abroad. Also like Walpole, after 1740, Fleury could not prevent France from entering a worldwide colonial conflict. (See Chapter 16.)

CENTRAL AND EASTERN EUROPE

WHAT WERE the main characteristics that defined the Polish, Austrian, and Prussian states in the seventeenth and eighteenth centuries?

Central and eastern Europe was economically much less advanced than western Europe. Except for the Baltic ports, its economy was agrarian. It had fewer cities, many more large estates worked by serfs, and no overseas empires. Its political authorities were weak because the almost constant warfare of the seventeenth century encouraged temporary and shifting loyalties among princes and aristocracies.

In the late 1600s, three strong dynasties, whose rulers aspired to the absolutism then being constructed in France, emerged in central and eastern Europe and would dominate the region until the end of World War I in 1918. The Austrian Habsburgs began to consolidate power outside Germany, while Prussia under the Hohenzollern dynasty emerged among the north German states. Most important, Russia under the Romanov dynasty at the opening of the eighteenth century became a major military and naval power. By contrast, in the eighteenth century Poland failed to establish a viable centralized government.

POLAND: ABSENCE OF STRONG CENTRAL AUTHORITY

In no other part of Europe was the failure to maintain a competitive political position so complete as in Poland. The fault lay with the Polish nobility, who blocked every attempt to establish an effective central government. The Polish monarchy was elective, and rivalries among the noble families prevented them from choosing one of their own as king. Most of Poland's monarchs, therefore, were outsiders and puppets of foreign powers. The Polish nobles belonged to a central legislative body called the **Sejm**, or diet. It specifically excluded representatives from corporate bodies, such as towns, and was virtually powerless. A practice known as *liberum veto* allowed any one of its members unilaterally to disband its meetings. The need to achieve unanimous agreement before taking any action made it extremely difficult for the diet to do much. Government as it was developing elsewhere in Europe simply was not tolerated in Poland, and during the last half of the eighteenth century, Poland temporarily disappeared from the map of Europe.

THE HABSBURG EMPIRE AND THE PRAGMATIC SANCTION

The close of the Thirty Years' War marked a fundamental turning point in the history of the Austrian Habsburgs. They had hoped, in alliance with their Spanish cousins, to bring Germany under their control and back to the Catholic fold. They failed, and with the decline of Spanish power, were on their own.

After 1648, Habsburg influence grew in three areas. The dynasty still had a firm hold on the title of Holy Roman Emperor, but the power of this crown depended less on the force of arms than on the cooperation it could elicit from the various political bodies in the empire, which included large German states (such as Saxony, Hanover, Bavaria, and Brandenburg), as well as scores of cities, bishoprics, principalities, and territories. The Habsburgs also consolidated power outside the empire, in Bohemia, Moravia, Silesia, Hungary, Croatia, and Transylvania. Lastly, under the Treaty of Rastadt in 1714, they claimed the former Spanish Netherlands and Lombardy in northern Italy. Thereafter, Habsburg power and influence would be based primarily on the territories outside of Germany. (See Map 13–2.)

The diversity of the Habsburgs' empire limited its ability to unify. In each of the many territories, the Habsburgs ruled by virtue of a different title—king, archduke, duke—and needed the cooperation of the local nobility, which was not always forthcoming. Various languages, customs, and faiths hindered political unification, and most of the governmental bodies dealt with only a portion of the Habsburg holdings.

Despite these internal difficulties, Leopold I (r. 1658–1705) managed to resist the aggression of the Ottoman Empire in the south and of Louis XIV in the west. He achieved sovereignty over Hungary in 1699 and took control of much of the Balkan Peninsula and western Romania, including access to the Adriatic and Mediterranean seas through the port of Trieste. Joseph I (r. 1705–1711) continued Leopold's policies.

Charles VI (r. 1711–1740) succeeded Joseph and added a new problem to the chronic one of territorial diversity. Charles had no male heir and only a very weak precedent for a female ruler of the Habsburg domains. He feared a breakup of the empire after his death—the fate that had befallen the Spanish Habsburgs in 1700. Therefore he devoted most of his reign to seeking the approval of his family, the estates of his realms, and the major foreign powers for a document called **Pragmatic Sanction**, which provided the legal basis for a single line of Habsburg inheritance through his daughter Maria Theresa (r. 1740–1780). He did indeed

Sejm   Central legislative body to which the Polish nobles belonged.

Pragmatic Sanction   Document recognizing Charles VI's daughter Maria Theresa as his heir.

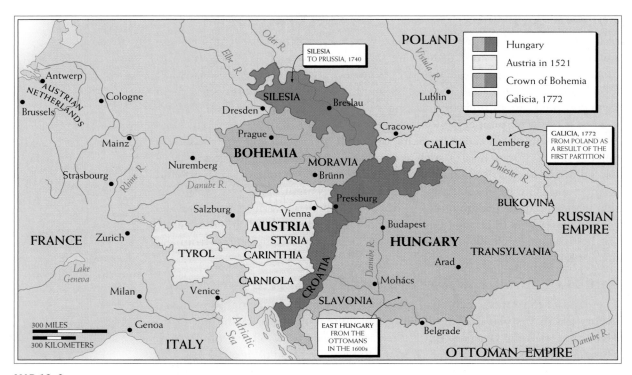

MAP 13–2

The Austrian Habsburg Empire, 1521–1772   The empire had three main units—Austria, Bohemia, and Hungary. Expansion was mainly eastward: eastern Hungary from the Ottomans (seventeenth century) and Galicia from Poland (1772). Meantime, Silesia was lost after 1740, but the Habsburgs remained Holy Roman Emperors.

WHY WAS expansion of the Austrian Hasburg Empire mostly eastward?

secure the legal unity of the empire, but had to make various concessions to nobles and other rules. Maria Theresa inherited the line of succession, but had neither a strong army nor a full treasury. This invited foreign aggression, and within two months of Charles VI's death, Frederick II of Prussia invaded the Habsburg province of Silesia in eastern Germany.

PRUSSIA AND THE HOHENZOLLERNS

The rise of Prussia occurred within the German power vacuum created by the Peace of Westphalia of 1648. The Hohenzollern family, which had ruled Brandenburg since 1417, inherited a series of disconnected German lands, including Cleves, Mark, Ravensburg, and East Prussia. Although their territories lacked good natural resources, by the late 1600s, within the Holy Roman Empire the Hohenzollern holdings rivaled only those of the Habsburgs.

The person who began to forge these areas into a modern state was Frederick William (r. 1640–1688), who became known as the Great Elector. He established himself and his successors as the central uniting power by breaking the medieval parliaments or estates, organizing a royal bureaucracy, and building a strong army. He collected taxes by force, using the money to build an army, which allowed him to enforce his will without the approval of the nobility.

To obtain the support and obedience of the **Junkers**, or German noble landlords, the Elector allowed them to have almost complete control over the serfs on their estates. Frederick William co-opted potential noble opponents by choosing Junkers as administrators and army officers, with the tax burden falling

Junkers   (Prussian nobles) They were allowed to demand absolute obedience from the serfs on their estates in exchange for their support of the Hohenzollerns.

most heavily on the peasants and urban classes. All officials and army officers took an oath of loyalty directly to the Elector. This system made the army and the Elector the unifying components of the state.

Despite Frederick William's accomplishments, the house of Hohenzollern did not possess a crown. The Great Elector's son, Frederick I (r. 1688–1713) achieved this status during the War of the Spanish Succession by putting his army at the disposal of the Habsburg Holy Roman Emperor Leopold I, who permitted Frederick to assume the title of "King of Prussia" in 1701.

His successor, Frederick William I (r. 1713–1740), was one of the most effective Hohenzollern rulers. He instilled military priorities and values throughout Prussian government, society, and daily life, and increased the Prussian army's size from about 39,000 in 1713 to over 80,000 in 1740. This made the army Europe's third or fourth largest, even though Prussia's population, in contrast, ranked thirteenth in size. Laws, customs, and royal attention made the officer corps the highest social class of the state, attracting the sons of Junkers to military service. The army, *Junker* nobility, and monarchy were thus forged into a single political entity. It has often been said that whereas other states possessed armies, the Prussian army possessed its state.

Frederick William I built the best army in Europe, but he also avoided conflict. The army was a symbol of Prussian power and unity, not an instrument for foreign adventures. However, on succeeding to the throne, his son Federick II (Frederick the Great, r. 1740–1786) almost immediately invaded Silesia, thereby upsetting the Pragmatic Sanction and crystallizing the Austrian-Prussian rivalry for control of Germany.

RUSSIA ENTERS THE EUROPEAN POLITICAL ARENA

*T*he rise of Prussia and the consolidation of the Austrian Habsburg domains doubtless seemed to many at the time only one more shift in the old game of German politics. Russia's entrance into the European political arena was, however, something wholly new. Russia had long been considered a part of Europe only by courtesy. Hemmed in by Sweden on the Baltic and by the Ottoman Empire on the Black Sea, it had no warm-water ports. Its chief outlet to the West (the port of Archangel on the White Sea) was closed by ice during part of the year. Russia was a land of vast but unexploited potential.

THE ROMANOV DYNASTY

The reign of Ivan IV, "the Terrible," (1533–1584) was followed by a period of anarchy and civil war. In 1613, an assembly of nobles tried to end the confusion of this "Time of Troubles" by uniting in support of Michael Romanov (r. 1613–1654). His dynasty remained in power in Russia until 1917.

Michael Romanov and his two successors. Alexis I (r. 1654–1676) and Theodore III (r. 1676–1682), maintained order, but their country was weak and poor. Its government was dominated by an entrenched hereditary nobility (the *boyars*), and it was only barely able to meet the challenges posed by peasant revolts and raids by Cossacks (horsemen who lived on the steppe frontier). The *streltsy*, Moscow's garrison, was also prone to mutiny.

PETER THE GREAT

In 1682, the *streltsy* decided a bloodily disputed succession by placing two boys on Russia's shaky throne: Peter I, "the Great" (r. 1682–1725) and Ivan V. The boys' elder sister, Sophia, served as their regent until Peter overthrew her in 1689.

QUICK REVIEW

Frederick William's Army
- Each district required to contribute men
- Exhaustive training produced the best army in Europe
- Frederick William refrained from using the army he built

HOW DID Peter the Great transform Russia into a powerful, centralized nation?

QUICK REVIEW

Peter I (r. 1682–1725)
- Resolved to increase power of the monarchy
- Imported products and people from the West in pursuit of this goal
- After 1697 tour of Europe, returned to Russia determined to westernize country

Peter the Great (r. 1682–1725), seeking to make Russia a military power, reorganized the country's political and economic structures. His reign saw Russia enter fully into European power politics.

The Apotheosis of Tsar Peter the Great 1672–1725 "by unknown artist, 1710. Historical Museum, Moscow, Russia E.T. Archive

He ruled thereafter, although theoretically sharing power with his co-tsar the sickly Ivan's death in 1696.

Like Louis XIV of France, who, as a boy, experienced the upheaval of the *fronde,* Peter resolved to establish an overwhelmingly powerful monarchy, and he turned to the West for help in doing this. Products and workers from the West had filtered into Russia, and Europe's culture, particularly its military science, intrigued Peter. In 1697, Peter made a famous tour of Europe. For convenience, he traveled officially incognito rather than as a head of state. (This minimized the ceremonial functions that diplomatic courtesy would otherwise have required.) The European leaders he visited regarded their almost seven-foot-tall guest as crude, but Peter was thoroughly at home in their shipyards and munitions factories. These places offered him what he had come to find.

Peter returned to Moscow determined to westernize Russia. He set himself four objectives and pursued them ruthlessly. He tamed the *boyars* and the *streltsy.* He brought the church under royal control. He reorganized governmental administration, and he promoted economic development. His goal was to increase Russia's military power and strengthen its monarchy.

TAMING THE *STRELTSY* AND *BOYARS*

As Peter was returning to Russia in 1698, the *streltsy* rebelled. Peter violently suppressed the revolt by torturing and executing about a thousand men and exhibiting their corpses as a warning to future dissidents. Peter then set about building a new military. He drafted an unprecedented 130,000 soldiers, and by the end of his reign he had a well-disciplined army of 300,000.

Peter also launched a campaign to wean the *boyar* nobility from Russian customs that Europeans ridiculed. He personally shaved their long beards and sheared off the dangling sleeves of their shirts and coats. His tendency to make major policy decisions without consulting the *boyars* offended them and prompted them to plot against him. He controlled them by playing factions off against each other.

DEVELOPING A NAVY

Peter built Russia's first navy, and it greatly increased his country's visibility on the world stage. In the mid-1690s, he constructed a fleet with which to challenge the Ottomans, and in 1696, he detached the Black Sea port of Azov from the Ottoman Empire. A major reason for his subsequent tour of Europe was to learn how to build warships that would win him a foothold on the Baltic. His chief competitor on this front was Sweden.

RUSSIAN EXPANSION IN THE BALTIC: THE GREAT NORTHERN WAR

Sweden's reward for being on the winning side in the Thirty Years' War was control of the Baltic Sea, and it was able, for a time, to deny Russia a port and permit Poland and Germany access only on its terms. Sweden's economy was, however, not equal to its military ambitions. In 1700, Peter began the Great Northern War (1700–1721), a campaign to win Russia a foothold on the Baltic coast. His opponent, King Charles XII (r. 1697–1718) of Sweden, initially succeeded in stopping him, but Russia's superior resources gradually won Peter the upper hand. The Peace of Nystad, which ended the war, confirmed Peter's conquest of Estonia, Livonia, and part of Finland and gave Russia ice-free ports and permanent access to western Europe.

FOUNDING ST. PETERSBURG

In 1703, Peter began construction of St. Petersburg, a new capital for Russia on the Gulf of Finland. In imitation of Louis XIV, he built palaces in the style of Versailles and compelled the *boyar* nobles to construct townhouses and gather about him in the new city. St. Petersburg was, however, more than a seat for an imperial court. It was a western European city transplanted to the Russian environment, and it indicated the seriousness of Peter's intent to westernize his homeland. Many of his subjects resented it as a symbol of autocracy and an attack on their native culture.

THE CASE OF PETER'S SON ALEKSEI

Peter feared that opposition to him would coalesce into support for his son, Aleksei. Aleksei was not particularly intelligent or ambitious, and Peter openly berated him for his shortcomings and quarreled with him. Resentment of his father may have driven him to compromise himself. In 1716, while the Great Northern War was still raging, Aleksei made a secret journey to Vienna to meet with the Habsburg emperor, Charles VI. The two men (probably with Sweden's encouragement) discussed conspiring against Peter, but nothing materialized. When Aleksei returned to Russia in 1718, his father opened an inquiry into his conduct and that of various nobles and members of the Senate. A six-month-long investigation led to Aleksei's condemnation, and he died under mysterious circumstances on June 26, 1718.

REFORMS OF PETER THE GREAT'S FINAL YEARS

Aleksei's case was more than a family dispute. It taught Peter that opposition to him was more widespread than he had realized. The tsar understood he could not simply exterminate his many opponents, as he had the *streltsy*. Instead, he implemented administrative reforms designed to bring the nobles and the church under closer control of persons he trusted.

Administrative Colleges   In 1717, Peter reorganized his administration to enhance his personal authority and fight corruption. He adopted a Swedish model—a system of eight *colleges*, or bureaus, charged with managing tax collection, foreign relations, war, and the economy. Peter staffed these colleges with persons of proven loyalty and each was advised by a foreign expert. The colleges moderated the influence of the Senate, in which Aleksei had sympathizers.

Table of Ranks   In 1722, Peter drew the nobles into state service by issuing a **Table of Ranks**. It made rank in the bureaucracy or military, not lineage, the determinant of an individual's social status. Earlier tsars had sometimes conferred

Events and Reigns

1533–1584	Ivan the Terrible
1584–1613	Time of Troubles
1613	Michael Romanov becomes tsar
1640–1688	Frederick William, the Great Elector
1643–1715	Louis XIV, the Sun King
1648	Independence of the Netherlands recognized
1682–1725	Peter the Great
1683	Turkish siege of Vienna
1688–1713	Frederick I of Prussia
1697	Peter the Great's European tour
1700–1721	The Great Northern War
1703	Saint Petersburg founded
1711–1740	The Great Northern War
1703	Saint Petersburg founded
1711–1740	Charles VI, the Pragmatic Sanction
1713	War of the Spanish Succession ends
1713–1740	Frederick William I of Prussia
1714	George I founds England's Hanoverian dynasty
1715	Louis XV becomes king of France
1720–1741	Robert Walpole dominates British politics
1726–1743	Cardinal Fleury
1727	George II
1740	Maria Theresa succeeds to the Habsburg throne
1740	Frederick II invades Silesia

15.6
Peter the Great: Correspondence with His Son

Table of Ranks   Issued by Peter the Great to draw nobles into state service, it made rank in the bureaucracy or military, not lineage, the determinant of an individual's social status.

nobility as a reward for service, but Peter envisioned pulling all the nobles into government service. The tsars, however, never won the kind of loyalty from Russia's nobles that the Junkers felt for their Prussian ruler.

Achieving Secular Control of the Church   Peter moved to suppress the independence of the Russian Orthodox Church, where some bishops and clergy had displayed sympathy for the tsar's son. In 1721, Peter abolished the office of patriarch and put the church under the control of a government department, the *Holy Synod*. It was staffed by several bishops and chaired by a layman, the *procurator general*. A Lutheran model guided the recorganization of the church—the most radical transformation of a traditional institution undertaken by Peter.

Peter had not, by the time of his death in 1725, decided on a successor, and a disputed succession gave the soldiers and nobles the opportunity they needed to reassert their influence. For the next thirty years, they decided who ruled Russia. Peter laid foundations for a modern state, but not stable one.

SWEDEN: THE AMBITIONS OF CHARLES XII

Sweden had seized the opportunity of the Thirty Years' War to make a bid for empire. During the seventeenth century, it controlled the Baltic, and Russia and Germany had access to that sea only on Sweden's terms. Sweden's economy was not strong enough, however, to underwrite its political ambitions.

In 1697, the headstrong and possibly insane Charles XII (r. 1697–1718) ascended Sweden's throne. Three years later the Great Northern War (1700–1721) began as Russia made a bid to win a base on the Baltic. Charles XII fought vigorously, but he mismanaged the campaign. After an initial victory and a distracting foray into Poland, he invaded Russia. His army bogged down in the brutal environment of winter and suffered decisive defeat at Poltava in 1709. The war ended in 1721, when Sweden ran out of resources. Russia occupied a large section of the eastern Baltic coast and broke Sweden's hold on the sea. After Charles's death, the Swedish nobles limited the power of the monarchy, and Sweden abandoned foreign adventures.

THE OTTOMAN EMPIRE

WHAT WAS the attitude of the Ottoman rulers toward religion in their empire and how was this reflected in their policies?

The **Ottoman Empire** was the largest and most stable state to appear in and near Europe Turks who conquered Constantinople and ended the Byzantine Empire in 1453. By the early seventeenth century, only the emperor of China had a larger territory and larger cities under his sway than the Ottoman sultan. (See Map 13–3.)

RELIGIOUS TOLERATION AND OTTOMAN GOVERNMENT

In 1516, the Ottomans took control of the sacred cities of Mecca, Medina, and Jerusalem and became the dominant power in the Muslim world. Their empire was diverse ethnically, linguistically, and religiously, and it offered more religious freedom than could be found anywhere in Europe. Thousands of Jews found refuge in Ottoman lands after they were evicted from Spain at the end of the fifteenth century, and the empire had a significant number of Christian subjects. The empire was governed through units called **millets** (communities of the officially recognized religions). The millet to which people belonged (not the territory they inhabited) determined which laws applied to them. *Dhimmis* (members of legal non-Islamic groups) managed their own community affairs through their religious leaders, but they paid a special tax, could not serve in the army or the administrative hierarchy of the empire, and were compelled in various ways

Ottoman Empire   The authority Instanbul's Ottoman Turkish sultan exercised over the Balkans, the Middle East, and North Africa from the end of the Middle Ages to World War I.

millets   Communities of the officially recognized religions that governed portions of the Ottoman Empire.

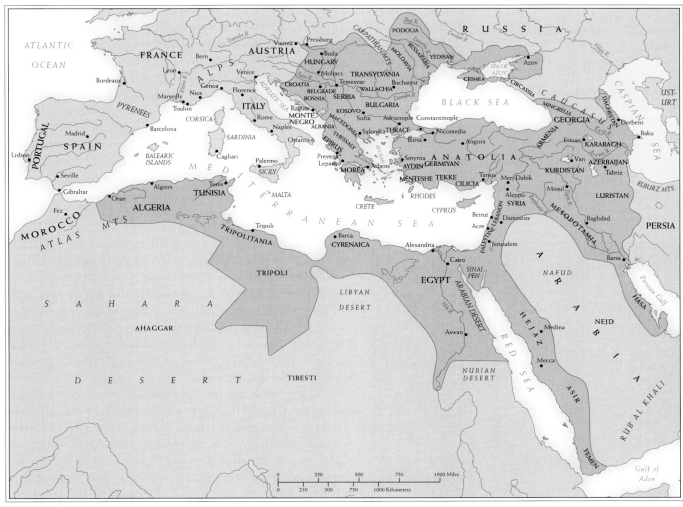

MAP 13–3

The Ottoman Empire in the Late Seventeenth Century   By the 1680s the Ottoman Empire had reached its maximum extent, but the Ottoman failure to capture Vienna in 1683 marked the beginning of a long and inexorable decline that ended with the empire's collapse after World War I.

FROM THE late 1600s until 1918, which non-Turkish peoples would rise up against Turkish rule in the Ottoman Empire?

to acknowledge their inferiority to Muslims. The Ottomans discouraged Muslims from mixing with *dhimmis,* and this prevented Muslims from acquiring the valuable skills and learning that these people possessed.

The sultan tried to prevent the rise of aristocratic competitors for his office by drawing his soldiers and administrators from groups that were expected to be especially loyal to him. Until the end of the seventeenth century, the Ottomans, utilizing a practice called *devshirme,* recruited their elite troops from Christian communities. By separating young Christian boys from their homelands and converting them to Islam, the sultan created a group of rootless men who were totally dependent on him. The most famous unit of the Ottoman infantry, the *Janissaries,* was formed in this way. The practice had the effect of excluding native Islamic peoples from the military and administrative structures of the empire. The thousands of men who filled influential government posts were largely recruited from the outer reaches of the empire. Technically they were the sultan's slaves, but their power made them the envy of many free subjects.

The Role of the *Ulama*   A group of Muslim scholars, the *Ulama*, dominated the empire's schools and courts as well as its religious institutions. The sultan and his administrators consulted with them to ensure that government policy accorded with Islamic law and the Qur'an, and they, in turn, supported the sultan as the chief protector of *Shar'ia* (Islamic law) and Sunni Islam. At a time when Europe was modernizing, the *Ulama* persuaded the sultan to preserve the empire's traditional way of life. As a result, Muslim civilization, which had helped medieval Europe rebuild its civilization, began to stagnate and to fall behind Europe—particularly in science and technology. The Ottomans attempted to catch up in the eighteenth century by importing European advisers, but the conservative *Ulama* and the lack of cultural grounding prevented foreign customs and ideas from taking root in Muslim soil.

THE END OF OTTOMAN EXPANSION

The Ottomans made their deepest foray into European territory in 1683. Their failure on that occasion to take Vienna signaled the beginning of their empire's slow decline. Rivalries within the military and administrative bureaucracies diminished the efficiency of its central government, and elites in the provinces and cities seized the opportunity to assert themselves. The sultan's authority was not so much repudiated as renegotiated by subjects who paid tribute but exercised considerable autonomy.

European explorers, meanwhile, charted sea routes that diverted world trade around the Ottoman territories. By the seventeenth century, the Dutch and Portuguese were importing great quantities of items directly from South Asia that formerly had passed through (and enriched) the Ottoman Empire. European naval power and weaponry improved at a comparable rate. The effects of all this became apparent in the 1690s, when war broke out between the Ottomans and a European league (Austria, Venice, Malta, Poland, Tuscany, and Russia). In 1699, the Ottomans were forced to retreat from Hungary, and Russia then began to challenge their hold on the northern shores of the Black Sea. A gulf steadily widened between the Ottomans and the Europeans, the former continuing to think of themselves as culturally superior and the latter regarding them as a declining, backward-looking people.

Devshirme. An Ottoman portrayal of the *Devshirme.* This miniature painting from about 1558 depicts the recruiting of young Christian children for the Sultan's elite Janissary corps.

Arifi, "Suleymanname," Topkapi Palace Museum. II 151, fol. 31b, photograph courtesy of Talat Halman

SUMMARY

The Netherlands Golden Age to Decline By the mid-eighteenth century, Britain and France had emerged as the dominant powers in western Europe and Spain had lost influence. The United Netherlands had enjoyed a Golden Age in the seventeenth century, and it was more urbanized than any other area of Europe. Dutch agriculture and financial systems were models for the rest of Europe, and the Dutch were the leading traders of Europe. After the death of William of Orange in 1702, the loose republican system that had given the Netherlands valuable flexibility turned into a handicap in the absence of leadership.

Two Models of European Political Development In the seventeenth century, England and France developed two different forms of government that served as models for other European countries in the eighteenth century. In England, nobles and the wealthy were politically active and had a tradition of broad liberties, representation, and bargaining with the monarch through Parliament. The English nobility felt little admiration or affection for the Stuart monarchs. In France, members of the French nobility believed the strength of Louis XIV served their personal interests as well as those of the king. This led to the so-called absolutism of the French monarchy, which became the country's sole significant national institution.

Constitutional Crisis and Settlement in Stuart England In the first half of the seventeenth century, many of the English suspected that their leaders were Catholic sympathizers. Oliver Cromwell led opposition in a civil war from 1642 to 1646, and then ruled until 1658. In 1660, the Stuart monarchy was restored under Charles II. His relationship with Parliament was testy. His brother and successor, the Catholic James II, was not as astute as Charles II. In 1688, members of Parliament invited William III of Orange to invade England and take the throne. After the success of the "Glorious Revolution," in 1689 William and Mary recognized a Bill of Rights, limiting the monarchy's powers, guaranteeing civil liberties to some, formalizing Parliament's role, and barring Catholics from the throne. The 1689 Toleration Act allowed Protestants freedom to worship, but denied Catholics similar privileges. The monarchy in Great Britain passed to the house of Hanover, and George I sought support from the Whigs. Robert Walpole functioned as George's prime minister. Parliament checked royal influence, and provided strong central political authority. Britain's economy was strong, and political life was remarkably free.

Rise of Absolute Monarchy in France: The World of Louis XIV Louis XIV's monarchy gathered unprecedented power on the national level in the area of foreign and military affairs, domestic administration, and economic regulation. At the same time, Louis was careful to allow nobles to retain their local power and privileges. He ensured loyalty to the crown by employing nobles in his administration, and crafted a political image as the "Sun King" based at Versailles. At this palace, Louis built a system of patronage that effectively excluded many nobles from government, even as it occupied them in ritual and ceremony all designed to promote Louis's personal rule and divine right monarchy. Louis's armies instilled fear in its neighbors, prompting several alliances to be formed against France throughout his reign. He repressed the anti-Jesuit Jansenists and revoked the Edict of Nantes, which had ensured toleration of French Protestants. These policies reinforced Europe's image of Louis as a repressive fanatic and sowed the seeds of domestic opposition to the monarchy, not only among Jansenist sympathizers, but also in noble and judicial bodies. The Habsburg Empire expanded so much that by the eighteenth and nineteenth centuries, Habsburg power and influence were based more on territories outside of Germany than within. Political unity was in short supply. The Hohenzollerns created a Prussian army that, according to an axiom, possessed the nation, rather than the other way around.

IMAGE KEY
for pages 312–313

a. Gold Fleur De Lys with Gold Crown

b. Hyacinthe Rigaud (1659–1743), "Portrait of Louis XIV" Louvre, Paris, France. Photograph copyright Bridgeman-Giraudon/Art Resource, NY

c., i. A pair of mid-17th century point de France lappets, lace. c. 1650

d. Jean Warin III (1604–1672). Foundation medal of Val-de-Grace. Verso: Anne of Austria her son Louis XIV. Bronze medaillon. 1638. Musee de la Ville de Paris, Musee Carnavalet, Paris. Bridgeman-Giraudon/Art Resource, NY

e. Portrait of Peter the Great in a gold frame with a crown on top, artist unknown

f. Detail, "An Eyewitness Representation of the Execution of King Charles I (1600–49) of England, 1649 (oil on canvas) by Weesop (fl. 1641–49). Private Collection/Bridgeman Art Library, London

g. Pierre Mignard (1612–1695), "Portrait of Francoise d'Aubigne, marquise de Maintenon (1635-1719), mistress and second wife of Louis XIV", c. 1694. Oil on canvas, 128 x 97 cm. Inv.: MV 3637. Chateaux de Versailles et de Trianon, Versailles. Bridgeman-Giraudon/Art Resource, NY

h. Pierre Patel, "Perspective View of Versailles." Chateaux de Versailles et de Trianon, Versailles, France. Photo copyright Bridgeman-Giraudon/Art Resource, NY

j. Portrait of Philip V

k. Suleyman I (Kanuni); Shehzade by Talikizade Suphi. Folio 79a of the Talikizade Shehnamesi, Library of the Topkapi Palace Museum, A3592, photograph courtesy of Talat Halman

Central and Eastern Europe The economies and political structures of central and eastern Europe were weaker than those of the west. Late in the seventeenth century, Poland could not develop a strong central authority, while Austria, Prussia, and Russia emerged as political and military powers.

Russia Enters the European Political Arena In the seventeenth century, Russia became one of the nations of Europe, and the Romanov dynasty was founded. Russia's old nobility. the *boyars,* retained considerable authority until Peter (later Peter the Great) assumed personal rule in 1689. Peter was zealous in his efforts to westernize Russia, to curb the power of the *boyars* and Moscow garrison guards (the *streltsy*), and to increase the nation's military strength. He was remarkably successful in most of his efforts. His critical failure was that, when he died in 1725, he had not appointed as successor; for decades after his death, power reverted to nobles and soldiers.

The Ottoman Empire The Ottoman Empire conquered Constantinople and ended the Byzantine Empire in 1453, and dominated the Muslim world after 1516. The Ottomans' empire was diverse ethnically, linguistically, and religiously, and offered more religious freedom than could be found anywhere in Europe. Social and political structures prevented leading families from interacting meaningfully with the ruling elite, which limited the infusion of new ideas and personalities into government. Military defeats in the late seventeenth century marked the beginning of the end for the Ottoman Empire.

REVIEW QUESTIONS

1. Why did Britain and France remain leading powers while the United Netherlands declined? How did the structure of British government change under the political leadership of Walpole?

2. What similarities and differences do you see between the systems of government and religious policies in place in England and France at the end of the seventeenth century? What accounts for the path each nation took?

3. Why did the English king and Parliament come into conflict in the 1640s? What was the "Glorious Revolution"? How did England in 1700 differ from England in 1600?

4. How did Louis XIV consolidate his monarchy? How successful was his foreign policy? What were the domestic and international consequences of his religious policies?

5. How did Peter the Great's plan for building a greater Russia compare with the conduct of the Ottoman leaders who allowed their empire to decline?

6. How was the Hohenzollern family able to forge a conglomerate of diverse land holdings into the state of Prussia? How do the Hohenzollerns and the Habsburgs compare in the ways they dealt with the problems that confronted their domains?

7. What sorts of political and diplomatic problems did questions about successions to thrones create for various states between 1685 and 1740?

KEY TERMS

absolutism (p. 315)

"divine right of kings" (p. 324)

Fronde (p. 323)

Gallican Liberties (p. 325)

"Glorious Revolution" (p. 322)

Jansenism (p. 325)

Junkers (p. 330)

millets (p. 334)

Ottoman Empire (p. 334)

parlements (p. 315)

parliamentary monarchy (p. 315)

Pragmatic Sanction (p. 329)

Puritans (p. 316)

Sejm (p. 329)

Table of Ranks (p. 333)

 For additional study resources for this chapter, go to:
www.prenhall.com/kagan3/chapter13

14 New Directions in Thought and Culture in the Sixteenth and Seventeenth Centuries

CHAPTER HIGHLIGHTS

The Scientific Revolution Copernicus proposed a heliocentric model of the universe. Kepler used data collected b̶ show that the planets have elliptical orbits. Galileo was a strong advocate of the heliocentric model and a believer i̶ rationality of nature. Newton derived laws of motion and the theory of universal gravitation.

Philosophy Responds to Changing Science Philosophers were profoundly influenced by the scientific revolution. Bacon, Descartes, Hobbes, and Locke all articulated philosophies influenced by the models suggested by the new science.

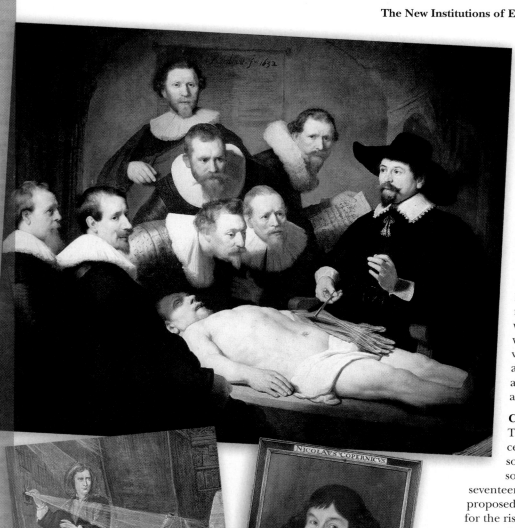

The New Institutions of Expanding Natural Knowledge The expansion of natural knowledge changed existing centers of learning and led to the creation of new "institutions of sharing." Scientific societies encouraged the exchange of ideas.

Women in the World of the Scientific Revolution Women were more often the subject of study and description than participants in early modern science. However, some noblewomen and female artisans were able to overcome the obstacles placed in their way and contribute to the scientific revolution.

The New Science and Religious Faith The new science challenged religion. Most natural philosophers worked hard to reconcile their work with mainstream religious views. Galileo's condemnation was an exception to the rule of accommodation between science and religion.

Continuing Superstition Throughout the seventeenth century, most Europeans believed in some form of magic. Witch hunts soared in the late sixteenth and early seventeenth centuries. Scholars have proposed a number of possible explanations for the rise and fall of witchcraft prosecutions during this period.

Baroque Art Depictions were naturalistic rather than idealized and sought to involve the observer on an emotional level through dramatic portrayals and contrast of light and darkness.

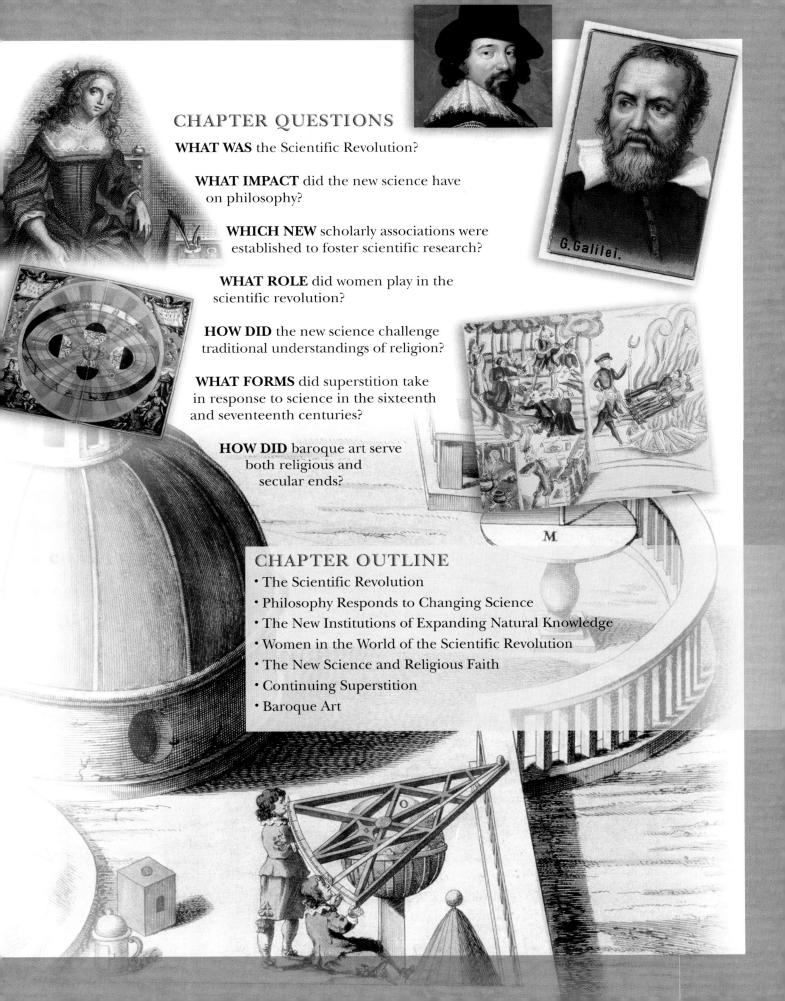

CHAPTER QUESTIONS

WHAT WAS the Scientific Revolution?

WHAT IMPACT did the new science have on philosophy?

WHICH NEW scholarly associations were established to foster scientific research?

WHAT ROLE did women play in the scientific revolution?

HOW DID the new science challenge traditional understandings of religion?

WHAT FORMS did superstition take in response to science in the sixteenth and seventeenth centuries?

HOW DID baroque art serve both religious and secular ends?

CHAPTER OUTLINE

- The Scientific Revolution
- Philosophy Responds to Changing Science
- The New Institutions of Expanding Natural Knowledge
- Women in the World of the Scientific Revolution
- The New Science and Religious Faith
- Continuing Superstition
- Baroque Art

G. Galilei.

IMAGE KEY

Image Key for pages 340–341 is on page 356.

During the sixteenth and seventeenth centuries, science created a new view of the universe that challenged many previously held beliefs. Earth moved from the center of the universe and became only one of several planets orbiting a sun that was only one of countless stars. This new cosmology forced people to rethink humanity's place in the larger scheme of things. The new scientific ideas came into apparent conflict with traditional religion and raised doubts about the grounds for faith and morality. Europeans discovered the world was a much more complex place than their ancestors had imagined. The telescope opened the heavens to them while the microscope disclosed the existence of a realm of microorganisms. A spate of scientific discoveries added to the intellectual dislocation already created by the Reformation and contact with the New World.

THE SCIENTIFIC REVOLUTION

WHAT WAS the scientific revolution?

The intellectual breakthroughs of the sixteenth and seventeenth centuries are said to constitute a **scientific revolution**, but that metaphor may be misleading if it implies a rapid, widespread transformation of culture. The development of science was a slow process that never involved more than a few hundred people, and these pioneers called themselves "natural philosophers," not scientists (a term that originated in the 1830s). Progress in science also owed much to the inventiveness of artisans and craftspeople as well as a few brilliant minds. Some individuals worked at universities or had the patronage of kings, but many pursued their studies informally from their homes or private workshops. It was not until the second half of the seventeenth century that learned societies and academies were established to promote research.

Despite this rather casual approach to scientific work, by the end of the seventeenth century the new ideas and research methods that were emerging were so impressive that they were setting the standard for testing the validity of all knowledge in the West. Science was achieving the cultural supremacy over other forms of intellectual activity that it still enjoys, and it was becoming a major defining characteristic of modern Western civilization. The discipline that did most to initiate these developments was astronomy.

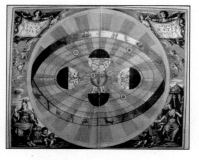

Scenographia: Systematis copernicani
Astrological Chart, ca. 1543.

British Library, London, UK/Bridgeman Art Library

NICOLAUS COPERNICUS REJECTS AN EARTH-CENTERED UNIVERSE

Nicolaus Copernicus (1473–1543), a respected Italian-educated Polish astronomer, had a reputation as a fairly conventional thinker until he published *On the Revolutions of the Heavenly Spheres* (1543). The book did not create a revolution, but it laid the groundwork for one by providing Copernicus's successors with material for critiquing the widely accepted view of Earth's place in the universe.

The Ptolemaic System The maps of the universe in use in Copernicus's day were variants of one found in the ancient Greek astronomer Ptolemy's *Almagest* (ca. 150 C.E.). They assumed Earth was the center point of a ball-shaped universe composed of concentric layers of rotating crystalline spheres to which the heavenly bodies were attached. Beyond these spheres lay the realm of God and the angels. Ptolemy's model was based on assumptions about the laws of physics made by the Greek philosopher Aristotle. Earth was at the center of the universe because it was presumed to be the heaviest of objects. Rest was thought to be the natural state of all objects. Therefore, an explanation had to be found for the motion of the heavenly bodies. They were said to be attached to invisible rotating spheres, each moved by the one above it. At the highest level, the "prime mover" imparted motion to the system. Christians equated Aristotle's "prime mover" with God.

scientific revolution The emergence in the sixteenth century of rational and empirical methods of research that challenged traditional thought and promoted the rise of science and technology.

Medieval astronomers were aware of problems with the **Ptolemaic system**. Chief among these was the fact that the planets did not appear to move in circular orbits. Sometimes they actually seemed to go backward. Ptolemy and his disciples explained this by proposing the existence of *epicycles*—that is, planets moving in short circular cycles that travel the orbits of much larger cycles. This accounted fairly well for what astronomers observed, but it was a very cluttered model for the universe.

Copernicus's Universe   Copernicus's *On the Revolutions of the Heavenly Spheres* was not meant to refute Ptolemy's model but to propose a refinement that would provide a more elegant solution to some of the mathematical problems it created. Copernicus suggested that if Earth was assumed to rotate about the sun in a circular orbit, the epicycles could be eliminated or reduced in size, and the apparent retrograde motion of the planets could be explained as an illusion created by viewing other planets from a planet that was itself in motion. Except for modifying Earth's position, Copernicus retained most of the other assumptions of Ptolemaic astronomy, and his system was no better than older ones at predicting movements of the planets. The Copernican model of the universe was, therefore, slow to attract adherents, and the initial importance of his work lay in the encouragement it gave people to think in new ways about scientific problems.

TYCHO BRAHE AND JOHANNES KEPLER MAKE NEW SCIENTIFIC OBSERVATIONS

Tycho Brahe (1546–1601), a Danish astronomer, spent most of his life trying to refute Copernicus and defend a revised version of Ptolemy's Earth-centered model for the universe. He thought the moon and the sun revolved around Earth and the other planets revolved around the sun. To make his case, Brahe collected the most accurate astronomical data that had ever been acquired by observation with the naked eye.

When Brahe died, his astronomical tables passed to Johannes Kepler (1571–1630), a German astronomer and a convinced Copernican. After much work, Kepler discovered that if the planets were assumed to move in elliptical, not circular, orbits, Brahe's data supported the Copernican theory that Earth revolved about the sun. Kepler published his findings in *The New Astronomy* (1609), but their acceptance was hampered by the fact that no one could explain why planets were locked in orbits of any shape rather than spinning out into space. That remained a mystery until Isaac Newton proposed his theory of universal gravitation.

GALILEO GALILEI ARGUES FOR A UNIVERSE OF MATHEMATICAL LAWS

By Kepler's day, little was known about the universe that could not have been known to Ptolemy, for all data had been gathered with the naked eye. In the year Kepler published his work, however, an Italian scientist, Galileo Galilei (1564–1642), turned a Dutch invention called a telescope on the heavens and saw things that had never been seen before. Unknown stars appeared, mountains were seen on the moon, spots passed across the face of the sun, and moons were discovered orbiting the planet Jupiter. Galileo argued that a Copernican model of the universe provided the simplest explanation for what the telescope revealed.

Galileo did not pursue science in the seclusion of an ivory tower. He worked at the court of the Medici Grand Duke of Tuscany, and his livelihood depended on promoting his discoveries in ways that enhanced his patron's reputation. Galileo, therefore, publicized his findings in literate treatises that were accessible to a wide audience. This made him appear to be the leading advocate for the Copernican

QUICK REVIEW

On the Revolutions of the Heavenly Spheres
- Copernicus's work meant as a revision of Ptolemy's model
- If Earth assumed to rotate around sun then model would be vastly simplified
- Model slow to attract adherents

Ptolemaic system   Astronomical theory, named after Greek astronomer Ptolemy, that assumed Earth was the center point of a ball-shaped universe composed of concentric layers of rotating crystalline spheres to which the heavenly bodies were attached.

Sir Isaac Newton's experiments dealing with light passing through a prism became a model for writers praising the experimental method.

CORBIS/Bettmann

model of the universe and caused problems for him with the Roman Catholic Church (discussed later).

Galileo did more than popularize Copernicanism. He fostered belief in a universe governed by rational laws stated in mathematical formulas. The mathematical regularity that Copernicus saw in the heavens, Galileo believed, was characteristic of all nature. This conviction encouraged scientists to look for explanations for things by focusing primarily on phenomena that could be quantified. They sought mathematical models to account for qualities such as color, beauty, and taste—and even to explain social relationships and political systems. When viewed from such a perspective, nature appeared to be a cold, mechanistic system, and only things that could be measured mathematically seemed real or significant. This attitude portended a major intellectual shift for Western civilization.

ISAAC NEWTON DISCOVERS THE LAWS OF GRAVITATION

The puzzle that Copernicus, Kepler, and Galileo left unsolved was why the heavenly bodies moved in the orderly fashion described by the new astronomy. It was the mystery that lay behind the laws of planetary motion that led Isaac Newton (1642–1727), an English mathematician, to make the discoveries that established a new understanding of physics—one that worked well as a basis for scientific research for over two centuries.

In 1687, Newton published *The Mathematical Principles of Natural Philosophy* (or *Principia Mathematica*). He shared Galileo's faith that reality could be described mathematically, and he was influenced by Galileo's theory of inertia. Earlier scientists had assumed that rest (motionlessness) was an object's natural state and movement had to be explained. Galileo suggested that what physicists ought to ask is not why there is motion instead of rest, but why there is a change in an existing state—either stillness or movement.

Newton theorized that the revolutions of the heavenly bodies were controlled by gravity, a pull that every physical object exerts on the objects around it. The strength of this force is proportional to the mass and proximity of each object, and the order that exists among the planets can be explained as the balance they have achieved among their mutual attractions. Newton demonstrated the effects of gravity mathematically, but he did not attempt to explain what gravity itself is.

Newton believed that mathematics held the key to understanding nature, but, like other advocates of the new science, he also believed the ultimate test of a theory was its ability to explain empirical data and observation. The worth of a hypothesis depended on its ability to describe what could be observed. Science began and ended with empirical observation of what was actually in nature, not with a rational argument about what ought to be there. Religious dogma, therefore, could not dictate conclusions to science.

WHAT IMPACT did the new science have on philosophy?

PHILOSOPHY RESPONDS TO CHANGING SCIENCE

he progress of science prompted major rethinking of the Western philosophical tradition. The religious assumptions that guided the thought of the medieval Scholastics were abandoned in favor of mathematics and mechanical metaphors. The universe was envisioned as a kind of gigantic clock. This dispelled much of the mystery of existence and reduced God to the role of an observer—a great mechanic who had constructed the machinery of the universe but who did not participate in its operation. Philosophers had previously assumed an understanding of the natural order would reveal divine mysteries and yield transcendent insights, but now they concluded that knowledge of nature revealed nothing beyond itself. Such knowledge might lead to physical improvements for living beings, but it could not disclose a divine purpose for life.

FRANCIS BACON: THE EMPIRICAL METHOD

Francis Bacon (1561–1626), the English lawyer, statesman, and author who is often honored as the father of the scientific method of research, was not a scientist. He contributed to science by fostering an intellectual climate conducive to its growth. In books such as *The Advancement of Learning* (1605), the *Novum Organum* (1620), and the *New Atlantis* (1627), Bacon attacked medieval Scholasticism's reverence for authority (its belief that truth had already been discovered or revealed and only needed to be explicated). He urged his contemporaries to strike out on their own and search for a new understanding of nature. Bacon was a leader among the writers who shifted the attention of European intellectuals from defending tradition to promoting innovation and change.

Bacon believed knowledge was not just an end in itself but should improve the human condition. He claimed Scholasticism had nothing useful to contribute, for its practitioners only rearranged old ideas. Real progress required that thinkers go back and reexamine the foundations of their thought. If they relied on empirical observation more than logical speculation, Bacon promised they would discover things that would open new possibilities for humankind.

Bacon's rejection of past methods of inquiry sprang from his awareness that the world was becoming a much more complicated place than it had been for his medieval forebears. Like Columbus (and partially because of him), Bacon claimed a new route to intellectual discovery had to be charted. The lands new to Europeans that were being explored around the globe were opening new vistas for the Western mind. Most people in Bacon's day assumed the best era in human history lay in antiquity, but Bacon disagreed. He anticipated a future of material improvement and better government achieved by empirical examination of natural phenomena.

RENÉ DESCARTES: THE METHOD OF RATIONAL DEDUCTION

René Descartes (1596–1650), the gifted French mathematician who invented analytic geometry, popularized a scientific method that emphasized deduction, and thinkers all over Europe eagerly applied his techniques to all kinds of subject matters. Descartes's *Discourse on Method* (1637) proposed a technique for putting all human thought on a secure mathematical footing. In order to arrive at truth, Descartes said it was necessary for us to doubt all our ideas except those that were clear and distinct. An idea was worthy of trust not because some authority vouched for it but because the ever rational mind intuited its validity. Descartes began his search for truth by seeing if he had any ideas he could not doubt (any

Sir Francis Bacon (1561–1626), champion of the inductive method of gaining knowledge.

By courtesy of the National Portrait Gallery, London

13.1
Francis Bacon: from *First Book of Aphorisms*

QUICK REVIEW

The Empirical Method
- Francis Bacon believed Scholasticism did nothing more than arrange old ideas
- Thinkers should reexamine the foundations of their thought
- Reliance on empirical evidence would yield the best results

Queen Christina of Sweden
(r. 1632–1654), shown here with the
French philosopher and scientist René
Descartes, was one of many women
from the elite classes interested in the
new science. In 1649 she invited
Descartes to live at her court in
Stockholm, but he died a few months
after moving to Sweden.

Pierre-Louis the Younger Dumesnil (1698–1781),
"Christina of Sweden (1626–89) and her Court: detail of the Queen and Rene Descartes (1596–1650)
at the Table." Oil on canvas. Chateau de Versailles,
France/Bridgeman Art Library

13.4
Thomas Hobbes:
Chapter XIII from
Leviathan

ideas that were self-substantiating). He concluded it was
not possible to question his own act of thinking without
first assuming he existed. To doubt doubting, one could
not doubt the existence of the doubter. With this clear and
distinct idea as his premise, Descartes was able to construct
arguments deducing the existence of God and a real world
external to the human mind.

Descartes divided existing things into two basic categories: things in thought and things in space. Thinking was
a characteristic of the mind and extension (occupying
space) of the body. Because space is mathematically mea-
surable, mathematical laws govern the world of extension.
Its laws are discoverable by reason, for mathematical truths
form coherent systems in which each part can be deduced
from some other part. Spirits, divinities, and immaterial
things have no place in the world of extension, which belongs exclusively to scientists. They explain it by using
mathematics and rational inference to discover the mechanical properties of matter.

Natural scientists eventually abandoned Descartes's
deductive method for induction, the process of generaliz-
ing from discrete bits of empirical data to formulate a hypothesis (and then devising an experiment to test that
hypothesis). Deduction, however, remained popular with
people who pondered subjects for which little empirical
data was available (political theory, psychology, ethics,
and theology).

THOMAS HOBBES: APOLOGIST FOR ABSOLUTISM

The new scientific attitudes greatly altered thinking about politics, as is apparent
in the work of Thomas Hobbes (1588–1679), the most original political philosopher of the seventeenth century. Hobbes was an urbane, much-traveled man and
an enthusiastic supporter of the new scientific movement. He visited Paris and
made Descartes's acquaintance. He spent time in Italy with Galileo, and he was
interested in the work of William Harvey (1578–1657), the man who first recognized that blood circulates through the human body. Hobbes was also a superb
classicist. He made the first English translation of Thucydides' *History of the Peloponnesian War,* and his dark view of human nature probably owed something to
Thucydides.

The turmoil of the English Civil War colored Hobbes's thinking about politics. *Leviathan,* the famous book he published in 1651, offered a thoroughly materialistic, mechanistic explanation for human behavior (and brutality). Hobbes
claimed that all mental states derive from sensation and all motivations are ego-
istical. The driving force behind human life is the quest to increase pleasure and
minimize pain. Human beings, Hobbes said, have no spiritual ends and serve no
great moral purpose. They simply strive to meet the needs of daily life, and this is
why they form governments. A sovereign commonwealth is all that prevents a society of egotists from tearing itself apart.

Hobbes used a mythical description of human origins to illustrate his political philosophy. He claimed that nature inclines people to a "perpetual and
restless desire" for power. In the state of nature (before civilization intervenes),

all people want and have a right to everything. This breeds enmity, competition, diffidence, and perpetual quarreling: "a war of every man against every man." Philosophers and theologians have often imagined the original human condition as a lost paradise, but Hobbes saw it as a corrupt, chaotic battleground that drove people, who were desperate for order, to organize societies. Unlike Aristotle and Christian thinkers such as Thomas Aquinas, Hobbes did not believe human beings were naturally sociable. He claimed they were self-centered beasts who were utterly without discipline unless it was imposed on them by force.

People escape their terrible natural state, Hobbes said, by making a social contract that obligates them to live in a commonwealth ruled by law. A desire for "commodious living" and a fear of death drives them to accept the constraints of communal life. The social contract obliges every person, for the sake of peace and security, to agree to set aside his or her right to all things and be content with as much liberty against others as he or she would allow others against himself or herself. Because words and promises are insufficient to guarantee this agreement, the social contract authorizes the coercive use of force to compel compliance.

England's Civil War convinced Hobbes that the dangers of anarchy were greater than those of tyranny. This being so, he concluded that rulers should have unlimited power. He did not think it mattered much what form a government took (monarchy or democracy) so long as there could be no challenge to its power. There is little room in Hobbes's political philosophy for protests motivated by an individual's conscience, for Hobbes insisted that suppression of a few individuals was preferable to the suffering the outbreak of civil war imposed on everyone. Both Catholics and Puritans objected to his subordination of spiritual authority to a secular sovereign, but he maintained that only a single, uncontested head of state could preserve order.

JOHN LOCKE: DEFENDER OF MODERATE LIBERTY AND TOLERATION

The most influential critic of the kind of political absolutism Hobbes favored was another Englishman, John Locke (1632–1704). Locke's sympathies were with the leaders of popular revolutions. His father fought with the parliamentary army during the English Civil War, and in 1682, Locke himself joined a rebellion led by Anthony Ashley Cooper, the earl of Shaftesbury, against Charles II. Its failure forced him to seek asylum in Holland.

Locke's two *Treatises of Government* were written after Charles II restored the English monarchy. The first was a devastating critique of the traditional argument for royal absolutism that equated states with families and rulers with the heads of patriarchal households. Locke argued that both fathers and rulers are bound by the law of nature that creates everyone equal and independent. In his *Second Treatise of Government,* he made the case for government's obligation to be responsive to the wishes of the governed. He disagreed with Hobbes's assumption that people are driven only by passion and selfish interests, and he noted they are also endowed by nature with reason and goodwill. They are able to cooperate and live together in peace on their own, and Locke claimed it is the desire to facilitate social life that leads them to establish governments. Governments are based on social contracts that are meant to protect human liberty, not restrain it. If rulers fail to honor the terms of such contracts, subjects have a right to replace them.

Locke believed governments should limit themselves to protecting property and should not interfere in the religious lives of their citizens. His *Letter Concerning Toleration* (1689) argued that each individual is responsible for working out his or her own salvation. Differences of opinion are likely, but unanimity cannot be imposed, for faith is a matter of conscience. Locke denied religious liberty to two groups—to atheists on the ground that their oaths (lacking divine sanction) could not be trusted, and to Roman Catholics on the ground they were pledged to serve a foreign prince (the pope).

Of all Locke's works, his *Essay Concerning Human Understanding* (1690) attracted the most immediate attention from his contemporaries, for it offered a scientific explanation for human psychology. Locke claimed the mind of a newborn is a blank tablet on which nothing is yet inscribed. No knowledge is innate. All ideas come from sensory experience. All human beings are, therefore, products of their environments, and they can be reformed and perfected by transforming the world that shapes them. Locke claimed that religious knowledge is acquired like other kinds of knowledge. Reliable spiritual information comes, however, only from studying the Scriptures and observing the natural order. Private revelations lead to fanaticism and superstition.

WHICH NEW scholarly associations were established to foster scientific research?

THE NEW INSTITUTIONS OF EXPANDING NATURAL KNOWLEDGE

*M*edieval scholars assumed that learning was a process of recovering what had already been discovered by ancient authorities (such as Aristotle) or revealed to the authors of the Bible and the founders of the church. Even the Protestant reformers saw themselves only as restoring the original Christian message and not as discovering something new in it. As science took root, however, confidence grew that genuinely new discoveries about nature and humanity were possible. Learning implied progress and a growing fund of information.

Science fostered a kind of intellectual faith that had wide-ranging social implications. Advocates of the new science were highly critical of Europe's universities, where traditional scholastic and Aristotelian modes of thought were deeply entrenched. This was not always fair, for the new ideas penetrated the universities, and a few natural philosophers (notably Newton) held university chairs. The slowness of the schools to assimilate scientific advances, however, persuaded scientists they had to establish different kinds of institutions to advance their work.

Colbert was Louis XIV's most influential minister. He sought to expand the economic life of France and to associate the monarchy with the emerging new science from which he hoped might flow new inventions and productive technology. Here he is portrayed presenting members of the French Academy of Science to the monarch on the founding of the French Academy.

Henri Testelin (1616-1695), (after Le Brun). Minister of Finance Colbert presenting the members of the Royal Academy of Science (founded in 1667) to Louis XIV. Study for a tapestry. Photo: Gerard Blot. Chateau de Versailles et de Trianon, Versailles

The most prominent of the new scholarly associations was the Royal Society of London. It was founded in 1660 to promote research and the sharing of scientific information. Similar organizations on both the local and national level sprang up in most European countries. Members of these societies met to hear papers and witness experiments. Many society "fellows" were men of high social standing, and their reputations lent credibility to reports of scientific discoveries. Their polite exchange of ideas also helped promote a culture of civility that elevated science above the kinds of religious and political squabbles that tore communities apart.

Members of these societies were drawn from the intellectual elite, but their interests led them to cooperate with laborers, craftspersons, and sailors whose skills, work experience, and travels made them invaluable sources of aid and information. Learned societies were eager to demonstrate what science could do to solve practical problems, advance the aims of government, and grow economies. Persons who had ideas for improving navigation, agriculture, engineering, and military technology turned to the societies for support, and the societies sponsored practical inventions, urged religious toleration, and promoted political liberty. They were the harbingers of a new and optimistic confidence in the future.

WOMEN IN THE WORLD OF THE SCIENTIFIC REVOLUTION

The traditions that made intellectual activities difficult for women in the ancient and medieval worlds blocked them from doing scientific work in the early modern era. With a few exceptions, universities did not admit women until the end of the nineteenth century. Women were also not welcomed into the new scientific societies and academies. A few women from the noble and artisan classes managed, however, to do some scientific work—with the help of male members of their families.

The husband of Margaret Cavendish (1623–1673), duchess of Newcastle, introduced her to a circle of natural philosophers with whom she debated the theories of Descartes and Hobbes. She was the only woman admitted to a meeting of the Royal Society, an organization she criticized for doing too little to explore science's practical applications. Her major scientific publications were *Observations upon Experimental Philosophy* (1666) and *Grounds of Natural Philosophy* (1668). She also wrote a text to introduce women to the study of science: *Description of a New World, Called the Blazing World* (1666). A few men wrote popularizations of scientific theories for female readers.

WHAT ROLE did women play in the scientific revolution?

QUICK REVIEW

Women and Science

- Significant obstacles stood in the way of women doing scientific work
- A few elite women, notably Margaret Cavendish, were allowed to make contributions
- Women from the artisan classes had more opportunities than other women

Women from the artisan classes had more opportunities to pursue science than other females, for they were trained to work in their families' businesses. Several German astronomers were assisted by their wives and daughters, and some of these women (most notably Maria Cunitz, Elisabetha Hevelius, and Maria Winkelmann) wrote books or made discoveries on their own. After the death of her astronomer husband in 1710, Maria Winkelmann (the discoverer of a comet) applied to the Berlin Academy of Sciences for permission to continue her husband's work. She was denied because of her gender. Years later she tried to return to the academy as an assistant to her son, but she was forced out and had to abandon astronomy.

In the 1730s, the French philosopher Voltaire drew on the mathematical expertise of Emilie du Châtelet for help in writing a book on Newton, but few women were admitted to the fields of science and medicine before the late nineteenth century. Some psychologists even argued that differences between male and female brains made women incapable of scientific work. The pursuit of natural knowledge was said to be a male vocation.

HOW DID the new science challenge traditional understandings of religion?

13.6
Rethinking the Bible:
Galileo Confronts his
Critics

Margaret Cavendish, who wrote widely on scientific subjects, was the most accomplished woman associated with the new science in seventeenth-century England.

ImageWorks/Mary Evans Picture Library Ltd.

THE NEW SCIENCE AND RELIGIOUS FAITH

The new science challenged traditional understandings of religion on at least three fronts. Biblical descriptions of the heavens disagreed with scientific discoveries. Scientists threatened to undermine the authority of clergymen, and science tended to promote an exclusively materialistic view of the universe.

THE CASE OF GALILEO

The Roman Catholic Church was going through a particularly difficult period in its history when, in 1633, it took the infamous step of condemning the Copernican theory and Galileo. The Council of Trent asserted the church alone had the authority to interpret the Bible, and to counter Protestant accusations that Catholicism had strayed from the Scriptures, the church's interpretations had become narrowly literal. Galileo's views on biblical interpretation, which he published in 1615 (*Letter to the Grand Duchess Christina*), sounded suspiciously Protestant to some Catholic leaders, and the astronomer's discoveries seemed to support the Copernican view of the universe, which the church had officially condemned as unbiblical in 1616.

Galileo apparently won the church's permission to write about Copernicanism so long as he did not assert its truthfulness but only entertained it as a theoretical possibility. In 1623, the newly elected Pope Urban VIII, who was an acquaintance of Galileo's, allowed him to publish his research. The result was a book, *Dialogue on the Two Chief World Systems* (1632), which clearly implied the correctness of the Copernican model of the heavens. The pope felt betrayed and mocked by Galileo's work and condemned him for breaking his promise to the church. Galileo was forced to repudiate his theories, and he spent the last nine years of his life under house arrest. The incident troubled the relationship between science and Catholic faith for a very long time. In 1992, the church finally admitted that errors had been made by Pope Urban's advisers.

OVERVIEW   MAJOR WORKS OF THE SCIENTIFIC REVOLUTION

Year	Work	Author
1543	*On the Revolutions of the Heavenly Spheres*	Copernicus
1605	*The Advancement of Learning*	Bacon
1609	*The New Astronomy*	Kepler
1610	*The Starry Messenger*	Galileo
1620	*Novum Organum*	Bacon
1632	*Dialogue on the Two Chief World Systems*	Galileo
1637	*Discourse on Method*	Descartes
1651	*Leviathan*	Hobbes
1687	*Principia Mathematica*	Newton
1689	*Letter Concerning Toleration*	Locke
1690	*An Essay Concerning Human Understanding*	Locke
1690	*Treatises of Government*	Locke

BLAISE PASCAL: REASON AND FAITH

Blaise Pascal (1623–1662), a French mathematician and physical scientist, made the most famous attempt to reconcile faith with the new science. Pascal was a deeply religious man who turned his back on wealth and chose a life of austerity. He, however, opposed both religious dogmatism and the skepticism of atheists and rationalists. He was drawn to Jansenism, the French Catholic movement that was based on the Augustinian teaching that grace alone brings salvation and knowledge of God. He was never able to integrate his insights into a fully developed system, but he published a collection of provocative reflections on the human condition entitled *Pensées*.

Pascal believed reason could reveal humanity's utter corruption, but that it was too weak to comprehend life's fundamental mysteries. They belonged to the realm of religion, and religion operated beyond reason. It involved a "leap of faith," absolute trust in divine grace. Pascal proposed an ingenious "wager" to demonstrate the unreasonableness of skepticism. He noted it is a better bet to believe that God exists than to doubt. If God does exist, the believer wins everything. If it turns out God does not exist, the believer has not lost much by believing. Furthermore, Pascal argued that, whether God exists or not, religious faith is still valuable in and of itself, for it motivates self-discipline and strengthens moral character. Pascal urged people to pursue self-awareness through "learned ignorance" (contemplation of the implications of human limits). This, he hoped, would counter what he saw as the false optimism of the new scientific rationalism.

THE ENGLISH APPROACH TO SCIENCE AND RELIGION

Francis Bacon tried to reconcile religion and science by suggesting divine revelation could come through both the Bible and the study of nature. Because both were created by God, it followed logically, he said, that the truths each disclosed would ultimately be discovered to constitute one consistent whole.

QUICK REVIEW

Blaise Pascal (1623–1662)
- French mathematician and physical scientist
- Drawn to Jansenism
- Believed reason could lead humans to religion, but that religion operated beyond reason

The mechanistic view of the universe that the new science supported convinced Newton and many others that nature's rational order implied reason was a characteristic of nature's Creator. To study nature was to study the Creator and to move by stages from knowledge of phenomena to an understanding of their ultimate cause. This faith underlay *physico-theology,* a popular ideology that appealed to Europeans who were tiring of wars of religion. It held out the hope that science might end such conflicts by developing a new understanding of God on which all parties could agree. Faith in a rational God had the additional appeal of encouraging faith in human rationality and humanity's ability to overcome the errors of its past. The new way of life that was emerging in response to the new science was increasingly justified as part of a divine plan. It seemed obvious that because God had given human beings reason and placed them in a rational world, it was their duty to master it. The pursuit of scientific and economic progress were religious missions.

CONTINUING SUPERSTITION

Despite the optimistic confidence some European intellectuals had in the ultimate triumph of reason, many of their sixteenth- and seventeenth-century contemporaries continued to believe in magic and the occult. Almost all Europeans believed to some degree in the devil and the power of his demons.

WHAT FORMS did superstition take in response to science in the sixteenth and seventeenth centuries?

WITCH-HUNTS AND PANIC

The trust in traditional certainties that began to fade in the late Middle Ages inspired some people to look for ways to ground truth in reason and science, but there was a darker alternative. Many people responded to the era's intellectual challenges with fear and suspicion, and their desperate search for security sent them across the line that divides religion from superstition. This was as true for the learned as for the less educated. Between 1400 and 1700, from 70,000 to 100,000 people were sentenced to death in the West for practicing *malificium* (harmful magic) and diabolical witchcraft. Between episodes of persecuting their neighbors, witches were said to fly off to conventions called *sabbats* where they engaged in sexual orgies with the devil and practiced every imaginable indecency. The Reformation contributed to this development by emphasizing the power of demons and the devil while eliminating many of the traditional sacraments and rituals that had once offered a defense against these powers of darkness.

VILLAGE ORIGINS

Belief in witchcraft pervaded both elite and mass cultures, but it was deeply rooted in rural areas. Village societies have customarily dealt with the threats and terrors of life by turning for help to "cunning folk," to people who are believed to have special powers to avert or mitigate natural disasters and ease problems caused by disease and infertility. The witch cultures of medieval and early modern village societies may also have been a form of peasant self-assertion. They subverted oppressive urban Christianity authorities by perpetuating ancient, pre-Christian religious practices.

Because a reputation for possession of magical powers gave a person standing in a village society, such powers tended to be claimed by people who were most in need of influence—the elderly, the impoverished, and single or widowed women. Should any of their neighbors claim, however, that they used their powers for evil rather than good, they were also the members of society least able to defend themselves. (See "History's Voices: Why More Women Than Men Are Witches.")

HISTORY'S VOICES

WHY MORE WOMEN THAN MEN ARE WITCHES

*I*n 1486, two Dominican monks, Heinrich Krämer and Jacob Sprenger, published The Hammer of Witches, *a guide to the detection and punishment of witches that was sanctioned by Pope Innocent VIII. It is a classic expression of misogyny.*

WHAT PROOF do the authors offer that women are more prone to witchcraft than men? What kinds of evidence do they regard as convincing?

Why are there more superstitious women than men? The first [reason] is that women are more credulous. … The second reason is that women are naturally more impressionable and ready to receive the influence of a disembodied spirit. … The third reason is that they have slippery tongues…; and since they are weak, they find an easy and secret manner of vindicating themselves by witchcraft. … [Therefore] since women are feebler both in mind and body, it is not surprising that they should come more under the spell of witchcraft. …

But the natural reason [for woman's proclivity to witchcraft] is that she is more carnal than a man, as is clear from her many carnal abominations. And it should be noted that there was a defect in the formation of the first woman, since she was formed from a bent rib. … And since through this defect she is an imperfect animal, she always deceives. …

As to her other mental quality, her natural will, when she hates someone whom she formerly loved, then she seethes with anger and impatience in her whole soul. …

Just as through the first defect in their intelligence women are more prone [than men] to abjure the faith, so through their second defect of inordinate affections and passions they search for, brood over, and inflict various vengeances, either by witchcraft or by some other means. Wherefore it is no wonder that so great a number of witches exists in this sex. … Blessed be the Highest who has so far preserved the male sex from so great a crime.

From *Malleus Maleficarum*, trans. by Montague Summers (Bungay, Suffolk, U.K.: John Rodker, 1928), pp. 41–47. Reprinted by permission.

INFLUENCE OF THE CLERGY

The widespread faith in magic that was the essential precondition for the great witch-hunts of the sixteenth and seventeenth centuries was not confined to ordinary people. It was shared by intellectuals and the Christian clergy whose sacramental powers had something in common with magic. The church invoked fear of demons and the devil to persuade people to accept its discipline, and priests claimed the power to exorcise demons.

Inasmuch as magical power was not human in origin, theologians reasoned it had to come either from God or from the devil. In the thirteenth century, the church declared that its priests alone were entitled to exercise supernatural powers. It followed, therefore, that all other wonder workers had to have acquired their magical potency through pacts with the devil. The church sincerely believed it was its duty to root out the servants of the devil, but such work was also self-serving. By destroying the "cunning folk," the church cleansed villages of the people who competed with its priests for spiritual authority.

WHO WERE THE WITCHES?

Roughly 80 percent of the victims of witch-hunts were women, most of whom were single and between forty-five and sixty years of age. It is possible that persecution of witches provided a male-dominated society with a means for ridding itself

Three witches charged with practicing harmful magic are burned alive in Baden in southwest Germany. On the left, two of them are feasting with demons at a *sabbat.*

Bildarchiv Preussischer Kulturbesitz

of unconventional women who were not under some man's control. Or it may simply be that older single women were attacked not because of their gender but because they were perceived to be, with other poor people, burdens on society. Some female professions, such as midwifery and nursing, exposed women to suspicion of malfeasance by associating them with mysterious deaths. (See "Encountering the Past: Midwives.") Economic need may also have driven more women than men to risk claiming powers to heal and cast spells.

END OF THE WITCH-HUNTS

The great witch panics occurred in the second half of the sixteenth and early seventeenth centuries. They were, in part, a response to the suffering caused by the religious divisions and wars that were ravaging Europe. Increasing levels of violence exacerbated fear and hatred and inspired a search for scapegoats on which to vent these emotions. Witch-hunts also helped the authorities of church and state enforce conformity and eliminate dissidents.

By the end of the seventeenth century, some people began to fear things were getting out of hand, and the witch trials ceased when it became evident that witch hunting was destabilizing society, not establishing order. The emergence of the new scientific worldview also undercut belief in witches, and the improvements science brought to fields like medicine gave people greater confidence in their ability to solve their problems without resorting to the supernatural. The Reformation may also have helped end the witch craze by declaring God's absolute sovereignty and ridiculing the sacramental magic of the old church. For Protestants, God's freely offered grace, not magic, was the only defense against the power of evil.

BAROQUE ART

HOW DID baroque art serve both religious and secular ends?

The term *baroque* denotes a variety of related styles associated with seventeenth-century painting, sculpture, and architecture. Baroque painters depicted their subjects in a thoroughly naturalistic, rather than idealized, manner; this focus paralleled the interest in natural knowledge that was associated with the new science and deeper understanding of human anatomy. Baroque painters such as Michelangelo Caravaggio (1573–1610) showed sharp contrasts of light and darkness. Baroque painting and sculpture is dramatic and theatrical, drawing the observer into emotional involvement with the subject.

Baroque art served both religious and secular ends. Especially in Roman Catholic countries, baroque painters often portrayed Biblical scenes as a form of religious instruction. Artists also used this style to depict everyday life in realistic detail. Dutch painters, for example, portrayed elaborate foodstuffs, while artists such as Louis LeNain (ca. 1593–1648) painted scenes of French peasant life.

Rightly or wrongly, baroque art became associated with Roman Catholicism and absolutist politics. The style first emerged in papal Rome, where Gian Lorenzo Bernini's great Tabernacle—situated under the dome of St. Peter's basilica, above the space where St. Peter is said to be buried—is the most famous example, along with the two vast colonnades outside the church. Bernini also created the dramatic sculpture of the Spanish mystic St. Teresa of Avila (1515–1582), depicting her in religious ecstasy.

baroque Artistic and architectural Styles that were naturalistic rather than idealized to involve observer on an emotional level through dramatic portrayals.

ENCOUNTERING THE PAST

MIDWIVES

Although women were excluded from formal medical training until well into the nineteenth century, the delivery of children was largely left to professional women called midwives. Midwifery was a trade often pursued by elderly or widowed women of the lower social classes. They underwent years of apprenticeship, but were not permitted to organize themselves into guilds. They were licensed by civil and church authorities who were invariably men. Sometimes upper-class women were appointed to supervise them.

A reputation for respectability and discretion was essential for a midwife, for she witnessed some of life's most private moments and was privy to the intimate affairs of families. Her character was also assumed to have an effect on the outcome of a birth. A bad character was said to produce stillbirths and imperfectly formed infants. Carelessness or incompetence could, of course, void her license.

Midwives had religious and civic duties associated with births. In emergencies they could baptize failing infants. They registered births, and they were required to report to the authorities any suspicion of abortion or infanticide. A trusted midwife might also be called on to testify to a child's legitimacy.

Male physicians began to replace midwives in the eighteenth century, and civil authorities increasingly required persons who assisted at births to have a formal medical training that was not available to women. Midwives, however, never ceased to serve the poor and rural populations of Europe.

WHY WAS midwifery long considered a female activity? Why did men eventually take charge of supervising the birthing process?

Until well into the eighteenth century, midwives oversaw the delivery of most children in Europe.
© CORBIS

In the secular world, England's Charles I (r. 1625–1649) ruled as a near-absolute monarch without Parliament. He employed the Roman Catholic Flemish artist Peter Paul Rubens (1577–1640), the leading religious painter of the Catholic Reformation, to decorate the Banqueting Hall's ceiling at his London palace in honor of his father, James I (r. 1603–1625). As a result, Puritans were suspicious of the king's Catholic sympathies, and not by coincidence was Charles I led to his execution in 1649 through the Banqueting Hall. In France, the interior of Louis XIV's palace at Versailles was decorated with vast, dramatic paintings of Louis as the Sun King. The Hall of Mirrors, gardens, and fountains reflected the power of the king. Monarchs across Europe imitated Louis's ostentatious displays and hoped to replicate his absolutist power.

SUMMARY

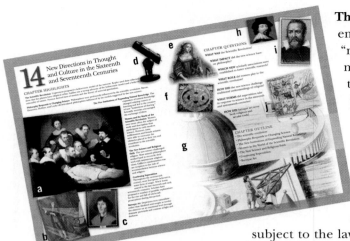

IMAGE KEY
for pages 340–341

a. Rembrandt van Rijn (1606–1669). "The Anatomy Lesson of Dr. Tulp." Mauritshuis, The Hague, The Netherlands.   Scala/Art Resource, NY

b. Newton analyzing the ray of light. Engraving by Loudan

c. Portrait of Astronomer Copernicus ca. 16th century

d. Newton's First Telescope

e. Margaret Cavendish, Duchess of Newcastle, writer

f. Scenographia: Systematis Copernicani Astrological Chart, c. 1543, devised by Nicolaus Copernicus (1473–1543)

g. Detail of "Tycho Brahe's Observatory on Ven" by Joan Blaeu ca. 2003 Ven, Denmark

h. Sir Francis Bacon (1561–1626). By Courtesy of the National Portrait Gallery, London

i. Portrait of the Italian Astronomer Galileo Galilei (1564–1642)

j. Three witches suspected of practicing harmful magic are burned alive on a pyre

The Scientific Revolution What we now call "science" emerged as a field of inquiry in the seventeenth century as "natural philosophy." Copernicus, hoping to simplify Ptolemy's geocentric system, had tentatively proposed in the sixteenth century that the sun might be the center of circular planetary motion. Brahe disagreed and performed extensive observations attempting to support the geocentric model. Brahe's assistant Kepler used Brahe's data to propose, in a 1609 book, that the sun was at the center of elliptical planetary orbits. Also in 1609, Galileo was the first to study astronomy through a telescope. Galileo became a strong advocate for the heliocentric universe and popularized the idea that the universe is rational and subject to the laws of mathematics. Finally, Newton combined mathematical modeling and scientific observation to derive his famous laws of motion and theory of universal gravitation.

Philosophy Responds to Changing Science Scientists of the seventeenth century were called natural philosophers, and there was some overlap between philosophers and natural philosophers. For this reason, and because of the challenges to traditional thinking posed by scientific work in this period, philosophers were profoundly influenced by the scientific revolution. Galileo's mathematical modeling of the physical world translated into a mechanistic worldview that was widespread among philosophers. Bacon, Descartes, Hobbes, and Locke all articulated philosophies that took aspects of the new science into account and also had implications for social and political organization.

The New Institutions of Expanding Natural Knowledge Through the Reformation, most intellectuals had believed their task was to recover and elaborate on knowledge from the Classical/biblical period. The expansion of natural knowledge changed universities and existing centers of learning, and it led to the creation of new "institutions of sharing." Scientific societies encouraged new kinds of social mingling and the cross-fertilization of ideas.

Women in the World of the Scientific Revolution European universities had offered little room for scholarship by women; the institutions of science soon turned out to be even more exclusionary. Not only were women prevented from becoming members of scientific societies and discouraged from practicing science on their own, but also women became objects of study and description—under the assumption they were inferior beings! Two categories of women were occasionally able to work around these constraints: noblewomen and female artisans. Women did write important scientific works and popularizations.

The New Science and Religious Faith The new science challenged religion in three ways: some scientific observations contradicted biblical descriptions (e.g., of the heavens); it was unclear who should resolve any potential conflicts between science and religion, natural philosophers or church authorities; and the new philosophy's materialism seemed to some to preclude spirituality. Most natural philosophers worked hard to reconcile their work with religious views, and they were generally successful. Galileo's condemnation by the church, however, was a dramatic exception to the general rule of accommodation between science and religion.

Continuing Superstition Through the seventeenth century, most Europeans believed in some form of magic and in the power of demons. "Magic," in the form of transubstantiation, was indeed at the heart of Christian ritual. Although such beliefs had been present for centuries, witch-hunts and panics soared in the late sixteenth and early seventeenth centuries. Possible explanations for this phenomenon include the impact of wars and upheaval, spiritual insecurity in the aftermath of the Reformation, and villagers' sublimated hostility toward urban leaders. There are also a variety of possible explanations for why witch-hunts died out in the seventeenth century.

Baroque Art In the seventeenth century, styles of painting, sculpture, and architecture collectively known as *baroque* came to prominence across Europe. Baroque depictions were naturalistic rather than idealized, and sought to involve the observer on an emotional level through dramatic portrayals and contrasts of light and darkness. Catholic baroque art and architecture aimed to instruct and impress. Secular artists depicted everyday life, but also created grandiose monuments to political absolutism, such as Louis XIV's palace at Versailles.

REVIEW QUESTIONS

1. What contributions to the scientific revolution were made by Copernicus, Brahe, Kepler, Galileo, and Newton? Was the scientific revolution truly a revolution? Which has a greater impact on history, political or intellectual revolution?

2. How do the political philosophies of Hobbes and Locke compare? How did each view human nature? Would you rather live under a government designed by Hobbes or by Locke? Why?

3. What prevented women from playing a greater role in the development of the new science? How did family connections enable some women to contribute to the advance of natural philosophy?

4. What things account for the church's condemnation of Galileo? How did Pascal try to reconcile faith and reason? How do you explain the fact that witchcraft and witch-hunts flourished during an age of scientific enlightenment?

5. What purposes and goals did baroque painting, sculpture, and architecture serve in the religious and secular spheres?

KEY TERMS

baroque   (p. 354)   **Ptolemaic system**   (p. 343)   **scientific revolution**   (p. 342)

  For additional study resources for this chapter, go to:
www.prenhall.com/kagan3/chapter14

Visualizing The Past...

Science, Art, and the Printing Press in Early Modern Europe

WHAT ROLE did art play in disseminating the discoveries of the scientific revolution? Why was the printing press especially important in this process?

O ne of the most important developments in the early modern period of European history (1450–1750) was the scientific revolution. Europeans, having finally absorbed the science of the ancient Greeks, lost to them until the close of the Middle Ages, were now ready to move beyond that legacy and, through exploration and experimentation, to make new scientific discoveries.

A new medium in Europe, the printing press, a machine Europeans developed in the fifteenth century, based on ideas originating in China, became the primary means of disseminating the new science. Images were as important as text in this process, and lavishly illusurated scientific works made scientific knowledge accessible to greater numbers of people than ever before. Science became a popular theme for European books and works of art.

This image is the title page to the sixteenth-century *Nova Reperta*, by Flemish artist Joannes Stradanus. *Nova Reperta* was a set of drawings celebrating the explosion of scientific discoveries, new technology, and new geographical discoveries of the sixteenth century. In this image we see depicted cartography and geography symbolized by the map of the New World, and gun powder, and the printing press.
The Newberry Library. Title page, *Nova Reperta*, 16th century engraving.
Photo courtesy of John M. Wing Foundation, The Newberry Library, Chicago
▼

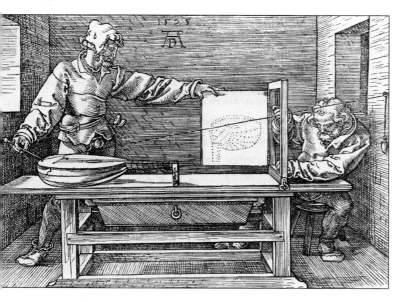

▲ **Engraving and woodcuts** became an especially important art form in the early modern period because they could be reproduced easily in books. Albrecht Dürer (1471–1528), one of the greatest artists of the Renaissance, was especially skilled at these art forms. Here we see a Dürer woodcut from the 1525 work *The Artist's Treatise on Geometry,* illustrating an artist using the technique of perspective to draw a lute.

Albrecht Durer, German, (1471–1528). *Artist Drawing a Lute,* demonstration of perspective from "The Artist's Treatise on Geometry," 1525, Woodcut. The Metropolitan Museum of Art, Harris Brisbane Dick Fund, 1941. (41,48.3)

This oil painting, Jan Vermeer's *The Astronomer,* is an excellent example of Dutch realism of the seventeenth century. Vermeer (1632–1675) painted many works for wealthy bourgeois households in Holland. What is interesting here is that the subject, an astronomer examining a globe of the heavens, would have attracted Vermeer's bourgeois clients. Science had become a central aspect of the cultural world and identity of ordinary Europeans by the second half of the seventeenth century. ▼

Jan Vermeer Van Delft (1632–1675). *The Astronomer.* Oil on canvas, 1668, 51.5 × 45.5 cm. RF 1983–28. The Louvre, Dpt. des Peintures, Paris, France, Photograph ©Erich Lessing/Art Resource, NY

▲ **Medicine also advanced** in the early modern period. One of the greatest physicians of the era was the Flemish doctor Andreas Vesalius. This image is an engraving, "De Humani corporis Fabrica," from Book II of Vesalius's *The Seven Books on the Structure of the Human Body (De humani corporis fabrica libri septem).* This landmark medical text used the artistic techniques developed in the Renaissance to depict the human form. It illustrated with great accuracy the human muscular system, in a format, the printed book, available to a relatively wide audience.

Andreas Vesalius (1514–1564), "Plate 25 from 'De Humani Corporis Fabrica,' Book II." Engraving. Courtesy of the New York Academy of Medicine Library

Europe in Transition 1300–1750

1300–1648

1648–1781

POLITICS AND GOVERNMENT

1309–1377 Popes reside in Avignon
1337–1453 Hundred Years' War
1356 *Golden Bull* creates German electoral college
1455–1485 Wars of the Roses in England
1519 Charles V crowned Holy Roman Emperor
1555 Peace of Augsburg recognizes the legal principle, *cuius regio, eius religio*
1558–1603 Reign of Elizabeth I of England
1572 Saint Bartholomew's Day Massacre
1588 English defeat of Spanish Armada
1598 Edict of Nantes gives Huguenots religious and civil rights
1624–1642 Era of Richelieu in France
1642 Outbreak of civil war in England

1648 Peace of Westphalia
1649–1652 The *Fronde* in France
1649 Charles I executed
1660 Charles II restored to the English throne
1661–1715 Louis XIV's years of personal rule
1682–1725 Reign of Peter the Great
1685 Louis XIV revokes Edict of Nantes
1688 "Glorious Revolution" in Britain
1700–1721 Great Northern War between Sweden and Russia
1701–1714 War of Spanish Succession
1740–1748 War of the Austrian Succession
1756–1763 Seven Years' War
1772 First Partition of Poland
1776 American Declaration of Independence

SOCIETY AND ECONOMY

1347–1350 Peak of Black Death
1450 Johann Gutenberg invents printing with movable type
1492 Christopher Columbus encounters the Americas
1498 Vasco da Gama reaches India
1519–1522 Ferdinand Magellan circumnavigates the Earth
1525 German Peasants' Revolt
1540 Spanish open silver mines in Peru, Bolivia, and Mexico
1550–1600 The great witch panics
1600–1700 Period of greatest Dutch economic prosperity
1607 English settle Jamestown, Virginia
1608 French settle Quebec
1618–1648 Thirty Years' War devastates German economy

1619 African slaves first bought at Jamestown, Virginia
1661–1683 Colbert seeks to stimulate French economic growth
1719 Mississippi Bubble in France
1750s Agricultural Revolution in Britain
1763 Britain becomes dominant in India
1763–1789 Enlightened absolutist rulers seek to spur economic growth
1765 James Hargreaves's spinning jenny
1769 Richard Arkwright's waterframe

RELIGION AND CULTURE

1300–1325 Dante Alghieri writes *Divine Comedy*
1302 Boniface VIII issues bull *Unam Sanctam*
1375–1527 The Renaissance in Italy
1378–1417 The Great Schism
1390–1430 Christine de Pisan writes in defense of women
1492 Expulsion of Jews from Spain
1513 Niccolo Machiavelli, *The Prince*
1516 Thomas More, *Utopia*
1517 Martin Luther's *Ninety-five Theses*
1534 Henry VIII declared head of English Church
1540 Jesuit order founded
1541 John Calvin becomes Geneva's reformer
1543 Copernicus, *On the Revolutions of the Heavenly Spheres*
1545–1563 Council of Trent

1549 English *Book of Common Prayer*
1609 Kepler, *The New Astronomy*
1632 Galileo, *Dialogue on the Two Chief Systems of the World*
1637 Descartes, *Discourse on Method*
1651 Hobbes, *Leviathan*
1687 Newton, *Principia Mathematica*
1689 English Toleration Act
1690 Locke, *Essay Concerning Human Understanding*
1748 Montesquieu, *Spirit of the Laws*
1751 First volume Diderot's *Encyclopedia*
1762 Rousseau, *Social Contract* and *Émile*
1763 Voltaire, *Treatise on Tolerance*
1774 Goethe, *The Sorrows of Young Werther*
1776 Smith, *Wealth of Nations*
1781 Kant, *Critique of Pure Reason*

Enlightenment and Revolution 1700–1850

1713–1824

1809–1848

POLITICS AND GOVERNMENT

1713 Treaty of Utrecht
1713–1740 Frederick William I builds Prussian military
1720–1740 Walpole in England, Fleury in France
1740–1748 War of the Austrian Succession
1756–1763 Seven Years' War
1772 First Partition of Poland
1775–1783 American Revolution
1789 Gathering of the Estates General at Versailles; fall of the Bastille, Declaration of the Rights of Man and Citizen
1793 Louis XVI executed, Second Partition of Poland
1793–1794 Reign of Terror
1795 Third Partition of Poland
1799 Napoleon named First Consul in France

1804 Napoleonic Code; Napoleon crowned emperor
1805 Third Coalition formed against France, battles of Trafalgar and Austerlitz
1806 Napoleon establishes the Continental System
1808 Spanish resistance to Napoleon stiffens
1812 Napoleon invades Russia; meets defeat
1814 Congress of Vienna opens
1815 Napoleon defeated at Waterloo
1821 Greek Revolution begins
1825 Decembrist Revolt in Russia
1829 Catholic Emancipation Act in Great Britain
1830 Revolution in France, Belgium, and Poland, Serbia gains independence
1832 Great Reform Bill in Britain
1848 Revolutions sweep across Europe

SOCIETY AND ECONOMY

1733 James Kay's flying shuttle
1750s Agricultural Revolution in Britain
1763 British establish dominance in India
1763–1789 Enlightened absolutist rulers seek to spur economic growth
1765 James Hargreaves's spinning jenny
1769 Richard Arkwright's waterframe
1773–1775 Pugachev's Rebellion
1787 Edmund Cartwright's power loom
1789–1802 Revolutionary legislation restructures French political and economic life
1794–1824 Wars of independence in Latin America break the colonial system

1810 Abolition of serfdom in Prussia
1825 Stockton and Darlington Railway opens
1828–1850 First European police departments
1833 English Factory Act to protect children
1834 German Zollverein established
1846 Corn Laws repealed in Britain
1848 Serfdom abolished in Austria and Hungary

RELIGION AND CULTURE

1721 Montesquieu, *Persian Letters*
1733 Voltaire, *Letters on the English*
1738 Voltaire, *Elements of the Philosophy of Newton*
1739 Wesley begins field preaching
1748 Hume, *Inquiry into Human Nature*
1748 Montesquieu, *Spirit of the Laws*
1751 First volume of Diderot's *Encyclopedia*
1762 Rousseau, *The Social Contract* and *Émile*
1763 Voltaire, *Treatise on Tolerance*
1774 Goethe, *The Sorrows of Young Werther*
1776 Smith, *Wealth of Nations*
1779 Lessing, *Nathan the Wise*
1781 Joseph II adopts toleration in Austria
1781 Kant, *The Critique of Pure Reason*

1790 Civil Constitution of the Clergy; Burke, *Reflections on the Revolution in France*
1792 Wollstonecraft, *Vindication of the Rights of Woman*
1802 Napoleon, *Concordat with the Papacy*
1806 Hegel, *Phenomenology of Mind*
1807 Fichte, *Addresses to the German Nation*
1808 Goethe, *Faust, Part I*
1817 Ricardo, *Principles of Political Economy*
1819 Byron, *Don Juan*
1829 Catholic Emancipation Act in Great Britain
1830–1842 Comte, *The Positive Philosophy*
1830 Lyell, *Principles of Geology*
1843 Kierkegaard, *Fear and Trembling*
1848 Marx and Engels, *Communist Manifesto*

The Foundations of Western Civilization in the Ancient World 1,000,000 B.C.E.–400 C.E.

1,000,000 B.C.E.–539 B.C.E.	750 B.C.E.–275 B.C.E.	431 B.C.E.–312 B.C.E.	46 B.C.E.–400 C.E.

POLITICS AND GOVERNMENT

2700–2200 B.C.E. Egyptian Old Kingdom	**612–539 B.C.E.** Neo-Babylonian (Chaldean) Empire	**338 B.C.E.** Philip of Macedon conquers Greece	**46–44 B.C.E.** Caesar's dictatorship
ca. 2370 B.C.E. Sargon established Akkadian Empire	**594 B.C.E.** Solon's constitutional reforms, Athens	**336–323 B.C.E.** Reign of Alexander III (the Great)	**43 B.C.E.** Second Triumvirate
2052–1786 B.C.E. Egyptian Middle Kingdom	**586 B.C.E.** Destruction of Jerusalem; fall of Judah (southern kingdom); Babylonian Captivity	**330 B.C.E.** Fall of Persepolis; end Achaemenid rule in Persia	**31 B.C.E.** Octavian and Agrippa defeat Anthony at Actium
1792–1750 B.C.E. Reign of Hammurabi; height of Old Babylonian Kingdom; publication of Code of Hammurabi	**559–530 B.C.E.** Reign of Cyrus the Great in Persia	**323–301 B.C.E.** Ptolemaic Kingdom (Egypt), Seleucid Kingdom (Syria), and Antigonid Dynasty (Macedon) founded	**27 B.C.E.–14 C.E.** Reign of Augustus
ca. 1700 B.C.E. Hyksos' Invasion of Egypt	**546 B.C.E.** Persia conquers Lydian Empire of Croesus, including Greek cities of Asia Minor	**287 B.C.E.** Laws passed by Plebeian Assembly made binding on all Romans; end of Struggle of the Orders	**14–68 C.E.** Reigns of Julio-Claudian Emperors
1575–1087 B.C.E. Egyptian New Kingdom (or Empire)	**539 B.C.E.** Persia conquers Babylonia; temple at Jerusalem restored; exiles return from Babylonia	**264–241 B.C.E.** First Punic War	**69–96 C.E.** Reigns of Flavian Emperors
ca. 1400–1200 B.C.E. Height of Hittite Empire	**521–485 B.C.E.** Reign of Darius in Persia	**218–202 B.C.E.** Second Punic War	**96–180 C.E.** Reigns of "Good Emperors"
ca. 1400–1200 B.C.E. Height of Mycenaean power	**509 B.C.E.** Kings expelled from Rome; Republic founded	**215–168 B.C.E.** Rome establishes rule over Hellenistic world	**284–305 C.E.** Reign of Diocletian; reform and division of Roman Empire
ca. 1100–615 B.C.E. Assyrian Empire	**508 B.C.E.** Clisthenes founds Athenian democracy	**133 B.C.E.** Tribunate of Tiberius Gracchus	**306–337 C.E.** Reign of Constantine
ca. 800–400 B.C.E. Height of Etruscan culture in Italy	**490 B.C.E.** Battle of Marathon	**123–122 B.C.E.** Tribunate of Gaius Gracchus	**330 C.E.** Constantinople new capital of Roman Empire
ca. 700–500 B.C.E. Rise and decline of tyranny in Greece	**480–479 B.C.E.** Xerxes invades Greece	**60 B.C.E.** First Triumvirate	**376 C.E.** Visigoths enter Roman Empire
	431–404 B.C.E. Great Peloponnesian War		
	392 B.C.E. Romans defeat Etruscans		
	362 B.C.E. Battle of Mantinea; end of Theban hegemony		

SOCIETY AND ECONOMY

ca. 1,000,000–10,000 B.C.E. Paleolithic Age	**ca. 750–700 B.C.E.** Rise of *Polis* in Greece	**431–400 B.C.E.** Peloponnesian War casualties cause decline in size of lower class in Athens, with relative increase in importance of upper and middle classes	**ca. 150–400 C.E.** Decline of slavery and growth of tenant farming and serfdom in Roman Empire
ca. 8,000 B.C.E. Earliest Neolithic settlements	**ca. 750–600 B.C.E.** Great age of Greek colonization	**ca. 300 B.C.E.–150 C.E.** Growth of international trade and development of large cities in Hellenistic/Roman world	**ca. 250–400 C.E.** *Coloni* (Roman tenant farmers) increasingly tied to the land
ca. 3500 B.C.E. Earliest Sumerian settlements			
ca. 3000 B.C.E. First urban settlements in Egypt and Mesopotamia; Bronze Age begins in Mesopotamia and Egypt			
ca. 2900–1150 B.C.E. Bronze Age Minoan society on Crete; Helladic society on Greek mainland			
ca. 2000 B.C.E. Hittites arrive in Asia Minor			
ca. 1200 B.C.E. Hebrews arrive in Palestine			
ca. 1100–750 B.C.E. Greek "Dark Ages"			

RELIGION AND CULTURE

ca. 30,000–6000 B.C.E. Paleolithic art	**ca. 500–400 B.C.E.** Great age of Athenian tragedy	**106–43 B.C.E.** Life of Cicero	**325 C.E.** Council of Nicaea
ca. 3000 B.C.E. Invention of writing	**469–399 B.C.E.** Life of Socrates	**70–19 B.C.E.** Life of Vergil	**348–420 C.E.** Life of St. Jerome
ca. 3000 B.C.E. Temples to gods in Mesopotamia; development of ziggurat temple architecture	**ca. 450–385 B.C.E.** Great age of Athenian comedy	**65–8 B.C.E.** Life of Horace	**354–430 C.E.** Life of St. Augustine
2700–2200 B.C.E. Building of pyramids for Egyptian god-kings, development of hieroglypic writing in Egypt	**448–432 B.C.E.** Periclean building program on Athenian acropolis	**59 B.C.E.–17 C.E.** Life of Livy	**395 C.E.** Christianity becomes official religion of Roman Empire
ca. 1900 B.C.E. Traditional date for Hebrew patriarch Abraham	**429–347 B.C.E.** Life of Plato	**43 B.C.E.–18 C.E.** Life of Ovid	
ca. 750 B.C.E. Hebrew prophets teach monotheism	**ca. 400 B.C.E.** Thucydides' history of the Peloponnesian War	**9 C.E.** Ara Pacis dedicated at Rome	
ca. 750 B.C.E. Traditional date for Homer	**384–322 B.C.E.** Life of Aristotle	**ca. 4 B.C.E.** Birth of Jesus of Nazareth	
ca. 750 B.C.E. Greeks adapt Semitic script and invent the Greek alphabet	**342–271 B.C.E.** Life of Epicurus	**ca. 30 C.E.** Crucifixion of Jesus	
ca. 570 B.C.E. Birth of Greek philosphy in Ionia	**335–263 B.C.E.** Life of Zeno the Stoic	**64 C.E.** Christians persecuted by Nero	
539 B.C.E. Restoration of temple in Jerusalem; return of exiles	**ca. 287–212 B.C.E.** Life of Archimedes of Syracuse	**ca. 70–100 C.E.** Gospels written	
	ca. 275 B.C.E. Founding of museum and library make Alexandria the center of Greek intellectual life	**ca. 150 C.E.** Ptolemy of Alexandria establishes canonical geocentric model of the universe	
		303 C.E. Persecution of Christians by Diocletian	
		312 C.E. Constantine converts to Christianity	

Global Conflict, Cold War, and New Directions 1939–2005

1939–1980

1980–2005

POLITICS AND GOVERNMENT

1939 World War II begins
1941 Japan attacks Pearl Harbor, U.S. enters war
1942 Battle of Stalingrad
1945 Yalta Conference; Germany surrenders; atomic bombs dropped on Japan; Japan surrenders; United Nations founded
1947 Truman Doctrine
1948 Communist takeover in Czechoslovakia and Hungary; State of Israel proclaimed
1949 NATO founded; East and West Germany emerge as separate states
1950–1953 Korean War
1954 French defeat at Dien Bien Phu
1955 Warsaw Pact founded

1956 Khrushchev denounces Stalin; Suez crisis; Soviet invasion of Hungary
1961 Berlin Wall erected
1962 Cuban Missile Crisis
1963–1973 Major U.S. involvement in Vietnam
1968 Soviet invasion of Czechoslovakia
1975 Helsinki Accords
1979–1988 Soviet troops in Afghanistan
1985 Gorbachev comes to power in the Soviet Union
1989 Revolutions sweep across Eastern Europe
1990 German reunification; Yugoslavia breaks up
1991 Persian Gulf War; Soviet Union dissolved
2001 U.S. attacked by terrorists
2003 U.S. invades Iraq
2005 Angela Merkl becomes first female chancellor in German history

SOCIETY AND ECONOMY

1945–1951 Attlee ministry establishes the Welfare State in Great Britain
1947 Marshall Plan to rebuild Europe instituted
1949 Europe divided into Eastern and Western blocs
1957 European Economic Community founded
1960s Rapid growth of student population in universities; migration of workers from eastern and southern to northern and western Europe; migration of non-European workers to northern and western Europe
1972 Club of Rome founded
1973–1974 Arab oil embargo

1980s and 1990s Internal migration from Eastern to Western Europe; racial and ethnic tensions in Western Europe
1990s Changes in Eastern Europe and Soviet Union open way for economic growth and new trade relations across Europe

RELIGION AND CULTURE

1940 Koestler, *Darkness at Noon*
1943 Sartre, *Being and Nothingness*
1947 Camus, *The Plague*; Gramsci, *Letters from Prison*
1949 de Beauvoir, *The Second Sex*; Crossman, *The God That Failed*
1958 Pasternak forbidden to accept Nobel Prize for *Dr. Zhivago*; John XXIII becomes pope
1960s The Beatles take world by storm
1962–1965 Second Vatican Council
1963 Solzhenitsyn, *One Day in the Life of Ivan Denisovich*
1968 Student rebellion in Paris
1974 Solzhenitsyn expelled from Soviet Union

1978 John Paul II becomes pope
1980s Growth of the environmental movement
1990s Expanding influence of Roman Catholic Church in independent Eastern Europe
1990s Feminists continue the critical tradition of Western culture
1990s Era of the Internet begins
2005 Benedict XVI becomes pope

Toward the Modern World 1850–1939

1850–1900

1900–1939

POLITICS AND GOVERNMENT

1854–1856 Crimean War
1861 Proclamation of the Kingdom of Italy
1867 Austro-Hungarian Dual Monarchy founded
1869 Suez Canal completed
1870 Franco-Prussian War; French Republic proclaimed
1871 German Empire proclaimed; Paris Commune
1880s Britain establishes Protectorate in Egypt
1882 Italy, Germany, Austria form Triple Alliance
1894 Dreyfus convicted in France; Nicholas II becomes tsar of Russia
1898 Germany begins to build a battleship navy
1904 Britain and France in Entente Cordiale
1908–1909 Bosnian crisis

1911 Second Moroccan crisis
1912 Third Irish Home Rule Bill passed
1912–1913 First and Second Balkan Wars
1914–1918 World War I
1917 Russian Revolution; Bolsheviks seize power
1919 Paris Peace Conference; Weimar constitution proclaimed in Germany
1922 Mussolini takes power in Italy
1923 France invades the Ruhr; Hitler's Beer Hall *Putsch*; first Labour government in Britain
1931 National Government formed in Great Britain
1933 Hitler appointed chancellor of Germany
1935 Nuremburg Laws; Italy invades Ethiopia
1936 Popular Front in France; purge trials in the Soviet Union; Spanish Civil War begins
1938 Munich Conference; *Kristallnacht* in Germany
1939 Germany invades Poland, starts World War II

SOCIETY AND ECONOMY

1850–1910 Height of European outward migration
1853–1870 Haussmann redesigns Paris
1857 Bessemer steelmaking process
1861 Serfdom abolished in Russia
1870 Education Act and first Irish Land Act, Britain
1875 Public Health and Artisan Dwelling Acts, Britain
1881 Second Irish Land Act
1886 Daimler invents internal combustion engine
1894 Union of German Women's Organizations founded
1901 National Council of French Women founded
1903 Third Irish Land Act; British Women's Social and Political Union founded; Wright brothers fly the first airplane

1906 Land redemption payments canceled for Russian peasants
1907 Women vote on national issues in Norway
1918 Vote granted to some British women
1921 Soviet Union begins New Economic Policy
1923 Rampant inflation in Germany
1926 General strike in Great Britain
1928 Britain extends full franchise to women
1928–1933 First Five-Year Plan and agricultural collectivization in the Soviet Union
1929 Wall Street crash
1932 Lausanne Conference ends German reparations
mid-1930s Nazis stimulate German economy through public works and defense spending

RELIGION AND CULTURE

1850–1880 Jewish emancipation in much of Europe
1853–1854 Gobineau, *Essay on the Inequality of the Human Races*
1857 Flaubert, *Madame Bovary*
1859 Darwin, *On the Origin of Species*
1864 Pius IX, *Syllabus of Errors*
1867 Mill, *The Subjection of Women*
1871 Darwin, *The Descent of Man*; Religious tests abolished at Oxford and Cambridge
1872 Nietzsche, *The Birth of Tragedy*
1873–1876 Bismarck's *Kulturkampf*
1879 Ibsen, *A Doll's House*
1880s Growing anti-Semitism in Europe
1880 Zola, *Nana*
1883 Nietzsche, *Thus Spake Zarathustra*
1892 Ibsen, *The Master Builder*
1896 Herzl, *The Jewish State*
1899 Bernstein, *Evolutionary Socialism*

1900 Freud, *The Interpretation of Dreams*; Key, *The Century of the Child*
1902 Lenin, *What Is to Be Done?*
1905 Weber, *The Protestant Ethic and the Spirit of Capitalism*; Termination of the Napoleonic Concordat in France
1910 Pope Pius X requires anti-Modernist oath
1920 Keynes, *Economic Consequences of the Peace*
1922 Joyce, *Ulysses*
1924 Hitler, *Mein Kampf*
1929 Woolf, *A Room of One's Own*
1936 Keynes, *General Theory of Employment, Interest, and Money*
1937 Orwell, *Road to Wigan Pier*
1938 Sartre, *Nausea*

A Chronological Survey of Western Civilization

The Middle Ages 476 C.E.–1300 C.E.

476 C.E.–843 C.E.

850 C.E.–1275 C.E.

POLITICS AND GOVERNMENT

330 Constantinople becomes new capital of Roman Empire	918 Saxon Henry I becomes first non-Frankish king in Germany
410 Visigoths sack Rome	987 Capetians succeed Carolingians in France
451–453 Attila the Hun invades Italy	1066 Battle of Hastings (Norman Conquest of England)
455 Vandals overrun Rome	1071 Seljuk Turks defeat Byzantine armies at Manzikert
476 Odovacer deposes the last Western emperor	1099 Jerusalem falls to Crusaders
489–493 Theodoric's Ostrogoth kingdom established in Italy	1152 Frederick I Barbarossa first Hohenstaufen emperor
527–565 Reign of Justinian	1187 Saladin reconquers Jerusalem from West
568 Lombard invasion of Italy	1204 Fourth Crusade captures Constantinople
632–733 Muslim expansion and conquests	1214 Philip II Augustus defeats English and German armies at Bouvines
732 Charles Martel defeats Muslims at Poitiers	1215 *Magna Carta*
768–814 Reign of Charlemagne	1240 Mongols dominate Russia
843 Treaty of Verdun partitions Carolingian empire	1250 Death of Frederick II (end of Hohenstaufen dynasty)
	1257 German princes establish electoral college to elect emperor

SOCIETY AND ECONOMY

400 Cities and trade begin to decline in the West; Germanic (barbarian) tribes settle in the West	850 Muslims occupy parts of Spain
533–534 *Corpus juris civilis* compiled by Justinian	880s Vikings penetrate central Europe
632–733 Muslims disrupt western Mediterranean trade	900 Introduction of the horseshoe
700 Agrarian society centered around the manor predominates in the West	900–1100 Rise of towns, guilds, and urban culture in West
700–800 Moldboard plow and three-field system in use	1086 *Domesday Book*
700 Islam enters its Golden Age	1130 Gothic architecture begins to displace Romanesque
800 Byzantium enters its Golden Age	1200 Shift from dues to rent tenancy on manors
800 Introduction of collar harness	

RELIGION AND CULTURE

312 Constantine embraces Christianity	910 Benedictine monastery of Cluny founded
325 Council of Nicaea	980s Orthodox Christianity penetrates Russia
395 Christianity becomes the official religion of the Roman Empire	1054 Schism between Eastern and Western churches
413–426 Saint Augustine writes *City of God*	1075 Pope Gregory VII condemns lay investiture
451 Council of Chalcedon	1095 Pope Urban II preaches the First Crusade
496 The Franks embrace Christianity	1122 Concordat of Worms ends investiture controversy
529 Saint Benedict founds monastery at Monte Cassino	1158 First European university founded in Bologna
537 Byzantine Church of Hagia Sophia completed	1210 Franciscan order founded
590–604 Pope Gregory the Great	1216 Dominican order founded
622 Muhammad's flight from Mecca (Hegira)	1265 Thomas Aquinas's *Summa Theologica* begun
725–787 Iconoclastic Controversy in East	ca. 1275 *Romance of the Rose*
ca. 775 *Donation of Constantine*	
782 Alcuin of York runs Charlemagne's palace school	
800 Beginning of Carolingian Renaissance	

absolutism   Government by a ruler with absolute authority.

Academy   School founded by Plato in Athens to train statesmen and citizens.

Acropolis   At the center of the city of Athens, the most famous example of a citadel.

Act of Supremacy   Act of 1534 proclaiming Henry VIII "the only supreme head on earth of the Church of England."

agape   Common meal, or "love feast," that was the central ritual of the church in early Christianity.

agora   Place for markets and political assemblies.

Ahura Mazda   The chief deity of Zoroastrianism, the native religion of Persia. Ahura Mazda is the creator of the world, the source of light, and the embodiment of good.

Albigensians   Heretical sect that advocated a simple, pious way of life following the example set by Jesus and the Apostles, but rejecting key Christian doctrines.

Anabaptists   ("rebaptizers") The most important of several groups of Protestants forming more radical organizations that sought a more rapid and thorough restoration of the "primitive Christianity" described in the New Testament.

anarchists   Those who opposed any cooperation with industry or government.

anti-Semitism   Prejudice against Jews often displayed through hostility.

Anschluss   Union of Germany and Austria.

apostolic succession   Special powers that were passed down from one generation of bishops to another.

appeasement   Allied policy of making concessions to Germany based on the belief that Germany's grievances were real and Hitler's goals limited.

Aramaic   Semitic language spoken widely throughout the Middle East in antiquity.

Arianism   Belief that Christ was the first of God the Father's creations and the being through whom the Father created all other things.

Areopagus   Council heading Athens's government comprised of a group of nobles that annually chose the city's nine *archons*, the magistrates who administered the *polis*.

arete   The highest virtue in Homeric society: the manliness, courage, and excellence that equipped a hero to acquire and defend honor.

aristocratic resurgence   Eighteenth-century resurgence of nobles that mantained the exclusiveness of noble rank, made it difficult to obtain, reserved powerful posts to nobles, and protected nobles from taxation.

Attica   Region (about 1,000 square miles) that Athens dominated.

Augsburg Confession   Moderate Protestant creed endorsed by the Schmalkaldic League (a defensive alliance of Lutherans).

Augustus   ("revered") Name by which the Senate hailed Octavian for his restoration of the republic.

Avignon Papacy   Period from 1309 to 1377 when the papal court was situated in Avignon, France, and gained a reputation for greed and worldly corruption.

Axis   Forces (opposed to the Allies) joined together in Europe, including Germany and Italy, before and during World War II.

banalities   Monopolies maintained by landowners giving them the right to demand that tenants pay to grind all their grain in the landowner's mill and bake all their bread in his oven.

baroque   Artistic and architectural Styles that were naturalistic rather than idealized to involve observer on an emotional level through dramatic portrayals.

Beguines   Sisterhoods of pious, self-supporting single women.

Black Death   Virulent plague that struck in Sicily in 1347 and spread through Europe. It discolored the bodies of its victims. By the early fifteenth century, the plague may have reduced the population of western Europe by two-fifths.

Bolsheviks   ("majority") Lenin's turn-of-the-century Russian faction favoring a party of elite professionals who would provide the working class with centralized leadership.

boyars   Wealthy landowners among the freemen in late medieval Russia.

Brezhnev Doctrine   Asserted the right of the Soviet Union to intervene in domestic politics of communist countries.

Bronze Age   (3100–1200 B.C.E.) Began with the increasing importance of metal that also ended the Stone Ages.

Caesaropapism   Emperor acting as if he were pope as well as caesar.

caliphate   Office of the leader of the Muslim community.

categorical imperative   Kant's view that all human beings possess an innate sense of moral duty, an inner command to act in every situation as one would have other people act in that same situation.

catholic   ("universal") As in "universal" majority of Christians.

censors   Men of unimpeachable reputation, chosen to carry the responsibility for enrolling, keeping track of, and determining the status and tax liability of each citizen.

Chartism   The London Working Men's Association's 1838 proposal for political reform featuring the Six Points.

Christian Democratic parties   Postwar parties that welcomed non-Catholic members and fought for democracy, social reform, and economic growth.

civilization   Stage in the evolution of organized society that has among its characteristics urbanism, long-distance trade, writing systems, and accelerated technological and social development.

Cold War   Period between the end of World War II (1945) and the collapse of the Soviet Union (1991) in which U.S. and Soviet relations were tense, seemingly moments away from actual war at any time during these years.

coloni   Tenant farmers who were bound to the lands they worked.

condottieri   Military brokers from whom one could hire a mercenary army.

Congregationalists   The more extreme Puritans who believed every congregation ought to be autonomous, a law unto itself controlled by neither bishops nor presbyterian assemblies.

conquistadores   "Conquerors"

conservatism   Form of political thought that, in mid-nineteenth-century Europe, promoted legitimate monarchies, landed aristocracies, and established churches.

Consulate   A republican facade for one-man government by Napoleon.

consuls   Elected magistrates from patrician families chosen annually to lead the army, oversee the state religion, and sit as judges.

containment   American foreign policy strategy (beginning in 1947) for countering the communist threat and resisting the spread of Soviet influence.

Convention   The newly elected French body that met on September 21, 1792, whose first act was to declare France a republic—a nation governed by an elected assembly without a king.

corporatism   Fascist policy organizing major industries as syndicates of labor and management devised to steer an economic course between socialism and a liberal laissez-faire system.

Counter-Reformation   A reorganization of the Catholic Church that equipped it to meet the challenges posed by the Protestant Reformation.

Creole   Merchants, landowners, and professional people of Spanish descent.

Crusades   Campaigns authorized by the church to combat heresies and rival faiths.

Cubism   Autonomous realm of art with no purpose beyond itself. Includes as many different perspectives, angles, or views of the object as possible.

culture   Way of life invented by a group and passed on by teaching.

cuneiform   Developed by the Sumerians as the very first writing system ever used, it used several thousand characters, some of which stood for words and some for sounds.

deism   The *philosophes'* theology. A rational religion, a faith without fanaticism and intolerance that acknowledged the sovereign authority of reason.

Delian League   Pact joined in 478 B.C.E. by Athenians and other Greeks to continue the war with Persia.

détente   Relaxation of tensions between the United States and Soviet Union that involved increased trade and reduced deployment of strategic arms.

"divine right of kings"   The belief that God appoints kings and that kings are accountable only to God for how they use their power.

domestic system of textile production   Means by which urban merchants obtained their wares. They bought wool or other unfinished fiber for distribution to peasant workers who took it home, spun it into thread, wove it into cloth, and returned the finished product to the merchants for sale.

ego   Among Freud's three entities of the mind, the *ego* mediates between the impulsive id and the self-denying superego.

émigrés   French aristocrats and enemies of the revolution who fled to countries on France's borders and set up bases for counterrevolutionary activities.

encomienda   Legal grant of the right to the labor of a specific number of Indians for a particular period of time. This was used as a Spanish strategy for exploiting the labor of the natives.

Epicureans   People who believed the proper pursuit of humankind is undisturbed withdrawal from the world.

equestrians   Men rich enough to qualify for cavalry service.

Estates General   Assembly of representatives from France's propertied classes.

eucharist   ("thanksgiving") Celebration of the Lord's Supper in which bread and wine were blessed and consumed.

euro   Launched in 1999 by the EU, a single currency circulating in most of Western Europe.

European Constitution   Treaty that would transfer considerable decision-making authority from governments of the individual states to the Union's central institutions.

European Economic Community (EEC)   European nations as members of the "Common Market" pledging to eliminate traiffs, guarantee unimpeded flow of capital and labor, and establish uniform wage scales and social benefits.

European Union (EU)   Formerly the European Economic Community (EEC), renamed in 1993.

existentialism   Maintains that the human condition is greater than the sum of its parts and can only be grouped as whole.

fascism   System of extreme right-wing dictatorial government.

fiefs   ("Lands") Granted to cavalry men to fund their equipment and service.

Fourteen Points   President Woodrow Wilson's idealistic principles articulated as America's goals in World War I, including self- determination for nationalities, open diplomacy, freedom of the seas, disarmament, and establishment of a league of nations to keep the peace.

Fronde   Widespread rebellions in France between 1649 and 1652 (named after a slingshot used by street ruffians) aimed at reversing the drift toward absolute monarchy and preserving local autonomy.

Gallican Liberties   The French Roman Catholic Church's ecclesiastical independence of papal authority in Rome.

Gaul   Area that is now modern France.

ghettos   Separate districts in cities and entire villages in the countryside where Jews lived apart from Christians in eighteenth- century Europe.

glasnost ("openness") Gorbachev's policy of opening the way for unprecedented public discussion and criticism of Soviet history and the Communist Party. Censorship was relaxed and dissidents were released from prison.

"Glorious Revolution" Parliament's bloodless 1688 declaration of a vacant throne and proclamation that William and Mary were its heirs.

Golden Bull Arrangements agreed to by the Holy Roman Emperor and the major German territorial rulers in 1356 that helped stabilize Germany.

Great Purges The arrests, trials, Communist Party expulsions, and executions—beginning with the assassination of Politburo member Sergei Kirov in December 1934—that mainly targeted Party officials and reached its climax from 1936 to 1938.

Green movement Made up, in part, of members from the radical student groups of the 1960s, this movement was anticapitalistic, peace oriented, in opposition of nuclear arms, and condemned business for producing pollution. Unlike earlier student groups, though, the Greens opted to compete in the electoral process.

hacienda Large landed estate that characterized most Spanish colonies.

Hegira Forced flight of Muhammad and his followers to Medina, 240 miles north of Mecca. This event marks the beginning of the Islamic calendar.

Hellenistic Term that describes the cosmopolitan civilization, established under the Macedonians, that combined aspects of Greek and Middle Eastern cultures.

Helots Slaves to the Spartans that revolted and nearly destroyed Sparta in 650 B.C.E.

heretics "Takers" of contrary positions, namely in Christianity.

hieroglyphs ("sacred carving") Greek name for Egyptian writing. The writing was often used to engrave holy texts on monuments.

Holy Roman Empire The domain of the German monarchs who revived the use of the Roman imperial title during the Middle Ages.

home rule Government of a country or locality by its own citizens.

hoplite A true infantry soldier that began to dominate the battlefield in the late eighth century B.C.E.

Homo sapiens Our own species, which dates back roughly 200,000 years.

hubris Arrogance produced by excessive wealth or good fortune.

Huguenots French Protestants, named after Besançon Hugues, the leader of the revolt that won Geneva its freedom at that time.

humanitas Wide-ranging intellectual curiosity and habits of critical thinking that are the goals of liberal education.

iconoclasm Opposition to the use of images in Christian worship.

id Among Freud's three entities of the mind, the *id* consists of innate, amoral, irrational drives for sexual gratification, aggression, and sensual pleasure.

Iliad Homer's poem narrates a dispute between Agamemnon the king and his warrior Achilles, whose honor is wounded and then avenged.

imperator "Commander in chief."

imperialism Policy of expanding a nation's power by seeking hegemony over alien peoples.

imperium Right held by a Roman king to enforce commands by fines, arrests, and corporal and capital punishment.

Impressionism Focuses on social life and leisured activities of the urban middle and lower- middle classes, a fascination with light, color, and representation of momentary experience of social life or of landscape.

indulgence Remission of the obligation to perform a "work of satisfaction" for a sin.

Industrial Revolution Term coined by early nineteenth-century observers to describe the changes that the spreading use of powered machinery made in society and economics.

Inquisition Formal ecclesiastical court dedicated to discovering and punishing heresy.

Intolerable Acts Series of laws passed by Parliament in 1774 that closed the port of Boston, reorganized the government of Massachusetts, quartered soldiers in private homes, and transferred trials of customs officials accused of crimes to England.

Ionia Western coast of Asia Minor.

Islam New religion appearing in Arabia in the sixth century in response to the work of the Prophet Muhammad.

Jacobins The best organized of the political clubs, they embraced the most radical of the Enlightenment's political theories, and they wanted a republic, not a constitutional monarchy.

Jacquerie (From "Jacques Bonhomme," a peasant caricature) Name given to the series of bloody rebellions that desperate French peasants waged beginning in 1358.

Jansenism Appearing in the 1630s, it followed the teachings of St. Augustine, who stressed the role divine grace played in human salvation.

jihad A struggle; interpreted as a call for religious war.

Junkers (Prussian nobles) They were allowed to demand absolute obedience from the serfs on their estates in exchange for their support of the Hohenzollerns.

jus gentium Law of all peoples as opposed to the law that reflected only Roman practice.

jus naturale Law of nature that enshrined the principles of divine reason that Cicero and the Stoics believed governed the universe.

Ka'ba One of Arabia's holiest shrines located in Mecca, the birthplace of Muhammad.

Keynesian economics Economic theories and programs ascribed to John M. Keynes and his followers advocating government monetary and fiscal policies that increase employment and spending.

Kulturkampf ("cultural struggle") An extreme church-state conflict waged by Bismarck in Germany during the 1870s in response to a perceived threat to German political unity from the Roman Catholic Church.

laissez-faire Policy of noninterference, especially the policy of government noninterference in economic affairs or business.

latifundia Great estates that produced capital-intensive cash crops for the international market.

Latium Region located in present-day Italy that included the small town of Rome.

Lebensraum German for "living space."

levée en masse Order for total military mobilization of both men and property.

Lower Egypt The Nile's 100-mile deep, triangularly shaped delta.

Luftwaffe The German air force.

Lyceum School founded by Aristotle in Athens that focused on the gathering and analysis of data from all fields of knowledge.

Magna Carta ("Great Charter") Document spelling out limitations on royal authority agreed to by John in 1215. It created foundation for modern English law.

Magna Graecia ("Great Greece") The areas in southern Italy and Sicily where many Greek colonies were established.

mandate Territory under the aegis of the League of Nations but actually ruled as a colony.

mannerism Reaction against the simplicity, symmetry, and idealism of High Renaissance art. It made room for the strange, even the abnormal, and gave free reign to the subjectivity of the artist. The name reflects a tendency by artists to employ "mannered" ("affected") techniques—distortions that expressed individual perceptions and feelings.

manor Communal farm considered to be early medieval Europe's chief economic institution.

manor A self-sufficient rural community that was a fundamental institution of medieval life.

Marshall Plan The U.S. European Recovery Program introduced by George C. Marshall, American secretary of state, whereby America provided extensive economic aid to the European states, conditional only on their working together for their mutual benefit.

Marxism Socialist movement begun by Karl Marx in the mid–nineteenth century that differed from competing socialist views primarily in its claim to a scientific foundation and in its insistence on reform through revolution.

Mein Kampf (*My Struggle*) Strategy dictated by Adolf Hitler during his period of imprisonment in 1923 outlining his political views.

Mensheviks ("minority") Turn-of-the-century Russian faction that wanted to create a party with a large mass membership (like Germany's SPD).

mercantilism Economic theory in which governments heavily regulated trade and promoted empires in order to increase national wealth.

Messiah Redeemer who would vindicate faith and establish the kingdom of God on earth.

Methodism Movement begun in England by John Wesley, an Oxford-educated Anglican priest, the first major religion to embody romanticism. It emphasized religion as a "method" for living more than a set of doctrines.

millets Communities of the officially recognized religions that governed portions of the Ottoman Empire.

Minoan Civilization of Crete (2100–1150 B.C.E.), and the Aegean's first civilization, named for a legendary king on the island.

modernism Movement of the 1870s criticizing middle-class society and traditional morality.

Monophysites Believers in a single, immortal nature of Christ; not both eternal God and mortal man in one and the same person.

monotheism Having faith in a single God.

Mycenaean Civilization occupying mainland Greece during the Late Helladic era (1580–1150 B.C.E.).

nationalism The belief that the people who share an ethnic identity (language, culture, and history) should also be recognized as having a right to a government and political identity of their own.

NATO North Atlantic Treaty Organization, a mutual defense pact.

natural selection Darwin and Wallace's theory that those species with a unique trait that gives them a marginal advantage in the struggle for existence change the nature of their species by reproducing more successfully than their competitors; the fittest survive to pass on their unique characteristics.

naturalists Authors who tried to portray nature and human life without sentimentality.

Nazis Members of the National Socialist German Workers' Party that formed in 1920 and supported a mythical Aryan race alleged to be the source of the purest German lineage.

neo-gothic Style that idealized nature and portrayed it in all its power.

Neoclassicism Style that embodied a return to figurative and architectural models drawn from the Renaissance and the ancient world.

Neolithic "New stone" age, dating back 10,000 years to when people living in some parts of the Middle East made advances in the production of stone tools and shifted from hunting and gathering to agriculture.

nomes Egyptian districts ruled by regional governors who were called nomarchs.

Odyssey   Homer's epic poem tells of the wanderings of the hero Odysseus.

Old Regime   Eighteenth-century era marked by absolutist monarchies, agrarian economies, tradition, hierarchy, corporateness, and privilege.

optimates   ("the best men") Opponents of Tiberius and defenders of the traditional prerogatives of the Senate.

orthodox   ("correct") As in "correct" faith in Christianity.

Ottoman Empire   The authority Instanbul's Ottoman Turkish sultan exercised over the Balkans, the Middle East, and North Africa from the end of the Middle Ages to World War I.

Paleolithic   Greek for "old stone"; the earliest period in cultural development that began with the first use of stone tools about a million years ago and continued until about 10,000 B.C.E.

Panhellenic (All Greek)   Sense of cultural identity that all Greeks felt in common with one other.

papal infallibility   Assertion that the pope's pronouncements on matters of faith and morals could not be questioned.

Papal States   Central part of Italy where Pope Stephen II became the secular ruler when confirmed by the Franks in 755.

parlements   Regional courts allowed considerable latitude by Louis XIV to deal with local issues.

parliamentary monarchy   English rule by a monarch with some parliamentary guidance or input.

patricians   Upper class of Roman families that originally monopolized all political authority. Only they could serve as priests, senators, and magistrates.

Peloponnesian Wars   Series of wars between Athens and Sparta beginning in 460 B.C.E.

Peloponnesus   Southern half of the Greek peninsula.

perestroika   ("restructuring") Means by which Gorbachev wished to raise his country's standard of living.

petite bourgeoisie   New lower middle class made up of white- collar workers such as secretaries, retail clerks, and lower-level bureaucrats.

phalanx   Tight military formation of men eight or more ranks deep.

pharaoh   The god-kings of ancient Egypt.

Pharisee   Member of a Jewish sect known for strict adherence to the Jewish law.

Phoenicians   Seafaring people (Canaanites and Syrians) who scattered trading colonies from one end of the Mediterranean to the other.

plebeians   Commoner class of Roman families, usually families of small farmers, laborers, and artisans who were early clients of the patricians.

polytheists   Name given to those who worship many gods and/or goddesses.

politique   Ruler or person in a position of power who puts the success and well-being of his or her state above all else.

populares   Politicians who followed Tiberius's example of politics and governing.

positivism   Comte's philosophy that all knowledge should be the kind of knowledge common to the physical sciences.

Post-Impressionism   Focuses more on form and structure to bring painting of modern life back in touch with earlier artistic traditions.

Pragmatic Sanction   Document recognizing Charles VI's daughter Maria Theresa as his heir.

Presbyterians   Puritans who favored a national church of semiautonomous congregations governed by representative presbyteries.

proconsulships   Extension of terms for consuls who had important work to finish.

Ptolemaic system   Astronomical theory, named after Greek astronomer Ptolemy, that assumed Earth was the center point of a ball-shaped universe composed of concentric layers of rotating crystalline spheres to which the heavenly bodies were attached.

Puritans   English Protestants who wanted simpler forms of church ceremony and strictness and gravity in personal behavior.

Qur'an   Sacred book comprised of a collection of the revealed texts that God had chosen Muhammad to convey.

racism   Belief that some peoples are innately superior to others.

realists   Authors who tried to describe human behavior with scientific objectivity, rejecting the romantic idealization of nature, poverty, love, and polite society, and portraying the hypocrisy, physical and psychic brutality, and the dullness that underlay bourgeois life.

regular clergy   Those clergy living under a *regula*, the rule of a monastic order.

Reign of Terror   Extreme measures employed by the French government in an effort to protect the revolution.

Rococo   Style that embraced lavish, often lighthearted decoration with an emphasis on pastel colors and the play of light.

romanticism   Reaction against the rationalism and scientism of the Enlightenment, insisting on the importance of human feelings, intuition, and imagination as supplements for reason in the human quest to understand the world.

sans-culottes   Parisians (shopkeepers, artisans, wage earners, and factory workers who had been ignored by the Old Regime) who, along with radical Jacobins, began the second revolution in France.

Scholasticism   Method of study associated with the medieval university.

scientific revolution   The emergence in the sixteenth century of rational and empirical methods of research that challenged traditional thought and promoted the rise of science and technology.

Second Industrial Revolution Started after 1850, it expanded the production of steel, chemicals, electricity, and oil.

secular clergy Clergy, such as bishops and priests, who lived and worked among the laity in the *saeculum* ("world").

Sejm Central legislative body to which the Polish nobles belonged.

September Massacres The execution ordered by the Paris Commune of approximately 1,200 aristocrats, priests, and common criminals who, because they were being held in city jails, were assumed to be counterrevolutionaries.

serf Peasant bound to the land he worked.

Shi'a The "party" of Ali. They believed Ali and his descendants were Muhammad's only rightful successors.

social Darwinism Spencer's argument (coming close to claiming that might makes right) used to justify neglect of the poor and the working class, exploitation of colonial peoples, and aggressive competition among nations.

socialist realism Doctrine of Soviet art and literature that sought to create figurative, traditional, optimistic, and easily intelligible scenes of a bold socialist future of prosperity and solidarity.

spinning jenny Invented by James Hargreaves in 1765, this machine spun sixteen spindles of thread simultaneously.

Stoics People who sought freedom from passion and harmony with nature.

studia humanitas **(humanism)** Scholarship of the Renaissance that championed the study of Latin and Greek classics and Christian church fathers as an end in itself and as a guide to reforming society. Some claim it is an unChristian philosophy emphasizing human dignity, individualism, and secular values.

Sturm and Drang ("Storm and Stress") Movement in German romantic literature that emphasized feeling and emotion.

suffragettes Derisive name for members of the Women's Social and Political Union, who lobbied for votes for women.

Sunnis Followers of the *sunna*, "tradition." They emphasize loyalty to the fundamental principles of Islam.

superego Among Freud's three entities of the mind, the *superego* internalizes the moral imperatives that society and culture impose on the personality.

symposium A men's drinking party at the center of aristocratic social life in archaic Greece.

Table of Ranks Issued by Peter the Great to draw nobles into state service, it made rank in the bureaucracy or military, not lineage, the determinant of an individual's social status.

tabula rasa (a blank page) John Locke's *An Essay Concerning Human Understanding* (1690) theorized that at birth the human mind is a tabula rasa.

ten lost tribes Israelites who were scattered and lost to history when the northern kingdom of Israel fell to the Assyrians in 722 B.C.E.

tetrarchy Coalition of four men, each of whom was responsible for a different part of the empire, established by Diocletian.

Thermidorian Reaction Tempering of revolutionary fervor that led to the establishment of a new constitutional regime.

Third Estate Members of the commercial and professional middle classes, or everyone but the clergy (the First Estate) and the nobility (the Second Estate).

Third Reich Hitler's regime of Nazis.

three-field system Developed by medieval farmers, a system in which three fields were utilized during different growing seasons to limit the amount of nonproductive plowing and to restore soil fertility through crop rotation.

transistor Miniaturized electronics circuitry making the vacuum tube obsolete.

transubstantiation Christian doctrine which holds that, at the moment of priestly consecration, the bread and wine of the Lord's Supper become the body and blood of Christ.

tribunes Officials elected by the plebeian tribal assembly given the power to protect plebeians from abuse by patrician magistrates.

ulema ("Persons with correct knowledge") Scholarly elite leading Islam.

Upper Egypt Narrow valley extending 650 miles from Aswan to the border of Lower Egypt.

Utilitarianism Maintained that people should always pursue the course that promotes the greatest happiness for the greatest number.

utopian socialists Early critics of industrialism whose visionary programs often involved plans to establish ideal societies based on noncapitalistic values.

vassal A person granted an estate or cash payments in return for rendering services to a lord.

Vulgate Latin translation of the Bible that became the standard text for the Catholic Church.

Warsaw Pact Mutual defense agreement among Albania, Bulgaria, Czechoslovakia, East Germany, Hungary, Poland, Romania, and the Soviet Union.

water frame Invented in 1769 by Richard Arkwright, this water-powered device produced a 100 percent cotton fabric rather than the standard earlier blend of cotton and linen.

Weimar Republic German republic that came to power in 1918 embodying the hopes of German liberals.

Zionism Movement based on the theory that if Jews were unacceptable as citizens of European nations, their only safety lay in establishing a nation of their own.

Chapter 1

ALLDRED, C. *The Egyptians* (1998). Probably the best one-volume study.

BRYCE, T. *The Kingdom of the Hittites* (1998). A fine new survey.

EHRENBERG, M. *Women in Prehistory* (1989). An account of the role of women in early times.

HALLO W. W. and SIMPSON W. K. *The Ancient Near East: A History*, rev. ed. (1998). A fine survey of ancient Egypt and Mesopotamia.

KAMM, A. *The Israelites: An Introduction* (1999). A good brief, accessible account.

POSTGATE, J. N. *Early Mesopotamia* (1992). An excellent study of Mesopotamian economy and society from the earliest times to about 1500 B.C.E.

RUDGLEY, R. *The Lost Civilizations of the Stone Age* (1999). A bold thesis asserting that many features of civilization existed during the Stone Age.

SAGGS, H. W. F. *The Might that Was Assyria* (1984). A history of one of the ancient world's great empires.

SANDARS, N. K. *The Sea Peoples* (1985). A lively account of the peoples who disrupted the Mediterranean's civilized states in the thirteenth century B.C.E.

SNELL, D. C. *Life in the Ancient Near East, 3100–332 B.C.E.* (1997). A social history focusing on culture and daily life.

Chapter 2

BURKERT, W. *The Orientalizing Revolution: Near Eastern Influence on Greek Culture in the Early Archaic Age* (1992). A study of the eastern impact on Greek literature and religion in the years 750 to 650 B.C.E.

CHADWICK, J. *The Mycenaean World* (1976). A readable account by a man who helped decipher Mycenaean writing.

DREWS, R. *The Coming of the Greeks.* (1988). A fine study of the arrival of the Greeks as part of the Indo-European migration.

FINLEY, M. I. *World of Odysseus*, 2nd. ed. (1978). A fascinating attempt to reconstruct Homeric society.

HANSON, V. D. *The Western Way of War* (1989). A brilliant description of the hoplite phalanx and its influence on Greek society.

HANSON, V. D. *The Other Greeks* (1995). A revolutionary account of the invention of the family farm by the Greeks and the role of agrarianism in the *polis*.

MANVILLE, P. B. *The Origins of Citizenship in Ancient Athens* (1990). An examination of the concept of citizenship in Solon's generation.

OSBORNE, R. *Greece in the Making, 1200–479 B.C.* (1996). An up-to-date illustrated account of early Greek history.

PRICE, S. *Religions of the Ancient Greeks* (1999). A fine discussion of the religious practices of the Athenians.

THOMAS, C. G. and CONANT, C. *Citadel to City-State: The Transformation of Greece, 1200–700 B.C.E.* (1999). A good account of Greece's emergence from the dark ages into the world of the *polis*.

YOUNG, D. C. *The Olympic Myth of Greek Athletics* (1984). A lively challenge to the orthodox view that Greek athletes were amateurs.

Chapter 3

BURKERT, W. *Greek Religion* (1985). A fine general study.

CARTLEDGE, P. *Spartan Reflections* (2001). A collection of valuable essays by a leading scholar of ancient Sparta.

CAWKWELL, *Philip of Macedon* (1978). A brief but learned account of Philip's career.

COOK, J. M. *The Persian Empire* (1983). A solid history that makes good use of archaeological evidence.

FOX, J. R. L. *Alexander the Great* (1973). An imaginative account that does more justice to the Persian side of the problem than is usual.

GARLAND, R. *Daily Life of the Ancient Greeks* (1998). A good account of the way the Greeks lived.

GREEN, P. *From Alexander to Actium* (1990). A brilliant new synthesis of the Hellenistic period.

HAMILTON, C. D. *Agesilaus and the Failure of Spartan Hegemony* (1991). An excellent biography of the king who was the central figure in Sparta during its era of domination.

HAMMOND, N. G. L. *The Genius of Alexander the Great* (1998). A new biography by the dean of ancient Macedonian studies.

KAGAN, D. *Pericles of Athens and the Birth of Athenian Democracy* (1991). An account of the life and times of the great Athenian statesman.

KAGAN, D. *The Outbreak of the Peloponnesian War* (1969). A study of the period from the foundation of the Delian League to the coming of the Peloponnesian War that argues that war could have been avoided.

PATTERSON, C. B. *The Family in Greek History* (1998). An interesting interpretation of the relationship between family and state in ancient Greece.

POLLITT, J. J. *Art and Experience in Classical Greece* (1972). A scholarly and entertaining study of the relationship between art and history.

POLLITT, J. J. *Art in the Hellenistic Age* (1986). An extraordinary analysis that places the art in its historical and intellectual context.

STRAUSS, B. S. *Athens after the Peloponnesian War* (1987). An excellent discussion of Athens' recovery and history in the 4th century B.C.E.

Chapter 4

BAUMAN, R. A. *Women and Politics in Ancient Rome* (1992). A useful study of women's role in Roman public life.

BOARDMAN, J., GRIFFIN, J. and MURRAY, O. *The Oxford History of the Roman World* (1990). An encyclopedic approach to the varieties of the Roman experience.

CORNELL, T. J. *The Beginnings of Rome: Italy and Rome from the Bronze Age to the Punic Wars* (1995). A fine new study of early Rome.

DAVID, J-M. *The Roman Conquest of Italy* (1997). A good analysis of how Rome united Italy.

GRUEN, E. S. *The Hellenistic World and the Coming of Rome* (1984). An explanation of Rome's conquest of the eastern Mediterranean.

LANCEL, S. *Carthage, a History* (1995). A good account of Rome's great competitor.

MEIR, C. *Caesar* (1995). A recent scholarly biography of Rome's great dictator.

MILLAR, F. G. B. *The Crowd in Rome in the Late Republic* (1999). A challenge to the interpretation that only aristocrats counted in the Roman Republic.

MITCHELL, T. N. *Cicero, the Senior Statesman* (1991). An intelligent study of Cicero's later career.

SCULLARD, H. H. *A History of the Roman World 753–146 B.C.E.*, 4th ed. (1980). An unusually fine narrative history with useful critical notes.

WILLIAMS, G. *The Nature of Roman Poetry* (1970). An unusually graceful and perceptive literary study.

Chapter 5

BARNES, T. *The New Empire of Diocletian and Constantine* (1982). A study of the character of the late empire.

BIRLEY, A. R. *Hadrian the Restless Emperor* (1997). A biography of an important emperor.

BROWN, P. *The Rise of Western Christendom: Triumph and Diversity, 200–1000* (1996). A vivid picture of the spread of Christianity by a master of the field.

FERRILL, A. *Caligula: Emperor of Rome* (1991). A biography of the monstrous young emperor.

GALINSKY, G. *Augustan Culture* (1996). A work that integrates art, literature, and politics.

JOHNSTON, D. *Roman Law in Context* (2000). A work that places Rome's law in the context of its economy and society.

KAGAN, D. ed., *The End of the Roman Empire: Decline or Transformation?* 3rd edition (1992). A collection of essays discussing the problem of the decline and fall of the Roman Empire.

LENDON, J. *Empire of Honour: The Art of Government in the Roman World* (1997). A brilliant study that reveals how an aristocratic code of honor led the upper classes to cooperate in Roman rule.

MILLAR, F. G. B. *The Roman Near East, 31 B.C.–A.D. 337* (1993). A valuable study of Rome's relations with an important part of its empire.

RUDICH, V. *Political Dissidence under Nero: The Price of Dissimulation* (1993). A fine exposition of the lives and thoughts of political dissidents in the early empire.

SYME, R. *The Roman Revolution* (1960). A major study of Augustus, his supporters, and their rise to power.

Chapter 6

ARMSTRONG, K. *Muhammad; A Biography of the Prophet* (1992). Substantial popular biography.

BARRACLOUGH, G. *The Origins of Modern Germany* (1963). Originally published in 1946 and still the best survey of medieval Germany.

BARTLETT, R. *The Making of Modern Europe* (1993). How migration and colonization created Europe.

COLLINS, R. *Charlemagne* (1998). Latest biography.

HOURANI, A. *A History of the Arab Peoples* (1991). Comprehensive with overviews of the origins and early history of Islam.

LEWIS, B. *The Middle East: A Brief History of the Last 2000 Years* (1995). Authoritative overview.

MCKITTERICK, R. *Carolingian Culture: Emulation and Innovation* (1994). The culture from which western Europe was born.

NORRIS, J. J. *Byzantium: The Decline and Fall* (1995).

SAWYER, P. *Kings and Vikings: Scandinavia and Europe A.D. 700–1100* (1994). Raiding Vikings and their impact on Europe.

Chapter 7

BALDWIN, J. W. *The Government of Philip Augustus* (1986). An important scholarly work.

FLANAGAN, S. *Hildegard of Bingen, 1098–1179: A Visionary Life* (1998). Latest biography.

HALLAM, E. M. *Capetian France, 987–1328* (1980). Very good on politics and heretics.

HAMBLY, G. R. G. ed., *Women in the Medieval Islamic World* (1998). Elite women from Mamluk and Ottoman court records.

HOLT, J. C. *Magna Carta*, 2nd ed. (1992). Succeeding generations interpret the famous document.

LEYSER, K. *Medieval Germany and Its Neighbors, 900–1250* (1982). Basic and authoritative.

RICHARD, J. *Saint Louis: Crusader King of France* (1992).

RILEY-SMITH, J. *The Oxford Illustrated History of the Crusades* (1992). Sweeping account.

Chapter 8

ARIÈS, P. *Centuries of Childhood: A Social History of Family Life* (1962). Pioneer effort on the subject.

BALDWIN, J. W. *The Scholastic Culture of the Middle Ages: 1000–1300* (1971). Best brief synthesis available.

CLANCHY, M. T. *Abelard: A Medieval Life* (1998). The biography of famous philosopher and seducer of Héloise.

HANAWALT, B. A. *Growing Up in Medieval London* (1993). Positive portrayal of parental and societal treatment of children.

HASKINS, C. H. *The Rise of Universities* (1972). A short, minor classic.

HOPKINS, A. *Knights* (1990). Europe's warriors and models.

LOPEZ, R. *The Commercial Revolution of the Middle Ages* (1971). A master's brief survey.

MÂLE, E. *The Gothic Image: Religious Art in France in the Thirteenth Century* (1913). An enduring classic.

OZMENT, S. *Ancestors: The Loving Family in Old Europe* (2001). A sympathetic look at families past.

SHAHAR, S. *The Fourth Estate: A History of Women in the Middle Ages* (1983). A comprehensive survey, making clear the great variety of women's work.

Chapter 9

ALLMAND, C. *The Hundred Years' War: England and France at War, c. 1300–ca. 1450* (1988). Good overview of the war's development and consequences.

BACKSCHEIDER, P. R. ET AL. (eds.) *A Journal of the Plague Year* (1992). Black death at ground level.

GILLETT, E. H. ET AL. *Life and Times of John Huss: The Bohemian Reformation of the Fifteenth Century* (2001). The latest biography.

KAHN, R. ET AL. *Secret History of the Mongols: The Origins of Chingis Kahn* (1998).

OZMENT, S. *The Age of Reform, 1250–1550* (1980). Highlights of late medieval intellectual and religious history.

PERROY, E. *The Hundred Years' War*, trans. by W. B. Wells (1965). Still the most comprehensive one-volume account.

RENOVARD, Y. *The Avignon Papacy 1305–1403*, trans. by D. Bethell (1970). The standard narrative account.

ZIEGLER, P. *The Black Death* (1969). Highly readable account.

Chapter 10

BARON, H. *The Crisis of the Early Italian Renaissance*, vols. 1 and 2 (1966). A major work, setting forth the civic dimension of Italian humanism.

BURCKHARDT, J. *The Civilization of the Renaissance in Italy* (1867). The old classic that still has as many defenders as detractors.

CONRAD, R. E. *Children of God's Fire: A Documentary History of Black Slavery in Brazil* (1983). Not for the squeamish.

EISENSTEIN, E. L. *The Printing Press as an Agent of Change: Communications and Cultural Transformations in Early Modern Europe*, 2 vols. (1979). Bold, stimulating account of the centrality of printing to all progress in the period.

HERLIHY, D. and KLAPISCH-ZUBER, C. *The Tuscans and Their Families* (1985). Important work based on unique demographic data.

KRISTELLER, P. O. *Renaissance Thought: The Classic, Scholastic, and Humanist Strains* (1961). A master shows the many sides of Renaissance thought.

MARTINES, L. *Power and Imagination: City States in Renaissance Italy* (1980). Stimulating account of cultural and political history.

PANOFSKY, E. *Meaning in the Visual Arts* (1955). Eloquent treatment of Renaissance art.

PARRY, J. H. *The Age of Reconnaissance* (1964). A comprehensive account of exploration in the years 1450 to 1650.

SKINNER, Q. *The Foundations of Modern Political Thought; I: The Renaissance* (1978). Broad survey, including every known political theorist.

VEZZOSI, A. *Leonardo da Vinci, Renaissance Man* (1996). Updated biography.

WHEATCROFT, A. *The Habsburgs* (1995). The dynasty that ruled the center of late medieval and early modern Europe.

Chapter 11

BLOOM, H. *Shakespeare: The Invention of the Human* (1998). A modern master's complete analysis of the greatest writer in the English language.

DURAN, M. *Cervantes* (1974). Detailed biography.

EVENNETT, H. O. *The Spirit of the Counter Reformation* (1968). Essay on the continuity of Catholic reform and its independence from the Protestant Reformation.

GREGORY, B. S. *Salvation at Stake: Christian Martyrdom in Early Modern Europe* (1999). Massive can't-put-down study covering a wide spectrum.

JOHNSTON, P. and SCRIBNER, R. W. *The Reformation in Germany and Switzerland* (1993). Reformation from the bottom up.

OBERMAN, H. A. *Luther: Man Between God and the Devil* (1989). Perhaps the best account of Luther's life, by a Dutch master.

O'MALLEY, J. *The First Jesuits* (1993). Extremely detailed account of the creation of the Society of Jesus and its original purposes.

OZMENT, S. *The Age of Reform, 1250–1550: An Intellectual and Religious History of Late Medieval and Reformation Europe* (1980). A broad survey of major religious ideas and beliefs.

OZMENT, S. *Flesh and Spirit: Private Life in Early Modern Germany* (1999). Family life from courtship and marriage to the sending of a new generation into the world.

STARKEY, D. *Elizabeth: The Struggle for the Throne* (2000).

STARKEY, D. *The Reign of Henry VIII* (1985). Portrayal of the king as in control of neither his life nor his court.

WENDEL, F. *Calvin: The Origins and Development of His Religious Thought*, trans. by Philip Mairet (1963). The best treatment of Calvin's theology.

WILLIAMS, G. H. *The Radical Reformation* (1962). Broad survey of the varieties of dissent within Protestantism.

WUNDER, H. *He is the Sun, She is the Moon: A History of Women in Early Modern Germany* (1998). A model of gender history.

Chapter 12

BRAUDEL, F. *The Mediterranean and the Mediterranean World in the Age of Philip the Second*, vols. 1 and 2 (1976). Widely acclaimed work of a French master historian.

DUNN, R. *The Age of Religious Wars, 1559–1689* (1979). Excellent brief survey of every major conflict.

GEYL, P. *The Revolt of the Netherlands, 1555–1609* (1958). The authoritative survey.

GUY, J. Tudor England (1990). A standard history and good synthesis of recent scholarship.

HAIGH, C. *Elizabeth I* (1988). Elizabeth portrayed as a magnificent politician and propogandist.

LOADES, D. *Mary Tudor* (1989). Authoritative and good storytelling.

MATTINGLY, G. *The Armada* (1959). A masterpiece and resembling a novel in style.

WORMALD, J. *Mary, Queen of Scots: A Study in Failure* (1991). Mary portrayed as a queen who did not understand her country and was out of touch with the times.

Chapter 13

ASHTON, R. *Counter-Revolution: The Second Civil War and Its Origin, 1646–1648* (1995). A major examination of the resumption of civil conflict in England that ended with the abolition of the monarchy.

BEIK, W. *Absolutism and Society in Seventeenth-Century France* (1985). An important study that questions the extent of royal power.

BLACK, J. *Eighteenth Century Europe, 1700–1789* (1990). An excellent survey.

BONNEY, R. *Political Change in France Under Richelieu and Mazarin, 1624–1661* (1978). A careful examination of the manner in which these two cardinals laid the foundation for Louis XIV's absolutism.

BREWER, J. *The Sinews of Power: War, Money and the English State, 1688–1783* (1989). An extremely important study of the financial basis of English power.

BURKE, P. *The Fabrication of Louis XIV* (1992). Examines the manner in which the public image of Louis XIV was forged in art.

BUSHKOVITCH, P. *Peter the Great: The Struggle for Power, 1671–1725* (2001). Replaces all previous studies.

COLLINSON, P. *The Religion of Protestants: The Church in English Society, 1559–1625* (1982). The best recent introduction to Puritanism.

DAVIS, N. *God's Playground*, vol. 1 (1991). Excellent on prepartition Poland.

DOYLE, W. *The Old European Order, 1660–1800* (1992). The most thoughtful treatment of the subject.

INGRAO, C. J. *The Habsburg Monarchy, 1618–1815* (1994). The best recent survey.

ISRAEL, J. I. *The Dutch Republic, Its Rise, Greatness, and Fall, 1477–1806* (1995). The major survey of the subject.

KANN, R. A. and DAVID, Z. V. *The Peoples of the Eastern Habsburg Lands 1526–1918* (1984). A helpful overview of the subject.

MCKAY, D. *The Great Elector: Frederick William of Brandenburg-Prussia* (2001). An account of the origins of Prussian power.

MCKAY, D. and SCOTT, H. M. *The Rise of the Great Powers, 1648–1815* (1983). Now the standard survey.

MONOD, P. K. *The Power of Kings: Monarchy and Religion in Europe, 1589–1715* (1999). An innovative examination of the roots of royal authority.

RUSSELL, C. *The Fall of the English Monarchies* (1991). A major revisionist account.

SCHAMA, S. *A History of Britain: The Wars of the British, 1603–1776* (2001). A highly accessible narrative (originally designed for television) that explores the major themes of British development during this period.

SUGAR, P. F. *Southeastern Europe Under Ottoman Rule, 1354–1804* (1977). An extremely clear presentation.

TREASURE, G. *Louis XIV* (2001). The best, most accessible recent study.

UNDERDOWN, D. *A Freeborn People: Politics and the Nation in Seventeenth-Century England* (1996). A lively reply to C. Russell above.

Chapter 14

ASHCRAFT, R. *Revolutionary Politics and Locke's Two Treatises of Government* (1986). A major study emphasizing the radical side of Locke's thought.

BARRY, J., HESTER, M. and ROBERTS, G. eds. *Witchcraft in Early Modern Europe: Studies in Culture and Belief* (1998). A collection of recent essays.

DEAR, P. *Revolutionizing the Sciences: European Knowledge and Its Ambitions, 1500–1700* (2001). A broad-ranging study of both the ideas and institutions of the new science.

FINOCCHIARO, M. A. *The Galileo Affair: A Documentary History* (1989). A collection of all the relevant documents and introductory commentary.

GAUKROGER, S. *Francis Bacon and the Transformation of Early-Modern Philosophy* (2001). An excellent, accessible introduction.

HARRIS, I. *The Mind of John Locke: A Study of Political Theory in Its Intellectual Setting* (1994). The most comprehensive recent treatment.

HEILBRON, J. A. *The Sun in the Church: Cathedrals as Solar Observatories* (2000). A remarkable study of the manner in which Europe's great church buildings were used to make astronomical observations and calculations.

KUHN, T. S. *The Copernican Revolution* (1957). Remains the leading work on the subject.

LEVACK, B. *The Witch Hunt in Early Modern Europe* (1986). Lucid survey.

PYENSON, L. and SHEETS-PYENSON, S. *Servants of Nature: A History of Scientific Institutions, Enterprises, and Sensibilities* (1999). A history of the settings in which the creation and diffusion of scientific knowledge have occurred.

SHAPIN, S. *The Scientific Revolution* (1996). A readable brief introduction.

THOMAS, K. *Religion and the Decline of Magic* (1971). Provocative, much-acclaimed work focused on popular culture.

TUCK, R. *Philosophy and Government 1572–1651* (1993). A continent-wide survey.

WESTFALL, R. S. *Never at Rest: A Biography of Isaac Newton* (1981). The major study.

Chapter 15

BLUM, J. *Lord and Peasant in Russia from the Ninth to the Nineteenth Century* (1961). Remains a classic discussion.

DEANE, P. *The First Industrial Revolution* (1999). A well-balanced and systematic treatment.

EARLE, P. *The Making of the English Middle Class: Business, Community, and Family Life in London, 1660–1730* (1989). The most careful study of the subject.

HOBSBAWM, E. *Industry and Empire: The Birth of the Industrial Revolution* (1999). A survey by a major historian of the subject.

KERTZER, D. I. and BARBAGLI, M. *The History of the European Family: Family Life in Early Modern Times, 1500–1709* (2001). A series of broad-ranging essays covering the entire continent.

KING, S. and TIMMONS, G. *Making Sense of the Industrial Revolution: English Economy and Society, 1700–1850* (2001). Examines the Industrial Revolution through the social institutions that brought it about and were changed by it.

MANUEL, F. E. *The Broken Staff: Judaism Through Christian Eyes* (1992). An important discussion of Christian interpretations of Judaism.

OVERTON, M. *Agricultural Revolution in England: The Transformation of the Agrarian Economy, 1500–1850* (1996). A highly accessible treatment.

STEARNS, P. *The Industrial Revolution in World History* (1998). An extremely broad interpretive account.

VICKERY, A. *The Gentleman's Daughter: Women's Lives in Georgian England* (1998). A richly documented study.

Chapter 16

BAILYN, B. *The Ideological Origins of the American Revolution* (1967). Remains an important work illustrating the role of English radical thought in the perceptions of the American colonists.

BLACKBURN, R. *The Making of New World Slavery from the Baroque to the Modern, 1492–1800* (1997). An extraordinary work.

BRADING, D. *The First America* (1991). A major study of colonial Latin America.

COLLEY, L. *Britons: Forging the Nation, 1707–1837* (1992). A major work with important discussions of the recovery from the loss of America.

DAVIS, R. *The Rise of the Atlantic Economies* (1973). A major synthesis.

HARMS, R. *The Diligent: A Voyage through the Worlds of the Slave Trade* (2002). A powerful narrative of the voyage of a French slave trader.

MACDONAGH, G. *Frederick the Great* (2001). Now the standard biography.

MAIER, P. *American Scripture: Making the Declaration of Independence* (1997). Replaces previous works on the subject.

MCNEIL, J. R. *Atlantic Empires of France and Spain: Louisbourg and Havana, 1700–1763* (1985). An examination of imperial policies in terms of two key overseas outposts.

PAGDEN, A. *Lords of All the World: Ideologies of Empire in Spain, Britain, and France, 1492–1830* (1995). One of the few comparative studies of empire during this period.

THORNTON, J. *Africa and the Africans in the Making of the Atlantic World, 1400–1800*, 2nd ed. (1998). A discussion of the role of Africans in the emergence of the transatlantic economy.

WOOD, G. S. *The Radicalism of the American Revolution* (1991). A major interpretation.

Chapter 17

BEALES, D. *Joseph II: In the Shadow of Maria Theresa, 1741–1780* (1987), The best treatment in English of the early political life of Joseph II.

CHARTIER, R. *The Cultural Origins of the French Revolution* (1991). A wide-ranging discussion of the emergence of the public sphere and the role of books and the book trade during the Enlightenment.

DOCK, T. S. *Women in the Encyclopédie: A Compendium* (1983). An analysis of the articles from the *Encyclopedia* that deal with women.

GAY, P. *The Enlightenment: An Interpretation*, 2 vols. (1966, 1969). A classic.

GOODMAN, D. *The Republic of Letters: A Cultural History of the French Enlightenment* (1994). Concentrates on the role of the salons.

LANDES, J. B. *Women and the Public Sphere in the Age of the French Revolution* (1988). An extended essay on the role of women in public life during the eighteenth century.

LEDONNE, J. P. *The Russian Empire and the World, 1700–1917* (1996). An exploration of the major determinants in Russian expansion from the eighteenth to the early twentieth century.

MACMAHON, D. *Enemies of the Enlightenment: The French Counter-Enlightenment and the Making of Modernity* (2001). A very fine exploration of French writers critical of the philosophes.

DE MADARIAGA, I. *Russia in the Age of Catherine the Great* (1981). The best discussion in English.

RAHE, P. A., CARRITHERS, D. and MOCHER, M. A. *Montesquieu's Science of Politics: Essays on "The Spirit of the Laws"* (2001). An expansive collection of essays on Montesquieu and his relationship to other major thinkers.

ROTHCHILD, E. *Economic Sentiments: Adam Smith, Condorcet, and the Enlightenment* (2001). A sensitive account of Smith's thought and its relationship to the social questions of the day.

SPADAFORA, D. *The Idea of Progress in Eighteenth Century Britain* (1990). A major study that covers many aspects of the Enlightenment in Britain.

STAROBINSKI, J. *Jean-Jacques Rousseau: Transparency and Obstruction* (1971). A classic analysis of Rousseau.

SULLIVAN, R. E. *John Toland and the Deist Controversy: A Study in Adaptation* (1982). An important and informative discussion.

WOLFF, L. *Inventing Eastern Europe: The Map of Civilization on the Mind of the Enlightenment* (1994). A remarkable study of the way in which Enlightenment writers recast the understanding of this part of the continent.

Chapter 18

BAKER, K. M. and LUCAS, C. eds., *The French Revolution and the Creation of Modern Political Culture*, 3 vols. (1987). A splendid collection of important original articles on all aspects of politics during the revolution.

CENSER, J. R. and HUNT, L. *Liberty, Equality, Fraternity: Exploring the French Revolution* (2001). A major survey with numerous documents available through a CD-ROM disk.

COBB, R. *The People's Armies* (1987). The best treatment in English of the revolutionary army.

DOYLE, W. *The French Revolution* (2001). A solid brief introduction.

HIGONNET, P. *Goodness beyond Virtue: Jacobins during the French Revolution* (1998). An outstanding work that clearly relates political values to political actions.

KENNEDY, E. *A Cultural History of the French Revolution* (1989). An important examination of the role of the arts, schools, clubs, and intellectual institutions.

LEVY, D. G., APPLEWHITE, H. B. and JOHNSON, M. D. eds. and trans., *Women in Revolutionary Paris, 1789–1795* (1979). A remarkable collection of documents on the subject.

Melzer, S. E. and Rabine, L. W. eds., *Rebel Daughters: Women and the French Revolution* (1992). A collection of essays exploring various aspects of the role and image of women in the French Revolution.

Ozouf, M. *Festivals and the French Revolution* (1988). A pioneering study of the role of the public festivals in the revolution.

Proctor, C. *Women, Equality, and the French Revolution* (1990). An examination of how the ideas of the Enlightenment and the attitudes of revolutionaries affected the legal status of women.

Tackett, T. *Becoming a Revolutionary: The Deputies of the French National Assembly and the Emergence of a Revolutionary Culture (1789–1790)* (1996). The best study of the early months of the revolution.

Van Kley, D. K. *The Religious Origins of the French Revolution: From Calvin to the Civil Constitution, 1560–1791* (1996). Examines the manner in which debates within French Catholicism influenced the coming of the revolution.

Chapter 19

Asprey, R. *The Rise of Napoleon Bonaparte and the Reign of Napoleon Bonaparte* (2001). an extensive two-volume narrative.

Beiser, F. C. *Enlightenment, Revolution, and Romanticism: The Genesis of Modern German Political Thought, 1790–1800* (1992). The best recent study of the subject.

Bentley, G. E. *The Stranger from Paradise: A Biography of William Blake* (2001). Now the standard work.

Boyle, N. *Goethe* (2001). A challenging two-volume biography.

Brookner, A. *Romanticism and Its Discontents* (2001). Exploration of French romanticism by a leading novelist.

Broers, M. *Europe under Napoleon, 1799–1815* (2002). Examines the subject from the standpoint of those Napoleon conquered.

Brown, D. B. *Romanticism* (2001). A well-illustrated overview.

Chandler, D. G. *The Campaigns of Napoleon* (1966). A good military study.

Chapman, T. *Congress of Vienna: Origins, Processes, and Results* (1998). A clear introduction to the major issues.

Johnson, P. *Napoleon* (2002). A brief, thoughtful essay.

Lefebvre, G. *Napoleon*, 2 vols., trans. by H. Stockhold (1969). The fullest and finest biography.

McGann, J. J. and Soderholm, J. (eds.), *Byron and Romanticism* (2002). Essays on the poet who most embodied romantic qualities to the people of his time.

Muir, R. *Tactics and the Experience of Battle in the Age of Napoleon* (1998). A splendid account of the experience of troops in battle.

Pinkard, T. *Hegel: A Biography* (2000). A long but accessible study.

Reardon, B. M. G. *Religion in the Age of Romanticism: Studies in Early Nineteenth-Century Thought* (1985). The best introduction to this important subject.

Woloch, I. *Napoleon and His Collaborators: The Making of a Dictatorship* (2001). A key study by one of the major scholars of the subject.

Chapter 20

Anderson, B. *Imagined Communities*, rev. ed. (1991). An influential and controversial discussion of nationalism.

Archer, C. I., Maclachlan, C. M. and Beezley, W. H. (eds.), *The Wars of Independence in Spanish America* (2000). Broad selection of essays based on most recent scholarship.

Athanassoglou-Kallmyer, N. M. *French Images from the Greek War of Independence, 1821–1830: Art and Politics under the Restoration* (2000). Explores both the Greek War of Independence and French politics.

Berdahl, M. *The Politics of the Prussian Nobility: The Development of a Conservative Ideology, 1770–1848* (1988). A major examination of German conservative outlooks.

Briggs, A. *The Making of Modern England* (1959). Classic survey of English history during the first half of the nineteenth century.

Brock, M. *The Great Reform Act* (1974). The standard work.

Craig, G. A. *The Politics of the Prussian Army, 1640–1945* (1955). A splendid study of the conservative political influence of the army on Prussian development.

Fortescue, W. *Revolution and Counter-Revolution in France, 1815–1852* (2002). A helpful brief survey.

Hobsbawm, E. J. *Nations and Nationalism since 1780: Programme, Myth, Reality*, rev. ed. (1992). The best recent introduction to the subject.

Jelavich, C. and B. *The Establishment of the Balkan National States, 1804–1920* (1977). A standard, clear introduction.

Kroen, S. *Politics and Theater: The Crisis of Legitimacy in Restoration France, 1815–1830* (2000). Examines how French theater reacted to the climate of changing political regimes.

Levinger, M. B. *Enlightened Nationalism: The Transformation of Prussian Political Cultures, 1806–1848* (2002). A major work based on the most recent scholarship.

Lynch, J. *The Spanish American Revolutions, 1808–1826* (1973). An excellent one-volume treatment.

Palmer, A. *Alexander I: Tsar of War and Peace* (1974). An interesting biography that captures much of the mysterious personality of this ruler.

Riasanovsky, N. V. *Nicholas I and Official Nationality in Russia, 1825–1855* (1959). A lucid discussion of the conservative ideology that made Russia the major opponent of liberalism.

Rubinstein, W. D. D. *Britain's Century: A Political and Social History, 1815–1905* (1999). Based on the most recent scholarship.

Sheehan, J. *German History, 1770–1866* (1989). A very long work that is now the best available survey of the subject.

Chapter 21

Anderson, B. S. and Zinser, J. P. *A History of Their Own: Women in Europe from Prehistory to the Present*, vol. 2 (1988). A wide-ranging survey.

Berlin, I. *Karl Marx: His Life and Environment* (1948). A classic introduction.

BROCK, P. *The Slovak National Awakening* (1976). A standard work.

HARRISON, J. F. C. *Quest for the New Moral World: Robert Owen and the Owenites in Britain and America* (1969). The standard work.

HIMMELFARB, G. *The Idea of Poverty: England in the Early Industrial Age* (1984). A major work covering the subject from the time of Adam Smith through 1850.

IGNATIEFF, M. *A Just Measure of Pain: The Penitentiary in the Industrial Revolution, 1750–1850* (1978). An important treatment of early English penal thought and practice.

KERTZER, D. I. and BARBAGLI, M. (eds.), *Family Life in the Long Nineteenth Century, 1789–1913: The History of the European Family* (2002). Wide-ranging collection of essays.

LANDES, D. *The Unbound Prometheus: Technological Change and Industrial Development in Western Europe from 1750 to the Present* (1969). Classic one-volume treatment of technological development in a broad social and economic context.

MERRIMAN, J. M. *The Agony of the Republic: The Repression of the Left in Revolutionary France, 1848–1851* (1978). Study of how the Second French Republic and popular support for it were suppressed.

PERKIN, H. *The Origins of Modern English Society, 1780–1880* (1969). A provocative attempt to look at the society as a whole.

RANDERS-PHERSON, J. D. *Germans and the Revolution of 1848–1849* (2001). An exhaustive treatment of the subject.

SORKIN, D. *The Transformation of German Jewry, 1780–1840* (1987). An examination of the decades of Jewish emancipation in Germany.

THOMPSON, E. P. *The Making of the English Working Class* (1964). A classic work.

WINCH, D. *Riches and Poverty: An Intellectual History of Political Economy in Britain, 1750–1834* (1996). A superb survey from Adam Smith through Thomas Malthus.

Chapter 22

BLACKBOURN, D. *The Long Nineteenth Century: A History of Germany, 1780–1918* (1998). An outstanding survey based on up-to-date scholarship.

BLAKE, R. *Disraeli* (1967). Remains the best biography.

BUCHOLZ, A. *Moltke and the German Wars, 1864–1871* (2001). Explains how Prussian leaders invented many aspects of modern warfare.

CUNNINGHAM, M. *Mexico and the Foreign Policy of Napoleon III* (2001). Explores one of the most controversial subjects in French foreign policy.

EDGERTON, R. B. *Death or Glory: The Legacy of the Crimean War* (2000). Multifaceted study of a badly mismanaged war that transformed many aspects of European domestic politics.

KEE, R. *The Green Flag: A History of Irish Nationalism* (2001). A vast survey.

LIEVAN, D. C. *The Russian Empire and Its Rivals* (2001). Explores the imperial side of Russian government.

MAY, A. J. *The Habsburg Monarchy, 1867–1914* (1951). Narrates in considerable detail and with much sympathy the fate of the dual monarchy.

O'BRIEN, C. C. *Parnell and His Party* (1957). An excellent treatment of the Irish question.

PFLANZE, O. *Bismarck and the Development of Germany*, 3 vols. (1990). A major biography and history of Germany for the period.

PLESSIS, A. *The Rise and Fall of the Second Empire, 1852–1871* (1985). A useful survey of France under Napoleon III.

RIDLEY, J. *Garibaldi* (2001). An extensive biography of a remarkable personality.

SKED, A. *Decline and Fall of the Habsburg Empire, 1815–1918* (2001). A major, accessible survey of a difficult subject.

VENTURI, F. *The Roots of Revolution* (trans. 1960). A major treatment of late nineteenth-century revolutionary movements.

WETZEL, D. *A Duel of Giants: Bismarck, Napoleon III, and the Origins of the Franco-Prussian War* (2001). Broad study based on most recent scholarship.

ZELDIN, T. *France: 1848–1945*, 2 vols. (1973, 1977). Emphasizes the social developments.

Chapter 23

ARONSON, I. M. *Troubled Waters: The Origins of the 1881 Anti-Jewish Pogroms in Russia* (1990). The best discussion of this subject.

ASCHER, A. and STOLYPIN, P. A. *The Search for Stability in Late Imperial Russia* (2000). A broad-ranging biography based on extensive research.

BIRNBAUM, P. *Jewish Destinies: Citizenship, State and Community in Modern France* (2000). Explores the subject from the French Revolution to the present.

HAMILTON, R. F. *Marxism, Revisionism, and Leninism: Explication, Assessment, and Commentary* (2000). A contribution from the perspective of a historically minded sociologist.

HAUSE, S. C. *Women's Suffrage and Social Politics in the French Third Republic* (1984). A wide-ranging examination of the question.

HIMMELFARB, G. *Poverty and Compassion: The Moral Imagination of the Late Victorians* (1991). The best examination of late Victorian social thought.

HOBSBAWM, E. J. *The Age of Empire: 1875–1914* (1987). A stimulating survey that covers cultural as well as political developments.

HOLPEN, T. *The Mid-Victorian Generation, 1846–1886* (1998). The most extensive treatment of the subject.

MALIA, M. *Russia under Western Eyes: From the Bronze Horseman to the Lenin Mausoleum* (2000). A brilliant work recording the manner in which intellectuals in western Europe understood Russia.

MOOSE, G. L. *German Jews Beyond Judaism* (1985). Sensitive essays exploring the relationship of Jews to German culture in the nineteenth and early twentieth centuries.

NORD, P. G. *The Republican Moment: Struggles for Democracy in Nineteenth-Century France* (1996). A major new examination of nineteenth-century French political culture.

PINKNEY, D. H. *Napoleon III and the Rebuilding of Paris* (1958). A classic study.

ROGGER, H. *Jewish Policies and Right-Wing Politics in Imperial Russia* (1986). A very learned examination of Russian anti-Semitism.

SERVICE, R. *Lenin: A Biography* (2002). Based on new sources and will no doubt become the standard biography.

SMITH, B. G. *Ladies of the Leisure Class: The Bourgeoises of Northern France in the Nineteenth Century* (1981). Emphasizes the importance of the reproductive role of women.

STONE, N. *Europe Transformed* (1984). A sweeping survey that emphasizes the difficulties of late-nineteenth-century liberalism.

THORPE, A. *A History of the British Labour Party* (2001). A survey from its inception to the present.

TOSH, J. *A Man's Place: Masculinity and the Middle-Class Home in Victorian England* (1999). A pioneering work.

Chapter 24

ALLEN, C. *The Human Christ: The Search for the Historical Jesus* (1998). A broad survey of the issue for the past two centuries.

BOWLER, P. *Evolution: The History of an Idea* (1989). An outstanding survey of the subject.

BOWLER, P. *Reconciling Science and Religion: The Debate in Early-Twentieth-Century Britain* (2001). A superb survey of the cooperation between religious and scientific writers during the period.

BURROW, J. *The Crisis of Reason: European Thought, 1848–1914* (2000). The best overview available.

COPPA, F. J. *The Modern Papacy since 1789* (1999). A straightforward survey.

DALSIMER, K. *Virginia Wolfe: Becoming a Writer* (2002). A psychoanalytic study.

DESMOND, A. and MOORE, J. *Darwin* (1992). A brilliant biography.

GAY, P. *Freud: A Life for Our Time* (1988). The new standard biography.

HELMSTADTER, R. ed., *Freedom and Religion in the Nineteenth Century* (1997). Major essays on the relationship of church and state.

HOURANI, A. *Arab Though in the Liberal Age 1789–1939* (1967). A classic account, clearly written and accessible to the nonspecialist.

KATZ, J. *From Prejudice to Destruction: Anti-Semitism, 1700–1933* (1980). An excellent and far-reaching analysis.

KÖHLER, J. *Zarathustra's Secret: The Interior Life of Friedrich Nietzsche* (2002). A controversial new biography.

LACQUER, W. *A History of Zionism* (1989). The most extensive one-volume treatment.

POLIAKOV, L. *The Aryan Myth: A History of Racist and Nationalist Ideas in Europe* (1971). The best introduction to the problem.

STERN, F. *Einstein's German World* (1999). An exploration of German science from the turn of the century to the rise of Hitler.

TURNER, F. M. *Contesting Cultural Authority: Essays in Victorian Intellectual Life* (1993). Essays that deal with the relationship of science and religion and the problem of faith for intellectuals.

VITAL, D. *A People Apart: The Jews of Europe 1789–1939* (1999). A remarkably broad and deeply researched volume.

WILSON, A. N. *God's Funeral* (1999). Explores the thinkers who contributed to religious doubt during the nineteenth and twentieth centuries.

Chapter 25

BALFOUR, M. *The Kaiser and His Times* (1972). A fine biography of William II.

BOSWORTH, R. *Italy and the Approach of the First World War* (1983). A fine analysis of Italian policy.

FERGUSON, N. *The Pity of War* (1999). An analytic study of important aspects of World War I with controversial interpretations.

FIELDHOUSE, D. K. *The Colonial Experience: A Comparative Study from the Eighteenth Century* (1966). An excellent study.

FISCHER, F. *Germany's Aims in the First World War* (1967). An influential interpretation that stirred an enormous controversy by emphasizing Germany's role in bringing on the war.

HALE, O. J. *The Great Illusion 1900–1914* (1971). A fine survey of the period, especially good on public opinion.

HAYNE, M. B. *The French Foreign Office and the Origins of the First World War* (1993). An examination of the influence on French policy of the professionals in the foreign service.

HERWIG, H. *The First World War: Germany and Austria, 1914–18* (1997). A fine study of the war from the loser's perspective.

KEEGAN, J. *The First World War* (1999). A vivid and readable narrative account.

LANGER, W. L. *European Alliances and Alignments,* 2nd ed. (1966). A splendid diplomatic history of the years 1871 to 1890.

LIEVEN, D. C. B. *Russia and the Origins of the First World War* (1983). A good account of the forces that shaped Russian policy.

STEINER, Z. *Britain and the Origins of the First World War* (1977). A perceptive and informed account of the way British foreign policy was made before the war.

WILLIAMSON, S. R. JR. *Austria-Hungary and the Origins of the First World War* (1991). A valuable study of a complex subject.

Chapter 26

BEREND, I. T. *Decades of Crisis: Central and Eastern Europe before World War II* (2001). The best recent discussion of a remarkably troubled region of the early twentieth century.

BESSEL, R. *Political Violence and the Rise of Nazism: The Storm Troopers in Eastern Germany, 1925–1934* (1984). A study of the uses of violence by the Nazis.

BOSWORTH, R. *Mussolini* (2002). A major new biography.

BULLOCK, A. *Hitler: A Study in Tyranny,* rev. ed. (1964). Remains a classic biography.

FURET, F. *The Passing of an Illusion: The Idea of Communism in the Twentieth Century* (1995). A brilliant account of the manner in which communism shaped politics and thought outside the Soviet Union.

HELD, J. ed., *The Columbia History of Eastern Europe in the Twentieth Century* (1992). Individual essays on each of the nations.

JELAVICH, B. *History of the Balkans,* vol. 2 (1983). The standard work.

KERSHAW, I. *Hitler, 1889–1936: Hubris* (1998). The best treatment of Hitler's early life and rise to power.

LINCOLN, B. *Red Victory: A History of the Russian Civil War* (1989). An excellent narrative account.

McKIBBIN, R. *Classes and Cultures: England, 1918–1951* (2000). Viewing the era through the lens of class.

POLLARD, J. F. *The Vatican and Italian Fascism 1929–32: A Study in Conflict* (1985). Provides the background to the Lateran Pacts.

STERNHELL, Z. *The Birth of Fascist Ideology: From Cultural Rebellion to Political Revolution* (1994). A controversial examination of the roots of Mussolini's ideology.

TUCKER, R. *Stalin as Revolutionary, 1879–1929: A Study in History and Personality* (1973). A useful and readable account of Stalin's rise to power.

WOHL, R. *The Generation of 1914* (1979). An important work that explores the effect of the war on political and social thought.

Chapter 27

ALLEN, W. S. *The Nazi Seizure of Power: The Experience of a Single German Town, 1930–1935,* rev. ed. (1984). A classic treatment of Nazism in a microcosmic setting.

CHASE, W. *Enemies within the Gates?: The Comintern and Stalinist Repression,* 1934–1939 (2001). Examines how Soviet policies destroyed the Comintern.

CONQUEST, R. *The Great Terror: Stalin's Purges of the Thirties* (1968). Remains the most useful treatment of the subject to date.

CONQUEST, R. *The Harvest of Sorrow: Soviet Collectivization and the Terror-Famine* (1986). A study of how Stalin used starvation against his own people.

EICHENGREEN, B. *Golden Fetters: The Gold Standard and the Great Depression, 1919–1939* (1992). A remarkable study of the role of the gold standard in the economic policies of the interwar years.

GELLATELY, R. *Backing Hitler: Consent and Coercion in Nazi Germany* (2001). Controversial study emphasizing widespread support for Hitler.

GETTY, J. A. and NAUMOV, O. V. *The Road to Terror: Stalin and the Self-Destruction of the Bolsheviks, 1933–1939* (1999). A major collection of newly available documents revealing much new information about the purges.

JACKSON, J. *The Politics of Depression in France, 1932–1936* (1985). A detailed examination of the political struggles prior to the Popular Front.

JACKSON, J. *The Popular Front in France: Defending Democracy, 1934–1938* (1988). As extensive treatment.

KERSHAW, I. *Hitler,* 2 vols. (2000). The best biography now available.

KERSHAW, I. *The Nazi Dictatorship: Problems and Perspectives of Interpretation* (2000). A very accessible analysis.

KINDLEBERGER, C. *The World in Depression, 1929–1939* (1973). An account by a leading economist whose analysis is comprehensible to the layperson.

PEUKERT, D. J. K. *Inside Nazi Germany: Conformity, Opposition, and Racism in Everyday Life* (1987). An excellent discussion of life under Nazi rule.

PROCTOR, R. *The Nazi War on Cancer* (2000). A fascinating study.

PULZER, P. *Jews and the German State; The Political History of a Minority, 1848–1933* (1992). A detailed study by a major historian of European minorities.

STEPHENSON, J. *The Nazi Organization of Women* (1981). Examines the attitude and policies of the Nazis toward women.

Chapter 28

ADAMTHWAITE, A. *France and the Coming of the Second World War, 1936–1939* (1977). A careful account making good use of the newly opened French archives.

BARTOV, O. *Mirrors of Destruction: War, Genocide, and Modern Identity* (2000). A collection of remarkably penetrating essays.

BECK, E. R. *Under the Bombs: The German Home Front, 1942–1945* (1986). An interesting examination of a generally unstudied subject.

BOTWINICK, R. S. *A History of the Holocaust,* 2nd ed. (2002). A brief but broad and useful account of the causes, character, and results of the Holocaust.

BROWNING, C. *Ordinary Men* (1993). Examines a single Nazi death squad.

BULLOCK, A. *Hitler: A Study in Tyranny,* rev. ed. (1964). A brilliant biography.

GADDIS, J. L. *We Now Know: Rethinking Cold War History* (1998). A fine account of the early years of the Cold War, making use of new evidence emerging since the collapse of the Soviet Union.

GILBERT, M. *The Holocaust: A History of the Jews of Europe During the Second World War* (1985). The best and most comprehensive treatment.

IRIYE, A. *Pearl Harbor and the Coming of the Pacific War* (1999). Essays on how the Pacific war came about including a selection of documents.

KEEGAN, J. *The Second World War* (1990). A lively and penetrating account by a master military historian.

KNOX, M. *Mussolini Unleashed* (1982). An outstanding study of fascist Italy's policy and strategy in World War II.

MARKS, S. *The Illusion of Peace* (1976). A good discussion of European international relations in the 1920s and early 1930s.

MURRAY, W. and MILLETT, A. R. *A War to Be Won: Fighting the Second World War* (2000). A splendid account of the military operations in the war.

THOMAS, H. *The Spanish Civil War,* 3rd ed. (1986). The best account in English.

WANDYCZ, P. *The Twilight of French Eastern Alliances, 1926–1936* (1988). A well-documented account of the diplomacy of central and eastern Europe in a crucial period.

WEINBERG, G. L. *A World at Arms: A Global History of World War II* (1994). A thorough and excellent narrative account.

Chapter 29

ANSPRENGER, F. *The Dissolution of Colonial Empires* (1989). A broad survey.

BOTTOME, E. *The Balance of Terror: Nuclear Weapons and the Illusions of Security, 1945–1985* (1986). An examination of the role of nuclear weapons in the Cold War climate.

ELLMAN, M. and KONTOROVICH, V. *The Disintegration of the Soviet Economic System* (1992). An overview of the strains that the Soviet Union experienced during the 1980s.

FEIS, H. *From Trust to Terror: The Onset of the Cold War, 1945–1950* (1970). A useful general account.

GADDIS, J. L. *The United States and the Origin of the Cold War, 1941–1947* (1992). A major discussion.

GLENNY, M. *The Balkans, 1804–1999: Nationalism, War and the Great Powers* (1999). A lively narrative by a well-informed journalist.

HITCHCOCK, W. *Struggle for Europe: The Turbulent History of a Divided Continent, 1945–2002* (2003). The best overall narrative now available.

JARAUSCH, K. H. *The Rush to German Unity* (1994). Examines the events and background of the reunification of Germany.

JOHNSON, L. *Central Europe: Enemies and Neighbors and Friends* (1996). Examines the various nations of central Europe with an eye to the recent changes in the region.

KEEP, J. *Last of the Empires: A History of the Soviet Union, 1945–1991* (1995). An outstanding one-volume survey.

MANDELBAUM, M. *The Ideas That Conquered the World: Peace, Democracy, and Free Markets* (2002). An important analysis by a major commentator on international affairs.

MANN, R. *A Grand Delusion: America's Descent into Vietnam* (2001). The best recent narrative.

PAREKH, B. *Ghandi: A Very Short Introduction* (2001). A very useful introduction to Ghandi's ideas.

ULAM, A. *The Communists: The Story of Power and Lost Illusions: 1948–1991* (1992). Narrative of the story of the passage from Soviet Communist strength to collapse.

WALKER, M. *The Cold War and the Making of the Modern World* (1994). A major new survey.

Chapter 30

AMBROSIUS, G. and HUBBARD, W. H. *A Social and Economic History of Twentieth-Century Europe* (1989). An excellent one-volume treatment of the subject.

ANDERSON, B. S. and ZINSSER, J. P. *A History of Their Own: Women in Europe from Prehistory to the Present,* vol. 2 (1998). A broad-ranging survey.

BERNSTEIN, R. *Out of the Blue: The Story of September 11, 2001 from Jihad to Ground Zero* (2002). An excellent account by a gifted journalist.

BRAMWELL, E. *Ecology in the 20th Century: A History* (1989). Traces the environmental movement to its late nineteenth-century origins.

CROSSMAN, R. (ed.), *The God That Failed* (1949). Classic essays by former communist intellectuals.

GOLDSTINE, H. H. *The Computer from Pascal to von Neuman* (1972). A clear history of the technological development of the computer.

JENKINS, P. *The Next Christendom: The Coming of Global Christianity* (2002). A provocative analysis.

KEPEL, G. *Jihad: The Trail of Political Islam* (2002). An extensive treatment by a leading French scholar.

LANDAUER, T. K. *The Trouble with Computers: Usefulness, Usability, and Productivity* (1997). An informed skeptical commentary on the impact of computers.

MALTBY, R. ed., *Passing Parade: A History of Popular Culture in the Twentieth Century* (1989). A collection of essays on a topic just beginning to receive scholarly attention.

MONTEFIORE, G. *Philosophy in France Today* (1983). A good introduction to one of the major centers of contemporary thought.

NAIMARK, N. *Fires of Hatred: Ethnic Cleansing in Twentieth-Century Europe* (2002). A remarkably sensitive treatment of a tragic subject.

VIORST, M. *In the Shadow of the Prophet: The Struggle for the Soul of Islam* (2001). Explores the divisions in contemporary Islam.

Part 1 Timeline, Page xlvii and page 1, top to bottom, left to right: (1) Scala/Art Resource, N.Y./Royal portrait head ("Head of Sargon the Great"). From Nineveh (Kuyunjik). Akkadian, c. 2300–2200 B.C.E. Bronze, h: 12" (30.7 cm). Iraq Museum, Baghdad, Iraq. Scala/Art Resource; (2) Giraudon/Art Resource, N.Y./Stele of Hammurabi—detail of upper part: The sun god dictating his laws to King Hammurabi. Babylonian relief from Susa, c. 1760 B.C. (diorite, height of stele c. 2.1 m, height of relief 71 cm). Louvre, Paris, France. Copyright Giraudon/Art Resource; (3) Gary Cralle/Getty Images Inc.–Image Bank; (4) Peter Harper/Dorling Kindersley Media Library/Dorling Kindersley/British Museum; (5) *The She-Wolf Suckling Romulus and Remus*, late 15th–early 16th century. The National Gallery of Art, Washington D.C., the Samuel H. Kress Collection. Photograph © Board of Trustees, National Gallery of Art, Washington, D.C.; (6) The Oriental Institute Museum/Courtesy of the Oriental Institute of the University of Chicago; (7) Museum of Natural History; (8) Gustavo Tomsich/Corbis/Bettmann/ ©Gustavo Tomsich/CORBIS; (9) Anderson/Rudolf Lesch Fine Arts Inc.; (10) Ministere de la Culture et des Communications/Ministere de la Culture et de la Communication. Direction Regionale des affaires Culturelles de Rhone–Alpes. Service Regional de l'Archeologie; (11) Winfield I. Parks Jr./National Geographic Image Collection/Winfield I. Parks Jr./National Geographic Image Collection; (12) Robert Frerck/Woodfin Camp & Associates; (13) The Granger Collection.

Part 1, Page 2 and page 3, top to bottom, left to right: (1) Liz McAulay/Dorling Kindersley Media Library/Dorling Kindersley/British Museum; (2) Max Alexander/Dorling Kindersley Media Library; (3) Christopher Rennie/Robert Harding World Imagery; (4) Getty Images Inc.–Hulton Archive Photos; (5) Scala/Art Resource, N.Y./"Battle of Alexander the Great at Issus." Roman mosaic. Museo Archeologico Nazionale, Naples, Italy. Scala/Art Resources; (6) Robert Frerck/Woodfin Camp & Associates; (7) Art Resource, N.Y; (8) Library of Congress; (9) Art Resource, N.Y; (10) Liz McAulay/Dorling Kindersley Media Library/Dorling Kindersley/British Museum; (11) Christopher Rennie/Robert Harding World Imagery.

Chapter 1 a. © Stephen Hayward; b. © Judith Miller/Dorling Kindersley/Ancient Art; c. Robert Frerck/Odyssey Production/Woodfin Camp & Associates; d. © Dorling Kindersley; e. © Judith Miller/Dorling Kindersley/Ancient Art; g. © Jean Clottes and French Ministry of Culture and Communication, Regional Direction for Cultural Affairs - Rhone-Alps - Regional Department of Archaeology; i. Belly handled amphora, Kerameikos, Height 1.55 m., National Museum, Athens; j. Archaeological Museum, Amman, Jordan, kingdom. Photograph © Erich Lessing, Art Resource, NY.

Chapter 2 b. © Gianni Dagli Orti/CORBIS; c. National Archaeological Museum, Athens, Greece/Ancient Art and Architecture Collection Ltd./The Bridgeman Art Library International Ltd.; e., f. and g. © Roger Wood/CORBIS; h. © Foto Marburg/Art Resource, NY; i. Photograph © Eric Lessing/Art Resource, NY; j. © Gianni Dagli Orti/CORBIS; k. "Hydria (water jug)". Greek, Archaic period, ca. 520 B.C. Athens, Attica, Greece the Priam Painter. Ceramic, black-figure, H: 0.53 cm Diam (with handles): 0.37 cm. William Francis Warden Fund. © 2004 Museum of Fine Arts, Boston. Accession #61.195.

Chapter 3 a. Chas Howson © The British Museum; c. © 2004 Christie's Images, Inc.; d. Nick Nicholls © The British Museum; f. Louvre, Dept. des Antiquites Grecques/Romaines, Paris, France. Photograph © Erich Lessing/Art Resource, NY; g. John Serafin/SBG; j. Library of Congress.

Chapter 4 a. Walter S. Clark/Photo Researchers, Inc.; b. Dorling Kindersley Media Library; c. Christi Graham and Nick Nicholls © The British Museum; d. © Sandro Vannini/CORBIS; f. © Araldo De Luca/CORBIS; h. Nick Nicholls © The British Museum; i. Alinari/Art Resource, NY; j. Portland vase, 3rd c. A.D. Cameo-cut glass. British Museum, London; l. North Wind Picture Archives.

Chapter 5 a. Vatican Museums & Galleries, Vatican City/Superstock; b. Andy Crawford © Hessischen Landesmuseums, Darmstadt, Germany; c. Christi Graham and Nick Nicholls © The British Museum; d. Scala/Art Resource, NY; f. Roger Wood/Corbis/Bettmann; h. © Burstein Collection/CORBIS; i. Ruggero Vanni/Vanni Archive/Corbis/Bettmann.

Part 2, Page 144 and page 145, top to bottom, left to right: (1) Canali Photobank/Justinian, detail. c. 547. Mosaic technique. Canali Photobank, Capriolo, Italy; (2) Gianni Dagli Orti/Corbis/Bettmann/Gianni Dagli Orti/Corbis; (3) The New York Public Library/Art Resource/Picture Collection, The Branch Libraries, The New York Public Library, Astor, Lenox and Tilden Foundations; (4) Giraudon/Art Resource, N.Y./Bayeus, Musee de l'Eveche. "With special authorization of the City of Bayeux". Giraudon/Art Resource; (5) Corbis/ Bettmann; (6) Marvin Trachtenberg/Marvin Trachtenberg; (7) Unidentified/Dorling Kindersley Media Library; (8) Scala/ Art Resource, N.Y./(c)Scala/Art Resource, NY; (9) Corbis/ Bettmann; (10) Robert W. Madden/National Geographic Image Collection; (11) Gavin Hellier/Robert Harding World Imagery; (12) Foto Marburg/Art Resource, N.Y./Copyright Foto Marburg/Art Resource, NY; (13) Bonaventura Berlinghieri/Art Resource, N.Y.

Chapter 6 a. The New York Public Library/Art Resource, NY; b. © Stapleton Collection/CORBIS; c. © Stapleton Collection/CORBIS; d., f. and j. © Dorling Kindersley; e. Kunsthistorisches Museum, Wien oder KHM, Wien; i. Scala/Art Resource, NY; k. Werner Forman/Art Resource, NY; l. By Permission of the British Library. (1000102.021).

Chapter 7 b. Centre Guillaume Le Conquerant. Detail of the Bayeux Tapestry-XIth century. By special permission of the City of Bayeux; c. Neil Lukas © Dorling Kindersley;

d. Geoff Brightling © Dorling Kindersley; f. Image Works/Mary Evans Picture Library Ltd.; i. Photograph © Foto Marburg/Art Resource, NY; j. The Bridgeman Art Library International Ltd./Private Collection/The Bridgeman Art Library, London; k. Alan Williams © Dorling Kindersley

Chapter 8 a. The Granger Collection, New York; b. © Museum of London; c. Art Resource, NY;/©Giraudon/Art Resource, NY; d. Bildarkiv Preussischer Kulturbesitz; e. The Art Archive/Picture Desk, Inc./Kobal Collection; f. Corbis/Bettmann.

Part 3, Page 216 and page 217, top to bottom, left to right: (1) Max Alexander/Dorling Kindersley Media Library; (2) Art Resource/Reunion des Musees Nationaux/Reunion des Musees Nationaux/Art Reesource, NY; (3) The Granger Collection/ The Granger Collection, New York; (4) Art Resource, N.Y./Lauros-Giraudon/Art Resource, NY; (5) The Granger Collection; (6) Arthur Hacker, The Cloister of the World./The Bridgeman Art Library; (7) The Bridgeman Art Library International Ltd./Elizabeth I, Armada Portrait, c. 1588 (oil on panel) by George Gower (1540–96) (attr. to). Woburn Abbey, Bedfordshire, UK/Bridgeman Art Library, London/New York; (8) Getty Images Inc.–Hulton Archive Photos; (9) Tim Booth/Dorling Kindersley Media Library; (10) Library of Congress/Courtesy of the Library of Congress; (11) Giraudon/Art Resource, N.Y.

Chapter 9 a. Victoria & Albert Museum, London/Bridgeman Art Library; b. © ARPL/HIP/The Image Works; c. Geoff Dann © Dorling Kindersley, Courtesy of the Wallace Collection, London; e. UNESCO/Ann Ronan Picture Library/The Image Works; g. British Library, London. The Bridgeman Art Library Ltd.; h. Hacker Art Books Inc.

Chapter 10 b. The Granger Collection; c. By Permission of The British Library; d. Scala/Art Resource, NY; f. Vatican Museums and Galleries, Vatican City, Italy/Giraudon/Bridgeman Art Library; g. The Mariners' Museum, Newport News, VA; h. This item is reproduced by permission of The Huntington Library, San Marino, California.

Chapter 11 a. © Scala/Art Resource, NY; b. Musee Unterlinden, Colmar, France/SuperStock; c. Geoff Dann © The British Museum; d. Bildarchiv Preussischer Kulturbesitz/Art Resource, NY; e. National Gallery of Ancient Art, Rome, Italy/Canali PhotoBank, Milan/SuperStock; f. Painting-Flemish-17th cent. Peter Paul Rubens (1577–1640) The Miracle of Saint Ignace Loyola. Oil on canvas (1617–1618). Size: 535 × 395 cm. Cat. 313, Inv. 517 Kunsthist. Museum, Gemaeldegalerie, Vienna, Austria. Art Resource, NY; h. From Max Geisberg, "The German Single-Leaf Woodcut, 1500–1550", edited by Walter L. Strauss. Hacker Art Books, 1974. Used by permission of Hacker Art Books, Inc.

Chapter 12 a. © Dorling Kindersley; b. The Granger Collection; c. Geoff Dann © Dorling Kindersley, Courtesy of the Wallace Collection, London; d. © Dorling Kindersley; e. © Dorling Kindersley; f. Getty Images, Inc. - Liaison; g. Queen Mary I, 1554 (oil on panel) by Sir Anthonis Mor (Antonio Moro) (1517/20 - 76/7). Prado, Madrid, Spain/Bridgeman Art Library; h. Oliver Benn/Getty Images, Inc.; i. The Granger Collection, New York.

Chapter 13 a. Neil Lukas © Dorling Kindersley, Courtesy of l'Etablissement Public du Musee et du Domaine National de Versailles; c. and i. © Judith Miller/Dorling Kindersley/ Mendes Antique Lace and Textiles; e. State Historical Museum, Moscow, Russia/Leonid Bogdanov/SuperStock; j. © Bettmann/CORBIS.

Chapter 14 b. Corbis/Bettmann; c. © Paul Almasy/CORBIS; d. ©James A. Sugar/CORBIS; e. Image Works/Mary Evans Picture Library Ltd.; f. British Library, London, UK/Bridgeman Art Library; g. Philip Spruyt/Corbis/Bettmann; h. Sir Francis Bacon (1561–1626), champion of the inductive method of gaining knowledge. National Portrait Gallery, London; j. Bildarchiv Preubischer Kulturbesitz.

Chapter 15 b. J. B. S. Chardin, "The Washerwoman". Nationalmuseum med Prins Eugens Waldemarsudde. PHOTO: The National Museum of Fine Arts; c. Andrew McRobb © Dorling Kindersley; d. Mike Dunning © Dorling Kindersley, Courtesy of the National Railway Museum, York; f. Geoff Brightling © Dorling Kindersley, Courtesy of the Museum of English Rural Life, The University of Reading; i. © Scala/Art Resource, NY.

Chapter 16 a. © Bettmann/CORBIS; b. Getty Images Inc. - Hulton Archive Photos; c. © Bettmann/CORBIS; d. © National Maritime Museum, London; e. and f. Dave King © Dorling Kindersley; g. © Royalty Free/CORBIS; h. Martin van Meytens: "Kaiserin Maria Theresia mit ihrer Familie auf der SchloBterasse von Schobrunn". Kunsthistorisches Museum, Vienna, Austria; i. North Wind Picture Archives; j. © Dorling Kindersley.

Part 4, Page 404 and page 405, top to bottom, left to right: (1) The Granger Collection; (2) Doug Scott/AGE Fotostock America, Inc.; (3) North Wind Picture Archives; (4) The Bridgeman Art Library International Ltd.; (5) Bibliotheque Nationale de France; (6) Musee de la Legion d'Honneur Des Ordres de Chevalerie; (7) Ron_Case/Getty Images Inc.–Hulton Archive Photos; (8) Giraudon/Art Resource, N.Y.; (9) Getty Images Inc.–Hulton Archive Photos; (10) The Granger Collection.

Chapter 17 b. Corbis/Bettmann; d. Bildarchiv Preubischer Kulturbesitz; e. The Granger Collection; f. Library of Congress; g. The Granger Collection; h. © Archivo Iconografico, S.A./CORBIS; i. © Bettmann/CORBIS.

Chapter 18 a. Image Works/Mary Evans Picture Library Ltd.; c. © The Wallace Collection, London; d. Musees des Beaux-Arts, Lille. Bridgeman-Giraudon/Art Resource, NY; e. Bildarchiv Preubischer Kulturbesitz; f. Giraudon/Art Resource, NY; g. Corbis/Bettmann; j. © Bettmann/CORBIS.

Chapter 19 b. © Historical Picture Archive/CORBIS; c. Bildarchiv Preubischer Kulturbesitz; e. © Bettmann/CORBIS; f. The Granger Collection, New York; i. © Bettmann/CORBIS.

Chapter 20 a. Andy Crawford © Dorling Kindersley ; c. Jose Gil de Castro, Chilian, (1786–1850). General Jose de San Martin, 1818. Museo Historico Nacional Buenos Aires, Argentina; d. Bibliotheque des Arts Decoratifs, Paris, France/Archives Charmet/Bridgeman Art Library; g. © Bettmann/CORBIS; h. Tretiakov Gallery; i. Dave King © Dorling Kindersley, Courtesy of Robin Wigington, Arbour Antiques, Ltd., Stratford-upon-Avon.

Chapter 21 a. Mike Dunning © Dorling Kindersley, Courtesy of the National Railway Museum, York; b. The Art Archive/Picture Desk, Inc./Kobal Collection; c. © Dorling Kindersley, Courtesy of the Coors Visitor Centre, Burton Upon Trent; d. Private Collection/The Bridgeman Art Library, London/New York; e. and i. Neil Fletcher and Matthew Ward © Dorling Kindersley; f. © Bettmann/CORBIS; g. Bildarchiv Preubischer Kulturbesitz; h. Bildarchiv Preubischer Kulturbesitz; i. Peter Newark's Pictures.

Part 5, Page 534 and page 535, top to bottom, left to right: (1) NASA/John F. Kennedy Space Center; (2) Library of Congress; (3) Library of Congress; (4) Corbis/Bettmann; (5) Liaison Agency, Inc.; (6) Getty Images Inc.–Hulton Archive Photos; (7) The Bridgeman Art Library International Ltd.; (8) Brown Brothers; (9) Corbis/Bettmann; (10) Corbis/Bettmann; (11) Corbis/Bettmann.

Chapter 22 a. Bildarchiv Preubischer Kulturbesitz; b. © Hulton-Deutsch Collection/CORBIS; c. Private Collection/The Bridgeman Art Library, London; d. © Bettmann/CORBIS; e. Getty Images Inc. - Hulton Archive Photos; g. Bildarchiv Preubischer Kulturbesitz; h. Getty Images Inc. - PhotoDisc; i. Bildarchiv der Osterreichischen Nationalbibliothek, Wien; j. Corbis/Bettmann.

Chapter 23 b. © Bettmann/CORBIS; c. © Scheufler Collection/CORBIS; d. Corbis/Bettmann; g. Image Works/Mary Evans Picture Library Ltd.; h. Private Collection/Bridgeman Art Library; i. UPI/Lewis W. Hine/Corbis/Bettmann; j. The Granger Collection.

Chapter 24 a. National History Museum, London, UK/Bridgeman Art Library; b. Dave King © Dorling Kindersley, Courtesy of Down House/Natural History Museum, London; c. and d. Prentice Hall School Division/Laurie O'Keefe; e. National Archives and Records Administration; f. © Hulton-Deutsch Collection/Corbis; g. Stone/Hulton/Getty Images Inc.; h. Clive Streeter © Dorling Kindersley; i. Bildarchiv Preubischer Kulturbesitz; j. Clark University, Special Collections/Archives; k. Ullstein Bilderdienst; l. English Heritage Photo Library.

Chapter 25 a. © Dorling Kindersley; b. © Bojan Brecelj/CORBIS; c., d., e., f., g., h. and i. Karl Shone © Dorling Kindersley; j. Imperial War Museum, London; k.

Richard Ward © Dorling Kindersley; l. © Swim Ink/CORBIS; m. ©CORBIS; o. © Bettmann/CORBIS; p. The Granger Collection.

Chapter 26 a., Bildarchiv Preubischer Kulturbesitz; b. Clive Streeter © Dorling Kindersley, Courtesy of The Science Museum, London; c. Underwood & Underwood/CORBIS/Bettmann; d. Archivo Iconografico, S.A./CORBIS; f. © Copyright 2003 CORBIS; g. Andy Crawford © Dorling Kindersley, Courtesy of the Imperial War Museum, London; h. Bildarchiv Preubischer Kulturbesitz; i. UPI/CORBIS/Bettmann; j. Bettmann/Hulton Deutsch/CORBIS/Bettmann.

Chapter 27 a. © Leonard de Selva/CORBIS; b. Art Resource/Bildarchiv Preussischer Kulturbesitz; c. © Leonard de Selva/CORBIS; d. © Scheufler Collection/CORBIS; e. Andy Crawford © Dorling Kindersley, Courtesy of the Museum of the Revolution, Moscow; f. The Granger Collection; g. Getty Images Inc.—Hulton Archive Photos; h. AP Wide World Photos; i. CORBIS/Bettmann.

Part 6, Page 688 and page 689, top to bottom, left to right: (1) Getty Images Inc.–Hulton Archive Photos; (2) Corbis/Bettmann; (3) FPG/Getty Images, Inc.–Taxi; (4) AP/Wide World Photos; (5) Stevens/SIPA Press; (6) Brooks, Richard A./Getty Images Inc.–Image Bank; (7) Franklin D. Roosevelt Library; (8) Tony Korody/Corbis/Sygma; (9) Corbis/Sygma; (10) Getty Images, Inc–Liaison; (11) John Launois/Black Star; (12) Getty Images Inc.–Hulton Archive Photos; (13) Reuters/ Natalie Behring/Getty Images Inc.–Hulton Archive Photos.

Chapter 28 a. © CORBIS; b. Andy Crawford/Dorling Kindersley © Imperial War Museum, London; c. © Dorling Kindersley; d. CORBIS/Bettmann; e. © Bettmann/CORBIS; f. Getty Images Inc. - Hulton Archive Photos; g. © Bettmann/CORBIS All Rights Reserved; h. The Granger Collection; i. © Swim Ink/CORBIS.

Chapter 29 a. R. Bossu/Sygma/CORBIS; b. © Owen Franken/CORBIS; c. © Reuters NewMedia Inc./CORBIS; d. CORBIS/Bettmann; e. © Jacques Langevin/CORBIS SYGMA; f. Masatomo Kuriya/CORBIS/Bettmann; g. Charles Fenno Jacobs/Getty Images, Inc.; h. Les Stone/CORBIS/Sygma; i. © Robert Maass/CORBIS.

Chapter 30 a. Geoff Dann © Dorling Kindersley, Courtesy of the Imperial War Museum, London; b. AP Wide World Photos; c. © JOUANNEAU/CORBIS; d. © Reuters NewMedia Inc./CORBIS; e. Steve Gorton © Dorling Kindersley; f. © Bettmann/CORBIS; g. © Bettmann/CORBIS; h. Tom Prettyman/PhotoEdit Inc.; i. Andy Crawford © Dorling Kindersley; j. © Reuters NewMedia Inc./CORBIS; k. © CORBIS.

A

WESTERN CIVILIZATION DOCUMENTS CD-ROM

SINGLE PC LICENSE AGREEMENT AND LIMITED WARRANTY

READ THIS LICENSE CAREFULLY BEFORE OPENING THIS PACKAGE. BY OPENING THIS PACKAGE, YOU ARE AGREEING TO THE TERMS AND CONDITIONS OF THIS LICENSE. IF YOU DO NOT AGREE, DO NOT OPEN THE PACKAGE. PROMPTLY RETURN THE UNOPENED PACKAGE AND ALL ACCOMPANYING ITEMS TO THE PLACE YOU OBTAINED THEM.

1. **GRANT OF LICENSE AND OWNERSHIP:** THE ENCLOSED COMPUTER PROGRAMS <<AND DATA>> ("SOFTWARE") ARE LICENSED, NOT SOLD, TO YOU BY PEARSON EDUCATION, INC. PUBLISHING AS PEARSON PRENTICE HALL ("WE" OR THE "COMPANY") AND IN CONSIDERATION OF YOUR PURCHASE OR ADOPTION OF THE ACCOMPANYING COMPANY TEXTBOOKS AND/OR OTHER MATERIALS, AND YOUR AGREEMENT TO THESE TERMS. WE RESERVE ANY RIGHTS NOT GRANTED TO YOU. YOU OWN ONLY THE DISK(S) BUT WE AND/OR OUR LICENSORS OWN THE SOFTWARE ITSELF. THIS LICENSE ALLOWS YOU TO USE AND DISPLAY YOUR COPY OF THE SOFTWARE ON A SINGLE COMPUTER (I.E., WITH A SINGLE CPU) AT A SINGLE LOCATION FOR ACADEMIC USE ONLY, SO LONG AS YOU COMPLY WITH THE TERMS OF THIS AGREEMENT. YOU MAY MAKE ONE COPY FOR BACK UP, OR TRANSFER YOUR COPY TO ANOTHER CPU, PROVIDED THAT THE SOFTWARE IS USABLE ON ONLY ONE COMPUTER.

2. **RESTRICTIONS:** YOU MAY NOT TRANSFER OR DISTRIBUTE THE SOFTWARE OR DOCUMENTATION TO ANYONE ELSE. EXCEPT FOR BACKUP, YOU MAY NOT COPY THE DOCUMENTATION OR THE SOFTWARE. YOU MAY NOT NETWORK THE SOFTWARE OR OTHERWISE USE IT ON MORE THAN ONE COMPUTER OR COMPUTER TERMINAL AT THE SAME TIME. YOU MAY NOT REVERSE ENGINEER, DISASSEMBLE, DECOMPILE, MODIFY, ADAPT, TRANSLATE, OR CREATE DERIVATIVE WORKS BASED ON THE SOFTWARE OR THE DOCUMENTATION. YOU MAY BE HELD LEGALLY RESPONSIBLE FOR ANY COPYING OR COPYRIGHT INFRINGEMENT THAT IS CAUSED BY YOUR FAILURE TO ABIDE BY THE TERMS OF THESE RESTRICTIONS.

3. **TERMINATION:** THIS LICENSE IS EFFECTIVE UNTIL TERMINATED. THIS LICENSE WILL TERMINATE AUTOMATICALLY WITHOUT NOTICE FROM THE COMPANY IF YOU FAIL TO COMPLY WITH ANY PROVISIONS OR LIMITATIONS OF THIS LICENSE. UPON TERMINATION, YOU SHALL DESTROY THE DOCUMENTATION AND ALL COPIES OF THE SOFTWARE. ALL PROVISIONS OF THIS AGREEMENT AS TO LIMITATION AND DISCLAIMER OF WARRANTIES, LIMITATION OF LIABILITY, REMEDIES OR DAMAGES, AND OUR OWNERSHIP RIGHTS SHALL SURVIVE TERMINATION.

4. **LIMITED WARRANTY AND DISCLAIMER OF WARRANTY:** COMPANY WARRANTS THAT FOR A PERIOD OF 60 DAYS FROM THE DATE YOU PURCHASE THIS SOFTWARE (OR PURCHASE OR ADOPT THE ACCOMPANYING TEXTBOOK), THE SOFTWARE, WHEN PROPERLY INSTALLED AND USED IN ACCORDANCE WITH THE DOCUMENTATION, WILL OPERATE IN SUBSTANTIAL CONFORMITY WITH THE DESCRIPTION OF THE SOFTWARE SET FORTH IN THE DOCUMENTATION, AND THAT FOR A PERIOD OF 30 DAYS THE DISK(S) ON WHICH THE SOFTWARE IS DELIVERED SHALL BE FREE FROM DEFECTS IN MATERIALS AND WORKMANSHIP UNDER NORMAL USE. THE COMPANY DOES NOT WARRANT THAT THE SOFTWARE WILL MEET YOUR REQUIREMENTS OR THAT THE OPERATION OF THE SOFTWARE WILL BE UNINTERRUPTED OR ERROR-FREE. YOUR ONLY REMEDY AND THE COMPANY'S ONLY OBLIGATION UNDER THESE LIMITED WARRANTIES IS, AT THE COMPANY'S OPTION, RETURN OF THE DISK FOR A REFUND OF ANY AMOUNTS PAID FOR IT BY YOU OR REPLACEMENT OF THE DISK. THIS LIMITED WARRANTY IS THE ONLY WARRANTY PROVIDED BY THE COMPANY AND ITS LICENSORS, AND THE COMPANY AND ITS LICENSORS DISCLAIM ALL OTHER WARRANTIES, EXPRESS OR IMPLIED, INCLUDING WITHOUT LIMITATION, THE IMPLIED WARRANTIES OF MERCHANTABILITY AND FITNESS FOR A PARTICULAR PURPOSE. THE COMPANY DOES NOT WARRANT, GUARANTEE OR MAKE ANY REPRESENTATION REGARDING THE ACCURACY, RELIABILITY, CURRENTNESS, USE, OR RESULTS OF USE, OF THE SOFTWARE.

5. **LIMITATION OF REMEDIES AND DAMAGES:** IN NO EVENT, SHALL THE COMPANY OR ITS EMPLOYEES, AGENTS, LICENSORS, OR CONTRACTORS BE LIABLE FOR ANY INCIDENTAL, INDIRECT, SPECIAL, OR CONSEQUENTIAL DAMAGES ARISING OUT OF OR IN CONNECTION WITH THIS LICENSE OR THE SOFTWARE, INCLUDING FOR LOSS OF USE, LOSS OF DATA, LOSS OF INCOME OR PROFIT, OR OTHER LOSSES, SUSTAINED AS A RESULT OF INJURY TO ANY PERSON, OR LOSS OF OR DAMAGE TO PROPERTY, OR CLAIMS OF THIRD PARTIES, EVEN IF THE COMPANY OR AN AUTHORIZED REPRESENTATIVE OF THE COMPANY HAS BEEN ADVISED OF THE POSSIBILITY OF SUCH DAMAGES. IN NO EVENT SHALL THE LIABILITY OF THE COMPANY FOR DAMAGES WITH RESPECT TO THE SOFTWARE EXCEED THE AMOUNTS ACTUALLY PAID BY YOU, IF ANY, FOR THE SOFTWARE OR THE ACCOMPANYING TEXTBOOK. BECAUSE SOME JURISDICTIONS DO NOT ALLOW THE LIMITATION OF LIABILITY IN CERTAIN CIRCUMSTANCES, THE ABOVE LIMITATIONS MAY NOT ALWAYS APPLY TO YOU.

6. **GENERAL:** THIS AGREEMENT SHALL BE CONSTRUED IN ACCORDANCE WITH THE LAWS OF THE UNITED STATES OF AMERICA AND THE STATE OF NEW YORK, APPLICABLE TO CONTRACTS MADE IN NEW YORK, EXCLUDING THE STATE'S LAWS AND POLICIES ON CONFLICTS OF LAW, AND SHALL BENEFIT THE COMPANY, ITS AFFILIATES AND ASSIGNEES. THIS AGREEMENT IS THE COMPLETE AND EXCLUSIVE STATEMENT OF THE AGREEMENT BETWEEN YOU AND THE COMPANY AND SUPERSEDES ALL PROPOSALS OR PRIOR AGREEMENTS, ORAL, OR WRITTEN, AND ANY OTHER COMMUNICATIONS BETWEEN YOU AND THE COMPANY OR ANY REPRESENTATIVE OF THE COMPANY RELATING TO THE SUBJECT MATTER OF THIS AGREEMENT. IF YOU ARE A U.S. GOVERNMENT USER, THIS SOFTWARE IS LICENSED WITH "RESTRICTED RIGHTS" AS SET FORTH IN SUBPARAGRAPHS (A)-(D) OF THE COMMERCIAL COMPUTER-RESTRICTED RIGHTS CLAUSE AT FAR 52.227-19 OR IN SUBPARAGRAPHS (C)(1)(II) OF THE RIGHTS IN TECHNICAL DATA AND COMPUTER SOFTWARE CLAUSE AT DFARS 252.227-7013, AND SIMILAR CLAUSES, AS APPLICABLE.

SHOULD YOU HAVE ANY QUESTIONS CONCERNING THIS AGREEMENT OR IF YOU WISH TO CONTACT THE COMPANY FOR ANY REASON, PLEASE CONTACT IN WRITING: LEGAL DEPARTMENT, PRENTICE HALL, 1 LAKE STREET, UPPER SADDLE RIVER, NJ 07450 OR CALL PEARSON EDUCATION PRODUCT SUPPORT AT 1-800-677-6337.